D0206231

DICTIONARY

OF

EXISTENTIALISM

DICTIONARY

OF

EXISTENTIALISM

Edited by Haim Gordon

GREENWOOD PRESS
Westport, Connecticut

Library of Congress Cataloging-in-Publication Data

Dictionary of existentialism / edited by Haim Gordon.
    p.   cm.
  Includes bibliographical references and index.
  ISBN 0–313–27404–5 (alk. paper)
  1. Existentialism—Dictionaries.   I. Gordon, Haim.
B819.D455   1999
142'.78'03—dc21   98–30495

British Library Cataloguing in Publication Data is available.

Library of Congress Catalog Card Number: 98–30495
ISBN: 0–313–27404–5

First published in 1999

Greenwood Press, 88 Post Road West, Westport, CT 06881
An imprint of Greenwood Publishing Group, Inc.
www.greenwood.com

Printed in the United States of America

The paper used in this book complies with the
Permanent Paper Standard issued by the National
Information Standards Organization (Z39.48–1984).

10 9 8 7 6 5 4 3 2 1

ADVISORY COMMITTEE

Fred R. Dallmayr

Sonia Kruks

Robert L. Perkins

CONTENTS

ACKNOWLEDGMENTS

Many people helped me in the long years required to bring this book into being. My wife, Rivca, was a constant source of encouragement and support. The editors at Greenwood Publishing Group were patient and most helpful. Professor Jimmy Weinblat, the Dean of Humanities and Social Sciences, and Professor Nahum Finger, the Rector of Ben Gurion University of the Negev, were personally supportive and gave funds to complete this project. The advisory committee gave much time reading items. My sincere thanks to all of you.

INTRODUCTION

Although the term "existentialism" gained prominence only after World War II, it describes an exciting area of philosophical activity and original thinking that emerged in the nineteenth century, particularly in the writings of Friedrich Nietzsche, Søren Kierkegaard, and Fyodor Dostoyevsky. What unites these nineteenth-century existentialists with the many thinkers of the twentieth century who contributed to this area of philosophy is their focus on the existence of each human being, especially on the whole being of each person. Such an approach to human existence differs substantially from the approach of many human sciences, especially the behavioral sciences. The sciences that deal with humans direct their research to a particular aspect of human existence; for instance, a physiologist may study the anatomy of males and females, while a sociologist may research the behavior of certain groups. In contrast, existentialist thinkers and writers relate to the person as a whole being as he or she exists in the world.

Yet, existentialism is not only an attempt to think beyond the models and approaches developed by the positive sciences, even while learning from these sciences. It is also a rebellion against the rationalism that commenced in the modern period with the writings of René Descartes and reached a peak in the philosophy of Georg Wilhelm Friedrich Hegel. Existentialists reject the emphasis placed by these rationalists on the human being as primarily a thinking being. Many existentialists hold that freedom, not thinking, is ontologically prior when relating to human existence. While relating to freedom as central to human existence, existentialists differ on the results and implications of this priority. Thus, one finds religious and atheist existentialists arguing with, and learning from, each other—even as they differ on some of their most basic conclusions.

A result of the priority of freedom is that existentialists believe that many human relations and encounters cannot be reduced to thinking; what is more, they argue, the whole person is engaged in such relations and encounters. Love, genuine dialogue, a leap of faith, profound joy, creativity, anguish, nausea, guilt, and resoluteness when facing one's death are merely a few of the relations and encounters of the whole free person that different existentialists describe and discuss. The implications of this approach emerge in a wide spectrum of philosophical fields, ranging from ontology and epistemology to theology and philosophy of religion, and also to ethics, aesthetics, and political thinking.

This dictionary is intended to serve four purposes. First, it provides a primary reference for scholars and students seeking information on particular thinkers, writers, terms, and ideas developed by, or linked to, existentialism. Second, in relating to a specific topic, it briefly describes the profound and original thinking of a few of the existentialists, while showing the significance of the topic for other thinkers. The emphasis on originality and profundity should be of great help to the scholars and students who turn to this book. Third, the discussion of a term frequently shows the different and even clashing approaches to a topic by existentialist writers. It thus reveals that the ideas and thoughts of existentialists present the challenge of further thinking and elucidation. Fourth, it points to the influences of other thinkers on existentialist writers and to the influence of existentialist thinkers upon each other. Choices of entries for inclusion in the dictionary have been made with these aims in mind.

Since existentialism is a close-knit field of thinking, presenting the bibliography at the end of each entry presented a problem. Quite a few major existentialist texts, such as Sartre's *Being and Nothingness*, Buber's *I and Thou*, Heidegger's *Being and Time*, Kierkegaard's *Fear and Trembling*, Nietzsche's *Thus Spoke Zarathustra*, Dostoyevsky's *The Brothers Karamazov*, Kafka's *The Trial*, Merleau-Ponty's *Phenomenology of Perception*, and Camus' *The Myth of Sisyphus*, would probably need to be listed for at least a third of the entries. Some of these texts would even need to be listed for more than half the entries. To avoid such repetition, I have decided *not* to list the major texts following the individual entries. For these and other major texts of existentialism, often mentioned in the entries, I refer the reader to the general selected bibliography at the end of the dictionary. Cross-references to relevant entries are capitalized the first time they appear in an entry.

AESTHETICS
Mathew Rampley

Aesthetics is frequently confused with the philosophy of art, given that an aesthetic experience is frequently equated with the experience of a work of ART; indeed, a work of art is seen as exemplifying an aesthetic experience. Undoubtedly, there is a close relation between aesthetics and the philosophy of art, but the two are not identical. Existentialist aesthetic thinking inevitably has to be traced back to the aesthetic theory of Kant, in particular, his concept of the disinterested aesthetic judgment. As a reaction to this tradition, a recurrent motif of existentialist thought is the stress on the profound intertwining of aesthetic experience and lived reality. Indeed, for many, the aesthetic is the basis of the lived, not a mode of experience detached from it. One exception to this approach is SARTRE, whose insistence on the irreality of the objects of the IMAGINATION seems to give his thought a Kantian flavor. This impression is tempered, however, by Sartre's interest in committed writing.

Ironically, as the founder of a tradition that inverts the philosophical denigration of art, KIERKEGAARD views the aesthetic as a stage to be overcome. There is a further IRONY, given that his writing, with its adoption of various literary genres and use of various pseudonyms, has an aesthetic quality. His work is suffused with self-reflective irony, but he is not merely successor to those romantics for whom irony was the symbol of the infinite. For Kierkegaard irony is only a means to an end, namely, the authentic LIFE of FAITH. It is like the via negative: not the TRUTH, but the way; the establishment of an authentic life will thereby represent the suppression of the ironic. He thus implicitly criticizes the privileging of irony in romantic POETRY, in that Romanticism values irony as an end. The aesthete lacking any higher ethical VALUES exists in a state of perpetual passivity; one is dependent on the contingent and immediate and is enmeshed in continual boredom. To counter this state, the aesthete, fearful that life will lose its diverting multifariousness, either seeks ever greater and novel stimuli or is plunged into a profound self-absorption. Both responses include the constant dread of NOTHINGNESS. Art, too, is often only a beautiful transfiguration of human dread, without resolving it, since art may remain subject to the same logic of CONTINGENCY, boredom, and immediacy and therefore can fail to point beyond itself to the ETHICAL or the RELIGIOUS STAGES.

NIETZSCHE is consistently hostile to Kantian aesthetics and criticizes two major aspects: its predominantly female character and the issue of disinterestedness. He attacks the emphasis on analyzing aesthetic experience from the position of the passive, hence feminine spectator. Strictly speaking, this is misleading since Kant does give some attention to questions of CREATIVITY and genius. In contrast, Nietzsche seeks to introduce a productivist aesthetics that emphasizes the creative artist and views the aesthetic experience as intimately bound up with the WILL to POWER. The sense of aesthetic form marks the will's striving for organizational control through creative intervention in the world. He admires the aesthetic form of tightly disciplined bodies such as the Jesuit order or the Prussian officer corps. The Romantic dissolution of form is a sign of an enfeebled will to power. Regarding the question of disinterestedness, Nietzsche grounds the aesthetic attitude in the physiological functioning of the human organism, specifically, human sexuality. Beauty is always erotic, as the myth of Pygmalion suggests, and, indeed, in the most pious of religious paintings such as those of Raphael, he sees an erotic drive. Also, theoretical KNOWLEDGE is guided by the aesthetic through their common grounding in will to power.

Although art is of central importance in HEIDEGGER's philosophy, the aesthetic experience is much less central. In the essay "The Origin of the Work of Art," the traditional orientation of aesthetics toward subjective sensuous experience is criticized. The work of art is viewed as a disclosing of truth. Heidegger views van Gogh's painting of a pair of peasant shoes as disclosing their essential being, together with the lived reality of an individual peasant woman and the truth of her peasant existence. Truth and beauty thus merge in the specificity of the aesthetic experience. Heidegger does not discuss at any length the aesthetic imagination. He returns to the concerns of the ancient Greek philosophers, specifically, Plato, to work through once more the problem of art and truth.

The basis of Sartre's aesthetics is his theory of the imagination. In *The Psychology of the Imagination*, Sartre mobilizes HUSSERL's concept of INTENTIONALITY to explain both the place of images in CONSCIOUSNESS and their relation to their OBJECT. Criticizing the philosophical tradition that saw the image as a content of consciousness, Sartre sees the image as a mental event, distinguished by the manner in which its object is intended. While all conscious events intend an object, the imagination, in contrast to PERCEPTION, intends its objects as nonexistent. Hence, the imagining consciousness engages in a process of quasi observation since its objects are posited either as absent, nonexistent, or as making no particular claim to existence or nonexistence. At the heart of the image, therefore, is the element of NEGATION, of nothingness; somewhat problematically, Sartre concludes that the imagining consciousness necessarily negates the real WORLD. Yet it is precisely the irreality of the image that permits its spontaneity, since it is not related to the transcendent objects of the perceiving consciousness.

Sartre's theory of the image forms the thrust of his theory both of the aesthetic object and of the work of art. The work of art is the prime example of the aesthetic object; as the product of creative imagination it is subject to the same intentional mode as the image. Hence, the work of art qua aesthetic object, although manifest in physical terms, is nevertheless experienced as a nonreality. The movements of the dancer and the performance of a Beethoven symphony are merely physical analogues of the aesthetic object of dance or Beethoven's music that exist nowhere. Similarly, a painting works as an aesthetic object precisely as the negation of the real world. Sartre's view of the aesthetic object, the creative imagination, and, finally, the artist is somewhat bleak. The aesthetic attitude comprises a shutting out of the Other, exemplified by the withdrawal into subjectivity of Genet or Flaubert or, indeed, by the obsession with nothingness that Sartre observes in Giacometti. Sartre's extension of the theory of the imagination to that of the work of art is also vulnerable to criticism since it excludes all nonrepresentational art. Certain types of abstract painting, for example, that draw attention to their very materiality would not count as works of art or as aesthetic objects. Also Sartre's theory of the nihility of the aesthetic object runs counter to a better-known aspect of his thought on artistic production, namely, the notion of the committed writer articulating the dialectic of lived reality.

MERLEAU-PONTY's approach is the antithesis of Sartre's in that the aesthetic is the basis of perception. Of key significance is the distinction, first drawn in his *Phenomenology of Perception*, between primary and secondary expression. Primary expression designates the articulation of the primordial encounter between the lived body and the world. It denies the objective givenness of the world, which is, more properly, an environment or milieu. The character of this given environment is determined by the interplay of BODY and world. Hence, primal perception is always already aesthetic in ESSENCE, both because of the role of the body as the locus of perception and also because of its creative CHARACTER. Secondary expression is, by contrast, the articulation of the experience of BEING as already constituted by bodily engagement. Such would be, for example, the discourses of science and technology. Given that primordial experience is fundamentally aesthetic in character, it follows that Merleau-Ponty privileges art, especially painting, as a primary mode of articulating the experience of being. Painting does not merely represent the visible as a neutral spectacle; instead, through its sensuous nature, it also reenacts the carnal engagement with the world. That it should fall to art to re-create most faithfully the intertwining of SUBJECT and world indicates the crucial role that aesthetic experience plays, albeit implicitly, in his thought.

Primary Works

Heidegger, Martin. *Poetry, Language, Thought.* Trans. Albert Hofstadter. New York: Harper and Row, 1971.
Sartre, Jean-Paul. *The Psychology of the Imagination.* Trans. Bernard Fretchman. New York: Washington Square Press, 1966.

Bibliography

Johnson, G., ed. *The Merleau-Ponty Aesthetic Reader.* Evanston, IL: Northwestern University Press, 1993.
Lacoue-Labarthe, Philippe. *Heidegger, Art and Politics.* Trans. Chris Turner. Oxford: Basil Blackwell, 1990.

AESTHETIC STAGE
Robert L. Perkins

The aesthetic stage of EXISTENCE is associated primarily with KIERKE-GAARD. The aesthete claims to live poetically: by optimizing possibility and denying the claims of others upon one's own autonomy and WILL, the person poeticizes his or her LIFE. Denying social and moral RESPONSIBILITY, the aesthete lives for the moment and manipulates others. To admit the claim of another upon oneself would be to submit to the other, to be dominated. Rather, the aesthete seeks to dominate, and IRONY is the principal tool. Domination and manipulation may be a combination or variation of two forms, either sensual immediacy (Don Juan) or reflective sensuality, as portrayed in Kierkegaard's "Diary of the Seducer." Understanding commitment and passionate relations to another to be the basis of being dominated, the aesthete ironically urges that passion, particularly, LOVE, and all forms of COMMUNITY are illusions. Because the aesthete sees others as objects to be manipulated for one's perceived benefit, he or she does not enter into upbuilding and supportive relations with others. The aesthete is, indeed, lonely and melancholic. The inner result is despair and hopelessness even if the outer appears as glitter, laughter, and enjoyment.

Primary Work

Kierkegaard, Søren. *Either/Or*. Vol. 1. Trans. David F. Swenson and Lillian Marvin Swenson. Princeton: Princeton University Press, 1959.

ALIENATION
Phyllis Kenevan

Alienation, as recognized by existentialists, may be evoked by an absurd universe, silent in regard to passionate human questioning, or by the failure of humans to make the leap of FAITH needed to relate to their creative source. It may also be the response to NIHILISM as religious, cultural, and social paradigms fail and begin to disintegrate. Since the self is a temporal process, one can be alienated from oneself, say, through self-deception about one's past or denial of RESPONSIBILITY for one's future; one can also lose oneself in the absorption and preoccupation of everyday public EXISTENCE.

In "Letter on Humanism," HEIDEGGER describes human existence as homeless, because we have abandoned BEING. What Marx recognized as alienation has roots in the homelessness of modern man, which is coming to be the destiny of the WORLD (see MARXISM). The thinking of the West has fallen behind the course of the world destiny, which demands thoughtful reflection about the dimension in which human existence would be at home. That dimension is determined by Being. The way to approach coming destiny is through contemplative thinking, which precedes the differentiation of theoretical and practical thinking and is more rigorous than conceptual thinking. The rootedness of human existence is threatened at its core by the loss of caring about Being; we have even forgotten the meaning of the question concerning Being. Much of this loss stems from the path taken by traditional Western PHILOSOPHY. Modern technology has created a new technical relation between humans and the world. All of NATURE has become an energy source for modern technology and industry. Technological advance will move faster and faster. In this crisis we have been unable to confront meditatively what is dawning in this age.

With this technological perspective, spiritual goals are no longer meaningful, and MYSTERY has no VALUE. Humans become raw material, merely resources to be used.

We need to find a new ground and foundation so as to meet this crisis. Through meditative thinking, Heidegger claims, we can confront the problem and try to understand the significance of the uncanny, increasing dominance of technology. He is not advocating turning away from modern technology; rather, he urges that although we affirm technology, we also deny it the right to dominate us to the point that it destroys us as thinking beings. The greatest danger is to be captivated and bewitched by calculative thinking and embrace it as the only way of thinking. The way out of homelessness would then be lost, for we can reach the truth of Being not through becoming standing reserve for technology but only through an openness to the mystery. Only then may we find the way of dwelling in the world without being alienated.

Being-*in*-itself, for SARTRE, is absurd rather than mysterious; it speaks to us neither through the heavens nor through the silence. It simply is, is-in-itself, and is what it is. It is contingent, as is consciousness, or being-*for*-itself. Listening to the silence or opening ourselves to Being is useless. Both the meaning of the world and our ESSENCE as humans are without justification. In his novel *Nausea*, existence appears to the protagonist, Roquentin, as an undifferentiated stuff, without purpose or meaning. As a conscious being in an undifferentiated plenitude of being, Roquentin is a stranger in the universe, alienated by the failure of finding a meaning for himself or for the world. That absence of meaning is why the human condition is forlorn or abandoned. CONSCIOUSNESS desires to be what it is and to know itself as such, but this is an impossible desire since the for-itself is a temporal process always unfinished; furthermore, to know itself would mean to be at a distance from itself, which would make self-identity impossible. The attempt to know oneself through the LOOK of the other also fails since that look objectifies me but misses my TRANSCENDENCE. That alienating look can also objectify me as a member of a class. The *Critique of Dialectical Reason* suggests that social alienation can be healed through the group-in-fusion, through its unity of common PROJECTS. When the group-in-fusion is at its strongest, and there is activity in common, FREEDOM is not alienated; alienation can return when the group-in-fusion deteriorates. A concluding section of *Being and Nothingness* summarizes that consciousness is contingent, in a contingent universe, alienated because always other than what it knows, alienated from its self-identity, and unable to found its NOTHINGNESS. Despite its metaphysical impotence, consciousness as creative freedom has the opportunity and responsibility to structure a world made meaningful through its projects and intentions.

Number 377 in NIETZSCHE's *The Gay Science*, entitled "We Who Are Homeless," describes the free spirits who are homeless because they are ahead of their time and have faced the breakdown of BELIEF in an absolute. That absolute may be in terms of Western philosophy or of the Christian GOD. A pathological nihilism is the consequence of the loss of the absolute; it can be overcome if and when humanity incorporates healthy categories to interpret the world. Before that could happen, the shadows of God, our contemporary values and meanings, having lost their foundation in the absolute, would lose their significance. The madman in the marketplace proclaiming the death of God is conveying the threat of metaphysical alienation. The breakdown of belief in the Christian absolute was inevitable, since CHRISTIANITY was doomed to perish of its own value system, primarily its belief in absolute truth; for when claims about a moral world order were put to the test, they proved not to be true. Western philosophy, also dominated by Judaic-Christian values, fails in the same way. The outcome of this failure, a conviction of the worthlessness of existence, was the greatest danger. Those unable to overcome the alienation caused by nihilism remain within the ascetic ideal; they would rather aim at the void than be void of a goal. Only the future SUPERMAN will have the WILL and vitality to overcome homelessness and alienation, to face time and finitude with joyful affirmation and live in harmonious continuity with all of nature. The cure for alienation requires a superhuman answer, but that answer could come from no transcendent source but rather from the creative human will.

Metaphysical alienation is understood by KIERKEGAARD as spiritual alienation. Its cause is a self alienated from itself as SPIRIT and therefore lacking personal relation to God. Spiritual alienation can be recognized in boredom, melancholy, and despair. In boredom, one sees the nothingness of human existence when one fails to find meaning in anything one pursues. A gnawing emptiness and tedium pervade one's life, which no diversion can relieve; nor can the world of everyday concerns free one from the profound emptiness. Melancholy is another response to meaninglessness. The melancholic person cannot explain the ground of one's affliction, precisely because one is alienated from its cause. Such is a spiritual ailment and a universal condition of existence. With both melancholy and boredom, there is a genuine threat to one's being, since one is not bored with a particular object or person. The cause of alienation is one's existence. In boredom or melancholy, all activities and relationships lose their significance. No distraction or diversion can dispel their meaninglessness because the cause is an inability on the part of the self to face its finitude and freedom. The only solution is to resolutely attempt to face up to one's life as eternal spirit and to make the choice one can no longer evade.

In *The Sickness unto Death*, Kierkegaard shows through a dialectic of despair how the attempt to escape from the real self follows certain patterns. Ultimately, there is no escape from this sickness except through faith. In all forms of despair the individual is alienated from one's real self. That self can be attained only when it relates itself, through a personal act of faith, to its creator. Only the individual can make the leap of faith. In the case of the exceptional individual whose leap of faith may involve a teleological suspension of the ethical, it is paradoxical that one's relation with God that ends one's spiritual alienation may alienate the individual from one's fellow humans.

Primary Works

Heidegger, Martin. *The Question concerning Technology and Other Essays*. Trans. William Lovitt. New York: Harper and Row, 1977.

Kierkegaard, Søren. *Fear and Trembling and The Sickness unto Death*. Trans. Walter Lowrie. Princeton: Princeton University Press, 1954.

Bibliography

Barret, William. *Irrational Man*. London: Heinemann, 1961.

Kruks, Sonia. *Situation and Human Existence: Freedom, Subjectivity and Society*. London: Unwin Hyman, 1990.

Laing, Ronald David. *The Divided Self*. Harmondsworth: Penguin, 1979.

ANGUISH

Phyllis Kenevan

Existentialists describe anguish as a MOOD or state of MIND, revealing one's BEING-IN-THE-WORLD in its immediacy. It is a universal possibility of human EXISTENCE and an abiding threat. Anguish is different from FEAR, which is an unreflective apprehension of something definite in the WORLD that can be met with action. Anguish, on the other hand, is reflective apprehension of the self, essentially, of one's FREEDOM. This concept of anguish originated with KIERKEGAARD, who described it as universal and, in its theological context, to be understood as the consequence of original SIN. Anguish is on a lower level than despair, which involves SPIRIT and KNOWLEDGE of the eternal; it is characterized by a dizziness of freedom before the possibility of CHOICE and the dreaded possibility of nonbeing. It is turned toward the future, where choices have to be made. But the past also causes anguish because past failures and misfortunes are viewed as repeatable possibilities in one's present existence. The self is in anguish over what it may become as well as what it has been. Choices have to be made between GOOD and EVIL, between salvation or perdition, yet there are no external signs to guide one. We experience this ambiguity as anguish or the dizziness of freedom. The freedom of possibilities both fascinates and repels because freedom brings with it the responsibility of choice, especially the choice for or against GOD.

In *The Sickness unto Death*, Kierkegaard defines the self as a synthesis of the temporal and the eternal; we are not only finite physical-psychological BEINGS but also spiritual beings who become most fully ourselves in relating to the God who created us. Until we attain that awareness of spiritual identity, we are not able to see that our anguish masks an underlying despair that can be cured only by Christian FAITH. When that realization comes, what was anguish before the possibilities of freedom becomes a spiritual awareness, a recognition of the choice between remaining in despair or making the leap of faith.

Anxiety in HEIDEGGER's philosophy reveals our thrownness, meaning the brute fact of our presence in the world. It breaks the spell of the anonymous public mode in which, for the most part, we lose ourselves. In the public mode I am disburdened of the RESPONSIBILITY for my LIFE since I interpret myself as THEY do and therefore choose whatever they choose. The they-self being everyone and no one is actually in flight from itself as unique and individual. When anguish emerges, I am stripped of the tranquilizing effect of lostness in the anonymous public mode and am recalled to the self. Individualized through the awareness of myself as finite, knowing I am going to die, and responsible for how I live, anguish can bring me to the awareness of my freedom and to the obligation to assume responsibility for myself. Anxiety can also reveal Being, however, only as no-thing, when the meaning that I have given to beings falls away, leaving me with the question of why there is something rather than nothing. Anguish reveals the nothing because it robs me of the everyday meanings that make the world familiar. What remains is only an uncanny nothing veiling Being. This unsettling experience does not last, although it remains an ever-present possibility. In anguish I am anxious about the nothing. The experience of NOTHINGNESS is fundamental.

SARTRE claims that through anguish I become conscious of my freedom, in the face of both the future and the past. The gambler who resolves not to gamble ever again discovers the next day in anguish that one is free to honor one's resolve or to betray it. Nothing binds one to it other than present free choice. The fear one feels on the edge of a precipice is not fear of falling; it is the anguish of realizing that one may decide the next moment to jump. Present resolve does not determine the future; I am condemned to be free. I am freedom. Why, then, is the experience of anguish rare? Because when I act, I am not reflecting; I act in accordance with meanings and expectations that guarantee against the anguished realization that I confer those meanings on the world. Thus, ordinary, everyday experience, falling into the-midst-of-the-world, allows me to hide my anguish. Furthermore, I hide from ethical anguish. My freedom is anguished at being the foundation of VALUES while itself without foundation. When I am aware of creating values, I see how unjustifiable those choices are. To escape that insight, I may fall into BAD FAITH: I may claim that the values I hold are not my inventions but are given. One mode of consciousness permits the possibility of good faith: an authentic apprehension of oneself as a CONSCIOUSNESS in temporal dispersion, accepting responsibility for one's past actions and assuming responsibility for one's choices in the future. Thus, one acknowledges the anguish of freedom. As with Heidegger, the burden of anguish is the path to authentic, responsible action. Anguish is the recognition of freedom.

Bibliography

Schrag, Calvin. *Existence and Freedom*. Evanston, IL: Northwestern University Press, 1961.
Wahl, Jean. *Philosophies of Existence*. New York: Schocken, 1969.

ANXIETY
Constance L. Mui

In existentialism, anxiety and concepts such as ANGUISH, FEAR, and dread point to a human condition stemming from FREEDOM. For JASPERS, anxiety is experienced in boundary situations, such as death, in which I confront extreme limits. NIETZSCHE considers anxiety an original and most fundamental feeling through which everything, including original virtue and SIN, is explained. He insists that virtue could stem only from anxiety. KIERKEGAARD distinguishes between fear and anxiety: fear takes on a definite object; anxiety has no proper object. As such, it is an anxiety of nothing, yet it constitutes a positive and necessary step toward self-fulfillment. Since self-fulfillment always involves a personal, spiritual transformation, anxiety is understood as a condition unique to conscious humans. He maintains that you may attain self-fulfillment by entering a succession of stages: the AESTHETIC STAGE, where you indulge in the senses; the ETHICAL STAGE, where you conform to absolute principles; and the highest, the RELIGIOUS STAGE, where you become an authentic, spiritual BEING standing alone before GOD. The move toward this final stage involves not a gradual evolution but a decisive LEAP in freedom, a plunge into the unknown. The future into which I leap is an undetermined possibility: I could open myself to a spiritual commitment or could give in to sin. At the threshold of this new stage, I vaguely anticipate a spiritual rebirth, while experiencing my vulnerability to sin. This ambivalent, unsettling state—a conflict that reveals freedom—is the source of anxiety. Kierkegaard says that dread is a sympathetic aversion and an averse sympathy. As an anxiety of some undetermined possibility with no concrete object, it is quite aptly an anxiety of nothing.

Central to Kierkegaard's view is his understanding of anxiety in light of the Christian doctrine of sin and REDEMPTION. For him, anxiety is a means of salvation in conjunction with FAITH. It is not a psychological state to be diagnosed but a spiritual state to be disclosed through inward reflection. He confers a positive VALUE on anxiety as that which compels me to lift myself from my everyday EXISTENCE so as to confront my most infinite possibility: my personal commitment to God where I freely choose faith over sin.

HEIDEGGER also distinguishes between fear and anxiety, maintaining that the latter has no definite object. The objects of fear are BEINGS-IN-THE-WORLD, while anxiety relates to my being-in-the-world. Anxiety constitutes the integral structure of DASEIN, the human entity. As the conscious being capable of questioning its own being, Dasein is aware of its existence as both being-in-advance-of-itself and being-in-the-world. Dasein is being-in-advance-of-itself in that it exists by projecting toward its own still-to-be-realized being. Thus, it confronts its being not as a static endowment but as a task to be fulfilled. Dasein finds itself already situated in a WORLD amid other beings, as having been thrown into existence in a world where things are ready at hand—they serve a purpose in relation to Dasein. As such, Dasein is not merely located in the world but is always in a given state or MOOD. A worthy mood is that of CARE: Dasein cares for other beings. However, to be caught up with everyday affairs is to run the risk of inauthenticity. Specifically, Dasein could lose sight of its real-self as the locus of the disclosure of Being by falling into the impersonal THEY, thoroughly absorbed by the crowd.

Against fallenness as Dasein's fundamental mood, Heidegger introduces anxiety as a mood of Dasein's being-in-the-world as being-toward-possibility. Anxiety can lift Dasein out of fallenness and make it confront the elusive sources of anxiety, for instance, the stark reality of Dasein's ultimate, but most unique, possibility of DEATH. In anxiety Dasein can wrench away from the preoccupation with things, pull itself out of fallenness, and focus on the NOTHING-NESS of its own being, which reveals to Dasein the nullity of human existence as thrown-being-unto-death. Sprung from Dasein's internal relation to its own being, anxiety is an ontological structure. As the mood that can bring out Dasein's resoluteness vis-à-vis its being-toward-death, anxiety commands much strength and fortitude and is the necessary first step toward AUTHENTICITY. Through anxiety Dasein becomes aware of death as the single most personal possibility that sums up the uniqueness and wholeness of its existence.

In *Being and Nothingness*, SARTRE analyzes anxiety in light of freedom: I anguish over the threat that my freedom poses and also over the threat others pose to my freedom. To exist as freedom is to exist as nothingness—he, too, understands the object of anxiety as nothing. To exist as a conscious, free being is to exist by projecting beyond yourself toward some future possibility. Thus, CONSCIOUSNESS is always a step ahead of what it has made of itself; its identity can never be fully defined. This constantly pulling away from itself makes it clear that consciousness does not possess substantial, thinglike qualities associated with inanimate objects. It exists as nothingness. Nothingness is present in the heart of consciousness, which is not opaque but translucent. It is pure spontaneity that reveals its perpetual failure to be in perfect unity with itself. As pure lucidity to be filled by an object that would give it some content, consciousness could direct itself outward to an object in the world, or it could turn inward, in a reflective moment, toward its own existence as freedom. Anguish enters in two ways. First is the anxiety when consciousness becomes aware of its exteriority through the other's look, which reveals to it that it has a BODY and is in danger, a being-for-others that exists for another consciousness in a way that is not accessible to itself. To overcome this anxiety, one could attempt to retrieve its objectness-for-others by looking back at the look, thus turning the other into an object. Whereas such anxiety concerns the other's threat, freedom could itself be a source of anxiety, arising in consciousness' reflective apprehension of itself as freedom, with its RESPONSIBILITY and insecurity. In fleeing anxiety, consciousness resorts to self-deception by appealing to psychological or theological determinism. However, fleeing anxiety can never succeed. Anxiety over my existence is indicative of the fact that I am free. Thus, anxiety constitutes an authentic moment that grounds me in freedom.

Primary Work

Kierkegaard, Søren. *The Concept of Anxiety*. Trans. Reider Thomte. Princeton: Princeton University Press, 1980.

Bibliography

Perkins, Robert L., ed. *The Concept of Anxiety: Volume 8 of International Kierkegaard Commentary*. Macon, GA: Mercer University Press, 1985.
Raymond, Diane Barsoum. *Existentialism and the Philosophical Tradition*. Englewood Cliffs, NJ: Prentice-Hall, 1991.

APPEARANCE
William Hurst

In *Being and Time*, HEIDEGGER attempted to draw some clear distinctions between a number of concepts, such as appearance, seeming or semblance, mere appearance, and phenomenon. It was important to identify the differences among these concepts because he had adopted PHENOMENOLOGY as his method, and he intended to argue that phenomenology is ONTOLOGY. If phenomenon were understood as appearance, how, indeed, could he claim that phenomenology is ontology, since ontology focuses on reality, and appearance and irreality are evidently distinct? It was necessary, therefore, to distinguish between appearance and phenomenon.

Heidegger argued that phenomenon should be understood in the manner that the ancient Greeks understood the concept. Etymologically, a phenomenon is "that which shows itself." An appearance, on the other hand, is that which does not show itself but rather announces its presence through something else that shows itself. As that which shows itself, a phenomenon is that which comes into the light or becomes present. This is precisely the ancient Greek understanding of BEING. Appearance, on the contrary, is a not showing or a not coming into the light as what it is. Whatever announces itself through a showing but without showing itself, therefore, is an appearance. Symptoms, symbols, indications, or presentations all have the same formal CHARACTER of appearance, even though each is different from appearance. Seeming, on the other hand, is quite different from appearance, in that in a semblance there is something that is showing itself or coming into the light, but it looks like something else. Underlying Heidegger's focus on appearance and phenomenon was his desire to keep his thinking free and independent of any purely subjectivist prejudice, which the concept of appearance, especially that of mere appearance, might entail. The phenomenon is that which shows itself in itself, and appearance is that which shows itself through whatever it is that shows itself but does not itself show itself. Even his way of distinguishing these two notions indicates his INTENTION to focus on whatever it is that is showing or hiding itself and his intention not to focus on whatever it is that might be subjectively grounding or forming the experience.

Heidegger's discussion of appearance led, at least, to the brink of a discussion about PERCEPTION. He wrote about how someone in a certain lighting can look as if his cheeks are red; and the redness that shows itself can be taken as an announcement of the Being-present-at-hand of a fever, which, in turn, indicates a disturbance in the organism. One might ask, however, about the possibility that what one sees is not really redness but a reflection caused by the particular lighting. In that case there would not be an appearance but rather a semblance, in which the cheeks seemed to be red but were, in fact, reflecting something red in the surroundings or even the peculiar lighting. In this case, there would be no announcement of the Being-present-at-hand of a fever but rather only a seeming of such an announcement.

In *Phenomenology of Perception*, MERLEAU-PONTY examined appearance while discussing CONSCIOUSNESS, the object of consciousness, illusion, TRUTH and falsity, and perception as the placing of one's FAITH in the WORLD. He addressed also the traditional opposition between appearance and reality. The argument has been made that in consciousness there is no difference between appearance and reality because, if such a distinction were made, one could not account for MYTHS, illusions, or dreams. According to this view, one would have to account for any difference between perception and illusion or hallucination on the basis of characteristics intrinsic to them. Indeed, the truth of the one and the falsity of the other would have to be equally apparent and to be based upon some structural difference. This view, relying on a belief that consciousness is transparent to itself, was not adequate, from Merleau-Ponty's perspective, to account for illusion, which requires, he wrote, that I should be able, if not to perceive an unreal object, at least to lose sight of its reality.

To account for this distinction between reality and appearance, without introducing a distinction within consciousness, Merleau-Ponty returned to the perceptual field. He claimed that there is a difference in the grasp of the OBJECT that my BODY is able to make if the object presented to me is, indeed, a real one and not simply an illusion. But the process of taking hold of an object within my visual field requires putting one's BELIEF or confidence in the world and in a future of experiences. Such faith does not guarantee the future, and it is impossible for me ever to have an all-embracing hold on an object or on the world, because I am not ever in a position to grasp all the horizons, both internal and external, of any object in my field. Thus, I may find, after continued exploration of an object that presented itself to me, that it is not what I first believed it to be and that what I had believed was, in fact, the product of an illusion—I took for real something that was not. Consciousness is not transparent to itself, and the objects of consciousness are not immanent to it but emerge gradually within the field of one's perception and thought and are always capable of being other than what they appeared to be as they present themselves to a process of exploration. Illusion, then, is part of a process of correction on the way to the unfolding of a solid appearance, which I can take hold of with my body, if the object is, indeed, something perceived. This consciousness is, moreover, not a subject or a self that is positing its object but is rather an awareness that there is significance. Thus, it entails neither the rationalist belief that everything has significance nor the radically skeptical view that nothing does. In *The Visible and the Invisible*, Merleau-Ponty developed the notion that consciousness is a field of Being, and the objects of consciousness are not posited in front of, or within, consciousness but are rather nuclei of significations. Such nuclei are in a position to change as the field unfolds; appearance and illusion are moments in the process of such an unfolding.

Primary Work

Merleau-Ponty, Maurice. *The Visible and the Invisible*. Trans. Alphonso Lingis. Evanston, IL: Northwestern University Press, 1968.

Bibliography

Kockelmans, Joseph J. *On Heidegger and Language*. Evanston, IL: Northwestern University Press, 1972.

Macann, Christopher. *Critical Heidegger*. London: Routledge, 1996.

HANNAH ARENDT
(1906–1975)
Mordechai Gordon

Hannah Arendt was born to Jewish parents in Hannover, Germany. At age two her parents moved to Königsberg, where her grandparents lived. Arendt's comfortable childhood was overshadowed by her father's deteriorating health; he died of syphilis when she was seven. In 1924 she began university studies at Marburg and came under the tutelage of HEIDEGGER. Later she moved to Heidelberg to write her doctoral dissertation on St. Augustine's Concept of Love, with JASPERS as her adviser. Arendt and Jaspers maintained a lifetime friendship, which was partially broken off in 1933 but renewed and deepened after World War II. She married twice, in 1929 to the philosopher and poet Gunther Stern and in 1940 to Heinrich Blucher, whom she met in France while involved in Zionist activities. In 1941 Arendt and Blucher immigrated to the United States. Arendt's writings were often controversial. Her book *Eichmann in Jerusalem* generated an international debate in which she was called a traitor and anti-Israel. Her portrayal of Eichmann as banal, her strong criticism of the prosecution of the trial, and her description of the role of the Jewish councils in the Final Solution led several friends and colleagues to denounce her.

Amor Mundi (love of the world) unites all of Arendt's works. In a collection of her essays about various persons, *Men in Dark Times*, it is safe to conclude that most, if not all, of these persons shared love of the WORLD. In the first essay she describes the humanity of Gotthold Ephraim Lessing and argues that, for Lessing, criticism is taking sides for the world's sake. Lessing's humanity consisted in friendship, in openness to the world, and in genuine love of mankind. *Amor Mundi* also informs *Between Past and Future* and *Crises of the Republic*. The former contains essays about authority and FREEDOM, which were previously experienced in public yet today have disappeared or have been relegated to the private realm. The world lost something essential, since freedom and authority are no longer experienced in public. *Crises of the Republic* deals with the eclipse of the public realm and the dangers for the republic when it no longer provides public SPACE for citizens. Late in life she began to write on the life of the MIND: thinking, willing, and judging.

In *The Origins of Totalitarianism*, Arendt shows how the total domination of totalitarian regimes tries to determine all individuals as superfluous and to abolish human spontaneity. It is the most terrible political existence, radically distinguished from all forms of despotism, since totalitarianism strives toward a system in which humans are completely superfluous. Such EXISTENCE was fully realized in the concentration camps; therefore, they are the most important institution of the Nazi and Soviet regimes. Three steps of total domination were perfected in these camps. The first was to kill the juridical person in the inmates by placing the camps outside the normal legal system in which a definite crime entails a predictable penalty and by abolishing the quality of GUILT or innocence before the law. The next step was to murder the moral PERSON in the individual by forcing inmates to be responsible for much of the administration of the camps, thus implicating them in the crimes of murdering their families, friends, and fellow prisoners. Through forcing victims to participate in crimes, the distinguishing line between murderer and victim was blurred; acts of CONSCIENCE became almost impossible. After annihilating the juridical person and murdering the moral person, there remained only to destroy human individuality, that is, a person's identity and distinctness. The monstrous conditions in transports to the camps, the shaving of the heads upon arrival, the torturing of the inmates were ways of destroying personal identity. Destroying individuality and spontaneity was the final step to total domination.

The ESSENCE of totalitarian rule is terror. Arendt insists that totalitarianism is unprecedented and should be distinguished from tyranny, whose essence is lawlessness. While both forms destroy the freedom to act, tyranny leaves intact a wilderness of FEAR in which desperate actions are still possible. Totalitarian rule strives to abolish this wilderness of fear and suspicion and its limited LIBERTY. By pressing humans against each other and destroying their individuality, total terror abolishes the space between them that guarantees human plurality and distinctness and is the prerequisite for political freedom. Total terror attempts to deny the fact that humans are essentially free, that is, capable of a new beginning.

IDEOLOGY is the political instrument through which totalitarianism mobilizes the masses to participate in crimes. Ideology explains the movement of history according to a specific logic. Racism is the belief that there is a motion inherent in the very idea of race, and communism is the conviction that a motion is inherent in the idea of class. Totalitarian rulers utilized the logical PROCESS that could be developed from an ideology: races that are unfit to live should be killed; dying classes consist of people who should be exterminated. Hitler and

Stalin discovered that the inner logic of an ideology can lead people to surrender their freedom of thought for the sake of a logical process of history or of nature. They used ideology to destroy the inner capacity of freedom much as they employed terror to destroy political freedom. The compulsion of total terror and the self-coercive force of an ideology correspond to each other and need one another in order to set the totalitarian movement into motion and keep it moving. Terror and ideology prepare each individual for a LIFE of lonely isolation. Terror ruins relationships between people; the logic of ideology ruins relationships with reality. Totalitarianism succeeds when people lose contact not only with fellow humans but also with reality. The result: both thinking and the ability to distinguish between fact and fiction vanish. The basic experience of living within a totalitarian regime is loneliness, which should not be confused with isolation—a political experience in which the capacity to be and act with others is taken away. Loneliness is the desperate situation in which a person feels deserted by all humans. Isolation concerns the political aspect of life; loneliness concerns human life as a whole. Totalitarianism is not content with the isolation that occurs when the political realm is destroyed but attempts to base itself on loneliness, on the terrible experience of not belonging to the world.

The Human Condition is Arendt's discussion of the significance of the public realm and the glory of worthy action in that realm. She views political existence from the vantage point of the person who acts in history, in the public realm with others, and tries to create a new beginning. The human condition is linked to the phenomenon of plurality, which is specific to political life; the political arena is the only realm that does not presuppose an interaction between individuals and the world but between individuals themselves. This interaction between individuals who are different from each other is of the essence of political life; political action includes debating issues of public concern and working together for a common cause. The Greek polis, the creation of the American republic, and various council systems that sprang up in modern Europe exemplify political action.

Political action is linked to natality, to the fact that each birth is a new beginning. The newcomer to the world has the capacity to begin something new, to act—to insert his or her self into the world with words and deeds. This insertion is neither moved by necessity, like labor, nor prompted by utility, like work. Action is often aroused by the presence of others whose company I may wish to join, but it is never conditioned by them. Action springs from the beginning that came into the world when I was born. Its worth is in the activity itself, unlike work and labor, which are instrumental. Thus, political action resembles the performing arts: both come to an end when the activity is over and leave only the memory of what was seen or heard. The worth of a certain action can never be reduced to a single deed with a definite outcome, since its consequences can grow and multiply. Furthermore, human action can never be completely conditioned or controlled. Like birth, action contains an element of surprise; its outcome can never be fully predicted because it comes about through the joint efforts of beings who are beginnings and beginners in the world and have the capacity to make the unexpected happen.

Speech is the actualization of the human condition of plurality. While action as beginning corresponds to the fact of birth, speech corresponds to the distinctness of each person, who differs from any person who was, is, or will be. Action and speech implicitly reveal who somebody is: your personal identity is based on your acts and words. What you are are the roles you assume. Yet, speech is more related to revelation, just as action has a closer affinity to beginning and human natality. Indeed, without the accompaniment of speech, action would lose not only its revelatory quality but also its SUBJECT. Speechless action cannot be considered action, because deeds become relevant only by disclosing the identity of the actor. Action without a name attached to it, a who, is meaningless. Finally, action is closely related to freedom as a political reality. Arendt distinguishes between freedom as a fact of life in the political realm and freedom as a philosophical problem. Only the former is related to action. Freedom is the raison d'être of politics, and it is experienced in action. It is not only one of the many political phenomena, such as justice, POWER, or equality, but rather the very reason that humans live together in political organizations. We cannot even conceive of action and politics as human activities and pursuits without presupposing that freedom exists, and we can hardly touch a single political phenomenon without raising the issue of political freedom.

Arendt's notion of freedom is different not only from the idea of inner freedom but also from liberty. Inner freedom, the freedom of the WILL or of thought, refers to an inner space into which individuals escape when their political liberty is threatened or limited. Thus, inner freedom is derivative, because it presupposes a retreat from the world in which freedom was denied into a private domain that is inaccessible to others. Genuine freedom requires a public space in which the opinions and actions of individuals can be seen and heard. A public space is created by humans in order to gather as equals to deliberate and decide on issues of common concern. It was established in the Greek polis and the town halls of the American republic at the end of the eighteenth century. *The Human Condition* calls this the space of APPEARANCE, where individuals can appear as equals in order to exchange opinions freely and make them public. Such a space is where people are free to initiate something new together with others. The public or political realm is the only realm where human action and speech can show themselves and where individuals are free to collaborate with their peers on common enterprises. The public space is not a particular physical location. Contrarily, this space is the organization of the people as it arises out of acting and speaking together. Public space lies between people whenever they come together in words and deeds. Action and speech create a space between the actors that is hardly bound by a specific location or time. Yet this space does not always exist, and most people, like the worker or the businessperson of our world, do not live in it. Although one cannot live in public space all of the time, to be deprived of it means to be deprived of a portion of reality, for, in politics, the reality of the world is guaranteed by the presence of others who view the same world from different perspectives. To exist in the political realm is the same as to appear to the many; whatever lacks this appearance has only a private significance but no political reality.

Action interrupts the irreversible and unpredictable course of human life in order to begin something new. Thus, action bestows meaning on human existence, which would otherwise resemble other natural processes. Action does not need to enlist a higher faculty to combat the irreversibility and unpredictability of human deeds, since the remedy for this predicament is one of the potentialities of action itself. The remedy for not being able to reverse what one has done is the act of forgiving, while the remedy for the uncertainty of the future is making and keeping promises. Without being forgiven, we could never be released from the harmful consequences of our actions, thereby greatly limiting our capacity to act. Without being bound to keep promises, we would never be able to master the chaotic future, which is simultaneously shaped by human freedom and plurality. Taking into account the power to initiate, to forgive and make promises, action seems like a miracle. This miracle not only bestows on human affairs faith and hope but also ensures that great words and deeds will always be a part of the political realm.

Arendt's reverence for action and freedom is evident in her analysis of modern revolutions from the American and French Revolutions to the 1956 Hungarian one. The common denominator for wars and revolutions is violence. Yet whereas wars are largely determined by violence, it is never a sufficient condition for revolutions and may play a marginal role in their unfolding. Far more important is that revolutions, in distinction from wars and political uprisings, ought to include the foundation of a radically new political order. Put simply, only where the liberation from oppression aims at least at the constitution of freedom (laws and institutions that guarantee the people the right to participate in government) can we speak of revolution. Revolutions are primary examples of the human capacity to act, because they enable the people to initiate new beginnings and to become politically active.

Arendt insists that every modern revolution has included not only the liberation from oppression and the demand for public liberties but also the spontaneous organization of the people in public spaces to debate on political issues and to work together for a common cause. Whether in the town halls of the American colonies, the French revolutionary societies, or the councils that sprang up in Russia and Hungary, ordinary people gathered to engage in political discussions and to partake in establishing the new political order. This spontaneous organization of people to participate in public affairs constitutes political freedom. Thus, political freedom should not be equated merely with civil rights or with freedom of movement, although the latter are a necessary condition for the former. Rather, political freedom is essentially positive. It requires a willingness to participate in political affairs and to initiate new enterprises that affect the public. It is based on the creative initiatives and actions of humans.

Primary Works

Arendt, Hannah. *The Human Condition*. Chicago: University of Chicago Press, 1968.
————. *The Origins of Totalitarianism*. New York: Harcourt Brace Jovanovich, 1951.

Bibliography

Canoven, Margaret. *Hannah Arendt: A Reinterpretation of Her Political Thought*. Cambridge: Cambridge University Press, 1992.
Kateb, George. *Hannah Arendt: Politics, Conscience, Evil*. Totowa, NJ: Rowman and Alanheld, 1984.
Young-Bruehl, Elizabeth. *Hannah Arendt: For Love of the World*. New Haven, CT: Yale University Press, 1982.

ART
Mathew Rampley

Within existentialist thought, art as an articulation of the concrete, singular, lived experience is placed in opposition to abstract conceptual thinking. This contrast occurs most explicitly in the discussion of POETRY. Poetic language is regarded as overcoming the perceived deficiencies of philosophic language in giving expression to EXISTENCE. HEIDEGGER, in particular, refers to Holderlin, RILKE, and Stefan George in near-oracular terms.

For KIERKEGAARD art is but a seductive activity to be overcome. It consists of a beautiful transfiguration of human ANXIETY that fails to resolve such anxiety, offering only an imperfect reconciliation with LIFE. It remains caught within the AESTHETIC STAGE, which is subject to CONTINGENCY, boredom, and passivity. In *Either/Or* he distinguishes between modern tragedy, which is oriented toward the inner suffering and GUILT of the protagonist, and ancient tragedy, where the sorrow is a function of a wider, cosmic fate. He offers a lengthy discussion of music, the art form par excellence, since its absolute subject is the genius of sensuality. He analyzes Mozart's opera *Don Giovanni*, whose eponymous hero exemplifies the aesthetic state.

NIETZSCHE views art as the final goal in the aesthetic REDEMPTION of modernity. Such is announced in *The Birth of Tragedy*, which describes the death of tragedy at the hands of the philosophical temperament of Socrates. The crisis of modernity stems from the fruitless search for metaphysical certitude intrinsic to the philosophical and scientific PROJECT. Its failure leads to the anxiety and indecision, later defined as NIHILISM, symbolized by Hamlet. In contrast, the tragic WISDOM of the Greeks, guided by the Apollonian WILL to form and the Dionysian impulse to dissolution, avoids such metaphysical speculation, remaining attached to the WORLD, though also acknowledging its precariousness. A return to the VALUES of the tragic is a means to avert the oncoming nihilistic crisis; the operas of Richard Wagner constitute a rebirth of Greek artistic culture. In later writings Nietzsche distances himself from Wagner, most dramatically in *Nietzsche contra Wagner*. However, the ideas of *The Birth of Tragedy* become, in altered form, the basis of his mature theory of art. At the heart of his work is the idea of KNOWLEDGE as metaphor, whereby perceptual experience is transformed by a series of metaphoric leaps from heterogeneous spheres into linguistic concepts. Knowledge has therefore, at best, a tenuous hold on reality; indeed, the idea of reality is a linguistic construct. Western philosophy has persistently misrecognized this fact, seeing concepts as corresponding to existing entities and not recognizing the metaphoric artistry involved in the construction of concepts. In contrast, art never loses sight of the constructed NATURE of knowledge and thus remains tied to surface APPEARANCES. It is the counter to PHILOSOPHY, RELIGION, and science. We have art so as not to perish from the TRUTH or from the obsession with truthfulness.

Heidegger values art for its disclosing a world. In his essay "The Origin of the Work of Art," he holds that art is the setting-into-work of truth. Since art could not come into being without LANGUAGE, it is essentially poetry. Such is not to be taken literally. Rather, art is poetry in that it acts as a locus where beings and BEING can emerge. Heidegger recalls the Greek term "poiesis," interpreted as "bringing forth." Art thus names beings and in so doing brings them into unconcealment. Underpinning Heidegger's view is his notion of poetic language, which resists the abstract circulation of ideas in metaphysical discourse. His essay "The Question Concerning Technology" outlines the Enframing, which is of the essence of technology and increasingly governs Western thinking. Enframing treats the world as a resource, or standing reserve, to be used. It subordinates everything to the demands of calculative reason and is consequently blind to the concrete singularity of things, their thingliness. Art stands outside this Enframing; it allows entities to appear in their true character. Van Gogh's painting of a pair of peasant shoes discloses the Being of the shoes, their essentially equipmental nature. Heidegger does not treat art as merely a true representation; art discloses the truth of the thing, the thing's general ESSENCE. Thus, the sculpture of a GOD in the temple of Aphaia at Aigina is not a simple likeness; rather, it makes the god be present.

Implicit in the manner of the artwork's bringing forth of the specific being is the bringing forth of an entire world that eludes the grasp of technological reason. Hence, art has a profound historical role; it discloses the essence of things, thereby opening up an entire historical world. In the Middle Ages beings were disclosed as God's creation, only later to be displaced by the notion of things as calculable, measurable OBJECTS. Consequently, true art's nature stems from the fact that it founds a world, rather than imitating the things disclosed in it. Art is historical not only in that it has a history but also because it grounds HISTORY; it founds a world. Today, art has a very particular historical resonance; it is involved in a struggle to wrest the world from the Enframing of technical reason.

In two essays, "Cezanne's Doubt" and "Eye and Mind," MERLEAU-PONTY explores the manner in which painting replicates one's primordial, that is, prereflective and prescientific, encounter with the world. Central to his thought is the role of the BODY as the basis of experience; the subject is always an embodied subject, and experience consists of the intertwining of the environment and the body, with its motor dispositions and habits. The embodied subject is always in the world, enjoying an aesthetic relation with the environment. Science and post-Cartesian metaphysics manipulate things and give up living in them. They see the world and others as alien objects, thereby misrecognizing the intimate intermeshing of SUBJECT and environment. In contrast, art, particularly painting, is truer to primordial, embodied experience, since it mimics the functioning of the body. Indeed, the key is the dependence of vision on the body, not merely through the physiological basis of the eyes but also by virtue of the fact that the world becomes visible through the body's moving in, and engaging with, the world. Painting repeats this intertwining of subject and world. The idea of art as a detached, purely optical rendering of the visible should be dismissed. By lending one's body to the world, the artist changes the world into paintings. It is impossible to imagine a disembodied painter. Central features of painting such as the rendering of SPACE and the use of light and color all function by way of the bodily echo they produce, an echo that would be meaningless to the disembodied subject of the Cartesian tradition.

As an expression of the subject's carnal living in the world, the painting possesses the same qualities as the expressive gestures of the human body. The whole body is the center of the perceptual encounter. Likewise, the painting is a totality, comprehended not as an aggregate of parts but as a whole; any separation of lines, colors, depth, or movement as elements of the painting is artificial, since all are dependent on each other. Merleau-Ponty mentions many artists—Delaunay, Matisse, Klee, Ingres, and Leonardo—yet his admiration is given to Cezanne. Cezanne is a philosopher in paint, attempting to render the experience of the visible, much as Merleau-Ponty is trying to describe it.

SARTRE's thought on art is directed primarily to LITERATURE, such as in his studies of Flaubert and Genet, in which he focuses on the creative tension between the objective forms of language and its use as the expression of an individual existence. He also deals with the dialectics of subjectivity, as expressed in the lives of these writers, in the manifold mediations of intersubjective relations by the social institutions of marriage, the family, and others. He wrote essays on artists such as Calder, Giacometti, and Tintoretto, but without any consistency of method. His essay on Tintoretto adopts a similar approach to his study of Flaubert, whereby attention is given to Tintoretto's place at the point of intersection of the different social, political, and art historical forces at work. In his essay on Giacometti, the near obsession in Giacometti's work with the representation of isolation and NOTHINGNESS is interpreted as emblematic of the creative imagination, which always works by negating its objects, assuring their irreality. In none of his writings is a coherent theory of art offered. Indeed, when dealing with the question of literature and commitment, Sartre expresses unease with writers who attempt anything other than a clear articulation of the real.

JOSÉ ORTEGA Y GASSET's essay "The Dehumanization of Art" offers both a theory of art and a critique of modern art as having come adrift from its moorings in human existence. At the root of his thinking is the primacy of lived experience embodied in SITUATIONS, PERSONS, things, all of which are invested with a profound engagement, be it emotional or practical. Thus, the aspect under which I first experience an apple is that in which I see it when I am about to eat it; all other ways of experiencing it are derived from that first engagement. In contrast science and philosophy require the suspension of such engagement. Art, which normally is grounded in the lived, has in the modern period become increasingly dehumanized; it has adopted the same inhuman attitude toward its object characteristic of the sciences. This dehumanization is manifest in, for example, the tendency of modern art to strive for mathematical purity, which is interpreted as a revulsion of living bodies. Likewise, dehumanization occurs in the adoption of ironic self-reflection, which strips away all elements of human pathos from an art that no longer takes itself seriously. Ironically, while modern art has lost its contact with the lived reality of its creators, it has thereby become more purely artistic, since attention is given to aesthetic form alone.

Although significant differences obtain between thinkers, the common pattern within existentialist thought on art is the idea of art as an expression of primary, prereflective engagement with the world.

Primary Works

Heidegger, Martin. *Poetry, Language, Thought*. Trans. Albert Hofstadter. New York: Harper and Row, 1971.

Kierkegaard, Søren. *Either/Or*. Vol. 1. Trans. David F. Swenson and Lillian Marvin Swenson. Princeton: Princeton University Press, 1959.

Nietzsche, Friedrich. *The Birth of Tragedy and The Case of Wagner*. Trans. Walter Kaufmann. New York: Vintage Books, 1967.

Bibliography

Johnson, G., ed. *The Merleau-Ponty Aesthetic Reader*. Evanston, IL: Northwestern University Press, 1993.
Lacoue-Labarthe, Philippe. *Heidegger, Art and Politics*. Trans. Chris Turner. Oxford: Basil Blackwell, 1990.

AUTHENTICITY
Thomas R. Flynn

HEIDEGGER introduces the term *Eigentlich*, rendered authentic, proper, or ownmost, to denote the condition of gathering one's EXISTENCE from its dissipated immersion in the WORLD of the THEY into one's most proper way of BEING. He denies the term moral significance; it is a purely descriptive expression. Yet he clearly advocates authentic existence and disvalues inauthenticity. The inauthentic PERSON is in flight from individuating CHOICES, especially from being-unto-death, one's ownmost possibility. Authenticity may be achieved but never permanently attained, because DASEIN is inevitably immersed in the average everyday and is continuously drawn toward the inauthentic.

The moral use of authenticity is clearer in the writings of SARTRE, who mentions the term in *Being and Nothingness*; an extensive discussion occurs in *Anti-Semite and Jew* and in his posthumously published *Notebooks for an Ethics*. In the former, authenticity means having a true and lucid CONSCIOUSNESS of the SITUATION, assuming the RESPONSIBILITY and risks it involves, accepting it in pride or humiliation, sometimes in horror and hate. There is a comprehensive aspect to authenticity: the concept of situation expands in the course of Sartre's writings to include all persons; you cannot live authentically without choosing FREEDOM for all. Authenticity carries a conative aspect: you own this choice, along with the self that results from it. Affirming the CONTINGENCY of your identity and VALUES and their dependency on your sustaining choice is what Sartre and BEAUVOIR mean by choosing freedom. The *Notebooks* associates authenticity with abandonment of the category of appropriation in which we seek to possess our reflected identities, our moral selves, as if we were things among things. The authentic person takes responsibility for the fact that he or she could act otherwise. Such a person repudiates the categories of being and having for that of doing. Moreover, the authentic individual can escape the hellish circle of BAD FAITH and sincerity by forming relations with self and others according to the models of generosity and appeal-response that characterize our communication with others via a work of ART. Thus, authenticity implies a solidarity with the other that fosters his or her freedom.

Bad faith is a major form of inauthenticity. But inauthenticity has a wider application, for it extends to those who lack the courage of their convictions as well as to those who are in error concerning their situations—for example, the worker whose consciousness has not been raised. Most commonly, the inauthentic person lives in bad faith. Sartre adds that when a person identifies with objective moral values, one lapses into the SPIRIT of seriousness, a form of bad faith and of inauthenticity that masks the responsibility implicit in our value judgments. Perhaps, the model of an authentic individual is Jean Genet. Poet, playwright, homosexual, and convicted felon, Genet was constituted a thief, in Sartre's account, by the objectifying gaze of his foster parents. His authenticity at that stage consisted in turning the tables on the possessive society of his peasant guardians by choosing the being that they had imposed on him. He became the thief that they perceived, inverting the values that their respectable SOCIETY demanded of its members. Ever the outsider, Genet subsequently chose the fine arts as a kind of murder, to lure right-thinking persons into the realm of the imaginary, the world of nonbeing, of freedom, where he would invert their values and unmask the freedom from which they were in flight. Neither pure consciousness nor simple FACTICITY, Genet lived the tension of pursuing both at once. Later, both Sartre and Beauvoir admitted the extreme difficulty of existing authentically in an inauthentic society. Both authors accepted the Marxist theory of class struggle, by which possessive individualism, fetishized commodities, and the like necessitate a society of exploitation, oppression, and self-deception. Only with the advent of a socialism of abundance could we expect an ETHICS of fraternity to be generally possible. In the meantime, we must rest content with an ethic of disalienation whereby we work to effect socioeconomic changes that will make objectively possible authentic choices.

In theistic existentialism, authenticity retains the characteristics of TRUTH, situation, and acceptance, but the object of these RELATIONS has changed. The individuating act is one of faithfulness or commitment to an Other or Thou. Such entails a LIFE of what MARCEL calls creative fidelity, not slavish rule-following, which would be inauthentic. BUBER speaks of the I–Thou relationship, as distinct from the impersonal I–It relation, that should emerge in encounters with others and with GOD. For both thinkers authentic interpersonal relations are dialogical, not manipulative or pragmatic.

Primary Works

Buber, Martin. *The Knowledge of Man.* Trans. Maurice Friedman and Ronald Gregor Smith. New York: Harper and Row, 1965.

Sartre, Jean-Paul. *Anti-Semite and Jew*. Trans. George J. Becker. New York: Schocken, 1974.

BAD FAITH
Thomas R. Flynn

In SARTRE's ONTOLOGY, this form of self-deception is based on the profound duality of in-itself/for-itself, of FACTICITY/TRANSCENDENCE, respectively, that characterizes human reality. Because I do not coincide with myself, because of the inner distance that marks CONSCIOUSNESS in relation to itself, I am able to lie to myself about the tension that this radical division entails. This truncated ignorance, an ignorance that knows better, can assume two forms: either I collapse transcendence into facticity (the more common case), or I volatilize facticity into transcendence. Sartre offers the example of the perfect waiter, who tries to be a waiter the way a stone is a stone. The ontological reality coupled with the self-transparency of prereflective consciousness brings it about that the waiter's attempt to efface his FREEDOM is in vain, and he is aware of doing so. This denial of RESPONSIBILITY is typical of the bad faith that infects all forms of determinism. Less common is the attempt to deny my facticity, as if I could live in the dreamworld of wish. This bad faith ignores the givens of my situation: my past choices, my embodiedness and what it entails. Both forms of self-coincidence fail, because consciousness is always aware of what it attempts to conceal. Although Sartre claims in *Being and Nothingness* that good faith is just another form of bad faith, in his posthumously published *Notebooks for an Ethics* he speaks of good faith as the positive acceptance of the choice to live the tension between facticity and freedom.

Primary Work

Sartre, Jean-Paul. *Notebooks for an Ethics*. Trans. David Pellauer. Chicago: University of Chicago Press, 1992.

SIMONE DE BEAUVOIR
(1908–1986)
Sonia Kruks

Simone de Beauvoir was born in Paris and resided there most of her life. After World War II she became a major figure in the WORLD of letters. Although some of her fame emanated from her association with SARTRE, she established herself as an intellectual presence in her own right as the author of several novels as well as philosophical and other nonfiction work—the most enduring has been her pathbreaking study of women, *The Second Sex*. Beauvoir's parents raised her as a Catholic, expecting that she would make a conventional marriage. A fall in her family's fortune made it impossible for her father to furnish a dowry, and Beauvoir was encouraged to study so that she could support herself as a teacher. She was among the first group of women to be allowed to study at the Sorbonne and to take classes at the École Normale Superieure. She taught PHILOSOPHY until 1943. As a student at the École Normale, Beauvoir met Sartre. Their initial free LOVE affair turned into a deep friendship that continued until Sartre's death in 1980. After World War II, with Sartre and a group of intellectuals that included MERLEAU-PONTY, CAMUS, and Aron, Beauvoir founded the journal *Les Temps Modernes* and published numerous articles in it.

Apart from several novels, a play, and short stories, Beauvoir wrote extensive nonfiction: political essays, travelogues, a study of old age, two volumes on ETHICS, *The Second Sex*, a multivolumed autobiography. The posthumous publication of volumes of letters that Sartre and Beauvoir wrote to each other has put into question the honesty of parts of the autobiography. Beauvoir regarded herself as developing applications of Sartre's philosophy, rather than being an original thinker. Her novels and major works draw on Sartre's insights. Pervasive Sartrean themes in her work include the centrality of FREEDOM to human EXISTENCE, RESPONSIBILITY for the VALUES we create, the possibility of BAD FAITH and inauthenticity. However, there are also significant shifts of emphasis within her work that make it more original. These include an account of freedom that concedes more POWER to SITUATIONS to shape freedom and an emphasis on intersubjectivity and social equality as necessary for a meaningful freedom.

Sartre ended *Being and Nothingness* with a promise to write a future volume that would develop ethical implications. In *Pyrrhus et Cineas*, written while *Being and Nothingness* was in press, Beauvoir addressed some of those ethical implications. The first part of the book follows Sartre in arguing that the world can have meaning only insofar as I act upon it as a freedom and make it mine. Whether I choose to go out and conquer the world, as Pyrrhus wished to do, or follow the advice of Voltaire's Candide to stay home and cultivate my garden, there are no preestablished connections between the world and myself. Nothing is decided before I act. Through my PROJECT, I take possession of the world, and values become possible. The second part goes beyond *Being and Nothingness* and argues that not all situations are equal from the point of view of freedom; inequality in the world matters to me, even if my own situation is privileged. My freedom is not wholly my own affair. A world in which other persons are less free than I am is a world in which the meaning of my actions becomes limited, for although I create meaning through my project, it can only endure beyond the moment, only escape being ephemeral, through being taken up in the projects of others. If my freedom cannot be meaningful except in interdependence with other freedoms, it must concern me that their situations be equal to mine. Others cannot assist in perpetuating my TRANSCENDENCE unless they are peers. Thus, I must attempt to create for all humans situations that will enable them to accompany and surpass my transcendence. Concretely, each PERSON must have access to the means of satisfying basic human needs, so that freedom does not consume itself in fighting sickness, ignorance, or misery.

In *The Ethics of Ambiguity* Beauvoir went further, asking what might be the responsible use of freedom in my conduct toward others. Human existence is profoundly ambiguous: while I am, indeed, a freedom, a pure internality against which external forces have no hold, I also experience myself as an OBJECT vulnerable to exterior forces. As CONSCIOUSNESS and BODY, SUBJECT and object, humans are both separate and interdependent. They have the capacity to support or to negate each other's freedom, to empower or to oppress each other. Social life is a realm of ambiguity because what I will do is never predetermined but is a result of my decisions and the values I create. Beauvoir paints a series of portraits of social actors in bad faith who attempt to evade responsibility. The serious man seeks to deny his freedom by subordinating himself to what he claims are absolute values or inevitable situations; he puts nothing into question and may become the ally of dictators and fanatics. When disappointed, the serious man can become the nihilist who, nihilating his own existence, rejects other existences that confirm him. Similarly, the adventurer and the passionate man deny the freedom of others. All such forms of bad faith fail to realize that we find a justification for our own existence only through that of others. To wish yourself free is to wish others free.

An authentic freedom chooses to realize itself in projects that unfold concrete possibilities for others: participation in science, artistic activity, or involvement in struggles for political freedom and equality. However, even such projects can be lived in bad faith. For example, in the name of an ideal of freedom, Marxism may descend into the serious, denying personal responsibility for EVIL by claiming that actions are justified by a supraindividual historical necessity. Only through fully accepting our finitude and contingency—the ambiguity of human existence—can the pursuit of freedom avoid congealing into its opposite: oppression. While many evade freedom and choose seriousness in bad faith, for the oppressed seriousness is an imposed condition. Slaves, those living under colonial regimes, and many women may be forced to live in such a restricted, infantilized situation that they cease to have the awareness that they are oppressed. Denied an open future by their oppressors, they are cut off from the possibility of transcendence. For such people, living is only not dying; human existence ceases to be more than an absurd vegetation. Ultimately, oppression is self-defeating, for the oppressors' actions undermine their own freedom. But oppressors do not usually give up privileges unless forced to do so. Thus, to extend the domain of freedom, you must help to create the conditions in which it is possible for the oppressed to comprehend and to resist their oppression.

The Second Sex is a case study of the oppression of women by men. The social inequality of women is not a natural or inevitable phenomenon. Although biological differences between the sexes are real, they have no intrinsic significance. Only when they are taken up and given meaning by men do they become a factor in women's oppression. Beauvoir criticizes Freudian accounts of women's psychological development as necessarily different from men's and rejects Engels' explanation of women's oppression as emerging inexorably from the development of private property. These explanations deny the role of human choices and values. The main source of women's oppression lies in the desire of men to assert themselves as subjects by defining women as their Other and reducing them to objects. A profound asymmetry emerges: woman is defined with reference to man, but not vice versa. Man is the subject, the absolute, against which woman is always judged and found to be lacking. Although it is ubiquitous in human HISTORY and in the contemporary world, the denial of women's subject-hood is not inevitable. The tendency to objectify other humans is in bad faith and is ultimately self-defeating. The self defines itself in its relations to others, yet such a self-definition does not have to be hostile. It can involve mutual recognition and respect—reciprocity between subjects—which has consistently been denied women. Woman's construction as man's Other— especially the identification of her existence with her sex—is the source of her oppression.

Volume 1 of *The Second Sex* examines the way men have constructed woman as their Other from prehistoric times to the modern period, from mythic and religious consciousness to exemplars of modern LITERATURE. As man's Other, woman is both feared and despised. She must be controlled. A world is created for her in which the free transcendence of which all humans are capable is difficult, at times impossible, to attain. Men constructed for woman a situation in which she discovers herself to be a free subject who is condemned always to live as an object. Volume 2 turns to an examination of the subjective experience of this situation: one is not born a woman; one becomes one. Drawing extensively on women's writings and voices recorded in memoirs and in psychiatrists' notebooks, she gives a composite account of what it feels like to grow up and live one's life as a female Other—to live a continual and painful contradiction between one's freedom and one's femininity. In this situation bodily and practical constraints very often deny women the grasp upon the world that is necessary for acts of transcendence.

Faced with an oppressive situation, different CHOICES are available to all but the most oppressed women. Many choices involve complicity with the oppressors, forms of bad faith. It may be less painful to accept one's objectification than continually to live the contradiction between freedom and IMMANENCE. In their versions of seriousness, many women try to escape the pain of their situation by assuming the role of sex object or by claiming as their own the irrationality and irresponsibility that men attribute to them. They choose feminine attributes: frivolity, flirtatiousness, docility. Others engage in RESENTMENT, in which they blame their oppressors but engage in no effective resistance. Yet others flee into narcissistic, amorous, or mystical fantasies, thus evading responsible action in the world. For those who attempt authentically to choose freedom, success will always be partial. By exploring obstacles encountered by the would-be liberated woman, Beauvoir presents the weight of the oppressive situation. Oppression is a social problem. An authentic, individual pursuit of freedom is not enough: it must be supported by that of others and by wider social transformations, such as greater economic power for women. Nor can relations of good faith between individual men and women achieve full reciprocity in a world where individuals of different sexes are unequally situated. The liberation of women must be part of a wider movement to end inequality and oppression.

Beauvoir's literature explores freedom, responsibility, bad faith, AUTHENTICITY. Her first novel, *She Came to Stay*, is a fictionalized account of a three-person relationship that resembles Sartre's and her friendship with Olga Kosakiewicz. *The Mandarins* treats many personal and political issues faced by the group around *Les temps Modernes*. *The Blood of Others*, set in a Resistance group during the German occupation, questions my responsibility for the DEATH of others. Her play *Who Shall Die?*, set in a medieval town under siege, probes the value of lives: you cannot legitimately claim that some lives are more valuable than others, even in a situation where starvation threatens. In this play and other writings Beauvoir includes women as central protagonists. Later stories, *Les Belles images* and *The Woman Destroyed*, explore patterns of bad faith in women.

Primary Works

Beauvoir, Simone de. *The Ethics of Ambiguity*. Trans. Bernard Fretchman. New York: Citadel, 1970.
———. *The Second Sex*. Trans. H. M. Prashley. New York: Vintage, 1989.

Bibliography

Bair, Deirdre. *Simone de Beauvoir: A Biography.* New York: Simon and Schuster, 1990.
Schwarzer, Alice. *After ''The Second Sex'': Conversations with Simone de Beauvoir.*
Trans. Marianne Howarth. New York: Pantheon, 1984.

BEING
Rivca Gordon

Questions concerning Being first appear among pre-Socratic philosophers, especially Parmenides. Since then, Plato, Aristotle, Leibniz, Hegel, and others responded to questions concerning Being, which they linked to questions about GOD, man, WORLD, KNOWLEDGE, TRUTH, and other topics. Many existentialists discussed Being: HEIDEGGER and SARTRE at length but also BERDYAEV, MARCEL, BUBER, and others.

Heidegger devoted much thought to elucidating and coping with the question of Being, which he viewed as the fundamental question of PHILOSOPHY, since Being encompasses and sustains all beings and entities. Yet, Being eludes our thinking. Despite its centrality in the HISTORY of philosophy, he held, today the question of Being has been forgotten, neglected, enveloped by silence. Those metaphysicians who raised the question since Aristotle, have, like him, dealt with the being of beings and not with Being. Thus, raising the question of Being requires returning to the pre-Socratics and overcoming centuries of silence. Due to this silence, Being, which is closest to a PERSON, closer than all other beings, including God, has remained the most distanced. To relate to this closest and most distanced question, we should not destroy or negate METAPHYSICS. Rather, we must remain on, and open up, that path of metaphysics upon which the question of Being can be raised. Traversing this path may require a long journey confined to one thought, with the hope that eventually Being will be illuminated.

In *Being and Time* Heidegger indicates that there *is* Being of beings, yet it differs from the meaning attributed to it in traditional metaphysics. In this tradition, Being was considered the most universal concept, yet such does not lead to a clear comprehension of Being. Being is not self-evident; it is most vague. One cannot define Being; in principle a definition must be derived from higher concepts, and no concept higher than Being exists. Nor is Being a plenitude of meanings, an object or substance with attributes, a logical abstraction, or a transcending of beings in the manner that transcendence is attributed to God. Categories applicable to beings cannot be applied to Being. In short, Being is not an entity and does not disclose itself in the manner that entities disclose themselves. Radical thinking that addresses the truth and meaning of Being can discover the open SPACE where the presence of beings and of Being is revealed. In that space Being is always the Being of beings. Basic ONTOLOGY reveals that the Being of an entity is partially disclosed in the defining, determining, and presenting of the essential characteristics of that entity; it already comprehends Being, even if very dimly. Only in such an ontology can the question of the Being of beings be directed to determining the a priori conditions for science, including its foundations. Put differently, in the manifold of entities within which humans exist, the question of Being asks about the unity and meaning of Being within this manifold, while always facing the dual, permanently interlinked presence of Being and beings.

DASEIN, the human entity, is the only entity through which the Being of beings can be disclosed. Being can be disclosed to Dasein, and only to Dasein, who has a preontological nearness to Being. Only Dasein can ask the question of Being. But when asking this question, Dasein is thrown back to the question who is Dasein, which can be answered by responding authentically and resolutely to the call to Dasein to realize a specific being. When Dasein responds thus to the call to realize one's being, the question of Being emerges to the foreground. Dasein is the only entity able to discuss, speak, understand its own being, which allows it to face authentically the meaning and truth of Being. Inauthentic Dasein is concerned with entities; the question of Being does not arise. When Dasein is authentic, Being can be disclosed, can become unconcealed; the Being of entities may show itself in its truth and in a manner that may be communicated to others. Through authentic LANGUAGE Dasein perceives its own Being and the Being of beings. Authentic seeing includes Dasein's longing to abide in truth and to wonder about Being; it is firmly linked to a striving for a resolute EXISTENCE and to CARE. The meaning of Being cannot be opposed to entities; rather, it is the ground that supports the entities; only as the ground of beings can Being reveal itself. Consequently, a phenomenological analysis of Dasein both leads to an understanding of Dasein and attains a grasp of the Being of beings. Still, Dasein's centrality in the possibility of raising the question of Being does not ensure that the question will be raised. It can be evaded. In daily life a person can flee the question of Being into inauthenticity and a life dictated by the inauthentic multitude, the THEY.

Only if Dasein exists are meaning and truth disclosed in their most primordial sense. Yet, it is not Dasein who presupposes truth. Rather, truth allows Dasein the possibility of presupposing, discovering, or understanding and, with it, the raising of the question of the Being of beings. The disclosing of truth is essential to the Being of beings. *Being and Time* attempts to show that the question of the truth and meaning of Being is linked to temporality, specifically, to Dasein as a being whose existential ontology is within TIME. Hence, the characteristics of Dasein's existence are revealed within temporality. Only when Dasein is resolute, active, and authentic can it face the question of Being and understand that the truth and meaning of the Being of beings are linked to temporality. Heidegger never answered the additional questions posed concerning the linkage of time and Being, nor did he complete his discussion of the link. Thus, the being of Dasein can disclose the foundation of the truth and the meaning of Being. This is one way of proceeding toward the goal of clarifing the question of Being. In writings after *Being and Time* Heidegger suggested other ways, through what can be disclosed by language, poetry, technology. Like the analytic of Dasein, every region of inquiry must seek a clear notion of Being. But his inquiries were never completed; they were on the way.

In *Being and Nothingness* Sartre suggested what can be described about Being with the help of a phenomenological ontology. The phenomenological approach grasps human CONSCIOUSNESS as ontologically central to any description of Being. It does not raise metaphysical questions. The question Why is there Being? does not enter the discussion; it is beyond what PHENOMENOLOGY investigates. Indeed, since human consciousness is always involved in Being, it can never see the totality of Being; hence, metaphysical questions lead to speculations. Being encompasses every thing that appears, every OBJECT of consciousness. There are two basic, linked realms of Being: Being-in-itself and Being-for-itself. Being-in-itself includes all beings that lack consciousness; Being-for-itself is the term Sartre uses for human consciousness. The linkage between the realms is not reciprocal. Being-in-itself is not dependent on consciousness, while consciousness is consciousness of something—very often of an entity from among the myriad of beings that constitute Being-in-itself.

Being-in-itself and Being-for-itself are separable only for the sake of inquiry. Through the relation of consciousness to it, Being-in-itself is determined as already there; it appears concretely as a world and as things in the world. Without consciousness, there is only Being, which is in-itself, forever what it is, and with no inclination to reveal itself to consciousness. Being-in-itself is limited by nothing, yet we sense its resistance; it is everywhere, yet we cannot touch it. Unnecessary, with no explanation, with no possibility to be its own cause, every being is contingent, for ETERNITY. Thus, there *is* only Being that can be disclosed, in various appearances, to a consciouness that is *not* this Being. Concretely, there are only Being and NOTHINGNESS, which allow Being and beings to appear and help to determine the basic relation between the two kinds of Being. Yet, Being-in-itself in its naked existence may sometimes appear to a person in the ecstasy of existential nausea. Being-in-itself without language, without names, meanings, determinations, relations, appears as already there: a pile of passive existents, an amorphic presence with no reason to be there, uncreated, with no change, with no relation either to itself or to what is not itself, opaque and full with itself; it is complete positivity and endless compression.

In contrast to Being-in-itself, consciousness is a total decompression of Being, a total emptiness of Being. Consciousness that achieves fullness of Being will no longer be consciousness. Consciousness is primordially a prereflective, immediate, spontaneous grasping *of* an object. It is directed toward an object that is other than itself and is a perpetual, concrete activity of negating Being, of transcending everything, including itself, toward Being. Being-in-itself is separated from consciousness by a film of Nothingness. If Being-in-itself is what it is, consciousness is what it is not: it is a being that is what it is not and is not what it is. Consciousness is very rarely present to the all of Being-in-itself. Yet, on the background of this all, consciousness, by an act of NEGATION, inscribes its being in the world and causes Being-in-itself to appear as a world with particular objects. Being-for-itself is an internal negation of this particular in-itself that the for-itself *is not*, on the background of Being. By inserting nothingness into the masses of Being, consciousness makes objects appear with their objective modes of being: causes, links, RELATIONS, order, quantity, temporality, potentiality, qualities. Being appears only through concrete appearances; every APPEARANCE points simultaneously toward this particular in-itself and to the ideal, unified synthesis of the totality, of the all of Being. Every effort of the for-itself to get closer to this ideal ends with the appearance of a world and things in the world that were already there as a pure collection of thises. Because Being is revealed as a resistance, as a coefficient of adversary, the for-itself can project itself toward the all of Being and, adding nothing to Being, without touching Being, bestow determinations and reveal a world and things in the world.

My prereflective comprehension of Being, Sartre holds, rejects any possibility of a radical dualism between the two realms of Being. Descartes' ontological proof is based on the reflective cogito, on knowledge that belongs to the second moment of the cogito. In contrast, consciousness has an immediate and concrete preontological, nonconceptual, but valid, understanding *of* Being. Even logically, you can refute the possibility of radical dualism between the two realms of Being. If Being *only is*, then, logically, Being necessarily precedes the being of the for-itself, which *is not* this being. To say that Being precedes the being of the for-itself means that *there is* another being—consciousness—that comes *after* Being in order to release it. We conclude that consciousness depends on Being and is supported by Being—which is not consciousness—and hence comes after Being. From a complementary perspective, dualism between the two realms of Being is rejected when Sartre suggests a metaphysical hypothesis. Through a single, unique modification, the for-itself emerged from Being-in-itself. A tiny nihilation caused a hole in the fullness of Being; by an absolute act of negation a part of Being established itself as for-itself. Being does not come from the for-itself. By self-negation or self-transcendence, the for-itself creates itself as fleeing from Being in order to be consciousness *of* Being, to be the assertion that there is Being. This assertion is a total upheaval: there is Being once there is another Being, the for-itself, which is not this Being, although it is immediately present to, and connected with, it by internal necessity and original relation.

Ontology cannot go beyond this determination: an endless, irreversible gap exists between the being of consciousness and Being-in-itself. However, the for-itself establishes a synthetic relation with the in-itself; it is an original project toward integration with Being-in-itself in order to create anew the totality of Being. The for-itself, which *is* a lack of Being and a constant transcendence beyond itself and everything else, desires to rid itself of the CONTINGENCY that characterizes its Being. It strives to eradicate the nothingness that separates itself and Being in order to reunite with the in-itself—while conserving itself as for-itself. Its *passion* is to gain the identity of Being and non-Being, of realizing itself as the Being-in-itself-for-itself. But this passion is a vain effort, a self-contradiction. This useless passion toward Being causes Being to be there. While Being does not need consciousness in order to be, without the latter, Being is only an abstraction. This passion shows that ontologically it is not possible to eliminate the gap that slipped into Being, that is, to reunite the two kinds of Being. It is impossible to eradicate the dual aspect of Being and Nothingness.

Berdyaev rejects any science of Being. A philosophy that posits Being as its starting point or views Being as an object, substance, universal, or absolute— as its basic concept—is not true. Being is a product of rational thinking. He rejects ideas of existentialists, especially Heidegger, who pretend to create a new science of Being, an elementary ontology. True existentialism is closer to KIER-KEGAARD, DOSTOYEVSKY, and NIETZSCHE and must be antiontological, radically opposed to an intellectual system that posits a closed totality of Being and to an ontology that asserts the primacy of Being. Despite the total rejection of Being, Berdyaev admits that his philosophy shows, at least implicitly, a vague view of Being. He is willing to accept the title metaphysician, if his reservations about the so-called science of Being be acknowledged. A true and primary Being is only a personal existence, a SUBJECT with its concrete FREEDOM and its SPIRIT. Being that is separated from the person has no existence; it is unreality. Being as subject or personal existence is original; there is no need to understand it conceptually or to infer it. Being that is posited by objectivization or by rational thinking has a secondary status. Its supposed primacy leads to determinism, to the destruction of freedom. Personal existence is outside this Being; it is not subject to Being; it constitutes an opposition to, and a radical rebellion against, Being. Personal existence is an acknowledgment of the superiority of freedom.

Freedom is without a base; it is ungrounded and cannot be derived from Being. Freedom always includes something new that cannot be determined by Being. The origin of freedom is in the principle of its irrational MYSTERY or in the principle that precedes every ontological determination: the desire of man for God, who desires for man. Berdyaev was against the all-embracing unity of

Being of abstract ontology, the ontological proofs of traditional THEOLOGY about the existence of God, and the attempts to apply to God categories of Being. God *is*: God exists; we can relate to him only symbolically and existentially. God is only in the sense of spirit, in the sense of Being who acts from within the principle of freedom and CREATIVITY. Berdyaev was criticized for positing an ontological and rational dualism that confirms the existence of two unrelated and disparate realms of Being: of humans and God. He answered that his radical personalism understands human existence only by relating to the unique character of a person and of God as PERSONALITY. Personal religious life occurs only when you stand in the presence of God and experience freedom as godly. Here is the deepest existential level, because here is revealed the concrete personality in its wholeness, as a microcosmos. Here is the spirit. Here dwells the mystery of the religious experience. God as a Being of spirit calls one to realize oneself to fulfill one's freedom and creative act as a response to God's creative act.

Thus, any effort to give personality characteristics of Being means its disappearance or its submission to the nonpersonal. This is ontological totalitarianism. In Berdyaev's radical ontology the human being is a personality, and God is a Being who is personality. Their Being as personality is revealed in the capacity to suffer, to love, to rejoice—in concrete existence with its contradictions. However, personality, whether of God or human, is never Being and does not share in Being. Being is always an objectivization, while personality belongs entirely to the subjective realm. These truths are at the basis of CHRISTIANITY, which stands on the principle of personalism.

Primary Work

Berdyaev, Nicolai. *Slavery and Freedom*. Trans. R. M. French. New York: Scribner's, 1944.

Bibliography

Allen, E. L. *Freedom in God: A Guide to the Thought of Nicolas Berdyaev*. New York: Philosophical Library, 1951.
Caputo, John. *The Mystical Element in Heidegger's Thought*. Athens: Ohio University Press, 1978.
Ellis, Robert Richmond. *The Tragic Pursuit of Being*. Tuscaloosa: University of Alabama Press, 1988.

BEING-IN-THE-WORLD
John Protevi

Being-in-the-world is HEIDEGGER's term for the immersed CHARACTER of DASEIN, or human EXISTENCE, insofar as it relates to BEING, in opening up the clearing in which beings can be encountered in meaningful RELATIONS. In *Being and Time* he analyzes the original, unitary phenomenon of Being-in-the-world into three constituent elements: (1) in the WORLD, (2) the being that is in the way of Being-in-the-world, (3) Being-in as such. He investigates the first element, in the world, under the rubric of the worldliness of the world. He distinguishes between being-present-at-hand, of OBJECTS just sitting there, and being-ready-to-hand, of tools ready to be picked up and used. Tools appear as tools when they unobtrusively fit into a system of references. This system of significant references makes up the worldliness of the world, which pivots on meanings projected by Dasein. The unity of the world is provided by the ultimate reference, Dasein, as that for the sake of which a tool is used in a PROJECT.

Dasein is the being that is in-the-world. Concerning Dasein, he asks, Who?, answered by an existential analysis, rather than the question, What?, which would be answered categorically. His answer investigates the way Dasein is with others. In the everyday, Dasein is submerged in the THEY, doing and thinking what they say is to be done and thought. Finally, Heidegger analyzes the Being of Dasein as it exists in the world, Being-in as such. He distinguishes three equiprimordial elements: moodfulness, understanding, and discourse. Moodfulness discloses Dasein's THROWNNESS, its being handed over to its existence as a not fully explicable task; understanding is the ability for Dasein to project its possibilities and thereby disclose partially meaningful future paths; and discourse is the underlying articulation of the world by projected meaning that allows for LANGUAGE as the performance of speech. The everyday Being-in-the-world of Dasein is falling, the inauthentic relation to Dasein's thrownness, in which idle talk corresponds to discourse, curiosity to moodfulness, and ambiguity to understanding.

Bibliography

Dreyfus, Hubert L., and Harrison Hall, eds. *Heidegger: A Critical Reader*. Oxford: Basil Blackwell, 1992.

BELIEF

Jacob Meskin

For KIERKEGAARD, Christian belief represents the ultimate stage of an individual's movement into the depths of one's own unique EXISTENCE. As a social BEING who shares a common reality with others, the individual must journey out of this condition along a path toward the inexpressibly personal TRUTH Christian belief brings. This belief is in a truth that exceeds conventional categories; it signifies the end point of an individual's uncertain and risky pilgrimage, one that leads you away from reliable, taken-for-granted things and carries you toward your innermost identity.

One of the most basic things I do in living a LIFE is to make choices. The publicly expressible factors I come up with when thinking about a CHOICE stop short of the idiosyncratic welling up of volition and action through which I concretely choose to do something. In this sense lived choice always involves what Kierkegaard calls inwardness, since my choice must spring from within me and only me. The reasons I may provide for a decision, which presumably help my choice make sense, still fail to capture my choice. I am always at least partially arbitrary, never completely determined by the objective reasons and causes I suggest to explain my choices. This distinction between reflection and lived life also crucially affects the understanding of TIME. When you think, you can assemble and arrange moments of time by reference to a rational order or necessary principle. From the perspective of reason we see each new moment in terms of the moment that immediately preceded it and how this earlier moment set the stage for the APPEARANCE of the new moment. But the arbitrary and individual features involved in making a choice cannot be reduced to elements of thought. Each moment of my life possesses an irreplaceable uniqueness: no single moment can be necessarily linked either to its predecessor or to its successor. Lived human time surges forth as a series of discrete, distinct moments, each new moment of the present enjoying something like a sovereign indifference to other moments. The present moment and the situation it defines are always radically open.

Yet we strongly resist this account of life, clinging to the reassuring, though falsified, picture of life that thought paints. We hide in the comforting, established concepts that thought uses to make decisions seem logical and determinable; we abide in the secure, ordered sequence of moments in necessary progression provided by thought. Religious belief may enter here. According to Kierkegaard, CHRISTIANITY offers a truth entirely different from that constructed by thought; it teaches a radical security, utterly distinct from the apparent safety found in familiar categories of thought. Christianity condemns our reliance on thought as the almost idolatrous elevation of a particular human capacity. It commands a way of life that cannot be coherently thought—it can only be lived. Reflection uses concepts to form intelligible, coherent experiences of which we can be conscious and which can be communicated. Dependence on reflection functions to mediate all experiences, forcing experience to be communicable, capable of being put into words, and temporally ordered. The truth of which Christianity speaks falls outside these mediations—it is immediate and does not and cannot have the characteristics of experiences mediated through reflection.

Kierkegaard's writings chart a life course whereby the individual gradually tries out and abandons different mediations, including that of thought, in order to come to have a direct experience of the being one is outside of reflective mediation. This deepest possible experience of self requires a relinquishment of reflection, a plunge into subjectivity beyond communication. At that point, an ultimately paradoxical juncture, religious belief becomes fully actualized in what he calls FAITH. Earlier moments of this life course make no reference to religious belief, even though they prepare the way. The three stages of progression are called aesthetic, ethical, and religious. In the AESTHETIC STAGE the individual attempts to find refuge in personal enjoyment and hedonism. Yet, even the most consistent and refined attempts at sheer enjoyment end in boredom and disappointment; using one's own personal pleasure as a standard generates a shifting, unstable, amorphous self-identity. In the ETHICAL STAGE, the individual obeys universally valid and binding ethical norms, yielding a stable, less idiosyncratic self. But ethics often fails to quiet the voice of FREEDOM. I may become aware that my choices are not necessitated, and they do not necessitate—I am free, even if the thought of the ethical stage tries to deny this.

A moment of ANGUISH may lead to the RELIGIOUS STAGE. Within the ethical stage, shared concepts and reflection connect you to others, but in the sphere of RELIGION, you directly contact the terrifying, yet reassuring, depths of your inexpressible subjectivity. IRONY and HUMOR may allow you, at times, to conceal your anguish. Yet, only when you have arrived at this vulnerable, indefensible, dangerous level of subjective life can you experience true faith. In an experience free of reflective shaping and conceptual protection, the Author of one's being becomes present. GOD is discovered in the immediacy of defenseless, naked selfhood; a grace-full pattern emerges from within, replacing your efforts to impose some kind of external form on life.

For BERDYAEV, the advent of Jesus points to a privileged kind of temporal moment: the inbreaking of the new, which represents a profound solution to the problem of dualism, reconciling the opposed worlds of matter and spirit. Instead of rejecting the plurality and change of the mundane world in favor of a higher, ideal unity or positing a gradual evolution of the material into the spiritual, he sees the spiritual bursting forth into the material in discrete moments. This is the new. The making of HISTORY, the work of genius, the achievement of politics and ETHICS all represent decisive spiritual transformations within the material WORLD. No evolution or comforting pattern guarantees these unforeseeable eruptions. This utterly unpredictable creative energy, which breaks forth into, and becomes, history, also resonates deeply within the individual, who can bring forth newness. The inward, lived dimension of temporal existence cannot be assimilated to scientific thought and may lead to religious belief and faith. Christ embodies the ultimate creative inbreaking of the new within both history and the individual.

MARCEL holds that you constantly create yourself by acts of fidelity, obligation, and commitment, thereby imparting to your life a distinctive pattern. These acts may seem incomprehensible when viewed from the perspective of rational, scientific reflection. Religious belief and the God it discloses provide an alternative framework within which to understand and validate the vital practices of fidelity and obligation. It seems that there could never be sufficient evidence to provide rational justification for making vows or promises. For it is possible that I will find myself in an emotional state in the future different from that which I now envision when I swear my unchanging devotion. Were I later to find myself in such a radically changed state, my continued fidelity to the other would become false, if not impossible. Yet, only from the stance of detached reflection, the successive moments of my life well up automatically one after the other naturally or mechanistically. From this external perspective it would seem problematic to make a promise at any particular moment, since this particular moment may well be succeeded by moments of a different CHARACTER. However, when I decide to vow fidelity to someone or something, I initiate an internal PROCESS that can influence and shape future moments so that they unfold in harmony with the decision I made.

Marcel emphasizes that the way in which you experience yourself as a creative PERSON must not be confused with the way you see yourself in reflection and analysis. This point is at the root of the distinction between problem and MYSTERY. A problem is properly approached and resolved through a scientific analysis of the component parts and factors involved. A mystery emerges in a situation in which the concrete existence of the person embodies the difficulty in his or her life. You cannot resolve a mystery through scientific analysis. Birth, fidelity, death, strife, love, conflict, and many other experiences challenge humans in ways that make scientific reflection inapplicable. We must understand faith, commitment, LOVE, belief, and grace as mysteries. Thus, you may discover God only in light of the risk undertaken in vowing fidelity to other humans, who may, of course, disappoint you. God is that ultimate Person who will never disappoint your fidelity and is, therefore, the root or ground of all the derivatives and fidelities in life. Faith in a person or cause refers to a primordial faith in God.

BUBER views religious belief as based on an experiencing of the WORLD different from analyzing and comprehending reality. Analytical reasoning is confined to the I–It and is vitally important if we are to understand the universe and ourselves. Yet the I–It is only one way of being. Another mode of existence is the I–Thou, a moment of grace in which I address and am fully present to the Other. I can relate as a Thou to a person, to a natural being, or to a spiritual reality. God is the Thou that can never become an It; he is the Eternal Thou: the One who endlessly addresses us. Relating to God as a Thou is the basis of religious belief. It is an addressing of God knowing that his presence is distinguished from the presence of things in the world.

Primary Works

Kierkegaard, Søren. *Training in Christianity*. Trans. Walter Lowrie. Princeton: Princeton University Press, 1967.
Marcel, Gabriel. *Creative Fidelity*. Trans. Robert Rosthal. New York: Farrar, Straus, and Giroux, 1964.

Bibliography

Bourgeois, Patrick. *The Religious within Experience and Existence*. Pittsburgh: Duquesne University Press, 1989.
Gordon, Haim, and Jochanan Bloch. *Martin Buber: A Centenary Volume*. New York: Ktav, 1984.

NICOLAS ALEXANDROVICH BERDYAEV (1874–1948)
Douglas Kellogg Wood

Berdyaev was born near Kiev of parents in the Russian nobility. Approaching adolescence, he experienced his first conversion, which led him to embrace PHILOSOPHY and the search for TRUTH and meaning. At the time he was attending the military academy of Kiev. He found military life disageeable, left the academy, and entered the University of Kiev, where he became an active Marxist. His growing disaffection from the mundane WORLD led him to adopt Fichte's philosophy, which he maintained simultaneously with his Marxist views. He believed in the GOD of objective idealism, a God struggling to achieve self-consciousness through historical TIME, who is more of an evolving moral principle than a transcendent deity. He addressed the apparent contradiction of accepting the Marxist theory of HISTORY and the ethical God of German Idealism in his first book, *Subjectivism and Individualism in Social Philosophy*, written while in exile in the province of Vologda. Berdyaev had joined a social democratic cell at the university, and after participating in that movement's first big demonstration in 1898, he was arrested and confined to northern Russia for two years.

After his exile Berdyaev moved to St. Petersburg to become coeditor (with Sergy Bulgakov) of the journal *New Way*. When this enterprise folded, he and Bulgakov associated themselves with the periodical *Problems of Life*, which was published into the early days of the Russian Revolution. Preoccupation with his spiritual struggle made Berdyaev oblivious to events leading to the 1905 revolution. His anguish and confusion were partially dispelled after the summer of 1907, when he experienced a second conversion, which delivered him from atheism—a term he now applied to Idealists as well as Marxists—and steered him into Russian orthodoxy. He later acknowledged in his book *Dostoievsky* that his turn to CHRISTIANITY would have been inconceivable without the great author's inspiration. Berdyaev welcomed the Russian Revolution in 1917 and participated in Kerensky's government. When that government was ousted in October, he supported the Bolsheviks, although he disagreed with their interpretation of RELIGION. His commitment to radical social change and his FAITH in the messianic vocation of the Russian people persuaded him that the economic and political policies of the Bolsheviks were (for the moment) essentially correct.

In 1918 Berdyaev established the Free Academy of Spiritual Culture in Moscow; two years later he was appointed to the chair of philosophy at the University of Moscow. Shortly thereafter he was arrested and subsequently exiled in 1922. With his wife, he went to Berlin, where he worked for the Young Men's Christian Association (YMCA) and founded an academy devoted to the study of religious philosophy. Four years later he moved to Paris, where he reestablished his academy, started a review, *The Way*, and met many leading intellectuals. After World War II, which he spent uneventfully in his home in Clamart, he resumed his educational work.

Berdyaev believed that the disastrous consequences of modern history were primarily the results of the Fall, of humankind's original severance from the divine—its loss of spiritual wholeness and subsequent enslavement in the space-time categories of an objectified world. This Fall had shattered humankind's primordial state of divine-human perfection and forced it to externalize and forsake the spiritual FREEDOM it enjoyed before the creation of the cosmos. Although humans may have fallen from God, every person can achieve REDEMPTION; men and women, who are created in the image of God, can achieve divineness. Redemption necessarily entails divinization. The primary obstacle and EVIL in the way of humankind's return to God is externalization, objectification, or thingification of the SPIRIT. When the spirit of humankind fell, it was objectified. EXISTENCE, in a sense, represents the lapse of the eternal into time, the transmogrification of timelessness into becoming. In its pure form, spirit is not concretely manifested; it is nonbeing rather than being. To avoid misunderstanding, we must distinguish between the traditional meanings of nonbeing. In Greek philosophy nonbeing was defined in two ways: as *ouk on* or *me on*, nonbeing that represents a complete negation of being and nonbeing that can enter into a dialectical relationship with being. Berdyaev uses nonbeing in the second sense: anything that is objective is ultimately unreal. BEING as objective reality—which is static, restrictive, and defining—is therefore devoid of reality. Spiritual or authentic reality is found in *me on* in dynamic meonic freedom. He denies the Parmenidean world of Being and the Platonic world of Forms or Ideas. The realm of Being is the objectified world of the Fall, which exists only as a painful illusion in the minds of PERSONS estranged from God.

Berdyaev's iconoclastic equation of Being with the phenomenal rests on his repudiation of essentialist philosophy and his aversion to ephemerality. It enabled him to dispose of ontological METAPHYSICS and empirical EPISTE-MOLOGY in one blow. To refute empiricism, he accepted Kant's conception of an active MIND that formulates the content of its thought and rejected the correspondence theory of truth. It rests on a passive conception of mind and a BELIEF that the external world of objects represents the ultimate source of reality and the sole criterion of validation. Though Kant remained agnostic about the noumenal world, Berdyaev used the noumena to undermine the empiricist's belief in the reality of the perceptual universe. The distinction between a phenomenal universe and an unknowable, noumenal dimension deprived phenomena of ultimate reality. It is possible to speak of the reality of the object-world in only a pejorative sense. This contention parallels the argument of post-Kantian idealists, who maintained that since noumena are ultimately real, it is misleading and useless to regard phenomena as constituents of KNOWLEDGE. While idealists thought that they could penetrate the inscrutable veil of the thing in itself by reason, Berdyaev believed that a priori logic prevented humankind from reaching spiritual reality. Reason distorted noumena. Only ecstasy and concrete mystical experience transcend the spatial and temporal limitations of the world of OBJECTS.

Berdyaev believed that discursive thought represents an aspect of humankind's fallen NATURE. He repudiates the a priori as the way to truth and emphasizes the importance of the individual, the SUBJECT, and the particular over the general, the object, the universal. Existence is prior to ESSENCE; a person's life is not predetermined by an abstract definition of humanity. This position dovetails with his belief that reality, including spiritual reality, can be described only in terms of potentiality, meonic freedom, or CREATIVITY. Humankind possesses a divine image and is a microcosm as well as a microtheos. Men and women are involved in a divine-human DRAMA and play a decisive role in realizing the return to ETERNITY. Both the Being of the idealist and the ephemeral, "blooming, buzzing confusion" of the empiricist were anathema to Berdyaev. Whereas the abstract reality of the ontologists implied the elimination of existence and the congealing of the spirit, the fluctuating universe of the anti-Eleatics entailed the equally inimical notion of DEATH—the inevitable exhaustion of all life forms in the devouring time-process. Since he believed in the eventual abolition of the objectified universe—since he had faith in an eschatological resolution of the historical PROCESS—he skillfully provided for the inevitable destruction of both the logical reality of the idealist and the empirical universe of the scientist.

Persons need not wait until the end of time to transcend the ontological limitations of the objectified world; a person can soar above the dimensions of the universe at a given moment, in the time-dissolving fire of creative ecstasy. Eternity or the Kingdom of God can be reached before the end of historical time because it is possible to transcend time by mystical intuition. Thus, there are two means of communing with eternity: through the absolute timelessness of the eternal present or the eschatological destruction of time at the end of the world. Berdyaev's conception of MYSTICISM, his belief in the possibility of transcending time in the intensity of the moments in an eternal now, derives from his notion of creativity. In *The Meaning of the Creative Act* he argued that creativity is a form of temporal TRANSCENDENCE, a way of liberation from the crushing absurdity of the universe. Creativity cannot be identified with its objectified product. Creative expression rises above the finite to the infinite; it is what the ancient Greeks termed an *ekstasis*, an experience of freedom from the mundane that leads to the eternal.

Humans possess a subconscious, a conscious, and, most significantly, a supraconscious. The subconscious, as a remnant of humankind's primitive biography, expresses itself in nondiscursive symbols and creates fantasies, dreams, and MYTHS. Berdyaev believed in the VALUE and, in some cases, in the reality of myth far more than in the products of reasoning. Verbal expression of concepts was analogous to the Fall of humankind. Just as the Fall externalized spirituality, the concrete articulation of thought in discursive symbols objectifies and debases the spirit. Words are divisive; they destroy the harmony and unity of religious insights by dividing them up into syntactical categories—subjects, objects, predicates. They are demonstrative of humanity's loss of WHOLENESS, of its disrupted and dissociated nature. Words take place in time, in the temporal process, which is likewise a reflection of the severed and shattered character of the objectified universe. Hence, conscious reasoning is far inferior to subconscious perception; unlike the symbols of dream and myth, rational thought is incapable of grasping reality in its entirety. Mythology, however, is not superior to the form of PERCEPTION of the supraconscious, which expresses itself in images and not only is capable of rendering a unitary vision of reality but can attain communion with eternity. The supraconscious carries on the creative activity that allows a person to transcend the limitations of the finite world.

Although creative ecstasy enables a person to transcend time and SPACE and to achieve communion with eternal Reality or God, it is ultimately an unsatisfactory experience: it allows an individual to escape from time only temporarily. Berdyaev, however, distinguished between two types of creativity. While insisting that all creative acts are eschatological and bring this world to an end, he differentiated between the temporary abolition of time, attained through mystical experience, and the permanent destruction of the temporal process achieved through the joint creative cooperation of God and humankind. The realization of the end of time—the creation of the supreme work of art—will mark the pinnacle of the divine–human partnership. All creative activity points in this direction. Our creative acts in the present participate in the existential time of the third, final phase of world history, an epoch of religious creativeness or aeon of the Holy Spirit. Creative ecstasy, which transcends time, happens in existential time. The results of every authentic creative act enter the Kingdom of God. Humankind's creative acts occur both in existential time—that timeless time of the last historical epoch that, though not identical with eternity, nevertheless participates in moments of eternity—and in the Kingdom of God, or eternity. The creative act takes place in existential time as well as eternity because it is assigned a special role in the historical drama. It permits humankind to destroy time in the depth of the moment and prepares the way for a spiritual transformation that will be marked by an awareness of supraconsciousness. Creativity is a transforming agent that effects the awakening of supraconsciousness—a spiritual awakening that enables human beings to create, with God's help, the third, final epoch of world history, the Age of the Spirit. Creativity includes eschatological energy that allows humankind to transcend time in the immediate present. The creative act participates in existential time as well as the Kingdom of God: it is united with the final epoch through creative anticipation and preparation of the irrevocable end of time and joined to God, or eternity, through personal, mystical communion.

In *The Meaning of the Creative Act*, Berdyaev believed that the third, or creative, epoch of world history was at hand. Subsequently, he revised his optimism. Although he may have lost hope for the immediate realization of a creative religious epoch, he insisted that after his ecstasy in writing *The Meaning of the Creative Act*, he never lost faith in the creative vocation of humankind. Even though spirit had been degraded into objectivity on every level of existence—psychological, ontological, and social—Berdyaev fervently believed that by sharing in the creative nonbeing of God, by turning from the objective world of actualized being to living meonic freedom, humans could prepare the way for a new outpouring of the spirit that would end spiritual alienation and objectification. To realize this new era, humankind must change the present structure of its CONSCIOUSNESS. At the moment, PERSONALITY is enslaved in the external world. To free themselves, humans must become persons as opposed to individuals. A person prevents the objectification of one's CONSCIENCE and judgment. The individual, on the other hand, has lost one's religious moorings, has compromised with collective society, and, hence, has lost one's spiritual dignity. Individuality is a state of incompleteness, a condition of slavery in which temporal obsessions, cravings, and revulsions of the EGO eclipse spirituality. Personality is the spiritual wholeness that accompanies religious enlightenment or the awakening of supraconsciousness. This spiritual condition characterizes the existence of a person who has renounced exclusive attachment to material objects by grounding one's life in God. A person, in contrast to an individual, is ultimately free—undetermined by forces of objectified existence. Within the context of the temporal world the person is a law unto oneself.

The complexity of modern SOCIETY has externalized personality by creating spiritually deracinated individuals. Berdyaev recognized that humans needed society for the practical necessities of life and developed a theory of society that preserved the integrity of personalism. He distinguished between collective socialism, which makes the state and society supreme over the personality, and personalist socialism, which is established on the unconditional predominance of the personality over state and society. In the latter, the personality preserves its freedom and dignity, while living in communion with others. Personalist socialism maintains that economics can be socialized, whereas the spiritual life cannot. While personalist socialism is the model of a society free enough to preserve spiritual integrity, it is not a perfect society, since nothing in time or the objectified universe can attain that state of perfection. Although perfection is realizable only outside the phenomenal universe, the establishment of a personalist society, a communality of spiritually free humans, is of central importance for the resolution of the divine–human drama as a staging ground for the return to eternity—for the realization of the age of the spirit and the achievement of the End of the historical process.

Berdyaev's apocalyptic theory of history drew inspiration from the Russian eschatologist Nicolas Fedorov and the Calabrian monk Joachim of Floris, who interprets history as a trinitarian drama. Three historical dispensations occur within three successive epochs, each identified with a member of the Trinity: the Father, Son, and Holy Ghost. The last epoch is now beginning and is proceeding toward the end of history and the triumph of spiritual freedom. This temporal genealogy is similar to Berdyaev's scheme in which the first epoch, the age of the Father, is identified with the Old Testament and corresponds to the first stage of revelation. The second epoch, the Age of the Son, is identified with the New Testament and the second stage of revelation. A third epoch, the aeon of the Holy Spirit, corresponds to the last stage of eschatological revelation and is characterized by apocalyptic expectation. It prepares the world for a return to eternity by achieving the meonic freedom of humanity and ushering in the Kingdom of Heaven. Berdyaev's philosophy of history, however, rests upon a critical analysis and complex interpretation of time: cosmic, historical, existential.

Cosmic time measures the movement of the planets around the sun. It is the universal metric from which calendars and clocks are derived; its symbolic image is the circle. Historical time, which is composed of unique, unrepeatable events, can be spatialized into periods (ages, centuries, millennia). Its symbol is a line moving into the future. Existential time is not susceptible to calculation. Within this special form of time creative ecstasy occurs, which includes the mystical transcendence of cosmic and historical time. It is symbolized by the point, which suggests the profundity of spiritual freedom. Berdyaev believed that the future Aeon, the new Spiritual epoch of the Holy Ghost, would occur in existential time, not in the cosmic or historical time that characterized the Ages of the Father and the Son. This imminent Age of the Spirit lies in the future. It is to be preceded by our stage of Godforsakenness, by the mechanization and secularization of life, and by transition through a period of atheism. Yet, we are swiftly approaching ''the beginning and the end'' and must not despair. Humans may still exist in time; they may be forced to suffer the horrors of historical tragedies in the future. But if they can create a society anarchic enough to preserve spiritual integrity, and if they accept the burden of freedom that demands the end of time, they will be able to participate in the meonic freedom of God and to receive the Aeon of the Spirit. They will overcome their personal dichotomies; they will regain their androgynous spirituality, their pneumocentricity—as all manifestations of the objectification of spirit cease to exist.

Thus, Berdyaev, while believing that we are fallen spirits, degraded souls enmeshed in the net of objectivity, still believed that humankind, by spiritually regenerating itself, by changing the structure of its consciousness, could prepare for, and achieve, a much better world in which persons would not have to compromise the integrity of their spirit.

Primary Work

Berdyaev, Nicolai. *The Meaning of the Creative Act*. Trans. Donald Lowrie. New York: Collier, 1962.

Bibliography

Allen, E. L. *Freedom in God: A Guide to the Thought of Nicolas Berdyaev*. New York: Philosophical Library, 1951.
Clarke, Oliver Fielding. *Introduction to Berdyaev*. London: Geoffrey Bles, 1957.
Wood, Douglas, K. *Men against Time: Nicolas Berdyaev, T. S. Eliot, Aldous Huxley, and C. J. Jung*. Lawrence: University Press of Kansas, 1982.

LUDWIG BINSWANGER
(1881–1966)
Roger Frie

Binswanger was born in Kreuzlingen, Switzerland. He attended the universities of Lausanne, Heidelberg, and Zurich and received his medical degree from the University of Zurich in 1907. He trained as a psychiatrist under Eugene Bleuler and Carl Jung at the Burgholzli Hospital in Zurich and became acquainted with the burgeoning field of psychoanalysis. In 1907 he accompanied Jung to meet Sigmund Freud. From 1910 to 1956 Binswanger directed the Bellvue Sanatorium in Kreuzlingen, which was founded by his grandfather.

Binswanger was initially attracted to psychoanalysis because of the insights it provided into human EXISTENCE and behavior. However, he was critical of the protophysiological basis on which Freud's drive theory and models of the mind were based. While Binswanger did not question the explanatory potential of natural science, he sought to develop an account of human existence that was not reductionist. He wished to formulate a philosophical as well as scientific basis for psychoanalysis, holding that PERSONALITY could not be wholly accounted for in terms of PROCESS, functions, or occurrences determined by natural causality. His objective was to understand and explain humans in the totality of their existence, not simply as natural OBJECTS constructed from various parts. HUSSERL's PHENOMENOLOGY provided Binswanger with a method to explain the visual reality of the mentally ill person. It was, however, HEIDEGGER's *Being and Time*, especially its fundamental ONTOLOGY, that enabled Binswanger to develop a philosophically oriented approach to psychiatry that could account for the PERSON's total existence.

Heidegger argued that DASEIN is neither autonomous nor self-contained but always already situated in the WORLD. Dasein exists as BEING-IN-THE-WORLD. For Binswanger, this conception of humans and world provided the psychiatrist with a key conceptual tool for understanding and describing human experience. He enlarged Heidegger's ontological conception of the world to include the horizon in which humans live and through which they understand themselves. Binswanger recognized three simultaneous modes of being-in-the-world: the *Umwelt*, constituting the environment within which a person exists; the *Mitwelt*, or world of social relations with other persons; and the *Eigenwelt*, the private world of self. The three modes together constitute a person's world-design—the context of meaning within which a person exists. For Binswanger, the main goal of psychopathology was to achieve KNOWLEDGE and scientific description of the world-designs of persons. In the first of his existential analytic studies, *Traum und Existenz*, he described dreams in terms of the dreamers' world-designs, rather than psychic processes. Similarly, in his studies on schizophrenia, he used the notion of world-designs of patients to elaborate manic experiences and the spatial and temporal structures of schizophrenic existence.

Binswanger also criticized Heidegger, specifically in his chief work, *Grundformen und Erkenntnis menschlichen Daseins*. He held that Heidegger's treatment of the interhuman dimension in *Being and Time* failed to account for the role of humans in the achievement of AUTHENTICITY and entirely omitted the importance of interpersonal LOVE. Heidegger's failing lay in his holding that Dasein achieved authenticity in isolation from others. Binswanger's specific concern was to show that self-realization could be achieved through reciprocity in relationship with another person. He turned to BUBER's writings on the nature of relation, especially to *I and Thou*, for a basis for his theory of intersubjectivity. Following Buber, Binswanger emphasized the dialogical NATURE of human existence. Such allowed him to develop a theory, beginning from Heidegger's thinking, with a phenomenology of love, that describes the possibility of a love relationship based on equality and mutuality. He applied this theory in his psychoanalytic work and also influenced other existentialists such as MERLEAU-PONTY.

Primary Work

Foucault, Michel, and Ludwig Binswanger. *Dream and Existence*. Ed. Keith Hoeller. Atlantic Highlands, NJ: Humanities Press, 1993.

Bibliography

May, Rollo, Ernest Angel, and Henri F. Ellenberger, ed. *Existence: A New Dimension in Psychiatry and Psychology*. New York: Basic Books, 1958.

BODY
Constance L. Mui

Existentialists reject the Cartesian mind–body split, which regards the body simply as "res extensa," an OBJECT among objects in the WORLD. They dismiss as unintelligible any ontological notion of a pure MIND that would exist apart from the body. For existentialists, the body, as it is lived, is thoroughly intertwined with CONSCIOUSNESS and can never be reduced to an object for consciousness. Thus, the body-as-lived provides the foundation, for instance, of the central theme in BUBER's thought: the I–Thou relationship, which is the most authentic relationship between PERSONS, in which the other is not an object at my disposal but a Thou who is completely and genuinely present to me. Such a relationship requires that I open myself to the other and allow the other to communicate his or her whole BEING to me. To be sure, the other cannot be wholly a Thou insofar as I still regard this person's body as an It. Yet, in the I–Thou relationship neither my body nor the other's body can be regarded simply as an extended object.

Viewing the body as more than a physical entity forms the cornerstone of SARTRE's thought. In *Being and Nothingness*, he outlines three ontological dimensions of the body, three different aspects in which the body exists. There is an outward dimension of the body that emerges when I encounter my body as the object that it is for the other. Usually, this is achieved through LANGUAGE or after referring to the other's body conceptually, as in the study of anatomy. I understand the workings of my body by reading about the human body in an anatomy book; it enables me to associate the pain I experience with an ulcer-related stomach pain by picturing the stomach in its spatial and organic composition. This apprehension of my body is one step removed from lived experience of pain and is a product of reflection in which I grasp my body first by analogy with another's body and second as an object or instrument known to any other. This dimension of the body serves an important purpose, yet it is not the primary dimension of the body. This body as it is known by me through the other is derivative of the more immediate and prereflective lived body, as I exist it as Being-for-itself.

Sartre asserts that the body-for-me is not to be understood in terms of the subject-to-object relation that exists between consciousness and a thing in the world. The body, as I live it, is not out there in the world. It is, on the contrary, the frame of reference around which the world is organized, making all objective RELATIONS in the world meaningful. Indeed, that the tree is standing there next to the house has no meaning to a disembodied mind. To exist my body is to open out into the world as situated consciousness; it is to exist my FACTICITY. The body as my facticity is the very being of the prereflective cogito as it concretely surpasses itself toward a future. To say that my body constitutes my being is to affirm my prereflective awareness of it. This prereflective awareness of my body-as-lived precludes it from completely being made into an object, as it also provides the necessary point of reference for my reflective awareness of other things. Thus, when I am painting a picture, my attention is directed solely toward the strokes of my paintbrush on the canvas. While engrossed in painting, my body does not appear in my field of consciousness, even though I am prereflectively aware of my bodily movements in accomplishing the task. Thus, the body is not an object of consciousness but is precisely that which is silently passed over by consciousness in pursuit of its concrete possibilities. Furthermore, there can be no psychic distance between me and my body-as-lived. Put simply, I am my body; I exist as I project toward my possibilities in the world. This intuitive, unobjectifiable relation is reflected in everyday language. The sentence "I am painting a picture" explains my hand movements. It would be awkward, if not unintelligible, to say that my hand is painting a picture. Existentially and conceptually, my body is in complete unity with my PERSON; lived experience is the primary dimension of the body.

Another aspect of the body is my body-for-others, which Sartre describes in his discussion on the LOOK, and in his revision of the traditional theory of intersubjectivity whereby the subject becomes aware of the other through the other's body. In contrast, my subject-to-object relation to the other is founded on the other's turning me into an object through his or her look. My making an object of the other lies subsequent to the other's making an object of me. I become aware of the other not through the other's body but through my awareness that I have a body that is being looked at. The look is a threat to consciousness; it makes me aware of the fact that a dimension of my being is out there and in danger. As the other's privileged possession, my body-for-others is neither accessible to, nor controlled by, me. This terrifying awareness prompts me to retaliate by turning the other into an object for me—through the same mechanism: I look back at the look so as to seize the other's body-for-me. This desire to rescue the body-for-others from the other is the ontological basis for conflicts in concrete human relations.

The theme of the body as lived is echoed throughout MARCEL's works, particularly in the first volume of *The Mystery of Being* and in his *Metaphysical Journal*, in which he distinguishes between a body and my body. *The Mystery of Being* cautions that any reference to the body as mine must not be construed as a relation of possession. My body is understood not in the sense of having but in the sense of being able to fulfill possibilities. My body-qua-mine is my embodiment, that nonintellectualizable connection between consciousness and the body, which makes possible the many ways I can be present and open to the world. To be embodied is to externalize myself. As ground for my possibilities, this unmediated, primary experience of my embodiment forms the nucleus of all of my mediated experiences involving objects in the world. *Metaphysical Journal* proclaims that I am my body insofar as I am a being who feels. I must initially experience or feel my own embodiment before I can feel or attend to anything else in the world. To feel embodied is to be in touch with how my body is present to me, whether I feel invigorated, sluggish, or restless. This inner perception of embodiment is given to me as an absolute priority over and above all other kinds of PERCEPTION. This original or archetypal feeling makes possible and shapes my participation in the world. Thus, to exist is to be embodied; to be embodied is to feel and be present to oneself in ways that actualize participation in the world.

The body is an integral part of MERLEAU-PONTY's theory of perception.

He discredits the orthodox, mechanistic approach to sense perception. Advocates of this position have reduced the phenomenon to a passive event in which the body serves as a receptacle of sense data transmitted by various objects. According to this view, the melody I hear becomes a function of sound waves that, by striking the tympanic membrane, cause sensuous excitations in my ear. But sensuous excitations cannot be explained solely in terms of mechanical interactions; they must be seen as the active, spontaneous, and sense-bestowing ways in which my body attends to an object and forms its data. Accordingly, an objective description of perception in terms of sound waves cannot capture the phenomenon of hearing as a unique way in which I, as embodied consciousness, am attuned to the world. Sensible qualities, such as the melody I hear, are not some predetermined entity. Rather, each sensible quality becomes the quality that it is by virtue of the action being performed upon it, as well as the perceptual milieu defined by my PROJECT at hand.

Merleau-Ponty is sketching a theory of perception as a form of lived experience. It is inevitable that the body plays a prominent role in perception because lived experience is embodied experience. The body represents a corporeal scheme in which all of its organs and members form a synchronized and coordinated unity with respect to its projects and movements. Due to the inner workings of my body as a corporeal scheme I have an intuitive sense of the spatial relations between various parts of my body, as well as their spatial relations to things around me. This can be seen when I ease slightly to the right as I pass someone on the street. The same organized scheme is at work with sensory objects. Thus, the body is an intersensory system that provides the common ground for unifying the senses. This unity is seen in the perception of a rose. One could analyze the perceptual act by breaking it down into sight, smell, and touch, each giving a mode of access to the rose. But these divisions do not emerge in my encounter with the rose. The rose is a red, fragrant, and prickly object that I experience all at once, prior to any objective thematization. While encountering the object, I do not experience my senses as divided but as simultaneously referring to one another. Each sense implicates my entire body.

Inherent in Merleau-Ponty's theory of perception is the perennial role of the body as a unified system: perception has less to do with HUSSERL's idea of sperforming syntheses upon the object than with the visceral encounter of the object. With emphasis being placed on the body's concrete presence before the object, he characterizes the body as BEING-IN-THE-WORLD. He rejects the treatment of consciousness as complete interiority and also the assumption of a strictly noumenal world. To be conscious of anything is to be embodied. The body is the expression of consciousness much as language is an expression of thought. He accentuates the intimate, inseparable bond between embodied consciousness and the world. As being-in-the-world, my body belongs to the world and is thoroughly caught up with all the things in it. The world forms the indispensable context for all my possibilities, encompassing all possible ways I can be. Whereas the world exists beyond my consciousness of it, because

augural lecture, "Humanity in Contemporary Phi-
as presented two weeks later. In 1930 he became a
eological Seminary in New York. Returning to Ger-
was appointed lecturer in theology at Berlin University
tthias Church, Berlin, the following November. Out of
e two publications, *Creation and Fall* and *Christology*.
onhoeffer and Martin Niemoller helped to start the Pastors'
, a forerunner to the Confessing Church, organized in May
to National Socialism's deepening control of Christianity. In
nhoeffer moved to London to serve as pastor in two churches.
tion of the preachers' seminary of the Confessing Church at
pril 1935, he returned to Germany to head this experiment in
UCATION. His authorization to teach at the University of Berlin
in August 1936; the seminary was closed by the Gestapo in Sep-
7, after almost two years of illegal operation. Two books were the
s period: *The Cost of Discipleship* and *Life Together*, which portrayed
LIFE at the seminary.
oeffer made contacts with leaders of the political resistance. He was
those who refused in April 1938 to take the oath of allegiance to Hitler
mmemoration of Hitler's fiftieth birthday. He used contacts in the European
menical movement to garner support for the Confessing Church's opposition
Nazism. He traveled to New York in June 1939 at the invitation of friends
who hoped he might remain there during this period of crisis in Germany. But
in July he returned to Germany. In August he was made a civilian agent of the
German military intelligence; he worked for the next four years to subvert the
Nazi regime and, ultimately, participated in the attempt to assassinate Hitler. By
September 1940 Bonhoeffer was prohibited from speaking in public and was
required to report his activities to the authorities. He began work on *Ethics*,
which was published posthumously. He continued to travel outside Germany
during 1941 and 1942—to Switzerland, Norway, and Sweden—making contacts
for the Resistance movement and helping to arrange the escape of a group of
Jews to Switzerland in October 1941. On 5 April 1943, less than three months
after his engagement to Maria won Wedemeyer, Bonhoeffer was arrested and
sent to prison in Berlin. The failed attempt on Hitler's life on 20 July 1944 by
Klaus von Stauffenberg and the discovery of files incriminating the Bonhoeffer
family indicated that Dietrich was involved in the Resistance. He was moved
finally to Flossenburg concentration camp, and, with other members of the Resistance movement, he was hanged on 9 April 1945.

The WORLD in which Bonhoeffer came of age was on the brink of collapse,
reeling with the loss of World War I. Two strands of this crisis shaped his
intellectual climate. First was the *volkisch* movement, which had grown out of
German nature MYSTICISM, Protestant Pietism, nationalism, and Romanticism.
It subordinated the formation of individual self-identity to a need to belong
to the *Volk*, a natural, organic, national social totality. Second was the anti-

Dietrich Bonhoeffer

I exist my body as a diver
diversity that it is. Sens~~
cause I exist as embo~~
than this bond or ν

Primary W~~   54

Marcel, Ga.
Henry .

Bibliography

Fell, Joseph P. *Heidegger an.*
   bia University Press, 1~~.
Madison, Gary. *The Phenomenolo~~.*
   sciousness. Athens: Ohio Univ

DIETRICH BONH~~
(1906–1945)

Wayne Whitson Floyd, Jr.

The work of Bonhoeffer, the Protestant theologian executed by the Nazi~~ participating in a plot to assassinate Hitler, resonates with a number of theme~~ (1) a fascination with personalist PHILOSOPHY; (2) an emphasis upon the ethical motifs of suffering, FREEDOM, RESPONSIBILITY, decision, and DEATH; (3) a desire to articulate the dialectic of individual and COMMUNITY, particularly as it comes to expression in Christian theological anthropology, and (4) a moral commitment to the unfinished tasks of humanity's striving toward maturity. He noted that religionless CHRISTIANITY may be necessary in order to give voice not only to the failings of traditional RELIGION but also to the promise of authentic faithfulness.

Dietrich was one of eight children—including a twin sister, Sabine—in the family of Kari Bonhoeffer, a noted neurologist and professor of psychiatry at the Friedrich Wilhelm University in Berlin, and his wife, Paula. He studied at Tübingen University from 1923 to 1924 and at Berlin University from 1924 to 1927, where he received his licentiate in THEOLOGY for his doctoral dissertation "The Communion of Saints." His *Habilitationsschrift*, *Act and Being* was

Enlightenment spirit of positive philosophy that reigned in Berlin in the late nineteenth century. Other influences ranged from the Protestant Reformers, especially Luther, to philosophical contemporaries, such as HEIDEGGER. From Luther he learned of the evils of egocentrism, the wiles of the heart turned in upon itself and oblivious to all that does not lie within its pretensions to omnipotent POWER. The distrust of Idealism placed Bonhoeffer in the camp of KIERKEGAARD. He was also attracted to the way PHENOMENOLOGY had attempted to analyze human EXISTENCE. The phenomenological framework of INTENTIONALITY, its themes of possibility vis-à-vis reality—of inauthenticity and fallenness, in Heidegger's terms—as well as openness to the future found resonances in Bonhoeffer's early writings. But even when embodied in such theological forms as the philosophy-of-limits of TILLICH, Bonhoeffer judged existential phenomenology's attempt to surmount the all-embracing subjective totality of Idealism to have failed, since its boundaries and limits remained drawn by the human SUBJECT—succumbing to an ultimate SOLIPSISM, however finely nuanced.

In the works of Grisebach, GOGARTEN, and BULTMANN, Bonhoeffer discovered a philosophical-theology-of-limits that understood its central problem to be as much ethical as epistemological. The Other is not an ''It'' but a ''Thou''—an approach that provided the long-sought-for, concrete limit to the rational pretensions of Idealism. The desire to articulate a limit beyond the arbitrariness of choosing and willing also led him to the crisis-theology of Karl Barth. Yet he suspected that the divine initiative in REVELATION had been carried to such an extreme by Barth that GOD can be conceived only as tangential to HISTORY, not in graspable, haveable particularity. In his dissertation, ''The Communion of Saints,'' he tried to engage not only the theological categories of PERSON and community but the concepts and methodology of contemporary sociologists. He sought to develop a theology of community that is concerned with the integrity of the person-as-Other. You know that your I is real only in the relation with a Thou, who confronts you with his or her Otherness. Yet he feared the danger in trying to save the idea of an asocial core of personal being—it might lead to atomistic thinking. His position was that the individual SPIRIT lives solely by virtue of sociality, and the social spirit becomes real in individual embodiment. You cannot speak of the priority of the personal or the social. Humanity's sociality demands individuality. Yet he often formulated the social dimension of human existence as an analogue of the individual, rather than vice versa. He believed that the community can be viewed as a collective person, with the same structures. The concept of person can be used to interpret the collective dimensions of social life. Communities have an objective spirit.

In *Act and Being*, Bonhoeffer turned to the category of revelation in order to articulate the sense of boundary and Otherness. He felt that Barth had given up on philosophy and posed an alternative, revelational positivism. He wished to retain both the ability to respect the constitutive activity of the thinking subject and the MYSTERY of finite reality hinted in the recalcitrance of the ethical demand placed on the self by the concrete Other. *Act and Being* asks, What sort of thinking would theology be if it could avoid the pitfalls of Idealism, particularly its propensity toward totalities that enforce the absolute reign of subjectivity by obliterating Otherness? What can such Idealist thinking learn from Christianity's theology of the revelation of God in the person Jesus? Does not the concreteness of revelation constitute an authentic particularity that provides the creative limit to the human EGO's desires to reign supreme? Can such a theology of revelation be understood as genuine thinking, rather than an irrational submission to a heteronomous divinity?

Two short works, *Creation and Fall* and *Christology*, reveal Bonhoeffer's wrestling with such questions. He draws upon traditional sources and norms: in the first book, the narratives of origin and corruption found in Genesis; in the second, Christianity's particular claims about the person and work of Christ. He laments that critical philosophy has lost sight of the significance of human beginnings before the Fall. What has been lost is an ability to recognize, much less participate in, the original freedom of human existence described in mythological form in Genesis—a freedom to let-be the Other, a freedom born of human encounter by the Other. We no longer can imagine that freedom is a relationship between two persons. Indeed, the Fall is a Promethean attempt to be God, to exist in the place of God, to become limitless, all-powerful, one whose very existence comes to be defined by the violent transgression of the limit of the Other, as in the Cain and Abel story. *Christology* began to reconstruct the traditional theological understanding of Christ's significance by refusing to engage in a speculative, metaphysical conjecture about how or why God chooses to come in the midst of the created order. What is crucial is not how or why but the question, Who? Jesus is the person-par-excellence, the sought-for limit to human pretensions, the center of human existence, history, and NATURE. Jesus' messianic act is not merely to come into the midst of the world, showing that world to be God's *proper* place. Jesus is God-who-is-our-boundary, the creative limit that allows humanity to be authentically human, rather than a demonic usurper of divine power. God lets violence be done to God's very self, so that an authentic limit or boundary—the absolute futility of human power and domination—might be encountered in its concreteness. Therefore, we must speak of Jesus as this weak man among sinners, of his manger and his cross. To deal with the deity of Jesus, we must speak of his weakness.

Bonhoeffer's *The Cost of Discipleship* explores what is at stake, for the individual and the Christian community, in a theology of costly grace. What does it mean for the Christian to claim that human freedom (from violence-to-the-other and for the-sake-of-the-Other) comes only at a great cost to God's BEING? To be a Christian means to become authentically human precisely by doing as God-in-Christ has done—by suffering and being rejected for the sake of others. His critique of religion is harsh. The church of his day does not want costly grace but cheap grace. Humanity does not wish to pay the cost of the loss of its power, its privilege, its domination. In its misanthropism, in its support of warfare, and in its refusal to protest genocide, the church has forgotten that the brother's life is a boundary that we dare not pass. In refusing such costly grace, humanity risks ceasing to be authentically human. The One who destroys the Other is not what God created humanity to be. *Life Together* is Bonhoeffer's prophetic challenge to his young seminarians at their illegal house of studies at Finkenwalde to move beyond false religiosity to authentic discipleship. The test of a community and its LOVE is that self-centered love cannot love an enemy.

The book Bonhoeffer most wanted to write was his *Ethics*, left uncompleted when he was arrested. He returns to the theme of humanity's desires to be God, to be its own creator and judge. Wishing to understand itself only according to its own abstract possibilities rather than the concrete reality of our creatureliness—mistaking freedom for the ability to transgress all boundaries—humanity finds itself alone, cut off from authentic life with God and with one another. ETHICS begins with the honest confession before God and other humans of the desire for mastery, dominion, and revenge and with shame for one's desire to make the Other into one's own image. It demands of humans a genuine turning away from the domination of the Other to a life lived precisely for the sake of that very Other. Bonhoeffer declares: Ecce homo!—Behold the man! In him the world was reconciled with God. We hear the theme that appears in his *Letters and Papers from Prison*: the turn toward authentic religiosity is a turn toward the world, for whose sake God-in-Christ suffered and died. Ethics thus means formation, or conformation with the crucified God, which is to have the right to be the person one really is since God loves the real person. God became a real person. To be a real person is to turn from the desire to be God and to turn toward, and embrace, in love and forgiveness, our humanity. Christianity is the story of how God becomes most God-like in suffering-love for creation and how humanity becomes most human in being Christ for others. This is consummated in self-giving, vicarious action for the sake of the Other.

In *Letters and Papers from Prison*, Bonhoeffer's final, fragmentary vision of human existence emerges. What would a theology be like that was no longer based on God conceived as a deus ex machina? What if the TRANSCENDENCE of God has to do with this world and how one lives in it, rather than with otherworldly affairs? Such questions led to the intensification of two themes: the worldliness of the Christian gospel and the suffering Jesus as hermeneutical key to a nonreligious human existence that is transformed by the divine presence among humanity. One implication of such Christian worldliness was a movement to a theology of human action and the insight that action comes not from thought but from a readiness for responsibility. He came to this insight through a renewed interest in the Hebrew Bible. What if Christianity, he queried Eberhard Bethge, understands REDEMPTION in entirely finite terms, as historical, on this side of death instead of as concerned to overcome the barrier of death? What if Christianity takes for its model the fact that in *Exodus* Israel is delivered out of Egypt so that it may live before God as God's people on earth? Once Christian theology makes this move, it recognizes the difference between Christianity and all religions. Humanity's religiosity makes persons look in their distress to the power of God in the world: God is the deus ex machina. The Bible directs people to God's powerlessness and suffering; only the suffering God can help. This is genuine maturity, the doing away with false conceptions of God for the sake of an authentic, faithful worldliness.

Primary Works

Bonhoeffer, Dietrich. *The Cost of Discipleship*. Trans. R. H. Fuller. New York: Macmillan, 1949.
———. *Ethics*. Trans. Neville Horton Smith. New York: Macmillan, 1955.

Bibliography

Floyd, Wayne Whitson, Jr., and Charles Marsh, eds. *Theology and the Practice of Responsibility: Essays on Dietrich Bonhoeffer*. Valley Forge, PA: Trinity Press International, 1994.

MARTIN BUBER
(1878–1965)
Rivca Gordon

Martin Buber was born in Vienna. When he was three, his mother left home with a lover. Martin met her again only after thirty years. His father sent him to Lemberg to live with affluent, scholarly grandparents, Solomon and Adele Buber. In 1896 he commenced studies at the University of Vienna. He also studied at the Universities of Leipzig, Berlin, and Zurich, receiving a doctoral degree from the University of Vienna in 1904. In 1899 in Zurich he met Paula Winkler. They married and had two children. Buber enthusiastically joined the Zionist movement in 1898. In 1901 he accepted Herzl's proposal that he become editor of the major Zionist publication, *Die Welt*. In 1902, during the fifth Zionist Congress in Basel, Buber joined the opposition against Herzl, which demanded that, together with political and economic goals, the Zionist movement undertake EDUCATION and cultural and spiritual goals. Herzl rejected this demand as interfering with the struggle to attain political goals. Soon Buber resigned as editor of *Die Welt*. In 1916 he helped to establish the journal *Der Jude*, dedicated to Jewish spirituality and to Zionism. In 1921 at the first Zionist Congress after World War I, Buber spoke out for a just treaty with the Arab inhabitants of Israel. His motion was diluted until it became almost meaningless. After the congress Buber again retreated from political activity.

In 1904 Buber began research into Hasidism. From 1906 to 1911 he edited *Die Gesellschaft*, a series of monographs on social topics; forty were published. He also published two books that presented Hasidism as a utopian mystical movement. In 1909 he gave three lectures on JUDAISM to the Bar Cochba Zionist youth group in Prague. The lectures, published in 1911, showed many young Jews a way to relate to Judaism in the modern world. From 1916 until 1923 Buber worked on *I and Thou*. During the rest of his LIFE he continued to publish books and studies that clarified and extended the discoveries presented in *I and Thou*. In 1921 Buber met FRANZ ROSENZWEIG. Shortly after their meeting Rosenzweig took ill and suggested that Buber be called, instead of him, to the chair of Jewish PHILOSOPHY and ETHICS at the University of Frankfurt. It was Buber's first academic position, held until fired by the Nazi regime in 1933. In 1938 Buber immigrated to Israel and joined the faculty of Hebrew University in Jerusalem. In 1925 a young publisher, Lambert Schneider, asked Buber to undertake a new translation of the Hebrew Bible. Buber asked Rosenzweig to assist him. Until Rosenzweig's death in 1929, they worked together. Buber continued alone until 1938. After World War II he again took up the translation, completing it in 1961.

Buber holds that persons can speak two basic words, which express distinct attitudes. Speaking the I–It relates to the Other or the thing that I encounter as an object. Speaking the I–Thou can establish the world of relation between the I and a human partner, natural creatures, or spiritual beings such as works of ART or GOD. A PERSON who relates dialogically may, in a moment of grace, encounter the Other as a Thou. The highest human challenge is to be guided in one's life by I–Thou encounters and to realize in the everyday what one has learned from such encounters. If persons strive to live such a life, it will revolutionize human EXISTENCE. From an ontological perspective, neither the I nor the EGO is primary. The I is developed through the attitudes that it develops to other beings in the WORLD. Through these attitudes persons relate to the encompassing world and bestow meaning upon it. Your ability to distance yourself from the beings of the world, Buber wrote three decades after *I and Thou*, allows you to be present to these beings and to relate to them. If, after such distancing, you adopt an I–It attitude, your I is separated from the objects of the world; it knows them as It, as objects. Such an attitude impoverishes the I and the objects to which it relates, even if it is at the basis of the scientific endeavor. If a person is guided by the I–Thou attitude, the I is able to relate wholly in full presence to the beings of the world and to spiritual beings. Saying Thou is a relating with your whole BEING; your I becomes a being who can relate wholly to the beings encountered.

The realm of the It includes feelings, habits, behaviors, responses, thoughts—the psychological and also scientific knowledge: causality, classification, selection, explanation. VALUES and ideas reside in the realm of the It, as do experiences in TIME and SPACE. Human relations are explained on the basis of past actions. In an I–Thou encounter, the separation that allows objective KNOWLEDGE between the partners vanishes; there are presence and direct knowledge. This presence and direct knowledge are a relating in FREEDOM and the basis of the spiritual realm. The I–Thou encounter does not negate reality or go beyond it. Rather, it encompasses the entire living SITUATION as a presence and influences the whole being of the participants. Dialogue occurs in the between that comes into being when two partners relate wholly to each other. The between is characterized by reciprocity, tension, a longing to encounter the partner fully, giving and receiving, choosing and being chosen. My full presence confronts the full presence of the Thou. This between vanishes with the return of the I–It. In "Elements of the Interhuman" written thirty years after *I and Thou*, Buber distinguishes between an I–Thou encounter and genuine dialogue. The I–Thou is a moment of grace, of MYSTERY. Genuine dialogue can be established by acts in which partners learn to live fully in the interhuman. It requires no manipulation of the Other and an honest sharing of what is relevant at this specific moment. Such dialogue can be stuttered or include moments of silence. Buber points to three chief forms of dialogue: friendship, in which a person's entire reality is involved; abstract dialogue, when an intellectual topic is discussed, perhaps disputed, while there is full recognition of the legitimacy of the Other's views; and the educational relationship, in which the educator, while relating to the whole being of the pupil, experiences momentarily the influence of one's being on the pupil. Such a moment may occur if the educator endeavors to help the pupil bring into being one's unique potentials. Buber calls this one-sided giving in the educational relationship a lofty asceticism. The pupil cannot experience a similar dialogical moment.

Human freedom is the discovery of choices and possibilities. Freedom is that point from which two paths open. One leads to a renewed bondage, to lack of direction through continual manipulations of yourself and of others in the realm of I–It. The other path directs you to dialogue, to WHOLENESS, spontaneity, and innocence, to personal RESPONSIBILITY for others and for that part of the world in which you find yourself. In this world, where necessity and chance constantly intermingle, only a life guided by dialogue is a fulfilling of freedom. Freedom is the answering to a call, to an address, to a demand for responsibility in all spheres of life. You cannot learn to live your freedom fully by following norms or values. Buber can only point the way by describing genuine dialogue. True freedom is courageously doing what needs be done now in this specific situation within these guidelines. Such a doing helps you relate authentically to the Eternal Thou, to God.

GOOD and EVIL are not two poles, Buber holds; they relate to concrete existence and intermingle in your life. Within each situation you are called to decide upon your direction. God calls upon the Israelites to walk in his ways; in each situation each Israelite must decide. The choice of a single direction in which a person's soul is unified is the choice of good. Evil is characterized by directionless being. It is a choosing of irresponsibility within the chaos of existence. Later, such a person can decide to be evil, to realize evil intentions: Cain murdered Abel. Buber stresses that only good can be done with your whole being. An example of such good is concrete LOVE of a person, which can also open you to the possibility of loving God. The greatness of human existence is the knowledge of the distinction between good and evil. This greatness reaches fulfillment when a person unites one's evil inclinations and directs them to doing good. Existential GUILT arises from the choice to be irresponsible, to evade dialogical, responsible decisions in concrete situations. An act of CONSCIENCE in which a person relates authentically to one's existential guilt requires three steps: first, a courageous illuminating of the guilty act; second, a confession of one's guilt; third, a persistent attempt to correct the evil by engaging in redeeming deeds, which need not be linked to the guilt.

Faith includes the two basic ontological attitudes. You can relate to God as an It or as a Thou. An I–Thou encounter with the Eternal Thou transcends time and space. Furthermore, the lines of all I–Thou encounters converge in the Eternal Thou. An I–Thou encounter with the Eternal Thou may include such an encounter with a nondivine being. It is overwhelming. Holiness is therefore not beyond the concrete but includes it and can be reached only through concrete actions and attitudes. God, as described in the Bible, intervenes in concrete historical situations. Belonging to the Jewish COMMUNITY of faith requires going beyond the mutual past and daily accepting the duty to act unconditionally within the world. The Bible repeatedly shows God's demands that you live justly within the historical situation in which you find yourself, in which you are engaged. Daily struggling to fulfill this demand is central to biblical FAITH. Israel was chosen by God to be a living example for all humankind of true faith and of living justly. Freedom is necessary but not sufficient for this worthy task. You must engage your freedom in going beyond the sordid situation that you encounter toward a universal goal that will lead to justice and TRUTH for all of humanity. To undertake such a challenge, RELATIONS of dialogue and communion must prevail within the Jewish community of faith. These relations will endow members of this community with the creativeness and profundity needed for such a challenge. Moreover, Israel, as a nation chosen by God, will disintegrate if in daily life it betrays this divine challenge.

A genuine religious community expresses its unity of faith in all realms of life: the ethical, the national-political, the social, the interhuman. Individual acts within such a community require relating dialogically to others and to God. The Torah given by God to Israel is not a group of abstract laws or universal values. It indicates—to each Israelite—a direction, a teaching for concrete life that demands justice and rejects evil. Realizing the Torah requires the personal responsibility that can be attained only by relating dialogically to others and to

God. Moses accepted the mission of struggling to establish a community of faith. The Bible records his few successes and many failures. Hebrew judges and prophets followed Moses' arduous path. These biblical leaders had little political POWER, if any. They relied on the truth of the godly message expressed in their spoken word.

Buber believes that the Hasidic movement established genuine communities of faith in Eastern Europe in the middle of the eighteenth century. The emerging of Hasidism in the harsh conditions of oppression in the Diaspora testifies to the possibilities of enhancing humanity and of the joy in life in a genuine religious community, even in adverse conditions. Furthermore, historical studies that ignore genuine communities of faith and leaders, like the Hebrew prophets, who struggled for a life of communion, exclude a major dimension of human existence and hence falsify HISTORY. This dimension—of religiosity, which transcends organized religion and relies on the spoken word of the prophet who brings the divine message—is established upon genuine dialogue and an I–Thou relationship to God. In contrast, organized RELIGION frequently relates to God as an It and often serves as a function of established SOCIETY or of the prevailing political regime. Religion becomes a static, inert institution whose main goal is to serve and to impose certain psychological, ethical, or political needs.

In *Two Types of Faith* Buber points to the distinction between the original faith of Israel, which is a relationship of trust in God, and the faith propounded by Paul during the early days of Christianity, which is based on acknowledging the truth of the good tidings brought by Jesus. Trust is based on dialogue; hence, a faith whose source is trust demands the fulfilling of the teaching through relations of communion in everyday life. The Torah is a teaching, a direction. Although it includes laws, they are secondary to the teaching of a genuine communal life. Jesus related thus to the Torah. In contrast Paul established a faith as a new beginning of history, which demanded acknowledging the truth of the good tidings. He appealed to individuals, detached from their historical community, who converted to faith in Jesus and the truth of his message. Gradually, these individual, separated converts established a community whose relationship to God is not of mutual trust and responsibility but of submission to a distanced alien power. Instead of following the teaching, the Torah, Paul demands submission to law. SIN becomes the center of human existence; humanity is imprisoned in sin. REDEMPTION and grace are gifts that only Jesus can bestow upon the faithful.

Buber's ONTOLOGY is linked to his understanding of society. A person belongs to a specific society. Within society the two basic relationships, I–Thou and I–It, are possibilities. Individualism and collectivism are manifestations of the I–It. The former disregards the possibility of dialogical encounter with the Other, stressing reliance on oneself; the latter deifies the social realm, demoting the person to the status of an object within society. Both manifestations thwart the possibility of genuine meetings with the Other; ALIENATION and aloneness prevail, and mediocre masses thrive. The religious establishment, the political party, the state are all manifestations of the I–It. In contrast, the I–Thou can occur in a genuine commune in which actual encounters between members are a real possibility. In such a commune autonomous, responsible persons who share a center and a direction create an encompassing mutuality. Some historical Hasidic communities and revolutionary groups are examples of such communes. In *Paths in Utopia* Buber presents the vision of a religious, socialistic commune, primarily based on the writings of nineteenth-century utopian thinkers. These visionaries related to a worthy element of human existence, the wish for true community and renewal of society, upon which justice and peace can be established. We should attempt to realize their thought and establish true communes, based on free people sharing together in all realms of social existence. This sharing must be continually renewed in the everyday, concrete life as members strive to fulfill their lives and forward communal goals. Thus, a genuine commune is never a final product; it is always in the process of being fulfilled and rejuvenated by acts of its individual members.

The political realm that is centralized and in which people strive to obtain power is the great enemy of the possibility of dialogue. Buber distinguished between the political principle, which stresses means and ends and the struggle for power, and the society principle. A genuine society is a community of genuine communes that develop together in a worthy direction. Today, the centralized political principle reigns; communes have surrendered to the state, which is an artificial negative being. Hence, we must strive to diminish the influence of the state and of politics. Administration by specialists accords with the society principle, which is noncentralized, nonpolitical, while the political principle serves only those in power, even in a democracy. Governments have attained too much power; they stifle spontaneity, autonomy, and the vitality of society. Buber advocates an existential revolution that will terminate the state and its power. In its stead a community of communes will be established, guided by chosen professional administrators. Interaction between nations will follow this approach, bringing about a civilization of dialogue.

Primary Works

Buber, Martin. *Between Man and Man*. Trans. Ronald Gregor Smith. New York: Macmillan, 1965.
———. *The Knowledge of Man*. Trans. Maurice Friedman and Ronald Gregor Smith. New York: Harper and Row, 1965.

Bibliography

Gordon, Haim, and Jochanan Bloch, eds. *Martin Buber: A Centenary Volume*. New York: Ktav, 1984.
Schilpp, Paul Arthur, and Maurice Friedman, eds. *The Philosophy of Martin Buber*. La Salle, IL: Open Court, 1967.

RUDOLF KARL BULTMANN
(1884–1976)
Houston Craighead

Bultmann was born at Wiefelsted, near Bremen, Germany. His academic background included studies at Marburg, Tübingen, and Berlin. He taught first at Marburg, then Breslau and Giessen. He returned to Marburg as New Testament Professor in 1921 and taught there until 1951. Probably best known for his project of demythologizing, Bultmann attempted to interpret the New Testament and Christian FAITH in existentialist terms, specifically in the LANGUAGE of HEIDEGGER's *Being and Time*. Bultmann was convinced that unless faith is articulated to the modern WORLD in concepts that can be understood, people living today would not have the opportunity to decide for or against it; they would not even know what the Christian faith is. He defines MYTH as a mode of thinking that is ignorant of NATURE's operations, takes place in a prescientific age, and conceives of GOD as a divine BEING existing in the TIME-SPACE continuum alongside other beings. Mythical thinking does not know of scientific explanations for natural phenomena and attributes natural events to supernatural causes; the world of myth is a realm of struggle between supernatural powers that intersect nature and human EXISTENCE.

Bultmann holds that the New Testament is essentially mythological. It presumes a three-storied universe with Heaven above, Hell below, and Earth as a battleground for angels and demons. HISTORY and nature are intervened by them, miracles occur, and humans are not in control of their lives. There is demon possession; the age is held in bondage to Satan. But a catastrophic end will soon come, inaugurated by woes of the last time, when the Judge will return from Heaven, the dead will rise, and Heaven or Hell will be assigned as each PERSON's ultimate destiny. The New Testament includes the account of a preexistent, divine being appearing as a man, whose DEATH atones for human SIN and whose resurrection marks the beginning of cosmic catastrophe. Death, viewed as the consequence of Adam's sin, is abolished, the demonic forces are deprived of POWER, and the risen Christ is exalted to God's right hand in Heaven as Lord and King. Christ will return to complete his redemptive work. This will happen soon; Paul thinks he himself will live to see it. Members of Christ's church by baptism and Eucharist will be in Heaven and enjoy the first fruits of this now.

That mythological picture, says Bultmann, is obsolete. Modern people cannot be expected to accept it for two reasons: (1) there is nothing specifically Christian about it; it is the cosmology of a prescientific age, and (2) we cannot choose our worldview by volition. One's worldview is defined by one's place in history. We live in the scientific age, and our thinking is shaped accordingly. To accept this mythological view would be a sacrifice of the intellect. One's religious worldview would deny one's everyday world. Hence, Christian theologians must engage in the task of demythologizing the New Testament. They cannot pick and choose some features to demythologize while leaving others; the entire mythological picture must go; theologians and parish priests must make clear what hearers are expected to accept and what not.

Myth expresses the human conviction that the origin and purpose of the world lie beyond the world. This conviction is not mythological or scientific. It is the fundamental conviction of Christian faith and authentic existence. In pointing to the beyond, myth speaks of it in terms of this world. God becomes a particular being acting to suspend the laws of nature and perform miracles. A way of describing the human predicament and the Christian answer for that predicament in nonmythological language is needed. If you center your attention on the literal occurrence of New Testament stories, you miss their point. One must get at the message, the *kerygma*, that those stories intend to proclaim. Rather than centering on sin as the fundamental human problem, Bultmann speaks of ANXIETY as central to the human predicament. Anxiety as an objectless dread. The human self is caught between its FREEDOM and RESPONSIBILITY and the accidents of history that prevent one from ever being in complete control. It lives in a transitory world where all persons, institutions, and goals are constantly shifting and passing away. Further, the human self anticipates its own death. People know that their ultimate end is always with them. Anxiety is the fundamental human feeling that results from the human SITUATION. It must receive a viable existential answer. Many deal with anxiety through self-understanding, which is of two types: authentic or inauthentic.

Inauthentic self-understanding views oneself as able, through whatever means, to control one's destiny by expanding one's power. Science is often an integral part of an inauthentic self-understanding, as is a mythological view that tries to manipulate the gods through prayers and sacrifices. Such an outlook fails because anxiety cannot be controlled by human ingenuity. The realization of the futility of this approach and the move to authentic self-understanding hold promise for humans to experience salvation, to be able to live freely, joyfully, and creatively with the ever-present anxiety. The *kerygma*, the central proclamation of the New Testament, when properly separated from its mythological expression, claims that people must recognize their finitude and helplessness in the world. There is an act of God that occurs in the inner LIFE of a person. Trusting that act and forsaking inauthentic self-understanding lead to resurrection into a new life.

Bultmann demythologizes the act of God; it is not a supernatural interference in the natural order. It is, rather, an event in the life of a person that fundamentally calls into question that person's self-understanding and brings one to see the presence of a transcendent power in the world. Any such event, viewed from the outside, from the scientific or objective point of view, can be interpreted as a natural occurrence. Yet the person who experiences such an event or encounter may respond to it as a transcendent act within one's existence. A sermon, for example, becomes the word of God when its hearers find their egocentric self-understanding called into question and the possibility of a new understanding opened for them. The word is not a BODY of doctrine but a happening in the life of an individual.

This new, authentic self-understanding is a natural possibility open to humans, but it cannot become actual by your willing it; you must encounter it as given; such can happen only in response to the New Testament proclamation about the particularity of Jesus as the Christ. That proclamation is essential. This authentic self-understanding is the life of faith. A person in this new life has died to the old self-understanding and has been resurrected to a new self-understanding. Authentic self-understanding involves freedom from the GUILT and slavery to a past life. One sees the past for what it is. One's PERCEPTION of the future is changed because one is no longer trying always to control that future but is open to whatever it may bring. The person of faith has a new freedom for loving others in the present. They are no longer loved primarily as objects to relieve one's anxiety; one is able to LOVE them for who they are. Such a person remains in the midst of the world in a state of detachment. One enters into the world with all one's might but always knows, now, that ultimate meaning is not contingent upon success or failure. The world can be reclaimed in a new sense. Is this proclamation true? Nonmythologically understood, it is clear that whether the proclamation is true or false is not an objective question that can be decided by rational, empirical means. Such a proclamation is experienced as true by those who trust it and give their lives to it. There is no evidence to compel you to call it true. But until the proclamation is freed from its mythical expression in the New Testament, modern people never have an opportunity to hear it. They will have to reject it as in conflict with the way science tells them the world operates. But grasped as a message to the inner life of the person, this proclamation has the possibility of being heard and accepted as true. Whether it is existentially true is a question only a person can answer in his or her interiority.

Consider the walking-on-the-water account in Matthew 14:22–32. The disciples are in a boat in the middle of the lake when a storm arises and threatens to capsize them. Jesus walks to them on the water, at first frightening them because they think he is a ghost. Peter asks if he, too, can walk on the water; Jesus bids him to step out of the boat and walk. Peter does so, keeping his eyes on Jesus. But when Peter looks down at the waves, his faith falters, and he begins to sink. He cries: Help me, Lord! Jesus pulls him back with the reprimand: Why did you lose your nerve? From Bultmann's perspective the lake could represent the uncertainty of life: sometimes calm, sometimes dangerous, unpredictable. The disciples are in a safe boat; they have what they need for security. The storm threatens to destroy that security; they fear for the meaning of their lives. In the midst of the storm comes one who has no boat. He walks on the water. Their first response is that he must be a ghost. Jesus replies that it is he. Peter, then, wants to do thus, and Jesus issues the fundamental challenge: get out of the boat (die to your inauthentic self-understanding that says you can save yourself). Peter, keeping his gaze on Jesus, finds himself walking on the water (resurrected into a new self-understanding where he is open to the future and focuses on the presence of God). But when he looks at the waves, not at Jesus, Peter begins to sink (he slips back into the inauthentic self-understanding of focusing on things in the world). One, then, must forsake whatever one's boat is; that forsaking is true existential death. One must trust that giving up one's boat will enable genuine life, where one walks on the water, where one moves into the future free from anxiety because one knows that life's meaning is from beyond the transitoriness of this world.

A criticism of Bultmann is that he does not go far enough in getting rid of myth; he clings to mythological residues. Since authentic existence is a fundamental possibility for all persons, it is ludicrous to make it contingent upon the specifics of a particular historical RELIGION. Why not see this as an essential human possibility realizable by any person apart from Christian details? Bultmann replies that his view must be distinguished from existentialist PHILOSOPHY. For the Christian, this possibility becomes actual by an act of God, which took place in Jesus as the Christ and continues to take place when Christian preaching is properly received by its hearers. God speaks in specifics to individuals, not in general to humanity. Conservative critics see Bultmann's attempt to remove the historicality of biblical stories as subversive and heretical. They insist on a literal, bodily resurrection of Jesus. Bultmann's turning of this into an existential event in the life of the present believer is seen to sever Christianity from its historical roots. Others accuse Bultmann of absolutizing the scientific worldview, of mistakenly swallowing the closed universe portrayed in twentieth-century physics. They insist that science gives a no more literal account of reality than any worldview constructed by human reason.

Primary Work

Bultmann, Rudolf. *History and Eschatology.* New York: Harper and Row, 1957.

Bibliography

Johnson, Roger. *The Origins of Demythologizing: Philosophy and Historiography in the Theology of Rudolf Bultmann.* Leiden: E. J. Brill, 1974.
———. *Rudolf Bultmann: Interpreting Faith for the Modern Era.* London: Collins, 1987.

ALBERT CAMUS
(1913–1960)
Gene Blocker

Camus was born of a French-Alsatian father and a Spanish mother in the Algerian town of Mondovi. His father was killed in World War I shortly after Camus' birth. As a cleaning woman in the working-class district of Belcourt, Algeria, his mother struggled alone and in great poverty during Camus' and his brother's childhood. Although his parents were illiterate, Albert showed promise in public school. One teacher, Louis Germain, helped him attain a scholarship to the lycee; Camus entered the University of Algiers in 1932 to study PHILOSOPHY, writing a thesis on the relationship of Augustine to Neoplatonism. His political involvement, briefly in the Communist Party and later in the French Resistance during the Nazi occupation of France, was seriously curtailed by a recurring tubercular condition. Before the war he worked as a reporter and editor for *Alber-Republicain*. After the German occupation, he edited the Resistance newspaper, *Combat*. In 1957 he received the Nobel Prize in literature. He died in a car crash.

Camus' absurdist writings represent an early phase, from 1935 to 1945, in which he wrote *Caligula, The Myth of Sisyphus*, and *The Stranger. The Myth of Sisyphus* is one of the clearest statements of the problem of absurdity; nonetheless, Camus never wrote a philosophy of absurdity. He was concerned to express and communicate with ordinary people the widespread experience of the social and psychological dislocations resulting from the collapse of European ideals of reason and humanity. He rejected the cynicism, NIHILISM, and pessimism associated with popular existentialism and absurdism, views alien to his robust LOVE of LIFE and FAITH in human dignity. For Camus the love of life was always more important than the meaning of life. He constantly upheld, in the face of life's stark absurdity, the human refusal to be completely defeated by life's ultimate meaninglessness. His earliest writings are two collections of short stories-cum-essays, *The Wrong Side and the Right Side* and *Nuptials*, written between 1936 and 1938. *The Wrong Side and the Right Side* contains five highly personal, probably autobiographical narratives. Each is a balance between a highly particularized narrative anecdote, a short story, and a moral reflection, an essay. In "Irony," for example, as a young man abandons an old woman for an evening with his friends at the cinema, he notices the light in her window go out; after two other similar anecdotes the narrator explains that while on the one side of the balance is the painful reality of old age and DEATH, on the other side is the light of the world, natural joy of life. *Nuptials* introduces a thematic element that prefigures much of his later work, the Mediterranean culture. The great weight of the fallen empires of ancient HISTORY, now visible only as ruins, reveals the tension between NATURE and human history and the ultimate triumph of the former. There is a need for balance between an honest confrontation with death, both of the individual and of mighty civilizations, and the Epicurean delights of sensual life in the here and now, which nullify both cultural HUMANISM and any ultimate religious hope.

Relating to, and going beyond, the problem of absurdity are the beginning of WISDOM. *Caligula* explores the apparent limitlessness of senseless, selfish cruelty as an act of rebellion against the meaninglessness of life, in the absence of a transcendent source of VALUE, such as GOD or a universal human reason. But this is merely an honest statement of the problem—it is neither a solution nor a cynical rejection of possible solutions. After the war Camus worked steadily toward a limited humanism within an absurdist framework—without transcendent guarantees. Even in his absurdist period, absurdity cannot be properly analyzed in purely negative terms. The problem of absurdity must be confronted honestly and truthfully. The central theme of *The Myth of Sisyphus* is whether absurdity requires SUICIDE. Yet, Camus does not see absurdity as entirely negative. Absurdity is always a tragic response; in "On the Future of Tragedy," he argues that tragedy is born of the irreconcilable opposition between an unacceptable reality and an unlimited hope. In *The Myth of Sisyphus*, the tragedy of absurdity depends equally on two factors: the human expectation and the world's refusal to meet that expectation. Without the former there could be no failure or refusal of the world to honor human demands upon it. Thus, the tragedy of absurdity ironically requires a sense of the great elevating side of life to balance its grim opposite. Life also can be magnificent and overwhelming.

Absurdity is also the perception of the unbridgeable gap between the human desire to understand the world and the refusal of the world to accommodate that desire. Stripped of the idealized garb that we PROJECT on it, the world confronts us as an alien, hostile force. Still, absurdity is always a dialogue between a PERSON and the world, a communication, however strained. It is not a neutral vision of reality independent of thought, since it implies a PERCEPTION of the world as lacking what human thought demands. To see the world in this light is to see it through a human, indeed, a Romantic point of view. Even as the gap between a person and the world widens, the Romantic outlook tries more and more desperately to establish a sympathetic link with this estranged, hostile world. However useless the attempt, we refuse to accept the world's rebuff and continue looking to the world for that sympathetic response we know we will never receive. Out of loyalty to ourselves and respect for humanistic ideals, we continue the impossible task, like Sisyphus, whose eternal punishment was again and again to roll a stone to the mountaintop only to have it roll down.

Camus recognizes that without some link, however tenuous, between thought and reality, we would have no awareness of a world, much less a worry over understanding it. To see that thought does not correspond with reality presupposes that thought does correspond with reality at least some of the time. Only if the world is partially comprehensible can doubt about its total comprehensibility arise. The experience of absurdity exists within a prescribed balance between understanding the world and failing to understand it. By understanding reality partially and knowing it is partial, we see the fundamental difference between an understanding of reality and the reality that is understood. There is no transcendent reality of which we are completely ignorant; indeed, what understanding we do possess is of various facets of reality. We understand realty, but not as it is in itself.

Camus' novel *The Stranger* indicates what it is like to face the world without humanly projected illusions. Meursault, the hero, appears incapable of ordinary human feeling; he is indifferent both to his mother's death and to the death of the Arab he senselessly, almost accidentally killed. No one understands Meursault's attitude. People despise him, not so much as a murderer, for whom they might in certain circumstances feel a degree of sympathy, but for his cold, unfeeling lack of concern. But Meursault is unfeeling only in his refusal to conform to social conventions of what is considered appropriate: one should weep at one's mother's funeral and be contrite after killing another person. Thus, Meursault courageously and honestly faces the TRUTH; he is an absurdist hero who separates reality from human projection. Usually, we myopically accept conventional interpretations that members of our society create, and thus we share with them a common reality. Achieving this comfortable social conformity requires, of course, that each person relinquish the peculiarities of his or her perspective. Most persons do this quite willingly, internalizing social conventions, never realizing that these stereotyped responses are anything but expressions of one's unique self. The absurdist hero realizes this hypocrisy and, like Meursault, refuses to participate in the pretense. Meursault adopts an odd sort of heroic posture that honestly and courageously faces the truth about a reality stripped of its familiar social guise. At the end of *The Stranger* and in *The Notebooks* Camus refers to a rare and momentary experience of natural beauty that overcomes the tragic frustration of trying to remake the world in our own image. In this Romantic, aesthetic, almost mystical vision, the world is accepted on its own terms, neither meeting nor denying our demands but transcending those demands—a stranger to us as we are to it.

In *The Rebel* and *The Plague* Camus moves toward an existentialist kind of humanism, as a sense of solidarity with all humans equally and uniquely capable of realizing and rebelling against the injustice of life. *The Plague* extends this humanistic reverence for life from an individualistic stance to group solidarity. The doctor, Rieux, continues treating his patients, though he knows the outcome is quite hopeless, as a gesture of solidarity with the human demand for meaning and justice. This humanistic solidarity, together with his mystical and aesthetic delight in nature and in physical well-being, defines for Camus a constructed meaning in the midst of the fundamental and unavoidable absurdity of life. In

The Myth of Sisyphus Camus argues that suicide is an inappropriate response to absurdity because it admits the self-defeat of humans and the conquest of absurdity over them. In *The Rebel* and *The Plague* he extends this argument against the prima facie wrong of murder. If suicide is wrong because of the sanctity of life, then so is wanton murder. The great problem for any political revolution, especially armed struggle against injustice, is precisely that it often destroys the value of the human life that it sets out to protect and preserve. Camus asks how we are to express and act out this rebellion without damaging or disparaging the attempts of other human beings in their acts of rebellion. If God is dead, is everything possible? If religious and philosophical guarantees are no longer possible, what is left with which to condemn the absolute rebellion of the Caligulas or Hitlers of this world? Is there nothing to fall back on but bourgeois conventionality, against which Camus felt a particular antipathy, second only to his contempt for religious absolutes? Rebellion against the injustice of life is an essentially human rebellion and must therefore always be tempered and moderated by solidarity with other people, even enemies. Rebellion is a difficult, morally serious undertaking. To help humankind is necessarily to hurt people, and for this one must accept RESPONSIBILITY.

The vehemence of the attacks on the central argument of *The Rebel* stunned Camus into a prolonged depression. Before 1952 SARTRE and Camus had been linked in the minds of readers. But the extremely negative review of *The Rebel* that appeared in Sartre's *Le Temps Modernes* precipitated a break between the two that never healed. Sartre rejected Camus' soft, liberal humanism, implying a belief in universal human nature—that all humans share an inherently ennobling sense of reason, beauty, and justice. He criticized Camus' moderate balance and his rejection of clear alternatives, especially on political issues, and rejected Camus' romantic assertion of the eventual POWER of nature over history, diametrically opposed as that was to Marxist dialectics. To Sartre this implied a lack of firm commitment; to Camus political IDEOLOGY was never absolutely certain and could never be more important than the individual humans it was meant to serve. Sartre thought Camus was naive in uncritically embracing bourgeois values of truth, justice, and love of fellow humans at face value. Of course, we have been socialized to accept these values, he argued, but only because these values empower the bourgeoisie, enabling them to remain in power and to continue to exploit the working class. Nonetheless, Camus honestly and truthfully affirms these values as his own—from whatever unconscious or socially constructed source they may have come.

Camus' response to the almost completely negative critique of *The Rebel* was *The Fall*. The novel may be read as a parody of Northern Europe, negative, life-denying values. Increasingly, he developed an opposition between the values of the Mediterranean south and those of the cold and austere north of Europe. The south he associated not only with the relaxed sensual hedonism and love of nature but also, during the war years, with the rejection of ideological extremism, which he began more and more to associate with Northern Europeans.

In *The Fall* the life-affirming, humanistic celebration of the sunny south is contrasted with the life-denying and humanistic negation of the bleak north. *The Fall*, set in cold and foggy Amsterdam, concerns the confessions, spread over several days and nights, of the Parisian expatriate lawyer Clemence to a stranger he meets in a bar. It soon becomes clear that the point of Clemence's confession of his sins over many years is not to cleanse his soul but rather to generalize his guilt into a universal condemnation of humanity, as doomed beyond all hope.

The last years of Camus' life were consumed with Algerian political affairs. He did not produce major works after *The Fall*. He devoted much time and energy in an unsuccessful effort to effect a political conciliation between France and the growing Algerian Muslim rebellion. Two years before his death France granted Algeria independence.

Primary Work

Camus, Albert. *The Rebel*. Trans. Anthony Bower. New York: Knopf, 1967.

Bibliography

Blocker, Gene. *The Metaphysics of Absurdity*. Washington, DC: University Press of America, 1979.
Bree, Germaine. *Camus and Sartre: Crisis and Commitment*. New York: Dell, 1972.
Thody, Philip. *Albert Camus: A Study of His Work*. New York: Grove Press, 1957.

CARE
John Protevi

Care is a Heideggerian term for the BEING of DASEIN. In *Being and Time* he defines Dasein; namely, Dasein exists as a threefold, unitary structure named care. Three existentials make up the everyday Being of Dasein: thrownness, possibility, and falling. Thrownness is revealed in moodfulness, and possibilities are projected by understanding. The third existential, falling, is the inauthentic relation to thrownness. Moodfulness discloses Dasein's thrownness, its being handed over to its existence as a not fully explicable task. Understanding is the ability for Dasein to project its possibilities and thereby disclose partially meaningful future paths. Falling is the fleeing from the revelation of Being-in-the-world caused by the uncanny withdrawal of things in the mood of anxiety;

falling Dasein flees this mood by its absorption with things in everyday tasks and preoccupations. HEIDEGGER determines care as possibility that is thrown and falling. He explains that the unitary phenomenon of temporality is revealed as the ontological sense of care. Temporality accounts for the original phenomena of the parts of time we know as future, past, and present. Care, the thrown and falling possibility, is thus made possible by temporality, a future that makes present on the basis of having-been. The three temporal ecstases are a unified process, a phenomenon of our existence that makes possible the experience of any thing.

Bibliography

Guigon, Charles, ed. *The Cambridge Companion to Heidegger.* Cambridge: Cambridge University Press, 1993.

CHARACTER
Abrahim H. Khan

This concept shares certain aspects of the meaning-complex for the concept PERSONALITY, which includes the idea of role or personage. A shared element is the notion of mask, face, or image superimposed on the individual and through which he or she becomes publicly recognizable. The word "character" among the Greeks denoted both a tool for making a distinctive scratch or mark and the engraved mark or impression itself. The Greek tendency toward exact observation and sharp delineation to represent human types is evidenced by Homer's interest in individuals who took difficult decisions. This perception of human types and action was sharpened in the late classical period, to judge from the work on Moral Characters attributed to Theophrastus. Clearly, the meaning of the word had been enlarged in Greek antiquity, from signifying a distinctive physical mark (as on coins) to connoting also human types. Its meaning-complex was extended in the Middle Ages to include a spiritual or religious aspect. From the time of Augustine, character became a term in ecclesiology for spiritual signs indelibly imprinted on the soul by sacraments such as baptism, confirmation, and ordination. Aquinas developed this technical usage, or idea of *character sacramentalis.* This technical usage still persists today alongside its signifying a conscious self-direction given to daily living and correlated with conduct. Kant's distinction between moral and physical character heightened the ethical significance of the concept and provided impetus for enlarging the meaning-complex to include an existential aspect. According to Kant, character is determined by self-activity, that is, by what an individual makes out of oneself with respect to the question of the kind of PERSON one wills to become in accordance with certain principles. An individual has the RESPONSIBILITY of determining his or her character by free decisions throughout LIFE.

Character as being correlative with conduct or formation of a self through choosing emerges in KIERKEGAARD's early writings: *Either/Or* and *Two Ages*. He writes that morality is character and adds that character is engraved; neither the sea nor the sand nor abstract common sense has it since essentially character is inwardness. He sought to underscore that character had a conceptual tie to the idea of passion or inwardness without which a self or personality never becomes enervated and gets shaped. Becoming a genuine self is by virtue of the infinite passion of inwardness, which is also a condition for an individual's becoming related to GOD. The indelible mark on the human soul is the infinite or SPIRIT within the self and not that infused in the self through certain sacraments. Character must include at least a spiritual and a volitional aspect. FAITH brings together the two aspects, passion and act, and is heightened through appropriating the absolute paradox of Jesus as God-in-man. To become properly related to God implies conducting one's life as a member of a COMMUNITY with civic obligations and simultaneously relating infinitely to the eternal.

MARCEL's and SARTRE's writings also acknowledge that a personal act or choice with respect to the nature of a person's existence is at the formative center of one's character. Marcel does not require a crucifixion of the understanding, in the way that Kierkegaard's absolute paradox implies, for the formation of character. Sartre's emphasis on an unconditionally free act for which the self takes responsibility without having to postulate a deity clearly recognizes no spiritual aspect in the meaning-complex of character. Action that is lucid and acceptance of responsibility for others are the essentials for character formation, Sartre thought. The meaning-complex for the concept character, therefore, might be distinguished minimally as requiring of a SUBJECT a free passional activity from within the self and responsibility for others with respect to that activity, rather than by artificial or external habits or inherited dispositions.

Passionate activity and responsibility as constitutive of the formative center of character resound in BUBER as well. Character is a task, the link between what the individual is and the sequence of one's actions and attitudes. The individual chooses from the multifarious form-giving and opposing forces in NATURE and SOCIETY those forces that one will allow to interpenetrate one's BEING, to stimulate one's interest, desire, and agreement and thereby to mold for community living as well. To live in community is to take personal responsibility for life and for the WORLD. Thus, character is the expression through a sequence of action and attitude of the unity of what a person is and hopes to become. This conception of character implies a preference for, and a recognition and acknowledgment of, absolute VALUES.

Primary Works

Buber, Martin. *Between Man and Man*. Trans. Ronald Gregor Smith. New York: Macmillan, 1965.
Kierkegaard, Søren. *Two Ages*. Trans. Howard V. Hong and Edna H. Hong. Princeton: Princeton University Press, 1978.

CHOICE
Lawrence J. Hatab

Choice in existential PHILOSOPHY is connected with the question of FREEDOM and the ultimate openness and groundlessness of the human condition. Existentialism rejects all forms of determinism that explain human actions as governed by forces beyond the control of the individual—as exemplified in religious, naturalistic, behavioristic, biological, or social forms of determinism. This robust sense of freedom leads to a strong sense of RESPONSIBILITY that is placed on the individual and marks the particular ethical dimension adopted by many existentialists.

KIERKEGAARD's notorious claim that TRUTH is subjectivity spotlights the importance of choice. It is not that all truth is subjective but that human matters—represented by the three stages of existence: the AESTHETIC, ETHICAL, and RELIGIOUS STAGES—are governed not by objective criteria that ground decisions in universal truth conditions but by the subjective commitment to choose to live a certain way. He holds that traditional philosophical systems—even those that defended freedom—ignored or suppressed the concrete conditions of human EXISTENCE in favor of objective criteria that ameliorate or deflect the difficulties involved in choices. He argues that we cannot purge from choice its characteristic exclusiveness and ambivalence—exclusiveness in the sense that a choice faces more than one alternative and must affirm one and deny others, ambivalence in the sense that each alternative has some attraction, and so there will never be certainty that the course chosen was the right one. Significant choices—particularly the decision to move from aesthetic indulgence to an ethical LIFE and from ethical worldliness to religious FAITH—force us to decide between two important, but conflicting, options. Dialectical philosophers such as Hegel had attempted to incorporate opposing conditions in an overarching system, but for Kierkegaard, such systems obviate the very conditions of human choices as lived phenomena. Passage between the stages of existence can be accomplished only by an individual act in the midst of exclusive alternatives. ETHICS demands the sacrifice of personal indulgence in favor of a commitment to the common GOOD, and RELIGION demands the sacrifice of worldly concerns in favor of a LEAP to the promise of ETERNITY. Traditional philosophy addressed these matters in terms of rational justification. Kierkegaard insists that such approaches are incapable of expressing these matters, especially with respect to the ANXIETY that accompanies choice. Anxiety is a simultaneous attraction and repulsion in the midst of a decision. This ambivalent suspension, together with the temporal structure of choice that includes an uncertain future and an irretrievable past, reveals that choice is not susceptible to rational demonstration, organization, or integration.

The subjectivity of choice means that there is nothing to which an individual can point to justify or guarantee a decision. PERSONS usually want to ground their choices in some determined reference so as to escape the discomfort of self-determination. Wanting to escape this discomfort is tantamount to rejecting the human condition, since our concrete finitude and the dilemmas surrounding life choices are not expendable. Consider the choice of marriage. For Kierkegaard, marriage is an ethical situation, where one faces a decision to exchange individual freedom and indulgence for a commitment to a spouse and family. The two spheres are, in many respects, mutually exclusive, and it is no wonder that people experience anxiety on the threshold of such a decision. Nevertheless, I can resolve the disparities only by an exclusive choice, and no one can make it for me. Moreover, the ambivalence and ambiguities surrounding marriage will not disappear after a choice has been made. Kierkegaard offers a strong affirmation of ethics and of traditional ethical norms. He stresses that ethics is a choice, a commitment to a way of life. The aesthetic stage is marked by moral indifference; the ethical stage is marked by choosing to live by the distinction between good and evil.

In SARTRE's philosophy, choice is shown in the correlation of CONSCIOUSNESS, NEGATION, and freedom. Human consciousness is essentially a negativity that is not bound by objective conditions. Such negativity is displayed in the capacity for denial, in the pervasiveness of possibility, and in various forms of distance that consciousness creates between itself and extant things. The human self is capable of resisting and refusing any compelling force, even unto DEATH. Sartre's famous proposition that ''existence precedes essence'' insists that existing individuals have no prior ESSENCE. Rather, they bring their NATURES into BEING through their choices to live a certain way. The responsibility for who and what I am is solely a result of my choices. This fundamental responsibility is the source of human anxiety and also of BAD FAITH—the various attempts to deny my responsibility by deflecting it to other forces, a strategy that aims to cover up the abyss of freedom that marks human consciousness. Choice and freedom are not absolute. Objective conditions, biological properties, and natural laws are not within the power of the self to choose. If one contracts a terminal disease, this is an element of FACTICITY that is not subject to choice. But how one will live with this fact, whether one is stoical, despairing, or cheerful, is up to the individual. The meaning of, and our response to, various life conditions are a matter of choice and are not fixed by material or social conditions. The priority of choice is both ennobling and frightening. Human life is not a causal product of biological processes, environmental forces, or instinctual drives but rather its choices in the midst of factical conditions, not something bound by these conditions. Thus, hunger as a biological event is not chosen, but fasting, even unto death, shows that desire for food is not an objective condition that compels action but rather a matter of choice. If someone is force-fed, that is one thing; but a conscious person in normal circumstances can create a PROJECT that calls for fasting or restraint in eating. Even bad faith is a choice to evade responsibility and seek a determined cause for one's action. Thus, choice is ineluctable in human consciousness; we are condemned to be free.

The priority of choice leads Sartre to reject an objective, absolute moral standard. Nevertheless, the way in which one chooses in a moral SITUATION can be judged in terms of whether or not the choice was made in bad faith. Freedom means that the chooser is totally responsible for the choice and for how this choice influences the WORLD. This approach cannot tell us what to do, but it insists on elements crucial to any morality: freedom, responsibility, and commitment. As Sartre did, one can judge Nazism to be a moral evil and take a stand against it, despite the fact that one cannot point to an absolute standard that rules out Nazism. Even if there were an absolute standard, that would not change the fact that one would still face the choice of whether or not to comply.

The individual, for HEIDEGGER, is always caught up in forces and circumstances greater than itself, this despite the fact that he agrees with Kierkegaard and Sartre in rejecting deterministic explanations of the human condition. The problem for Heidegger is that the model of consciousness and the rhetoric of choice are too reductive on the side of the human subject. Human activity is better rendered as a complicated interplay of individuated paths within social, historical, and natural conditions. The authentic life is not something fully chosen by an individual at the expense of, or in disregard to, extraindividual circumstances but rather the discovery of a specific path within these circumstances, a path that has been clarified and liberated from encrusted habits and superficial cultural norms that conceal the depth and import of a person's existential concerns.

Primary Works

Kierkegaard, Søren. *Concluding Unscientific Postscript*. Trans. David F. Swenson and Walter Lowrie. Princeton: Princeton University Press, 1968.

Sartre, Jean-Paul. *Existentialism and Humanism*. Trans. Philip Mairet. London: Methuen, 1973.

Bibliography

Gordon, Haim, and Rivca Gordon. *Sartre and Evil*. Westport, CT: Greenwood Press, 1995.

CHRISTIANITY
Thomas B. Ommen

Christian existentialism includes, in addition to KIERKEGAARD's work which is a seminal influence, the work of MARCEL, BERDYAEV, and UNAMUNO. These later thinkers distinguished their work from THEOLOGY and tried to avoid identification with institutional Christianity. They shared Kierkegaard's distaste for Christendom and the conformity and rote FAITH it can produce; his critique of Hegelian rationalism became, in their work, a critique of more recent varieties of theological rationalism in neo-scholastic and Eastern Orthodox forms. Theology based on Christian existentialism also originated in the work of Kierkegaard and culminated in this century in the thought of BULTMANN, TILLICH, and other Protestant theologians. These writers spoke from within the Christian faith and addressed their work primarily to a Christian audience. Such thinkers may be quite critical of traditional forms of theology, but they were engaged in what Tillich called the theological correlation of Christian message and contemporary SITUATION. Tillich and Bultmann employed HEIDEGGER's ideas to interpret the Christian message and to reexpress it in terms relevant to contemporary culture. The influence of existentialism on Roman Catholic theology is less evident. Pius XII's critical remarks on existentialism in his encyclical *Humani Generis* of 1950 made it unpopular among traditional Catholics. Yet, RAHNER and other Catholic theologians used Heidegger's thoughts to describe the structures of human existence.

Christianity has played the role of what Marcel called a fertilizing principle even in the work of atheists like SARTRE whose rejection of GOD involves an interpretation of, and reaction against, Christian faith. For Marcel, Berdyaev, and Unamuno, Christian faith played a positive role. Theological themes like MYSTERY, grace, faith, hope, and LOVE abound in their work, although they were reluctant to be associated with any particular theological understanding of such themes. Marcel was anxious to avoid confusing mysteries revealed in hu-

man experience with theological mysteries such as incarnation and REDEMP-
TION. His ONTOLOGY was open to REVELATION, and he hoped to prepare
the way to its acceptance. But PHILOSOPHY cannot presuppose revelation nor
even claim fully to understand it. Berdyaev considered revelational authority not
an external but an internal fact. The philosopher may acquire the MIND of
Christ, and that leads to a philosophy different from one constructed on non-
Christian foundations. Marcel felt a fraternal alliance with nonbelievers and
sought to work on a threshold between unbelief and BELIEF. He strove to
develop a philosophy acceptable to non-Catholics and even nonbelievers. Unlike
the theologian, the philosopher, in Berdyaev's view, must maintain an autonomy
from ecclesiastical authorities and traditional theology. Philosophy adopts a critical stance toward religious belief and is, in contrast to theology, more an
individual than a COMMUNITY enterprise. Unamuno sought to avoid identification with dogmas, harshly criticized Spanish Catholic orthodoxy, and spent
years in exile largely as a consequence of his thorny relationship with ecclesiastical authorities.

The religious character of existential philosophy has appeared in a hunger for
God and immortality and, in addition, in a mysterious sense of divine presence.
The negative form of TRANSCENDENCE is captured in images of the Fall and
original SIN. As Kierkegaard put it, because of the Fall, the individual cannot
take oneself back into the eternal by way of recollection. In Marcel's image,
the fundamental human experience is that we live in a broken WORLD, in need
of salvation. All hope is ultimately hope of salvation. Only in God, Berdyaev
argued, does humanity overcome a fundamental solitude and discover a purpose
commensurate with human EXISTENCE. Nonreligious existentialism leaves humans trapped in the world, facing the absurdity of DEATH. For Unamuno, death
is the most threatening situation humans face, and it prompts a hunger for immortality that survives even if reason rejects it as an illusion. One can say, in
a sense, that the longing for immortality led humans to create God, although
this is possible only because God beforehand created Himself in us.

The positive sense of God's presence is harder for Christian existentialists to
identify and articulate, in part because of a reluctance to appeal to revelation.
For Marcel, the experience of God takes the form of a participation in BEING,
even though we are unable to know or to say in what we participate. The
presence of God is found in a spiritual dimension of human existence, an ontological point where the divine and the human meet. This mysterious presence
of the divine cannot be objectified; it takes the form of a blind INTUITION.
The heart of philosophy lay, for Berdyaev, in the idea of the reciprocal action
of the divine and human, of the penetration of the supernatural into the natural
most fully captured in the divine incarnation in Christ. Only when Unamuno
had been reduced by rational doubt to skepticism did he attain a sense of God's
presence, more as a hope than a fact. God is most present in moments of spiritual
suffocation, in the tragic sense of human destiny. To believe in God is to wish
for Him and to be unable to live without Him.

Christian existentialists distrust rationalist approaches to God. Kierkegaard stressed the gap between reason and the paradox of the eternal in TIME. No form of human knowledge can grasp the claim that the Eternal is the historical. Christian TRUTH is appropriated subjectively, in an appropriation-process of the most passionate inwardness. Marcel argued against attempts to rationalize the experience of God. He did not like to speak even of God's existing, because this seems to reduce the divine to the status of an OBJECT. Whatever knowledge we have of God is in the form of participation, in an immediate awareness that cannot be verified. Mystery, unlike a problem, cannot be objectified. Berdyaev stressed that God cannot become an object of thought. Reason stands, for Unamuno, over against a human longing for immortality; it contradicts, in a sense, human feeling. The God of natural theology is no more than reason hypostatized and projected into infinity, not a reality that can be encountered. Reason leads to the nothing-God, to a depersonalized divinity far removed from the living God and father of Jesus.

Through the 1970s existentialism provided the most influential philosophical framework for Christian theological work, particularly in the Protestant tradition. Such a theological reliance on philosophy was an additional attempt to carry out what Tillich called the correlation of Christian message and changing cultural situation. Every theology is dependent for the clarification of its concepts upon a pretheological understanding of human existence that reflects implicitly or explicitly a philosophical tradition. Theologians have regularly turned to philosophy to find new ideas in which to express a Christian understanding of existence. For many theologians, existentialist ideas provided an adequate philosophical framework.

Bultmann found existentialist philosophy to express an understanding of the basic structure of human existence and of the existence of the Christian believer in particular. To critics who accused Bultmann of distorting the Bible to fit a Heideggerian mold, he responded that they should rather be surprised that philosophy already sees what one finds in the New Testament. For Tillich, existentialism was a natural ally of Christianity. It offered the most appropriate ideas for describing the most important questions generated by the human situation and in showing that the symbols contained in the Christian message provide answers to those questions. Existentialism powerfully describes human existence under the old aeon, in a state of estrangement from authentic existence. At the center of existential theologies is a stress on the historicity of human existence. To be human is to be constantly confronted with the question of who we are and the choice of AUTHENTICITY or inauthenticity. We are offered the possibility of losing ourselves in the past or in the crowd or of seizing new possibilities, especially those opened up by faith in God. The innermost reality of humans, our sense of self, completely transcends not only the outside world but also the interior world shaped by subjective feelings and experiences. The continual possibility of self-transcendence makes us fully human. We can close ourselves off from the future or remain open to it by preserving a distance or FREEDOM from the world and what lies within it. The true ground of such freedom is found in the grace of God. A stress on historicity is supported by the decisional understanding of human life portrayed in the Bible. New Testament parables, for example, always confront the reader with a summons to decision.

Tillich is critical of attempts to consider God an object alongside other objects. Self-affirmation in spite of the ANXIETY of GUILT and condemnation presupposes participation in something that transcends the self. Christ offers an embodiment of the New Being in which human estrangement is overcome. In this New Being, the negativities of existence are overcome, and unity with God and our ESSENCE is regained. Christ offers an example of a human who within the world conditions of existential estrangement was one with the Father. Because humans exist in a state of estrangement from their essential nature, a strictly philosophical understanding of existence is for existentialist theology insufficient. A PHENOMENOLOGY of authentic human existence requires a movement from philosophy to theology. Existence without God is marked ultimately by despair and a sense of meaninglessness. Tillich's question-answer paradigm captures the distinction. Life without God is marked ultimately by a questionableness that philosophy can illuminate but not overcome. Anxiety is finally countered only through divine revelation and grace. The answer to the questions of human existence cannot be derived from existence. It is spoken to human existence from beyond. Revelation and the gospel provide a definitive clarification of life that is not visible to philosophy.

The understanding that philosophy produces is distinguished from the experience of God as personal event in one's LIFE, which is mediated by faith and by an encounter with Christian proclamation. Philosophy can offer a clarification of the notion of justification, but for the individual to actually experience justification, an inner realization is essential, made possible by a faithful response to the word of God. Authentic existence is not a work of human effort, produced by human courage or resolve. Rather, it arises from a response to divine forgiveness and release from attempts at self-justification.

A faithful response to the Christian kerygma, essential to authentic existence, is often endangered by the mythical form the message takes. In Bultmann's thought, existentialist theology includes DEMYTHOLOGIZING. The nonobjective reality of God, experienced only in the existential experience, is objectified in MYTH. God becomes an object and is thus experienced as another aspect of the external world. What is needed, Bultmann argued, is not the selection or elimination of myth, which is at the center of New Testament proclamation, but demythologization or interpretation in existentialist terms. What is important in myth is the understanding of human existence it expresses; the self-understanding expressed in myth is in harmony with, and can be reexpressed with the help of, existentialist philosophy. Life according to the flesh, for example, in Pauline terms, can be expressed in terms of estrangement and anxiety. Existentialism offers an effective approach for making the biblical message relevant to a contemporary understanding of the human condition.

Demythologizing is one aspect of a broader theory of theological hermeneutics developed by Bultmann and his students. The interpretation of any text depends on a living relationship to the subject matter expressed. In the case of serious LITERATURE, like Scripture or the classics of philosophy, the proper relationship and preunderstanding are a recognition of the existential claim they make on the reader. The object of interpretation in such instances is interest in HISTORY as the sphere of life in which human existence moves, in which it attains understanding of itself and its particular possibilities and develops them. Such texts emerge in the framework of historicity as possibilities of self-understanding that must be seized and repeated. For a scientific and critical interpretation of biblical texts, preunderstanding is raised to thematic and explicit awareness with the aid of philosophy. A philosophical examination of the meaning of existence serves as the basis for theology.

Thus, theologians like Bultmann and Tillich have found in existentialism a way of posing the questions of existence. Theological questions are treated primarily as questions of humanity's existence in relationship to God. The sacred writings are seen as statements that primarily express an understanding of human existence. Existentialism also offers a system of basic concepts that make possible an analysis of the understanding of existence.

Primary Works

Berdyaev, Nicolai. *The Divine and the Human*. Trans. R. M. French. London: Geoffrey Bles, 1949.

Kierkegaard, Søren. *Attack upon Christendom*. Trans. Walter Lowrie. Princeton: Princeton University Press, 1968.

Marcel, Gabriel. *Presence and Immortality*. Trans. Michael A. Machado and Henry J. Koren. Pittsburgh: Duquesne University Press, 1967.

Bibliography

Kelsey, David H. *The Fabric of Paul Tillich's Theology*. New Haven CT: Yale University Press, 1967.

COMMUNITY
Richard Polt

The individualist strain in the existentialist tradition would seem to militate against a positive conception of community. In *The Present Age*, KIERKE-

GAARD rails against the predominance of the public, which disregards the infinite importance of the individual soul. NIETZSCHE shows nothing but contempt for the herd and extols great, creative individuals who stand on solitary peaks. In SARTRE's *Being and Nothingness*, the group is merely a surface phenomenon; the underlying reality is one of individual subjectivities that freely posit their own values. Relations with others are inherently combative: I struggle to objectify others while avoiding objectification myself. In contrast, BUBER has searched for genuine communion with others, which demands a distinction between inauthentic and authentic coexistence; he believed in the distinction between SOCIETY and community originated by Tonnies: a society is a calculative, contractual arrangement in which interpersonal relations are means to an end; a community is bound together by shared convictions that permeate its members' lives; in it interpersonal relations help to constitute the identities of the members.

Of the many forms that solicitude can take, HEIDEGGER singles out two. I can inauthentically LEAP in for others, dominating them and taking over their responsibilities; or I can authentically leap ahead of others in order to point the way and reveal their responsibilities in a liberating manner. He mentions two types of shared involvement. Being with one another can be based on doing the same thing, as when several hired hands work in tandem. It can also be based, more authentically, on each person's free commitment to the task at hand. Thus, he delineates an authentic Being-with, or community. Everyday existence, however, is inauthentic—I am not myself but simply the THEY: I do what one does, as one does. DASEIN exists for the sake of its own Being: my activities are given sense and orientation by their contribution to my ability to be. However, I ordinarily fail to acknowledge this condition: I do not take RESPONSIBILITY for my existence but simply exist in an average way that conforms to the prejudices of my group. The they is a permanent feature of Dasein, although the extent to which it dominates existence is variable. I can break free (temporarily) from the they only when I accept ANXIETY, mortality, and GUILT and resolutely take responsibility for my choices. However, this does not mean that I become separate from the they: the authentic choice is but a way of taking hold of the everyday self. My possibilities for action are always drawn from the public culture that I have inherited: only in my heritage can I find my fate, which is not ultimately solitary but wrapped up in the destiny of a group. Thus, a generation can be bound together through communication and struggle, under the guidance of a freely chosen hero or role model.

In the 1930s and 1940s Heidegger asserts that the polis is the foundation of Dasein—the site where HISTORY can occur, where BEING can have a meaning. This community is sustained by great, creative individuals: poets, thinkers, priests, rulers. The essence of a people lies in its historical response to Being, a response preserved in the sayings of thinkers and poets. His vision of community seems to be oriented toward an elite who are capable of interpreting and regenerating the experience of Being entrusted to a people.

Buber rejects both atomistic individualism and collectivism in which the self is surrendered to a leader or to an abstract concept of the people. Individualism is mistaken because genuine personhood does not lie in self-discovery or self-assertion but rather in an encounter with the Thou. Collectivism obscures the fact that although the individual belongs to a group, the group can never absorb the PERSON. Genuine reciprocity requires recognition of the distance between persons. Authentic RELATIONS must form the basis of community. The shared goods and interests that bind together a community are sustained not by political programs but by personal encounters, animated by a spirit of mutuality that enables the members to be present for each other. Such mutuality is a living, reciprocal relationship among the members of the community and between each member and the living center that gives focus to the community. Community requires a personal transformation that brings about a common dedication to realizing an ideal of justice. It would be impossible to establish an unjust community: means must be consistent with ends.

Buber understands community also in religious terms. One model for an authentic human group is the historic Hasidic community, which is united by reverence for, and celebration of, GOD. A theophany can occur in everyday situations of mutual responsibility and reciprocity. By saying Thou to our fellow humans we become capable of saying Thou to God; community is the only site in which the divine plan for humanity can be realized. Community involves both a commitment to implementing ideals and an acknowledgment of the difficulty of this process. It remained a goal often reached only tentatively and sporadically. Buber found the possibility of genuine solidarity in the kibbutz and the ideal of the halutz as a model builder of a community.

MARCEL develops his concept of community in opposition to an inauthentic human group—society or mass society. His understanding of community is closely related to, if not founded on, his relational view of selfhood. The origin of the EGO and of the higher type of self, the person, is found in the realm of the interpersonal and is based on an acceptance of the EXISTENCE of others: I am myself rather than others; this difference must be recognized by another. I become myself by acquiring possessions that are acknowledged by others as mine and by identifying myself with persons whom I LOVE and with groups of which I am a member. My self-development is intrinsically social; within an authentic community my PERSONALITY can fully flourish.

However, one's relations to others are often inauthentic in the contemporary world. I can seek recognition through posing, fawning, or manipulation and fail to do justice to the other as a person; simultaneously, my development as a person is hampered. A human group in which inauthentic relationships predominate is a mere mass society, a collective held together by calculable, impersonal relations. A false egalitarianism prevails: humans are viewed as measurable by the same official classifications and criteria and thus as fundamentally interchangeable. This process of abstraction and leveling works against authentic personality and FREEDOM. Marcel identifies two forms of mass society. First, society can be ruled by competitive, egocentric individualism. This form promotes selfishness at the expense of genuine personal development, since competition is ruled by a single, impersonal measure of achievement, for example, the market VALUE of one's labor. Marcel also denounces totalitarian alternatives to capitalism even more vigorously: fascism and communism crush and degrade individuals in the name of a false collective ideal.

Much of Marcel's positive concept of community must be inferred from his sustained criticisms of mass society; he also provides direct descriptions of, and prescriptions for, authentic groups. A community must be bound together by an authentic intersubjectivity. Members of a community must be open to each other and CARE about each other, thus allowing each other to be persons. Egocentrism is to be overcome through recognizing that personality and freedom are gifts, rather than achievements of the WILL. We must also assume responsibility in service of a common cause, engaging ourselves with commitment and creative fidelity. This cause should be understood in terms of its meaning for living persons; community cannot be built around an abstraction but only around a universal—a profound experience that can speak to all humans. The loyal engagements that unite people in a community must be animated by the spirit of availability, that is, a responding with concern to human situations that present themselves and an engaging in genuine communication. These authentic relationships make a community more tightly integrated than a mass society, while leaving room for differences among the members and a sphere of individual privacy. Marcel's CHRISTIANITY emerges in his view that individuals transcend the group thanks to their connection to a transcendent reality, acknowledged in the ideal community. Members of the community are linked by fraternity, that is, by grasping themselves as children of the same Father. Interpersonal communion is guided by an attempt to commune with the ultimate unity of love, TRUTH, and justice. He encourages communities formed on a local level, little aristocracies devoted to what is best, bound together by fraternity and love. His model is a religious community. He warns against dogmatism and fanaticism: the community must remain available to other communities and open to fresh discoveries. Small-scale associations may assist us to resist the forces of impersonal massification.

It is not easy to resolve the ontological questions that underlie the difference between a Heideggerian and a Buberian-Marcelian conception of community. How important is the I–Thou relation in human coexistence? Is authentic community founded on Heideggerian individual resoluteness or on openness to the other? From Buber's perspective, Heideggerian authenticity remains too solitary and monological to serve as the basis of genuine encounters and of community. But Heidegger claims that his statement that Dasein exists for the sake of its own being is not an endorsement of selfishness; rather, it describes a formal, ontological condition for the possibility of both egoistic and nonegoistic stances. If Heidegger is correct, the position proclaimed in *Being and Time* is not inconsistent with the positions of Buber and Marcel, whose accounts of interpersonal relations could be seen as elaborations of the authentic and inauthentic modes of Being-with, briefly described by Heidegger.

Primary Works

Buber, Martin. *Paths in Utopia.* Trans. R.F.C. Hull. Boston: Beacon Press, 1958.
Marcel, Gabriel. *Creative Fidelity.* Trans. Robert Rosthal. New York: Farrar, Straus, and Giroux, 1964.
————. *The Mystery of Being.* Vols. 1 and 2. Trans. G. S. Fraser. Chicago: Henry Regnery, 1960.

CONSCIENCE
Daniel O. Dahlstrom

Existentialist thinkers contrast conscience as it presents itself in an inauthentic manner, namely, a conscience that has let itself be fully assimilated to public or ethically rational considerations, with conscience in the proper sense of the term, namely, one that is an accomplishment and individual. For KIERKE-GAARD, this contrast amounts to the difference between a conscience that one has relative to other humans and a conscience that one has before GOD, which is not given but must be achieved. In *Fear and Trembling* he rejects Hegel's argument that, because conscience takes the form of the particular individual judging oneself, it must be annulled in the process of realizing an ethical LIFE, the validity of which is derived precisely from its universality. A genuine conscience, Kierkegaard holds, is concerned not with some future outcome of action in this WORLD but with the judgment of ETERNITY; hence, the means to an end are as important to conscience as the end itself.

NIETZSCHE in *The Gay Science* contrasts a strictly ethical or communal conscience, as elaborated in the tradition of Kant and Hegel, with a higher, intellectual conscience, overseeing one's ordinary conscience. That superior form of conscience unmasks the irresoluteness and self-deception attaching to the all-too-facile and firm belief in the judgments of an ethical conscience and, in the process, its capacity to enable a PERSON to overcome oneself. Nietzsche's appeal to a higher conscience is at odds with Kant's account, which equates conscience with the CONSCIOUSNESS of an unerring internal court within each individual; contrarily, Nietzsche assigns to an intellectual conscience precisely the task of questioning why a person listens to his or her conscience and finds its judgments to be true and honest. Probing the genealogy of an ethical conscience in this manner means raising the question of whether the rigidity with which a person obeys one's conscience does not betray a lack of self-understanding, a failure of nerve, or even an inability to create new ideals. Nietzsche observes that most people lack an intellectual conscience. Anyone who genuinely feels what the latter requires—anyone who experiences the demand for certainty as the most intimate of one's desires and the most urgent of one's needs—has a sense of being utterly alone, as though one were in the desert, even when one is, in fact, surrounded by others and involved with them. In *On the Genealogy of Morals* he demonstrates that conscience is an instinct for cruelty turned inward after no longer being able to be released outwardly. He introduces this theme by asking how it was possible to breed an animal with a capacity to remember and keep promises—a human with a sense of RESPONSIBILITY. The sovereign individual who is responsible and conscious of one's FREEDOM as the POWER over oneself and one's fate is the product of a lengthy, historical process of mnemotechnics, usually taking the form of painful customs in an attempt to render certain ideas unforgettable—on the supposition that the only things that do not fade from our memory are the things that caused pain. Conscience is described as the resulting, dominating instinct of such an individual.

Nietzsche locates the basis of the moral conception of conscience, of GUILT and duty, in the sphere of legal obligations; such notions derive their force ultimately from the pleasure of punishing, the pleasure of participating in a right of masters and—above all—quenching a thirst for cruelty, as compensation for an unpaid debt. He holds that a bad conscience is nothing other than the consciousness of guilt, a mechanism invented by humans filled with RESENTMENT—quintessentially by Christians—for the purpose of inflicting pain on themselves once the more natural way to vent this desire was blocked. Hence, his hypothesis: bad conscience is the gravest and uncanniest illness, the phenomenon of the animal soul turning against itself, something that became inevitable as soon as humans, having undergone the most fundamental change in their experience, found themselves enclosed within the walls of SOCIETY and of peace. The high point of this invention is that Christian stroke of genius: the sense of an unatonable guilt before God, an absolutely unprecedented example of madness of WILL. Nevertheless, while bad conscience is a sickness, it is a sickness in the sense that pregnancy is a sickness, holding out the promise of a SPIRIT capable of reversing the bad conscience.

HEIDEGGER'S analysis of conscience presupposes an inauthentic and an authentic EXISTENCE. Inauthentic existence is the phenomenon of letting oneself be determined by a group. To reverse the process of being lost to the group an individual must retrieve himself or herself from it or, in other words, take back a choice that had been relinquished to the group and decide for oneself both on the basis of, and for the sake of, one's own potential to be. Since, however, a person always finds that one has, from the outset, fallen into some group behavior and let one's self be appropriated by the group's mentality, a retrieval of an authentic self is possible only if something attests to a potential to be oneself, that is to say, a potential to be what and how one authentically is. Conscience is what attests to the potential to be oneself in this sense. Conscience is to be investigated exclusively as an existential, that is, as a phenomenon that is distinctive of, and distinctively self-discloses, human existence. This analysis purports to rule out psychological descriptions or theological interpretations for which the distinctiveness of human existence is either not at issue, ignored, or even passed over in favor of some generic sense of BEING. Traditional attempts to interpret conscience by tracing it to the intellect, the will, a feeling, or some mixture of the same all prove inadequate because they overlook its fundamental, existential CHARACTER. Moreover, the aim of the investigation is not to accomplish a genuine conscience (whether the latter be understood as one's conscience before God or as an intellectual conscience) but to unpack what "to be" means in the case of DASEIN.

Heidegger elaborates who is addressed by conscience, to what the person is called, what is said in the call, and who does the calling. Conscience is a call to Dasein itself; the call of conscience is directed at Dasein's way of understanding itself in its everyday concerns. Conscience does not call Dasein to its standing or validation in the public domain or to what it can do or procure in that arena. Indeed, the call of conscience is devastating to those who, having identified themselves with a group, are passionately attached to the respect they enjoy in the public arena. However, conscience also does not call Dasein to the self of some sort of interior life or private WORLD of the soul. Rather, conscience simply calls Dasein back to the potential to be most proper to it as a BEING-IN-THE-WORLD. Finally, the call of conscience need not be articulated or verbalized. Indeed, its call is silent without sacrificing understandability or clarity. Nor is the call of conscience something to which we can remain indifferent; it has a jolting, unsettling effect.

Heidegger insists that the call of conscience is the call of Dasein to itself, even though it is neither planned nor prepared nor willfully carried out by that Dasein. He explains this apparent anomaly by noting that Dasein, for the most part, flees the fact that it has been thrown into the world, taking solace in a group-self. This flight is a flight in the face of the uncanniness of Dasein's individualized being-in-the-world, an uncanniness revealed in ANXIETY. Uncanniness is the basic way of being-in-the-world, even though it is obscured in Dasein's everydayness. What is uncanny is the fact that I am at all, the sense that I am not at home, that I am no one in the world, that my individuality and my being thrown into the NOTHINGNESS of the world are utterly alien to the group, presenting it with nothing that might be publicly discussed and passed on. What Dasein has to report from out of the depths of this uncanniness of its having been thrown into the world are not facts or events but solely the potential to be, revealed in anxiety. It does not verbalize this communique; its call is a beckoning out of the public gossip of the group and into the reticence of its potential to be. The certainty of the caller is due to the fact that Dasein, in the utter individuality of its uncanniness, is completely unexchangeable. The call of conscience, a call that Dasein makes to itself in a state of anxiety, is what first makes it possible for Dasein to project itself onto and toward the potentiality most distinctive to it alone. The call of conscience is the call of CARE; the caller is Dasein, anxious as it is, in its thrownness, about its potential to be; the called is Dasein, summoned to the potential to be what is most distinctively its own, hence, a summons to it to emerge from its descent into the group and exist as care. What makes conscience possible in an ontological sense is the fact that care is the basis of what Dasein is.

Given this analysis, there is no need to appeal to some alien power; indeed, the latter is a sign that Dasein is taken not on its own terms but in terms of something other than Dasein. These interpretations are attempts to find a way out from, or to flee in the face of, conscience. Conscience is always a private, individual affair, coming to me from myself about myself or, more precisely, from an existential point of view, about the potential to be what distinguishes me as Dasein from other ways of being. Anything like a public conscience or the world's conscience is a fabrication, the voice of the group, which can be sustained only if I make it my conscience. Only by stepping outside domination by the group is conscience genuinely free and legitimately objective.

The guilt to which conscience on an existential level calls Dasein is an original guilt. Dasein is the thrown ground or basis of its potential to be, its existence. Inasmuch as it is thrown into the world, Dasein can never become master of what it is, and, yet, insofar as it exists, projecting itself as a possibility, Dasein exists to take control of itself. Dasein is faced with the dilemma of having to take control of, to master, or simply to take responsibility for what it is never fully responsible for: its life. Dasein ultimately is what it cares about-and-for, and what Dasein cares about-and-for is, in the last analysis, its potential to take responsibility for the potential that it is, precisely as a possibility existing as thrown into the world. At the same time, in taking over being the basis for itself, Dasein must constantly choose certain possibilities while ignoring others and, accordingly, bear responsibility. Dasein is inauthentic when it conceals these two basic senses of thrownness and projecting that constitute its very being. Dasein's original guilt consists in this concealment, which, in turn, makes conscience possible. Conscience is possible at all only because Dasein, having been thrown into the world and continually falling prey to the world's demands, conceals itself from itself and, hence, in that respect, is guilty at the very core of its being. Thus, uncanniness and guilt are combined by Heidegger into an existential definition of conscience. On the basis of the uncanniness of being-in-the-world and from out of the depths of the feeling of this uncanniness, Dasein summons itself to the potential to be guilty in the sense most proper to it; conscience is this summons or call.

Primary Works

Nietzsche, Friedrich. *The Gay Science*. Trans. Walter Kaufmann. New York: Random House, 1974.
————. *On the Genealogy of Morals and Ecce Homo*. Trans. Walter Kaufmann and R. J. Hollingdale. New York: Vintage, 1969.

Bibliography

Aloni, Nimrod. *Beyond Nihilism: Nietzsche's Healing and Edifying Philosophy*. Lanham, MD: University Press of America, 1991.
Barnes, Hazel. *An Existentialist Ethics*. Chicago: University of Chicago Press, 1967.

CONSCIOUSNESS
Adrian Mirvish

NIETZSCHE views consciousness as a late, unreliable, and weak manifestation of the WILL to POWER, but it is also associated with the emergence of a higher form of humanity. Regarding the genesis of consciousness, think of a state of NATURE in which humans coped with their environment on the basis of instincts, finely tuned for survival. Nietzsche sees our forebear acting spontaneously, living on the basis of cunning, strength, and the ability to wage war. With the advent of SOCIETY, humans become divorced from their ferocious past; the structure of instinct is undermined and partially replaced by the demands and constraints of a new form of EXISTENCE. Here consciousness arises first as a social phenomenon whose origin lies in the need to communicate efficiently, given human vulnerability. Drawing inferences and setting up interpretations—for instance, cause and effect to order experience—take the place of action on the basis of instinct. It is no longer possible to act merely on instinct and dispositions prevalent at the moment. Social constraints demand an operationally fixed identity for viable interactions. Instincts are turned to create an inner WORLD instead of being discharged outward.

In spite of its utility, consciousness is a late, poorly developed arrival. Nietzsche insists that our most important activity is unconsciousness and that there would be no hope for human survival without instincts since consciousness is unreliable and gullible. What we experience consciously are the most superficial sequences of events. To these we often ascribe a causal relation that, even if convenient, may be fictional. For instance, dreams are the resultant interpretation of physical sensations: nerve excitations or impulses, the end product of the movement of the blood, external noises, the pressure of the bedclothes. If my feet are bound with a rope, I may dream that snakes are coiled around my ankles and say that the mental image was the cause of my SENSATIONS. He even says that there may be no difference between waking and dreaming states. LIFE may be a strange commentary on a text that cannot be known or may not even exist. His book *Twilight of the Idols* points to four great errors: hypostatizing imaginary causes, confusing cause and effect, the error of false cause, and the error of free will. Yet so endemic are these errors to consciousness that the herd is doomed to a life of illusion. Mastery over oneself means having a mastery over one's circumstances, nature, and the herd. In order to exercise the Will to Power creatively, with finesse, the SUPERMAN needs to channel the dynamic, raw energy of his passions. However, it cannot be reason in a traditional sense that serves this ordering function. Instead, this must be due to that part of the SPIRIT that, if not objectively distanced from the passions, is nevertheless able to hold them in check and channel them with a vision to the future. CREATIVITY involves foresight, patience, self-mastery, and the ability to hold oneself in check. This points to consciousness playing an important role in the dynamic constitution of the superior PERSON.

Concomitantly, ART offers respite from the harshness of life, an aesthetic justification of human existence that, though an illusion, makes it a valuable artifice. This aesthetic justification is not blind but needs consciousness, which is hence tied up with the ability to have a higher-quality appreciation of life. So we are presented with two conflicting views of consciousness. How can they be understood? Nietzsche tells us that the soul is only a word for that which has to do with the BODY, that the entire evolution of the spirit is tied up with questions about the body, and that what we take to be spiritual is a sign of the LANGUAGE of the body. The unity of the body is far more complex than that of consciousness. Even if one does not wish to attribute a type of physicalist reductionism to Nietzsche, the preceding approach differs from what he says elsewhere about consciousness. Recall the strong claim that self-mastery entails having a mastery over one's circumstances, nature, and the herd. This is possible because life's most fundamental instinct aims at the constant expansion of power. But mastery of oneself involves making creative and conscious use of one's passions. He even talks about an unreasonable drive of a Will to KNOWLEDGE pushing relentlessly so that one transcends one's TIME to gain radically new understanding. The driving force here is the Will to Power, but it takes consciousness as a catalyst to be able to move humankind to new heights and vistas. Thus, the discrepant views of consciousness are due to an asymptotic shift between the limits of two opposing tendencies: the proclivity toward a physicalist account where consciousness is seen as a superficial and fallible latecomer and a tendency to a sort of vitalism of the Will to Power. Nietzsche claims that it is not the particular organic entity but rather struggle via the Will to Power that motivates the drive to continue, grow, and become self-conscious in life. Consciousness becomes the necessary catalyst for art, insight, and the emergence of a new, superior human.

SARTRE's approach to consciousness is descriptive. Consciousness is intentional: it is directed to a transcendent OBJECT. In PERCEPTION an object as figure is always constituted on a ground. As intentional, consciousness is consciousness of a figure. The ground is made up of other thises or objects, undifferentiated by virtue of not being focused on. The genesis of a new figure results in the disappearance into the ground of the one preceding it. Consciousness is selective: individuated objects cannot appear all together on the ground of the world, while the appearance of a selected group results in the fusion of others with the ground. No set of objects is automatically designed to be organized as figure or ground; that depends on the direction of the subject's attention. The object of consciousness is given immediately, but it is also the result of the PROJECT I pursue at the time. There is not first an isolated consciousness that is only subsequently thrown into existence. Instead, consciousness arises in enterprises and knows itself first insofar as it is reflected in them.

Sartre also holds that what constitutes the BEING of consciousness is lack, which serves as the foundation of its own NOTHINGNESS. What is lacking is the outline of a presence-to-itself, which points to a project or goal ontologically. Projects or goals are future-directed phenomena. But as "literally not" yet existing, they introduce the factor of nothingness into the very heart of consciousness as a dynamic PROCESS. Sartre distinguishes between two types of negating, constitutive mechanisms. External NEGATION merely allows a person to judge that objects already existing in one's perceptual field are not the same as each other. By contrast, in internal negation what consciousness denies about an entity qualifies the former by its absence. What consciousness becomes for the moment is the absence of what it intends. He further subdivides the internal negation into concrete and radical negations. The former is what groups off a specific, individuated entity or figure. That is, the concrete negation constitutes in the mode of not-being-its-object. In addition to external, transcendent objects, one's experience of self can be delineated as figure by the concrete negation. For instance, saying, "I am not handsome" does not merely negate a positive quality while I manage to keep the totality of my being intact. Instead, it is a real, negative feature characterizing me from within, one that, for example, explains my melancholy and failures.

Radical negation delineates the undifferentiated ground of the subject's experience. While the type of awareness usually generated by the latter negation is vague, it can under unusual circumstances become strangely highlighted. For instance, Sartre asks what would happen if, on being caught peeking, I wheel around only to discover that I have made a mistake; no one is looking at me. Far from having disappeared, he says, the Other remains present everywhere, below me, above me, in the neighboring rooms, so that in trepidation I continue profoundly to experience my being-for-the-Other. What gives rise to this presence? The concrete negation does not apply since it is what groups off a specific figure. But because of being everywhere, the Other is constantly in the ground of my experience, behind, below, or above any figure I happen to be focusing on, but in an indefinite mode. Its presence is diffuse or undifferentiated. Thus, radical negation delineates the experience of the Other's undifferentiated presence in the ground of my experience. Hence, even if it is free, consciousness operates through, and in terms of, a set of definite structures.

Any viable, philosophical methodology, Sartre holds, must start by expelling things from consciousness in order to establish its true relation to the world. Consciousness has no contents. But even if one wishes to fight traditional theories where consciousness contains sensations, ideas, or representations, what sense does it make to say that there is nothing in it? The key is to understand the idea of consciousness as embodied, which Sartre develops by making use of Kurt Lewin's idea of hodological SPACE. For the latter the individual is characterized by means of intentional, goal-directed activity. Objects functioning as goals or valences can be positive when the agent is attracted to them or negative when they serve as things to be avoided. By six months a rattle suspended above a baby's crib may lead the child to extend hands, feet, and head in a unified movement toward it. In moving to, or away from, valences, paths or vectors are traced out, a function of direction and strength on the part of the subject. But over a given period of time valences also change in value or move out of focus, as they shift from figure to ground depending on the SUBJECT'S needs. Valences, and vectors as the means of attaining or avoiding them, fluctuate during the normal process of experience. Together vectors and valences make up what Lewin calls a field of force.

Sartre talks about hodological space as a qualitative and magnetic field that is traversed and in which one pursues and flees in the process of unveiling what is new. Unlike Euclidean space with fixed sets of coordinates, the hodological frame of reference is generated relative to each subject as an embodied consciousness and is constantly fluid. The lived body is coextensive with its range of possibilities and field of force. My body is everywhere; it is out in the world, extending across the tool that it uses. This same is true about my relation to others. Hodologically, what happens when the Other looks at me is that he or she is contained in my field of force, generating an alien field of force within my own. A total space is grouped around the Other, made with my space, and this space is alien to me. For a different scenario, when I am caught peeking at the keyhole and frozen by the Other's look, what happens hodologically is that my field of force, at least momentarily, implodes as I become an object for the Other. The Other's LOOK unfolds its distances while denying my own. Hence, when Sartre says that consciousness has no contents, this is because it is out in the world. Rather than being an absorbing container, consciousness has to be understood as embodied, as an active agent interacting with things and others.

Primary Works

Nietzsche, Friedrich. *Twilight of the Idols and The Anti-Christ.* Trans. R. J. Hollingdale.
    Harmondsworth: Penguin, 1968.
Sartre, Jean-Paul. *The Transcendence of the Ego.* Trans. Forrest Williams and Robert
    Kirpatrick. New York: Farrar, Straus, and Giroux, 1987.

Bibliography

Madison, Gary. *The Phenomenology of Merleau-Ponty: A Search for the Limits of Con-
    sciousness.* Athens: Ohio University Press, 1981.

CONTINGENCY
Patrick Bourgeois

The meaning of contingency in existential PHILOSOPHY can be seen both
within the uniqueness of its essential themes as well as in contrast to various
traditional senses. One of its main traditional senses is the nonnecessity of BE-
ING, which is dependent on the necessary Being, GOD, and which therefore
does not itself necessarily exist. In the context of the mechanism of NATURE
in modern philosophy, that which is contingent is that which is not determined.
The logician basically means by contingency a depending on some condition or
on the TRUTH of something else. It is distinguished from that which is possible
since that also can include what is necessary. Contingency takes on a uniqueness
and intensity, especially as expressed by SARTRE.

SIMONE DE BEAUVOIR convinced Sartre to write his philosophical notion
of contingency, which came to expression in *Nausea.* Although many interpreters view the treatment of contingency as mainly expressed in the account
of the chestnut tree, it is clear that contingency is an all-pervasive theme dealt
with throughout the novel. Roquentin, the protagonist, undergoes progressive
experiences of EXISTENCE in nausea as one of possible ways of experiencing
existence. The nonnecessity of existence, of his own as well as that of things,
is experienced by Roquentin; it reaches a certain popular and descriptive intensity in the experience of the chestnut tree and its roots. In other early writings,
when Sartre moves away from the transcendental dimension of HUSSERL's
phenomenology to the existential and the prereflective cogito, he throws into
focus the contingency at the heart of human existence and, indeed, of all exis-

tence. Thus, with human FREEDOM at the core of existence, whatever meaning there is in human existence is due to the responsible freedom of humans and not dependent on some absolute being. Within the relation between WORLD and CONSCIOUSNESS, consciousness bestows meaning. Sartre incorporates this notion of contingency into his more mature thinking on INTENTIONAL-ITY, modes of being, prereflective cogito, and freedom.

For Sartre there are two modes of being: the in-itself as the mode of things and the mode of human being that has awareness of itself and is therefore for-itself. The intentional dimension of human existence puts it essentially in relation to the in-itself, so that, even on a prereflective level of awareness, there is an awareness of that which is not human, of an OBJECT, of things in the world, a relation to something other than myself. For-itself can exist only in relation to in-itself; it cannot be without the in-itself. The two modes of being are intentionally correlated; human consciousness, as constitutively TRANSCEN-DENCE, is supported by a being that is not itself. The prereflective cogito is the primary and originary consciousness, foundation for all reflection, primordially involving a primacy of being rather than a primacy of KNOWLEDGE. Furthermore, the contingency of human existence takes on a more intense and central sense when one recalls that in the intentional relation a certain priority is given to the in-itself, from which, in a sense, it can be said to emerge. Hence, as ''being what it is, and not being what it is not,'' in-itself is positive, while for-itself, as ''being what it is not, and not being what it is,'' is negative—it is not a thing. Thus, for-itself is not merely nonnecessary and contingent, without cause, without reason (without God) but is dependent on the other mode of being, being in-itself, thus intensifying contingency in human existence. In addition, the being of for-itself and of in-itself come to light as not necessary, giving rise to the perplexity of a contingent being without a necessary being on which it is dependent: humans and things exist without cause or reason and have been referred to as absurd.

Although contingency is not an explicitly developed focus of HEIDEGGER's thought, it is a consequence of his view of the finitude of human existence. He seems, in *Being and Time*, to relegate contingency to the derived and narrowed present-at-hand mode, as a characteristic according to which this or that present-at-hand being can come to pass. However, there is a deeper sense of contingency, less focused on but essentially there, in his account of DASEIN. Finitude of humans is central to the sense of human existence, thus meaning that human existence, as the projection of possibilities from the finitude of human being, may be, but does not necessarily have to be. In this context, dread is the basic ONTIC aspect of the ontological openness as moodness, overtaking Dasein on first coming to realize the contingency of its own BEING-IN-THE-WORLD. Dread is likewise the privileged mode of its dispositional openness or way of finding oneself vis-à-vis being-in-the-world: it is about, and in the face of, being-in-the-world, relating to possibilities toward future and those thrown from our past. In this context of felt possibility, taking into consideration the nonfixity of possibility and its contingency, dread is the experience of the ethereal and the awesome. The aspect of felt possibility in the concrete here and now is manifest in the sense that the affective in Dasein, more ontologically conceived as the openness in finding oneself, or moodness, incorporates felt possibility at the heart of human being. Dread, in some sense, is the experience of possibility as not closed, as openness; in this sense, it leads to the Nothing side of Being. Actually, dread in the face of, and about, being-in-the-world must be seen to be in relation to the NOTHINGNESS of Being—or of Dasein. So dread can be tied to nothing as an aspect of Being. In this sense, then, one could include contingency as experienced in dread, but as a privileged, ontological disclosure of Dasein's Being.

The response of humans to the contingency of the world, including themselves, is not terror of annihilation but a sense of our Otherness and distance from Being. It is dread before the withdrawal of Being. A sense of the deliberate absence of Being is founded on a certain manifestation of the presence of Being. The possibilities that dread encounters have the sense of nonnecessity; they are not possibilities of a necessary being but actual and existential possibilities of Dasein, of a contingent being that is a thrown PROJECT. Later, Heidegger carries his analysis of dread to the analysis of birth and DEATH, the latter of which is the unfolding and appropriating of the possibility of no longer having possibilities. This understanding he expresses ontologically as being-toward-death, a constitutive possibility of Dasein from birth. In this extended sense, contingency can be seen to be at the very heart of Dasein analysis.

In Christian existential philosophy the contingent is related to an Other that is not contingent; this Other is a presence of a personal God and thus quite different from the absolute being of pre-Kantian philosophy, as seen in the writings of KIERKEGAARD and MARCEL. For Kierkegaard, the human, even as contingent, stands before God in a mature response of faith in purity of heart, relating to God, the absolute Good, first and foremost as the Father in a personal RELATION in the sense of Abraham and St. Paul. Marcel accentuates the notion of presence of a personal God but adds the notion of an indirect access through images and MYTHS in order to prevent idolatrizing that which is reflected upon here in what he calls second reflection, a reflection that returns to the primordial and lived existential level beneath that of a derived and more scientific reflection, what he calls primary reflection. In none of these is contingency of the human brought into finitude of human existence as the essential dimension of human being or an ontological character, as it was seen by Sartre and Heidegger, nor is there an absurdity derived from it.

Although, in Heidegger's analysis of human existence as Dasein, the depth of its significance and its pervasive influence are seen, clearly, the more popular and explicitly stated sense of contingency is in the writings of Sartre, where existence is contingent in the sense of not necessary and of not having a divine, necessary Being as cause.

Primary Works

Heidegger, Martin. *What Is a Thing?* Trans. W. B. Barton, Jr., and Vera Deutsch. South Bend, IN: Regnery/Gateway, 1967.
Sartre, Jean-Paul. *Nausea.* Trans. Lloyd Alexander. New York: New Directions, 1959.
———. *Search for a Method.* Trans. Hazel E. Barnes. New York: Knopf, 1963.

CREATIVITY
Doug Mann

In existentialist thought one discovers two principal senses of the concept of creativity: (1) its ontological sense and (2) its aesthetic sense. In the ontological sense, thinkers are interested in how we create ourselves as free human existents. The focus is on the production of the unique, individual self and the processes that hinder this production. In the aesthetic sense, existentialists are interested in creation of works of ART, of LITERATURE, and of VALUES.

In his early work *The Birth of Tragedy*, NIETZSCHE celebrated the aesthetic over the moral and saw creativity as residing primarily in the realm of the former. He declares that only as aesthetic phenomena are LIFE and the WORLD eternally justified. He sees two sources of the creative impulse in the ancient Greeks, which echo throughout the history of Western art: the Apollonian and the Dionysian. The Apollonian artist draws the veil of Maya over APPEAR-ANCES and creates an ideal world through such forms as the epic poem and the plastic arts, especially sculpture. The Dionysian creates by way of embracing life in its darkness, frenzy, sensuality, and primitive depth and thus favors tragedy and music as creative forms. The Apollonian dreams, while the Dionysian engages in intoxicated revelry. The Apollonian artist aims at the divine glory of the principle of individuality, while the Dionysian seeks to collapse this individuality into a more primordial unity. In song and dance, the Dionysian artist becomes a work of art, with Nature revealing itself in the artist's intoxicated revelry, in the free play of the creative process. The Apollonian element in Greek culture created the world of the Olympian gods as an antidote to the terror and horror of life, as a seduction to life. Under the "bright sunshine" of these gods, EXISTENCE was desirable. Music had a strong Dionysian current and provided a cosmic symbolism that stands in a relation with the primordial unity that is prior to all surface phenomena. As the Dionysian artist contacts this primordial unity through both music and tragedy, Nietzsche concludes that the birth of tragedy can be found in the spirit of music.

Nietzsche admired great artists for having created themselves. They triumphed over the values of the herd and let loose their own vision of reality. Great artists are able to express their WILL to POWER by creating values. The highest exemplar of this creation of the self is the SUPERMAN, who is able to organize the chaos of one's passions and thereby overcome animal NATURE. The superman best exemplifies the process of creating oneself by giving oneself laws and thereby becoming what one is. In his *amor fati* he accepts responsibility for all his actions as part of the PROCESS of imposing order on drives, passions, and sensations. He dwells far from the marketplace and fame, for absorption into the general public strips the individual of creativity in its noblest sense. In *On the Genealogy of Morals* Nietzsche recounts a dialectic of noble and herd MORALITY. The nobles are the most creative; they produce values out of a sense of the abundance of life. In creating themselves they create values for others. Against this abundance the herd reacts by creating its own values—of RESENTMENT, produced by transvaluating the GOOD of the nobles into EVIL or SIN and their own weakness into a distinct good. An example of herd morality is CHRISTIANITY, which is the religion of resentment. Tied to this supreme expression of the creativity of the herd are phenomena like democracy and socialism, which are expressions of the herd's creative will to power. However, GOD is dead; hence, humankind is its own legislator and creator of values. Leading this effort are genuine philosophers, commanders, and legislators of values who reach for the future with a creative hand. In seeking knowledge, in their will to truth, they create, expressing a will to power.

SARTRE holds that in the primary, ontological sense, humans are free; our CONSCIOUSNESS, the for-itself, is opposed to the in-itself BEING of nonconscious entities. The for-itself creates itself by thought and action out of the existential void, but always from a given, objective starting point. When I create myself through thought and action, I simultaneously create an image of humanity. This is equally true of morality. There is no luminous realm of values; we are condemned to be free, to create values in a godless universe. The moral choice resembles the construction of a work of art. This aesthetic view of creativity is linked to his attack on HUSSERL's notion of the Transcendent Ego. Sartre suggests that the EGO, or self, is the creation of reflective consciousness and is in reality no more than the sum of our mental states and actions. This created ego is a being in the world, not, as Husserl thought, a concrete I that inhabits each conscious act. The ego is an OBJECT of consciousness that is created by a poetic production, a continuous creation ex nihilo. When we reflect on our past states and actions, we posit an ego as their center. Each moment of consciousness feeds back on the ego by reconstituting it on new grounds. The self is forever in a state of renewal. Hence, Sartre calls the ego fugitive, always in flight from its congealment into hardened form. The illusion that such a congealment of the self into a hardened form has actually occurred constitutes BAD FAITH.

In ''Why Write?'' Sartre shows how a literary text is constituted not just by writing but also by reading. The writer appeals to the FREEDOM of the reader to share in the production of a work of LITERATURE. The author only guides the reader: reading is a sort of directed creation. As with the ontological impulse to create the ego as the unity of past states and actions, the reader of a novel, play, or poem is led to create the work of literature in the act of appropriating the literary object. In *Being and Nothingness*, Sartre finds one of the greatest expressions of human freedom in our creation of NOTHINGNESS. Humans bring Nothingness into the world. Consciousness is an emptiness that projects meaning onto itself and into the world and can thus be said to create being, by launching itself out of its emptiness and into the world through one's PROJECT.

In *Being and Time*, HEIDEGGER hints at a notion of creativity: one of the central ways that DASEIN exists is through projection of itself upon objects and other Daseins by caring. Dasein resigns its right to authentic projection when it falls under the sway of the THEY and accepts their edicts as to its nature. It can recover its possibilities for authentically creating itself when it squarely faces its Being-toward-Death. In later works, poetic creation brings us closer to Being, the ground of all existence. Heidegger felt that this unity was first clearly perceived by the great pre-Socratic thinkers. His essay ''On the Origin of the Work of Art'' says that a work of art should be seen as a bringing of TRUTH into the light of Being. Artistic creation is a revealing of truth. It is an unconcealing of Being through the revelation of Beauty in the work of art. This work of art reveals Truth insofar as it reveals a world; thus, van Gogh's painting of the peasant's shoes leads us into a world of the peasant, of open fields, hard labor, and a blazing fire in the hearth. The truth of the peasant's world gazes out at us through van Gogh's colors and brush strokes. The artist reveals the truth of this world and thus reveals a certain relation of a human to the Earth and the sky above.

In ''Building Dwelling Thinking'' Heidegger suggests that artistic creation is essentially POETRY, for poetry is an opening up of the concealedness of beings, the saying of Truth. He privileges LANGUAGE as a mode of creativity, thereby privileging poetry. Poetic creation is a kind of building that gives us a place to dwell; thus, we can say that, poetically, man dwells. In art, we find truth setting itself to work. Creation opens up Being to us, and the beauty produced by art shows us Truth as unconcealed. In short, through artistic creation Truth comes into being. Thus, we create ourselves in freedom through the spoken word, through relating to the work of art and literature, through new tables of values, through action, work, and play.

Primary Works

Heidegger, Martin. *Poetry, Language, Thought.* Trans. Albert Hofstadter. New York: Harper and Row, 1971.

Nietzsche, Friedrich. *The Birth of Tragedy and The Case of Wagner.* Trans. Walter Kaufmann. New York: Vintage Books, 1967.

Sartre, Jean-Paul. *What Is Literature?* Trans. Bernard Fretchman. London: Methuen, 1978.

DASEIN

John Protevi

Dasein, the German word for EXISTENCE, became a technical term in HEIDEGGER's PHILOSOPHY, determined by the structure of his enterprise. His study *Being and Time* was not, in Heidegger's eyes, a philosophical anthropology but rather the preliminary investigation oriented toward the proper horizon for the question of BEING. Hence, a new term for the OBJECT of that preliminary investigation needed to be coined. Since that being traditionally named human is the only one who has access to a variety of ways of Being and is the one where the question of Being is enacted, the Being of that being must be clarified. But our Being, through and through historical, has interpreted itself in ways that hide the original phenomena of its Being, so a preliminary analysis of our Being must also be a destruction of the HISTORY of ONTOLOGY. Wishing to free the phenomenon of our Being from sedimented preconceptions, Heidegger adopts Dasein to designate what used to be called human being.

Dasein is not to be equated with SUBJECT, for, as the place where the Being question occurs, Dasein is the locus of the encounter between subject and object, the opening within which a subject can come to address an object. Da-sein, ''there-being,'' marks the opening up or clearing within which beings are encountered. Dasein is thus less a thing than a PROCESS in which things appear to one another.

Primary Work

Heidegger, Martin. *The Basic Problems of Phenomenology.* Trans. Albert Hofstadter. Bloomington: Indiana University Press, 1982.

DEATH
Constance L. Mui

Existentialist writers treat death as a personal event in the context of FREEDOM and AUTHENTICITY. What concerns them is not the natural phenomenon of death or the actual encounter with death but the more important and perennial problem of how one chooses one's EXISTENCE in view of, and in spite of, the fact that one must die. My awareness of my death affords me a compelling grip on my existence as a conscious BEING who is free and limited. This focus on my finite existence is rooted in the claim that self-KNOWLEDGE is fundamentally different from knowledge of the empirical world. For instance, HEIDEGGER's analysis of death in *Being and Time* considers death as an ontological structure, a constitutive element of human existence.

Heidegger insists that it is the philosopher's task to explain the Being of beings. The proper starting point is to investigate the Being of a human, DASEIN, by which the problem of Being can come into focus; this being alone raises and attempts to understand the question of Being. What is the specific mode in which being manifests itself in Dasein? The being of Dasein is existence. All other entities merely *are*; Dasein alone exists. It has to be in the sense that its being is a task to be fulfilled. It stands over and against itself, assuming an attitude toward its own being. To exist is to be responsible for your being without being responsible for being there. As already BEING-IN-THE-WORLD, Dasein did not cause itself to be there. But once there, Dasein is responsible for its being; its being is not a static endowment but a PROJECT that only it can carry out. Dasein exists by projecting toward possibilities, always stretching out to its own still-to-be-realized-being. This stretching out paths the way for Heidegger's formulation of temporality, in which death is explained. Dasein is not in TIME. It exists as a temporal being; its existence assumes a temporal, or "ekstatic," structure. Time is not something external that Dasein encounters. Rather, Dasein brings time into the world by existing. Dasein does not move linearly from the past through the present to the future. Dasein achieves its present first by projecting into the future and then turning back to assimilate the FACTICITY of its past. Existential time is primordially futural. Yet Dasein's having-been must be brought to bear since Dasein projects itself only on the condition of its already-being-in-the-world. The temporal structure of Dasein is the unity of a future that makes present in the process of having been.

The prominent role of futurality underscores the significance of possibility: Dasein is precisely being-toward-possibility. Of all the possibilities it faces, death (as the possible impossibility of Dasein's existence) stands out as the single most unsurpassable and ultimate possibility through which existential time is revealed as finite. To be a being-toward-possibility is to exist as being-toward-death. Death is not an independent agent or outside force with no intrinsic relation to Dasein. As a possibility, it is an ever-present, ever-impending potentiality that forms the structure of human existence. We should avoid the familiar portrayal of death as a pointlike event of ceasing to be in the world and instead understand it as Dasein's way of being, since temporality and finitude are inseparable components in Dasein's constitution. Existential time is finite. Like temporality, finitude must be understood in the ontological sense: Dasein exists finitely, as a temporal being-toward-death.

The ontological structure of finitude reveals itself to Dasein through ANXIETY. Unlike fear, which is of a definite object, anxiety is an awareness of NOTHINGNESS, of Dasein's imminent possibility of the impossibility of existence. Whereas the object of fear is beings-in-the-world, the object of anxiety is being-in-the-world. Heidegger cautions that anxiety is not a human weakness and therefore something to be avoided or overcome. Through anxiety Dasein becomes aware of death as the one possibility that makes its existence unique and whole. Since no one else can experience it in my place, death instantiates my uniqueness; it affords me ultimate isolation from the anonymity of the THEY. Death is Dasein's own-most possibility, enabling Dasein to grasp its existence as a whole. LIFE in its entirety is life facing death. To assume a unified existence Dasein must posture itself in relation to its ending, its death. Experiencing anxiety may also be a calling upon Dasein to choose an authentic life, to lift itself out of triviality and return to the knowledge of itself as being-toward-death.

Far from being a weakness, anxiety commands considerable strength and fortitude. Dasein could ignore the call to authenticity and persist in its inauthentic attitude toward death by seeking comfort and shelter in the they and get caught up in the everyday, mundane world where death becomes impersonal and inconspicuous. Dasein thus exists in false security, in a reality that conceals death as its most unique possibility. On the other hand, Dasein could resolutely confront what anxiety reveals. Authentic selfhood requires that Dasein take death upon itself and, without illusion, accept that its whole life is facing death. This confrontation reveals that death gives existence its fullness and uniqueness. Death sets Dasein apart and restores it to its individuality, enabling it to engage in freely chosen possibilities. Furthermore, by resolutely advancing toward death, Dasein may become authentically present to other beings. All false sense of security and illusion of evasion disappear at the moment Dasein recognizes death as its ultimate possibility, as its most proper, most distinctive, nonrelational, unsurpassable, and irretrievable possibility. Death throws Dasein back upon its resources and invites it to assume responsibility for its authentic selfhood.

SARTRE rejects Heidegger's attempt to incorporate death into the internal structure of human existence and his attempts to recuperate death by interiorizing and humanizing it. According to Sartre, Heidegger offers a consoling view in which death is seen as the last part of a series. Like the final note of a melody, death is internal to human existence and gives it its constitutive meaning. Sartre warns against being seduced by this comforting hypothesis. He rebukes the idea that death obtains its uniqueness from the fact that no one else can undergo my death—the same could be said of life and LOVE. If my actions are considered merely in terms of their function and efficacy, other people can always repeat them. If to love Dennis means to make him happy by being his constant companion, it is conceivable that someone else can do the same. If to die is to be a martyr giving witness to a cause, certainly others can do such. Love, life, and death become mine only from the perspective of subjectivity. My subjectivity makes my love, life, and death unique and induplicable; hence, subjectivity rather than death makes my existence unique. Death does not confer meaning upon life because any meaning I assign to my life can come only from my subjectivity, my freedom. A second flaw in Heidegger's position is that to expect death is not the same as to wait for it. To expect death is to anticipate it vaguely, knowing that I am mortal; to await death is to anticipate it on the specific knowledge of its occurrence at a relatively definite time—imminent execution, terminal disease, old age. While it is possible to expect death, one cannot, in principle, await it because even in the event of a scheduled execution, the prisoner could die beforehand by accident. Thus, if there were no sudden and premature deaths but only orchestrated ones, it would be possible to wait for death and intelligible to talk, as Heidegger does, about authenticity in terms of resoluteness. In reality, more often than not, death occurs by chance abruptly and surprises even those who are resolved to advance toward it. For this reason, death cannot be likened to the final note delivering the entire melody to its harmonious conclusion. Sartre's example is a young man who aspires to become a great writer but dies before embarking on his magnum opus. This untimely death nullifies the meaning of his life projects. Hence, death cannot confer meaning upon life.

Sartre makes a categorical distinction between conscious and nonconscious beings. Objects designated as in-itself are simply what they are, such as a rock, whose being is self-contained; it cannot exist as anything more or other than what it is. Its identity as a rock is congealed and determined. By contrast, for-itself is the PERSON, a conscious being who exists as freedom. To exist as freedom is to exist by disobeying the principle of identity. For-itself is constantly engaged in becoming, in perpetually adding to its identity; it is always a step ahead of being defined. Its basic existential structure is dynamic and future-oriented: for-itself exists by moving beyond what-it-is toward what-it-is-not. Every moment in for-itself's existence is characterized by a simultaneous flight and LEAP, as it nihilates its past toward future possibilities. To exist as freedom means that one is never in perfect coincidence with, but always exists at a distance beyond, itself. For-itself is a constant moving-toward-possibility that validates its existence as flight-from-self, as internal relation of identity denied.

For-itself as flight continues until death, which brusquely stops it in the midst of its project. At death, I become completely my past with the full substantiality of a thing. Since for-itself is freedom, death is not included in its ontological structure. If it were, it would have to be rooted in freedom. But death represents the total destruction of freedom. Death defeats for-itself's existence as internal relation of denied identity by turning it into a corpse, an inert in-itself with a fixed identity. In short, death lies outside my possibilities and can in no way constitute the internal structure of my existence. Sartre acknowledges that finitude underlies every human possibility insofar as I make a particular choice only by excluding others, and the choice once made will necessarily be part of my history. But death is not to be confused with finitude, since my existence would still be finite in the sense described even if I were immortal. Finitude entails that concrete human freedom is both limited and limiting. Death is not merely the limitation of freedom but the very elimination of it.

Sartre insists that in order to take seriously Heidegger's invitation to face death without illusion, we must expose it for what it is. Death abruptly terminates my project of self-creation without giving meaning to my life. Freedom gives meaning to life. Because there is no GOD who endows me with intrinsic VALUE, any meaning attributed to my life must originate from me, inferred from my actions, rooted in my freedom. Actions have meaning only in reference to my project, which is always subject to change. Consequently, I do not have a fixed identity or meaning, not even with respect to my past. To be sure, the facts of my past cannot be changed, but I can change their significance in light of a new project. Thus, I may consider the years spent in graduate school as wasted if I decide to become an artist. The future determines the meaning of the present, since humans exist as flight, as free beings who perpetually move toward new possibilities. Thus, death cannot be a source of meaning for life even if it comes about through SUICIDE. Since the future discloses the meaning of my actions, suicide, being the last act of my life, nullifies my future; its meaning remains undetermined. I cannot look back on my suicide and consider myself a martyr. All told, death is utterly absurd: it is simply there, devoid of intrinsic meaning. Not only does it fail to add meaning to my life, but it ultimately betrays any meaning I manage to attain therein. All my life I strive toward self-determination, only to have this project terminated for no reason and often without warning. Life, too, is absurd since it ends in such absurdity.

Death is uniquely mine. It is an aspect of my facticity, along with my birth, my environment, and fellow human beings, which together form my SITUATION. It alone presents the ultimate destruction of freedom. It is inevitable, beyond my control and escapes me in principle. In Sartre's story ''The Wall,'' a character condemned to face the firing squad imagines himself escaping at the final moment by retreating into the wall behind him. Despairingly, he acknowledges that such thoughts are futile. The facticity of death undermines his attempts in BAD FAITH to merge with the other so as to mitigate the burden of freedom and to deny his contingency in a godless world. Each person stands alone facing death. The three condemned prisoners are put in a room where they are to confront death together. But, never before have these men been more alone and forlorn. Death is also the ultimate NEGATION of freedom from the vantage point of my being-for-others. So long as I have a body, a dimension of my being is accessible only to others: I cannot see myself as others see me. That my body has an externality that exists only for the other poses an inherent threat to my freedom. Having no control over how others perceive me, I am at their disposal. At death, my entire being collapses into being-for-others. I become a corpse with a HISTORY, a mere property possessed by others. At death, my life does not become complete but fixed; its meaning is congealed in the other's CONSCIOUSNESS. Death is the ultimate threat to freedom.

Life's absurdity provides the basis for CAMUS' ethic of revolt against death. Camus contends that, while we may turn to RELIGION or PHILOSOPHY for meaning, we nevertheless experience life as absurd when we face the fact that all humans are ultimately condemned to death. In *The Myth of Sisyphus* he considers whether suicide is the answer to the absurdity of human existence—as the only serious philosophical question of our time. He rejects suicide, calling it a defeatist act of faithlessness that gives an undue importance to death while denying the existence we do have. We must revolt against death by embracing life defiantly and passionately and struggling to find happiness in spite of the absurd. We have a duty to be happy because happiness is the strongest affirmation of life. It is a moral imperative to revolt against death, accept life's absurdity, and in so doing find happiness. By giving up any romantic notion about death and accepting life on its own terms, we appreciate our existence as precious.

The atheistic, stark portrayal of death is vehemently rejected by Christian existentialists such as MARCEL, who insists that death fully brings out the transcendent and immortal NATURE of our being. To be is not merely to exist but to delve into the inexhaustible and to open ourselves to the Absolute—God. Humans share an impulse toward TRANSCENDENCE, which is not above or beyond us; it is fully present. We emerge as transcendent beings in the basic, yet most penetrating, experiences of love and fidelity. Nowhere is the transcendent nature of a person's being revealed more strongly than in the experience of the death of a loved one. The MYSTERY of death cannot be understood apart from the mystery of love, which refers not merely to romantic union but also to friendship and filial love. These relationships attest to the reciprocal presence of the lovers through spiritual participation in each other's life. Presence is a deeply personal and unobjectifiable reality: lovers enter into a communion in which the ordinary self–other RELATION is transcended. In this communion of the WE, the beloved becomes a Thou, a personal being rather than a BODY to be possessed and objectified. My profound experience of intersubjectivity is predicated on a primordial urge toward communion with the Absolute. The we experience becomes the ground for disclosing the Absolute Presence; love transcends finite experience and raises us above the world of vicissitude. Through love, we are united with the infinite in ourselves and in others.

Hence, Marcel's position that the more fully I experience the beloved as a Thou, the more I affirm her immortality. To love someone is to attain for her the Absolute; it is to say, You shalt not die. Love transforms the very reality of my friend's death. Because my friend is not an object but a Thou, I suffer no loss upon her death since one may lose a possession but never a Thou. And because my friend is not merely a physical body but a presence, she is not destined for utter deterioration as material objects are. At death, my friend's being continues to be present to me, an interior presence that remains as strong a reality as it ever was. What remains is not merely a memory but an active communion. My continuing to evolve and mature even in my friend's physical absence gives witness to her immortality; her presence enables me to develop as a being. Thus, the communion attained with a friend is the guarantee of her immortality. Death is the greatest testimony of the transcendent nature of my being.

Echoing Spinoza that it is the essence of every being to endeavor to persist in its own being, UNAMUNO contends that human ESSENCE is possessed by the hunger for being, an insatiable appetite for immortality. We endeavor not simply to continue breathing, but to continue to be this concrete person of flesh and bone—the relational being with a history and an identity who has yearned and felt, striven and struggled. Hunger for immortality drives us toward theism. Not because we believe in God do we affirm immortality; rather, desire for immortality affirms our belief in God. Given our yearning for immortality, we must live as if God exists. This conception of religion reflects the tension between FAITH and reason: we are pulled toward faith because nothing is more horrible than not being. On the other hand, we fall back on reason, which exposes the limitation of faith. Even if faith convinces you of the soul's immortality, reason makes you aware of the tragic fact that the concrete person of flesh and bone, my embodied existence, will someday cease to be. But I don't want to die; I refuse to die; I struggle on, even with my last breath. Why are we such hopeless romantics? The alternative of total passivity is even more unacceptable. Life is one big contradiction, a tragedy marked by a perpetual struggle between faith and reason. At the heart of human existence there are the dreadful, haunting consciousness of finitude and the resoluteness with which you strive to overcome that finitude.

While these different accounts of death set the existentialists apart, they also show a common thread: the significance that death takes on for the individual, the wide range of emotions and experiences one faces, and the challenges and choices that one must confront in the consciousness of one's impending death.

Primary Works

Marcel, Gabriel. *Creative Fidelity.* Trans. Robert Rosthal. New York: Farrar, Straus, and Giroux, 1964.
Unamuno, Miguel de. *Tragic Sense of Life.* Trans. J. E. Crawford Flitch. New York: Dover, 1954.

Bibliography

Barret, William. *Irrational Man.* London: Heinemann, 1961.
Lauer, Quentin. *The Triumph of Subjectivity.* New York: Fordham University Press, 1958.

DEMYTHOLOGIZING
Houston Craighead

The principal relevance of demythologizing for existentialist thought is connected with the efforts of RUDOLF BULTMANN to remove the mythical elements from the Bible. He contends that the genuine proclamation of the New Testament has to do with the possibility of authentic human EXISTENCE. In the New Testament this proclamation is expressed in the worldview of first-century Judea, a prescientific, mythological worldview in which supernatural events occur and in which humans are driven by supernatural POWERS. People with the worldview of twentieth-century science cannot accept such a mythical picture as a literal account of the way the universe operates. Further, there is no need for them to accept it because it has nothing essentially to do with the Christian FAITH but only happens to be the view that prevailed when the New Testament writers were living. Unless the Christian proclamation is articulated in a way twentieth-century people can understand and accept it, Christian faith will not be a possibility for them. They will simply dismiss it together with the mythical picture in which it was expressed.

In order to free the Christian message from its mythical New Testament surroundings, Bultmann proposes to use HEIDEGGER's thought, particularly, ideas and concepts in *Being and Time.* The question to be asked of the New Testament stories is not, Did they occur?; so far as they are supernatural, they certainly did not. That is to miss their point. Rather, one ought to ask what they are saying about the issues of human existence and the questions of meaning and possibility for individual PERSONS. Freed from its mythical expression, the New Testament message is that humans, if they place their faith in the final reality beyond the WORLD, if they cease to cling to all forms of meaning and security within the world, will experience the DEATH of their old, inauthentic, futile striving and the birth (resurrection) of a new self-understanding in which the future is received gladly and openly. This new LIFE is in the world but not of the world. It is authentic life in Christ.

The historical Jesus has significance for Bultmann so far as it was in the experiences that some of Jesus' contemporaries had of him that this authentic self-understanding came into HISTORY. Whether and to what extent Jesus himself was aware of this understanding are not important; what is important is the significance of this understanding for persons now. The existential significance, not the historical happening in the past, is at issue. The availability of this present existential meaning depends on the freeing of its proclamation from the mythological setting found in the New Testament.

Primary Works

Bultmann, Rudolf. *Existence and Faith*. Trans. Schubert M. Ogden. London: Hodder and Stroughton, 1961.
———. *History and Eschatology*. New York: Harper and Row, 1957.

DIALECTICAL REASON
Thomas R. Flynn

SARTRE's *Critique of Dialectical Reason* was envisaged as a defense of historical rationality on the model of Kant's three critiques of scientific, moral, and aesthetic teleological reasoning. Following the regressive method of Kant's *Prolegomena to Any Future Metaphysics*, Sartre argues from the fact to the conditions of its possibility. The fact is that classes exist in our social experience; the condition for its possibility includes the mechanism of praxis, practico-inert, PROCESS, series, powered by need and the transcendental fact of material scarcity. Sartre adopts the Hegelian–Marxist account of dialectic as both the processive nature of reality and our logical grasp of the same. Thus, dialectic is both objective (the metaphysical glue of history) and subjective (the instrument we utilize to comprehend this social reality in the act of contributing to it).

Unlike traditional analytic reason, dialectical rationality *mediates* contradictions, raising them to a higher viewpoint from which their partial TRUTH and falsity become apparent. Analytic logic is based on the principle of noncontradiction: mutually contradictory propositions cannot be true or false together. Hegelian logic subsumes analytic logic as a moment or phase in its totalizing advance. Following Marx, Sartre reads dialectic in practical terms, as the logic of human praxis in its material and social context. Whatever understanding of the meaning/direction of HISTORY we might achieve by its means will be a practical accomplishment, consonant with our commitment to the struggle at hand. Sartre acknowledges a circularity here, but, he insists, it is not vicious. It is the inevitable self-referring of committed KNOWLEDGE. Its truth will lie in its success in making sense of the class struggle, which is itself a conflict of rationalities. Bourgeois analytic reason, for example, is blind to the solidarity that links individual FREEDOMS to their social conditions and to one another.

Dialectical reason is organic and totalizing. The famous double negation (- - a = a) of analytic reason that restores the original affirmation in dialectical reason produces a *new* affirmation because the original NEGATION is recognized to be internal, modifying the negated term in its very meaning. Hence, the second negation affects the previously negated whole, which it, too, internally negates. These negations of negations are cumulative: whether it be a bone, a contract, or a friendship that is broken, you can never return to the status quo ante. In other words, dialectical reason is also temporalizing, and TIME is progressive and cumulative.

Primary Work

Sartre, Jean-Paul. *Critique of Dialectical Reason*. Trans. Alan Sheridan. London: Verso, 1982.

FYODOR MIKHAILOVICH DOSTOYEVSKY
(1821–1881)
Malcolm Jones

Dostoyevsky was born in Moscow in the Mariinsky Hospital for the Poor, where his father was a doctor. He was a day boarder at various schools. In 1838 he entered the Military Engineering Academy in St. Petersburg. Ill suited to the study of engineering and military life, he read European LITERATURE with great enthusiasm. In 1839 his father was murdered by his serfs. In 1844 he resigned his commission to devote himself to literature. His first publication was a translation of Balzac's *Eugenie Grandet*. In 1846 with the publication of his novel *Poor Folk* he was hailed by the leaders of the Natural School—V. G. Belinsky and others—as a new Gogol. The bubble of his reputation soon burst. Advocates of social realism, led by Belinsky, were confounded by his interest in the fantastic and in abnormal PSYCHOLOGY.

In 1847 Dostoyevsky frequented the home of M. V. Butashevich-Petrashevsky, where progressive ideas, including those of French utopian socialism, were discussed. His membership in this circle and its political offshoots, the Durov and Speshnyov circles, led to his arrest in April 1849. Dostoyevsky's involvement in subversive activities was minimal, but, with a number of others, he was condemned to death by firing squad. Only after the ritual preparations had been carried out to the last letter was it announced, at the place of execution, that the sentence had been commuted to four years in the penal fortress of Omsk, followed by four years in exile as a soldier of the line. He spent the latter years in Semipalatinsk, where he met and married Mariya Dmitriyevna Isayeva. Dostoyevsky received permission to return to St. Petersburg in 1859; in 1861, with his brother Mikhail, the critic Apollon Grigoryev, and the philosopher N. N. Strakhov, he initiated the periodical *Time*, whose aim was to reconcile progressive, Western tendencies in Russian thought with those of the Slavophiles and their allies. The journal was suppressed in 1863. In 1864 Dostoyevsky suffered a triple blow: his wife, his brother Mikhail, and Apollon Grigoryev died. That year *Notes from Underground*, the first of his great works, was published. The following years saw the publication of the novels that made his reputation: *Crime and Punishment, The Idiot, The Devils, The Adolescent*, and *The Brothers Karamazov*. In 1867 he married Anna Grigoryevna Snitkina, his shorthand typist; their marriage was mutually enhancing. During his adulthood Dostoyevsky suffered from epilepsy, particularly in the mid-1860s.

Dostoyevsky was inclined to reject the claims of rationalism and to conform to the Slavophile tradition. In the 1840s he flirted with utopian socialism and with the thought of the left-Hegelians. On his return from Siberia, he courted the company of people influenced by Hegel's PHILOSOPHY. This was when the Russian progressive movement was in the thrall of the natural sciences, utilitarianism, and Feuerbachian materialism. The influence of German Idealism in Dostoyevsky's work was not deep, except in one respect: ideas were no less real to him than the material WORLD, perhaps more so.

Dostoyevsky's novels present many existentialist themes: the rejection of determinism, rationalism, and abstract philosophical systems; the affirmation of individual FREEDOM, passion, and the WILL; RESENTMENT and rebellion; alienation from the self, from other people, from SOCIETY; confrontation with one's own imminent DEATH and its impact on individual CONSCIOUSNESS; LIFE in a world in which GOD is dead; dread in the face of a vast and hostile universe. He portrays a world of extreme personal stress and interpersonal tension, of humanity under intense pressure; his characters often exist on the margins between aggressive assertion of the individual will and total breakdown. His narrators, it seems, are sometimes in danger of losing control of their narrative. The plots of his major novels pivot on murder and/or suicide. Psychological thinkers of different schools, including Nietzsche and Freud, considered him a precursor.

Dostoyevsky has been seen as the originator of the polyphonic novel in which all voices have equal weight, including that of the narrator. His novels create an arena in which questions concerning human EXISTENCE are fought out—principally through male CHARACTERS, many of whom represent and express philosophies of life and engage in intense disputes about freedom, beauty, the political order, RELIGION and atheism, ETHICS, the NATURE of the universe, history, the meaning of life. These characters are possessed by idea-feelings; they disregard abstract discussions. The Underground Man attempts to refute the claims of reason to legislate for human actions. But he is himself the prisoner of a rationalistic creed and feels unfree: hence, the desperation of his protest. Raskolnikov in *Crime and Punishment* discusses the right of great men to step over the moral code if they have a new word for humanity. But after he commits murder, he fails to sustain his posture and finds himself drawn into a dialogue on spiritual resurrection as conveyed in the Christian gospel. Myshkin in *The Idiot* engages in discussions on the ability of beauty to save the world, on the existence of God, on the experience of the condemned man before his execution and the effect on him if he is reprieved, on ALIENATION from nature, on life in a society without a central binding idea, and on spiritual VALUES that may restore humanity to a state of harmony. But Myshkin, himself apparently the embodiment of compassion, humility, and beauty of PERSONALITY, is reduced, by the pressures of life in St. Petersburg, to a state of idiocy. In *The Brothers Karamazov* Ivan presents arguments for rebelling against a divine order that permits suffering of innocent children and claims that if there is no God, everything is permitted. A stepbrother takes this as a hint that Ivan wishes his father murdered. Ivan wrestles with the consequences, eventually succumbing to brain fever.

Many of Dostoyevsky's texts are significant to the existentialist tradition. Those most often discussed by later commentators are *Notes from Underground* and *The Brothers Karamazov*. Part I of *Notes from Underground* has been called the best overture for existentialism ever written. The book directs a glaring spotlight onto its hero's deepest ANXIETIES, never glossing over their ugliness, never concealing their contradictions, never seeking to justify them or to place them in a more favorable light by allusion to subsequent conversion, and never seeking to prescribe a way out of humanity's essential depravity. To take refuge in romantic fantasy, to find meaning in unreflective social conventions are revealed as deceptions, as a flight from living life, a flight that sometimes tempts the hero of the narrative but that he ultimately scorns. The primary butt of the hero's onslaught is Nikolay Chemyshevsky, the leader of the progressive movement in Russian philosophy of the time, who presented humans as (potentially) rational and perfectible, who have only to be shown their true interests so as to act in accordance and who live in a world where rational laws operate in the moral as well as the natural sphere. The Underground Man is intellectually oppressed by this doctrine and feels emotionally impotent in his relations with other people. At first he reacts by petty expressions of resentment, which turn eventually into a torrent of intellectual protest. He protests that never in history have humans acted rationally. Nor could anyone who looks within himself possibly take his conflicting emotions for rationality. He rejects reason as the dominant faculty, on both historical and psychological grounds, and posits the free exercise of individual will as most important, even if it is whimsical or exercised in the service of destruction—hence, the famous passage in which the hero claims that the prospect of a perfect society of the socialist anthill is so intolerable that humanity would wantonly destroy it just so as to send all these logarithms to hell so that we can once again live according to our own foolish will.

The chapters of *The Brothers Karamazov* that received most attention for their contribution to existentialism are ''Rebellion'' and ''The Legend of the Grand Inquisitor.'' In both chapters Ivan Karamazov is the protagonist. In the first he narrates a series of episodes about the innocent suffering of children and protests that if this is the sort of world God created, and if it is the price to be paid for harmony in the next, then he respectfully returns his ticket of admission. ''The Legend of the Grand Inquisitor'' is a discussion of freedom and of the inauthentic versus the authentic. Ivan relates his poem-story of how Jesus returns to earth in sixteenth-century Seville, just as the Grand Inquisitor is supervising the burning of heretics. Jesus is recognized immediately and performs miracles of healing, reminiscent of the Gospels. The Grand Inquisitor has Jesus arrested; that night he visits him in his cell and attempts to justify himself. The gist of his long apologia is that Jesus made a fundamental mistake in giving the gift of freedom. It is too heavy a burden for humanity. Hence, the Catholic Church corrected his message and based it on the three principles of authority, MYSTERY, and miracle, which can be derived from the story of Jesus' temptations in the wilderness. Humanity craves strong government (authority), the guarantee of the satisfaction of its basic material needs (miracle), and something to worship (mystery). Satan offered these gifts to Jesus, who mistakenly rejected them. The Catholic Church accepted Satan's offer.

''The Legend of the Grand Inquisitor'' plays a seminal role in the development of the thought of BERDYAEV, who is partially on Ivan's side in what he sees as a revolt against the false conception of a God of progress in favor of the more humane conception of God implicit in his protest. He asks whether this more humane conception is embodied in the Grand Inquisitor, who accuses Jesus of placing impossible demands on humanity, or in Jesus, who will not relieve humanity of suffering at the cost of freedom and dignity. CAMUS saw in the Grand Inquisitor the successful rebel who demands the domination and unification of the world, in order that a handful of men may preside over the bringing in of the kingdom of heaven on earth. It was Dostoyevsky's declared intention to refute Ivan's arguments against God by artistic means. Freedom was to be found in a life of active, Christian LOVE based on the Gospels and the traditions of the Orthodox Church.

Crime and Punishment continues the Underground Man's rejection of rationalism and utilitarianism; the hero rebels in deed as well as word. Compared to Ivan Karamazov, who argues that "if there is no God then everything is permitted," Raskolnikov has a limited agenda. He argues that it is permitted to great men with a new word for the world to step over conventional morality, provided that their message is thereby advanced. Thus, Raskolnikov's act of murder is not an *acte gratuit* but a deed carefully planned according to a theory of life in which humans may be classified as ordinary or extraordinary, each class being subject to different ethical rules. The novel describes the failure of the theory.

The Idiot and *The Devils* give prominence to another theme: SUICIDE. Raskolnikov contemplated suicide but rejected the idea. Ippolit, a minor character in *The Idiot*, reads to a throng of St. Petersburg citizens gathered at Prince Myshkin's dacha in Pavlovsk a last explanation in the form of a confession, designed as a prelude to his own suicide. He is dying of an incurable disease and argues that suicide is the last act of free will left to him. If he had been given the choice, he would never have agreed to being born on such ridiculous terms. His PERCEPTION of life's absurdity is brought into focus by Holbein's picture of Christ's body taken down from the cross. Here the most priceless being, for whom Nature's laws were perhaps created, seems to have been overcome by a dark, insolent, machinelike, and senselessly eternal POWER. For Kirillov in *The Devils* suicide is linked to the belief that Jesus lived and preached a tragic illusion. Kirillov wishes to replace him as a savior, by demonstrating through his suicide that FEAR can be overcome. Once that has happened, the "man-god" will replace the "god-man," for if there is no God, then Kirillov is God, and the most extreme form in which he can manifest his divinity is in terminating his own life. A chief character of *The Devils*, Stavrogin, comes nearest, among Dostoyevsky's heroes, to being a hero of the *acte gratuit*. Having created and passed on to other characters a series of distinctive worldviews that they adopt and translate into action, he finds himself steeped in contradictions and doubt. He is reduced to petty acts of aggression and manipulation and declares that he can never take his own life because he lacks the magnanimity needed. In the end he hangs himself.

Dostoyevsky's heroes often indicate that despair underlies the senselessness of life without God. This view of life helped to generate the emotional power and vision of his great novels. But it should be granted that Dostoyevsky also depicted the crucible of doubt through which true Christian faith must pass.

Primary Works

Dostoyevsky, Fyodor. *The Brothers Karamazov*. Trans. Richard Pevear and Larissa Vo-
    lokhonsky. New York: Vintage, 1991.
————. *Notes from Underground; White Nights; The Dream of a Ridiculous Man*. Trans.
    Andrew R. MacAndrew. New York: Signet, 1961.

Bibliography

Berdyaev, Nicolai. *Dostoievsky*. Trans. Donald Atwater. New York: Sheed and Ward,
    1934.
Carr, Edward Hallet. *Dostoevsky*. London: Unwin, 1962.

DRAMA
Peter Royle

There are existentialists who write drama; others write about it. The first group
includes SARTRE, BEAUVOIR, and MARCEL; the second includes these three
authors but also KIERKEGAARD and NIETZSCHE. The most important existentialist dramatist is undoubtedly Sartre, but in "Forgers of Myths" he seems
to indicate that the best French dramatists of his generation subscribe to his
conceptions of drama. Such are Beauvoir, Anouilh, and CAMUS. However, the
plays of Beauvoir and Camus, while dealing with themes such as FREEDOM,
the absurd, and the moral conundrums posed by political action, are rather un-
dramatic and verbose. Also, apart possibly from *Antigone*, Anouilh's plays have
less in common with existentialism than a play like *Nights of Anger* by Armand
Salacrou or *Biedermann and the Arsonists*, written by Max Frisch. The hallmark
of these plays is a preoccupation with particular SITUATIONS, described in the
context of a soul-searching probing of the limits of the human condition. CHAR-
ACTERS choose themselves freely in situations that tend to be extreme. Thus,
Antigone in Anouilh's play chooses to die rather than compromise, and Kaliayev
in Camus' *The Just Assassins* refuses to throw his bomb because this would
mean killing innocent children, opting for revolutionary action that remains true
to humanist origins. Orestes in Sartre's *The Flies* is often considered to be the
archetypal existentialist hero, choosing as he does, even at the cost of the as-
sassination of his mother and her husband, freedom for himself and the liberation
of his fellow citizens.

Apart from *Kean*, a brilliant adaptation of a play by Dumas, Sartre's best plays are not his most ambitious, such as *The Devil and the Good Lord* and *Altona*, but his earlier plays, *No Exit, Men without Shadows*, and *The Respectful Prostitute*. Many claim that his masterpiece is *Dirty Hands*. Many of Marcel's plays precede by decades French existentialist theater, in the years immediately following World War II. His writing for the theater is steeped in religious thought. In ''Religion and Blasphemy in the Contemporary French Theater'' he expresses surprise and satisfaction at the receptivity of modern audiences to religious themes and wonders if there is a chance of drama's returning to its religious roots. Marcel favors a subtle approach and has little sympathy with Sartre's theory of a LITERATURE of commitment. His existentialism is based on a mistrust of systems, including systematizing philosophies, and a belief in the intuitive POWER conferred by participation in BEING. The atmosphere of his plays is of deep seriousness; he is masterly in his detection of moral and psychological ambiguities and his ability to elicit dramatic tensions in ordinary, everyday situations and to see hidden, less than reputable motives in the most apparently saintly behavior. He explains the widespread angst of his generation by an equally widespread need for grace; he attempts to illustrate this need, indirectly, in his plays.

Although Kierkegaard does not present a full-fledged theory of drama, his writings include references to theater and indications of what such a theory might be. He regards the tragic hero as belonging to the universal, as opposed to the knight of FAITH, specifically, Abraham, who renounces the universal in order to become a particular man. He often uses dramatic techniques, for instance, the dialogue in the banquet scene in *Stages on Life's Way*. His thoughts on drama are opposed to Hegel's theory in which Greek tragedy, which is his paradigm, rests upon a conflict of forces, both of which, as in Antigone, may be GOOD but both of which, in the interests of absolute justice, must be condemned for their one-sidedness. In the inevitable tragic resolution of the drama wholeness is restored. Kierkegaard rejects the both/and of Hegel in favor of what he calls either/or; but he would agree that in the final resolution of theatrical drama, which is different in this respect from real-life drama, there is a reconciliation consistent with the idealism of Hegel.

In *The Birth of Tragedy* Nietzsche dismisses the dialectical tradition, which he sees as a sign of decadence to be traced back to Socrates. It is fundamentally opposed to the SPIRIT of tragedy, and its first major dramatic representative is Euripides, whose main faults, according to him, are the relegation of the chorus to a subsidiary, storytelling role and the stress placed on dialogue to the detriment of genuine audience participation. Tragedy is born of music, which is a direct expression of the nonphenomenal world of universals. It is an affirmation of collective vitality; its GOD is Dionysus. The true role of the chorus is, as Schiller had said, that of a screen for the dramatic action or of an intermediary between the WORLD of the spectator and the world depicted on the stage. The Dionysian affirmation of LIFE, expressed immediately in music, needs the cooperation of an aesthetic, Apollonian element to give rise to the images of tragedy. Whereas the Dionysian principle is associated with intoxication and ecstasy, the Apollonian is linked to dream and rationality. Although there is no dialectical synthesis of the two principles, tragedy can be seen as illustrating, paradoxically, both reconciliation and a force diametrically opposed to it. Later, Nietzsche partially repudiated *The Birth of Tragedy*, claiming that he had not gone far enough in his rejection of the dialectics of reconciliation and in the affirmation of the intrinsic VALUE of life, including suffering. He rejects Kantian and Schopenhauerian categories, and his new enemy, the greatest enemy of life and art, is Jesus, the human representation of the triune God, victim, executioner, and comforter in one and the same person. Whereas CHRISTIANITY preaches original sin in an attempt to explain human suffering, the Dionysian spirit exemplified in tragedy is a glorious affront to such notions, and the tragic hero triumphantly accepts one's own annihilation and reabsorption into the collective life force.

Sartre subscribes to the doctrine of the total freedom of the individual; but in his drama there are elements that are Nietzschean, in particular, in *The Flies*. Nietzschean themes include the following. Persons are creators of values, which they affirm in opposition to God. But despite Sartre's statement in *Being and Nothingness* that conflict is the ESSENCE of human RELATIONS, Orestes is genuinely concerned with the well-being of his fellow humans, including those whom Nietzsche would have regarded as inferior. *The Flies* is not a tragedy in the Greek or Nietzschean sense and, in many ways, is not a tragedy at all: it contains a comic element, it celebrates an extreme form of individualism incompatible with the spirit of music, it is anti-idealist, and it enshrines an ONTOLOGY of freedom and not of fatality. Furthermore, the dialogue, like that, according to Nietzsche, in the plays of Euripides, is generally considered to be often too theoretical and obtrusive. Sartre subsequently came to this view. The play is nevertheless an existentialist landmark, because Sartre chooses in it perhaps the most fatalistic of all Greek MYTHS to illustrate a doctrine of freedom that is the most radical denial of fate. Sartre held that the classical theater, based on an essentialist vision of the world, must give way to a theater of situations that explores the limits of the human condition and in which characters are identical with the choices they make.

A major achievement of existentialist drama is to have brought philosophical themes to the attention of a much wider public than could be reached by philosophical argument, while illustrating their existential significance through an implicit appeal to the audience's humanity. Existentialist theories of drama not only are a contribution to AESTHETICS enabling traditional works to be seen in a new light but show the roots of aesthetics itself in metaphysical considerations of life and DEATH that can be seen as intrinsically dramatic.

Primary Works

Marcel, Gabriel. *3 Plays: A Man of God; Ariadne; The Votive Candle*. New York: Hill and Wang, 1965.
Sartre, Jean-Paul. *No Exit and Three Other Plays*. New York: Vintage, 1949.

Bibliography

Contat, Michel, and Michel Rybalka. *Sartre on Theatre*. Trans. Frank Jellinek. New York: Pantheon, 1976.

EDUCATION
Nimrod Aloni

Existentialism shares with classical and Romantic philosophies of education a commitment to the enhancement of FREEDOM and growth, to the realization and perfection of human potentialities, and to an ethical code that places the highest VALUE on the dignity of humanity, in relation to which all political, religious, economic, and ideological doctrines are regarded as means. It differs from classical and romantic approaches in its fundamental conceptions. A basic premise of existentialism is that humans, unlike OBJECTS in the WORLD, have no given ESSENCE that governs or ought to govern their lives and from which a particular program of LIFE can be inferred. It rejects the classical notion of humans as primarily rational beings capable of grasping—by means of proper education—intellectual INTUITIONS that are objectively valid concerning the NATURE of reality, MORALITY, and beauty. It also rejects the romantic, naturalistic assumption of an inner nature or fixed self in every PERSON that is fundamentally GOOD and unique and that pushes to unfold and actualize itself toward healthy EXISTENCE and full humanity.

The Romantic attempt to ground human conduct and education in nature and the classical attempt to ground them in the dictates of reason are considered by existentialists to be intellectually wrong because they both base their views on metaphysical assumptions that, if not fictitious, are at least unverifiable. They are morally wrong because such attempts manifest BAD FAITH: the attempt to escape the distinctively human condition of freedom and RESPONSIBILITY. The alternative advanced by some existentialists is that humans can appeal to no external authority, either natural or supernatural, and are therefore destined to choose, define, and create themselves as the true and responsible authors of their life PROJECTS. SARTRE held that man is nothing else but what he makes of himself.

Concerning human perfection, existentialists identify it, as do many other humanists, with the process of humanization; yet their understanding of this notion differs significantly. For classical humanists, wisdom is the highest virtue; its cultivation produces both moral CHARACTER and happiness: the rational person is necessarily also morally good and blessed. The road to such perfection is education, understood as the ART of turning the soul from the world of becoming to the world of BEING. Romantic educators conceive the road to perfection as the turning of the soul not to the universal and objective but, rather, to the inner world and unique self of the individual. True education consists of a careful drawing out and attentive actualization of the individual's inner nature. In contrast, existentialists appeal neither to the general order of things nor to the particular nature of the individual. Humans find in the world, NIETZSCHE stated, only what they have inserted into it earlier. Meanings, values, and ideals are not there in the objective world to be discovered; they are the products of the distinctively human capacity for creative form-giving, sense-making, and self-molding. Hence, the process of humanization, perfection, and education is identified by many existentialists with personal authenticity. They seek to inspire and empower students to exercise their freedom, self-concern, moral agency, and CREATIVITY. Achieving these goals requires challenging the individual to account for one's existence, to recognize one's freedom in the face of alternative and competing ways of life, and to courageously accept responsibility for one's CHOICES and deeds.

Existentialist educational theory entails a revolt against the predominant tendency to identify the good life solely with the mastery of formal KNOWLEDGE, morality of principles, rationalization of experience, and reliance on science and technology as the chief furtherers of human excellence and happiness. It has reconstructed the ancient Greek outlook that considers the worth of one's life in terms of one's ethos-character or mode of existence. The existentialist image of great character or of the desirable mode of existence is, of course, very different from the image held by the ancient Greeks. It has been shaped, to a large degree, by the secularization and demystification of the world. KIERKE-GAARD, for example, has complemented the traditional notion of TRUTH as an essence that is objective and universal, with truth as subjectivity, which involves one's relations to oneself in concrete existence—passions, feelings, volitions, moods, insights, and aspirations. Education, Kierkegaard holds, is primarily self-education. It consists of free and often anguishing self-choosing and self-creation, molding oneself into a true SUBJECT. In this process one confronts not only the alienating effect of abstract impersonal thought but also the dehumanizing power of the crowd's conventions and habits.

Nietzsche advanced a quite similar concept of education. GOD is dead, reality is meaningless and purposeless, there are no objective facts and values but only perspectives and interpretations. Human dignity lies in authentic, creative acts of self-formation and self-overcoming. Formulated negatively, the more you betray these virtues in favor of conventional ways of life—be they religious, ideological, social, political, or technological—the less human you become. This conception of AUTHENTICITY differs significantly from that of Romantic naturalism. Nietzsche refers the pupil not to a true self that lies deep inside but rather to a life project that lies high above.

Positing authenticity and the recognition and the exercise of one's freedom and responsibility as a major goal of education also implies that education should be grounded not in EPISTEMOLOGY, PSYCHOLOGY, or sociology but in a person's relation to Being. The difference between the lowest and the highest ways of life should be understood not in terms of knowledge or morals but in relation to the modes of existence that are open to every person. The existential educational surmounting from the lesser to the more authentic has been pictured in different ways. For Nietzsche and ORTEGA it meant the overcoming of inertia and passivity toward powerful self-formation and self-assertion; JASPERS contrasted the being of a person as an object with one's existence as a subject; CAMUS scolded against succumbing to the absurd and endorsed an enthusiastic, conscious rebellion against it; BUBER contrasted the I–It with the open and dialogical relations of the I–Thou; and TILLICH pictured the challenge of authentic self-affirmation as the facing of a threefold anxiety: DEATH, meaninglessness, and condemnation. These images of authentic life constitute educational challenges.

Collectivism is one among many elements that, in the eyes of existentialist educators, cripple personal authenticity, freedom, responsibility, and creativity. Among these dehumanizing, miseducating trends we find deification of external authority in the religious, intellectual, political, moral, and professional domains; conformist assimilation in the crowd and unreflective immersion in computers and gadgets; fragmentation of the individual into his or her role playing as well as subordination to ideological groups and bureaucratic hierarchies; reducing all issues to their technical, calculative dimension. These pervasive cultural trends are held as hindrance to the development of PERSONALITY, moral agency, responsibility, and creativity. Hence, genuine education should consist, first, of awakening individuals to their condition, especially to the ways in which their existence is shaped and conditioned by the economic, religious, intellectual, and political trends. Second, students should exercise their freedom, responsibility, and moral agency. Third, educators should encourage and assist students—in formal and informal activities—to form their subjective vantage point, personal voice, and creative and responsible life project.

The goal of personal authenticity should share in determining the nature of the curriculum. Teaching and learning should aim neither at absolute and eternal truths in the classical sense nor at the mastery of subject matter, in the contemporary sense, but rather at personal emancipation and empowerment. Knowledge of past and present cultures is considered a necessary, yet insufficient, condition for the exercise of freedom and responsibility, because for a culturally illiterate person the given reality would most often seem the only possible reality, and the predominant attitude toward life would thus be conceived as natural. Hence, the broadening of the student's intellectual horizons is essential for the development of true individuality or authenticity. Knowledge is held by some existentialist educators not as a final authority but as a resource. The way we relate to knowledge and incorporate it to redefine and create ourselves is regarded as important as the cultivation of knowledge itself. We are free in the face of knowledge. Appealing to one or another frame of reference, BODY of knowledge, or method always involves an act of choice and thereby of personal commitment and responsibility, hence, the importance of relating knowledge to existential challenges in the student's concrete life. Thus, teaching and learning become forms of self-formation and self-assertion.

Finally, in opposition to functionalism, existentialist education cultivates dialogical relations between teachers and students in which they exist as whole humans. The pedagogical encounter between the teacher and the pupil is as important as the direction or content associated with it. In dialogues between a teacher who grounds one's practice in one's whole being and a pupil whose authenticity stands for him or her as a possibility and task, the essence of existialist education manifests itself and becomes apparent.

Primary Work

Buber, Martin. *Between Man and Man*. Trans. Ronald Gregor Smith. New York: Macmillan, 1965.

Bibliography

Aloni, Nimrod. *Beyond Nihilism: Nietzsche's Healing and Edifying Philosophy*. Lanham, MD: University Press of America, 1991.
Gordon, Haim. *Dance, Dialogue, and Despair: Existentialist Philosophy and Education for Peace in Israel*. Tuscaloosa: University of Alabama Press, 1986.

EGO
Patrick Bourgeois

The ego in existential PHILOSOPHY is somewhat enigmatic. Its legacy emerges from the modern tradition of philosophy as reflection and likewise from the egology of Husserlian PHENOMENOLOGY. Within the existential tradition, the deepening of philosophy as reflexive to the depth of EXISTENCE, the focus on FREEDOM at the core of human existence, and the extension of reflection from its epistemological limits to the whole of human existence put the ego in its place—which can best be seen in light of contrasting, yet similar, roles given to it by SARTRE and MERLEAU-PONTY.

In stark contrast to HUSSERL's egology, in which the enterprise of phenomenology is interpreted in RELATION to the acts and OBJECT arising within CONSCIOUSNESS, oriented to that which transcends consciousness, Sartre's earliest account of the ego is an attempt to overcome what he called the SOLIPSISM of phenomenology. The first transcendental dimension for Sartre is exclusive of the ego; the ego is a unity produced from the essentially temporal structure of consciousness, the activity and states of which are derived from this founding flux. It is the unity of acts and states, a derived and produced unity, based on a more primordial unity of the temporal consciousness. Thus, the transcendental level is the temporal flux of consciousness, which is the founding level of the ego and all else in consciousness. This flux becomes the prereflective cogito in *Being and Nothingness*, which is in diametrical opposition to Descartes and Husserl alike, putting the founding level of the cogito within concrete human existence. This primordial level of existence as INTENTIONALITY contains a primordial level of self-awareness. All awareness, besides being intentional, is also self-awareness on a prereflective level. This two-directional awareness, which is prior to the level of an explicit act of awareness, is prepersonal in the sense of prior to "I" or "you," thus giving a common denominator for intersubjectivity that is prepersonal and lived.

It is precisely this level of the prepersonal that Merleau-Ponty's thought places in central focus for affording a common ground for intersubjective coexistence. For Sartre, this level of the prereflective cogito is considered to be the mode of BEING of human existence as for itself; it is freedom at its core. In this context he develops the defining expression for the mode of being of prereflective consciousness: I am what I am not, and I am not what I am. This expression captures the characteristics of the prereflective cogito and expresses the temporal dimension of human existence around which all themes, even freedom, get articulated. The human is not any fixed determination but is rather the negating of any determination in the form of for-itself as role, objectivity, or identifying trait. I am not my present determining qualities or characteristics, and I am in orientation to possibilities not yet actualized as my determinations. But Sartre is not naive: in his account of human existence, there is the expression of the tension between the in-itself and the for-itself. This tension is lived out in the negating of a fixation, a prerequisite for any possibility of authentic existence. The only determination is the freedom, lived out and preserved as being what I am not and not being what I am. Sartre's philosophy brings the ego down to earth, giving flesh, bone, and life to the Cartesian cogito. Merleau-Ponty's incorporation of the ego as cogito in his phenomenology is meant to overcome some of the insurmountable difficulties with this account.

Although Merleau-Ponty has no full-fledged account of the self, his latent view includes implicitly a view of the ego, which is deepened and brought down to earth as an existential cogito. Merleau-Ponty, as his thought matures, comes to deny any trace of a Cartesian cogito, even the tacit cogito of his early works, as a prereflective self-presence. Such a self-presence prior to the unity and bond of WORLD and lived BODY is forfeited. His latent view of an existential self, in the *Phenomenology of Perception*, has its ground prepared in the account of the emergence of the human level of behavior in relation to levels of behavior that precede it, dealt with in *The Structure of Behavior*. There, he emphasized that the higher, human, or symbolic level of signification emerges from the lower level but is not reducible to, or explainable only in terms of, it. This human level of behavior, as essentially symbolic and as entailing the comprehension of possibilities latent within its situation, is incarnated in the lived body. This notion of the lived body indicates the body that is owned and proper to an individual, with its prepersonal and personal dimensions, individual and general levels. The concrete subject's generality and individuality are two stages of a unique structure between which there is a certain reciprocity of receiving and giving. The prepersonal dimension of the lived body prior to the personal level is that to which the personal is receptive and that which constitutes the world with a pregiven meaning in relation to personal constitution. Hence, the prepersonal dimension of the lived body also mediates the personal aspect of the other, since on that level there is already a corporeal unity in a common world.

For Merleau-Ponty, as the parts of my body together constitute a system, so my body and the other's body are one whole, two sides of one and the same phenomenon. There is a commonness between my body and the bodies of others, which are constituted as an internal relation, so that corporeal INTENTIONS exist at this level prior to any explicit distinction between individual bodies. Because these are internal relations between my consciousness and my body and between my lived body and that of others, one cannot be complete or adequately understood without the other. There is a certain completion achieved in the system in the interrelation among the self and others on this level of the lived body. On the prepersonal level, precisely as lived, entailing the lived world and the lived body, there is a oneness with others and with the world more basic even than the personal level. Consequently, solipsism is a fallacy, for that others and my body are engendered together means that there is no level prior to this intersubjective carnal life, that there is neither individuation nor numerical distinction prior to this level. Being alone in this sense requires lack of awareness of being alone. Thus, an anonymous life of primordial, prepersonal coexistence, rather than solitude, is basic. Anonymity must not be overextended at the expense of differentiation from others, for, even prior to an explicit development of a reflective, personal level, anonymity of the lived body already contains the principle of differentiation from others. It is both one with, and bound to, theirs and, at once, differentiated from them. Once the personal dimension has emerged, it appropriates the whole of the lived body as its own, encompassing even that primordial level in its concrete existence, finding therein the foundation for the differentiation between individuals. Yet, my primordial PERCEPTION as corporeal self-awareness is not "my" perception, since I am conscious only on the basis of my natural, cultural, already acquired prepersonal body, the originary operating intention of which constitutes the horizons of my perceptual field, prior to the emergence of the personal level.

For BUBER the personal becomes the central matrix of his philosophy, which he develops before applying it to the religious at the heart of existence. His fundamental insight is the difference between relating to a thing or to an object that is observed and to a person or a "Thou" who addresses one and to whom one responds. He shows that one can relate to another as a thing and entirely miss the personal dimension of the personal relation. Such an objective attitude toward another PERSON puts the person in an "I–It" relationship, which is not a genuine personal relationship since it does not transpire between an "I" and a "Thou." Rather, it involves an "I" with merely an "It," even though the "It" is another person. Within such a relation, the "I" is entirely alone; the personal dimension is lacking. In the genuine "I–Thou" relation it is very different, being a relationship between persons who are present to one another in a real address and response. This person "Thou" now becomes the perspective on the universe in the light of which it is now interpreted; likewise, the "I" is different now from its former relation to the it. Not only is the "I" different in this unique relation, but the "I" of the "I–It" and the "I" of the "I–Thou" are different "I's," since in the personal relation it is the relation that is primordial and not the "I." Further, the whole being is involved in the "I–Thou" and thus involves a risk not entailed in the "I–It" relation. This takes on special significance in the religious context. According to Buber, the essence of biblical RELIGION is the dialogue between a person and GOD in which each is the other's "Thou." God is the only "Thou" who cannot become an "It," as much traditional THEOLOGY attempts to do. When this fundamental insight of Buber is applied to other areas, such as psychotherapy, the dialogical relation is emphasized.

The conflation of these various traditions toward existential phenomenology and hermeneutic ONTOLOGY passes through the sieve of phenomenological intentionality, the deepening of which has been the background for the consideration of the deepening of the ego from the modern tradition, with its abstract view of the ego.

Primary Work

Sartre, Jean-Paul. *The Transcendence of the Ego*. Trans. Forrest Williams and Robert Kirkpatrick. New York: Farrar, Straus, and Giroux, 1987.

Bibliography

Madison, Gary. *The Phenomenology of Merleau-Ponty: A Search for the Limits of Consciousness*. Athens: Ohio University Press, 1981.

Schroeder, William Ralph. *Sartre and His Predecessors: The Self and the Other*. London: Routledge, 1984.

EMOTIONS
William Hurst

Emotion is rooted in the concept of EXISTENCE; it is not a private, inner psychic state but rather a mode of BEING-IN-THE-WORLD. SARTRE argued that emotion is primarily a CONSCIOUSNESS of the WORLD or a mode of apprehending the world. Psychologists seem to assume that when one speaks about an emotion, such as FEAR or LOVE, one is identifying a self-conscious inner state. On the contrary, Sartre holds, emotion belongs to unreflective consciousness. Emotion is a consciousness that is not primarily an awareness of itself but is rather, and more fundamentally, a mode of grasping the world. As such a mode of being aware or apprehending of the world, an emotion is the context within which OBJECTS in the world become present for an unreflective consciousness. Often, in experiencing an emotion, one will not be aware of the emotion itself. It may happen that the emotion becomes an object for consciousness and thereby enters into self-consciousness, but at that moment it enters the domain of the abstract; it is named and identified and has lost its primary connection with the world. What is made present for reflective consciousness is the emotion itself.

As an emotion makes objects present, it endows them with a quality that they would otherwise not have, and it remains attached to those objects in a way that it seems as if it is feeding off those very objects. Fear endows objects with a CHARACTER that is different from that endowed by joy or lust. This endowment and attachment are magical, Sartre holds; they render the world a frightening or joyful or attractive place, depending on the emotion. Consciousness is a spontaneous presence that has neither a prior nor an originary source. To the extent that emotion is a fundamental and essential dimension of consciousness, it has no cause outside itself. Conceived in this way, emotion is a primordial aspect of consciousness.

Thus, consciousness, which is an apprehension, a transformation, and, in a sense, a creation of the world as it comes into BEING, is emotional consciousness. The passive quality of the emotion appears as something that simply happens to a PERSON. Sartre suggested that this aspect of emotion is accounted for by its fundamentally unreflective character and by its emergence into a condition available for reflection. Thus, an emotion seems to happen to a reflective consciousness, while it is, in fact, coextensive with the fundamental mode of unreflective consciousness. In addition to magically endowing objects with qualities, an emotion is linked to action and to the attempt to transform the world in accordance with the possibilities outlined by the emotion. Thus, one cannot examine fully the NATURE of emotion without attending to the role of action in sustaining the emotion and in giving expression to its view of the world. It is not as if the emotion impels to action, since action itself results from a CHOICE that a person makes of oneself and the world. Rather, the emotion, as a consciousness of the world, is a choice of oneself and the world. Although it may seem as if a person is impelled to action by passions, it is rather the case that one chooses one's passions. The choice of passions is a part of the fundamental choice that one makes of oneself. Thus, Sartre accounts for the observation that some people seem to be impelled to action without having a clear consciousness of an inner emotional state. Such occurs because emotion is fundamentally and primordially an unreflective consciousness of the world, which is only secondarily conscious of itself. As it makes the world present, it entails an action that serves to maintain or transform the world magically created or endowed by emotional consciousness.

For HEIDEGGER, emotion is a mode of disclosure, included within the broader concept of state of MIND. The most important emotional state, from the point of view of the revelation of DASEIN to itself, is ANXIETY, in which Dasein is genuinely moved by its recognition that it exists, that it has nothing as a support for its existence, and that it is responsible for itself. Thus, emotion is a state that is indistinguishable from being-in-the-world and constitutes the way in which Dasein is given to itself and the way in which the world and being come to be. Emotional states are states of REVELATION. At any given moment Dasein is in such a state. To the extent that Dasein's mode of being is authentic, that it recognizes itself in the opening of Being and takes hold of itself in the anxiety through which it grasps its own most precarious mode of being, to that extent Dasein recognizes that emotion as its own. If Dasein exists as the THEY, or impersonal being, to the same extent its states of mind, including its emotions, are not recognized and not grasped as its own but are attributed to conditions that surround it.

In inauthentic existence Dasein's emotions do not belong to itself or at least are not accepted and recognized as its own. Authentic existence is a process in which Dasein takes as its own all that truly belongs to it. The first barrier to AUTHENTICITY is the fallenness of Dasein and its forgetfulness of itself in the dispersal that follows its state of fallenness. To come to itself out of this fallenness, it is necessary that Dasein pass through anxiety. Without coming to know and experience the fullness of anxious existence, Dasein will continue to live in the impersonal, where anxiety fades but where Dasein does not recognize itself. Thus, emotion is very closely linked with the essential nature of Dasein, with its fundamental structure. Dasein is always characterized by an emotion;

being-in-the-world is always shot through with emotion. Emotion is part of the structure of one's mode of being at any given moment. It would seem that the most fundamental emotion through which Dasein becomes aware of itself as being-in-the-world is anguish. Through this emotion Dasein becomes aware of its own potentiality for being, even as it confronts the void that surrounds its existence, a void from which it came and into which it seems to be projecting itself, as toward a future possibility that is at the same time its own origin. In this state Dasein is in a position to take RESPONSIBILITY for itself. This dimension of existence is not accessible to intellectual analysis but yields only to the emotional dimension of being-in-the-world.

What, then, is emotion in an existentialist context of thinking? Emotion is existential; it is a mode of presence, or of being-in-the-world. It is a primordial mode of being present, since it is not dependent on consciousness, and not an aspect of thinking. It is a primitive, ontological mode of presence.

Primary Works

Heidegger, Martin. *Basic Writings*. Ed. David Farrell Krell. New York: Harper and Row, 1977.
Sartre, Jean-Paul. *Sketch for a Theory of Emotions*. Trans. Philip Mairet. London: Methuen, 1971.

EPISTEMOLOGY
Adrian Mirvish

Within existentialism, epistemology involves a move away from the attempt to delineate universal TRUTHS or principles, plus a concomitant shift from reflection to a concern with KNOWLEDGE operating in the WORLD that one constitutes spontaneously. But how can one discuss this topic in terms of immediate experience and prior to explicit forms of categorization? What will this change in emphasis reveal about the basic structure of human existence?

In HEIDEGGER's *Being and Time*, DASEIN has epistemic concerns as the unique BEING that questions its Being. The concern is not with knowledge in an abstract sense. By questioning, Heidegger wants to go beyond the intellectual process in which I deliberately ponder the MYSTERY of my own EXISTENCE. Humans live and question at a preontological level. Yet, Dasein's present existence is shaped by an intricate network of goals. These possibilities, although not yet literally existing, nevertheless shape present existence, for example, how to react to an estranged friend. Goals imply the existence of questioning by introducing uncertainty and CHOICE into one's LIFE. Possibility and questioning go hand in hand. Possibility is grounded in Dasein's past, which includes its culture. Dasein is first and foremost world-oriented in a cultural context. What is most basic, ontologically, is the commonality that one Dasein shares with another within the same world, as opposed to any private or idiosyncratic qualities. Concomitantly, Dasein's ESSENCE lies in its existence: what I am is what I make myself. But since my behavior is related to my obviously selective goals, which reflect my culture and past, my actions are always interpretive. What I am is a partial result of the way I question myself and the world.

Since my possibilities partially reflect my existential context, goals are going to reflect the bias of my culture. In addition, concern with a particular inquiry means that other matters will temporarily fade out of focus. Moreover, so definitive are the issues of interpretation that not only are my questions shaped by the constraints of context, but in the process of asking, I have already an inchoate, preontological understanding of the sort of answers that can be yielded. Hence, although Being reveals itself to Dasein, because of the preceding limitations, it also conceals itself; I can never gain a truly objective overview of the scope of my inquiries. I am involved in the world through the way I use instruments to accomplish goals. Usually, tools function transparently, in a ready-to-hand fashion. The instrument, such as a saw, is not individuated; much less is one aware of its operating in a necessary, codependent context. Not only sawing but doing advanced mathematical analysis are also practical when they function as a type of transparent, ready-to-hand activity: the mathematician is often immersed in a system that functions smoothly. Moreover, when eating, driving, or skiing, one remains involved in the use of numerous, often overlapping, instrumental complexes. For Dasein the world is pervaded by utensil PROJECTS and complexes. Here, the most basic mode of epistemic concern is manifest.

Equipment, however, can break down, jarring or dislocating the epistemic transparency of the ready-to-hand state. A context is created for the now-individuated problem; it does not exist isolated and in a vacuum. Thus, a broken or missing drill or hammer or any other breakdown induces the epistemic shift to an individuated OBJECT functioning in a specific context in the world. Beyond circumspection, at the point where one is further distanced, although still practically involved in the problem, there are present-at-hand modes of existence both ontical and ontological. In the first case one's concern is typically with the nature of science, including reflection. Ontologically, present-to-hand modes of existence involve delineating the domains of traditional ONTOLOGY, whether these happen to involve Plato's Forms, Leibniz's monads, or sense data. These sets of entities, traditionally, have been taken as the basic building blocks of reality and as a primary target for knowledge. Presence-at-hand considered ontically is a speculative activity that engenders abstractions. Epistemologically, one is dealing with mere constructs even if they happen to be useful. This points to a new orientation: for instance, in the case of mathematics it becomes more important to work transparently within a system, in effect, until there is a breakdown. What is significant epistemologically is the ready-to-hand doing of mathematics, with foundational issues taking on more of a practical cast. Or in therapy, instead of focusing on a diagnosis and forcing the patient into a categorical mold, the therapist focuses on relating interpersonally with a Dasein like oneself, who is in need. Knowledge on an ONTIC level lies in exercising understanding at a ready-to-hand level. In traditional ontology, Heidegger suggests, instead of looking for eternal truths, one should operate in an interpretive, ready-to-hand fashion. The optimal epistemic orientation is to grasp for understanding in a field of experience shot through with finitude as a result of one's not evading, but rather coming to terms with, DEATH as one's owmnost possibility. Being-in-the-world implies that, instead of trying to gain an objective point of view, a true understanding of Being will involve the recognition of constraints; Dasein operates within perspectives from which it is not possible to completely extricate itself.

SARTRE distinguishes between knowing as an experience that can be put in explicit terms versus immediate, prereflective CONSCIOUSNESS, where there is a far more inchoate grasp of objects. By counting the number of cigarettes in a case I disclose an objective property in the world. The fact that there are twelve is a clearly delineated phenomenon, distinguished from my counting. Of course, I could explicitly recall how I counted the dozen cigarettes: individually, by rows, by columns. However, my consciousness of counting could also be not well formed. Epistemically, my consciousness qua counting subject is nonthetic. To distinguish between reflective and prereflective consciousness, consider instrumentality. Objects encountered in one's environment are not generally experienced isolated, at a distance from the SUBJECT, but instead grasped in terms of their instrumentality. My pen usually functions transparently; I am not directly aware of it as long as it continues to write. When objects are experienced as tools, consciousness operates prereflectively. Consciousness in its reflective or contemplative form generally comes after the fact.

Consider an ace jet pilot performing a complex set of exercises coordinated with others at high speed. There is no time for reflection. The pilot's actions are prereflective and precise. Unlike the counting case, the pilot could, in retrospect, accurately delineate at least a discrete subset of his actions. Consequently, the pilot's actions were both prereflective and thetic, an explicit form of knowledge. For Sartre prereflective comprehension, both thetic and nonthetic, is epistemically prior to formal categorization. I have a prereflective comprehension of being, of others, and of my own existence. In a famous passage in *Nausea*, Roquentin describes the sudden REVELATION of brute existence. Objects as distinctly individuated, as possessing standard meanings—all this was suddenly revealed as superficial. With this order stripped away, what remains are formless, disordered masses, being-in-itself. Roquentin seems to have experienced the world apart from normal, cultural groupings or meanings. He sensed that the set identity of objects floundered, that their individuality was a veneer. Prior to his discovery Roquentin used to take things in his hands, using them as instruments, superficially catching a glimpse of their resistance. Moving beyond the veneer, he perceives an intrusive, overwhelming resistance apart from its conventional guise or context. Roquentin has a prereflective comprehension of being.

The thetic consciousness of an object demands the correlative existence of nonthetic self-consciousness. Grasping an object explicitly entails my also being nonthetically aware of my fundamental project by which I constitute a world in terms of an initial goal. How is it possible for me to become thetically aware of my fundamental project? The distinction between knowledge and nonthetic comprehension is crucial. Consistent with his claim that there is no unconscious, Sartre notes that normal, impure reflection can grasp the fundamental project but nonthetically. It is presented all at once, a confused conglomerate generally impervious to categorization. A reason for this obduracy is that as ontologically prior to reflective scrutiny, the fundamental project is going to skew the attitude that one can reflectively take, later, to that reflected on. Both effectively and conceptually one is already coming into the reflective attitude with a prior bias, precluding objective knowledge of self.

In *Notebooks for an Ethics* the theme of pure reflection and a true epistemic grasp of self is developed. This reflection demands courage. One becomes critically committed to one's prereflective enterprise instead of observing it. But even pure reflection is ontologically derivative to prereflective experience; it is not foundational; pure reflection grasps itself a posteriori. It must accept the CONTINGENCY of its situation but then create a critical sense of this given world by questioning and acting on whether the VALUES of its prereflective project should be accepted or rejected. There is a project sprung from the nonreflective project and a decision to suspend or pursue the project. What does this tell us about knowledge that one may have about one's fundamental project? Pure reflection can provide a comprehension of this prereflective phenomenon by emphasizing one's absolute contingency. For instance, Mathieu Delarue in Sartre's trilogy *Roads to Freedom* is an intellectual plagued by self-doubt, hesitant to take a stand. But, as a soldier who fights the Germans in the early days of the Nazi occupation of France, he is the last alive while holding off the enemy. What now defines Mathieu's life is a concrete project: to kill as many Germans as possible and hold out for fifteen minutes. Mathieu finds a purpose through giving assent to what he is doing prereflectively—not by positing an ideal. At any given instant he could have capitulated. The French army had been routed, and Mathieu was completely overwhelmed. Instead, each of his shots avenged some ancient scruple, indicating the existence of pure reflection as a constant reaffirmation of his prereflective project. This reflection is a dynamic state, intensifying the determination to realize a goal. Having opened himself to contingency, pure reflection lets Mathieu be free and give up the need to found himself. Thus, there is no knowledge about one's fundamental project through pure reflection; this phenomenon is dynamic so that it would be distorting to try to fix it categorically. However, by enhancing the motivation of the subject's initial project pure reflection provides a genuine comprehension of self that it comes to own reflectively.

Concerning my grasp of the Other, Sartre describes two paradigm cases: my being object for the Other as subject and my being subject for the Other as object. With the former I am an object for myself through the Other's eyes, and I seemingly grasp myself from without; subjectivity escapes me. Instead of comprehension I have an alienated perspective of myself. Concomitantly, the Other's grasp of me is skewed since my subjectivity escapes him too. He or she sees me as an object. There is no genuine comprehension. When I am subject for the Other as object, the same point applies mutatis mutandis for the inherently flawed understanding that I have of the Other. In addition, the other decentralizes the stability of the world that I constitute, due to my experiencing his or her taking a perspective on that world that will always escape me. The Other also provokes attrition in my experience, as a sentient agent who sucks my experience away from me. My grasp of self is undermined. In contrast, my prereflective comprehension of the Other is sure and immediate for the two cases. For instance, when I am caught out and made object for the Other as subject, my experience of being objectified by the Other's LOOK is immediate. I immediately apprehend a strange presence without question or equivocation. In the converse case, too, I immediately grasp the Other's presence as troubling. For both cases my flawed understanding is ex post facto as opposed to my immediate prereflective grasp of the Other.

What about the comprehension that I can have of the Other when we are subject for each other? In *Notebooks for an Ethics* Sartre writes that a common project reveals the Other's fragility. By opening oneself up to me via projects that are precious to him or her, I can find a common bond of humanity. I can experience a common finitude and go beyond radical alterity and genuinely comprehend the other as a finite being. I come to comprehend the Other in his or her relation to the world; he or she opens it up to me by means of enterprise and in the light of his or her fragility. The issue is not formal knowledge. Being open means that I do not insist on imposing categories on the Other precisely because spontaneity is valued. Genuine comprehension in an authentic interaction means being open to the Other as dynamic.

Primary Works

Sartre, Jean-Paul *Iron in the Soul*. Trans. Gerard Hopkins. Harmondsworth: Penguin, 1963.
———. *Nausea*. Trans. Lloyd Alexander. New York: New Directions, 1959.

Bibliography

Sallis, John, ed. *Radical Phenomenology: Essays in Honor of Martin Heidegger.* Atlantic Highlands, NJ: Humanities Press, 1978.

ESCHATOLOGY
Houston Craighead

Traditionally, eschatology refers to events that will occur at the end of chronological TIME, which will give HISTORY its meaning. The PERSON who knows what these events will be knows the meaning of history. Traditional Christian eschatology has to do with the return of Christ to judge the WORLD and the establishing of a heavenly kingdom for the redeemed. An existentialist interpretation of eschatology moves these events into the present, into the interior LIFE of human beings. Eschatology becomes personal, present, subjective. In his Gifford Lectures, *History and Eschatology*, RUDOLF BULTMANN traces the concept of eschatology through Jesus, Paul, John, and the early church. Jesus seems to have understood eschatology as coming in the future, at the end of the world order; he was going to return and bring in a new age. Paul saw Jesus as the eschatological event; the new age was now for those related to GOD through the Christ. However, Paul still looks for Jesus' historical return and expects it within his lifetime. John does not look for a future return of Jesus. The new order is now; the kingdom of God is within the believer. The eschaton is already real. The early church could not sustain this Pauline/Johanine understanding and returned eschatology to merely chronological time. SIN became immoral acts rather than inauthentic self-understanding; obedience became actions in accord with religious rules rather than the self-evident fruit of salvation.

Bultmann returns to the existential understanding of eschatology found in Paul and John. The true eschatological event, the true meaning of history, the apex of chronological time is the event that takes place in the interior life of a person. It is the movement of the person from the inauthentic self that strives to create its own meaning, to the new self that sees that the meaning of history lies beyond history and has been given in the event of Jesus as the Christ. He sees this as the paradox of the Christian message: an event that happens within history, beginning with Jesus' appearance as the Christ and continuing again and again, but is not confirmable by historical method. Jesus as the Christ, as the eschatological event, is not an established fact of the past but is repeatedly present. It addresses the individual here and now in the word of Christian preaching.

Thus, each moment is a possible eschatological moment in which the individual can be addressed and to which he or she can respond by opening oneself to the future and giving up one's striving to cling to ways in which one could create meaning for one's life. This event is eternal—though it happens in history, it happens over and over. It can never be confirmed or infirmed by empirical means; it is an affirmation made by a person on the basis of one's interpreting something in one's own inner life as an address from beyond, from God.

Primary Works

Bultmann, Rudolf. *History and Eschatology*. New York: Harper and Row, 1957.
———. *Jesus Christ and Mythology*. New York: Scribner's, 1958.

ESSENCE
Alfons Grieder

Since Plato and Aristotle the term ''essence'' and the closely related term ''idea'' have been key terms in Western PHILOSOPHY. They acquired a variety of meanings, and it is difficult to define them precisely. Ontologically, the essence of something is, roughly speaking, its NATURE, that is, what it is in itself or what necessarily constitutes its reality, as opposed to its contingent features or its mere APPEARANCE. Existentialists pointed out that human EXISTENCE did not seem to lend itself to a straightforward application of essence for at least three reasons. First, the received view was that the description of essences does not imply any claims concerning actual existence or nonexistence. But is not a PERSON's FACTICITY, the fact that one is in the WORLD, part of one's essence? Second, humans are free to choose themselves or make themselves. In what sense, therefore, could they have essences and be SUBJECT to necessity? Finally, some thinkers came to question the ontological opposition between what something is and that something is. Such may have led HEIDEGGER and JASPERS to use the term DASEIN for the human entity.

HUSSERL held that every individual real BEING has its essence or eidos. This essence, which is the characteristic constituting the individual's proper being, is contrasted with the individual's existence and the fact that it is real.

Essences can be intuited. In order to intuit an essence it is not required that it is the essence of a really existing individual; the essence of an individual that is a product of fantasy can also be intuited. General essences are obtained through a process of variation and on the basis of a dual unit consisting of (1) a series of individuals differing from each other with regard to what they are and (2) an identical, invariant content shared by them all. An essence that depends on other essences is called an abstractum and is contrasted with so-called independent essences, or concreta. A pure eidos is one for which it is irrelevant whether its possible instances are real; it is independent of what factually exists. Immanent essences pertain to possible experiences or acts of CONSCIOUS-NESS. All essences of transcendent OBJECTS, that is, objects that cannot possibly belong to, and inhere in, the flux of consciousness, are called transcendent. The general essence is called the eidos, the idea in the Platonic sense but conceived as pure and free of metaphysical interpretation.

Essences given in INTUITION may be described, and eidetic judgments may be formed on the basis of what is intuitively given. The eidetic sciences, for instance, ONTOLOGY, are free of factual judgments. On the other hand, all factual sciences are involved with, and depend on, eidetic judgments. Transcendental PHENOMENOLOGY, Husserl holds, is an eidetic science concerned with the description of the essential structure of possible experiences and of their noematic correlates, that is, the objects as they are meant to be in accordance with those experiences. Noemata have to be distinguished from essences, and their transcendental-phenomenological description has to be distinguished from ontological judgments concerning the objects themselves. For instance, a round square may be a noema, an object of consciousness, but it is not an essence, as it is contradictory. Phenomenology can provide an eidetic description of the senses in which objects are meant to be; such senses can be determined without resorting to factual considerations.

Heidegger's major work, *Being and Time*, presents itself as an ontology of Dasein, the human entity. It gives a phenomenological description of essential structures of Dasein's being, such as BEING-IN-THE-WORLD, understanding, attunedness, discourse, care, the temporal ecstases. The essence of Dasein lies in its "to-be," in its existence. In this statement the phrase "essence of Dasein" refers to Dasein's mode of being, and "existence" to Dasein's having to be and actually being its possibilities. What is more, Dasein's mode of being lies in its being toward possibilities in such a way that its own being and choice of possibilities are an issue for it. Existence is not so much something Dasein has but rather the way it is itself in the world and, hence, precisely what constitutes Dasein's essence. After *Being and Time* Heidegger used the term "essence" primarily to describe the unconcealment of beings in their entirety. With the essence, the truth of the specific being is also disclosed. Using this approach, he described the essence of a work of ART, the essence of dwelling, and the essence of technology. He pointed out that essence is historical in that each period is characterized by a particular way in which Being and beings are disclosed. Thus, the essence of modern technology, as standing reserve, greatly differs from the essence of technology in ancient or medieval times.

Among SARTRE's various claims concerning essence, the following seem particularly important. (1) There is no dualism of appearance and essence. Essences are not something behind or hidden behind appearances. They are revealed in the appearances. The essence of an existent is the manifest law or principle of its appearances—of the appearances' concatenation. (2) In the life of a person essence is ontologically preceded by existence. What each person is and becomes depends on his or her choices, which are a manifestation of his or her freedom. (3) The essence of a person is therefore his or her past. Thus, objects in the world have an essence that is a set of qualities or properties in terms of which each of them may be defined. In contrast, a person's essence is contingent; it is how that person makes or defines oneself by one's CHOICES.

Approaching the problem from a different perspective, MERLEAU-PONTY argues that the being of the essence is not primary and does not rest on itself but is bound up with the world: without the being of the world there are no essences, and without essences there is no being of the world. Facts and essences are abstractions. What there is, is the world. Essences constitute an inner, invisible framework of the world, which can be understood only through its relationship to speech.

Primary Works

Husserl, Edmund. *Ideas*. Trans. W. R. Boyce Gibson. New York: Collier Books, 1962.
Merleau-Ponty, Maurice. *Signs*. Trans. Richard C. McCleary. Evanston, IL: Northwestern University Press, 1964.
Sartre, Jean-Paul. *Existentialism and Humanism*. Trans. Philip Mairet. London: Methuen, 1973.

ETERNITY
Ernest Sherman

Shall we live primarily for this WORLD or the next? The Platonic tradition divides reality into a perfect transcendent realm of universal ESSENCE and an imperfect, everyday realm of particular EXISTENCE. When this doctrine was combined with JUDAISM, CHRISTIANITY, and Islam, it led to the notion of GOD's essence as the Highest GOOD. God's kingdom is that eternal, timelessly perfect Ideal toward which imperfect humans must strive. The finite creature must return to the infinite Creator. Existentialists challenge such an otherworldly view. The term "existentialism" refers to our unique, this-worldly existence over against lofty pretensions of Platonic essentialism. Although some existentialists retain the goal of eternity in modified form, they are united in urging us to live earthly LIFE as meaningfully as possible.

According to KIERKEGAARD, the modern, scientific picture of the world does not offer convincing proof of a transcendent order. When we behold ourselves as a natural thing among things, we face the objective uncertainty of any supernatural Creator. However, when a PERSON turns inward, one discovers a unique, choosing PERSONALITY who stands enigmatically apart from things and can never be reduced to them. Further, because I am never merely defined by things, I am alienated and in despair in a world that stresses things. To escape this SITUATION, I drift from thing to thing in a vain pursuit of meaning and fulfillment. The negativity of my condition bespeaks an absent God who is able to fill my void. As an infinitely yearning person, I stand in need of an infinitely divine SUBJECT. How is this need to be addressed?

Kierkegaard replies that you must commit yourself to nothing less than an absolute RELATION to the absolute. Once you admit forlornness and the impossibility of circumventing God's objective uncertainty, you have no recourse but to believe in him through a subjective LEAP of FAITH. Renouncing all outer things, you must plunge into your inner abyss with infinite passion and resignation and hope to attain a relationship to God. This leap of faith does not solve the riddle of human existence. The central MYSTERY of spirituality is that persons are summoned to live in the ambiguous intersection of TIME and eternity. Specifically, Christians must bind themselves to Christ, the God-man who, despite his eternal essence, was born, crucified, and resurrected. However, even though Christ plays the role of Mediator who joins Heaven and Earth, a concept of him will not overcome your alienation. His NATURE will always remain an absurdity to the understanding, an OBJECT of faith to be perpetually reaffirmed in the teeth of doubt. This apparent contradiction will strike us as an Absolute Paradox and never cease to pose a challenge to our loyalty. Like a swimmer in over 70,000 fathoms of water, you can hold to your faith only by persistent striving.

But faith merely provides the anticipation of the eternal in existence. To be sure, we take it on faith that Christ represents the fullness of time. His mediation is the eternalizing act that completes all time in an instant. Nevertheless, owing to his paradoxical appearance, we must struggle with the tension between the complete and the incomplete, the eternal and the temporal. To keep the faith is a lifelong task, assumed in the moment and renewed from moment to moment. If, lacking faith, we withdraw from the world and our responsibilities, we should be splitting the eternal and denying its immediate relevance to the temporal. Consequently, the true direction of faith is a double movement that leaps out of time only to return to time. Filled with the promise of eternal happiness, we then belong entirely to this world and entirely to the world to come. We embody a genuine, concrete eternity.

BUBER redefines worldly responsibility as the ability to respond to the Other in an I–Thou relationship. God is the ever-present Eternal Thou who directly addresses us and whom we may address. The Eternal Thou shines through every I–Thou encounter with a fellow creature. Whether in full explicitness in human relations or more implicitly in other relations, all extended lines of relation meet in the Eternal Thou. Therefore, our unremitting task is to open ourselves to the Thou. When we are not relating as a Thou, we deal with objects on the impersonal level of I–It. Yet no matter how necessary the I–It may be, a person must open oneself to the possibility of an I–Thou encounter, which may help to make holy and whole the everyday, genuinely uniting eternity and time. Thus, we may prepare the way for Messianic consummation that shall redeem all moments together.

God is dead! exclaims NIETZSCHE; RELIGION is a feeble escapism for those who prefer a heavenly Nothing to everyday reality. Nevertheless, Nietzsche's fundamental thought repeatedly invokes spiritual LANGUAGE. A vision came to him in an immortal moment in which he gave birth to his central notion of the eternal recurrence. From that time he was able to utter a sacred Yes to all aspects of life. How are we to understand his teaching? Starting out to undermine any belief in an eternal essence, Nietzsche sees the world as the self-expression of the WILL to POWER. To create is to excel, to show power by triumphing over other manifestations of Will. Nature is a system of competing forces that must overcome itself again and again. Those humans are most in tune with nature who are creative enough to engage in self-overcoming. They are the great masters who break old tablets and pioneer new ways and standards. Those less in tune are the herd, the mediocre conformists. All would be well if the aristocracy and herd kept their place. However, the natural aristocracy can be disturbed if the masses conspire against their betters and shape a culture of weakness in their own image. Such a life-NEGATION has taken place under the 2,000-year reign of Christianity that inverted the natural order, relying on the religious impulse that prefers death to life, an effete heaven to a vital earth. Happily, this era of decadence is coming to a close. With the dawning realization that God has perished, there is a major crisis in Western VALUES and an unprecedented opportunity for rebirth through a transvaluation of all values. Those who are strong enough must combat their very humanity and prepare the way for the SUPERMAN who can eliminate all vestiges of otherworldliness and found an unshakable, Earthbound WISDOM by which all eternal gods shall be permanently crushed.

Nietzsche seeks to demonstrate that the temporal movement of the Will is not open but closed. The flow of time is circular rather than linear. Two reasons are put forth. First, Nietzsche theorizes that the law of the conservation of energy reduces to the conservation of the Will to Power. From this reduction he infers that since the Will has a finite number of combinations, all possible mutations of the Will have already been produced, and every Will-event in nature has already happened innumerable times. Second, such a limited play of forces is clearly intelligible, whereas an unlimited, renewable force would be the old God of religion in a new disguise. Consequently, his insight into the eternal recurrence of the same must possess an eternal, superhuman importance. Unlike weaker expressions, his grasp of the truth ipso facto amounts to a supreme rapport with the Will to Power, an absolute mastery of its absolute cycle of self-overcoming and self-returning. Hence, the moment in which his fundamental thought occurred to him can be deemed an immortal moment, and the Yes to existence that it inspired can be deemed a sacred Yes.

Although he abandoned the Catholic faith as a young man, HEIDEGGER continued to be driven by a spiritual quest. Adopting prophetic phrases of the poet Holderlin, he speaks of our philosophizing in a time of need in which the gods have fled. To respond to this crisis, we must develop a radically new orientation, a fundamental ONTOLOGY that investigates BEING itself. By properly disclosing the nature of Being, we shall open ourselves to a fundamental, spiritual REVELATION. He claims that the Being-question has never been explicitly raised, even though it underlies Western philosophy from the beginning. When Plato gave decisive formulation to the split between eternity and time, essence and existence, he was merely consolidating a forgetfulness of Being that haunted Greek speculation at its inception. Plato was bringing to fruition an abstract, oversimplified approach to Being, while he remained systematically blinded to his limitations. What is now needed is a total dismantling of philosophy, a dismantling that re-collects the hidden, concrete TRUTH of Being.

Being is the ultimate, temporal context of things, the enfolding medium within which all facts arise, and all abstractions are constructed. Heidegger seems to consider it eternal. In setting out to re-collect Being and overcome our forgetfulness, he points to the tendency to get lost in facts and mistake the context for that which it makes possible. Whether we posit a supernatural essence like Kierkegaard's God or a naturally existent essence like Nietzsche's Will to Power, we are lapsing into an idolatrous reification, for, strictly speaking, Being itself is nothing (no thing). Neither essence nor existence, it abides as the negative background against which positive entities emerge. In later years Heidegger assumed a more chastened and reverential stance. Heidegger advocates meditative thinking that empties itself of preconceived notions and awaits the true awakening of the Holy and the Divine. Specifically, as a golden mean between the aggressive, calculative thinking of modern science and the submissive piety of modern religion, we should develop a letting-be that actively receives the sublime Gift of Being. Humans will be the shepherd of Being, the vessel through which Being pours forth.

Primary Works

Buber, Martin. *Eclipse of God*. New York: Harper and Row, 1952.
Kierkegaard, Søren. *Concluding Unscientific Postscript*. Trans. David F. Swenson and
    Walter Lowrie. Princeton: Princeton University Press, 1968.

Bibliography

Caputo, John. *The Mystical Element in Heidegger's Thought*. Athens: Ohio University
    Press, 1978.
Elrod, John W. *Kierkegaard and Christendom*. Princeton: Princeton University Press,
    1981.

ETHICAL STAGE
Robert L. Perkins

KIERKEGAARD's ethical stage of EXISTENCE is presented primarily in two letters addressed to the aesthete in *Either/Or*, Part II, and in an essay on marriage in *Stages on Life's Way*. Kierkegaard's author of these pieces is Judge William, who argues that the aesthete should choose despair, the ethical, and himself in his eternal validity. The choice of despair is a necessary first step because the aesthete did not choose to be an aesthete; aestheticism is the immediate form of LIFE and is based on selfishness and egoism. While exploiting others and SOCIETY, the aesthete conceives of oneself as a beautiful soul. To move beyond the AESTHETIC STAGE of life the aesthete must recognize the sort of PERSON one is, which causes despair. The aesthete becomes an ethical person by repenting for the waste of one's life in trivial pursuits and the manipulation and/or victimization of others. Repentance is an ethical continuum between aestheticism and the ethical life. The choice to become responsible for others permits one to enter into deep, personal relations with other persons. Such relations upbuild one. The most important relation is marriage. LOVE, rather than duty, inclination, or social arrangements, is the basis of marriage. Thus, there is no justified reason not to marry unless one is not asked or is always turned down. One must fulfill all ethical duties to other persons and society insofar as such depends on oneself.

Primary Work

Kierkegaard, Sren. *Either/Or*. Vol. 2. Trans. Walter Lowrie. Princeton: Princeton University Press, 1959.

ETHICS
David Detmer

Ethics addresses such fundamental questions as: What is goodness, and how does it differ from EVIL? What is the NATURE of VALUES, and what things are most valuable? What is justice, and how can one live responsibly? Can we justify our answers to these questions? Finally, ethics discusses applying, in our lives, such WISDOM as we are able to achieve in connection with these questions. For ethics, the goal is not simply to think well but to lead a GOOD LIFE. Even when existentialists examine topics such as ONTOLOGY and EPISTEMOLOGY, their discussions place in prominence value-laden concepts such as FREEDOM, individuality, CHOICE, passion, CREATIVITY, and subjectivity. While many themes of ethics unite them, nonetheless, differences between individual existentialists are evident. The following discussion pursues three themes of ethical interest that unite existentialists, before moving to a brief examination of the details of the ethical thinking of three thinkers.

Distinctive in the existentialists' position are their extreme claims on behalf of freedom. They claim that freedom is a radically pervasive feature of human experience—as much present in actions that strictly conform to societal norms as in those that seem to fly in the face of such constraints; as much a feature of inaction as of action; and as much a part of emotional life as of thinking or willing. Hence, they insist, one must honestly and lucidly face up to one's own freedom and recognize the importance of mutual recognition and support of the other's freedom; one must strive to expand the scope of practical or political freedom. A rationale for ascribing such value to freedom is that all values are created by free choices, and thus freedom, as the foundation of all values, is the chief value. The rationale for emphasizing practical or political freedom may be that ontological freedom, while not identical to political freedom, is foundational to it. Ontological freedom is an irreducible feature of the human condition. Because we are ontologically free, we should seek to preserve and to extend our practical or political freedom. Were we robots, lacking freedom, it would make no ethical difference whether or not we successfully completed our (programmed) PROJECTS. Were we omnipotent GODS, we would always succeed in our chosen projects. Since we are neither robots nor gods but finite, ontologically free, conscious beings, our practical freedom is a constant concern. SARTRE writes that "if man is not originally free, but determined once and for all, we cannot even conceive what his liberation might be . . . If man were not free, it would not be worth moving a finger for him."

Most other ethical themes that unite existentialists can be understood as flowing from ontological freedom. For example, if I am free, then it is at best a mistake to claim that I am not free. If it is also true that I know I am free, I deceive myself when I claim that I am not free. Since it is also true that a freedom that makes me responsible, a freedom that removes all possibility of appealing to deterministic excuses is frightening—then it is hardly surprising that the self-deception that claims that I am not free is common. Indeed, such BAD FAITH is a pattern of CONSCIOUSNESS. At birth, we are thrown into a WORLD in which others define reality and offer rewards for obeying or punishment for disobeying their directives. The passivity of inauthenticity entails the ability to shield myself from the nagging RESPONSIBILITY for the world defined by others without becoming engaged in the project of telling overt lies. A certain skill at selective attention is sufficient. Conversely, it takes courage, energy, and creativity to chart and to authentically follow one's own course in life, to the disapproval of the crowd.

What is AUTHENTICITY? To be authentic is to seek an accurate understanding of the human condition, to face up to that condition honestly, and to live accordingly. To be authentic, I must take responsibility for my choices and actions and gather my energies, POWERS, and passions so that they flow in a unified fashion in the direction of my choosing. Authenticity therefore involves integrity, WHOLENESS, and creativity. A lucid understanding of the inescapability of my freedom undermines my following others passively. The unity of my powers and passions gives me the strength to construct my project, where self-division and conflict weaken me and enable me only to drift along, following projects established by others. Existentialists often defend authenticity by appealing to the virtues of honesty and courage. It is dishonest to lie to oneself about the human condition; it is cowardly to hide from oneself the demanding aspects of that condition.

A PERSON often hides one's freedom and responsibility from oneself by immersing oneself in the anonymous crowd. This herd mentality and corresponding lifestyle are inauthentic. Yet, crowd-immersion is very popular; Heidegger calls it the THEY. Since freedom and responsibility can be tiring and intimidating, if not terrifying, I can always appeal to widely held views or actions in an attempt to avoid responsibility. I can believe what they believe and do what they do. In this way I attempt to avoid having to make a choice. Yet, to choose not to choose is still a choice. Choosing to follow a path laid out by others is still my choice, for which I am responsible.

Existentialists condemn the inauthentic life of the herd because for individuals who have undertaken different life projects, an uncritical adoption of popular beliefs and behavior will not enhance one's distinctive flourishing. Also, uncritical conformity results in a failure to correct popular BELIEFS and behaviors. Frequently, in the political sphere, what is uncritically accepted is cruel, unjust practice, such as the domination of women. Many horrors of contemporary politics stem from widespread cruelty and from common, cowardly conformism that uncritically accepts this cruelty. It is not clear that the critique of the inauthentic herd mentality need apply to all aspects of communitarian thinking. Could there be a community of authentic individuals? BUBER suggested that only an authentic individual can truly be present for one's fellow; one becomes authentic through genuine encounters with others. Moreover, a lucid awareness of my freedom reveals the importance of the freedom of others and of the need to band together with others in freely undertaken joint projects.

Much of KIERKEGAARD's work discusses the implications of his declaration: TRUTH is subjectivity. He shows that the very choice of committing oneself to ethics is subjective. If I encounter ethical norms and feel constrained by them, this is because I have already chosen the ethical life. If I had chosen some other life—the aesthetic or the religious life—I would not in the same way be constrained by ethical norms. This choice of a mode of EXISTENCE is subjective. There are no objective, neutral grounds for choosing one life over another. There are aesthetic reasons for making choices, just as there are ethical or religious reasons for other choices, but there are no objective reasons for choosing between modes of existence.

This does not mean that such a choice is arbitrary or capricious. Even if there are no external reasons for choosing one mode over another, such reasons may emerge in a person's experience. Thus, a person living the aesthetic life, with its absence of seriousness or personal commitment, may come to regard that life as shallow and unsatisfying and to choose the ethical mode, with its commitment to universal moral principles. In passage from one mode of existence to another, the self is altered: the change is basic and dramatically colors the ways one sees, thinks, and lives. Kierkegaard calls this transition a LEAP into the unknown. He thus reaches the conclusion that there is no objective basis for condemning the transgression of ethical principles when the rationale for the transgression flows from the adoption of the religious mode of existence. He defends the teleological suspension of the ethical, in which an individual violates an ethical norm and leaps into a religious commitment. Such is a highly individual affair, carried out with passionate intensity, having little in common with the passive conformity of organized RELIGION.

NIETZSCHE's MORALITY is of life-affirmation. Life is understood in the robust sense of vitality and vigorous thriving. He favors life and what enhances it and condemns whatever is antilife. He regards these views as a challenge to the long-prevailing moralities of the West, which are antilife. A morality that favors life will be this-worldly and will promote intelligence, POWER, freedom, creativity, and courage, which enhance life. It will esteem pride and oppose humility and shame as attitudes of self-hatred. It celebrates excellence and despises mediocrity and submediocrity and rejects egalitarian efforts to disguise or obliterate these distinctions. Life's struggles are joyful occasions for the courageous, nonresentful exercise of freedom. The predominant moralities of the West—CHRISTIANITY and the secular moralities influenced by it—reverse these valuations. Christianity, with its doctrine of original sin and emphasis on the afterlife, is an otherworldly morality that fosters self-hatred and hostility to life. It opposes intelligence in favor of faith, prefers meekness to power, praises humility, and condemns pride. Its otherworldly orientation, opposition to life, and fostering of self-hatred emerge clearly in its degrading of sexuality. It supports egalitarianism, promotes resentment of excellence, and glorifies this-worldly failure. It suggests that all humans are miserable; hence, distinctions that differentiate them are virtually meaningless; humans, far from being able to rely on their creativity, are utterly dependent on otherworldly salvation; the chief value of this life can therefore be found in preparing for the next one—a process that involves the nearly total sacrificing of those goods available to us in this life.

Nietzsche explains that this antilife morality has historically served the mediocre herd. Those who excel in intelligence, creativity, skill, and strength rejoice in life and respect themselves. However, for the many who are lacking in these excellencies, to acknowledge that such traits are valuable would be to admit that they themselves are failures. Unable to achieve success in straightforward competition, mediocre people employed the strategy of convincing their superiors to adopt a morality according to which this life is worthless, power and intelligence are evil, self-renunciation is a virtue, and all people are equal—and if any position of superiority is to be acknowledged, those assigned to it must be meek and humble. This strategy has proved an almost total success. However, this slave morality is falling apart. We cannot long survive, let alone thrive, if we devalue life, reject excellence, and renounce the life's goods. Moreover, we are aware that the values we support are self-destructive and based on lies. This is part of the meaning of his declaration: God is dead. We can no longer believe in God, as is evidenced by the tepid nature of much of religious FAITH. Many of the world's grievous ills stem from our continuing to think in terms of an antilife morality. We must smash the shabby values of this morality and replace it with a pro-life, pro-power, joyful morality of creative freedom.

Many themes of Sartre's ethics are illustrated in his discussion of a moral dilemma of a student who sought his help in deciding between two incompatible courses of action: either stay with, and help, his mother, who was dependent on him, or travel to England to join the forces fighting to liberate France from Nazi occupation. On the first option, the student's efforts would yield benefits, but to one person. On the second option, he would participate in an undertaking affecting a great number of people but one in which he could be certain neither of the nature and significance of his role nor of the eventual success of the cause. In his reply, Sartre claims that all ethical principles are broad and abstract and fail to anticipate the unique particularity of SITUATIONS confronting individuals. Consequently, he emphasizes the ineliminable dimension of subjectivity involved in choosing between rival ethical principles and in applying these principles.

While the values to which Sartre appeals—freedom, choice, authenticity—are central to existentialist ethics, they do not exhaust it. Thus, while he emphasizes freedom in interpreting and applying ethical principles and even uses the word "invention" in connection with this role, he would not regard every choice as morally acceptable. He emphasizes the importance of subjectivity because ethical principles are abstract and must be adapted creatively to individual circumstances. Morality is *not* subjective in the sense that any moral principle is valid or that any principle becomes valid once it is freely chosen. The dilemma of the student arises because no defensible ethical theory is sufficiently concrete to be able to decide between two such worthwhile activities as caring for one's mother and attempting to liberate a nation. However, Sartre would not regard a third option, that of murdering the mother and fighting for the Nazis, as defensible, for, as he puts it, although the content of morality is variable, a certain form of this morality is universal. What counts is whether the invention is made in the name of freedom.

Primary Works

Nietzsche, Friedrich. *On the Genealogy of Morals and Ecce Homo*. Trans. Walter Kaufmann and R. J. Hollngdale. New York: Vintage, 1969.
Sartre, Jean-Paul. *Notebooks for an Ethics*. Trans. David Pellauer. Chicago: University of Chicago Press, 1992.

Bibliography

Detmer, David. *Freedom as a Value*. La Salle, IL: Open Court, 1988.
Gordon, Haim, and Rivca Gordon. *Sartre and Evil*. Westport, CT: Greenwood Press, 1995.

EVIL
David Detmer

For existentialists, evil does not denote a unique negativity with a well-defined NATURE but functions as a synonym for bad, disvalue, unethical. Some thinkers ascribe a more specific sense to evil, distinguishing it from other forms of badness. NIETZSCHE distinguishes evil from bad. He holds that an analysis of the moralities that have prevailed throughout history reveals that they are variations on two basic types. In the original type, the master morality, the primary term is GOOD, and the negative term is bad. In contrast, in slave morality, which is fueled by RESENTMENT, the negative term, evil, is primary, and the corresponding positive term, good, has an entirely different meaning. In early societies in which moral codes first emerged, individuals who achieved positions of dominance tended to be intelligent, strong, creative, and proud and loved LIFE and the WORLD. Such individuals saw themselves as good and, by extension, saw their characteristics, which they regarded essential to excellence, as good. By contrast, almost as an afterthought, they considered the individuals occupying an inferior position in their SOCIETY, as well as their traits of stupidity, weakness, unoriginality, passivity, obedience, and humility, to be bad. The meaning of bad here is remote from wicked or immoral. Its meaning is contemptible, poor, not conducive to life.

Nietzsche believes that the slaves originally had the same goals as the masters: to achieve POWER. However, they lacked the traits necessary to compete successfully for worldly power. Their alternative strategy, which obtained a stunning success, was to persuade the masters to accept the claim that worldly success is unworthy and that intelligence, strength, pride, and the like are evil or immoral. The slaves redefined good so that it stood for meekness, humility, self-renunciation, and obedience and claimed that worldly concerns must be sacrificed in favor of preparation for the afterlife. Such a slave morality is CHRISTIANITY; its great popularity testifies to the astonishing success of the slaves' project. Today slave morality and its idea of evil should be overthrown; the phenomenon of NIHILISM—the widespread sense that the dominant VALUES are unworthy and unbelievable and the rootlessness, disorientation, and meaninglessness that pervade the lives of many people—is attributable to the long reign of slave morality. It is obvious that strength is better than weakness, intelligence better than stupidity, and self-love better than self-hatred. Hence, one must restore to strength, intelligence, and self-love the sense that they are good, and to weakness, stupidity, and self-hatred the sense that they are bad.

BUBER defines evil as lack of direction. This may be understood in both a religious and a secular sense, since the two meanings converge. The religious meaning of direction is movement toward GOD. The secular meaning is movement toward self-fulfillment, authentic decisions, and worthy goals. The important thing is that I make a decision with my entire BEING and with a deep awareness of my RESPONSIBILITY. When I do so, my being moves in a direction toward good and away from evil. Buber's position typifies existentialism in at least three respects. First, he suggests that the manner in which a decision is made is highly significant; the goodness of the content of a decision tends to be related to the goodness of the manner in which the decision is made. Second, he argues that a lack of decision is often worse than a bad decision; he suggests that a Devil would not be one who resolutely went against God but rather one who never came to a decision. This position accords with the existentialist critique of the passive obedience and mindless conformity prevailing in the present age. Finally, he proclaims that the dominant form of evil in our time is the conception and consequent treatment of other people as things, in his terms, as mere Its.

SARTRE agrees with Buber in recognizing the prevalence of evil without resorting to Manichaeism. Their position is that the reality of evil—as an OBJECT of experience, as a social phenomenon, as a possibility confronting a free consciousness—is undeniable, without supposing that evil exists as a self-sufficient ESSENCE. Beyond this recognition, however, their positions tend to diverge. Buber holds that evil can perhaps be redeemed by the grace of God, provided that one turns to God with the unity of one's entire being and asks God for such REDEMPTION. For Sartre, evil cannot and should not be redeemed but, rather, should be fought. He explicitly rejects all attempts to relativize evil. Such attempts threaten to drain evil of its manifest seriousness. He cites Dachau and Auschwitz as having conclusively demonstrated the EXISTENCE and the irreducible CHARACTER of evil. For Sartre evil is the purposeful destruction of human FREEDOM. Both good and evil flow from freedom: good flows from freedom to freedom, while evil flows from freedom against freedom. This distinction is likely to be misunderstood if one construes Sartre as referring solely to ontological freedom and never to political freedom. In moral matters, he often has the latter sense in mind, as when he defines practical freedom in terms of the right to eat and to be adequately clothed, and when he remarks that practical freedom, which he contrasts with metaphysical freedom, is conditioned by proteins. Moreover, corresponding to this distinction between different kinds of freedom, we find a distinction between different kinds of evil; he dismisses metaphysical evil as a luxury in comparison to the evil of hunger. Finally, one must not conclude that Sartre regards evil to be a simple, obvious matter. Rather, he emphasizes the myriad complexities of the intertwining of good and evil in lived experience, noting, for example, how moral scrupulousness might sometimes lead to the perpetuation of injustice; how antisocial character traits are often tied to CREATIVITY and can help to bring about advances that benefit people; how we tend to ignore the good aspects of people we consider evil; and how much of what we take for evil in other people is our projection of our own evil onto them. Such an insistence upon the recognition of complexity and ambiguity is necessary, for only if we understand evil accurately and with due acknowledgment of its complicated interactions with good can we hope to fight it successfully.

Primary Works

Buber, Martin. *Good and Evil*. New York: Scribner's, 1952.

Nietzsche, Friedrich. *On the Genealogy of Morals and Ecce Homo*. Trans. Walter Kaufmann and R. J. Hollingdale. New York: Vintage, 1969.

Bibliography

Gordon, Haim, and Rivca Gordon. *Sartre and Evil.* Westport, CT: Greenwood Press, 1995.

EXISTENCE
Stephen Tyman

Existence as a distinctive philosophical term was of early medieval derivation. When it was reappropriated in the nineteenth century, it was no longer in the context of the realism and substantivism that still tinctured the earlier concept. The old ESSENCE/existence distinction, which Aquinas adapted from Averroes, had spoken to the factor of creaturely being, which, eluding the criteria of essentiality, presented to the mind the stark facticity of the creation. But as to the question of how particular existential possibilities might recursively redound to the development of essence and upon this basis prove explorable in a personal way, Thomism remained silent. Into this area existentialism moved. The crux of difference lay in grasping existence as referring primarily to a radically individual SUBJECT both self-conscious and free. This latter acceptation, which KIERKEGAARD pioneered, JASPERS and HEIDEGGER sanctioned in the term EXISTENZ. However, with regard to the significance of this central point, the subsequent history of existentialism is mixed.

For Kierkegaard the reintroduction of the existence motif was designed to combat rationalism, especially that of Hegel, whose PHILOSOPHY had become too abstract, too absorbed in the reconstructions of science. But merely to supplement the deliverances of critical self-reflectivity with an awareness of the PROCESS CHARACTER of thought itself did not suffice to get to the existential core, nor, in principle, could any corrective of the preceding view. Existence remains as irreducible to socioeconomic determinants as to the historical development of the ideal; it is antithetic to the public realm, including LANGUAGE, and as such it is fundamentally resistant to direct conceptual rendering. Nevertheless, existence is self-accessible in the spiritual mode of reflection, which Kierkegaard designated as inwardness. The ultimate ontological moment is now grounded in an individual act of being remote from intersubjective mediation and thus is communicable to the self as to the other only through indirection. Even an individual seeker must brave the masking effect of PERSONALITY and point of view, as Kierkegaard did with his pseudonymous authorial perspective. What is possible for a PERSON depends on a primordial existential CHOICE, the making of which is representable only obliquely and after the fact.

Kierkegaard calls FAITH that moment when existence has been clarified to the point of transparency, realizing the potential for a self-accessible inwardness that he calls a second immediacy, to distinguish it from the unconscious immediacy of NATURE. But, like all immediacy, it is silent in its heart. The decisive determination of existence is characterized through the famous formula of selfhood: a relation that relates itself to itself, thereby relating itself to the power that constitutes it. He stresses three things: (1) the root factor of personal existence is not a possible SUBJECT of direct, conscious representation but is a dynamic movement into existence, reflectively available only as a double movement recoiling upon already bifurcated dimensions of itself; (2) therefore, an element of radical self-creativity, with the RESPONSIBILITY entailed, lies at the heart of personal existence, which (3) nevertheless is possessed of a derivative or received nature, carrying as an inescapable facet of its meaning an orientation to its sustaining POWER, the Creator.

The refractive effect of CONSCIOUSNESS upon underlying existence is highlighted by NIETZSCHE. A decidedly antireligious tone prevails; REVELATION or self-clarification through grace is absent. So strongly does he stress this point that he eventually subsumes the deliverances of consciousness under the polemical category of the lie. This indicates that the existential factor is impermeable to the concept, and in principle there can be no relation of adequation between the two. Lacking the measure of faith, when the mind turns back upon itself, it always misrepresents underlying existence. The deglorification of mind as a faculty of representation is followed by an exploration of the existential dimension under the rubric of power, which represents the compelling category of LIFE, the principle of vitality any inhibition of which amounts only to nihilistic self-denial. The WILL to power is taken to be the core of an individual's being. Individual existence arises as a stark and often brutal self-assertion, relentlessly swallowing up other centers of force in an ineluctable drive for self-augmentation through dominance.

Nietzsche provides an elaborate supporting psychostructure and an accompanying scathing moral and cultural critique of the VALUES of compassion, which he views as the embodiment of NIHILISM. In contradistinction to the morass of degenerate humanity, his image of the SUPERMAN or self-transcending individual developed in *Thus Spoke Zarathustra* is that of a toweringly self-reliant individual tragically torn by his still-human capacity to suffer, whose chief virtue is the ability to draw upon the forces of existence without stint of rationalization or supporting social apparatus. He also attempted to conceive a larger, more ontological context for his potentiation of individual existence. In this presentation, will, conceived as a fundamental unity immediately broken into indefinitely many incipiently self-moving centers of force, is given ontological standing. However, a fundamental ambiguity arises: individualized will is characterized as will to power in a localized version of itself, suggesting that the true element of its being is perhaps not individual at all. This is not to say that the larger, more oceanic repository of will is available to itself as a consciousness or bears any other mark of ownness or individuality for itself. Will to power, in itself, cannot constitute an individuality over against existing individuals for the simple reason that it is always irremediably decentered and infinitesimally fragmented. Nietzsche makes some attempt to contract the thought of all-embracing will into a stable cognitive structure. In the doctrine of Eternal Recurrence the primordial element of ontological integrity is situated in self-repetition. The primary thrust of the thought of Eternal Return lies in the salutary effect it has upon the individual who, attempting to reflect upon the root source of individuality, finds in the figure of self-repetition sufficient inspiration for continuance of the process of self-creation through self-assertion. Thus, only the manifest comes always and forever to speak for the unmanifest; individual will is the sole testament of the capacity of will-itself even to exist.

In Heidegger's thought existence was invoked in a way fundamentally ambivalent to modernism: it sought to appropriate and augment, even while limiting and largely forcing to an extracognitive register all the themes associated with free self-awareness—themes that, in the throes of the Enlightenment, had assumed authority and prominence. The Cartesian IDEOLOGY of self-transparency that had in the name of science laid aside all ways of unknowing was broadly challenged. Likewise challenged was Kantian ETHICS, where personal FREEDOM had become abstractly conceived and so closely aligned with the conditions of practical reason whose possibility defined it, that there was nothing personal left in it.

Existentialists, however, did not speak with one voice. A strong strain of Enlightenment humanism remained, deeply featured in the work of Jaspers, who retained a commitment to reason as the principal factor of right order in human existence. He recognized a tension: Existenz was not, properly speaking, a concept but rather a cipher lodged indissolubly and unfathomably at the heart of all rational life and discourse. Existenz represented the vertical dimension of TRANSCENDENCE always announcing its perpendicular relation to any given horizon of experience, thereby presenting its lack of closure, but never in such a way as to be commensurable with that horizon. Consequently, Existenz contains the paradox of an unfulfillable task that is nevertheless the defining moment of the human condition: it is the necessity to achieve a reconciliation of Existenz and Reason, which is fundamentally redefined in the context of this insight. No longer can it be regarded as the font of a self-contained intelligibility or a self-justifying matrix of explanations with regard to the WORLD. Instead, the core of reason is stripped to the barest presupposition required of intelligence registered in the experience of mutuality: the pure possibility of communication. The actuality of communication can never be proven. But the ideal of communication is ontologically prefigured in the nature of existence. Thus, the fulfillability of the existential impulse to communicate remains a matter of faith—in the efficacy of reason itself—which is equivalent to a faith in the ultimate mutuality of human concerns.

While Jaspers is committed to Enlightenment humanism, he radically redefines its central focus and scope. He proposes the paradox of an individual need to communicate beyond the boundaries of individuation. His famous boundary experience is an event that simultaneously reinforces the finitude and particularity of the existentially reflecting individual and, through the upsurge of inward pressure against these limits, the acknowledging of the primordiality of transcendence. He is careful to circumscribe the limit of authority to be granted to transcendence by insisting that it be situated, that is, subjected, to the finite conditions making possible its enactment. This radical humanism does not foreclose an openness to SPIRIT. Confidence in the integrity of one's humanity can be grounded only in faith. Because of his invocation of faith in support of humanism, he left himself open to the question of other mobilizations of faith.

The human-centered interpretation of existence was carried further by SARTRE, who shows how basic themes of existentialism can be seen in vigorous light when taken in concrete human terms. In *The Transcendence of the Ego*, he tried to wean phenomenology from the transcendental tendencies it had acquired in HUSSERL's later writings. When PHENOMENOLOGY (devoted to essence) and existentialism (devoted to existence) are properly construed, they point to a single matrix of interpretation focused upon the factical-experiential immediacies of human life. These must be approached, however, strictly on their own terms. Existence itself is shown in its true colors only when it is not forced into the conceptual framework of creationism. Thus, meaning being an event in existence rather than vice versa, existence cannot be said to be meaningful: it is, rather, absurd. This absurdity becomes a theme of PHILOSOPHY. But existence does not stand alone. It is always delineable against the background of an act of meaning directed to it, which presupposes human consciousness—which is not another dimension functioning in the same way as existence. Consciousness has the character of being something that is not. Using the categories of the in-itself and for-self, the former representing pure being-in-itself and the latter consciousness, Sartre situates existence in the intersection of the two. A person is never reducible to any finite set of conditions but is rather in the ontologically position of needing to assert itself out of the context of what it is not. Existence is condemned to restlessness, never at home in its world but never utterly free of it. The apex of human AUTHENTICITY is a celebration of existence that embraces its finitude to the point of understanding consciousness as thoroughly embodied. But an ambivalence prevails, for at the heart of the bodily is the upsurgence of desire, putting the person in a highly charged relation with another. Existence thus writhes in perpetual discomfiture, to which it is the earmark of authenticity to hold fast.

Thus, existence, whether thought of as a concept, a cipher, or a term descriptive of a unique experiential domain, remains a vexed issue within existentialism. Its meaning varies depending on whether it is appropriated in the transcendent context of spirit, the field of human activity, in a manner that resists or invites rational treatment, or in a variety of combinations of these approaches.

Primary Work

Jaspers, Karl. *Philosophy*. 3 vols. Trans. E. B. Ashton. Chicago: University of Chicago Press, 1969/1971.

Bibliography

Ehrlich, Leonard. *Jaspers: Philosophy as Faith*. Amherst: University of Massachusetts Press, 1975.
Lampert, Laurence. *Nietzsche's Teaching: An Interpretation of "Thus Spoke Zarathustra."* New Haven, CT: Yale University Press, 1986.
Perkins, Robert L., ed. *The Sickness unto Death: Volume 19 of International Kierkegaard Commentary*. Macon, GA: Mercer University Press, 1987.

EXISTENZ
Kurt Salamun

In JASPERS' thought Existenz is a sign pointing indirectly to a dimension of individual self-realization that is nonobjective and cannot be communicated by rational categories but only elucidated by PHILOSOPHY and experienced in one's LIFE. The framework of Existenz is the thesis that a PERSON realizes one's potentialities in four dimensions of BEING: (1) naive vitality or vital existence, where physical conditions, spontaneous emotions, egoistic interests, and instinctive impulses dominate; (2) logical thinking and rationality; (3) ideas that become manifest in personal ideals, principles of RELIGION, political ideologies, creative conceptions of the ARTS; (4) Existenz, which presupposes the other three but which is nonempirical and nonobjective. Existenz is the dimension of the actuality of self-being and true selfhood. It is the authentic ground of human being, the intimate dimension of personal humanity. Realization of Existenz in moments of life is possible under two conditions: the experience of boundary situations (DEATH, suffering, guilt, etc.) and/or mutual existential communication with a partner. Realization of Existenz is accompanied by the awareness of a TRANSCENDENCE; one experiences one's self-realization as a gift from a nonobjectifiable being. Certain moral attitudes are linked with Existenz: courage, patience, dignity, intellectual integrity, fidelity, solidarity, RESPON-SIBILITY.

Primary Work

Jaspers, Karl. *Philosophy*. 3 vols. Trans. E. B. Ashton. Chicago: University of Chicago Press, 1969/1971.

FACTICITY
Thomas R. Flynn

In HEIDEGGER's thought facticity designates the BEING-IN-THE-WORLD already of DASEIN, its coming on the scene with a past. Human reality in SARTRE's writings is being-in-situation. Facticity denotes the given dimension of any SITUATION, its resistance and obstacles, which Heidegger claims as well, as distinct from TRANSCENDENCE or the free surpassing of the given by CONSCIOUSNESS. There is no FREEDOM except in-situation, Sartre argues, and hence there is no freedom without facticity. Examples of facticity are my place, my past, my environment, my fellowman, my death. Viewed ontologically, facticity is being-in-itself, with the recalcitrance and thinglike opacity that the concept entails. It is the being of which I am the internal NEGATION or nihilation. Considered temporally, facticity is the past: my previous CHOICES and those of others, sedimented in the practico-inert. Under either aspect facticity contributes in an ambiguous degree to my freedom and identity. I am my existential PROJECT, which distinguishes me from other freedoms; but that project is the temporal surpassing of this facticity, the internal negation of this given. The exact contribution of the in-itself and of freedom in this relationship is undeterminable. Hence, Sartre calls situation an ambiguous phenomenon. As the social aspect of Sartre's PHILOSOPHY grew in importance, so, too, did the conditioning role of facticity in his understanding of freedom.

Primary Work

Sartre, Jean-Paul. *Critique of Dialectical Reason*. Trans. Alan Sheridan. London: Verso, 1982.

FAITH
Daniel O. Dahlstrom

For existentialist thinkers, whether theist or atheist, faith is not so much an intentional or epistemic attitude as it is a lived decision to commit oneself to, and to put one's confidence in, some PERSON, oneself and/or another—precisely as a Thou. UNAMUNO emphasizes that, inasmuch as persons tell us the TRUTH and give us hope, it is not in truth or in hope that we directly believe but in the person who gives us hope. Similarly, MARCEL distinguishes faith from the reflection that must precede it as well as from reflection on faith. He insists that faith is not a problem that the believer might comprehend with a suitable technique but a MYSTERY that involves the believer. Faith is a commitment that I make absolutely. I enter into faith with every fiber of my BEING or, at least, with that part of me that cannot be repudiated without repudiating my whole self.

KIERKEGAARD was partially provoked by attempts either to subordinate faith to philosophical reflection or to historicize faith or to identify it with the immediacy of certain religious feelings. He describes faith as a paradox and a miracle as well as a movement, more specifically, a double movement like a dancer's leap. He deems faith the highest human passion. One cannot go further than this passion, though it is also possible to fail to reach it by, among other things, pretending to dissolve the paradox. In *Fear and Trembling*, he contrasts Abraham, the knight of faith, with the knight of infinite resignation. The latter designates a purely philosophical movement and a necessary final stage on the way to faith but falls short of its passion. The knight of infinite resignation cannot understand Abraham's faith that, even when raising the knife, he would not lose Isaac but would once again have what he loved most. The knight of infinite resignation is aloof and detached from the world. He has resigned himself to the transiency and insignificance of everything finite in comparison with the infinite. He has renounced everything, removed himself to an infinite perspective, and gained a spiritual self-possession, together with the peace and rest of resigned disengagement.

By contrast, Abraham makes the double movement toward the infinite and then back to the finite, hence, a movement in which nothing is renounced, but everything is gained. Abraham never surrendered his claim to Isaac and through that same faith got Isaac back. This double movement is likened to the LEAP a dancer tries to make into a fixed posture without grasping or lurching. The knight of faith, like the dancer, makes the leap look like a walk, with no clumsy break in the natural rhythm of a movement of someone fully alive. Hence, the knight of faith is, on the surface, indistinguishable from the Philistine. When the knight of faith makes his leap, he recognizes intellectually its impossibility as does the knight of infinite resignation; but unlike the latter and like Abraham, he believes the absurdity that alone can save him. Thus, faith is the passion whereby, in the midst of the pain of resigning oneself to the impossibility of something, one dares to risk it as nevertheless possible.

Corresponding to the unintelligibility or absurdity of faith are its silence and solitude, its incommunicability and lack of mediation. There is in faith an inwardness that is posterior, not prior, to reflection and is incommensurable with anything external. Indeed, for the knights of faith, there cannot be any thought of a partnership. This faith is on a collision course with the Greek legacy of ETHICS insofar as the latter is based on universal principles. From the perspective of ethics, Abraham is a murderer. Yet herein lies the paradox of faith, namely, that the individual is not subordinate to the universal but in an act of true faith occupies a higher rank than the universal, over against the universal. By faith, Abraham puts himself in an absolute RELATION to the absolute, a relation that cannot be mediated and, thereby, justified by any universal. Faith does not abolish the universal viewpoint of ethics, but in faith the individual's relation to the absolute determines his or her relation to the universal rather than the reverse. Faith is a matter of free CHOICE, but it is not up to the individual to determine alone one's relation to the absolute; faith remains a miracle. Thus, only faith secures faith that is paradoxically both humanly willed and divinely bestowed.

While for Kierkegaard such faith brings certainty, for SARTRE this paradox is merely an instance of BAD FAITH, which is a basic phenomenon of human EXISTENCE. In *Being and Nothingness* Sartre introduces bad faith at the conclusion to his account of ANXIETY. Anxiety is my CONSCIOUSNESS of my FREEDOM, of being my own future; in a state of anxiety I recognize possibilities as my possibilities, detached from any realizations of them, past or future, and dependent on me alone to sustain. In anxiety I am aware of my self as free and, hence, of my NOTHINGNESS in relation to being-in-itself. Accordingly, it is impossible to overcome ANGUISH, since anguish is what, in the literal sense of the term, I am. Yet, anxiety is rare; the structure of our possibilities, especially in ordinary, active lives, commonly excludes anxious apprehension. People also attempt to elude anxiety. Fleeing anxiety typically means taking refuge in some form of determinism—regarding my choice as though it were engendered not by my freedom but by something or someone else. However, it is impossible to flee one's anxiety without knowing that one is anxious; the flight from anxiety is also a becoming aware of one's anxiety even in denying it. Bad faith is the attitude, born of anxiety, that flees anxiety and, simultaneously, denies the anxiety-ridden CHARACTER of this flight.

Bad faith is problematic. Whether I deny qualities that I possess or affirm qualities that I lack, it is unclear how such deception occurs where there is no duality of deceiver and deceived, as exists in lying. Refusing to appeal to the unconscious, Sartre describes how bad faith is rooted in complementary, yet contrasting, structures—notably, FACTICITY/TRANSCENDENCE and being-for-itself/being-for-others by virtue of which human reality, in the way that it most immediately is, must both be what it is and not be what it is. Bad faith is the ART of forming concepts that affirm the identity while preserving, without reconciling, such differences. For instance, the demand for sincerity, insofar as it is a demand that I acknowledge what I am for others, is a form of bad faith since it requires that I agree to consider myself as I am for-others, a fixed entity, and not a freedom. Put differently, bad faith is the spontaneous way consciousness is what it is not and is not what it is in many SITUATIONS. Sartre alludes to good faith as a way of radically escaping bad faith, presumably through critical thought and a steadfast refusal to accept nonpersuasive evidence. He also characterizes good faith as the attitude of immediate trust in some thing or person.

In *Two Types of Faith* BUBER contrasts trusting someone with acknowledging a thing to be the case, where, in each instance, there are less than sufficient reasons for doing so. While trust, in Hebrew *emunah*, presupposes a COMMUNITY, namely, that one finds oneself in contact with another, acknowledgment, in Greek *pistis*, presupposes a person confronting a truth, requiring acceptance of that truth or even conversion. Buber finds this contrast between communal trust and individual conversion exemplified in the difference between the faith of JUDAISM, a persevering trust in a covenant between a people and GOD, and the faith of CHRISTIANITY, the entrance into which requires a leap from the communal tradition and acknowledgment of what formerly was considered not true and, indeed, rather absurd. These differences between the faith of Judaism and of Christianity are essential, in keeping with their respective sociohistorical origins. Each type of faith faces a distinct crisis in the twentieth century. Nevertheless, Buber insists that, in their joint crises, the renewal of each type of faith has something to learn from the other, Judaism from the Christian emphasis on the decision of the person and Christianity from the Judaic emphasis on dialogue, communion, and a people as the locus of faith.

Primary Work

Buber, Martin. *Two Types of Faith*. Trans. Norman P. Goldhawk. New York: Harper and Row, 1961.

Bibliography

Huertes-Jourda, José. *The Existentialism of Miguel de Unamuno*. Gainesville: University of Florida Press, 1963.
Perkins, Robert L., ed. *Fear and Trembling* and *Repetition: Volume 6 of International Kierkegaard Commentary*. Macon, GA: Mercer University Press, 1993.

FEAR
Daniel O. Dalhstrom

In *The Concept of Anxiety* KIERKEGAARD points out that ANXIETY is completely different from fear, which refers to something definite. In *Being and Time* HEIDEGGER analyzes fear as a mode of the emotional state or state of MIND we find ourselves in that, along with, yet distinct from, understanding and discourse, is equiprimordially and prereflectively constitutive of human EXISTENCE. In contrast to fear, he introduces angst as the fundamental emotional state. Whereas the object of angst is not something ready-to-hand or present-at-hand within the WORLD, the object of fear is precisely such an entity.

Heidegger unpacks the structure of fear in terms of what is feared (the fearful), the fearing itself, and why one fears. What is feared can be encountered in one's environment, something ready-to-hand, an automobile or a knife, something present-at-hand, a bolt of lightning, or a fellow human. What is feared is a threat, which means something known to be detrimental to a specific sphere of things within a practical context in which we are involved. That the fearful OBJECT is a threat also means that it is coming closer, so close that it is near enough to imposing its detrimental effect. The closer the fearful object gets, the more the feeling mounts that it can affect us and yet in the end may not; awareness of this possibility enhances the fear.

Heidegger's account of fearing turns on his distinction between a MOOD and an emotional state. Fear as a mood is conceived as the ONTIC correlate to fear conceived as the ontologically disclosive, emotional state of DASEIN. Ontically, fear is a way in which an individual immediately experiences the approach of something threatening. But, from the ontologist's point of view, fearing is what lets something fearful effect Dasein, uncovering it precisely, yet prereflectively, in its mode of being as fearful. Moreover, from the same ontological perspective, fearing discloses the world in such a way that something fearful can emerge from it and thus discloses Dasein's way of being as that of BEING-IN-THE-WORLD. Fearing not only uncovers entities that Dasein fears or those for which it fears but also discloses to Dasein how it exists as something thrown alongside them. The third part of Heidegger's analysis of fear is directed at the reason why or that for which one fears. Dasein fears for itself as a being-in-the-world, which includes fearing for its BODY, its PROJECTS, and its relationships. Fearing discloses Dasein in its endangerment, in the fact that it has been left over to itself. Yet while fear is an emotional state, it is ultimately rooted in the more fundamental anxiety. Fear is anxiety that has fallen or lapsed into the world, and, as such, it is inauthentic and hidden from itself. In fearing, Dasein's chief concern is inauthentic; it is something other than its authentic being-in-the-world, resolutely anticipating its DEATH. From an ontological point of view, emotional states are ways in which Dasein is-and-discloses-itself as its pastness and the way in which it exists and projects itself already thrown into the world. Accordingly, both fearing and anxiety are distinctive ways of projecting and being there. In fear, the inauthentic emotional state, Dasein forgets itself in a preoccupation with what is or is about to be present; by contrast, in anxiety, Dasein is confronted with its genuine thrownness.

In *Being and Nothingness*, SARTRE describes fear as an immediate, unreflective way of apprehending something transcendent, provoked by the possibility of being changed or even destroyed by something outside me. Fear is the awareness that I am something transcendent among other things transcendent and that I am dependent on other things and capable of being destroyed. To counter this situation, I immediately take whatever steps possible to put distance between myself and the threat. Anxiety is the awareness that taking those steps is an open possibility resting upon my decisions; thus, in anxiety I am aware that I am free, responsible for my future, and nothing can compel me to take those steps. Emphasis on the unreflective character of fear and the manner in which it constitutes transforming relations to objects is a staple of Sartre's sketch of a theory of the emotions. In a state of fear, one is not originally conscious of being afraid; rather, one is conscious of the world; more precisely, the person who is afraid is afraid of something. Fear is a kind of EMOTION, a conscious, but unreflective, way we transcend ourselves and relate bodily to things within the world in the course of magically transforming those RELATIONS. Expressions of passive fear, such as fainting at the approach of a wild animal as a means of escaping it, and active fear, such as fleeing from the animal, are alike attempts at the unreflective level to transform the relation to the fearful object, not by canceling the object itself but by magically eliminating it as an object of CONSCIOUSNESS. When someone fears, one attempts, by means of magical behavior, to deny the existence of the fearful object in the external world. Indeed, the fear can be so great that the individual will attempt to destroy oneself in order, thereby, to destroy the object of its fear. In *Being and Nothingness* Sartre characterizes fear as nothing other than such magical behavior bent upon suppressing by a kind of incantation the frightening objects that we are incapable of keeping at bay. The origin of fear is said to be the discovery that I am an object transcended by possibilities that are not my possibilities. Hence, I am able to escape fear to the extent that I regard my BEING an object as nonessential.

As part of his effort to determine the way in which others are needed by a PERSON in order to realize completely the structures of a person's being, Sartre discusses fear of others. Fear confirms prereflectively not only the existence of others but also how I exist in my relations to them. The significance of fear consists in the fact that it is an original reaction, along with shame and pride, by virtue of which I come to recognize another as a SUBJECT beyond my reach. This recognition of the other as a being for-itself brings with it a recognition of myself as objectified; yet, it also brings a recognition of my selfness as a necessary basis for constituting the other as an object. Thus, fear is part of a process of regaining my subjectivity by objectifying others—making them into beings-for-others.

Primary Works

Kierkegaard, Søren. *The Concept of Anxiety*. Trans. Reider Thomte. Princeton: Princeton University Press, 1980.
Sartre, Jean-Paul. *Sketch for a Theory of Emotions*. Trans. Philip Mairet. London: Methuen, 1971.

Bibliography

Perkins, Robert L., ed. *The Concept of Anxiety: Volume 8 of International Kierkegaard Commentary*. Macon, GA: Mercer University Press, 1985.

FEMINISM
Sylvia Walsh Perkins

The influence of existentialism upon feminist thought is most apparent in the writings of SIMONE DE BEAUVOIR. Beauvoir's thought is especially influenced by her close relationship with SARTRE; influence by other thinkers such as HEIDEGGER and KIERKEGAARD also can be detected. In her major feminist text, *The Second Sex*, Beauvoir used the LANGUAGE and concepts of Sartre's PHILOSOPHY in her description of woman's existential SITUATION; this does not mean that her work lacked originality. Recent analyses of Beauvoir's writings view them as containing significant modifications of Sartre's philosophy that mark her perspective as being different from his views.

Sartre's influence is most apparent in the adoption of an ontological framework in *The Second Sex*. Finding biological, psychoanalytic, and historical materialist accounts inadequate for understanding human LIFE in its unity or totality and woman's concrete EXISTENCE in particular, Beauvoir poses questions that she seeks to answer: What is a woman? Whence comes the submission of woman? How did this submission begin, and why should man have won from the start? How can a human BEING in woman's situation attain fulfillment? She rejects the notion of a fixed human ESSENCE; in denying that woman can be equated with a particular gender or defined in terms of a feminine essence, she appeals to the biological and social sciences. Woman's situation is one in which she is defined, unlike man, in terms of her sex and always in relation to him, not as an autonomous being. Man sets himself up as the absolute, essential Self or SUBJECT over against whom woman is relegated to the position of the inessential Other or OBJECT.

Beauvoir follows Hegel in viewing one CONSCIOUSNESS as standing in fundamental hostility toward every other consciousness; the subject is able to pose or establish itself only in being opposed by an Other. While granting that otherness constitutes a fundamental category of human thought without which no individual or group is able to define itself, she nevertheless contests the notion that the duality of the self and the Other was originally attached to the division of the sexes. In asking how it is that woman, rather than man, came to be identified as the Other and why there is no reciprocity of subject and object roles between the sexes, Beauvoir cites, and seems to be incited by, the absolutizing of the feminine as the Other by LEVINAS, whose typically masculine point of view she seeks to refute.

Beauvoir adopts the Sartrean distinction between the in-itself, which she identifies with IMMANENCE, and the for-itself or PROJECT of TRANSCENDENCE and self-definition in FREEDOM, which is the task of every PERSON. This task, however, has been denied to woman, who is enslaved by NATURE to her reproductive function and restricted socially to the realm of immanence by male domination. The desire to dominate emerges in the attempt of a consciousness to establish itself through making an object of the Other, whom it oppresses toward that end. To explain the fact that it is always woman who is oppressed, Beauvoir appeals to what she regards as a deep-seated tendency toward complicity in women, a complicity grounded in an ambivalent relation to freedom, which is both desired and feared. Thus, much of the RESPONSIBILITY for woman's oppression is placed upon her willingness to forgo the difficult project of transcendence and comply with male demands in return for material advantages.

In *The Second Sex*, in the negative attitude manifested toward women's bodily functions, it is not clear whether Beauvoir is only giving a descriptive account of women's alienated relation to her embodiment under patriarchy or whether the point of view is her own. Some commentators interpret her as radicalizing Sartre's notion of embodied freedom or situated subjectivity in such a way as to reveal the masculinist concept of the autonomous subject to be a project of BAD FAITH in its flight toward disembodiment and separation from others. Beauvoir is far more optimistic than Sartre concerning the possibility of reciprocity in LOVE and freedom. Whereas *Being and Nothingness* views love as an impossible goal, Beauvoir regards woman's tendency in this direction as something she can and must overcome.

As the foremost feminist philosopher of the post–World War II period, Beauvoir may be regarded as the mother of contemporary feminism. While some argue that she had minimal impact on the feminist movement in North America, she is an important formative figure in its background and development. Her continuing presence is felt in the emergence of French and American postmodern feminists, for instance, in their attempts to affirm and articulate a sense of woman's difference in the face of phallologocentrism or the dominant, male-centered symbolic order. Postmodern feminists have been divided in their assessment of Beauvoir's thought. Some view her contribution as being undermined by the influence of Sartre's philosophy, which they perceive as sexist. Beauvoir is faulted for adopting male norms and VALUES, such as transcendence, autonomy, MIND over BODY, binary oppositions, and sameness, and for devaluing immanence, the female body, and female difference. This interpretation views postmodern feminism as completely breaking with Beauvoir's existentialism in favor of a gynocentric perspective that affirms, rather than seeks to transcend, woman's otherness or sexual difference in the articulation of a female-defined discourse and economy of relationships. In this view the maternal, the female body, and the plural nature of feminine eros are valorized and celebrated through autoerotic, lesbian, and heterosexual experiences of feminine body pleasure. Others view Beauvoir as anticipating postmodern feminism in her allusions to woman's sexuality or eroticism as being distinctively different from male sexuality, in her critique of the masculinist idea of the mother, and in her conception of a subjectivity that is socially, yet freely, constituted. Certainly, her central claim that femininity is a social construct rather than a fixed essence or biological destiny (''one is not born but rather becomes a woman'') remains fundamental to postmodern and other forms of feminism.

Two other existentialists who figure at least marginally in contemporary feminist theory are TILLICH and NIETZSCHE, aspects of whose thought and language are utilized in the formulation of a feminist ONTOLOGY and ETHICS by the American radical feminist Mary Daly. In her critique of patriarchal religion and morality in *Beyond God the Father*, Daly describes her work as being, like Tillich's, on the boundary between philosophy and THEOLOGY, since she speaks out of women's experience, which in her view had not been represented in either discipline. Daly objects to objectifying GOD as a being, preferring to speak of the divine as the ground or POWER of being. Rejecting the traditional conceptualization of the divine as a Noun, she adopts a dynamic conception of ultimate reality as a Verb, as an endlessly unfolding Be-ing in, and through whom the unfolding or participation of woman in being may occur. Contesting the traditional androcentrism of God-language, she seeks to transcend anthropomorphic symbolization altogether through the reconceptualization of God as Verb. Daly also appropriates Tillich's concept of New Being, but she is critical of an identification of Jesus as the New Being since, in her view, he constitutes a male symbol associated with the role of sacrificial scapegoat, traditionally imposed upon women. Hence, Christ cannot serve as a model for women's liberation. Rather, the bearers of New Being will be those who live on the boundary, that is, women. Daly looks forward to a Second Coming that is not a return of Christ but a new arrival of female presence that signals the end of humankind's attachment to the scapegoat mentality of the primordial victim as the Other. Like Nietzsche, Daly also looks forward to a transvaluation of VALUES, entailing the end of phallic morality and its attendant victimization of others through rape, genocide, and war. In its place she envisions an ethic that transcends gender stereotypes in the realization of psychic WHOLENESS or androgyny and a total elimination of sex roles, which would be redefined in value-free terms.

Primary Work

Beauvoir, Simone de. *The Second Sex*. Trans. H. M. Parshley. New York: Vintage, 1989.

Bibliography

Al-Hibri, Aziza Y., and Margaret A. Simons, eds. *Hypatia Reborn: Essays in Feminist Philosophy*. Bloomington: Indiana University Press, 1990.
Daly, Mary. *Beyond God the Father: Toward a Philosophy of Women's Liberation*. Boston: Beacon Press, 1973.

FREEDOM
Lawrence J. Hatab

Existential philosophers champion the freedom of individuals to define and choose their course in LIFE. Existential thought combines a conception of freedom that rejects deterministic systems and explanations of human behavior, whether these systems be defined in religious, biological, material, or environmental terms. Such a PHILOSOPHY of freedom is found in the writings of SARTRE. He defines freedom in negative terms since it follows from the intrinsic negativity of CONSCIOUSNESS, which exhibits a pervasive sense of possibility and becoming, a capacity for creation, denial, refusal, and multiple interpretations of the meaning of things. Such shows that human consciousness involves a negative TRANSCENDENCE that continually reaches beyond objective conditions of FACTICITY. Sartre's famous proposition that ''existence precedes essence'' sums up the transcendence of consciousness by rejecting all traditional conceptions that point to an essential human NATURE conceivable prior to the existence of individual humans. Humans, because of the negativity of consciousness, are nothing prior to individual CHOICES made in the course of life. The freedom of consciousness is accompanied by ANXIETY in the face of the groundlessness of the human condition. Moreover, with nothing to guarantee or warrant choices, humans are susceptible to BAD FAITH, to explaining choices in terms of fixed conditions or forces that relieve the self of the burden of RESPONSIBILITY. His philosophy calls us to renounce bad faith and various attempts to reify consciousness, so that we can affirm and nourish freedom, as the ennobling of humans as self-creating. His humanistic response to the death of GOD announces that the human self is its own creator.

Sartre argues that any attempt to surpass this freedom amounts to a denial of consciousness. Consciousness displays various negative relations to existing conditions, but these negative relations turn out to be valuable elements of human life: desire, IMAGINATION, anticipation, hope, CREATIVITY, projection, INTENTION—all such phenomena are constituted by a transcendence of facticity. If any philosophical proposal to ground human action were to be actually fulfilled, the kind of life we know human consciousness to be would be impossible. Indeed, even the positing of philosophical grounding is a free PROJECT of consciousness that is chosen. Bad faith is chosen—we choose to evade responsibility by tracing our action to factical forces. The radical freedom of consciousness is ineluctable. As he writes, we are condemned to be free. Freedom is not absolute, however. There are objective conditions of facticity that consciousness does not control: natural laws, physical states, and circumstances independent of my WILL. Freedom, however, is absolute in the sense that what we make of our circumstances, how we respond to them, the meanings we give to them are free projects that are not compelled or necessitated by objective forces. Thus, if in wartime a town is invaded by enemy forces, this is not a matter of free choice for the townspeople. Nevertheless, one could not say that people are compelled by FEAR or the threat of DEATH to obey the enemy. Resistance is a real option, even unto death. Or consider a child raised by abusive parents. There are any number of possible responses to such an upbringing on the part of mature individuals. Certainly, circumstances might make some choices more difficult than others, but circumstances never lock us into certain responses. In his later thought Sartre modified somewhat the degree to which people can choose their responses to circumstances. He acknowledged that there are factical limits and obstacles to human freedom. But even the idea of an obstacle is defined by the freedom of consciousness. If a locked door is impassable, its impassability is defined by the desire to go through it. Freedom of consciousness, then, is a pervasive project that accounts for the full range of human possibilities and impossibilities.

Although NIETZSCHE also defines freedom in terms of negativity—as a resistance to, and overcoming of, obstacles—he does not equate freedom with consciousness, and he does not offer a call for freedom. He is much more open to instinct and unconscious forces; he limits social freedom to certain types, to creative individuals who have the strength and impulse to break conventions and to establish new VALUES. Most people are not able to exercise creative freedom, and they should not be encouraged to do so. Consequently, he does not take freedom to mean the absence of constraint but, rather, a selective opportunity for cultural innovation. Convention is not something that Nietzsche regrets; the fact that most people are bound by rules and not free to follow their own path is an important part of cultural structure. Both the exception and the rule are necessary, the former for innovation, the latter for stability. Freedom is a privilege of cultural rank and personal endowment and should not be generalized to all humans. For Nietzsche, creative freedom and conformity are not a function of choice but rather of CHARACTER. The free and the unfree seem to be a consequence of strong and weak natures. The force of will is prior to objective, mechanistic schemes of causality.

In HEIDEGGER's thought there are a conception of social freedom and a rejection of metaphysical reductions that are implicit in deterministic explanations of human action. He does not abide a notion of freedom that is attached to individual consciousness because this perpetuates the error of modern philosophy since Descartes that centers thought and experience in the human SUBJECT. Human existence is subordinated to BEING, where Being indicates a holistic process of disclosure in which DASEIN finds its sense of being and relates to beings in the WORLD. Heidegger emphasizes a kind of negativity, but such negativity is not simply characteristic of consciousness but of Being itself. If freedom is connected with negativity, with not being bound or closed, then freedom is ontological and not anthropological; it is a characteristic of Dasein's being. Since NEGATION has a certain ontological priority, then no reduction to positive properties of beings can claim an ultimate status—and this includes human consciousness and subjectivity. Dasein's fundamental awareness of death, of nonbeing, is that dimension through which the very meaning of life and the meaning of things in the world are disclosed. This disclosive dimension of Dasein cannot be reduced to deterministic systems or metaphysical constructs because Dasein is primordially open to the nothing out of which Being is manifested.

In some writings, Heidegger calls this open ontological region through which Being is disclosed freedom. Such freedom, however, is not a property of subjectivity or consciousness; indeed, it is that region into which Dasein is thrown, out of itself, so to speak, so that the Being of beings can show itself to Dasein. The freedom of Dasein is less a human or psychological freedom and more the destiny of ontological freedom, in the sense that Dasein does not decide to disclose Being; rather, Dasein is the disclosive site of Being's emergence. With respect to social freedom, Heidegger does show some affinity with other thinkers in his notion of AUTHENTICITY. Upon experiencing the anxiety of death, the task of Dasein is to release itself from the grip of convention and the THEY for the project of an authentic EXISTENCE that is open to Dasein's own possibilities. authenticity, however, is not a break with sociality. Dasein is essentially

Mitsein, or being-with. Authenticity is never a strict departure from social life. It indicates an individuated adjustment in the social world that allows for a certain sense of social freedom.

What unites the different interpretations of freedom in existential philosophy is a radical conception of finitude, in the sense that existence runs up against, and is defined by, a negative limit. Any doctrine that presumes to reduce existence to positive states of being or closed conditions is disrupted in existential thought by the freedom of negativity.

Primary Work

Sartre, Jean-Paul. *Existentialism and Humanism.* Trans. Philip Mairet. London: Methuen, 1973.

Bibliography

Barnes, Hazel. *Sartre.* Philadelphia: Lippincott, 1973.
Raymond, Diane Barsoum. *Existentialism and the Philosophical Tradition.* Englewood Cliffs, NJ: Prentice-Hall, 1991.
Schrag, Calvin O. *Existence and Freedom.* Evanston, IL: Northwestern University Press, 1961.

GOD
Murray A. Rae

A defining characteristic of existentialist thought is the determination to commence the investigation of reality from the concrete situation of human EXISTENCE. The human BEING is to be understood as a being on the way, always confronted by possibility. Commensurate with this attitude, the question of God is not a question of conceptual coherence but of whether and how the divine being establishes, sustains, and addresses humans. Existentialists inquire whether and how I may encounter God in the concrete situations of human existence and how I may establish a personal RELATION with him. They may agree that this is the proper way to frame the question, but it certainly does not ensure any uniformity of response. In what follows four widely divergent responses are presented.

A substantial portion of KIERKEGAARD's work was published pseudonymously by supposed authors who represent a LIFE view that is often incompatible with Kierkegaard's position. Through this device we may assume that he wished to convey that the widespread, objective, and rationalistic epistemological PROJECT, favored by thinkers of his TIME, is a falsification of the way humans engage reality. Such is very true in the case of a PERSON's relation to God, to whom one must relate with FAITH and LOVE. His essay *Fear and Trembling* challenges the assumption of a simple identity between the deliverances of reason and the purposes of God, especially in relation to ethical demands. When Abraham takes his son, Isaac, to be sacrificed, hearkening to God's command, no rational defense of Abraham's actions is available. We must choose between reason and faith.

The particular fault of Hegel, in Kierkegaard's estimation, was the presumption that the whole of reality, including God, could be embraced within a rational system. To counter this ingrained philosophical approach, Kierkegaard repeatedly elucidated the fundamental distinction between the Idealist and the Christian accounts of how one learns the TRUTH or, more explicitly, how a person enters into a relation with God. He added that any proposed rational demonstration of the existence of God yields only a concept, the concept with which the demonstration began. He recommends that we recognize the impossibility of absolute objective certainty in respect of God and accept RESPONSIBILITY for the personal decision to believe or not. His point is that a personal, thus subjective relation of faith is the only means of access to the reality of God. If a person's relation to God is marred by SIN, thus rendering him or her incapable of attaining a sure KNOWLEDGE of God, then such a person stands in need not of good arguments but of deliverance from one's state of ALIENATION and error. Because of sin there is an absolute qualitative difference between God and humans, a difference that is overcome by personal reception of the gift of faith that draws the person into a relation of trust in God.

Kierkegaard admits that the confession of God's presence among us is paradoxical. Human estimations of what it is to be divine and what it is to be human preclude the two realities being given together in a single human being, such as Jesus. But, he asks, Should such presuppositions be accorded absolute authority in such a matter? Should our understanding of what it is to be divine not be formed in response to what God has actually done among us? God's address to humankind requires that we abandon every image of God that is self-contrived and be attentive to the God who gives himself to be known. Thus, he emphasizes, the understanding of God is based on the reshaping of the human relation to God, which takes place under the impact of REVELATION and which is available only through personal engagement with, and commitment to, the person of Jesus.

In his writing about the ways humans may encounter God, BUBER asserts that the Hebrew biblical tradition describes a God who is present to humans, encountering them in the reality of their day-to-day existence. God is not to be conceived as a principle or an idea but as the One who addresses us. To believe in God is to be conscious of oneself as addressed by God. Thus, BELIEF takes the form of personal relationship rather than assent to certain doctrines or propositions. The divine address is epitomized in the prophetic traditions of Israel but ultimately penetrates all the events of our lives. The openness of each person's future, emphasized by the Hebrew prophets, exists today, safeguarded by God, to the point of allowing even a rejection of God. The divine word of address does not compel allegiance. Rather, it invites relationship. It enables a genuine reciprocal meeting between one active existence, the divine, and another, the human. To be open to the possibility of such a meeting, which is a moment of grace, a person must abandon every image of God and listen anew to the word that is not of one's making but is given by God. As in the Hebrew Bible, the word of God is known as a word addressed to the individual in a dialogical encounter.

In *I and Thou* Buber distinguishes between the I–Thou and I–It relations. Every I–Thou encounter becomes an occasion through which a person relates to God, since the rays between the I and the Thou continue to the Eternal Thou, or God. He adds that the Eternal Thou can never become an It. Speaking of God as an It is betraying his uniqueness as an Eternal Thou. The concept of person is utterly inadequate for describing the nature of God, but to speak of God in personal terms affirms the reality of God's creative, revelatory, and redemptive involvement in human HISTORY, which establishes a mutuality. One learns the significance of mutuality in relations through interactions with other persons, specifically through addressing each person as a Thou. I enter into relation with God not by turning my back on others but by bringing them into the relation; one does not draw aside from others or from the world in order to enter a relation with God.

For SARTRE the rejection of God is linked to human FREEDOM, which is expressed in terms of the precedence of existence over ESSENCE and the denial of any essence to which we are somehow to conform. Human freedom is total. The idea of God as bestower and arbiter of meaning and VALUE is an imposition upon the stark meaninglessness of existence. In such a SITUATION, whereby one recognizes oneself as a freedom facing an absurd existence, many persons act as if they desire to become God. Like one of the broadly accepted ways of viewing God, these persons want to be eternally at rest, yet conscious and free. They are in BAD FAITH. Furthermore, Sartre contends, the actual existence of God would belie the reality of individual autonomy. Such occurs because belief in God entails an all-embracing determinism, since if a Creator exists, then both things and persons would be shaped according to the intention of the one who has caused them to be.

HEIDEGGER has sometimes been described as an atheist, but he explicitly rejected the atheism articulated by Sartre, and in his deliberations on Being many passages appear to have theological overtones. He describes DASEIN, the human entity, as thrown into the WORLD without apparent purpose or cause. The precariousness of human life and the NOTHINGNESS at the end of this life give rise to ANXIETY. Still, Dasein is unique in its capacity to raise the question of Being. Dasein can respond to the call of Being, and Being gives itself to be known. Humans can become the shepherds of Being. Such thinking led TILLICH and BULTMANN to find basic categories for their theological work in Heidegger's writings. Tillich equates God with the the ground of Being and moves beyond Heidegger's writings. Bultmann benefited from Heidegger's thinking when he presented his ideas on the need to demythologize the New Testament.

Primary Works

Buber, Martin. *Eclipse of God.* New York: Harper and Row, 1952.
Kierkegaard, Søren. *Training in Chrsitianity.* Trans. Walter Lowrie. Princeton: Princeton University Press, 1967.

Bibliography

Gordon, Haim, and Jochanan Bloch, eds. *Martin Buber: A Centenary Volume.* New York: Ktav, 1984.
Perkins, Robert L., ed. *Fear and Trembling* and *Repetition: Volume 6 of International Kierkegaard Commentary.* Macon, GA: Mercer University Press, 1993.

FRIEDRICH GOGARTEN
(1887–1967)
Theodore Runyon

Friedrich Gogarten was born in Dortmund, Germany. His father was imprisoned for his activity in socialist causes and died while Friedrich was a child. Gogarten began his university studies at Jena, where he was introduced to Fichte and Romanticism. Fichte's thought was the subject of his first book. He was soon greatly attracted to the writings of KIERKEGAARD. Continuing his theological studies in Berlin, he attended lectures of Harnack and Simmel; the latter influenced the young Gogarten to immerse himself in ART, which he did in Florence in the summer of 1910. He returned to Heidelberg to study with Troeltsch. After completing his examinations, he soon moved as pastor to a parish near Jena, where he could continue his studies, especially on Luther.

In the existential, interpersonal understanding of reality developed during that period in Europe by BUBER and others, Gogarten found an alternative to Fichte's egocentric definition of reality. Idealism had divided reality into the "I" and the "not-I." But Gogarten argued that the "I" comes to birth as it is called into being from outside itself by the Thou. Individuality is therefore secondary; the interpersonal is the primary mode of BEING.

In 1926 Gogarten published *Believe in the Triune God*, in which he sought to clarify how FAITH is related to HISTORY. The method of historicism had raised questions concerning the factual basis for religious traditions. The answer to this challenge by some of Gogarten's mentors was derived from Idealism. Even if religious texts and traditions prove questionable on historical grounds, CHRISTIANITY has given rise to noble ideas that are universal and eternal and thus transcend history. From Gogarten's perspective, this is to take Christian faith out of history, to make it an idea isolated from history. He argues, instead, that faith is nothing but history, a RELATION in TIME that is created by the existential dialectic between the past and the present and built on the model of the encounter between Thou and I. The past makes its claim upon us, confronting us with the possibility of GOD relating to us in the present in a way analogous to the way God has related to persons and nations in the past. If we allow ourselves to be drawn into this history, we may reproduce in the present the authentic history of the past. Then-history becomes now-history, but with its own concreteness and conditionedness in terms of the present context. The problem of relativity is thus resolved not by finding some universal above history that is not SUBJECT to particularity and conditioning but by living in history the responsible LIFE of faith. Yet faith is based on a kind of relativity, our relativity to God in every new moment of history.

Gogarten's next major work, *Political Ethics*, also addresses the problem of relativity. The cultural bias of supposedly universal ethical norms had been exposed, leading ethicists to seek new approaches. In Gogarten's view, although historical contingency may undermine an absolutist ethic, it need not be inimical to ETHICS, for the fact that history is full of contingent relationships is what makes it unavoidably ethical. Our BEING is always being-from-the-other and being-with-the-other. Ethical decisions and actions are not a matter of adhering to abstract, nonhistorical norms of behavior but responding to each SITUATION out of the being one has in relation to God and neighbor. He applies this approach to an ethic of the state as well. Western democratic theory, largely grounded in Rousseau's thought, rests sovereignty in the individual and makes social organization a secondary, artificial construct created by individuals for the more efficient realization of their private goals. In contrast, Gogarten sees the state as a fabric of interresponsibility in which each citizen has one's being in being-for-the-others. The state is vested with POWERS to ensure that the needs of the body politic will be met with enforced obedience, if necessary, to maintain order even when fallen humans do not will it. This last statement may partially explain his hesitance to criticize Nazism in its early stages. After 1935, however, when teaching in Göttingen, he came out against Nazism decisively, explaining that any human effort to achieve total control inevitably becomes demonic.

In the postwar period, in *The Reality of Faith*, Gogarten seeks to replace the substantialist categories traditionally used to define the divinity and humanity of Christ with ideas taken from interpersonal EXISTENCE. Descriptions of Christ as a combination of divine and human substance are replaced by the history of Jesus' relationship to the one he called "Abba," Father, and to his fellow humans. He receives his being-in-relation *fully* from the God who intends to reach out in LOVE to estranged humanity. At the same time, Jesus receives his being-in-relation *fully* from his fellow humans to whose plight he responds. His divinity and humanity are the result of the same divine WILL and describe the same history from two perspectives. Rather than an unintelligible MYSTERY, the doctrine of the two natures of Christ is meant to be an explication of Jesus' relational history—and therefore his very being—with God and humanity.

In *Despair and Hope for Our Time*, Gogarten distances himself from those who denounce secularization as an unmitigated EVIL that threatens the spiritual identity of Western civilization and asks whether a certain kind of secularization is not implicit within the biblical message. Prophetic faith is also "secularized" in that it denied to the gods of the nations and of NATURE the power and control over the WORLD that the ancients generally assumed they exercised. The New Testament continued this theme with the claim that the demonic "prinicipalities and powers" that once ruled over human destiny have been conquered by Christ, so that all relativities have been reduced to one. In Max Weber's term, the world has been disenchanted. Gogarten holds that this disenchantment should be placed in the context of stewardship. Humanity is no longer victimized by forces and powers once thought to have the world under their control, but we have been called upon by the Creator to exercise care of this inheritance that has passed into our hands. This world has thus been made an integral part of the relationship between humanity and God, a part of authentic existence-in-faith. Faith accords reason, exercised in science and technology, an important role within the context of this faith relationship precisely because reason assists in the management of what has been entrusted to us.

However, this genuine secularism is to be sharply distinguished from the secularism that claims that humanity has displaced the Creator, that human control in the world is absolute. Under the impact of this atheist secularism, the world is turned into the victim of exploitation as we seek from it our gratification without regard to our answerability for the world or our RESPONSIBILITY to future generations. The IRONY is that, having freed itself from accountability to God, this secularism quickly succumbs to ideologies that are, in effect, new RELIGIONS that unify the world in one overarching and comprehensive picture. To do so, they impose an arbitrary order and suppress all alternatives. Nazism was such an IDEOLOGY. Operating out of a quasi-mythical view, it systematically destroyed all opposition to its ordering of the world in conformity with its own image. The problem of ideologies, therefore, is not that they are secular but that they are *not secular enough*. According to Gogarten, Christian faith, as existence in answerability to the Creator, denies to ideologies their absoluteness and calls, instead, for the use of our rational capacities to carry out our account-ability to God as historical PERSONS.

Primary Works

Gogarten, Friedrich. *Christ the Crisis*. Trans. R. A. Wilson. Richmond, VA: John Knox Press, 1970.
———. *Demythologizing and History*. New York: Scribner's, 1955.
———. *Despair and Hope for Our Time*. Trans. Thomas Wieser. Philadelphia: Pilgrim Press, 1970.

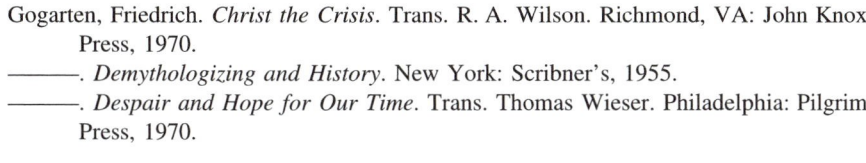

GOOD
David Detmer

Existentialists have presented analyses of the concept "good," discussed whether, or in what sense, good can be said to exist, and considered the extent to which judgments about what is or is not good state TRUTHS about the WORLD, as opposed to simply being expressions of attitudes and feelings. Their most substantial engagement with the good has been the treatment of central questions of ETHICS, namely, what things or states of affairs are good and what the nature of a good LIFE is. While existentialists differ in their answers to these questions, they all regard the affirmation of human FREEDOM to be most important in connection with any consideration of the good. This may seem paradoxical. If we are already free, why stress freedom as a good? In reply existentialists point to an intimate connection between freedom as an ontological condition and practical freedom in the social and political spheres. A life of social and political freedom harmonizes better with one's ontological freedom than does a life in which such alternative VALUES as security and stability dominate, for if freedom is a ubiquitous feature of the human condition, it would seem to follow that a political SITUATION in which many real options are present, in which change is a constant possibility, will suit the human condition better than a political situation in which these features are absent.

Another aspect of the good life that existentialists stress and that must be understood in relation to ontological freedom is AUTHENTICITY. To be authentic is to face up to the human condition frankly and lucidly and to live accordingly. Thus, authenticity demands an awareness of your freedom and a rejection of the temptation to hide from, and to deny, the RESPONSIBILITY it implies. Such recognition of your freedom and acceptance of the consequent responsibility for your CHOICES reveal also the necessity for individuality as an essential feature of the good life. They criticize the widespread tendency toward uncritical conformity as inauthentic. They claim that this tendency results from the ANGUISH that often accompanies an awareness of your responsibility for your choices, ideas, and actions. One way to escape from such anguish is to always think and do what ''THEY'' think and do—in short, follow the crowd. By this strategy you evade taking responsibility for your choices by attempting not to choose at all, by conforming passively to the choices of others. This choice of passive conformity is still a choice for which you are responsible. Authenticity reveals that there can be no escape from the obligation to choose and for the responsibility for choosing well. Those who frankly recognize this will tend, to some extent, to be nonconformists; they will not follow the crowd.

Authenticity also has a social dimension. It reveals to me not only my freedom but that of others as well. Indeed, in many ways my freedom is inextricably bound up with that of others. Thus, SARTRE explains that the free PROJECT of writing implies and demands freedom for prospective readers. To write is to appeal to the readers' freedom in interpreting and responding to one's words. A persistent social theme found in the works of JASPERS, BUBER, MARCEL, and HEIDEGGER, in addition to Sartre, is the significance of authentic, interpersonal communication that is open, honest, nonmanipulative, and characterized by receptivity and by a keen awareness that the other is a free BEING, rather than a means to my ends. The emphasis on dialogue as a basic good is significant for religious existentialists, such as Buber, for whom GOD is a participant in dialogue. Similarly, LOVE emerges most clearly as a fundamental good in the works of the religious existentialists BERDYAEV and DOSTO-YEVSKY, who regard God's love as crucial to our understanding of the good.

Many elements that existentialists consider central to the good life are strongly related to, if not derivable from, those mentioned. They place a high value on CREATIVITY, which they believe to be often linked to a life of authenticity. (For Berdyaev, God, through his creativity, gives us moral instruction.) Their praise of courage in the face of uncertainty and in enduring the ridicule of the crowd flows directly from the demands of authenticity. Similarly, Buber's call for direction—the creative gathering together and unifying of one's energies and passions so that they flow harmoniously together—is crucial to the personal courage necessary for authenticity. The same can be said of a resolute willingness to face anguish. Finally, the social dimension of freedom and of authenticity serves as the foundation for a strong political and economic concern, which must be brought creatively into balance with personal life.

Primary Works

Berdyaev, Nicolai. *Slavery and Freedom*. Trans. R. M. French. New York: Scribner's, 1944.
Buber, Martin. *Good and Evil*. New York: Scribner's, 1952.

Bibliography

Detmer, David. *Freedom as a Value*. La Salle, IL: Open Court, 1988.

GUILT
Peter Royle

Guilt ordinarily means RESPONSIBILITY for the dereliction of a duty or the infraction of a law, a notion that seems clear and simple but that poses many philosophical problems. It is normally defined in legal, moral, or psychological terms and is commonly associated with jurisprudence, THEOLOGY, PHILOSOPHY, and the social sciences. Existentialist thinking has added to our understanding of this term.

KIERKEGAARD stresses the importance of the individual as opposed to the system; he justifies his attitude by reference to religious FAITH. Individuals are in need of salvation, and individuals, all considerations of collective guilt notwithstanding, must be judged guilty or innocent. But the individual CHARACTER of guilt does not prevent him from subscribing to the Christian doctrine that all humans are born guilty by virtue of their implication in the disobedience of Adam. The SIN from which they need individual redemption is both universal and particular. We live in a fallen WORLD. The guilt at the heart of existence is an effect of our singular EXISTENCE; singularization is sin. The GOOD is one thing, and guilt is incurred by not willing it. To overcome it involves progressing beyond the first stage of human existence, the aesthetic, through the intermediate, moral stage, to the RELIGIOUS STAGE, in which guilt will be wiped out, through Christ, by the forgiveness of the loving GOD. Whereas guilt is the opposite of FREEDOM, the reality of freedom is ANXIETY.

For SHESTOV, Kierkegaard's God, whatever the nature of his aspirations, remains the God of the philosophers, perfect, immutable, and therefore a slave to his ESSENCE and autonomous rational laws. On the contrary, Shestov holds, God is absolute freedom and is capable of entering into dialogue with fallen, guilty men. The way to overcome guilt does not lie through increased KNOWL-EDGE, as the essence of human guilt is precisely the separation from God brought about by that knowledge of good and EVIL imparted by the forbidden fruit. Anxiety is not the reality of freedom but the expression of its loss; to overcome it means to enter into a dialogue with the living God. Shestov and, to a lesser extent, BUBER attack Spinoza, whom they accuse of taking away from God his capacity for being addressed. Dialogue between the human I and the divine Thou is central to Buber's thought. Whereas, for Christians, RE-DEMPTION from guilt comes from divine grace, for Buber each PERSON must initiate one's own redemption. Guilt has an ONTIC character obscured by antireligious thinking such as that of Freud. To overcome it, psychotherapy may help, but essentially what is required are self-illumination and perseverance, followed by an act of reconciliation with God, oneself, and the world.

For BERDYAEV, guilt is not the effect of a loss of primal freedom: it springs from the uses of freedom, which belongs to the mysterious realm of nonbeing out of which God created the world. Guilt, as the infraction of a law, must sometimes be resolutely assumed, since laws often conflict, and the genuine moral life is creative, not an existence based on mere obedience to authority. Ultimate redemption from guilt, in contradistinction to the doctrines of most Western Christians, can be only collective, as it is inconceivable that any truly loving BEING could countenance the eternal suffering of a single damned individual, let alone of a mass. It is necessary to go beyond redemption from guilt. The Fall, which makes redemption necessary, is an inevitable stage in the divine plan for the world, since innocence based on ignorance is not consonant with the dignity of free humans; but to make redemption the ultimate goal of creation would be to have a very limited view of the divine purpose. Beyond redemption there is the Third Epoch, in which humans will participate fully in the ongoing, divine creative process.

For UNAMUNO, Jesus came to redeem us not from guilt incurred by sin but from DEATH. Even evil deserves to be eternalized, since in becoming eternal, it would cease to be evil, the essence of evil consisting of a despairing turning away from the desire for immortality. Nevertheless, guilt exists, and it is collective. Since we must not ascribe guilt to the individual who is unaware of the evil that one does, it follows that the person who feels the guiltiest, for example, the saint, is the guiltiest, taking upon oneself the guilt of SOCIETY. Following World War II, JASPERS wrote on German guilt. The atmosphere of submission, such as existed in Nazi Germany, is one of the features of collective guilt. A person has always to choose between an alienating objectivity and a subjectivity in which it dissipates itself. In choosing, it limits itself, yet it would be guilty in failing to choose. Thus, we are guilty by the very fact of existing. Guilt is one of the limit-situations.

NIETZSCHE claims that the historical origin, the psychology, and the etymology of guilt have their origin in cruelty. Human propensity for cruelty, which progressive thinkers are loath to acknowledge, has been historically necessary for the creation of a memory capable of making and keeping promises. The bad CON-SCIENCE is a product of peace, in that hostility, joy in cruelty, and other aggressive emotions, when bereft of an external enemy, turn inward. Whereas redemption, he holds, which originated in buying back, seems to be clearly related to account-keeping, which, exemplified by the verb "ought," we find at the heart of conventional morality. Guilt is an account-keeping notion. Setting prices, determining values, manufacturing equivalencies, and exchanging are part of the self-definition of a human; the lawbreaker is simply a debtor who has attacked his creditor. The creditor may elect to treat the guilty person mercifully, but only insofar as the creditor feels one's superior power to be impregnable.

HEIDEGGER denies that guilt arises in the first instance from indebtedness. On the contrary, indebtedness becomes possible only on the basis of a primordial Being-guilty. Primordial guilt cannot be defined by MORALITY, since morality already presupposes it. Not only, therefore, are guilt and redemption not derivative from those financial and commercial conceptions to which they bear a semantic resemblance, but they are not even rooted in those intrinsic moral and spiritual values that could be seen as providing an analogue for the values of trade and finance. Guilt is incurred through error, which is merely one form of errancy, going astray. This errancy is exhibited by our civilization, which has turned away from Being. We are called by conscience to an authentic Being-guilty. Thrown at birth into an inauthentic existence, DASEIN is guilty; on the level of inauthentic, everyday reality we ordinarily hide the fact. Only on the basis of Dasein's resolutely facing death is the call of conscience answered.

In *Being and Nothingness* Sartre affirms that in the face of the other I am necessarily guilty. Even if I am tolerant toward the Other, I frequently deprive him or her of freedom. Either I experience myself in shame as an object under the Other's gaze, or, by affirming myself, I convert the Other into an OBJECT. In either case I am guilty. Remorse and responsibility are usually antithetical, a theme that emerges in his play *The Flies*. On the ontological level we are necessarily guilty, yet we should definitely not cultivate guilt feelings. Just as we are both responsible and not responsible—responsible, on the ontic level, for everything that happens in the world and yet not responsible, on the ontological level, for this responsibility itself—so we are simultaneously guilty and not guilty—guilty on the level on which we are not responsible and not guilty, at least to the extent that we assume this responsibility for which we are not responsible. Similarly, we may be condemned on one level to the enslaving dialectic of conflict, while being free on another level to work for the freedom of humankind.

For MARCEL an inescapable guilt springs from the seeming impossibility of reconciling sincerity, conceived of as faithfulness to myself, with fidelity to a freely espoused commitment to another, whether human or divine. Although he does not claim to be able to solve this MYSTERY, the solution is to be found along Buberian lines. True existence lies in my relation not with the Other but with a Thou. What the I reaches in the Thou is not NATURE but freedom; I apprehend the Thou as an enduring fidelity. The conflict between sincerity and fidelity is thereby overcome: both the I and the Thou remain free to respond to the solicitations of their original natures.

Guilt defined as responsibility for the dereliction of a duty or the infraction of a law is clearly a problem for all existentialists, which may hinder individuals who wish to act creatively in specific situations. Sartre appears to maintain the Kantian notion of the individual as universal legislator when he suggests that each of my decisions is also a decision on the way humans should act in the world. To be ontologically guilty is often grasped as involving a fall into existence such as is perhaps implied in Christian notions of original sin or at the moment of self-choice, which, while it may entail AUTHENTICITY, also may bring with it infringing upon the freedom of the Other. By relating guilt to the negativities introduced into Being by humans, existentialism has opened up a new perspective. For instance, Sartre has sensitized us to a new range of moral and political problems by forcing us to see them and assume a responsible attitude toward them where we would perhaps prefer not to think about them; thus, although there is undoubtedly exaggeration in his claim that we are all both executioners and victims, it is a judgment that contains an uncomfortable TRUTH. Many concrete stances adopted by existentialists and their commitment—a commitment necessarily entailed by their thought—have given them insights into guilt, both individual and collective.

Primary Works

Buber, Martin. *The Knowledge of Man.* Trans. Maurice Friedman and Ronald Gregor Smith. New York: Harper and Row, 1965.

Kierkegaard, Søren. *The Concept of Anxiety.* Trans. Reider Thomte. Princeton: Princeton University Press, 1980.

Shestov, Lev. *Athens and Jerusalem.* Trans. Bernard Martin. New York: Simon and Schuster, 1968.

MARTIN HEIDEGGER
(1889–1976)
John Protevi

All great thinkers, Heidegger once wrote, think only one thought. Heidegger's one thought was the question of BEING. His thinking over the decades was a long struggle with Being. The struggle yielded few answers; he proposed ways, not works. Heidegger was born in Messkirch, Germany. His early schooling came at the hands of the Jesuits, his university study at Freiburg. He taught at Freiburg from 1915 to 1923, at Marburg from 1923 to 1928, and again at Freiburg from 1928 to 1944. From 1945 to 1951 he was forbidden to teach by the French occupying forces because of his membership in the Nazi Party. As emeritus he taught at Freiburg from 1952 until 1957. His most visible involvement with Nazism was his rectorship at Freiburg in 1933–1934; he was an enthusiastic participant in the Nazi restructuring of the German university system. He remained a card-carrying member of the party until 1945. His postwar statements about his involvement with Nazism were self-serving at best. Perhaps most damning was his postwar silence over the Holocaust, especially given his lamenting the sufferings of displaced Germans. In discussing his works, one must distinguish between works published under Heidegger's supervision and the publication of his collected works, which include many lecture courses.

Heidegger burst upon the European philosophical COMMUNITY with the 1927 publication of *Being and Time*. It is credited by many with being the single greatest stimulus to the existentialist movement; its analyses of inauthentic EXISTENCE, ANXIETY, DEATH, CONSCIENCE, and historicality were among the most provocative affronts to the neo-Kantian and neo-scholastic philosophies that dominated the German universities of the 1920s. These analyses do not occur for their own sake, that is, not for the sake of a PHILOSOPHICAL ANTHROPOLOGY. They are preliminary to asking the question of Being. Since humans are the place where the question of the sense of Being is enacted, the Being of humans must be clarified so that the question comes into focus. But our Being, through and through historical, has interpreted itself in ways that hide the original phenomena of its Being, so a preanalysis of our Being must also be a destruction of the HISTORY of ONTOLOGY.

Heidegger adopts the term DASEIN to designate what used to be called human being. Dasein is not to be equated with SUBJECT, for, as the place where the Being question occurs, Dasein is the locus of the encounter between subject and OBJECT, the opening within which a subject can come to address an object. The preliminary analyses of Dasein that make up the first half of *Being and Time* reveal a variety of structural features, which he called existentials, to distinguish them from the categories appropriate to other beings. At first, only two characterizations of Dasein are given: existence and mineness. The essence of Dasein lies in its existence. Mineness entails that a Dasein cannot be analyzed as a particular instanciation of a species of beings that are constantly enduring, that are present-at-hand. Dasein must be personally addressed, as the use of personal pronouns shows. The mineness that characterizes Dasein can be authentic or inauthentic, but everyday Dasein is indifferent to this difference, so Dasein is to be examined in its everydayness.

The basic constitution of Dasein is BEING-IN-THE-WORLD. The analyses of worldhood destroy the opinion that conceives things as substances: the first encounter between Dasein and the entities encountered within the WORLD is practical, made possible by a network of referrals. A substantial presence of things is thus an intellectual production accomplished by ignoring the primary, practical encounter of entities in a network of referrals. The world holds together, however; it is not a pure dispersal. The referrals are gathered by a final reference, which has no further reference: Dasein. This final reference to Dasein is the for the sake of, which serves as the final reference in any laying out of the world within which Dasein lives. Yet, who is Dasein? Heidegger explodes the Cartesian epistemological subject and its political counterpart, the classical, liberal individual, by showing how Dasein is equally a with-Dasein. The examination of everyday Being-with reveals that the self is a task to be achieved.

The everyday self is hardly a self; it is the dispersed, anonymous THEY. To achieve authentic selfhood, one must gather oneself from out of scatteredness. Authentic selfhood is a modification of the they-self. Heidegger now addresses the ways in which a SPACE is opened within which a subject can confront an object. The first element in the existential constitution of the there of Dasein is attunement. This analysis reveals FACTICITY as thrownness. Dasein is as being-attuned, as being always in one MOOD or another, even if in bored everydayness. This being-attuned, this necessity of finding oneself in a mood, reveals Dasein's Being as a task, even though the they-self seeks to avoid this recognition. At this point, he coins the term ''thrownness,'' which means the facticity of being handed over. What is thrownness? To what are we handed over? His answer: We are handed over to our Being as a task, as something we must do, although the whence and wherefore of this being-handed over remain hidden. Facticity is the character of our Being as something to which we are handed over. Hence, one must achieve the proper RELATION to thrownness. Falling is one mode of thrownness, as being lost in the publicness of the they.

Heidegger analyzes understanding in terms of Dasein's ability to be. Dasein is able to be, in the variety of ways that it is, only by disclosing the there, by means of projections. Dasein projects a possibility of itself onto its for the sake of and onto the world. This projection is not free-floating, for Dasein's possibilities are thrown; hence, Dasein is thrown possibility. Existence is being possible in a way that allows the projection of those possibilities to remain possibilities. The projections disclose entities within the world—allow them to appear as objects for a practical or theoretical subject—on the basis of their relation to a possibility of Dasein. Anxiety testifies to the originary totality of the structure of Dasein. In anxiety things fall away to reveal the worldliness of the world and Dasein's insertion into it as Being-in-the-world. What one is anxious about is precisely this Being-in-the-world. Dasein is thus anxious about no-thing, about Being, which is not a being. In falling, one flees this isolating anxiety by immersing oneself in the things of the world. Thus, an avoiding of anxiety is the condition of FEAR—only by fleeing from anxiety is one able to be confronted by fearsome things.

With the analysis of anxiety and falling, Heidegger defines Dasein as CARE, determined as possibility that is thrown and falling. With the definition of Dasein as care, Heidegger offers a recapitulation of the analyses in terms of underlying temporal structures. He points out that the death of the other can be experienced only as an event in the world, never as such. While Dasein can certainly heroically sacrifice itself, can die instead of the other in a certain SITUATION, it can never take over the task of dying for the other. Such is linked to the possible totality of Dasein, characterized by its existentiality, its being out-ahead-of-itself. How can an entity that is essentially out beyond itself be thought of as a totality? Dasein is conceivable only as a totality as a Being toward death. Being toward death, which individualizes Dasein, is precisely that which is denied by scattered they-self with its falling absorption in the things of the world.

Dasein tends to conceive its own death in the terms it uses to conceive the death of the other—as an event in the world that has not yet occurred. Heidegger insists that Dasein's relation to its own death must be conceived as its nonrelation to the possibility of its own impossibility. Death is Dasein's most authentic, ownmost possibility, yet it is, at the same time, the possibility that Dasein need not be. The possibility of an authentic Being-toward-death lies in responding to the call of conscience, which is a calling of Dasein to assume its GUILT. But what could an ontological guilt be that could be analyzed prior to any instanciation, prior to any concrete, culturally determined content of the call of conscience? The phenomenon of the nothing in anxiety provides the proper perspective. Ontological guilt is being the null basis of a nullity. Dasein is the null basis of itself in that Dasein is handed-over to itself as a task. Dasein is responsible for its own projections, even though it is thrown as thrown possibility. The call of conscience is thus a calling Dasein out of its falling absorption in the things of the world to take up its possible Being-toward-death. Such a taking up occurs in the mode of resolute openness, which, in a confrontation with death as the possibility of the impossibility of Dasein's existence, renders Dasein authentic, stripping away the complacencies of the they-self and revealing to Dasein its true situation.

Possibility, projection, exsistence, understanding: all these phenomena are futural. Thrownness and guilt are made possible by an original having-been. Falling among objects of concern is presenting. All phenomena of Dasein are thus shown to be grounded in temporal structures. Care, the thrown and falling possibility, is thus made possible by temporality, a future that makes present on the basis of having been. The three temporal ecstases are a unified process, which is an original phenomenon of our existence that makes possible the experience of any thing. Historicity is a more concrete working out of temporality; it reveals the embeddedness of Dasein, its Being-with other Daseins in a common historical situation, whose possibilities lay out the concrete possibilities any Dasein can take up. Dasein's FREEDOM is thus a being-free for PROJECTS handed down in one's situation with one's fellows. The TRUTH of this being-with others must be wrested from the complacencies of the they, which congratulates itself on everyone's individuality at the very moment that it ensures rigid conformity by passing on received opinion. The emphasis on history is thus also revealed by the necessity of destroying the received opinions that mask the original structures of Dasein.

Heidegger's essay "Letter on Humanism" sketches various attempts at determining a human essence: Marxist, Christian, Roman, Greek. He concludes that every humanism remains metaphysical, because it is based on a prior determination of Being that determines the Being of beings. But the question of the truth of Being, revealed in pondering the difference between Being and beings, is not posed. As a refusal to ask about the truth of Being, META-PHYSICS remains in the grip of a forgetting of Being. Beings appear in different epochs in different manners—a gift of God for medieval European Christians; raw material for contemporary global technologists—but these appearances occur in structured processes of arrival into unconcealment. Consequently, the forgetting of Being is the forgetting of Being itself in order that the Being of beings might be determined. In our quest for a HUMANISM, the first question to be asked is, What is metaphysics? Following this question would lead not to a determination of the Being of beings but to ponder how there could be a history of different metaphysical systems. What allows for this multiplicity of metaphysical determinations of the Being of beings? The answer must be sought in terms of Being. The question of human existence becomes the question of the relation between Dasein and Being. The metaphysical answers to the question, What is a human? have distinguished humans from other animals on the basis of a special attribute: reason. But this approach closes itself to the fact that a person's true essence lies in one's relation to Being, one's being claimed by Being. Being is not an event that simply occurs out there. Rather, the appearing process addresses Dasein, calling for a response.

Heidegger holds that what is now termed humanism is to be opposed because it does not set the dignity of humans high enough. That dignity is to be the shepherd of Being. Dasein guards Being in that its Ek-sistenz establishes the clearing in which beings are allowed to appear. Being relates to each PERSON as nearness, and this nearness occurs as LANGUAGE, which is thus the house of Being. Humans can dwell in this house of Being. For humanism to regain its meaning, metaphysics is to be overcome, for it hides the original phenomenon of Dasein, our access to the question of Being. The question that is to replace, What is a human? is the thoughtful question, How is the claim of Being itself on Dasein to be thought in terms of its Ek-sistenz?

Heidegger's philosophy often took the form of evocative commentary on major Western thinkers. These works provide concrete examples of his position that historical situation is of the utmost importance to the structure of human existence. These studies present the unsaid intimations of the question of Being in the texts of great thinkers. Such saying of the unsaid can be brought about only by a destruction of the received opinions, the labels that slot thinkers into various compartments. For instance, in his essay on Anaximander, he tackles a most obscure couple of words and, with patient explication and brilliant insights, succeeds in articulating his notion of history of Being. He first brackets the hasty interpretations of Anaximander and asks us to ponder the possibility that the earliest works of the West provide a destiny for us in the modern age of forgetfulness of Being. The earliest works sketch a kinetic sense of the Being of beings as presencing, in which Being and Becoming are not set in opposition, but Being is rendered fluid enough to shelter Becoming. The Being of beings is then thought as the presencing of present entities in the open of unconcealment. This open is not a static stage but an event.

Patient meditation and careful working on these early texts are the key to much of Heidegger's later writings. Such care and patience, such listening break down the active, representing subjectivity that focuses on the manipulation of beings—which is, let us not be deceived (and Heidegger never was), an inescapable and essential mode of human being—to allow a thoughtful response to Being. Heidegger writes that thinking is the poetizing of the truth of Being in the historic dialogue between thinkers. His essays on Parmenides and Heraclitus stressed their common root in their ability to think the Being of beings as a process of coming into APPEARANCE of beings. Both thinkers thought this appearing process as a gathering into sameness; both were concerned with identity and difference as the principles regulating the appearing PROCESS. He indicates that the Greeks thought the ESSENCE of language together with the Being of beings, but this insight was forgotten in the turning of human attention to present beings.

Heidegger's work on Plato and Aristotle is no less stimulating. His "Plato's Doctrine of Truth" sketches a move from an early Greek notion of truth as unconcealment, *aletheia*, to the determination of truth as correctness in Plato. The neatness of this schema came under considerable criticism, and Heidegger retracted it at the end of his career in "The End of Philosophy and the Task of Thinking." He also devoted much attention to modern German philosophy from Leibniz to HUSSERL that seeks to free up from sedimented interpretations each thinker's experience with Being. Each confrontation also reveals the predominant approach of Heidegger's own thought. In *The Metaphysical Foundations of Logic* he investigates the Leibnizian notions of appetitus and the principle of reason in terms of Dasein's TRANSCENDENCE, an approach consonant with his project of fundamental ontology. Later, he again examined Leibniz' principle of reason, but this time in the context of a meditation on the happening of Being in the modern age of subjectivism. In his 1929 lecture course published as *Kant and the Problem of Metaphysics*, he counters the neo-Kantian appropriation of Kant as an epistemologist by insisting upon Kant's concern with Being. NIETZSCHE also came to represent for Heidegger a figure of immense historical importance, to whom he devoted several lecture courses, published in four volumes. For Heidegger's history of Being, Nietzsche represented a challenge: how to place in a history the thinker who claimed to trace the essential traits of that history.

Besides his historical commentary, Heidegger's writings in the 1950s and 1960s focused on the questions of technology and language, his titles for the essence of our global historical situation, and the possible remedy. In "The Question concerning Technology," he lays out his notion of standing reserve that reveals the modern turning of the Earth into a resource waiting to be put to use for human needs. This waiting for appropriation is the sense of Being for our age; things are said to be for us insofar as they can be represented by various procedures that render them accessible to manipulation. The extent of these representational procedures is global, and, although the threat of simple annihilation is ever-present, the threat to the essence of Dasein is perhaps even more insidious. The essence of mortals is to be protective of the call of Being, that is, to be aware of ourselves as the place where Being is known as that which, over and above beings, allows our access to them. But appropriated beings so crowd our attention that Being threatens to become completely overlooked. Heidegger offers no panaceas. Perhaps the danger safeguards a way out; perhaps the obviousness of our thoughtlessness will prompt some thought and allow some room for meditating Being. His late meditations on Being often come during the call to allow an experience with language or to meditate on the workings of language in POETRY. In a series of exquisite readings of German poets, Heidegger struggles to let his readers hear the sounding of language, that is, to escape from the contemporary technical view of language as a tool for communication. He calls on us to experience language as the process of coming to appearance of beings, the way in which beings are revealed to us.

This latter locution reveals the profound unity of Heidegger's work, the late meditations on language emerging out of the historical confrontations with the Greeks and the early, fundamental ontology's emphasis on historicity of existence. One of his essays on Heraclitus is entitled "Logos." Logos, Heidegger interprets, is the gathering into sameness that allows for the appearance of beings. Logos for the Greeks, then, is what language could be recognized to be for the moderns: Being as the way of coming into appearance of beings. The ancient Greeks, when read thoughtfully, let us think about our way of Being, our own existence and its historical situation.

Bibliography

Bernasconi, Robert. *The Question of Language in Heidegger's History of Being*. Atlantic Highlands, NJ: Humanities Press, 1985.

Dallmayr, Fred. *The Other Heidegger*. Ithaca, NY: Cornell University Press, 1993.

Dreyfus, Hubert L., and Harrison Hall, eds. *Heidegger: A Critical Reader*. Oxford: Basil Blackwell, 1992.

Sallis, John, ed. *Radical Phenomenology: Essays in Honor of Martin Heidegger*. Atlantic Highlands, NJ: Humanities Press, 1978.

HISTORY
Doug Mann

JOSÉ ORTEGA Y GASSET is one of many existentialists who attempted to understand human EXISTENCE as historical. In his essay *History as a System* Ortega announces that any diagnosing of human existence must include an ordered inventory of its system of convictions. He thus ties an analysis of human existence to human BELIEFS. The great turning point in modern history occurred around 1900, as the generation that lived then was the last one to accept a FAITH in Reason as a guide to LIFE. The science of the Renaissance that had ruled human investigations for centuries lost its power to enchant us by explaining human existence. Ortega concludes that we must shake ourselves free from the physical/mathematical approach to the human element, to recognize that the collapse of physical reason leaves the way clear for a vital, historical reason. The human element escapes physicomathematical reason because humans are not things and have no given NATURE. Thinking of human life requires radically different categories. He traces the dominance of physicomathematical reason to Parmenides' view of BEING as fixed and static; we moderns are still prisoners in the magic circle described by Eleatic ONTOLOGY. Eleaticism was the radical intellectualization of Being that paved the way for the appropriation of the human element by materialist concepts.

Physicomathematical reason looked for human nature in thinglike entities like BODY, soul, and SPIRIT but could not find it there. Humans are not things: we are DRAMAS, pure and universal happenings. We have no constitutive identity; we must constitute ourselves through personal and collective identities and thus act as novelists of ourselves. Our Eleatic being is what we have been, but our authentic being is non-Eleatic, what we have not been. Ortega wants us not to say that a PERSON is but that he or she lives. To approach the authentic being, we must substitute for the techniques of physicomathematical reason those of narrative reason. History is a system of human experiences. Living is accumulating being, of making your individual being through a dialectical series of experiments. He calls for recognizing that there is no human nature, just human history. What nature is to things, history is to persons.

NIETZSCHE also examines human life free from the restriction of abstract categories imposed by reason. In his meditation ''The Use and Abuse of History'' he muses over how history can slacken activity by acting as an excuse to avoid life and action. He makes two tripartite distinctions: between the historical, the unhistorical, and the superhistorical; and between monumental, antiquarian, and critical history. Although a sense of both the historical and the unhistorical is necessary for the health of an individual, COMMUNITY, or culture, the unhistorical is the cradle of all actions. Both artists and generals must act against the past in order to create something unique and unprecedented. The unhistorical is the creation of a limited horizon around oneself by means of forgetting. By contrast, the superhistorical recognizes the blindness of every individual deed and turns one away from the process of becoming toward what gives human existence an eternal and stable CHARACTER, toward ART and RELIGION. Both are natural antidotes to the historical disease, against the sapping of life by a constant turning to the past for models, inspiration, and KNOWLEDGE.

Monumental history provides example, teachers, and comforters to all who fight a great fight. Great moments and people from the past provide a high road for humanity. The lover of monumental history accepts false analogies and tempting comparisons with the great moments and actors in history to induce him or her to rashness and enthusiasm, if not fanaticism. Monumental history provides an expanded sense of the importance of present deeds but can also breed an admiration for the past as a masquerade for those hating present POWER. Antiquarian history is for conservative and reverent natures who look to the past with LOVE and trust for their origins. Reverence assigns too low a value to present growth, hindering the mighty impulse and paralyzing action. Critical history brings the past to the bar of judgment, interrogating it ruthlessly. These modes of history, the monumental, antiquarian, and critical, can be useful to life, although they suffer from the same weaknesses as does the historical life. Indeed, an excess of history endangers life. It leads to a weakened PER-SONALITY, for it parades before us a carnival of arts, worships, and MORAL-ITIES, a world-panorama that cosmopolitanizes yet leaves us bereft of a healthy, living culture. It excludes PHILOSOPHY from education and life, making the philosopher a lonely wanderer living apart from this world-panorama. It leads to a belief that the present has a superior justice to past ages and to a thwarting of the national instinct to create. The historical audit destroys many pious illusions, and we are creative only through love and in the shadow of love's pious illusions. A historical culture has a grayness, a belief that it lives in the old age of mankind. The inhabitants of such a culture nod like Chinese dolls to present power. Lastly, an excess of history produces a theory of action that sees egoism everywhere, leading to IRONY and cynicism, casting a sickly doubt on honesty and forthrightness of feeling.

The second half of HEIDEGGER's *Being and Time* confronts the issue of the temporality of DASEIN, of human existence. Humans have a historical nature because, instead of hopping along from moment to moment, my existence fills up a stretch of life that is unified by the projecting of my present moment into the future. Heidegger calls this stretching along of human existence historiciz-ing. To lay bare the ontological structure of historicizing, in order to understand human historicality, he uses key definitions and distinctions. The German words *Historie* and *Geschichte* distinguish between the study of history and the actual lived process, which the translators render as ''historiology'' and ''history,'' respectively. He distinguishes between four senses in which the term "history" is used: (1) something past, like the remains of a Greek temple; (2) a derivation from the past, a context of events and effects in the past, but where the pastness of these events and effects has no priority; (3) the totality of entities that change in TIME; (4) that which has been handed down to us. Dasein is primarily historical, whereas ready-to-hand things and the natural environment are secondarily historical. They become world-historical when they belong to the world where historical existents act.

When I grasp the finitude of my existence and resolutely face the reality of my DEATH, I bring myself to my Fate. As a fateful Dasein, as an authentic Being-in-the-World, I exist with others. My historicality is a cohistoricality. If my existing as a historical being involves existing at the same time as a fateful being, then my authentically historical nature comes not from the past or present but from my projecting into my future. An authentically temporal existent realizes its finitude and projects that which it takes from its individual and communal past onto the present and future. Equipment, things in our world that we use, has its fate, too, as does nature; buildings can house historical events, while a countryside can act as the site of a colony or religious cult. A Dasein who does not face up to the fateful nature of human existence can be inauthentically historical in that it fails to recognize the way that our lives are stretched along and loses itself in the present moment and the blindness of the inauthentic public. Heidegger criticizes those who wring their hands over the problem of historicism, which is not a problem at all, for human existence is historical whether or not a period leaves behind it a historical record.

In his essay "Existentialism and Humanism" SARTRE sees humans as the sum of their actions, which makes the self a historical product. His radical emphasis on FREEDOM seemed to point to history as an arena of freely chosen, individual human projects. His claim that existence precedes essence led to a view of a person's being entirely responsible for what one makes of oneself. Like Heidegger, Sartre sees human existence as radically temporal. Yet in the 1950s in his *Critique of Dialectical Reason*, Sartre attempted to integrate existential and Marxist interpretations of history, whereby historical materialism was the valid interpretation of this history, while existentialism was the only concrete approach to human reality. He strove to integrate the person as free with the idea of humans as part of the dialectical process of history. Against those Marxists who saw humans as passive products of economic circumstances, he restated the core of Marxist thought: just as we are the products of class and society, we also make history. Hence, contemporary MARXISM lacks a hierarchy of mediations that would allow us to understand the individual within his or her class and SOCIETY at a given moment in history. This hierarchy of mediations, of existential layers between the individual and one's socioeconomic position, allows the individual to emerge from the background of the contradiction between the forces of production and the relations of production that govern those forces. This recognition of historical agency, through an examination of the hierarchy of mediations between the individual and society, will prevent viewing humans as mere products of inhuman forces governing society.

Sartre introduces the progressive-regressive method, which allows an enriching cross-reference between the individual and one's society. The regressive part of this method seeks to study the historical particularity of an object; the synthetic or progressive part of the method seeks to recover the project of the individual as a totalization in a social context. We can regress from Marxist social structures to individual biographies to keep alive a sense of the CONTINGENCY of history, while later progressing from moment to moment in a totalizing movement of enrichment to an objectification of the project of the individual, which is best understood in terms of these structures. In his biographies Sartre attempts thus to combine Marxist interpretations of these lives with the freedom of the person.

Existentialist analysis retains its usefulness in analyzing human projects as it reaffirms the specificity of the historical event, refusing to see it simply as the battleground for abstract ideas. Existentialism, unlike a priori Marxism, retains a living sense that human projects are complex pyramids of meaning. Sartre looks forward to the day when all humanity will make its history in common, giving history only one meaning, consisting of the goals of those who live within it. But we need a margin of real freedom beyond the production of the necessities of life before a philosophy of freedom can take the place of Marxism, and thus both Marxism and existentialism remain necessary for those wishing to analyze human existence and history.

Existentialists relate history to everyday human existence. We interpret the past best in terms of the categories created by a phenomenological investigation of the way the individual exists. Sartre's invocation of Marxism attempts to escape this emphasis on the individual. Perhaps the greatest shortcoming of existentialist approaches to history is that the overemphasis on the individual causes a loss of the sense in which humanity moves as a mass. Still, existentialists have repeatedly shown how human existence is temporal and therefore historical; the making of an individual life within the temporal flux is simultaneously the making of history.

Primary Works

Nietzsche, Friedrich. *Untimely Meditations*. Trans. R. J. Hollingdale. Cambridge: Cambridge University Press, 1983.

Ortega y Gasset, José. *History as a System and Other Essays toward a Philosophy of History*. Trans. Helene Weyl. New York: Norton, 1962.

Sartre, Jean-Paul. *Critique of Dialectical Reason*. Trans. Alan Sheridan. London: Verso, 1982.

HUMANISM
Richard Polt

Attitudes known as humanism have roots in classical Greek culture, which celebrated human resourcefulness and logos (reason and discourse). The Greek educational ideal of *paideia* aimed at developing a full human LIFE; the Romans drew on this ideal in conceiving of *humanitas* as an EDUCATION focused on the liberal ARTS as disciplines suited to a free PERSON. The first "humanists" arose in fourteenth-century Italy; Renaissance humanists cultivated the "humanities," combated medieval otherworldliness, and explored the human potential for self-development and reasoned action in NATURE and SOCIETY. Modernity is often called humanistic, in the sense that persons seek to discover and alter their environment for their ends and to develop themselves as autonomous creators of meaning. Thinkers in the existentialist tradition are concerned with concrete human EXISTENCE, particularly the CHOICES that shape one's life. But humanism has two main currents: the first stresses the FREEDOM of humans; the second stresses the distinctive qualities of human nature (especially reason) that earn humans a privileged position in the universe.

One of KIERKEGAARD's characteristic reflections on being human is found in the opening of *The Sickness unto Death*. He writes that man is SPIRIT, and spirit is the self. He adds that man is not yet a self. Thus, human capacity for self-determination is both a gift and an unfulfilled demand. As one falls short of selfhood, one enters despair. Kierkegaard points to Christian FAITH—a turning to the eternal power that constituted the self—as an existential response to this predicament. In contrast, a worldly humanism is a deluded form of despair; it disregards our dependence on the absolute. Human existence is distinguished by the individual's problematic relation to the self and to GOD. Hence, we must avoid reducing existence to a set of formulas, for TRUTH is found in the subjective passion with which one commits oneself to a form of life. Concepts and systems fail to capture what it means to be human—they fail most comically to explain or justify the life of the individual who creates them.

NIETZSCHE's writings examine the hidden sources of human acts and ideas and discover a vital CREATIVITY or WILL to POWER. He admires the bold individuals of the Renaissance and uses philology as a path to the ancients, whom he often views as higher human types than self-negating Christians and modern democrats. His thought is a celebration of human greatness and an invitation to self-affirmation. Nietzsche's uneasiness with humans centers on the conflict between truth and human life. Up to now, our instincts and even our reason have primarily produced useful delusions such as a free will, a moral order in the universe, an afterworld, a God. Truth has had little value for life. Human life and culture have also produced a few seekers of truth who have distanced themselves from life as it is. Would it be possible to live and thrive with truth as a VALUE? This higher form of life would reject existing values, which negate either reality or life, and create values that affirm both life and truth. The model for such a life is often the artist; but a being who could combine life and truth should perhaps be seen as more than human—a SUPERMAN. In *Thus Spoke Zarathustra*, the superman is contrasted with the last men, who no longer look beyond themselves and are satisfied with petty comforts. Thus, humanism, as a glorification of our current nature, sets its sights much too low.

BUBER champions a distinctive form of religious humanism: Hebrew biblical humanism, which emerges from his interpretation of the insights of JUDAISM and his reflection on the potentials and failings of the European philosophical tradition. Modernity has brought about a situation of homelessness: we no longer inhabit a familiar place in the cosmos. Buber appreciates Nietzsche's vision of humans as unfinished and unsettled; however, he dissents from viewing our situation in terms of the will to power. Kierkegaard, who conceives of humans in terms of their lived predicaments and their potential relation to the divine, is closer to a genuine understanding of the human condition. As humans, we are free—distanced from the world rather than absorbed in it; but for this very reason, we are capable of openness and RELATION. Full human life is realized neither within an individual nor through a false collectivism but in the interhuman—the realm of dialogue. Persons must be understood through their relations to other persons and to God—which can be genuine or inauthentic at each historical moment. Dialogue and religious faith can help us experience the WORLD as a home and present a historical goal: to cooperate with God by taking RESPONSIBILITY for the world and working for justice. The covenant between God and the Jewish people obliges them to be exemplary in the pursuit of faith and justice. Genuine humanity requires a choice for truth and against lies, for right and against wrong, guided by a living, thoughtful relation to tradition. We can be enriched and transformed by opening ourselves to the voice of the Hebrew Bible and its call to justice and faith. Buber's humanism is a response to an address that comes from the past, from others, and from God.

SARTRE regards freedom as an absolute. He gives humans, as bearers of CONSCIOUSNESS, a central role as creators of a meaningful world. We can never encounter what is purely nonhuman: all encounters are shaped by meanings and values produced by human choices. No one is in a position to survey and judge any properties of humans as a whole; this would require a God's-eye point of view from which one could contemplate all humanity as an OBJECT, or being-in-itself. The human ''WE'' is an empty concept: hence, the human species can be neither loved nor hated. Roquentin, the protagonist of Sartre's novel *Nausea*, mocks humanists for their many varieties of abstract LOVE of man. Sartre grants that there are patterns of human relations that characterize the human race; but these patterns are established and given meaning by individual choices. Every human choice projects an ideal image of humanity, but this human ESSENCE is clearly dependent on the free choice of an existing individual. For humans, existence precedes essence. According to the well-known lecture "Existentialism and Humanism," existentialism precludes fatalism and pessimism by invalidating all appeals to a predetermined human nature. We must face the human condition: to acknowledge our freedom and responsibility by taking action. Individuals are responsible not only for themselves but for all humans, since our choices always project an image of humanity that posits a value as GOOD for everyone. I must ask myself whether I would accept the value I am positing if everyone lived by it; this universalization of my values leads to my respecting the freedom of all. Existentialism does not imprison us in subjectivity; rather, it makes possible a shared understanding of the human condition and the creation of true COMMUNITY. The self-enclosed humanism that puts human nature on a pedestal and treats it as an end is worthy of ridicule. We create human nature by reaching beyond ourselves and pursuing concrete goals in the world in which we are engaged. In subsequent writings Sartre pursues humanism as a social program of liberating humanity.

In *Being and Time* HEIDEGGER develops an ontology of DASEIN as the entity whose being is at issue and thereby has an understanding of what it is to be. He views Dasein in terms of its temporality: its THROWNNESS into a preestablished situation, its projection of future possibilities, and its dwelling within a familiar, present world. This discussion might appear humanistic; Heidegger seems to devote his attention to humans. However, his primary interest is the question of BEING. Thus, *Being and Time* is not an anthropology. Heidegger later underwent a change in his thinking during which he wrote the "Letter on Humanism," which is, in part, a response to Sartre's "Existentialism and Humanism." He dissociates himself from both these isms. His crucial objection is that every form of humanism involves a METAPHYSICS, an interpretation of beings as a whole that does not ask about the truth of Being. Metaphysics assigns properties to various regions of what is, including humans, without reflecting on how the "is" itself becomes manifest to us. In particular, humans are typically interpreted as the rational animal; but reason is grounded on our relation to Being, and this relation separates us radically from animals. Ironically, humanism fails to do justice to what is essentially human, which is the fact that the person is a "shepherd of Being." As calling for an appreciation of the proper dignity of humans and of the essence of humanity, Heidegger is a humanist. In contrast to Sartre, Heidegger rejects both the LANGUAGE of values and the attempt to set up a system of philosophical ETHICS: both are too closely connected to a humanism that views us as the judges and masters of beings. Genuine ethics can only be a return to the Greek sense of ethos as abode: we must learn to dwell in the truth of Being, which is the only possible source of directives and WISDOM.

Thus, existentialists depart from the type of humanism that exalts human nature. For Kierkegaard, human nature in the abstract is subordinate to the existing individual, and fulfillment is to be found in committing oneself to living for God. For Nietzsche, human nature as it stands is to be transcended because it is not yet worthy of exaltation. Buber finds human fulfillment in openness to what transcends both the individual and humanity. Sartre holds that there is no human nature to be exalted other than the essence we create for ourselves through our commitments in the world. For Heidegger, human nature is defined by its relation to what is higher than humanity: Being. These philosophers view us as beings who point beyond ourselves; the fulfillment of humanity depends on authentically recognizing that which transcends us and acting on this recognition.

Primary Works

Heidegger, Martin. *Basic Writings*. Ed. David Farrell Krell. New York: Harper and Row, 1977.
Sartre, Jean-Paul. *Existentialism and Humanism*. Trans. Philip Mairet. London: Methuen, 1973.

Bibliography

Schaeder, Grete. *The Hebrew Humanism of Martin Buber*. Trans. Noah J. Jacobs. Detroit: Wayne State University Press, 1973.

HUMOR
John Morreall

The ability to laugh is uniquely human; many existentialists appreciated its importance. DOSTOYEVSKY suggested that in watching people laugh, we can get a glimpse inside their souls. BERDYAEV compared humor to the ARTS and music in its POWER to rescue us from the monotony of daily EXISTENCE; he also saw its VALUE in puncturing the inflated gravity that we often assume. Humor and existentialism share themes such as the individual's struggle against the system, the difficulty we experience in communication, and the importance of extreme experiences. What HEIDEGGER called thrownness—finding ourselves in a world we did not choose—is the basis of much comedy, as in Charlie Chaplin's films. Absurdity is another common theme: many experiences and

LIFE itself are enigmatic, baffling, unexplainable; there is no ultimate ground for what we believe and do. Mark Twain observed that humor is based on suffering—there would be no laughter in heaven. NIETZSCHE suggested that a person is the only animal that laughs because he alone suffers so greatly.

Two themes of existentialism are at the basis of theories of humor. The first is the inability of reason to adequately capture lived experience. In this theory the cause of all laughter is the sudden perception of an incongruity between a concept and the real objects that the concept is supposed to cover. The pleasure of humor lies in the triumph of PERCEPTION over conception, in seeing that strict, untiring, troublesome governess—reason—fall flat on her face. The second is the categorical difference between a PERSON and a thing and the degradation of a person acting like a thing. To see the place of humor in existentialism, consider two main philosophical theories of humor. The Superiority Theory began in ancient Greece and holds that all laughter is laughter at; ridicule is the essential form of laughter, which expresses superiority. For Plato the proper object of laughter is some vice in a person, particularly self-ignorance, and our attitude toward that person is malicious pleasure. Aristotle agrees that all laughter is scornful—which, he says, is educated insolence. He claims, however, that the person who laughs at nothing is as deficient as the person who laughs at everything. Hobbes held that laughter is an expression of sudden glory felt as we compare ourselves with others or with our former selves and seem to be doing better.

In the Incongruity Theory, laughter expresses enjoyment at some lack of fit between our mental patterns and expectations and an OBJECT of perception or thought. Jokes typically lead our MINDS along one track and at the punch line shift them to another track, forcing us to reinterpret the first part. Laughter, Kant said, is an affection arising from having some expectation frustrated and liking the experience. For Schopenhauer, laughter is caused by a sudden perception of the incongruity between a concept and the real objects that the concept is supposed to embrace. In the most general form of the Incongruity Theory, humor is an enjoyment of incongruity. While existentialists have not proposed radically new theories of humor, they have adapted the two traditional theories in interesting ways.

SARTRE's most sustained treatment of humor appears in his biography of Flaubert, where, in attacking the bourgeois way of life, he presents the idea that scorn is the basic form of laughter. People hate to be laughed at because laughter is a powerful attack for which we have little defense or retaliation, either by reason or feeling. Laughter is primarily the social act of a group's humiliating an individual who has acted in a less than human way. The proper object of laughter is a person acting like a thing, and laughter is a substitute for lynching or banishment. The incongruity that evokes laughter is between vitalism and mechanism. Laughable people think that they are the source of their actions, when, in fact, their actions follow from previous circumstances and external factors. The laughable person is an object pretending to be a SUBJECT, being in-itself masquerading as being for-itself. What makes a person laughable is self-misunderstanding or self-deception. Sartre's characterization of laughter is reminiscent of Plato's *Philebus*, where Socrates defined the laughable as the vice that represents the opposite of the inscription at Delphi: know thyself.

In laughing at people, Sartre says, we see them as objects and break all solidarity with them. That is why it is perverse to offer oneself as an object of others' laughter—the comic actor is a traitor to oneself. Laughter's function is to protect the self-concept of those laughing by putting the ridiculed person outside their group, indeed, outside the human group. This is a protective strategy, allowing those laughing to maintain their noble conception of what it is to be a human. In Sartre's account, humor, instead of being opposed to seriousness, has a purpose to save the SPIRIT of seriousness. Mirth denounces false seriousness in the name of true seriousness. Laughter is a panic reaction, like shock, flight, or terror, which blows the whistle on subhumans' pretending to be human. Even stage comedy is the institutionalization of savage laughter, the characters with their thinglike behavior providing practice targets for our scorn.

KIERKEGAARD sees humor as the joy that has overcome the world. In his writing, he frequently favors IRONY and humor; his style is often satirical. Well aware of the traditional prejudice against humor, he criticizes the emphasis on seriousness. It is just as mistaken to be serious in the wrong place as it is to laugh in the wrong place. The primary element in the comic, as in the tragic, is contradiction, a notion roughly equivalent to incongruity. Life includes many contradictions and possibilities for humor; the more fully we exist, the more we discover the comic. Our experience of incongruities can be either comic or tragic: the comic perspective faces a contradiction and sees a way out; the tragic perspective despairs of a way out. Humor and irony relate to the three realms of human existence—the aesthetic, the ethical, and the religious. Irony marks the boundary between the aesthetic and ethical realms: irony transcends sensual experience for self-reflective and critical understanding, seeing the unreality of what looks real. Humor marks the boundary between the ethical and religious realms: the ethical person finds no resolution for life's contradictions and assumes a tragic outlook; the religious person believes in an ultimate resolution and can view the world comically. Religious faith involves contradictions that can be seen comically. The most fundamental is the believer's SITUATION as a finite creature face-to-face with an infinite GOD yet an abyss away. Kierkegaard calls CHRISTIANITY, with its paradoxes, the most humorous view of life in HISTORY. Just as the humorless person has a shallow understanding, viewing Christianity only seriously reveals a shallow appreciation of Christian FAITH.

Nietzsche's style reveals a sense of humor. He often advocates a humorous attitude toward the human condition. In *Thus Spoke Zarathustra*, laughter marks the liberated attitude of Zarathustra, who, in his speech to the higher men, calls himself the laughing prophet and urges them to learn to laugh at themselves as a man ought to laugh. The enemy that Zarathustra must destroy is the Spirit of Gravity. We are still in the age of tragedy, an age of morals and RELIGIONS; the comedy of existence has not become apparent. Nietzsche looks forward to an age of lightness when WISDOM will be united with laughter—joyful wisdom. This spirit of lightness may often be connected to laughter, most notably, dancing and singing. It is illuminating to contrast Nietzsche's ideas about destroying the Spirit of Gravity and laughing in the face of eternal recurrence with the gravity of CAMUS. In *The Rebel* and *The Myth of Sisyphus* Camus champions metaphysical rebellion—a protest against one's own state and the whole of creation—as the most authentic response toward the human condition. There is no fate that cannot be surmounted by scorn. But while defiance and scorn might make sense against the Greek gods, they seem to make no sense against an impersonal universe. Thus, Camus' protesting the human condition seems like a petulant two-year-old's shouting at the door in which he has pinched his fingers. Are we mistreated by the universe? Are we owed more than a human life? If groundlessness is an inherent feature of our life and, indeed, as many existentialists insist, is what makes our FREEDOM and dignity possible, then defiance and RESENTMENT against it seem silly and inauthentic. For the moment they may make the fist-shaker feel strong, courageous, proud. But such self-assuaging is unrealistic; it is childish posturing at best. As Thomas Nagel suggested, if the universe is absurd, and nothing matters objectively, then that fact does not matter either, and dramatic protests against one's fate betray a failure to appreciate the cosmic unimportance of our situation.

Grave, heroic responses to absurdity like Camus' seem like anachronistic carryovers of ancient heroic and tragic traditions, combined with the egocentric Romanticism of the last century. Nietzsche's higher men, by contrast, will be joyful, dancing heroes who transcend the tragic stance; the lesson they offer is that facing a world without epistemological or ethical foundations, our highest and most authentic response is not pointless rebellion but joy and laughter. If we are to take the absurdity of the human condition seriously, paradoxically, we must take it lightly.

Primary Works

Kierkegaard, Søren. *The Concept of Irony*. Trans. Howard V. Hong and Edna H. Hong. Princeton: Princeton University Press, 1989.
Sartre, Jean-Paul. *The Family Idiot: Gustave Flaubert 1821–1857*. Vols. 1–5. Trans. Carol Cosman. Chicago: University of Chicago Press, 1981–1993.

Bibliography

Morreal, John. *Taking Laughter Seriously*. Albany: State University of New York Press, 1983.

EDMUND HUSSERL
(1859–1938)
Paul Gorner

Husserl was born in Prossnitz, Moravia. From 1876 to 1878 he studied astronomy, mathematics, and PHILOSOPHY at the University of Leipzig. From 1878 for three years he studied mathematics under Carl Weierstrass and philosophy under Friedrich Paulsen in Berlin. In 1882 he became an assistant to Weierstrass. Although a mathematician, he became interested in philosophical questions concerning the foundations of mathematics. In 1884, following the advice of his friend and mentor Thomas Masaryk—later the first president of Czechoslovakia—Husserl went to Vienna to study philosophy under Franz Brentano. In 1886 he moved to Halle, where he wrote his habilitation thesis on the concept of number, under Carl Stumpf, a former pupil of Brentano. This formed the basis of his first published work, *Philosophie der Arithmetik* (1891). In 1901 he moved to Göttingen. This coincided with the publication of the work that made him famous, his *Logical Investigations*. In 1913 he founded the *Jahrbuch fur Philosophie und phanomenologische Forschung*, the first issue of which comprised his own *Ideas concerning a Pure Phenomenology and Phenomenological Philosophy*. In 1916 he succeeded Heinrich Rickert to the chair in Freiburg, where from 1919 to 1923 MARTIN HEIDEGGER was his assistant. He became an emeritus in 1928. Being Jewish, his life became difficult after 1933. However, he produced in the last years of his life his monumental *Crisis of the European Sciences and Transcendental Phenomenology*.

Husserl's *Philosophy of Arithmetic* shared the prevailing BELIEF in the foundational significance of PSYCHOLOGY. KNOWLEDGE is realized in mental acts and PROCESSES. Psychology is the discipline that studies the MIND and its operations; the foundations of all forms of knowledge are to be found in it. Hence, he sought to understand the basic concepts of mathematics by tracing their origin in certain mental acts. His book was devastatingly criticized by Frege, who accused Husserl of failing to recognize the fundamental difference between logic and psychology. Partly as a result of Frege's criticisms, Husserl's thought underwent a fundamental change. In *Logical Investigations* his approach to the foundations of mathematics of his *Philosophy of Arithmetic* is criticized as an instance of a general error about logic: psychologism. Thinking, inferring, recognizing contradiction are mental acts, but we must distinguish between mental acts and their content, that is, between the act of judging and the judgment. The subject matter of logic is not mental but ideal. Psychology as an empirical discipline that deals with facts, generalizations, and probabilities cannot provide the foundation for an a priori science that deals with strict laws and necessities and that does not describe and explain thinking as a psychological process but lays down norms for its validity.

Husserl believed that any claim to knowledge must be capable of rational justification. His critique of psychologism should be seen in the light of this rationalism. By making logic relative to psychology, psychologism is destroying rationality. Anthropologism, historicism, and sociologism have the same self-destructive, relativistic consequences. The objects of logic and mathematics are neither physical nor mental. As well as defending the existence of ideal entities Husserl also defends, in his doctrine of categorial INTUITION, a mode of access to such OBJECTS that is more than mere thinking. There is sensory seeing of particulars, but there is also a seeing or intuiting of universals, numbers, RE-LATIONS, states of affairs, ESSENCES. Although acts of categorial intuition are founded in sensory acts, their object is genuinely given; it is not produced by the act. The notion of the intuition of essences goes hand in hand with a considerable broadening in the scope of the a priori. States of affairs that are grounded in essences make synthetic a priori propositions true. Synthetic a priori TRUTHS are not restricted to forms of experience, as Kant claimed, but can pertain to anything.

Logical Investigations elaborates a phenomenological approach to CON-SCIOUSNESS in contradistinction to that of empirical psychology. Like everything else, consciousness has its essence and essential structures. PHE-NOMENOLOGY studies the essence of consciousness independently of the actual EXISTENCE of its objects, its causes, and its physical basis. The fundamental feature of consciousness is INTENTIONALITY, its being of or about something, its directedness-toward something. By virtue of what Husserl calls its matter, an act of consciousness is directed toward an object and intends it as such-and-such. In 1905 Husserl lectured on a feature of consciousness that he had neglected in *Logical Investigations*: its temporal structure. Items in consciousness, such as this auditory sensation, are not simply present. Intrinsic to the experience I have now is a reference to both the past and the future. It has a horizon of retention (which is not the same as actively remembering) and protention (which is not the same as active anticipation). Although TIME later came to play a crucial role in Husserl's version of transcendental idealism, his treatment of it in 1905 fits the realist tendency of the *Investigations*.

Given this realist tendency, or what was perceived as such, the appearance in 1913 of *Ideas* shocked some members of the phenomenological movement. In *Ideas* phenomenology is presented as perfecting the transcendentalism of Kant and as issuing in a form of idealism even more extreme. Kant had at least allowed for the existence of mind-independent things-in-themselves. For Husserl, everything either is consciousness or is constituted in consciousness. As before, phenomenology requires an eidetic reduction (roughly, disregarding the factual existence and particularity of something and focusing on its essence), but now it is presented as also requiring a transcendental reduction. In what he calls the natural attitude, we are directed toward items in the WORLD. We regard such items as existing and as having certain properties. Underlying all affirmations of particular items is the affirmation of the real existence of the world. Husserl calls this the general thesis of the natural attitude.

Phenomenology as Husserl now understands it involves the phenomenological epoche: the suspending, putting out of action of all such affirmations of real existence and real being-thus. What remains is pure transcendental consciousness. Transcendentally reduced consciousness is not an item in the world but that for which there is a world. There is no denial of intentionality. Despite the transcendental reduction consciousness still has the characteristic of being directed toward. Items in the world and the world as a whole remain, but as objects of consciousness, as pure phenomena. The task of phenomenology so construed is to describe the structured multiplicities of acts and APPEARANCES in which entities of the various ontological types are constituted. Whereas in the *Investigations* Husserl was unable to discover, and found it unnecessary to posit, an I or EGO over and above the stream of experiences, in *Ideas* he claims to have found it.

The remainder of Husserl's career is dominated by two aims: (1) the deepening of the conception of transcendental phenomenology and (2) its elaboration as a system. Regarding the first aim, phenomenology is concerned to lay bare not only the noetic-noematic structures of consciousness in which objects are constituted but also the genesis of the modes of consciousness themselves. Objects are constituted in experiences, but experiences themselves are constituted in inner time-consciousness. Final understanding is achieved only when this constitution is described. The second aim was never achieved. The nearest thing to it is his *Cartesian Meditations* (1928), but this remains schematic and programmatic. It includes an attempt to deal with a problem that his previously published work had neglected: intersubjectivity. The transcendental phenomenology presented in *Ideas* appears solipsistic, inasmuch as the carrying out of the transcendental reduction leaves a single consciousness and its intentional contents. Some of these contents will be other SUBJECTS, but only as intentional contents of my consciousness. In Meditation 6 Husserl seeks to remove this appearance of SOLIPSISM. He describes the constitution of the other. This involves a reduction of a different kind, what he calls the primordial reduction: the reduction to the sphere of own-ness, the removal from my consciousness and its objects of all reference to other subjects. I am not just a BODY but an animate body or body-subject. Among the items that figure in my sphere of own-ness are bodies that in appearance and behavior resemble my own. These I analogically interpret as being also other body-subjects. On this basis there is constituted in my consciousness a COMMUNITY of egos. The public world in which I reside is the product of this transcendental we-community. The world is constituted in transcendental intersubjectivity.

The final phase of Husserl's phenomenology is his *Crisis of the European*

Sciences and Transcendental Phenomenology. The key notion is the *LEBEN-SWELT*, the world of lived experience. Objectivism seeks to eliminate everything subjective from our representation of the world by allowing as real only those aspects of experience that can be represented by means of the concepts of the mathematical natural sciences. It dismisses the life-world as mere appearance. Such objectivism is absurd inasmuch as it calls in question the life-world from the standpoint of what is itself a construction formed on the basis of the life-world. The properties and structures attributed by the objectifying sciences to the objective world are themselves the product of a process of idealization and mathematization of life-worldly structures. The task of philosophy is not to downgrade the life-world but to remove from it the garment of ideas that science has thrown over it. This doesn't imply any abandonment of Husserl's ideal of absolute rationality. The claim of natural science to provide such rationality is rejected on the grounds of the rootedness of such science itself in the life-world. Husserl's emphasis on the life-world does not represent a fundamental change in his conception of phenomenology as transcendental philosophy. The life-world does not provide the ultimate foundation, for it is itself constituted in transcendental subjectivity.

At first sight it seems unlikely that Husserl might have had significant influence on existentialist thought. His phenomenology is motivated by the ideal of ultimate rational justification. In some ways existentialism represents a reaction against this Enlightenment ideal. Moreover, in Husserlian phenomenology theoretical modes of comportment are treated as basic, and practical modes as secondary. The subject that such phenomenology seeks to describe is not an embodied, engaged subject in the world but a transcendental ego outside the world. Also, he is concerned, to the point of obsession, with clarity, rigor, and precision. Yet Husserl influenced existentialism. Phenomenology is concerned to trace the origin of the objective in subjectivity. Although existentialists did not adopt the Husserlian doctrine of constitution, they were attracted by a philosophy that placed an emphasis on subjectivity. Although it might have been felt that Husserl's descriptions did not do justice to lived experience, the idea of a return to lived experience, of restoring an immediate contact with things by peeling away the concealing layers of scientific conceptualization, appealed to existentialists. Furthermore, although the three existentialist thinkers that I shall briefly discuss felt that Husserl placed too much emphasis on theoretical modes of intentionality, they saw in intentionality something that sets humans apart. Mention should also be made of the appeal of Husserl's emphasis on the temporal nature of consciousness, whereby the subject is inseparable from both its past and its future.

These features of Husserl's phenomenology influenced SARTRE. He adopts Husserl's Cartesian view of consciousness as essentially transparent and regards himself as employing the Husserlian method of phenomenological description. However, on some key points he is in sharp disagreement with Husserl. He rejects the notion of a pure ego and denies that it is required for the unity of consciousness. He also rejects the idea of transcendental consciousness. The being of consciousness is BEING-IN-THE-WORLD. The subjects MERLEAU-PONTY chose for phenomenological analysis are closer to those chosen by Husserl, such as PERCEPTION and the relation of scientific knowledge to the life-world. What makes his phenomenology existential as opposed to transcendental is that the subject whose comportment he describes is the concrete, situated, engaged subject in the world rather than a world-constituting transcendental ego.

In lectures delivered in Marburg in 1925 Heidegger lists what he regards as three fundamental discoveries of phenomenology: (1) intentionality, (2) categorial INTUITION, and (3) the meaning of the a priori. All three are evident in Heidegger's *Being and Time*, despite differences in vocabulary. The different kinds of intentionality are different modes of comportment to entities. Heidegger differs from Husserl in treating practical modes of comportment as fundamental and theoretical modes as derivative. Phenomenology, as Heidegger understands it, is a letting be seen of that which shows itself. That which it lets be seen is the being of entities. The phenomenological seeing of BEING must be an instance of the categorial intuition that Husserl defends in *Logical Investigations*. Heidegger follows the early Husserl in defending the universal scope of the a priori. He rejects the view that the a priori has something specially to do with subjectivity: the a priori concerns the being of entities.

What was Husserl's attitude to existentialism? In a word, it was dismissive. He regarded it as a form of irrationalism, a betrayal of the ideal of philosophy as a rigorous science. He did not object to Heidegger's analysis of DASEIN but to the suggestion that it could fulfill the philosophical role claimed for his analyses of consciousness. Without the transcendental reduction, he claimed, the philosophical dimension is not even entered. Heidegger's fundamental ONTOLOGY is just another form of self-destructive anthropologism. Yet, there seems little doubt that the *Crisis* reflects the influence of *Being and Time* on Husserl's thinking.

Primary Works

Husserl, Edmund. *Cartesian Meditations: An Introduction to Phenomenology*. Trans. Dorian Cairns. The Hague: Martinus Nijhoff, 1960.
———. *Ideas*. Trans. W. R. Boyce Gibson. New York: Collier Books, 1962.
———. *Logical Investigations*. Trans. J. N. Findlay. London: Routledge, 1970.

Bibliography

Kockelmans, Joseph J., ed. *Phenomenology: The Philosophy of Edmund Husserl and Its Interpretation*. Garden City, NY: Doubleday, 1967.

IDEOLOGY

Stephen Tyman

The concept of ideology arose originally in the Marxist school, representing the sense in which class interests come to predispose the point of view even of those who attempt to be rational and unbiased in their thinking. Thus, an outlook can be bourgeois, meaning that it is thoroughly suffused with unexamined values and presuppositions reflecting more the sociocultural mind-set of the class than any set of convictions freely and independently held. For the most part, however, the term "ideology" is invoked in view of a political role, with its hopes and ambitions, borne by a given ideational gestalt. "Writ large," the term then connotes the battlefield, as it were—where global points of view collide and conflict with one another in a struggle for control. In the Marxist analysis, political thought eventually transcends ideological deployment, but only after having passed through a necessary historical evolution involving ideological phases during which economic distortions and the dominance of the moneyed classes progressively fall away.

The existential response to ideology has been ambivalent. The fact that the whole program comes tied to a political agenda has been problematic. Second, where one political vision (say, the Marxist) has failed to win out, there arises the specter of several irreducible and unalterably opposed ideologies locked in perpetual death struggles with one another. In such a context, the traditional question of philosophical TRUTH gets subordinated to the issue of the conflict, with the standard of truth amounting to no more than the question of which ideology prevails. Most existentialists find little to recommend this last prospect. Nevertheless, considerable interest remains in the concept of ideology. Existentialists describe a core of human reality not reachable through conventional ratiocination that can accord with the recognition of ideological strains everywhere at work, rendering problematic and difficult of access all cognitive immediacies and hints at self-knowledge. This in turn, confirms the tension between human BEING and knowing that often animates existential thinking.

HEIDEGGER suggests in *Being and Time* that through the admission of something like an ideological dimension of one's PERSONALITY and self-recognitive categories, one is able to discern and subsequently to loosen the grip of alienated social criteria upon the deeper self. In this context, ideology becomes the name of what the existentialist seeks to surmount. However, when various ideological overlays have been stripped away from the PERSON, leaving what BUBER called the single one, one may get to the existential hub of CHOICE. On the other hand, Buber recognizes that what he called the COM-

MUNITY of opinion is forever in danger of succumbing to its ideological encrustations and must consequently be continually dissolved and reborn. Genuine dialogue can help withstand the onslaught of ideologies.

SARTRE sees in the problematics of ideology a dimension of the human PROJECT that is not to be got around. Seeking an ideology is a human tendency rather than the distortion of a few disgruntled intellectuals: all tend to view reality as if it could somehow be captured in a single tense or reflected in a single mirror. This self-asserting totalization of points of view expresses a fundamental human drive toward cognitive unification of all experiential strands. But Sartre declines to embrace any single actual or possible PHILOSOPHY; he declares that there are only philosophies and, therefore, irreducibly multiple points of view, where competing interests collide. But this exposé itself is the ideology of existentialism, the carrier of a historically important iconoclasm that is the precursor to a genuine recognition of a far-reaching human responsibility. This RESPONSIBILITY extends to the self-creation of a human ESSENCE, a process of creation so absolute that it can appeal to nothing outside itself.

In *Being and Nothingness*, Sartre had situated the core of the creative process in the factor of desire, a dizzyingly free, self-orienting hunger for BEING, set within being itself, which shows that in the heart of being there lurks a NOTHINGNESS, an ontological lacuna. From this point of view, the Marxist enterprise seemed too preoccupied with material strictures, thereby veering precariously close to determinism. Later, Sartre became convinced that his vision of radical FREEDOM had left the human project in too arbitrary a condition. He attempted to rectify his earlier ONTOLOGY of desire by acknowledging a core factor of need. This placed existentialism in the very closest proximity to the concerns characteristic of Marxist ideology: the predominance of class interests, the conditions of labor and production, and the alienating effects of domination. Sartre, however, remained wary of collapsing existentialism with MARXISM. He understood need as a limitation on human freedom, as an essential fragility in the human condition. An ideology that takes need into account would, therefore, in effect be grounded in a sense of the humane. Thus, he adapted the concept of ideology to the concerns he took to be most essential to existential thought, without sacrificing what he continued to believe to be human autonomy.

The problem of ideology leads into the heart of what for existentialism is central: the RELATION between the self and the other, especially as this relation is mediated by social factors and institutions. The concept of ideology shatters any individual pretension to autonomous intelligibility, suggesting instead that one way or another all thought of the self, as much as thought of the other, is mediated by broader social realities. It is a great challenge for existentialists to accommodate this point of view without giving up a commitment to the possibility of an authentic, solitary insight into the human condition. No clear answer emerges to the vexing question of how centrally the role of ideology might be placed.

Primary Works

Buber, Martin. *Between Man and Man*. Trans. Ronald Gregor Smith. New York: Macmillan, 1965.
Sartre, Jean-Paul. *Search for a Method*. Trans. Hazel E. Barnes. New York: Knopf, 1963.

Bibliography

McBride, William L. *Sartre's Political Theory*. Bloomington: Indiana University Press,
1991.

IMAGINATION
David J. Gouwens

For existentialists, the imagination is a category of understanding human EX-
ISTENCE. This emphasis on the imagination has been a protest against both
rationalism and empiricism. In place of rationalism's image of the self as primarily a rational animal or empiricism's image of the self as an observer of the
WORLD, existentialism's picture of the self as self-making rather than given
has placed the imagination at the center of the PERSON. The imagination is
the source of the possibilities that the unfinished self projects onto the undefin-
able future and is crucial to this dynamic process of self-creation.

KIERKEGAARD's reflections on the imagination are dialectically developed
against what he perceived to be an undue elevation of the imagination in which
the self is dissipated into the vapors of fantasy and also against Hegel's anti-
Romantic denigration of the imagination in favor of reason. In *The Sickness
unto Death* he describes the imagination as the capacity for all capacities. Because the self is not substantial but is the synthesis of possibility and actuality,
the imagination is central to the PROJECT of becoming a person: in it possibilities for the self are entertained that may be acted upon. The imagination is
the mirror in which a person reflects to oneself one's possibilities. The intensity
of these self-projections indicates the possibility of the intensity of the self, and
to lack imagination is to lack the condition for becoming a self. It is to remain
at the level of despair. Yet imagination by itself yields only possibility, while
any existing person also requires actuality so as to become a self. Hence, the
imagination is a necessary, but not sufficient, capacity for the project of a worthy
human existence.

For NIETZSCHE the Western philosophical tradition is premised upon attaining a TRUTH behind the APPEARANCES. This quest is at once illusory, a misuse of the imagination, and arbitrary, a limit on the imagination. The proper philosophical approach must recognize that categories or laws of thought are illusory, they are useful fictions. Hence, the true thinker will entertain different points of view, each disclosing an aspect of reality.

In *Being and Time* HEIDEGGER indicates that fundamental to human existence is the imaginative projecting of possibilities of authentic existence, which reveals the temporality of existence and its orientation to the future. Interpretation is an imaginative establishment and REVELATION of meaning within the world. Later, in *Kant and the Problem of Metaphysics*, he shows how the productive (as opposed to the reproductive) imagination is the root, the primordial identity of both understanding and sensibility, at once basic to the human positing of KNOWLEDGE and to the possibility of thingness of OBJECTS. The transcendental imagination opens up the NOTHINGNESS that allows a distinction between SUBJECT and object, the knower and the known; it opens up the horizon of the future within which DASEIN, receptively and spontaneously, encounters BEING. Later, he focuses on the originating function of poetizing as the revelation of Being.

In *Imagination* SARTRE criticizes discussions of the imagination in which the image is explained as a mental copy of the perceived thing. Throughout the HISTORY of modern philosophical thought, thinkers see the image as identical to, yet somehow different from, PERCEPTION. This, in turn, requires convoluted attempts to differentiate the image from the percept. As a way out of the conundrum he turns to HUSSERL's PHENOMENOLOGY. Instead of seeing the imagination as a kind of perception and as something within consciousness, Husserl sees imagination as an intentional activity, a CONSCIOUSNESS of something. The image is a type of consciousness directed toward an intentional object transcendent to consciousness. The imagination becomes an activity, a mode of consciousness. In *The Psychology of the Imagination*, Sartre holds that imaginative consciousness, in contrast to perception, posits its objects as nothingness. This indicates that imagination is essential to the FREEDOM of the person: consciousness is able both to establish the world and to escape from the world by means of this annihilation or surpassing capacity.

Sartre pursued the psychology of artistic imagination in his biographies of literary figures. In *Baudelaire*, he describes the poet as uncertain of his own existence, hating himself and his RESPONSIBILITIES for the future. Baudelaire evaded freedom by escaping into imaginative self-creation, but with the self-contradictory goal of possessing himself as an object, pathetically seeking to exist for himself as he was for others. POETRY was a means to avoid action and freedom by creating a spiritual reality that did not simply deny the world but absorbed it into linguistic symbol. Artistic imagination was a vehicle for BAD FAITH. In *Saint Genet: Actor and Martyr*, Sartre describes Genet's imagination and ART as corrosive, a strategy of survival that did not render reality into dream but dematerialized it in order to transcend it. Sartre traces Genet's various metamorphoses with the help of his imagination, from thief to aesthete to writer, and shows that his great writings accomplish the desperate attempt of his imagination to find the way out, to claim his humanity against society's disgust at him.

The culmination of Sartre's thought on artistic imagination is *The Family Idiot*, his study of Flaubert, which is an analysis of the relation between imagination and the real, both on the level of Flaubert's PSYCHOLOGY and on that of the collective imagination of his TIME. As with Baudelaire and Genet, Sartre sees Flaubert's artistic imagination as the attempt to resolve an intolerable situation into which he was thrown at birth. But the imaginary is not only refuge; it takes revenge by desituating the dreamer. What saved Flaubert was his discovery of writing with its recognition that a book may become a real center of derealization, a means by which the imagination's escape from reality is embodied in an object, which allows the artist to triumph by controlling the imagination of the others, his readers.

In *Good and Evil*, BUBER reflects on the Genesis MYTHS in order to discern the ancient Hebrew understanding of the NATURE of the origin of EVIL. He holds that these stories find the origin of evil not in a conscious decision between GOOD and evil but in imagination and indecision. In imagination, humans envision possibilities, imagery, in place of the good given by GOD, and in a dreamlike state rather than in conscious defiance they slip into that imagined evil. Hence, one must often strive to overcome the chaos of imagination that overwhelms the real. Buber goes on to affirm that this evil urge of the imagination can become good when linked to the passion of a life directed to God. In contrast, Berdyaev's stress on freedom and CREATIVITY is framed within a vision of creativity as grounded in God, who created the world through imagination, which is an absolute ontological power. Humans can partake in this creativity through their imaginations, for the faculty of imagination is the source of all creativeness. In the creative act the imagination rises above reality, affirming the priority of the self over the nonself, SPIRIT over nature, freedom over necessity. Thus, for BERDYAEV, human imaginative creativity does not merely mirror God's creation but contributes to God's creation and even to God's being, for imagination continues the work of God's creation in a way that God does not know.

Primary Works

Buber, Martin. *Good and Evil*. New York: Scribner's, 1952.
Sartre, Jean-Paul. *The Psychology of the Imagination*. Trans. Bernard Fretchman. New York: Washington Square Press, 1966.

IMMANENCE
Patrick Bourgeois

The role of immanence in existential PHILOSOPHY is related to TRANSCEN-DENCE, especially as expressed in the PHENOMENOLOGY of HUSSERL, and its finding, INTENTIONALITY. It is the reduction that is the entrance to phenomenology, as the science of APPEARANCES and of appearing, which become strict when the status of the appearing of things becomes problematical. The phenomenological *epoche* has put out of action or placed in brackets all transcendence of intentionality of consciousness, of all the fact WORLD, thus delivering us from the natural attitude to what is immanent in consciousness; this he calls the phenomenological residue. Stressing the immanent dimension, transcendence is reduced so that everything that is other than CONSCIOUS-NESS is there for it. Thus, with the *epoche*, the sense of the world, not the world itself, appears in the phenomenological bracketing, in which the natural attitude is relinquished, and the description is of what then appears, the *noema* in the *noesis*. The phenomena are immanent to consciousness. The phenome-nological reduction has yielded the phenomena of actual internal experience.

The role of immanence for SARTRE emerges in his attempt to overcome what he considers to be Husserl's SOLIPSISM. Although the EGO is within consciousness, it is not the transcendental unity presupposed for all conscious acts as it is for Husserl's egology. For Husserl, the ego is the pole from which all emerges within and for consciousness. For Sartre, there is an immanent unity to the flux of consciousness that constitutes itself as the basic unity of itself. There is no need for a transcendental ego. This flux is the unity more basic than any other unity, such as that of world or of the ego. The ego pole appears solely in reflection, as an ideal and indirect unity of the series of reflected conscious-ness. In *Being and Nothingness* the full existential import of immanence is seen, with the four characteristics of the prereflective cogito as intentionality, non-positing self-consciousness, prepersonal, as a mode of being constituted by a spontaneity of FREEDOM. This limitation of immanence to the unity of the flux of transcendental experience or of the prereflective cogito on the level of lived existence is strict in that Sartre wants to consider a great deal as transcen-dent to the original constituting consciousness.

MERLEAU-PONTY explicates the fundamental dimensions of human behav-ior and existence as immanent in the broad sense, as inclusive of all that with-stands the initial reduction. In this context, the thing is immanent in the sense of for us and transcendent in that we are always open to it, because no thing is ever given completely or exhaustively. His focus is mainly on the in-itself-for-us CHARACTER of the thing, but the correlation, immanence-transcendence, allows for the full meaning of both poles, thus preventing him from idealism or REALISM or from rationalism or empiricism. He focuses on a level below these distinctions, that between thing and consciousness. He reinterprets intentionality in such a way as to give transcendence more room than Husserl gives it. He deepens intentionality to the rich, fundamental prepredicative and prereflective level. At times it almost seems as though he cuts off transcendence with the unity of PERCEPTION, but it becomes clear that transcendence is such that the given in experience is never exhaustively given nor fully grasped.

Even the present OBJECT is not fully present but is mixed with absence. This aspect of absence in perspective does not deny the presence of those aspects of the perceived in the given that are not the direct object of focus. Rather, the hidden side, the wall, the rest of the room in which I am sitting but not facing, the hidden and invisible side of the lamp that is present to my look are also present, but in their own way. The unseen or invisible side of the perceived is not simply a possible perception or a necessary conclusion of analysis or reasoning. The nonvisible sides are not given by intellectual synthesis but by a practical synthesis—which means that I can touch it but also that I can react to it, since it is within my field of presence. Merleau-Ponty avoids the view according to which in this stratum of experience we restore the true from the apparent by analysis and conjecture.

In the perceptual paradox of immanence-transcendence, what appears in experience is never exhaustively given, and it must be for me. The thing given is open for further investigation. Each flowing profile of the sensible thing both reveals and, at the same time, conceals the other profiles. The apparition of the real is, at the same time, the other profiles and is possible because, as a perceiver, I am part of it in the sense that I belong to NATURE, to the realm of things that are experienced in perceptual FAITH as real. In opening human EXISTENCE to transcendence cut off by idealism, existential phenomenology opened immanence to a further sense of transcendence, which correlatively alters or deepens the sense of immanence. This sense of transcendence-immanence is, so to speak, the condition of possibility of a religious transcendence. Existential philosophy cannot demonstrate such a transcendent, but many of its writings take place with the context of its presence. This Transcendent, as intensely personal, somehow influences and alters the depth of immanence in the before GOD of KIERKEGAARD, in the I–Thou of BUBER, and in the presence of MARCEL. Such a Transcendent need not be an object or a BEING; our access may be only indirect in the LANGUAGE of symbol, metaphor, and narrative.

Marcel seems to hint at the need for an indirect access to the question of the whole, in thinking beyond the boundaries of knowledge and of problematic reflection. Most of his primary reflection on the MYSTERY of being takes place within a certain domain going beyond the boundaries of the Kantian limit—the total and full existence beneath and beyond the realm of primary reflection. Marcel speaks of the need for images, for MYTH, in order to prevent idolatrizing that which is reflected upon. Such treatments of philosophy, initiated by Marcel, allow for continual and ongoing reflection on the mystery of existence. Thus, one could perhaps say that philosophy culminates precisely in its attempt to stay attuned and to see or to interpret, at the limit, the ultimate significance of the mystery of being, in its various senses of immanence and transcendence.

Primary Works

Husserl, Edmund. *Ideas pertaining to a Pure Phenomenology and to a Phenomenological Philosophy*. Trans. F. Kerstein. Dordrecht: Kluwer, 1982.
Marcel, Gabriel. *The Mystery of Being*. Vols. 1 and 2. Trans. G. S. Fraser. Chicago: Henry Regnery, 1960.

IMMORTALITY
Sonya Sikka

Existentialist thinkers are oriented toward concrete, individual EXISTENCE and draw attention to the importance of DEATH as a constituent of LIFE. The common factor in their thought on immortality is a refusal to underrate the reality and gravity of death. Existentialist analysis tends to stay with what is revealed within experience, as opposed to producing theories through inference and hypothesis. The analysis of death in *Being and Time* is representative. HEIDEGGER remains with the actual experience of death, as that which DASEIN anticipates. This is not to say that he definitively excludes the possibility that some facet of the BEING of humans could survive death. But he notes that the this-worldly interpretation of death must be secured before this question can be appropriately raised. Hence, he never formulates a theory about what there might be on the other side of death. Although SARTRE does not provide a disproof of immortality, his position contrasts with Heidegger's deliberate neutrality. BELIEF in immortality can only be an illusion produced by the desire to escape finitude, an illusion that has the detrimental effect of shifting attention away from the real concerns of the present.

In contrast, MARCEL does not deny the validity of traditional, philosophical ways of addressing the question of survival after death and even claims that the hypothesis of immortality is required to explain certain empirical facts. The assurance of immortality that he describes is not based on hypothesis; rather, it arises from an experience in the face of death. The experience that reveals the deepest truth about death is not ANXIETY in the face of my own death, as

HEIDEGGER holds, but the loss of a loved one. To LOVE someone is to say, "Thou at least shall not die," where this hope and FAITH in the continued existence of the other are not a wish but a prophetic assurance that the being of the loved one—as opposed to the temporal life—cannot finally be destroyed. What grants this assurance is the bond to the other forged through genuine communion. In asserting immortality, one asserts that this bond is preserved in the beyond, which is not some other place but an unknown dimension or perspective. A testimony of this preservation is the presence of the loved one after death, when he or she is no longer objectively there. The presence in memory indicates a real presence and contains within it the promise of an eventual resurrection and reunion. It points to a transformation of which the human MIND can form only a dim image. Ultimately, the idea of immortality points to GOD and refers us to THEOLOGY.

JASPERS avoids any conception of immortality that might be linked to the idea of a continuing existence. The instinct to endure in TIME, he claims, is itself doomed to extinction. There is, however, an aspect of being human that he calls EXISTENZ and is pointed toward TRANSCENDENCE. Through the elevation of Existenz, it is possible to enter into immortality, understood not as infinite perdurance but as the depth of the present. Immortality is gained in the moment of fulfilled time, in those actions, decisions, and commitments where an elevated Existenz gains an assurance of its being that transcends any need for ongoing temporal duration. This assurance cannot be objectified and, hence, immortality can be neither demonstrated nor disproved. All attempts to objectify immortality, to view it in terms of ongoing temporal existence after death produce only symbols. These symbols may be granted some validity as long as they are taken as symbols. Taken literally, however, they tend only to confirm the desire for continued temporal existence, whether one's own or that of another, and such existence is mortal.

TILLICH also rejects immortality as an extension of temporal life. Eternal life is found not in the hereafter but in the here and now. It is not an endless being in time but a form of being that transcends time by fulfilling it. Immortality is achieved through "essentialization," a process whereby a being returns to its eternal origin by realizing its ESSENCE. This does not mean conforming to an abstract and universal exemplar but, rather, a fulfillment of individual potential within temporal existence. Precisely through this fulfillment an individual participates in eternal life. Immortality cannot consist in disembodied existence, where the soul is detached or abstracted from the BODY, but involves a spiritualization of the whole being of the PERSON. We have the right to hope for this existence, since we participate in it already, in a fragmentary fashion. But any further attempt to say what it is like would be POETRY.

Primary Works

Jaspers, Karl. *Philosophy*. 3 vols. Trans. E. B. Ashton. Chicago: University of Chicago Press, 1969/1971.

Marcel, Gabriel. *Creative Fidelity*. Trans. Robert Rosthal. New York: Farrar, Straus, and
    Giroux, 1964.

ROMAN INGARDEN
(1893–1970)
Peter Simons

Roman Ingarden was born in Kraców. He studied in Lvov with Kazmierz Twar-
dowski before going to Göttingen in 1912 to study with HUSSERL, whom he
followed to Freiburg in 1916, completing his doctorate in 1918. He returned to
Poland and achieved his Habilitation, becoming first dozent and later professor
at Lvov until 1939. During World War II he worked on his opus magnum, *The
Controversy over the Existence of the World*. From 1945 Ingarden was professor
at the Jagiellonian University in Kraców until his retirement in 1963. For a few
years during the Stalinist period he was forbidden to teach. He was the principal
exponent of PHENOMENOLOGY in Poland, yet he never accepted Husserl's
transcendental idealism. Much of his work is a concerted attempt to establish a
robust ontological REALISM. He is probably best known for his writings on
AESTHETICS, in particular, *The Literary Work of Art*.

Ingarden stressed the priority of ONTOLOGY over EPISTEMOLOGY. He
rejected Husserl's views, set forth in *Ideas*, that it is conceivable that the physical
WORLD be annihilated or fail to exist, while no concomitant difference need
be observed in our conscious experience. The physical world is thus dependent
on the mental, but not conversely. *The Literary Work of Art*, apart from being
an extended investigation into the multiply stratified ontological structure of
literary works, is intended to implicitly demonstrate that the mode of BEING
of literary characters, which Ingarden called purely intentional OBJECTS, is
different from those of physical things and independent Platonic ideas; hence,
the latter cannot plausibly be supposed to be involuntary products of mental
activity. Ingarden reserved the epistemology of LITERATURE for a later work,
The Cognition of the Literary Work of Art. He also published extensively on
the ontology, epistemology, and axiology of other forms of ART. Later writings
deal with the foundations of moral RESPONSIBILITY.

The Controversy over the Existence of the World, drawing on ideas Ingarden
developed for over twenty years and left uncompleted at his DEATH, was projected as an exhaustive investigation of the possible relationships of dependence

between the physical and the mental. He distinguished ontology from META-PHYSICS, which attempts to decide which ontological possibilities are actually realized. An ontological investigation, such as the *Controversy*, had to wade through a large number of possibilities concerning the dependence relations between the physical and the mental realms. Ingarden divided ontology into three branches. Existential ontology considers the modes of being of various categories of objects and the moments of EXISTENCE that comprise these modes of being. Formal ontology investigates objects according to their form. Material ontology considers their remaining characteristics. Thus, the mode of being of a PERSON is that of a self-existing, but generated, individual; its form is that of material substance existing and changing in TIME, while materially it is constituted in the manner investigated by anatomy and physiology; and it is physically dependent on suitable conditions in its surroundings. Despite the greater abstractness of existential and formal ontology, material ontology is the most basic.

Ingarden regarded himself as a continuer of Husserl's original essentialistic phenomenological method. He disagreed with Husserl's idealism and considered the later philosophy of the life-world in Husserl's *Crisis* to embody no novelty. He particularly disapproved of HEIDEGGER, whose PHILOSOPHY and influence were not beneficial to Husserl. He regarded the common view of existentialism as a form of phenomenology as wrong and considered Husserl to tower over all his successors quite radically and that the scientific seriousness and the exactness of Husserl's phenomenological analyses and the first generation of phenomenologists stood far above all Heideggerian and post-Heideggerian literature. Ingarden was also skeptical whether Heidegger's innovations in philosophy were so new.

In one respect only, Ingarden stands close to Heidegger: in his treatment of what he calls metaphysical qualities. In *The Literary Work of Art*, he writes in a remarkably forceful, heartfelt passage about these metaphysical qualities— such as the sublime, the tragic, the dreadful, the shocking, the inexplicable, the demonic, the holy, the sinful, the sorrowful, the wonderfully fortunate, the grotesque, the charming, the light, the peaceful. These qualities are neither properties of individual objects nor mental properties of humans but are associated with whole SITUATIONS or events, over which they, as it were, hover like an atmosphere and permeate or illuminate the situation and the participants therein. They occur rather seldom in everyday life, but they may through a sudden change of events, like an unforeseen accident or an unexpected kiss, suddenly break into our gray existence and transform it completely. They reveal a deeper sense of LIFE, sometimes an ecstatic, positive one, sometimes a brutal or tragic, negative one, and they, in turn partly constitute this sense of life. They throw the little cares and joys of our humdrum, everyday existence into relief and are what life is experienced as being lived for.

Here there is much affinity with Heidegger's specific account of the arresting effect of confronting our own finitude, which reveals itself not as an object we FEAR but as an atmosphere. Heidegger calls upon DASEIN to resolutely face his or her own impending annihilation in the authentic mode of being-toward-death, which is the secret sense behind its gray, everyday existence and which it strives to escape in the forgetful mode of the everyday. Ingarden differs from Heidegger in generalizing from the angst in the face of one's own death to a much wider range of metaphysical qualities, including positive ones such as communion with GOD and less dramatic ones such as the grotesque and the charming, and in claiming that we secretly crave rather than shun their realization. But the contrast between the peak experiences of metaphysical qualities and the humdrum of everyday life, the personal and existential importance of such experiences, their embodiment of the sense of life, and their inaccessibility to rational grasp are features shared by Heidegger's account and Ingarden's presentation. Ingarden sees the revelation of metaphysical qualities in manageable doses as being part of the raison d'être of art and of the quest for philosophy.

Primary Works

Ingarden, Roman. *The Literary Work of Art*. Trans. George G. Grabowicz. Evanston, IL: Northwestern University Press, 1973.
———. *Ontology of the Work of Art*. Trans. Raymond Meyer with John T. Goldthwait. Athens: Ohio University Press, 1989.

INTENTION
William Hurst

The concept of intention has a central role in existentialist PHILOSOPHY, most often dependent on HUSSERL's thought. In the emergence of existentialist thought, however, the concept underwent significant modifications. One of the earliest meanings is KIERKEGAARD's, whose focus on FREEDOM and on SITUATIONS of despair and ANXIETY implied that intention should be linked with a traditional philosophical affiliation of free WILL with the intentional act. An act that does not flow from a conscious intention of the SUBJECT could not be considered under the rubric of free will. Humans are capable of acting with or without an intention. An act committed without an intention would not be fully human and could not therefore be evaluated in the moral context of freedom, unless one had somehow put oneself in the position of deliberately acting unintentionally. But such a deliberate lack of intention would, of course, conceal an intention.

Some existentialists have employed the concept ''meaning'' almost as a synonym for intention. What one intends, in the sense of what one means, applies in the first case to speech acts or to other modes of expression, such as writing or sign language, but perhaps also to artistic and cultural artifacts. The meaning of an expression is thought to originate in the intention of the speaker, writer, gesturer, or maker. Thus, the meaning of the objective expression would be the manifestation of the subjective intention. From this usage, the subjective dimension of the intention is evident. A phenomenologist might wonder where such an intention originates. Does it flow from some hidden source in the subject? Must it appear only in conscious form and aim at an OBJECT of a CONSCIOUSNESS? What is the effect of having such subjective intentions? Are they derivative from outside or objective forces? Are they expressions of things deeper that do not have the same CHARACTER, like impulses or drives? What are the principal and unexcludable features of an intention?

SARTRE and MERLEAU-PONTY sought to expand the Husserlian meaning of intention far beyond a transcendental idealism; they sought at every juncture to understand subjectivity, experience, or consciousness as they are in the WORLD. Merleau-Ponty stated plainly that we have to give up the idea that our thoughts are somehow ways in which we invisibly come into contact with ourselves, as a kind of contact of self with self. They are outside ourselves, not in us, but rather in front of us always eccentric to us and outside us. Where, then, are they? They are in the world, even as they serve to open a world and to structure it and to provide a SPACE within which one comes to be and to recognize oneself as a BEING-IN-THE-WORLD. In a thought-provoking reflection, Merleau-Ponty compared the associations of psychoanalysis with what he called rays of TIME and of the world. Such rays indicated a kind of spatial and temporal opening in BEING, an opening that does not admit of a noema-noesis analysis and that ''does not even presuppose man.'' Might it be that these rays of time and the world, which create not only a space within which objects can become visible but also a time within which they can assume a significance for an experience of them, also convey a subtle meaning of the concept of intention, a meaning outside the noesis-noema schema, which sidesteps the questions about their source within or under the subject?

In bracketing the natural attitude and the world of the scientist, Merleau-Ponty and Sartre confronted issues about the nature of human intentions, without succumbing to a subjectivist idealism. For them, existentialism represented the solution to the alternatives of materialism and idealism. If the mechanistic explanations of human behavior and the scientific understanding of the objective human BODY can be opposed by the data of consciousness, which reveal a kind of absolute interiority and which imply, indeed, as Merleau-Ponty claimed, that I am the absolute source, this did not mean that such opposition entails a subjective idealism as the only way to preserve the integrity and reality of human intentions. The existentialist emphasis on the being of the world and that the world is always already there and that the subject is always already engaged in the world precludes the subjective idealistic solution. It also entails a rethinking of concepts such as intention, which can no longer be considered to emanate from a pure subject and to have a purely subjective existence, made manifest in various externalizations, whether those be gestures, words, monuments, or artifacts or memories, dreams, fantasies, and thoughts. Intentions, like thoughts, do not inhabit an inner space but are rather eccentric to the subject, existing in the world, much as the subject exists in the world, in an ecstatic RELATION to itself.

The Heideggerian notion of being-in-the-world permeates many existentialist concepts and transforms them into concepts that give expression to this most fundamental characteristic of human existence. The INTENTIONALITY of consciousness, as its most essential feature, its having objects, so that consciousness is always consciousness of something, receives an in-depth modification when consciousness is understood as in-the-world and as not a private, interior space. The intentions that gave consciousness objects now exist in the world and outside or in front of the subject, giving it a spatial and temporal world. Since the "I" is necessarily a kind of anonymous presence, these intentions cannot be conceived of as having a source in a personal presence in the world. The subject or the source from which they emerge is not the named I. These intentions are not subjective in the usual sense of the word but, rather, allow a world to come to be for a subject. In Merleau-Ponty's investigations they seem to emanate from Being. Certainly, for HEIDEGGER's thinking, they seem to emanate from Being or perhaps from whatever it is that gives Being such emanations. They provide the frameworks within which beings can come to be.

But where does this meditation on the meaning of intention end? How does the movement from a common, everyday understanding of intention as allied with the concept of free will, embodied in human acts, end with a reflection on the emanation of frameworks for being, from that which gives Being, according to Heidegger? Existentialists attempt to remove the purely subjective components of intention without, at the same time, converting it into an objective PROCESS, state, or condition. That move to what is between the subjective and the objective was a move into what gives rise to both and had ontological ramifications.

Similarly, Kierkegaard stated problems confronting the concrete individual. What ought one to do, in the face of absurdity and despair and perhaps in a state in which one is bereft of accustomed resources, either because of circumstances such as illness or because of overwhelming anxiety? Where does intention play a role in such a situation? To a very great extent, the world and the self that one experiences in such a situation result from one's intentions, since they cannot be conceived of as the consequences of objective processes. I am the absolute source, as Merleau-Ponty put it, or I am condemned to freedom, as Sartre said. Heidegger viewed such a situation as a possible call to authentic existence. One is being called out of everydayness and out of the inauthentic way of being in the THEY and into authentic existence, a mode of existing in which one assumes as one's own all one's own potentialities for being, including the potentiality for DEATH. One assumes the despair in the face of being, and one resolves to be oneself over against the possibility of death and of NOTH-INGNESS. Sartre and Merleau-Ponty suggest that one attempt to accept fully the being that one is, with the consequence that one will thereby fully realize the freedom that resides in not being what one is. JASPERS took the Kierke-gaardian ultimate situations of despair and pointed out that authentic existence is attained only in the midst of such situations. It is not so much a matter of attempting to look into oneself to know one's intentions or to purify them; it is, rather, a matter of looking into the world and attempting to assume RE-SPONSIBILITY for it, as if it were the product of one's intentions.

Primary Works

Husserl, Edmund. *Logical Investigations*. Trans. J. N. Findlay. London: Routledge, 1970.
Merleau-Ponty, Maurice. *The Structure of Behavior*. Trans. Alden Fisher. Boston: Beacon Press, 1963.

Bibliography

Sallis, John, ed. *Radical Phenomenology: Essays in Honor of Martin Heidegger*. Atlantic Highlands, NJ: Humanities Press, 1978.

INTENTIONALITY
Peter Simons

Intentionality is the characteristic of CONSCIOUSNESS whereby it is consciousness *of* something. Although the concept of intentionality was commonplace in the Middle Ages and goes back to Aristotle, it owes its modern prominence to the writings of Franz Brentano in the 1870s, in which it served as the defining characteristic of mental as against physical phenomena. Later, intentionality came to play a key role in the PHENOMENOLOGY of HUSSERL, from whence it influenced existentialist thinking.

In his *Logical Investigations* Husserl began a development of his conception of consciousness. The notion of intentionality was modified so that experiences count as intentional that, as we would say now, purport to present an OBJECT. This means that not all intentional experiences actually do successfully present transcendent objects. Those of fictional or illusory NATURE do not. Further, not everything mental or with content is intentional: SENSATIONS like warmth or pain are mental and have content, but they do not present or purport to present an object, though they may be caused by an object—as when I feel the warmth from the fire that I see. Husserl draws attention to two striking features of perceptual intentionality. One is its experienced directness: the perceived object is given bodily. The other is the aspectual nature of outer PERCEPTION. We are never presented with physical objects as a whole but only aspects, which nevertheless cohere as a unitary and are, as it were, surrounded by a haze of virtual ways in which the perception could go on. He holds that the data or sensory material of perception is informed by objectifying acts, so that we are conscious *through* them rather than *of* them. He also claimed that we are intuitively aware of abstract ESSENCES in acts that differ in nature from normal perceptual INTUITION; he called this categorical intuition.

Later, in *Ideas* Husserl concludes that we can grasp intentional consciousness as having its intentional structure in which something is given, independently of the question whether something transcendent exists, which is, in fact, targeted by consciousness. This indifference of the facts of the structure of consciousness to the existence or otherwise of a transcendent object was taken by Husserl as justifying the methodological priority of the descriptive theory of consciousness, phenomenology, over positive science, which has to suppose the existence of something outside consciousness. Phenomenology is thus able to fulfill the role of a rigorous science and to serve as the foundation for all other sciences.

When discussing intentionality, HEIDEGGER, SARTRE, and MERLEAU-PONTY acknowledged their debt to Husserl's thinking. Heidegger's replacement of the subject-object intentionality structure by the unified, but articulated, structure of BEING-IN-THE-WORLD is intended to overcome the schism between SUBJECT and WORLD to which Husserl's Cartesian assumptions had seemingly led. DASEIN is not a disembodied Cartesian observer but an active, embodied agent that is always already in an environment that is discovered rather than constituted. The impact of intentionality on Sartre's thought was tempered both by the influence of Heidegger and by the linking of other themes with that of intentionality. Sartre's essay *The Transcendence of the Ego* suggests that the EGO is not, as Husserl had thought, the subject fount of consciousness and therewith of the constituted world. Rather, Sartre holds, the ego itself is constituted or posited by consciousness. Merleau-Ponty also gave intentionality an important place in his *Phenomenology of Perception* but rejected Husserl's overintellectualist conception and stressed, instead, the bodily aspects of intentionality. These bodily expressions of intentionality, which Husserl had neglected, begin in motor activities such as reaching and grasping and are present in other-directed action such as gesture or in sexual relationships.

Primary Works

Husserl, Edmund. *Ideas*. Trans. W. R. Boyce Gibson. New York: Collier Books, 1962.
———. *Logical Investigations*. Trans. J. N. Findlay. London: Routledge, 1970.

INTROSPECTION
David J. Gouwens

A consistent theme of existentialist approaches is that introspection yields a distinct self-awareness and self-KNOWLEDGE. Existentialist thinking on introspection focuses on two broad issues: introspection as a source of the individual's knowledge of oneself and clarifying this knowledge by describing the structures of the self that account for introspection. In the thought of KIERKEGAARD, introspection is described primarily as a varying set of acquired capacities. CONSCIOUSNESS arises as a PERSON gains the capacity to stand over against the self in reflective self-awareness, including introspection. Introspection, however, is not an inborn or single activity; the kind of consciousness available to a person depends on one's commitments. In the aesthetic sphere of EXISTENCE, in which one is directed to the pursuit of pleasure, there are different levels of reflection, ranging from the immediate, nonreflective AESTHETIC STAGE to the highly self-reflective introspective. Governed by the pleasures of the moment or by the distancing of abstract reflection, the aesthete is plagued by rootless, contradictory feelings, lacks decisiveness, and possesses no self-continuity over TIME. In an eminent sense the aesthete has no self at all; aesthetic introspection is simply attending to ever-shifting moods or thoughts on these moods. Furthermore, the aesthete is unwilling to face ANXIETY and despair.

Kierkegaard holds that both the ethical and the religious spheres of existence include the elements necessary to genuine introspection. In these spheres a person chooses a limited number of goals and ideals and attempts to realize them as a SUBJECT. Thus, one becomes a self in the eminent sense who gains both continuity over time and a transparency, or personal clarity, to the ideal. Inwardness, which includes introspection, is at the heart of the ethical and religious tasks of attaining self-continuity and self-transparency: only by examining one's life in the light of the ideal can one criticize and reform it. Thus, ethical and religious introspection is an examination of the larger patterns of action in a person's life.

NIETZSCHE suspects that introspection is mostly self-deception, for it is often in one's interests to interpret oneself falsely. He is suspicious of what lies behind introspection: the myth of the self as a substantial SPIRIT. Much of our life, whether thinking, feeling, willing, remembering, or acting, takes place without self-consciousness. Soul and consciousness are social myths that arise late in human HISTORY, under the pressure of the need for communication. But the thinking that arises to consciousness under this pressure is the smallest part of our actions, thoughts, and feelings and often the worst part, for what we discover in knowing ourselves is what SOCIETY dictates. In addition, much of what is considered to be the inner life results from despising the BODY and ignoring the fact that humans are a complex multiplicity of bodily instinctual, social, and historical drives. The body shows how much of human LIFE is not self-conscious or self-reflective. However, he does not eliminate introspection but, rather, redefines it, suggesting that one can reach self-knowledge through self-creativity, through creative enhancement of human life. The SUPERMAN, Nietzsche's image of such a higher form of human existence, attains one's self-knowledge by carefully sublimating one's will to power into CREATIVITY.

HEIDEGGER's DASEIN in *Being and Time* is the self revealed within a WORLD. Heidegger points out that the everyday self is an inauthentic self, defined by the THEY. A true, authentic self-knowledge may emerge not by inspecting a point called the Self but by projecting possibilities as one's own possibilities. Authentic existence requires resoluteness, which allows authentic self-knowledge to emerge as a person comes to stand out from others. It also allows a self-awareness of one's temporal existence as thrown into a given world that includes other persons, in which one faces possibilities and one's DEATH. Thus, self-knowledge arises from a transparent, practical knowledge of projected meanings within time. Later, Heidegger pointed out that calculative thinking restricts self-consciousness and introspection to the interior or the heart; in contrast, thinking, which is in the neighborhood of POETRY, opens a space for self-consciousness and resoluteness to emerge.

SARTRE points out that consciousness, which is in itself nothing, comprises various modes of self-awareness in which it stands out from itself and becomes self-conscious. The first is nonpositional, prereflective awareness, when consciousness is intentionally directed to something outside. If I am counting cigarettes, I do not know myself counting; yet there is a kind of prereflective self-awareness of myself while I count. Second, reflection, which includes introspection, is consciousness standing over against itself, a positional self-consciousness. In counting the cigarettes, I can stand back from myself and attend to myself counting. Reflection gives rise to the distinction between the reflected consciousness, which knows itself as being observed, and the reflecting consciousness, the observer. Reflection explains the ideal possibility of authentic introspection and also the possibility of BAD FAITH. Reflection can ideally allow authentic introspection if one realizes that introspection discovers not the self but one's dual elements of FREEDOM and FACTICITY. One does not discover an inner self; one makes oneself known to oneself in CHOICES and commitments. For a person in bad faith, reflection can explain the dynamics of self-deception. Bad faith emerges not only in self-deceit but also in a person's being-for-others. For instance, the Other may define and set a CHARACTER for me that, if I accept it and embrace it in bad faith, will exempt me from the ANGUISH of freedom. Thus, what introspection may lead me to call my character is actually the reflection of how I am defined by the Other. Sartre also believes in purifying reflection, part of which is existential psychoanalysis. In contrast to Freudian psychoanalysis that explains the self and self-deception in terms of causes traceable to subconscious dynamics, Sartre's psychoanalysis sees bad faith and self-deception as conscious, free choices. The task of existential psychoanalysis is to uncover these choices through discussion and introspection.

Primary Works

Kierkegaard, Søren. *Concluding Unscientific Postscript*. Trans. David F. Swenson and Walter Lowrie. Princeton: Princeton University Press, 1968.
Sartre, Jean-Paul. *Baudelaire*. Trans. Martin Turnell. New York: New Directions, 1967.

INTUITION
William Hurst

Many existentialists have discussed intuition, usually assuming HUSSERL's view of intuition as the guarantor and foundation of all KNOWLEDGE, as synonymous with the experience of OBJECTS, be they things in the natural WORLD or other people or imaginary constructs, such as symbols and arithmetical concepts. Intuition in all such instances is understood as a making present of an object. In this making present, which constitutes the givenness of the object, one identifies the experience of the object. Husserl's principal injunction, in his famous statement, was the exhortation to "return to the things themselves." He believed that the things themselves present themselves in experience when one has freed oneself from both theoretical prejudices and the prejudice of the natural attitude. In performing the phenomenological epoche, one puts out of play all the BELIEFS and attitudes that would insert themselves between the things themselves and the SUBJECT experiencing them.

MERLEAU-PONTY pointed out that to understand a word or a concept like consciousness, one cannot simply develop a kind of word-meaning, which would include all the necessary ingredients and provide thereby an objective understanding of the concept or word. To understand the meaning of such terms, one must discover them within one's experience; thus, one must explore within one's own consciousness what it means to be conscious; one must discover one's actual presence to oneself. So it is with all existential concepts. They do not allow us to escape from EXISTENCE to the universe of things said. It is necessary to discover meanings within experience, by searching for the thing itself as it presents itself. Such definitions are not, however, purely arbitrary and constructive, as if they emerged out of a purely subjective experience. The attempt at definition has the purpose of rendering the experience more accessible to oneself and to others. It must be accompanied by exhaustive descriptions of the APPEARANCE of the object, rendering thereby some access to the experience in which the intuition occurred. Merleau-Ponty's remark about ideas, that if they are possessed, they are no longer ideas, might be significant with regard to this task of searching for intuitions within one's experience. Ideas always indicate some future grasp. To the extent that they can be clearly articulated, perhaps they no longer express the intuition one is seeking. Such expressions do not necessarily lead to the experience of the object, in which genuine knowledge and intuition occur.

Merleau-Ponty thought that philosophical thinking, to the extent that it seeks intuitions, might find itself looking for a kind of coincidence with the thing, or with BEING, which would, once and for all, eliminate all distance and solve all problems. Such an intuition would, however, be based on the pretense that it is possible to eliminate the distance from the thing and from Being that is essential to human perception and thought. Indeed, LANGUAGE comes into being at a distance from Being and exists only in such a region of distance. Immediacy eliminates that distance or precludes its coming into being. If the philosopher of coincidence were faithful to such an intuition, once it was attained, the philosopher would remain silent, enjoying the immediacy of Being. But the philosopher attempts to put that intuition into words, thereby displaying the distance that continues to exist, and indicating that the intuition is not one of coincidence. Intuition is rather a "privative non-coinciding, a coinciding from afar, a divergence, and something like a good error." Such a movement of thought does not culminate in a nostalgia for Being but, rather, in the attempt to attend to what he referred to as the dehiscence of the thing. Such attending in language reveals itself as an effort to articulate the coming to be of beings. It is called forth by the "voices of silence," and it opens upon things in whose presence it attempts to situate itself. Thus, the distance from Being is essential for our relation to Being, and the lack or loss of the immediacy of coincidence is a condition for thinking and speaking Being. That human being is a being of distances is the central truth of this reflection.

SARTRE ascribed noncoincidence to the for-itself as its essential characteristic. The for-itself seeks coincidence; it seeks to become what it is and thereby to become an in-itself. But such an achievement would, of course, destroy its own mode of being, which is characterized by noncoincidence with itself and with being. He cited Husserl when he wrote of intuition, claiming that there is only intuitive knowledge and that for Husserl such intuition is nothing but the presence of the thing "in person" for consciousness. But Sartre had already argued that presence is not a characteristic of the thing but can be ascribed only to the for-itself; indeed, it is the ecstatic mode of being of the for-itself. Thus, intuition is the presence of consciousness for the thing, rather than of the thing for consciousness. This inversion required an extended analysis of the NATURE of knowledge, which he claimed is rooted in negativity. There is presence, which is the for-itself, and knowledge consists fundamentally in the intuition that there is being. There is a known, but there is no knower, because the for-itself is pure negativity. It is not even the case that the for-itself can relate itself to any particular being or thing, because it is negativity that causes a this to exist. Thus, Sartre understood the relation of the for-itself and the in-itself to be the presence of the for-itself for the in-itself, by which presence, being is. The knowledge that is one with the negativity of the for-itself is the intuition that there is being.

For HEIDEGGER, intuition is rooted in one of the existentialia that characterize the structure of DASEIN. It does not have a primary role but is, rather, an aspect of the understanding of Being, which is constitutive of Dasein. Intuition, even the phenomenological intuition of ESSENCES, is rooted in understanding, which is to say that Dasein always already has an understanding of Being, by reason of its very structure of projection. As one of the existentialia, understanding, along with states-of mind, characterizes the primordial disclosedness of Being-in-the world. As rooted in that understanding, intuition is an aspect of Dasein's self-understanding, which is an aspect of its understanding of Being. From another perspective, it could be argued that intuition as the making present of what is, is not a derivative or secondary feature of the understanding of Being but expresses, rather, the most central dimension of Dasein's mode of being and is equiprimordial with the there in which Being discloses itself. While it is true that Heidegger took intuition out of the consciousness-being relationship by rooting it in understanding, which is an existential structure of Dasein and not a component of consciousness or subjective experience, note also that the making present of what is had a significant role to play in Heidegger's long attempt to think Being. If one went beyond his early existentialist writings and attempted to situate intuition in the context of his later attempts to think Being, it would have to be placed at the core of that very thinking that lets beings be and that attempts to think whatever it is that gives them being.

Primary Works

Heidegger, Martin. *On the Way to Language.* Trans. Peter D. Hertz. New York: Harper and Row, 1971.

Merleau-Ponty, Maurice. *The Visible and the Invisible.* Trans. Alphonso Lingis. Evanston, IL: Northwestern University Press, 1968.

Bibliography

Fell, Joseph P. *Heidegger and Sartre: An Essay on Being and Place.* New York: Columbia University Press, 1979.

IRONY
Daniel Berthold-Bond

Irony is a mode of indirect discourse where the intended meaning is concealed or contradicted by the literal meaning of what is said and serves to disclose an incongruity or disrelationship between what is and what ought to be. KIERKEGAARD and NIETZSCHE discussed a number of common themes: the role of irony in the exposure of dissonance and disparity, the central place of the figure of Socrates, the master ironist, and the relation of irony to indirect communication.

Kierkegaard's first major work was his master's dissertation later published as *The Concept of Irony: With Constant Reference to Socrates.* The SUBJECT continued to fascinate him throughout the subsequent fourteen years of his authorship. Commentators have remarked that Kierkegaard's preoccupation with Socrates was an indirect effort to come to terms with his own polemical, skeptical, ironic disposition, his attraction to the spirit of "infinite negativity." The definition of irony as "infinite negativity" was familiar to Kierkegaard through his study of Hegel. In applying this definition to Socrates, Kierkegaard interprets the essence of Socratic irony to be a polemical attitude toward conventional VALUES and certainties. The intention behind this destructive PROJECT, however, is constructive: by disclosing the infirmity of objective systems of value and the hollowness of the self that passively submits to custom, irony recalls us to our selves, to self-examination, and to a concern for our subjective possibilities and hence initiates the awakening of ethical self-CONSCIOUSNESS.

Kierkegaard depicts Socratic irony as "mastered irony" or "ethical irony," in contrast to two more common configurations. Nihilistic irony remains embroiled in the destruction of all claims to certainty, all absolutes, and all assertions of value and leads ultimately to paralysis and despair. Romantic irony represents the aesthetic outlook that negates actuality in order to project an imaginative, poetically produced world of ideality in which the self can escape the boredom and despair of LIFE. Its retreat into the imagination effects a movement of self-dispersion and flight from reality. Mastered irony incorporates and yet transforms the nihilistic and romantic gestures: it shares the nihilistic negation of the external and objective and the romantic turn inward to the exploration of ideality, but neither as a capitulation to despair nor as a flight from reality. Its purpose is to decisively transfigure the self through the ethical concern for self-TRANSCENDENCE. Mastered irony exposes the discrepancy and contradiction between what we are and what we might become, between our present actuality and highest possibilities—between our finitude and infinitude, our temporal and eternal selves, our being as embodied creatures and our being as SPIRIT. Finally, however, even mastered irony abandons us to incompleteness, since it can direct us only toward subjective possibilities without ever bringing us to resolute commitment. Socratic irony remains on the boundary of self-integration, but fully authentic EXISTENCE is possible only by FAITH, which leads us beyond the intrinsic indecisiveness and negativity of Socratic doubt. Kierkegaard is frustrated by the common attitude that it is a simple matter to go beyond Socrates. Indeed, he adopts the position of Socratic irony, which is ideally suited to calling attention to the incommensurability of the impoverished actuality of Christendom with the infinitely challenging demands of the Christian GOD.

Kierkegaard constructs a style of indirect communication for his pseudonyms that imitates the ironic phrasing and ethical power of Socratic speech, a LANGUAGE marked by elusiveness, secrecy, concealment, and paradox. The function of indirect communication is to emancipate the listener to think, just as the maieutic function of Socratic irony was to repel the interlocutor from Socrates and thereby throw him or her back onto one's own resources. While Kierkegaard knows that the ironic structure of his indirect communication will never bring his reader to faith—faith is beyond all irony—he hopes it will awaken his reader into subjectivity, which is the necessary propaedeutic to faith.

Nietzsche sought to embody a "Socrates who practiced music," who might redeem us from NIHILISM through artistic creation. He had deeply ambivalent feelings about Socratic irony whose rationalistic impulse stood in antithesis to the Dionysian-Apollonian union of ART, and his irony turned against the instincts, the BODY, and life itself, thus preparing the way for the Christian impoverishment of the world. Yet, he praises Socrates as the greatest of all "physicians of culture," as gadfly, and as midwife—traits grounded in his irony, which disclosed the hypocrisy and complacency of common MORALITY. Nietzsche not simply imitates his ironic critique of culture but also struggles to overcome Socrates by fighting the turn his irony takes against art and instinct. His relationship to Socrates has an ironic structure to it, where friendship is expressed as struggle, where invitation is concealed by denial. Moreover, this ironically ambiguous relation to Socrates is incorporated into Nietzsche's style of indirect communication: the reader emerges as the friend who is treated as an enemy, the confidant who is repulsed and turned away. Nietzsche's language scorns reliance on customary forms of expression, reveling in experimentation, the sheer joy of play, the continual exploration of masks, disguises, and camouflage. He constructs a deep level of secrecy in his texts and adopts as his strategy the flight into concealment, an evasion of direct communication, constantly taunting his reader, intentionally arousing suspicion and distrust. The purpose is again modeled on the Socratic maieutic art: the teacher must deny authority, emancipate the learner. The irony of indirect communication, constantly masking what it says, is suited to awakening the reader's own subjectivity so as to engage in self-examination and creation of value.

Although HEIDEGGER and SARTRE do not seriously discuss the concept of irony, they do help to underscore important points. Heidegger is almost silent about irony, but his view of the fundamentally mysterious and enigmatic CHARACTER of language recalls the ironic structure of indirect communication. In ''A Dialogue on Language between a Japanese and an Inquirer,'' Heidegger refers to language as an ultimate secret and MYSTERY that must be carefully safeguarded. To seek to analytically decipher the riddle of language is to effect the vanishing of the ESSENCE of what is said. Heidegger's writings imply that all thoughtful language is mysterious, not simply that mode of language that is consciously constructed as indirect communication. If it is fair to say that irony is a crucial element of enigmatic language—as Kierkegaard and Nietzsche would suggest—we might infer that Heidegger's way to language could be explored through attention to ironic discourse. Sartre helps reinforce the characteristic of irony to expose disparity and contradiction. *Being and Nothingness* discloses that, like BAD FAITH, irony is a negatite, a form of activity that discloses absence or NOTHINGNESS. What is said is not what is intended, what is affirmed is really denied, what is created is not what it appears to be. This description clearly may be applied to the self-concealing and self-revoking nature of indirect communication. When seen in the larger context of Sartre's anatomy of negatites as revealing consciousness as that BEING whose being is always in question, always other than itself, irony discloses the disparity between what is and possibility, the self as for-itself or FREEDOM.

Primary Works

Heidegger, Martin. *On the Way to Language*. Trans. Peter D. Hertz. New York: Harper and Row, 1971.
Kierkegaard, Søren. *The Concept of Irony*. Trans. Howard V. Hong and Edna H. Hong. Princeton: Princeton University Press, 1989.

Bibliography

Morreal, John, ed. *The Philosophy of Laughter and Humor*. Albany: State University of New York Press, 1987.

IRRATIONALISM
Peter Royle

Definitions of irrationalism vary according to ideas of what is rational. The term can apply to BELIEFS and actions; but what seems to contradict the principles of reason to a philosophical rationalist will not necessarily do so to a scientific empiricist, a romantic, or an existentialist. Whereas rationalism has a fairly well defined meaning, irrationalism has a much broader sense and is often used as a derogatory appellation for doctrines or behavior of which one disapproves. However, it may be appropriated by thinkers who wish to call into question the imperialistic ambitions of reason or, in extreme cases, to overthrow reason. Most of those who would accept the label "irrationalist" believe their position to be reasonable and put forward reasons to support it.

Existentialists would all be lumped together as irrationalists by positivists, linguistic analysts, most empiricists, and many in the Anglo-American philosophical tradition. In their antipathy to desiccated rationalism and the stress they lay on the irrational in human affairs, existentialists warrant and, indeed, lay claim to such a designation. Like Romanticism, existentialism is, in part, a revolt against certain aspects of the Enlightenment such as the emphasis placed on reason at the expense of other human faculties and the belief that increased scientific and technical KNOWLEDGE will bring progress in all spheres of importance to humankind. Existentialists exalt FREEDOM, WHOLENESS of BEING, and a light that, although it is not the abstract, disembodied reason of the Enlightenment, is, as HEIDEGGER's notion of a light in the clearance of BEING demonstrates, a rational light nevertheless, albeit a finite one.

Some questions that irrationalists ask are, Doesn't reason need a ground other than itself? Are rational motives not ultimately rooted in EMOTION and desire? Isn't there a logic of the emotions as well as of reason? Can VALUES be purely rational? Isn't the definition of madness, unreason, often a mere instrument of social control rather than the denotation of a disease? Must valid thinking result in universal concepts? Whatever the rules of logic decree, can there not be realms where self-contradictions, circles, and infinite regresses obtain? Can rationalism accommodate the notion of ontological FREEDOM?

There are many rationalist answers to these questions. Most European PHILOSOPHY since Plato has tended to be essentialist, universalist, idealist, and abstract, in a word, quintessentially rationalist, which existentialist philosophies would repudiate. Thus, KIERKEGAARD repudiated the hyperrationalism of Hegel and maintains that truth lies not in objectivity but in subjectivity. The rationality of the detached scientific observer is unreasonable in that individuals are not just passive observers or describers of ineluctable PROCESSES: they fall prey to irrational ANGUISH and have life-determining CHOICES to make. There are no necessary reconciliation of contradictory theses and no inevitable transcending synthesis, but an agonizing either/or. In the absence of any clear mandate from reason or reason alone, these choices must be made in conformity with the whole being of the individual, in the profound apprehension that error, EVIL, and damnation are real.

Heidegger holds that authentic choice of my self depends on my resolution in the face of my DEATH. As with Kierkegaard, I experience anguish in the face of the void; for Heidegger this void is the possibility of my nonexistence. Hence, philosophy has to return to the prerationalist meditations on Being of the pre-Socratics. Existence is not synonymous with being or actuality, as it is in the metaphysical traditions that he castigates, but is being outside oneself with all the negativities and paradoxes that that idea contains. Strictly speaking, outside the relation of Being with DASEIN, there is no WORLD at all. Being in the fullest sense should be seen not as the emptiest of rational categories, but as the ultimate reality and the focus of concern. It should be seen in opposition not simply to nonbeing but also, at the very least, in its relation to thinking, appearing, and becoming. Heidegger derives his categories from attention to things themselves, many of which fly in the face of established rationalist thought. Such are EXISTENCE, nothing, being, thrownness, and temporality. These categories, together with anguish and freedom, show themselves to be impervious to logical laws of identity and noncontradiction. They may be irrational, but they point to real entities or states that can be intelligibly described. Speech is primarily a naming that enables beings to appear in their TRUTH, or unhiddenness; POETRY takes precedence in this regard over prose. The poet's mission is to unveil what is but until now has been concealed. The true poet is a creator and a discoverer; to some extent this discovery may change the world.

Existence, a term that SARTRE uses in the traditional, metaphysical sense, is the stuff of the world, a world that cannot be explained, as it has no reason to be. Human SUBJECTS are obliged to perceive it as more or less rationally organized, as they are condemned to be free, which means to choose themselves in a way that the world will disclose itself as meaningful in the light of their PROJECTS. The essential feature of humankind is its negativity as consciousness stands outside being, into which it irrupts. My RELATIONS with the Other, rooted in the Other's look, are similarly negative and impervious to rationalistic explanation. In my encounter with the Other, whose existence cannot be proved but only experienced, there is a necessary conflict of freedoms. The phenomenological portraits of the lover, the masochist, and the sadist based on this insight are rich and cast a new light on these phenomena. Sartre's theory of human relations has the merit of solving two fundamental questions that Descartes, even with the help of his proof of the existence of GOD, could not resolve: How can I know that bodies I perceive in the world are people with souls like myself and not mere machines? How can I demonstrate the link between my own

BODY and my soul? Sartre's answer is that under the other's gaze I experience myself as the object of a transcendent subject, who therefore exists, even though I cannot prove or deduce him or her; at the same time, I acknowledge, in shame, the body that the Other perceives—as being myself. Sartre answers the two questions in one swoop, demonstrating the relevance of irrationalist descriptions to traditional philosophical concerns.

Sartre stresses that freedom in the ontological sense means autonomy of choice. He demonstrates that, although freedom always exists in a given situation, ontological freedom must be total or cannot be at all. I can choose not to choose, but this is still a choice for which I am responsible. As many determinists have charged, freedom, of which they conceive as motivelessness and therefore irrational, is or would be nothing. But for Sartre this nothing, or, rather, NOTHINGNESS, is real, being the specific domain of humankind, through whom negativity, without which specific things are inconceivable, is brought to undifferentiated being. Human reality is freedom. Anguish is to be explained not by the numinous or by death but by my reflective awareness that, just as if I am standing on the edge of a precipice, nothing stops me from hurling myself into the abyss, and nothing prevents me from completely botching my LIFE. Freedom is not motivelessness, but motives are not forces in the psyche of which I am the prisoner: they are aspects of the outside world revealing themselves as reasons to act through the free, prerational project that I am. AUTHENTICITY springs from an attitude not to death, which is an absorption into being, but to life.

One irrationalist existentialist is SHESTOV, who wishes to emancipate us from reason. For an individual to be rational in the traditional manner means, he holds, to resign oneself, like the stoics, to the tyranny of necessity. Even GOD, in the Western tradition, is not free, as He is also subject to reason and necessity, bound by the laws of logic. He cannot make two plus two equal anything but four. He cannot wipe out or change the past, and in the final analysis God is bound to remain eternally what He is. All genuine dialogue with such a Being, despite what priests and rabbis hold, is impossible. The real God, however, is a living God; His freedom is absolute. Furthermore, He made humans in His image. If we are bound by reason and necessity, it is because we have eaten from the Tree of Knowledge instead of nourishing ourselves at the Tree of Life.

Some maintain that existentialists are not philosophers but poets and, as such, irrational. It is certainly true that there is an important poetic vein in the works of many existentialists. Heidegger would maintain, however, that this poetic element is proof of the proximity of existentialists to the sources of truth, which is not to be found, in any sense that deeply matters, in prosaic linguistic propositions, which reflect and consecrate a human alienation growing more unremitting as civilization proceeds on its rationalist course. Similarly, true philosophy springs from a participation in the freedom and CREATIVITY of Being. Existentialists would regard certain romantic, symbolist, and surrealist writers as irrational in the pejorative sense of the term. Irrationalism, despite what rationalists think, is not like METAPHYSICS, according to Kant: it is feasible to distinguish between true and false irrationalist propositions on the basis of their existential claims and fundamental believability.

Another feature of what is regarded as existentialist irrationalism is its down-playing of moral notions of GOOD and evil. For Kierkegaard morality is transcended in the RELIGIOUS STAGE of an individual's development; the title of one of NIETZSCHE's works is *Beyond Good and Evil*; for Shestov good and evil are among the fruits of the Tree of Knowledge and must be superseded by a reunion with God, who, as the absolutely free Creator, is above and beyond any such notions; even Sartre, who devoted time and energy trying to devise an ETHICS, makes all ordinary moral imperatives, such as the injunctions not to kill or lie, subservient to the overriding need to liberate oneself by working for the liberation of others. Existentialist SITUATION-ethics is closely related to this idea of the need to supersede ordinary concepts of good and evil. It is also necessary to discriminate between valid and invalid varieties of irrationalism. Such discriminations can never be made from the vantage-ground of infallible knowledge but will always demand a personal judgment.

The achievements of antirationalist and irrationalist thinking are important. Such currents have brought to the fore, in a particularly acute form, many perennial problems of logic and metaphysics that more traditional Western philosophies have preferred to play down, such as the problems inherent in the notions of identity, alterity, and change. Sartre, for example, tries to show that ''A is A'' is not necessarily a simple tautology or analytic proposition, since, according to him, the for-itself, or consciousness, does not coincide with itself. This antirationalist line of thought, it may be claimed, has laid bare the ramifications of any coherent conception of genuine freedom. It is not necessary to fully agree with Shestov to contest the human legitimacy of reason. To be opposed to rationalism, at least in its life-denying forms, it is sufficient to denounce the principle at its root and to insist that reason be humanity's servant and not its master. Irrationalism, while rejecting scientism, can accommodate science, on the ground that science, which cannot explain but only describe, is opposed to the use of a priori rationalist deductions in the nonlogical and nonmathematical areas in which it holds sway. But the greatest achievement of irrationalism is the new light that it sheds on the human condition and on the possibilities for self-realization in an imperfect, yet wonderful, world.

Primary Work

Heidegger, Martin. *What Is Called Thinking?* Trans. Fred D. Wieck and J. Glenn Gray. New York: Harper and Row, 1968.

Bibliography

Barret, William. *Irrational Man*. London: Heinemann, 1961.
Raymond, Diane Barsoum. *Existentialism and the Philosophical Tradition*. Englewood
    Cliffs, NJ: Prentice-Hall, 1991.

KARL JASPERS
(1883–1969)
Kurt Salamun

Jaspers was born in north Germany in the city of Oldenburg. He studied law at
the universities of Heidelberg and Munich, then changed to the study of medicine at the universities of Berlin, Göttingen, and Heidelberg, graduating from
the University of Heidelberg in 1909. After a successful academic career in
Heidelberg—interrupted during the Nazi period—he accepted a professorship
at the University of Basel in 1948. He died in Basel. Jaspers worked for some
years as a voluntary research assistant at the Heidelberg psychiatric hospital
before becoming a professor of PSYCHOLOGY at the University of Heidelberg
in 1916. In 1920 he became professor of PHILOSOPHY at his university. His
former professions as psychiatrist and psychologist provided many subtle insights into psychological phenomena, which were influential in the development
of two key concepts: boundary SITUATIONS in human LIFE and existential
communication. In 1913, he published his first major book, *General Psychopathology*, followed in 1919 by *Psychologie der Weltanschauungen*. Suffering
from an incurable disease of the lungs and cardiac decompensation since childhood, Jaspers was eighteen years old when properly diagnosed; the prognosis
given was that his life expectancy would be very short. He invented procedures
of treatment for his disease and adapted his lifestyle accordingly. In his *Philosophical Memoir* he gives an account of the enormous restrictions of his everyday life. Jasper married Gertrud Meyer, of Jewish origin, in 1910. He had a
deep, personal relation with his wife.

    The confrontation with the Nazi regime brought radical changes in Jaspers'
life and thought. After the Nazis came to power in 1933, Jaspers was excluded
from administrative duties at the University of Heidelberg. In 1937 he was
denied the right to teach; a year later he was forbidden to publish. Until the end

of World War II, the danger for Jaspers and his wife of being deported to an extermination camp was very high. The experience of Nazi terrorism was one reason Jaspers and his wife left Germany and moved to Switzerland in 1948. These experiences also led Jaspers to dedicate more thought to POLITICAL PHILOSOPHY. Thus, while his prewar writings concentrated on individual EXISTENCE—human self-realization, personal FREEDOM, and intimate communication between PERSONS—his postwar writings discuss public affairs such as the question of German GUILT for the Nazi regime, totalitarianism, worldwide communication among nations, the possibility of peace, and the ideal of democracy.

Jaspers' early psychiatric studies oppose a dogmatized, methodological approach in psychiatry that concentrates on narrow neurobiological explanatory methods. He endeavors to integrate elements of a descriptive psychology and of hermeneutics into the methods of psychopathology. He found those elements in the phenomenological and hermeneutic works of HUSSERL and Dilthey. The antidogmatic attitude is also evident in his studies in the psychology of worldviews. Two lines of analysis became highly significant: the conception of system and the explanation of the function of worldviews in human life. A system implies a priori tendencies to dogmatization, stagnation, rigidity, and closed-mindedness. It is the opposite of everything advancing CREATIVITY, open-mindedness, spontaneity, and free activities. The function of worldviews in human life is a necessary condition of human world orientation and emotional stability. Everybody needs a framework, a set of rational schemes and categories for structuring the overwhelming complexity of the WORLD. By forming a worldview we also satisfy emotional needs and desires for constancy, security, simplicity, certainty. Worldviews are rational shells that prevent chaotic disorientation, neurotic unrest, feelings of despair and ANXIETY. Yet, those shells tend to become rational systems or iron cages that prevent self-reflection and self-determination. Then their function is dehumanizing; they eliminate personal freedom and repress spontaneous activities of the human MIND.

Thus, a worldview with its positive functions is in permanent danger of becoming a dehumanizing, repressive iron cage dominated by instrumental rationality. A necessary condition for realizing true humanity is to struggle against the dogmatizing tendencies of worldviews. The realization of true humanity is an everlasting dynamic and open process and must not be dogmatized. In *Psychologie der Weltanschauungen*, the dynamic elements that help us to resist the degenerating process of our worldviews by breaking up the closed iron cages of instrumental and technical rationality are the irrational forces and impulses of life. In later writings these dynamic elements are focused around the concepts EXISTENZ and existential freedom.

A crucial hypothesis in Jaspers' PHILOSOPHICAL ANTHROPOLOGY is that a person realizes his or her life and potentialities in four modes of BEING. The first dimension is naive vitality, the biological self, where physical conditions, spontaneous EMOTIONS, egocentric interests, and instinctive impulses dominate. This dimension of life is without self-reflection and self-consciousness. The second dimension he calls CONSCIOUSNESS in general. This is the dimension of logical thinking and rationality, where one has the intellectual capacity to reflect according to rules and to construct universal KNOWLEDGE about the world according to formal categories of the understanding. The third dimension of human BEING is that of SPIRIT, which is dependent on the logical correctness of understanding but goes beyond it. Its specific principles are ideas that allow one to see different phenomena in terms of unities and as parts of a meaningful whole. They are manifest in personal ideals, principles of RELIGION, political IDEOLOGIES, creative conceptions of the ARTS. Those ideas cannot be known as OBJECTS but only by a kind of empathic or hermeneutic understanding. These three modes of being represent the person as an empirical phenomenon. The fourth dimension of self-realization, as Existenz, is the nonobjective dimension of the actuality of self-being, of true selfhood, the authentic, genuine self, of existential FREEDOM, undetermined moral decision. It is the authentic ground of human being. This existential dimension of humanity cannot be explained by scientific approaches or by philosophical anthropology; it can be elucidated by a transcending philosophizing.

Analogous to the four dimensions of human self-realization Jaspers distinguishes four types of communication. In naive vitality and spontaneous instinctive life, the person lives in primitive communities; one's instincts tell one how to pursue one's advantage in satisfying basic needs. The second dimension, consciousness in general, corresponds with a type of communication that is based on logical and rational categories. Scientific discussions of experts with the aim of solving a technical problem are examples of this type of intellectual communication. In the third dimension, spirit, the person experiences a mode of communication in the close COMMUNITY of an idea of a whole, say, of a certain state, SOCIETY, family, university. While these three types of communication are objective forms of human interactions that can be studied by the sciences, the most valuable form of communication, where the person realizes Existenz, can be elucidated only by philosophy and experienced in one's private life. Existential communication is a very intimate personal relationship between two humans that cannot be verbally communicated in objectifying LANGUAGE.

To exist means to be in a SITUATION. A person can change most situations, but he or she can never get out of one situation without entering into another. One special type of situation that confronts each person in the process of living is the boundary situation, which cannot be dealt with by using the type of rational knowledge used to solve problems in everyday life. Boundary situations require a radical change in attitude and in one's way of thinking. The adequate way to react to boundary situations is to strive to become the Existenz I potentially am. A boundary situation is evident in the inevitable fact that I am always in situations and cannot escape the historicity of existence. I cannot live without struggling and suffering and cannot avoid guilt. I must die. Because of the antinomic structure of life and reality a person has two basic perspectives in confronting such situations: a pessimistic one and an optimistic one. In Jaspers' analyses of reactions to boundary situations, a number of moral attitudes are mentioned that are highly significant for his concept of Existenz and his ideal of humanity. He does not postulate these attitudes as moral norms and ethical rules for human interaction. Rather, he wants to stimulate such attitudes by his philosophy. He appeals to all persons in an indirect way, urging them to accept these attitudes in their lives and personal RELATIONS. The boundary situation of death can be the source of FEAR and anxiety as well as nihilistic despair, but it can also awaken the urgency of living authentically without self-deception. Consciousness of the inevitable presence of death can give courage and integrity and an authentic perspective on the things that matter most. The moral attitudes in the face of death are courage without self-deception; a profound serenity in spite of pain; peace in the face of death with the calm knowledge that this is the end; composure, patience, and dignity.

In response to the boundary situation of suffering, Jaspers postulates an attitude of active suffering. Such is the opposite of resignation and implies an effort to try to be happy despite suffering. The boundary situation of guilt suggests the insight that one's acting or not-acting in several situations has had unforseen and unintended consequences that make one guilty. The moral attitude correlated with guilt is a permanent readiness for taking personal RESPONSIBILITY for acting in the world. The boundary situation of inevitable struggle makes one conscious of the everlasting life-struggle. This struggle is obvious in the fight for material ends, for social status, and for prestige and power in society. In this struggle one's success is necessarily accompanied with the defeat and suppression of the demands of others. This violent, coercive struggle Jaspers contrasts with loving struggle—a nonviolent, noncoercive, and nonegoistic form of struggle with another person. Its dominant norm is solidarity.

Existenz is also possible through communication in an intimate relationship between two persons. Jaspers mentions moral attitudes that can be interpreted as necessary conditions of existential communication: (1) the nonegoistic intention to help a partner to realize his or her Existenz without using the other as an instrument for one's own self-realization—one should establish existential solidarity with one's partner, (2) an open-mindedness and frankness that enable a person to communicate with another person without prejudice and masked purposes—one must risk the empirical self, that is, risk a radical change in habits, opinions, and way of life, (3) an intention to accept the partner in his or her own personal freedom and specific possibility of self-realization. This means not forcing one's dogmatized standards of living on the other. Communication partners have to accept each other as completely equal in their personal freedom and chance to become Existenz, despite objective differences, (4) an intellectual integrity and truthfulness that allow an openness to criticize one's own failings with the same force as the failings and dogmatized opinions of others, (5) the willingness to bear loneliness and the dignity of solitude, which is not the same as social isolation; solitude is the sense of readiness in possible Existenz.

An important feature of human dignity is to dare to be lonely and to live in solitude. Jaspers urges one to risk the adventure of self-contemplation and self-reflection without directives. Dignity of solitude during self-reflection is linked to personal freedom. His appeal to lonely self-reflection can be interpreted as an opposition to the growing manipulative influences of persuasive clichés and stereotypes of human self-interpretation. Yet, the moral attitudes pointed out in the context of boundary situations and existential communication are necessary, but not sufficient, conditions of self-realization. In his writings after World War II, the concept of reason becomes a dominant feature of the human ethos. Reason was given the function of transferring the implicit moral ideals, basic to Existenz, from the private sphere of life to the public sphere; reason grounds these moral attitudes for a new, rational politics and world citizenship. Self-realization as Existenz is inextricably bound to an awareness of TRANSCENDENCE. In becoming Existenz by confronting boundary situations and by existential communication, a person learns that self-realization is not the result of rational planning or managing efforts. It is a gift from a transcendent source. Self-realization as Existenz means the realization of autonomy and freedom; yet one also becomes aware of one's fundamental limits and has to recognize that human being is not the absolute foundation of Being.

Jaspers rejects theism, atheism, pantheism, or religious conceptions of a revealed GOD. In *Philosophical Faith and Revelation*, he explains that he does not accept the Christian FAITH grounded in an objective REVELATION of God. Any conception of God's revelation necessarily implies a claim to the possession of an objectively guaranteed absolute certainty and an absolutely true knowledge of God. This claim breeds intolerance, various forms of fanaticism, and an incapacity for communication with others. Jaspers believes that transcendence manifests itself only through ciphers. Everything can become a cipher in existential contexts and have the function of a signpost to Transcendence. But no cipher can give information about a specific shape or content to Transcendence. In opposition to religious faith, he suggests a philosophical faith that has no objective, guaranteed certainty of the existence of Transcendence and is not bound to rituals, priests, and demonstrations of a revealed God. It is an optimistic credo and confidence in freedom, humanity, and transcendence that favors an attitude of openness for worldwide communication and confidence that human life is worth living.

Jaspers' early thinking influenced his later political philosophy in several areas, including the application of the concept of boundary situation to HISTORY and politics. He argued that the German people were in a boundary situation because of the Nazi regime. He demanded from the Germans an existential self-reflection concerning their moral and political guilt in having made no efforts to prevent the rise of Nazism and in having failed to conspire against it after the regime was established. This self-reflection on their moral and political failings in the boundary-situation of Nazi terrorism was meant to give the German people a chance for a radical change in their political opinions and attitudes. They should create a new politics in a new state with a democratic constitution, free of authoritarian leadership and citizen-submissiveness.

Jaspers also argues that mankind as a whole stands in a boundary situation. Two new dangers for the future of mankind confront us: the possibility of annihilating all life on earth with the atom bomb and the possibility of establishing a worldwide totalitarian regime. To overcome the universal boundary situation demands a radical change in human attitudes toward science, politics, MORALITY, and religion. A new style of politics must be governed by reason and an ethos of humanity. Politics must no longer struggle to dominate others or to impose interests. This new politics must encourage the promotion of all conditions leading toward a constant world peace and a kind of world federation, not in the form of a supergovernment but a league of free nations, made effective by treaties that guarantee unlimited freedom of speech and unrestricted communication, restrain violence, and bind all nations to renounce arbitrary force. Thus, the ethos of humanity that constitutes the moral basis of the conception of Existenz becomes the moral basis of the new, reasonable politics. Its transfer to the public sphere shall be done by reason. Freedom and personal autonomy, which are aspects of individual self-realization as Existenz, are bound to the political freedom of others. There can be no political freedom without the realization of existential freedom, and existential freedom is necessarily dependent on political freedom.

In Jaspers' PHILOSOPHY OF HISTORY, developed in *The Origin and Goal of History*, he presents a nondeterministic position. Humans are able to impose their will and intentions upon the historical PROCESS and to affect the specific directions of the course of history. History is not a teleological process that makes humans into instruments of historical laws, POWERS, or an inevitable fate or socioeconomic mechanism. Furthermore, there existed an Axial Period in history that lasted from around 800 B.C. to 200 B.C. In this period the fundamental categories of thought, culture, and religion developed that have continued the self-understanding of humankind up to the modern period (in China by Confucius and Lao-tse, in India by Upanishads and Buddha, in Persia by Zoroaster, in Israel by the prophets, in Greece by Homer, the great philosophers, and tragedians). The Axial Period thesis has the function of making us aware of a source common to humankind, beyond all differences of creed, political opinion, and political system. The historical consciousness of the Axial Period reminds us of cultural highlights of humankind and of the threefold origin in China, India, and the West. It reveals the importance of pluralism in universal history. This awareness is a necessary condition to change traditional political thinking about categories of national power, of domination, of claims for exclusiveness in the possession of TRUTH.

Jaspers intended to write a world history of philosophy; the main publication of this unfinished project is the book *The Great Philosophers*. This project was to have consisted of five distinct approaches to the history of philosophy corresponding to the following aspects: the historical, the thematic, the genetic, the practical, and the dynamic. For Jaspers, studying philosophy does not mean to acquire knowledge about ideas of past philosophers, but an encountering of great humans in our history, who can influence life orientations in all times because they make us aware of existential possibilities of human life.

Primary Works

Jaspers, Karl. *The Future of Mankind*. Trans. E. B. Ashton. Chicago: University of Chicago Press, 1961.
———. *Philosophy*. 3 vols. Trans. E. B. Ashton. Chicago: University of Chicago Press, 1969/1971.
———. *Way to Wisdom*. Trans. Ralph Manheim. New Haven, CT: Yale University Press, 1954.

Bibliography

Samay, Sebastian. *Reason Revisited: The Philosophy of Karl Jaspers*. Notre Dame, IN: University of Notre Dame Press, 1971.

JUDAISM
Michael Oppenheimer

Existentialism has contributed categories and a vocabulary to help Jews explore the meaning of Jewish EXISTENCE. Judaism's relationship to existentialism should be understood in the context of its encounter with modernity, which began in Central and Western Europe in the third quarter of the eighteenth century. This process, termed Jewish Emancipation, undermined earlier foundations of Jewish LIFE and identity, the autonomous Jewish COMMUNITY, and the comprehensive system of Jewish law. From that time, the meaning of BEING a Jew has been addressed and questioned by Jews and non-Jews. In response to these questions, Jewish philosophers have related to the Jewish experience with the help of major ideas and insights of Western thought.

The power of existentialism lay in its ability to speak to those who believed that Judaism was more than just a heritage, a fixed set of religious laws, or the basis of ethnic or national identity. The experience of freedom by post-

Emancipation Jews might have also contributed to the appeal of existentialist thought. The emphasis on the quest for human meaning and on personal experience as the arena where this quest is played out and where TRUTHS must be verified has had a catalytic role in the development of modern Jewish thought. Jewish philosophers have revealed the experiential reality behind such religious elements as the covenant, REVELATION, election, Jewish law, and the Bible. In exploring the power of these elements to provide direction to a life, they have argued that they are not a threat to FREEDOM and that they do not require the adoption of an uncritical literalism. A common core of existential themes is offered by FRANZ ROSENZWEIG, MARTIN BUBER, and EMMANUEL LEVINAS. The themes coalesce around the understanding that only through a life of sustained commitment to Judaism, as a religious and national reality, does the elemental fact of being born a Jew acquire its full meaning. They insist that the basis for communal and individual Jewish existence is the covenant between GOD and the Jewish people, which is portrayed as a dialogue. The dialogue began with the reciprocal exchange of pledges in biblical times, and it continues today as a living force. The individual Jew acquires direction by identifying with the covenantal experience and purpose of the Jewish people. A major element in this discussion of the covenant is the portrait of God as a PERSON whose voice is accessible in the present.

Rosenzweig identified two crucial issues that he believed were equally important for all modern Jews: Judaism's relevance in the modern WORLD and its power as a living religious tradition. He responded to the first with his philosophical exposition *The Star of Redemption* and to the second with discussions of areas of experience where God's voice remains fully accessible. Revelation constituted the foundation for his philosophical and theological reflections. He held that while God was revealed to the Jewish people at Mount Sinai, it is only through the personal experience of God's LOVE in the present that the individual discovers the truth and meaning of this earlier revelation. He wrote that FAITH based on authority is equal to unbelief. Thus, faith is not something one acquires or accepts out of loyalty to the past. Faith is authentic when it is a response to the present reality of God's revelation.

The Star of Redemption presents a PHILOSOPHY built upon the theological concepts of creation, revelation, and REDEMPTION. He intended to demonstrate that Judaism provides an orientation to the fundamental constituents of reality, God, man, and world. These elements, he believed, were the foundations of Western thought and experience; philosophy, however, was powerless to uncover the living relationships between the three. Judaism understands creation as the relationship between God and the world, revelation as the relationship between God and man, and redemption as the relationship between man and the world. Creation was God's sustained founding of the world, revelation was the event of God's transformative love given to humans, and redemption was humans' giving permanence to the world through loving the neighbor. Both Judaism and CHRISTIANITY were carriers of God's revelation. While

Christianity's role is to extend that revelation to all nations, Judaism lives outside the terrors of HISTORY, anticipating through its liturgy that ETERNITY that will come at the end of TIME.

Rosenzweig addressed the issue of the ongoing vitality of Judaism by uncovering those dimensions of Judaism that provide an experience of, or encounter with, God. In an essay published during the last year of his short life, he explored the meaning of the anthropomorphisms found in the Bible. He insisted that biblical anthropomorphisms were misunderstood as descriptions of God or characterizations of divine attributes. They were the record of meetings between God and humans. The biblical words about God's hearing or speaking document the manner that God was experienced by the human partner. The plethora of anthropomorphisms that cascade out of the biblical text not only indicate the multiplicity of past divine-human meetings but testify to the ways that God can be available in the present to those who seek Him. Hence, critical studies of the Bible and Jewish law never undermined their contemporary significance. He described the miracle of both text and law in terms of their ongoing revelatory power. In the essay, ''The Builders,'' Rosenzweig lay the foundation for a new appreciation of Halakah. He insisted on translating the word ''law'' as ''Gebot,'' or commandment. Law is not a stagnant feature of the past that is accepted or rejected in total. Rather, as a dynamic vehicle for the individual's relationship to God, its appropriation comes as one uncovers the personal meaning of individual laws, as one finds each law addressed to oneself, as one hears within this law the voice of God. Since God's commanding voice to the Jewish people is still sounding, Jewish law should not be restricted to the traditional 613 commandments but be extended to every realm where Jews respond to God's address.

Buber insisted that Judaism was not a faith centered on law and liturgy nor the life of a nation that has continuation and expansion as its primary goals. Judaism is a unique combination of faith and nation that was called into existence by God and that must always be ruled by the imperatives of covenantal existence. Many major themes in his *I and Thou* resound in his presentation of the nature of Jewish existence. For example, Buber believed that the Jews were the first people to respond to God as a Thou who is involved in the totality of life. The relationship to God does not pull individuals out of the world but binds them to the world and to other persons. Through exploring events recorded in the biblical text, he demonstrated that the basic doctrine that fills the Hebrew Bible is that our life is a dialogue between the above and the below. Biblical dialogue takes place between representatives of a nation and God. Creation establishes the foundation for this dialogue, revelation constitutes the specific moments of God's address and the people's hearing, and redemption refers to the attempt to realize God's kingship on earth.

Buber described currents within Jewish history that had broken out to contest the forces of stagnation and institutionalization. The periods of the biblical prophets, the rise of Hasidism, and the development of modern Zionism exemplify the highest spiritual forces within Judaism. From its emergence, Judaism's role in history has been to provide a model of the nature of true community. This model overturns the usual contrasts between the sacred and the profane and between private and public life. The essence of the prophetic word was found in the imperative that all of life, especially the realm of politics and social relations, are subject to the divine call for justice. The voice of God in the Bible calls upon Jews to distinguish, in their lives, between truth and falsehood and justice and injustice. Buber's studies of the Hasidic movement acted as a corrective to the prevailing view that made Judaism synonymous with rationalism. He demonstrated the power and purity in the teachings of Hasidism, which were of relevance for all persons. The core of the message of Hasidism was the call to release the sparks of the divine that lie in all that exist.

Buber saw in the Zionist movement a unique opportunity as well as test of Judaism's historic responsibility. He profoundly disagreed with Rosenzweig's depiction of Judaism that focused on its liturgical anticipation of eternity. For Buber, the covenant between the Jewish people and God could be realized only with a return to the land of Israel, where Jews could become responsible for all the dimensions of national life. He warned the newly emerging nation to guard against the egoism and imperialism that often dominated modern nationalism. The raison d'être of the Jewish nation could not be its own existence. Only by realizing the unity of all life under the direction of one God could Israel fulfill its destiny of bringing God's revelation to all persons and nations. In *Two Types of Faith* he characterized Jewish faith in terms of *emunah*, that is, as a relationship of trust in someone based on experience of that person. *Pistis* is the term used to describe Christian faith; it is a faith based on the acceptance of a proposition about the OBJECT of faith. He further distinguished between the communal orientation of Judaism and the more individual one of Christianity and wrote of the need for the two traditions to speak with, acknowledge the legitimacy of, and learn from each other.

Levinas sees an intimate tie between his thought and Judaism. He believes that Judaism teaches the priority of ETHICS over ONTOLOGY, of the GOOD over being, which constitutes the foundation of his critique of philosophy and Western thought. He finds in the divine commandment, Thou shalt not kill! and in the Bible's insistence on our obligations for the poor, the orphan, and the stranger the bases for his statement about the extreme RESPONSIBILITY that the self has for the other that is embodied in the face-to-face relation. The universal significance of Judaism's teachings about the interhuman constitutes a major part of his contribution to our understanding of Judaism. His examinations of the ways that these teachings are depicted in the Talmudic texts and embodied in Jewish law demonstrate the ongoing relevance of these elements of Jewish religious life. In the essay "Loving Torah More than God," Levinas sees Israel as both a historical people and a religious category, taking its sustenance from the Torah that teaches a life of law and MORALITY. The Torah also describes a specific relationship to God. While this is a relationship of intimacy, it is not a direct contact or emotional communion. The relationship to God comes through the ethical teachings of Torah, and the life with God emerges as Torah is taken into a world. Undoubtedly affected by the horror of the Holocaust, Levinas speaks of the tremendous conflict between the commitment to justice and the violence in the world. Faith is defined in terms of this situation of the passionate commitment to justice in the face of God's seeming absence from history. The people of Israel are a blend of the universal and the particular that stands for all humankind. It is universal in sharing with other monotheistic traditions, in speaking of the fraternity of all humans and responsibility for the other. Israel's particularity is found in the concept of election, which means not privileges but responsibilities.

Primary Works

Buber, Martin. *On the Bible*. New York: Schocken, 1968.
Levinas, Emmanuel. *Nine Talmudic Readings*. Trans. Annette Aronowicz. Bloomington: Indiana University Press, 1990.
Rosenzweig, Franz. *The Star of Redemption*. Trans. William W. Hallo. Boston: Beacon Press, 1972.

Bibliography

Schilpp, Paul Arthur, and Maurice Friedman, eds. *The Philosophy of Martin Buber*. La Salle, IL: Open Court, 1967.

FRANZ KAFKA
(1883–1924)
Jane Bennett

Franz Kafka was born in Prague, the son of a prosperous businessman. He studied law at the German University of Prague and at Munich and became an official in an insurance company. Between 1912 and 1917 he was twice engaged to Felice Bauer; they never married. In 1917 he was diagnosed with tuberculosis and soon resigned from his post. Other influential women in his life included Milena Jesenka-Pollak, with whom he had a rich correspondence, and Dora Dymant, who nursed him until his death in a sanatorium near Vienna. Kafka wrote a diary from 1910, many short pieces, and several novels but published little in his lifetime. He requested that his unpublished work be destroyed upon his DEATH; these wishes were disregarded by friend and executor Max Brod. Kafka's writing confounds conceptual and genre boundaries, in particular, those between waking and dream states, PSYCHOLOGY and PHILOSOPHY, the literal and the metaphorical, the political and the metaphysical. But this transgressive quality, far from preventing established disciplines and perspectives from claiming Kafka as one of their own, seems rather to have encouraged it.

Psychoanalysts have viewed Kafka's writing as a sublimation of his struggle with a domineering father. Sociologists, noting Kafka's double marginalization as a German-speaking Jew in Prague, find in his writing investigations of otherness, minority status, anomie. Theologians have read *The Castle, The Trial*, and even *Amerika* as allegories of SIN, divine grace, salvation. Political theorists have found "In the Penal Colony" to be an anticipatory account of totalitarian regimes or have treated Kafka's fiction as a supplement to their analyses of POWER, legitimacy, justice, bureaucracy, law. Existentialism finds a kindred spirit in Kafka. Themes such as paradox and uncertainty in the human condition, the quest for meaning, the inadequacy of conceptualization to experience, and RESPONSIBILITY and CHOICE appear regularly in his stories. Indeed, the psychological, literary, sociological, religious, and political insights in his texts are perhaps but parts of his project of illuminating the human condition.

No interpretation meshes fully with Kafka's texts. Just as one begins to formulate a thesis, develop a theme, or apply a framework of analysis, hitherto unthematized elements in the story jump out and call attention to themselves as inconsistent with it. This poetics makes an existentialist point: categories of analysis or interpretation seek to catch or hold experience, but even the best-built leak. Kafka seems to conceive LIFE as a liquid, as somewhat responsive to the human attempt to channel it, but never fully contained within those grooves. Thus, a WILL to meaning of the reader emerges via the textual resistance it confronts. Kafka's disturbing plots and CHARACTERS confound even the most careful hermeneutic examination; his chapters proceed not according to a coherent and determinate narrative but through nonlinear associations characteristic of dreams. Like the characters, Joseph K. or Karl Rossmann, the reader should assume not that life is liquid but that it can be comprehended through reason, logic, and common sense. A condition of meaning is the reduction of experience, and a blind eye must be turned toward some dimensions of life in order that sense be made of others. Moreover, if experience is always richer than, and exceeds, its interpretation, then the fantastic, the illusory, the false, and the dreamlike are ineliminable dimensions of the human condition.

K., the protagonist of *The Castle*, is summoned by letter to a distant locale to become its official land surveyor. But once he arrives, he is unable to confirm his appointment. One of his many attempts to do so concerns a visit to the home of Barnabas, who has brought K. letters from Klamm, allegedly a high Castle official. Barnabas is out, and his sister informs K. that Barnabas' status as official messenger is itself a matter of concern to the family, for he has never been issued a uniform. Moreover, Klamm himself may be only the villagers' wish for contact with a projection of those in power, for it turns out that their descriptions of Klamm vary significantly. None of the descriptions resemble the man Barnabas hears being called Klamm inside what Barnabas believes to be the Castle. Similarly, Joseph K. in *The Trial* awakes one morning to find himself under arrest. A respectable clerk, he wishes to respond to an apparent legal charge, but he is continually frustrated in his quest to determine the NATURE of his crime. His questions meet with an excess of words—extensive conversations with his lawyer, proclamations and proceedings by magistrates and court officials, advice and strategizing by sympathetic acquaintances. Characters in Kafka's stories divulge and confess, interpret and recount, endlessly elaborating the context of events. But none of the preferred explanations—although each an intelligent, sensible exploration of facts floating round a particular event—are determinate. None enable the reader to judge the event in question, to explain it adequately, or to predict the future of the story.

Despite inadequate information of dubious relevance, Kafka's characters continue to struggle to shape the course of their lives. They persist in their quests for meaning in the face of enormous obstacles and minute prospects for success, with some awareness that EXISTENCE precedes ESSENCE. These characters have a remarkable degree of toleration for the absurdity of their SITUATIONS. The attitude of the ape in ''A Report to an Academy'' is exemplary here. Caught and caged, he decides to become human, for then he will be let out. The ape does not seek unconditional FREEDOM, only a way to transform his situation into something more bearable. Because no unequivocal meaning to the human condition can be found, one does best to craft coincidences into a story that will help one cope with the disappointment. Resoluteness is grasped as a survival strategy in an uncertain and bizarre WORLD.

Kafka's stories lack the closure, logic, and analysis of systematic philosophical inquiry. But nonnarrative fiction turns out to be an apt vehicle for an existentialist perspective. What better way to expose the asymmetries, ambiguities, and open-ended possibilities in human life than through plots with gaps, missing information, unsuitable characters, uneasy juxtapositions? His fiction, moreover, highlights the question of the meaning of human life, which becomes linked to the question of the identity of the self. A modern answer to ''Who am I?'' may be ''I am SUBJECT not OBJECT, agent not effect, a free and rational rather than determined or contingent BEING.'' That the realization of this ideal is extremely difficult comes as no surprise to readers of Kafka, for he has a fondness for situations that express the tension between the single-mindedness required to discipline the self in accordance with the ideal of rational agency and the multiplicity of any given PERSON. The assistants in *The Castle* exemplify this point. They are exaggerated versions of the raw material modern selves have to work with: children in adult bodies who are much better suited for disrupting and derailing the PROJECTS of others than they are for conceiving and enacting their own. They have power over K. but little efficacy of their own. True, they act as if they seek to seduce K.'s fiancée and thus appear to possess a positive aim, but, strangely, success in this venture is of no concern to them. Neither do they possess stable identities. They blend into each other and into others around them and fade into piles of rags in a corner.

Kafka explores the possibilities for freedom not only of recalcitrant human bodies and wills but also within overbearing institutions. The Court and the Castle render free action futile or absurd, and yet, they continue to endorse the ideals of responsibility, INTENTIONALITY, efficacy, and rational agency—for their identity is wrapped up with them. Such ideals are chimeras, illusions. But that does not make them less central to human existence or lessen their impact upon the lives of individuals. Perhaps that is why HUMOR is a central ingredient in Kafka's vision. He not only frustrates the will to meaning but also allows us to laugh at it. The longing for a teleological world or a ready-made identity is strong, but that doesn't mean it isn't also downright silly. Because humor cannot be described but only experienced, his jokes lose much in the paraphrasing of them. They usually involve the liberalization of figures of speech or characters' investment of meaning in what turn out to be the most arbitrary and contingent of events. He pokes fun at the reader's longing for a final cause, for a source of authority, for a responsible agent, for someone or something to explain it all.

Despite the oppressive ubiquity of diffuse, bureaucratic power, despite the fact that somehow nearly every intention is thwarted or perverted, and despite characters' utter inability to challenge or even locate the precise source of the interference, their lives are still the product of their choices. Joseph K. could have responded differently to the warders who inform him of his arrest; K., the land surveyor, could have gone home after finding that the Castle had no need of surveying; the officer in the penal colony volunteered to take the soldier's place on the torture machine. Kafka explores the strangely familiar modern experience of the simultaneity of choice and overweening constraint, of bearing a degree of responsibility for one's life that far exceeds one's personal efficacy.

Primary Works

Kafka, Franz. *America*. Trans. Willa Muir and Edwin Muir. Harmondsworth: Penguin, 1967.
———. *The Castle*. Trans. Willa Muir and Edwin Muir. Harmondsworth: Penguin, 1957.

Bibliography

Gordon, Haim. *Dance, Dialogue, and Despair: Existentialist Philosophy and Education for Peace in Israel*. Tuscaloosa: University of Alabama Press, 1986.

SØREN KIERKEGAARD
(1813–1855)
Robert L. Perkins

Søren Aabye Kierkegaard was born in Copenhagen, Denmark, where he was educated, undertook his prolific literary, philosophical, and theological activities, lived the internal struggles of his outwardly bourgeois existence, and died. His father was a shrewd businessman who retired at forty and enjoyed being a dilettante in PHILOSOPHY and THEOLOGY. Young Kierkegaard was the apple of his father's eye. He was educated in the Latin school, and he occasionally taught there while a student at the University of Copenhagen. He seemed a perpetual student, lax and indolent. He passed his theological examination with honors in July 1840 and defended a master's thesis, later raised to a doctorate, "On the Concept of Irony with Continual Reference to Socrates," in 1841. About this time he terminated an engagement to Regine Olsen and made the first and longest of three trips to Berlin. His book *Either/Or* was followed by pseudonymous LITERATURE, which includes: *Fear and Trembling, Repetition, The Concept of Anxiety, Philosophical Fragments and Prefaces* (all in 1844) and *Stages on Life's Way* (1845). In *Concluding Unscientific Postscript* (1846) he acknowledged what everyone who cared already knew: that he was the author of the series. He soon became involved in a controversy with a scandal sheet, *The Corsair*. The notoriety caused by this controversy affected him adversely, making him an even more private person.

Kierkegaard began a second literature, which was increasingly critical of the religious establishment and Danish political and social conservatism. In the last years of his life he became embroiled with the Danish People's Church. His position was that official CHRISTIANITY had nothing to do with the Christianity of the New Testament. During this controversy he fell ill in the street and died a few weeks later. Five public thinking struggles engaged Kierkegaard: (1) the struggle against German Romanticism and hedonism, (2) the struggle against Idealism and Hegel, (3) the irresponsibility of the press, (4) critique of the age, and (5) the struggle against the use of Christian institutions by the power structure.

Regarding the first struggle, Kierkegaard did not explicitly criticize the philosophic hedonism of the ancients or the moderns. His target was the literary hedonism of the German Romantics, particularly, Friedrich Schlegel. He based his critique of Schlegel's novel *Lucinde* on Hegel's comments on Romanticism and characterized the Romantic lifestyle as the aesthetic mode of EXISTENCE.

Like Hegel, he perceived the Romantic movement as a threat to MORALITY and RELIGION. Literature is not morally neutral: it recommends a life-view, or none at all, which is the nihilist life-view. Romanticism begins with Fichte's view of the EGO, but the more the Romantics sought to exploit the metaphysical POWER of the ego as self-constituting, the more vacuous it became. They used the Fichtean ego to justify the willfulness and eccentricity of the empirical self. This arbitrariness they called IRONY, and from the self-assertiveness of the ego the Romantics criticized the common LIFE as philistine. Because of their adolescent exuberance and sexuality, they were particularly critical of the institution of marriage, which they wished to discard in favor of free LOVE. They opposed duties of any sort. Vegetative indolence was considered to be the best life. The ironist abandoned every objective principle by which life could be ordered and lived but, ironically, was dominated by the last mood or feeling. The Romantic poetizes the world in one's own image. In *Lucinde*, Schlegel had some justification in protesting the drabness that made marriage lazy, sluggish, apathetic, and utilitarian or reduced woman to a domesticated breeding animal. But this protest did not legitimate the destruction of fidelity, RESPONSIBILITY, caring, and promise-keeping. *Lucinde* offers no valid cures for the ills it deplores. If the conventional married PERSON is confined by the rules of marriage, the Romantic is confined by the omnipotence of whim. FREEDOM, however, is possible only with self-identity and continuity, both of which are rendered impossible by Romantic irony. The basic decision of life is to decide to master one's impulses and drives, to master irony and its powers to deceive oneself into thinking that oneself is ultimate. The first and ultimate decision constituting authentic human existence is the choice of the ethical, to recognize that there is an other with a validity equal to one's own.

In *Either/Or* Kierkegaard strives to refute Romanticism and to elevate the ethical life. The choice a person faces is either the aesthetic or the ethical. The religious enters only as an apparent afterthought. The modes of existence are also presented in *Stages on Life's Way*. These works show the self-destructiveness of the aesthetic mode of existence: its indolence, sensuality, self-indulgence, moodiness, arbitrariness, lack of continuity, and reduction of the Other to an instrument. The aesthetic life is natural, unreflective in some expressions, but capable of using reason for the basest ends. To be otherwise, you must choose. When a CHOICE is made, the person has chosen the ethical mode of existence and has chosen to become a self, capable of GOOD and EVIL.

Ethical existence is presented in three essays by the pseudonymous Judge William, who is married. His arguments rationalize marriage, which intellectually and emotionally legitimates the love shared between his wife and himself. Yet, the ethical is not the end of the matter, for evil has been mentioned. The last section is a sermon with the theme against GOD we are always in the wrong. This expression opens a world different from ethical or aesthetic modes of existence. Though a religious orientation emerges in Judge William's ethics, the thought there is that WE, in the ethical mode of existence, are justified. The sermon "Guilty/Not Guilty" in *Stages on Life's Way* examines the religious mode of existence through a love story where great evil is done without intent. That consideration focuses the ambiguity of life so far as reason and, literally, genius will permit and thrusts us into the religious mode of life as the final limit of the aesthetic and ethical modes of existence. The aesthetic mode of existence must lose its egocentricity, and the ethical mode of existence must lose its moral complacency if they are to be taken up into the religious. The aesthetic mode of existence ends in despair; the aesthete strives to live in a world of infinite possibility where everything is possible, and nothing is actualized. The aesthete attempts to escape suffering and finds only melancholy and isolation. Denying the actuality of one's evil, the aesthete cannot accept one's historical existence. Consequently, the aesthete has no self. The ethical mode of existence is expressed in a theory of the virtues, a moral law characterized by the universal, or a set of provincial social conditions that claim the authority of universal reason. Unless the person questions these laudatory philosophical terms, he or she cannot enter into the infinity of the religious. Both the aesthete and the ethical person suffocate in a one-story universe without the divine. The initial expression of the existential transformation of one's life is the simultaneous maintenance of an absolute relation to the absolute and a relative relation to the relative, the aesthetic, and the ethical. God's command to Abraham to sacrifice Isaac is Kierkegaard's paradigmatic challenge to the ultimacy of the ethical. The religious does not leave us without ethical guidance—it transforms the inclinations, the virtues, the legalistic moral systems, and the social codes into a command to love one's neighbor as one loves oneself.

In *Works of Love*, Kierkegaard explored the meaning of Christian or neighbor love in great detail using the locution, You shall love your neighbor as you love yourself. Neighbor love is different from conjugal love, though it in no way limits conjugal love. Love based on passions are preferential. Neighbor love is nonpreferential and universal. The spouse is the nearest neighbor and therefore is entitled not merely to passionate love but also to neighbor love. Neighbor love requires us to love as we love ourselves those we love preferentially as well as many people who we are not inclined to love and may hate us. Neighbor love, being a task, is commanded love. It is the only love that can be commanded. Loving the spouse is the paradigm of the ethical mode of existence; loving the neighbor is the paradigm of the Christian mode of existence. The different modes of existence intend different kinds of selves. The fundamental task the person has is to become what one is: a person. Paradoxically, that is the ART of life.

The dynamics of becoming a person is discussed in *The Concept of Anxiety* and *The Sickness unto Death*. The difficulty of the aesthetic mode is that it multiplies possibilities for itself but brings nothing to actualization. That false step is the despair of possibility, which is the lack of necessity. The ethical person may be stifled by the conventions of the SOCIETY or by habit, so that one suffers from the despair of necessity, which is the lack of possibility. The self is not a synthesis of these dialectical opposites such as BODY and soul, finitude and infinitude, temporal and eternal. Rather, the self is the center of activity that synthesizes these categories in the process of becoming itself. Only persons in the religious mode of existence come to the full realization of the self, for only over against the divine are the existential categories completely comprehended and experienced. To relate finitude, necessity, and temporality to God sounds paradoxical, but that may be because we think of the divine with a diminished set of categories. However, reflection on the modes of existence leads to a consideration of the divine.

Regarding the second struggle, Hegel's philosophy and the person of Socrates are at issue in Kierkegaard's struggle against Idealism. German Romanticism arose out of a misappropriation of Fichte's concept of the ego. Hegel, however, is no romantic. Kierkegaard disagreed with Hegel's confidence that reason was omnicompetent and could grasp reality and systematize it. Already in his dissertation, he recognized that one could not use Hegel's system of philosophy to understand an individual's life. This thought became the center of his rejection of Hegel's philosophy and his identifying thought and BEING. There is a certain plausibility to the identification, for to say something exists is to think it. But the issue is more profound since an individual cannot be explained by the system. Thought and being, in the sense of an existent, are not the same. Still, this is not the heart of the matter, for the being Hegel speaks of when he writes about the unity of thought and being is not some paltry existent. What other kind of beings does philosophy reflect upon?—pure ideas, logical RELATIONS, and such things as states and laws. Kierkegaard argues that for Hegel the concepts of thought and being are identical. However, existence is left out; his philosophy is irrelevant to existence.

Hegel thought that his system was inclusive: it contained the totality, and the totality was the TRUTH. This belief is amazing, given the limits of human KNOWLEDGE. Hegel's belief in the unity of thought and being, combined with his claim that his system contained the totality of logical categories and that totality is the truth, does suggest the presumption to divine knowledge. Kierkegaard discussed idealism generally under the figure of Socrates; he found much lacking in Hegel's system and little lacking in Socrates' existence. His Socrates is not the ironic Athenian but, rather, a man of moral and religious sensitivity and encompassing humanity. Socratic HUMANISM is the fundamental challenge to the Christian FAITH. In order to distinguish Socratism from Christian faith, Kierkegaard developed a series of thought experiments in *Philosophical Fragments* that highlight the differences between them through categories that are different from the Platonic. He builds upon Plato's notion of recollection to develop his view of Socratism in all its dimensions: psychological, moral, and religious. Instead of recollection, Kierkegaard assumes faith; instead of ignorance, the consciousness of SIN and the possibility of offense; instead of enlightened conversation, a decisive moment of repentance; instead of reason, paradox; and instead of the witty and ironic Athenian, the teacher in

TIME in the form of the servant. In *Concluding Unscientific Postscript* he presents the implications of Socratism for Christianity in detail. The description of Christianity is subordinated to the description of Socratism, which is taken as normative.

While presenting these thought experiments Kierkegaard attacked the ancient view held by Hegel that philosophy was the discovery of universal truths by means of reason. He accepts this understanding of philosophy but wishes to deny the universality of reason in a very few instances and claims that there is something that escapes being categorized in universal terms. To understand ourselves as existents and to understand that God exists are not to understand a universal truth but, rather, to understand the existence of radical individuality. This paradoxical view challenges the understanding of reason that held sway from Plato through Hegel. The passion of reason is to find something it cannot think; Socrates found something he could not think: himself. He discovered the paradox that the individual cannot be completely understood in universal categories; the individual eludes universal categories because of the singularity of one's existence. Kierkegaard also examined some traditional proofs for God's existence and found them logically faulty; they cannot give knowledge in the sense of universal truths or truth of any sort. An individual of whom we can assert no universal categories and the God whose existence we cannot prove would be unthinkable in an absolute sense. They would be an absolute paradox in an existential sense, but not in a logical sense. Logic and reason, having found what they cannot think, become silent. If, in its encounter with the absolute paradox, reason understands the absolute unlikeness, faith will result. Philosophy continues its proper activity of attempting to understand what can be subordinated to universal categories. If, however, reason insists on universality in the case of the radically paradoxical, offense is the result. Philosophy will continue its proper activity of thinking the universal and will begrudge this absolute individuality its uniqueness. It will attempt to reduce it to a universal, never recognizing that what is reduced to the universal is not the absolute individual or paradox, but some misstatement of it.

Regarding the third struggle, the *Corsair* was the most popular publication in Denmark in the period—popular for what Kierkegaard considered the wrong reasons. The paper was gossipy, satirical, irresponsible. Though there were press laws about slander, the *Corsair* managed to avoid most legal challenges by use of anonymity. It intimidated leaders of the COMMUNITY, for they did not have an organ through which to defend themselves; furthermore, defense against gossip and satire invites more of the same. Kierkegaard became involved with the *Corsair* when one of its writers, P. L. Moller, reviewed Kierkegaard's *Stages on Life's Way* in an elegant gift-book, *Gaea*, which Moller edited. Moller was a rake with some solid achievements in literature. Deeply offended that such a morally disreputable person would mock the moral dilemma artistically transmuted into *Stages on Life's Way*, Kierkegaard struck back in a newspaper article, rhetorically emphasizing that Moller was an editor and writer for the *Corsair*.

In response, the *Corsair* published a series of articles about Kierkegaard, accompanied by demeaning cartoons. Some articles were pure fiction, but most opined about the characteristics of his personality, his tragic engagement; the cartoons played on these and upon his curved spine, short leg, and uneven trousers. The public loved it.

Important issues emerged: the responsibility of the press and the nature of the comic. Kierkegaard was provoked to think about the nature of public communication, HUMOR, and the public. It is difficult now to realize the personal damage done by these attacks on his personal life, physical deformities, and the uneven length of his trousers. Public communication is difficult, at best, because it is directed to an unlearned public. To exploit the natural ignorance of the uninformed in order to demean and destroy the personal habitat of a person is not the vocation of the press and is indefensible. When humor is used as part of a debate on substantive matters, it should contain a higher point of view. Kierkegaard thought that the comic, including satire, should be well grounded in an ethical point of view and should serve that point of view and not be self-serving. Without a higher ethical stance, the comic becomes demoralizing and contemptible. The public, which enjoys malicious humor, measures itself by its own lowest standards. Kierkegaard achieved his goal of silencing the *Corsair*, but he did not succeed in silencing gossip.

Regarding the fourth struggle, the *Corsair* affair caused Kierkegaard to think about the NATURE of a public that enjoyed the level of humor it exploited. In his dissertation he had already criticized the Romantics for undermining the common life. Shifting focus, he examined the public that enjoyed the Romantics and bought and read the *Corsair*. He held that the Romantic movement, the irresponsible press, and the public are engaged in a struggle against common life. Anonymity and impersonal relations flourish. The press is published by people who have only a monetary interest in the writers; writers make copy for people they do not know; the reader knows neither the writer nor the publisher. Yet everything in modern public and political life depends on who operates the newspapers. New information did much to widen the perspectives of people, but the press created a body of persons holding a cache of predigested and preevaluated opinions, gossip, and rumor who are easily manipulated. Kierkegaard warned that the interests of the press owners and the political manipulation of the public boded no good. The constant delivery of fresh opinion, rumor, alarms led people not to respond simply as persons. Interest groups became the newly formed personas that play out their roles in HISTORY. Individuals become the instruments of classes and interests. The public has to be coddled and continually entertained with fresh episodes of sensate titillation and laughter. The Roman emperors furnished bread and circuses; in the modern age, the press replaces the circuses. The public can believe x today and not-x tomorrow, for the public is nothing, has no interests, continuity, or substance. Shaped by the press, accepting opinions created and endorsed by it, the public becomes intolerant of anyone who is different.

Leveling is the reduction of thinking to public opinion, art to entertainment, religion to a support of the public's desires for legitimacy, speech or discourse to chatter, courage to making a speech, cordiality to saying social pleasantries, love to marrying a well-to-do widow, piety to going to church once a year, and the reduction of ethical norms to community standards. This leveling debases the individual in one's task of becoming a person of CHARACTER. If anyone dares to be a person, the public subjects that person to its envious displeasure and censure. This critique of the public opposes the strains of modernity that enforce a homogeneity of taste, thought, and existence. The Romantic form of life with its indolence, pleasure, and sensuality has gone public; it has spread over the whole body politic and become what the age demands. The body politic has been reduced to quaking in face of the latest public opinion poll. Religion has become the sacred canopy over the whole. Kierkegaard's statements about the ownership of the press showed that he understood some of the rudiments of the capitalist tendency to reduce everything in a culture to serve its ends. Besides the press, the church and the pulpit were the other major media of communication in Denmark.

Regarding the fifth struggle, the People's Church was deeply involved in the main currents of Danish life. Due to the excellence of the preaching and the administrative and political skills of Bishop Jakob Peter Mynster, the pastor to two generations of Kierkegaards, the church in Denmark was the keystone of the Golden Age in literature and culture. Upon Mynster's death he was praised as a witness to the truth. Such puffery was too much for Kierkegaard. He published a series of articles and brochures in which he criticized the temporal power and the wealth of the church. The attack was on the church, but the church was a department of state, and so the attack was also on the state. Church ministers were paid by the state, and they held appointment from the state with the church as the intermediary. Kierkegaard called this cozy arrangement "Christendom." The collection of his articles and brochures has been called *Attack upon Christendom*. Kierkegaard felt that the service of the church as constituted by the state was a sin, and to refuse to partake in it made one answerable for one less sin. The church had compromised the teachings of Jesus and had accommodated itself to the Danish state and public. The clergy, though perhaps well intentioned but spiritually dense, thought that to seek first the kingdom of God was primarily to tidy up, improve, and enhance the worldly status of the church and to advance one's place in the church, rather than to imitate Jesus, who was a lowly servant. Such is the mendacity of the church that what it does to support the political and social arrangements is thought of as purifying and refining the idea of Christianity. In Christendom, Christian concepts are corrupted and reduced to twaddle by a mendacious clergy. Not only is Christianity compromised in such a situation, but those who would oppose Christendom are placed in a position where they must oppose the one institution that should question the ultimacy of the status quo.

In its struggle to assert the legitimacy of its status, the church has compromised its authority and forgotten the religious insight that questions all arrangements and persons: as against God we are always in the wrong. The question involved money. The clergy wanted positions and good salaries, while the rulers were willing to use the authority of the clergy to consolidate their rule. The church no longer suffered as its Savior did, under Pontius Pilate; it had made a deal with Pilate. The political, economic, and cultural establishment that was Christendom was united against Christianity. Kierkegaard adjures two things: the use of the police to collect the church's tithes and the system of property ownership that made the whole thing possible.

Primary Works

Kierkegaard, Søren. *The Concept of Anxiety*. Trans. Reider Thomte. Princeton: Princeton University Press, 1980.
———. *Concluding Unscientific Postscript*. Trans. David F. Swenson and Walter Lowrie. Princeton: Princeton University Press, 1968.
———. *Works of Love*. Trans. Howard Hong and Edna Hong. New York: Harper and Row, 1964.

Bibliography

Perkins, Robert L., ed. *Fear and Trembling* and *Repetition: Volume 6 of International Kierkegaard Commentary*. Macon, GA: Mercer University Press, 1993.

KNOWLEDGE
Andrew J. Burgess

Existentialist thinkers do not form an epistemological school; they do not share the same concept of knowledge. Indeed, even the use of the term "knowledge" is not as common among the existentialists as among many other modern philosophers. Where knowledge is explicitly discussed, it is often in a secondary role, as part of analyses of other central concepts within ETHICS, ART, RELIGION, or ONTOLOGY. Describing the existentialist concept of knowledge is thus as much a matter of identifying where and why it is present. Accordingly, the approach here is to discuss four representatives, KIERKEGAARD, BUBER, MARCEL, and HEIDEGGER.

The typical response of these thinkers to the question of radical skepticism about the EXISTENCE of the external WORLD is that such a skepticism is misguided. It conceals only a deeper dogmatism. Kierkegaard looks at several Hegelian-style versions of the Cartesian principle that everything ought to be doubted and finds them wanting. Who could be in a position to doubt absolutely everything? Ironically, he tells a story about an earnest young Hegelian philosopher, Johannes Climacus, who sets out to follow the skeptical program. After many vain attempts Climacus begins to wonder why it is that he never hears about philosophers who have been through the ordeal of radical doubt. Could the experience have been so horrifying that they did not dare speak of it? Finally, upon hearing that such doubt is a prerequisite for philosophizing, he gives up hope of being able to make sense of the claim and abandons PHILOSOPHY forever. Although Kierkegaard ridicules modern skeptics, he praises the ancient Greek skeptics, who, like Climcaus, put their doubting into everyday practice, even at the cost of personal inconvenience and ridicule. In *Philosophical Fragments* he draws an analogy between this Greek skeptical doubt, which resolutely rejects the apparent coming-into-existence of things, and the nonskeptic's equally resolute BELIEF, which affirms them. These remarks on EPISTEMOLOGY are not developed, however, and they chiefly preface a further analogy (and disanalogy) between the nonskeptic's belief and the Christian's FAITH.

Writing against the background of a neo-Idealist tradition, Marcel arrives at a similar judgment about skepticism. The appendix to his *Metaphysical Journal* declares that doubt does not occur in a vacuum. An act of doubting already presupposes an affirmation of some kind of experience, albeit confused, of the world. Heidegger's phenomenological investigations in *Being and Time* attack the same Cartesian misunderstanding of doubt in Kant. Against Kant's complaint about the scandal that there is still no cogent proof for the existence of things outside us, Heidegger insists that the true scandal is not that such a proof has eluded philosophers but that they keep trying to find it. If there had been a correct grasp of DASEIN as already BEING-IN-THE-WORLD, doubt about the existence of the world would never have arisen.

A significant epistemological point common to existentialists is a dichotomy between two ways of relating to the world—a way of knowing, on one hand, and a different way, variously identified as existing, relating, or BEING. These thinkers allow a legitimate role for traditional concepts of knowledge, yet they limit the scope of these concepts. Kierkegaard's well-known distinction between objectivity and subjectivity set the stage for later developments. Objectivity represents the methods for seeking historical and scientific knowledge, where the individual remains dispassionate and neutral in relation to the TRUTH. Subjectivity identifies those cases where one relates the truth to oneself and adopts it as ethical task. The first is the sort of knowledge modern epistemology focuses on, while the second is not. Kierkegaard sketched this distinction and applied it in terms of two kinds of communication—communication of knowledge, which gives information, and communication of capability, which provides the learner with a new competence. In different ways, communication of capability lies at the basis of communication of mathematics, physical training, artistic expression, ethics, and religion. The distinction between kinds of communication is nonetheless incomplete. He describes how nearly all the forms of capability-communication also require some kinds of knowledge-communication to be effective. Moreover, communication of information in the natural sciences also calls upon specific competencies that need to be acquired.

Buber's *I and Thou* contrasts two primary relations, the I–It and the I–Thou. The I–It includes all human relationships in which experience is categorized and thereby known. Within the I–Thou relationship, a PERSON neither labels nor categorizes but simply encounters the Other with one's whole being. It would be tempting to think of the I–Thou as providing a more basic knowledge than the I–It, but this inference Buber rejects. Because knowledge requires categorization, the I–Thou cannot be a kind of knowledge. Later, he clarifies the distinction he had drawn in *I and Thou*. He speaks simply of two movements within human LIFE, distance and RELATION. In the first movement, distance, we set ourselves over against the world and recognize that things are different from ourselves; in the second relation we enter into personal relationship with things. He stresses that the two movements are logically, rather than chronologically, related. If there is a priority, it belongs to distance, since relating to something presupposes a previous distancing from the OBJECT to which one is related. In the essay, ''Man and His Image Work,'' Buber tells a story of an ancient linden tree that once stood near his path. One day he set himself to abstract from the tree as given to him by his senses, until the tree became for him a bare ''x,'' like a Kantian thing-in-itself. Then he addressed himself to the tree, saying ''So it is you,'' entering into relation to it; with that relating the tree became for him again a living, green thing. What Buber learns from this experiment is that there is more than one sort of knowing. There is knowledge when a person knows something as a sensible object; one knows the tree as a green and leafy thing. That is knowledge through distance. There is, however, also another way of knowing the tree, through a personal encounter. This is knowledge through relation; this, too, is a powerful knowing.

In *Being and Having* and later in *The Mystery of Being*, Marcel distinguishes between having and being and between primary and secondary reflection. Within the activities of having, carried on through primary reflection, the investigator stands apart from the object of investigation and has control of it, treating it as a problem to be solved. Primary reflection works toward abstract, universal knowledge. Within the activities of being, approached through secondary reflection, the individual cannot be separated from the object of reflection. The object of reflection is not a problem to be solved but a MYSTERY to be contemplated. The reflecting individual is intrinsically a part of what is being reflected. The secondary reflection achieved is thus different in each individual case and cannot be fully recaptured in abstract, universal terms. In view of the traditional associations of the term ''know,'' Marcel is reluctant to say that the individual can know being, the arena of human relationships. Although he speaks of a blinded INTUITION of a mystery, he does not thereby appeal to some special path of knowing. To call the apprehension of being a knowing might suggest that it is a separate experience captured by some paranormal feeling, rather than a possible dimension of human life accessible to whoever is open to receiving it. Yet that does not mean that people need to be ignorant of being. Marcel himself strives to clarify the mystery of being concretely, in terms of paradigm situations that evoke the concept. The mysteries of being that he invites the reader to explore are drawn from fidelity, LOVE, family, fatherhood, and hope. Each of these turns out to have an element of mystery that goes beyond their commonplace function.

Marcel's distinction between having and being reflects a distinction between epistemology and ontology. He insists on the priority of being over knowing in order to restore to human life what he calls its neglected ontological weight. While Marcel and Buber limit themselves to using examples to evoke the mystery of being, Heidegger and SARTRE take up the apparently more formidable task of demonstrating the thesis of the priority of ontology over epistemology through systematic, phenomenological analysis. The differences between Marcel and Buber, on one hand, and Heidegger and Sartre, on the other, are more than mere variations in approach. For Marcel the matter is one of principle. Although he considers himself a phenomenologist, he does not think that being can be defined phenomenologically. Being, he says, is a mystery that can be approached only indirectly. Being is the dimension of unity underlying the diversity created by primary reflection. In *The Mystery of Being* he writes that whereas primary reflection tends to dissolve the primary unity of experience, secondary reflection helps us to recover that unity. The Cartesian divisions of soul/body and self/other are not the final answer. Beneath them lies a basic unity to which people need to return. On occasion Buber also speaks in terms much like those of Marcel on this point. For example, in his essay "What Is Man?" Buber sets out to describe the human condition in terms of the human capacity to enter into relationships with each other and with the mystery of Being, which can be apprehended through these relationships but which transcends them.

The main alternative to Marcel's and Buber's approach is provided by Heidegger's *Being and Time*. Ontology is the starting point of the book's argument; epistemological issues come up explicitly only once the framework has been built to allot them their proper place. The problem with Descartes' philosophy, Heidegger argues, is that it takes for granted a particular ontology without recognizing that it is doing so. Descartes' doctrine of things as res extensa is an example of this uncritical procedure, and Kant's critical method turns out no better. If one begins with an ontology of isolated selves and external things, there is no escape from it. Almost all modern philosophy is infected. Heidegger's approach is to begin from the vague understanding of Being with which people function. In everyday life we have a grasp of the Being of the World that, while inadequate and distorted, still provides a better guide for developing an ontology than Cartesian thought. Indeed, just because the everyday understanding is plainly confused, philosophers will not be tempted to adopt it uncritically, and they will probe it to find its ontological roots. Truth lies concealed in everyday life. The philosopher should strive to uncover it. The result of beginning ontology through an examination of the everyday is a far richer and more complex set of concepts than presented in modern philosophy. In later writings Heidegger argues that the cogito's mathematical ideal conceals the varieties of ways in which truth can be attained. Scientific investigation is not the only way something can be understood. Both the shepherd and the astrophysicist discover truth about the sun, but it is not the same truth. Yet this does not mean that the two truths are subjective in the sense of arbitrary. To call the variety of truths subjective is to retreat into a questionable philosophical position concerning the distinction between SUBJECT and object.

The existentialist contribution to understanding the concept of knowledge is shown at least as much by the ways they do not speak about the term ''knowledge'' as by the ways they do. Much of philosophy since Descartes has taken its lead from natural science and thereby conceived the term ''knowledge'' narrowly. To avoid misunderstanding, existentialists tend to shy away from such a potentially misleading term. The expressions they use to speak about knowledge—subjectivity, mystery, encounter, and truth as uncovering—are not proposed as an alternative vocabulary to say the same as traditional Cartesian epistemology. They rather restructure philosophical issues. One existentialist contribution to epistemology has been to explore the ethical implications of the quest for knowledge. The stories of Johannes Climacus' vain effort to doubt everything, Buber's encounter with the linden tree, and Heidegger's stargazing shepherd call attention to VALUE-laden contexts within which knowledge claims are made. Hence, these thinkers have opened up new ways of discussing areas of philosophy that had been marginalized because of a particular doctrine about the concept of knowledge.

Primary Works

Buber, Martin. *The Knowledge of Man*. Trans. Maurice Friedman and Ronald Gregor Smith. New York: Harper and Row, 1965.
Marcel, Gabriel. *The Mystery of Being*. Vols. 1 and 2. Trans. G. S. Fraser. Chicago: Henry Regnery, 1960.

Bibliography

Gallagher, Kenneth T. *The Philosophy of Gabriel Marcel*. New York: Fordham University Press, 1962.
Malantschuk, Gregor. *Kierkegaard's Thought*. Princeton: Princeton University Press, 1974.

LANGUAGE
Mathew Rampley

Chief among the recurrent motifs in existentialism is a distinction between authentic and inauthentic language. By inauthentic is frequently meant chatter, idle talk, and gossip. Chatter is inauthentic since language becomes a vehicle of rootless trivia. This distinction is predicated on the widespread recognition that language has both a private and a public CHARACTER; it consists of shared, socially mediated signs that persons employ in order to express their individual concerns. KIERKEGAARD repeatedly refers to the tension between EXISTENCE and language. Criticizing Hegel's view that reality can be accounted for by abstract KNOWLEDGE, Kierkegaard argues that while language uses universals, human existence has a subjective particularity irreducible to the generalizing qualities of language. He distinguishes between linguistic statements as oriented toward idealities and human existence as a concrete reality. CONSCIOUSNESS mediates between the two, thereby setting up the opposition between the individual and the general in language. Hence, abstract thinking is incapable of articulating major TRUTHS of existence; only a subjective LEAP of FAITH achieves what cannot be reached by objective knowledge.

In *Logical Investigations* HUSSERL makes a number of conceptual oppositions. The first is between the real and the ideal, or sense perception and abstract conceptuality. Conceptual thinking is based on an abstraction from the concrete world of INTUITION, for example, mathematical knowledge. The second opposition is of expression and sign; signs are lifeless until given meaning by the meaning-bestowing intentional act of consciousness. Of course, nonintentional signs do exist, for example, the canals on Mars. They merely indicate rather than mean; they have no intrinsic meaning. This contrast leads to a further opposition of meaning and reference. Expressions mean not only because of their semiotic character but also because they have an intentional OBJECT. The object need not actually exist, and an expression may have more than one object, but an expression cannot not have an object; an expression not only says something but also says it of something. Hence, the expression, as the marriage of the sign with an intentional mental act, has an intentional object, without which it would not be an expression.

In HEIDEGGER's *Being and Time*, language takes its place in a cluster of interrelated concepts including discourse, meaning, gossip, assertion, what-is-said-in-the-talk, and what-is-talked-about. Primary among these is discourse, which is one of the fundamental existentialia of BEING-IN-THE-WORLD. Discourse articulates the meaningfulness of existence. Being-in-the-world is always already immersed in meaning, but not always explicitly. Articulated in discourse are Dasein's dealings with the WORLD as an environment of meanings. Discourse thus has an intentional object. Language is separate from discourse, for while discourse is an existentialia of Being-in-the-world, language is merely its contingent historical vehicle. The lifeless signs of language are given meaning only when used as bearers of discourse through the intentional activity of DASEIN. The difference between meaning and reference has been maintained in his opposition of what-is-said-in-the-talk and what-is-talked-about, where the latter is the intentional object of discourse, and the former the content of historical language. This contrast introduces the notion of idle talk as the inauthentic mode of discourse. Idle talk designates the language prevalent when Dasein succumbs to the attraction of conformity; it is the understanding of Being that the THEY has. It is founded not in Dasein's concernful dealings with the world but instead in received views. This includes the knowledge of abstract disciplines such as science and mathematics. Common to these is a rootlessness devoid of any relationship to beings-in-the-world.

Heidegger's later thought rejects the idea of language as a tool. Language speaks through Dasein, possessing a primordial POWER exceeding the grasp of Dasein's intentional states. He privileges poetic discourse as the language of the disclosure of BEING. Contrasted with POETRY is METAPHYSICS, which, as abstract circulated knowledge, covers up Being. Western society has been immersed in metaphysics for so long that it is blind to Being. However, sedimented in language, particularly in Greek, is an indication of an authentic understanding of Being. His interest in language thus follows two routes: a concern with poetry and an investigation of early Greek philosophers such as Heraclitus and Parmenides in order to recall the Greek understanding of Being. His later thought is thus a conviction that language conceals Being as much as it reveals it. Certain Greek terms become privileged as indicative of a pre-Platonic recognition of the role of language in disclosing Being. Key among these are *aletheia, logos, physis, ousia*. He notes that *logos*, meaning discourse or argument, is etymologically related to the verb *legein*, meaning to collect, gather together. Implicit in this is recognition that discourse is primarily related to beings, and to gather is to disclose and to make manifest. Similarly, *aletheia*, translated as truth, is etymologically related to *lanthanein*, to conceal, hence, the original Greek understanding of truth as unconcealment. Thus, language not only refers to beings but also discloses beings, only afterward becoming a sign for already-existing beings. The privileged locus of such a disclosure is poetic discourse. Authentic language must be perpetually disclosing beings anew.

In SARTRE's *What Is Literature?*, an opposition is made between poetry and prose. The key to language is its grounding in intersubjective relations rather than its referential-disclosive function. As he notes in *Critique of Dialectical Reason*, words ''carry the PROJECTS of the Other into me and they carry my own projects into the Other.'' For Sartre there is no distinction between discourse and empirical language, nor one between Being-with-Others and the articulation of that RELATION, since the articulation facilitates intersubjective Being. He does admit that one can become alienated from language, even one's own. This is because of the intersubjective grounding of language and, hence, how the Other interprets one's utterances can never be controlled. The Other is always implicit in one's use of language, even when not actually present. The speaker treats language as a tool for self-expression, but the recipient can rely on the resulting words only to interpret what was meant, since the intentions expressed through language are not available. For this reason *What Is Literature?* presents a preference for prose as an expression of the writer's existential SITUATION, whereas poetry engages in a magical fetishization of language that interferes with understanding.

Language can become a tool of alienation. Sartre draws a contrast between the abstract, universal qualities of conceptual knowledge and language. The weakness of conceptual discourse is apparent in its inability to capture the lived; hence, he valorizes those forms of language that express the lived in nonabstract terms. Chief among these are literary forms; he reassesses poetic discourse given its capacity to subvert normal patterns of language. He commends the poetry of Genet, which attacks bourgeois SOCIETY and that of Cesaire since it subverts the habits of colonial discourse imposed upon Francophone Africa by providing an authentic expression of the lives of colonial African existence. Sartre recognizes that the lived singularity of the individual's existence is mediated by the generalities of race, class, and gender. A truthful use of language combines the individual and the social, the particular and the universal.

Sartre retains an attachment to the notion of a prelinguistic, conscious INTENTION on the part of the individual, which can sometimes be misrepresented in language, indeed, simply misunderstood by the addressee. In *The Phenomenology of Perception*, MERLEAU-PONTY criticizes the notion that thought somehow expresses itself in words, as if conscious thought consisted of a private mental language that was translated into the public language of intersubjectivity. Language informs cognition rather than merely expressing something anterior. The idea of a conflict between individual experience and its expression in language has little place in his thought, since that individual existence has no determinate form until given it by words. Meaning is a function of language, not anterior to it. The extent of the difference between Merleau-Ponty and other existentialists can be seen in his assertion of an intentionless flux of words speaking through the individual. There is no speaking subject, struggling to articulate its existential situation, since the subject is not an origin; the meaning of that existence is given shape by the inherited public language. The individual's existence is a social event, its meaning generated by the intersubjective HISTORY of the individual's culture. He distinguishes between authentic and inauthentic modes of language. At the base of this lies an opposition between the speaking word and the spoken word. With speaking word Merleau-Ponty means those linguistic practices that introduce new meanings into the world. It is authentic in that it makes explicit the fact that language produces meaning rather than merely representing it; indeed, he regards only the speaking word as the articulation of true thought. In contrast the spoken word consists merely of the expression that is already established and has become common currency. Its object appears to be always-already there, which encourages the illusion of a meaningful world anterior to language. Thus, the spoken word merely encourages speakers to forget the role of linguistic praxis in creating meaning in the world.

Primary Works

Heidegger, Martin. *On the Way to Language*. Trans. Peter D. Hertz. New York: Harper and Row, 1971.
Husserl, Edmund. *Logical Investigations*. Trans. J. N. Findlay. London: Routledge, 1970.

Bibliography

Kockelmans, Joseph J., ed. *On Heidegger and Language*. Evanston, IL: Northwestern University Press, 1972.

LEAP

Peter Royle

The leap, variously known as "the leap of FAITH" and "the existential leap," is usually interpreted as the act of self-definition and commitment, performed in ignorance of its consequences, whereby an individual gives meaning and direction to one's LIFE by transcending one's daily EXISTENCE. It is ordinarily associated with ANGUISH. CAMUS' *The Myth of Sisyphus* has done much to popularize the leap, which he regards as the defining characteristic of existential thinkers.

In *Stages on Life's Way* KIERKEGAARD's concept of the leap is most fully developed. Between the aesthetic and religious stages lies the ETHICAL STAGE, which is a bridge between the AESTHETIC STAGE of pure immediacy and orientation toward the outside WORLD and the RELIGIOUS STAGE of pure inwardness or inclosing reserve. A PERSON moves from stage to stage by a leap. To take an analogy from NATURE, the ethical is to the aesthetic and the religious what the chrysalis is to the caterpillar and the butterfly. Whereas the aesthetic is superseded in the ethical through finite reflection, the ethical is superseded in the religious through infinite reflection. Both the ethical, the sphere of the universal, and the religious, that of the singular, are dialectical, but whereas in the ethical we have something akin to reflection in a mirror, in the religious it is as if we had the infinite reflections of two mirrors that face each other. In nature movement from the chrysalis to the butterfly, other things being equal, is inevitable; in existence we have ontological discontinuity. There is no necessary synthesis. There are leaps or failures to leap.

For SHESTOV, the enemy of life and FREEDOM is not ignorance but KNOWLEDGE. Unlike JASPERS, for whom the leap of faith is the conclusion of a reverence for science, Shestov relates to GOD from the beginning. The seeker of TRUTH would be forced to admit that life is, in its very immediacy, full of contradictions incomprehensible to reason; it is absurd. But this absurd is, for Shestov, God, a Being whose freedom is so absolute that it is not even bound by reason and the laws of contradiction and identity. Not for him the God of the philosophers, who is not free to make two plus two equal five, to act in defiance of his nature or to alter the past; and not for him the age-old attempt of humankind to emancipate itself through reason instead of freeing itself from it. To continue to partake of the fruit of the Tree of Knowledge instead of that of the Tree of Life is to concede, with Hegel, that the serpent in Eden was right. God intended humans to share in his own freedom; to do it, they have to make the leap of faith.

For HEIDEGGER, the primordial leap is the leap into existence of DASEIN; human existence is, as the etymology of the word existence implies, BEING outside oneself. With Dasein ontological discontinuity and therefore leaping or its possibility come into the world. Thus, on the basis of LANGUAGE, all newness or emergence of fresh forms of being involves some sort of leap. But whereas newness in nature appears to be preprogrammed, and different beings lie side by side in spatial and temporal continuity, Dasein involves discontinuity both with the universe and with itself. If the coming into being of new forms were to be considered a leap, then the emergence of Dasein would have to be seen as a leap into leaping; but for Heidegger we are thrown into being; existence, or self-temporalization, irrespective of any progression to higher or lower existence-spheres, is a leap. But this leap is also a being-thrown, and it can also be a fall. My first state, from which AUTHENTICITY has to be wrested, is dispersion in the THEY. Instead of resolutely defining myself and my goals in relation to my own DEATH, I allow indifferent others to dictate my behavior, and I become like a thing in the middle of the world instead of engaged in things in the world. Authenticity, therefore, involves a leap out of the dreary, but comfortable, abyss into which I have fallen. It results in a gathering together and a taking root, allowing Being to be.

In SARTRE's ONTOLOGY, human reality, which irrupts into the world, is fundamentally a PROJECT, or a self-temporalizing leap into the future, generating those meanings and ends in the light of which external reality reveals itself. Without freedom and freely created goals the world could not be nihilated and would therefore remain unknown. But the project whereby meaning comes to the world, enabling me to see things as tools and obstacles and giving me reasons to act in a specific way, is necessarily beyond reason. Reason comes into being through the project and not vice versa. How my initial prerational project can be changed in the light of rational considerations is a theme of Sartre's ETHICS and political writings. Freedom always involves a break with the past and a leap into a largely unknowable future. If I wish to be fully human and free, I must continue to leap forward, like a constantly flowing river, toward a future that remains open, even though I know it will lead to my death. There are for Sartre existence-spheres through which the for-itself passes by means of leaps: ek-stases. The first ek-stasis is that of prereflective consciousness. The second is that of reflection proper. In the third ek-stasis the for-itself splits, and a real Other comes into being. The passage from one ek-stasis to another is effected by a leap, a sort of metaphysical leap into the void.

Camus holds that the movement from the absurd to TRANSCENDENCE in the philosophies is gratuitous and therefore irrational. Honesty demands that we remain within the realm of the absurd and the limits of human reason. But, irrationalists would maintain, this is not possible as long as reason is defined in the monolithic way it is. If even not to choose is a choice, then every human act must be ignorant of some of its consequences and involves risk. The difference between those who choose not to choose and those who choose to choose is that the latter make an explicit or implicit leap of faith; the former either remain on the edge of the precipice or fall into the abyss.

Primary Works

Kierkegaard, Søren. *Stages on Life's Way*. Trans. Howard V. Hong and Edna H. Hong. Princeton: Princeton University Press, 1988.
Shestov, Lev. *In Job's Balance*. Trans. Camilla Coventry and C. A. Macartney. Athens: Ohio University Press, 1975.

Bibliography

Perkins, Robert L., ed. *Fear and Trembling* and *Repetition: Volume 6 of International Kierkegaard Commentary*. Macon, GA: Mercer University Press, 1993.

LEBENSWELT
Phyllis Kenevan

The *Lebenswelt* or WORLD of everyday LIFE is the ordinary world of practical concerns. It is the world I am born into, which I assume existed before me, and the reality I take for granted in ordinary involvement with others in the affairs of practical life. It includes not only physical NATURE but also a common, shared social and cultural milieu that predates any philosophic or scientific articulation of epistemological problems. Because our preoccupied absorption in ordinary living is, for the most part, unreflective, philosophers have traditionally missed its ontological significance as a mode of knowing self and world and limited themselves to a derivative theoretical mode, which effectively barred access to knowledge of BEING. BERDYAEV pointed out that thinkers devoted to EPISTEMOLOGY seldom arrive at ONTOLOGY. Although there are differences between the philosophers identified with phenomenological ontology, there is nevertheless a similarity in method and basic concepts. The phenomenological method originated with HUSSERL; although he was committed to the philosophic pursuit of a pure descriptive science of ESSENCES, which meant bracketing the natural standpoint, in later writings he described the world as a totality of horizons of lived experience. He influenced the existentialists, who claimed that the ''I'' was not an isolated SUBJECT but was linked to a world.

KIERKEGAARD describes the failure of speculative PHILOSOPHY to focus on what really matters: how we ought to live. He ridicules the philosopher of abstractions, the systematizer who builds elaborate castles only to live in a shack nearby; he insists that what may be gratifying for abstract speculation in no way meets the need for an understanding that one can take into one's life. NIETZSCHE criticized philosophy for its obsessive attachment to epistemology and objectivity, to contemplation without interest, which he called nonsensical absurdity. He argued for a variety of perspectives and affective interpretations and offered a redefinition of objectivity as one encompassing multiple perceptions. Both SARTRE and HEIDEGGER begin their analysis of human EXISTENCE with this lived world, the ordinary world of our practical concerns. Heidegger describes the world of immediate experience as a surrounding environment experienced in terms of practical PROJECTS, a world of tools ready for our use. The world I experience is one that precedes any subject/object dichotomy; it is a world in which I am involved and dwell, a world I am familiar with. It is also a world that I share with others. Being the most primordial, this BEING-IN-THE-WORLD reveals most closely what humans are, as well as the direction to take for an ontology. In contrast, theoretical knowing takes us away from ontology. Since it never leaves the ONTIC meaning, it can give us facts only about entities but never the BEING of those entities. For that reason the Cartesian approach, which overlooked the immediacy of experience, could not answer questions about Being and generated unanswerable questions.

In the primordial environmental world, SPACE is not a dimension but a direction in which one experiences distance as remoteness or nearness. In lived space, my concern makes OBJECTS near or far. Paris may be closer to me than the adjoining suburb, and the stars I gaze at through a telescope may be closer than the glasses on my forehead. Measured space is derivative from primordial space. As Heidegger holds, the world is not in space, nor is space in the SUBJECT; space is in the world. By existing in the world, we spatialize it. Similarly, lived TIME is as we experience it; a visit can be long and tedious or pass in a flash. As humans we are historical beings-in-the-world from the moment of birth and understand ourselves from then on in terms of the world in which we find ourselves. The ordinary, everyday preoccupied self is, for the most part, a public self, an anonymous THEY, although that inauthentic mode is also capable of modification. AUTHENTICITY and inauthenticity are modes open to CHOICE.

In *Being and Nothingness*, Sartre describes being with others through patterns of BAD FAITH in which persons try to evade RESPONSIBILITY. Self-understanding in the everyday public mode is nonreflective. In this mode, according to Heidegger, one is disburdened of individual responsibility and falls into the anonymous they. This has a tranquilizing effect, allowing me not only to evade responsibility but also to evade an ever-present threat of ANXIETY, which, when it comes, breaks the hold of the anonymous self and frees me to hear the call of conscience. Sartre describes this modification as evoked by the anguishing recognition of my inescapable FREEDOM. In the ecstases of temporality both Heidegger and Sartre find the ontological ground of human existence. The disclosure of my being-in-the-world as one in which I already find myself, projecting possibilities ahead of myself, is possible because my being is, in Heidegger's terms, in temporal ecstases, an openness to Being. Sartre also interprets being-in-the-world in terms of the temporal ecstases.

Recognition of human existence as a temporalizing process already involved in a world is not possible from a Cartesian starting point. Trapped in a derivative theoretical mode, the Cartesian sees human existence as substance enduring through time, confined in one's subjectivity and questioning the validity of a world outside consciousness. Thus, the Cartesian misses the existentialist conclusion that the temporal horizon projected by the human existent is, at the same time, the horizon of the world, or, as Sartre puts it, the circuit of the self is possible only in terms of the world. Without self there is no world; without world there is no self.

Primary Works

Heidegger, Martin. *The Basic Problems of Phenomenology.* Trans. Albert Hofstadter.
    Bloomington: Indiana University Press, 1982.
Sartre, Jean-Paul. *Nausea.* Trans. Lloyd Alexander. New York: New Directions, 1959.

Bibliography

Barnes, Hazel. *Sartre.* Philadelphia: Lippincott, 1973.

EMMANUEL LEVINAS
(1906–1996)
Robert Bernasconi

Born in Lithuania, Levinas moved to the Ukraine in 1917. From 1923 he studied
philosophy at the University in Strassburg; he transferred to the University of
Freiburg, where from 1928 to 1929 he attended the lectures of HUSSERL and
of HEIDEGGER. Back in France, Levinas published *The Theory of Intuition in
Husserl's Phenomenology*, which rejected Husserl's concept of INTUITION as
tainted with intellectualism. During World War II he was imprisoned in a camp
for soldiers of the French army. His wife went into hiding; no members of his
family left in Eastern Europe survived. Because of Heidegger's collaboration
with Nazism, Levinas announced the need to depart from the climate of his
philosophy. During the 1950s he wrote a series of studies proclaiming the priority of ETHICS over ONTOLOGY, culminating in *Totality and Infinity* in
1961. Soon after, he became professor of philosophy at Poitiers before moving
to Paris-Nanterre in 1967 and to the Sorbonne in 1975. In 1974, Levinas published *Otherwise than Being or beyond Essence*. Whereas *Totality and Infinity*
stated its challenge to ontology in a language that was predominantly ontological, *Otherwise than Being* wrote of substitution, persecution, obsession, hostage,
and election. He wrote essays on Judaism, some of which were collected in
Difficult Freedom. His lectures on the Talmud were also published.

Drawing on Heidegger's ontological difference between Being and being,
existence and the existent, Levinas understood existentialism to be the experience and thought of EXISTENCE as an event. In these terms, Levinas never
was an existentialist, but there is a great deal of existentialism in his writings,
such as "Evasion," a twenty-page essay from 1935, and two short books pub-

lished in 1947, *Existence and Existents* and *Time and the Other*. "Evasion" is known for introducing the term "nausea" into philosophy, before SARTRE's novel of that title. Its starting point is the assertion of the finitude and burden of BEING. Perhaps he borrowed the notion of evasion from Heidegger's *Being and Time*, which holds that DASEIN evades the Being that is disclosed in its MOOD. Levinas recognized a need for evasion, a need for escaping oneself and going beyond the traditional model of being at peace with oneself. However, just as shame shows that we are unable to hide from ourselves, so the ANGUISH of nausea reveals that we are condemned to being. The value of European civilization lies in its search for a way of surpassing being, even though the fundamental ontologism of Western PHILOSOPHY makes it impossible. He speculates at the end of the essay about escaping being by a new route, even at the risk of going against common sense.

With its discussions of fatigue, indolence, effort, and horror, *Existence and Existents* can be seen as a continuation of "Evasion." The starting point was again the ontological difference, especially the existence of the human existent, but Levinas soon introduced the idea of an existing beyond or behind the opposition between being and NOTHINGNESS, which he called the "there is." He gave the name "hypostasis" to the upsurge of the existent within impersonal being. The analysis of this "hypostasis," which amounted to a suspension of the "there is," led him to focus on the BODY and its position. It also led to a criticism of Heidegger and Sartre: they sacrificed the substantiality of the SUBJECT in an attempt to develop a notion of the spirituality of the subject, as, for example, in Heidegger's account of the ecstasis of Dasein as a being outside of itself. Later, Levinas insisted that to lose sight of the substantiality of the subject was to exclude the basis for ethical RESPONSIBILITY.

Time and the Other seeks to overcome the Eleatic notion of being in which multiplicity is subordinated to a unity. Levinas appealed only to DEATH, fecundity, and eros. This same critique was repeated in *Totality and Infinity* in the name of ethics, but in *Time and the Other* the clearest anticipation of what was to come lay in his insistence that, fundamentally, TIME was always the time of the other, not that of a solitary EGO. Contesting Heidegger's analysis of Being-toward-death, Levinas resisted the anticipation of death and insisted instead that there is always hope; death is always in the future. Although Levinas presented his account of the feminine as part of an attempt to leave the dominant tendencies of Western philosophy behind, it left him open to the charge of remaining tied to traditional sexism. He characterized the feminine in terms of alterity, thereby assuming the male perspective. In the introduction to *The Second Sex* SIMONE DE BEAUVOIR pointed out this failing. Nevertheless, *Totality and Infinity* associates the feminine with habitation and dwelling in conformity with most traditional stereotypes, just as in his discussion of fecundity he continued to focus on paternity and the son.

In the 1951 essay "Is Ontology Fundamental?" Levinas gave the first totally unambiguous indication that his challenge to the tradition was henceforth to be issued primarily in the name of ethics. He rejected Heidegger's ontological account of the relation with the Other. The Other escapes comprehension and does not encounter me on the basis of being. The Other is approached as a face. The face has an ethical significance: the Other is the sole being I can wish to kill, and yet at the same time the face makes murder impossible. Levinas does not provide an ethics so much as an account of the condition of ethics. He often encapsulated his position with a saying from *The Brothers Karamazov*: "Each one of us is guilty before everyone, for everyone and for each one, and I more than the others." This claim is presented in detail in *Totality and Infinity* in the context of his account of the face-to-face relation in which the Other puts the I in question, depriving me of my self-assurance and imposing an infinite obligation upon me. The ethical relation is asymmetrical in favor of the Other for whom I can never do enough and who demands of me more than I could ever demand for myself. This responsibility is tempered only by demands made by the third party, the others of the Other. Levinas locates the third party, in the sense of the whole of humanity, already in the eyes of the Other. Hence, ethics is from the outset in a complex relation with justice. The Other appears only enigmatically as an interruption that serves to remind me that even if equality had been accomplished, that would still not satisfy one's ethical demands. Justice is questioned by ethics, just as ethics is corrected by justice. The third party is the embodiment of neutral reason. This sets up a contrast with the face-to-face, which can be approached only from within.

Many of Levinas' later works are a response to the difficulties of negotiating how one might articulate philosophically what seems to stand outside philosophy. This issue emerges in *Totality and Infinity* largely in terms of Descartes' notion of infinity as a thought that overflows the attempt to think it. Levinas disregards the way in which Descartes takes this as a proof of God's existence. He dismisses proofs of God as irreligious, much as an attempt to provide a foundation for ethics is unethical, insofar as it starts by denying ethics. He appealed to Descartes' account, first, because it supports his discussion of the thought of the Other as a reversal of Husserlian intentionality and, second, because Descartes approaches the idea of the infinite by first establishing the cogito. The conflict between the order of knowing and the order of being attracts Levinas. He employs it to articulate how the separation of the I from the Other saves the I from being overwhelmed by the Other. This structure safeguards the sphere of responsibility of the subject and so makes ethics possible. Levinas' use of the notion of infinity might seem an affront to the philosophy of finitude. Heidegger developed an account of the finitude of humans in the context of being toward death in *Being and Time* and of his reading of Kant. But, just as Hegel recognized that the notion of human finitude borrows its sense from its opposition to an idea of infinitude, so Heidegger recognized that talk of human finitude is parasitic on THEOLOGY and abandoned this formulation. As Levinas explained, infinity is located within the totality, within history, and not outside it. Even if the term "infinity" is not unproblematic, it is not related to finitude in a simply negative fashion.

There is debate as to the extent to which *Otherwise than Being* represents a new version of Levinas' thought. Certainly, many descriptions found in *Totality and Infinity* persist in later works. Nevertheless, a change of emphasis is unmistakable. This is most apparent in the central notion of substitution, which is defined in terms of Rimbaud's "I is an other." Whereas in *Totality and Infinity* the separation of the same from the Other was conceived spatially in terms of distance, here the emphasis shifted to proximity, with the difference between the self and the Other being thought as a temporal interval. He again resisted the denial of the substantiality of the subject found in the reduction of subjectivity to the Sartrean for-itself. Levinas also sought to go behind the CONSCIOUSNESS of the I. Although *Totality and Infinity* described a PROCESS in which the I was put in question by the Other, the concept of the I was never questioned. In *Otherwise than Being* the oneself finds its hypostatization in a responsibility for others called obsession. The putting into question of all self-affirmation comes to be expressed in such formulations as "I am in myself through the others," which brings together what *Totality and Infinity* sought to separate. I am accused not only by the poverty or need of the Other but also by the fact of my being persecuted. I am responsible for the persecutor at whose hands I suffer persecution. This is not hyperbole but the result of decades of reflection on Nazi persecution.

Heidegger is alluded to in almost every philosophical text Levinas has written. About other existentialists, he has been less forthcoming. This is especially true of Sartre. Apart from a short essay written on the occasion of Sartre's death in 1980, largely concerned with Sartre's relation to Judaism, Levinas has had little to say about him, beyond acknowledging his importance. Levinas read MERLEAU-PONTY. "Meaning and Sense," an important essay written between *Totality and Infinity* and *Otherwise than Being*, includes a discussion of Merleau-Ponty that relates the latter's philosophical position against Platonism to his political stance against colonization. By passing through anti-Platonism, Levinas attempted to return to a new Platonism that transcends culture and HISTORY but does so through the directionality of ethics. Levinas rejects KIERKEGAARD's account of the sacrifice of Isaac that suggests that the ethical level is surpassable. Although Levinas' critique of Hegel borrowed from Kierkegaard, it does not take the form of an appeal to subjectivity. ROSENZWEIG's critique of Hegel in *The Star of Redemption* was more decisive for Levinas, especially in directing him to creation as that which resists systematization. Although Levinas is sometimes considered a philosopher of dialogue, his approach is very different from that of MARCEL and BUBER. These thinkers characterize the I–Thou relation in terms of Being in the sense of presence; Levinas locates the face-to-face beyond being. Buber characterized the I–Thou relation as reciprocal, whereas for Levinas it is asymmetrical. He insisted on the ethical dimension; one could not approach the Other without attending to his or her needs or, as Levinas would say, with empty hands.

Primary Works

Levinas, Emmanuel. *Ethics and Infinity*. Trans. Richard Cohen. Pittsburgh: Duquesne University Press, 1985.
——. *Existence and Existents*. Trans. Alphonso Lingis. Dordrecht: Kluwer, 1978.
——. *Otherwise than Being or beyond Essence*. Trans. Alphonso Lingis. The Hague: Martinus Nijhoff, 1981.
——. *Totality and Infinity*. Trans. Alphonso Lingis. Pittsburgh: Duquesne University Press, 1969.

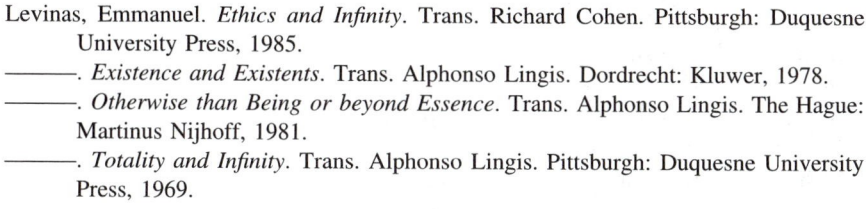

LIBERTY
Frank Schalow

For existentialists, the term ''liberty'' frequently includes a radical sense of FREEDOM—not only the distinctive potential and empowerment that humans possess but also the channeling of such freedom in order to promote the welfare of individual and SOCIETY. Thus, liberty harbors a teleological sense that supplies direction to the CHOICES humans make and yields a benefit in which all individuals can share. Liberty emerges as humans expand the scope of their freedom. If society provides the context for liberty, it also includes conditions of enslavement. A PERSON's relation with others can be as much an obstacle as a factor in one's liberation. In projecting possibilities, human EXISTENCE often reveals itself according to extremes of self-surpassing and BAD FAITH, of AUTHENTICITY and inauthenticity. Liberty becomes manifest when a person overcomes one's mode of deprivation or enslavement. The self does not acquire liberty as a possession but attains it through the struggles of life and the conflicts inherent in society. Thus, liberty corresponds to the possibility of choosing authentic selfhood.

HEIDEGGER coins the term ''resoluteness'' to describe the dynamics of choice by which an individual cultivates the possibilities of a common heritage or destiny. The authentic self thereby exhibits the heroism of overcoming the dominance of the status quo, of the anonymous THEY. The hero embodies the conflict and struggle required to inaugurate a deeper experience of historical TRUTH as unconcealment. Here Heidegger echoes NIETZSCHE's appeal to the exceptional human, the SUPERMAN, as elevating humanity to its highest creative peak. For both thinkers liberty emerges within a political arena through the empowerment of the individual. Thus, Nietzsche opposes the way educational institutions relegate the individual's pursuit of excellence to the standards of the masses, to the lowest common denominator. Self-empowerment, however, must extend to individuals whose historical circumstances seem to preclude that end. Indeed, liberty may develop in response to the various forms of political oppression in which different factions within society become oppressed and disfranchised. Thus, BEAUVOIR emphasizes the need to restore equality among the sexes. Those who are excluded from the mainstream of society also hold forth the possibility of a more radical exercise of freedom that can break the bonds of oppression. As with DOSTOYEVSKY's underground man, the quest for freedom requires an antiauthoritarian stance, which aims to rescue the integrity of the individual from the pressures of social conformity. As inseparable from its political embodiment, liberty arises in defiance of tyrannical structures. Freedom remains so irrepressible that even the reign of a totalitarian authority may not completely squelch the person's initiative to choose. Even when bereft of all other benefits and privileges, each person still can choose one's attitude.

Liberty becomes a crucial issue at that historical juncture where political hegemony reigns, and totalitarianism flourishes. A key existential motif suggests that liberty can be achieved only within a crucible of political struggle and decision. SARTRE draws upon his experience of participating in the French Resistance movement against Nazism. He considers the existential PROJECTS whose development would establish the social institutions through which the welfare of humanity can best be achieved. Sartre initially locates the origin of freedom in the individual. Yet he gradually acknowledges that the meaning of individual projects must be delineated on a social scale. No matter where or when totalitarianism may manifest itself, liberty can be achieved only through cooperative effort in which specific projects converge on a commonly held end. If the exercise of freedom can be construed as a POWER, then to avoid totalitarianism is to take steps to prevent the concentration of such power in the hands of a few. Liberty can be attained when individuals cooperate to extend the scope of freedom and take the necessary steps to counter totalitarian regimes.

The emphasis on liberty and fraternity, which sprang from the French Revolution, assumes a Marxist form in Sartre's political writings. He correlates liberty with the overcoming of economic and social oppression. Yet liberty cannot be identified with any simple, ideological formula. Revolutionary praxis that aims to liberate must be open to self-criticism and to the retrieval of its deeper roots in the meaning-engendering project of human existence. To promote liberty is to harness society's resources for the purpose of achieving justice through political activism and reform. Thus, existentialism equates liberty with emancipating the person through the development of a society that can maximize freedom for all.

Primary Work

Sartre, Jean-Paul. *Critique of Dialectical Reason*. Trans. Alan Sheridan. London: Verso, 1982.

Bibliography

McBride, William L. *Sartre's Political Theory*. Bloomington: Indiana University Press, 1991.

LIFE
Stuart Charme

Existentialists direct attention to the specific, concrete lives of humans. Our personal experiences of living must guide our reflections about life. Life must always be the beginning point from which all other thoughts, VALUES, or ideals are discussed. KIERKEGAARD and NIETZSCHE were disturbed by philosophical systems that drained the vitality out of human existence. Too often in the HISTORY of PHILOSOPHY, humans had been reduced to disembodied, rational MINDS that were alienated from their BODIES and much of their EXISTENCE or to interchangeable markers within a system in the movement of History.

Existentialists reject transcendent or supernatural models for explaining the meaning and purpose of human life. Acceptance of the paradigms of traditional religious SOCIETY is no longer viable. Nor does the purpose of life lie in the enjoyment of pleasure, the pursuit of happiness and security, or the detached exercise of reason. Rather, humans should eschew simple answers about life and passionately confront the radical absurdity at the core of their EXISTENCE. From birth, one discovers oneself thrown into a WORLD for which there is no obvious justification. Each life begins with no explanation for why it is occurring at this particular time, in this particular family and culture. These elements constitute the SITUATION in which one's life will occur and to which one must devise a response. This discovery of life's CONTINGENCY can be a source of ANGUISH. Likewise, one has immense FREEDOM to fashion a limitless range of responses to life's absurdity. For Kierkegaard, despair and dread are an indispensable platform from which authentic, religious FAITH can be launched.

To steer one's life between nihilistic despair and the hypocrisy of conventional RELIGION requires a personal commitment, a LEAP of faith that connects one to the reality that grounds one's life.

Because of their emphasis on the meaninglessness of human life, Nietzsche and SARTRE are considered nihilistic. However, their rejection of preexisting meanings for life is a prerequisite for CREATIVITY. Nietzsche portrayed life as dangerous and risky, punctuated by inevitable pain and suffering but also teeming with possibility. He emphasized the strength of those who can live in a meaningless world and the POWER of the human WILL to wrest meaning and values from random and accidental experiences. These thinkers demand an attitude of intense self-awareness and self-affirmation in the face of life's absurdity and meaninglessness—without the support of a divine guarantor of life's meaning and purpose. Humans must carve out significance for life in spite of its absurdity. One should become an active creator of one's life. Thus, each person must accept RESPONSIBILITY for what one makes of one's life. Only humans can choose the meaning of their lives, since human CONSCIOUSNESS creatively participates in the establishment of structure and meaning in the world. Nietzsche insisted that a PERSON can will his or her past, not by reversing the direction of TIME but by accepting the events of one's life as irreplaceable. Similarly, Sartre argued that people choose the lives they lead; he means that every person will determine the weight and meaning to give to each of the facts of one's existence, such as race or sex. Even identical twins can choose very different lives.

An authentic human life faces the absurdity of existence and embraces the freedom of human consciousness; an inauthentic life flees the anguish of freedom into illusions, superficial pleasures, and bogus identities. The mass thinking of the modern world leads people to conform their lives to the way one is supposed to think and act. Modern life has become dehumanized and depersonalized. Authentic life requires active engagement in the concrete reality of one's situation rather than passively suffering it. A life ruled by an endless cycle of production and consumption is ultimately empty, particularly if it distracts one from a serious struggle with the question of life's meaning. Nietzsche heroically demanded that a fully human person regard his or her life as a creative achievement that he or she would be willing to live through again and again in its most minute detail. Such a person accepts the critical contribution that every detail of one's life makes to who one is. REDEMPTION is not to be found in another realm but in the embrace of every aspect of one's life as worth reliving eternally.

For TILLICH, a fully human life requires that one grapple with the depth dimension of human existence. Authentic religion is not a separate, independent component of life but rather the sense of ultimate concern about the spiritual aspects of life that inform how one makes sense of, and acts in, the world. One must struggle with the meaning of one's life and commit oneself to what one feels to be ultimately real. One's ultimate concern is the lens through which a person's life can be understood, since it reveals the grounding of his or her sense of reality. Authentic life begins with an act of faith reaching out to GOD as a partner in encounter. Such faith is not a matter of affirming dogma or observing ritual but rather a way of life based on an absolute, personal relationship with God.

Human life is an unfinished project that continues to unfold in the future. Its meaning as whole can always be altered by events or CHOICES that have not yet occurred. One's life is like a creative work of ART in progress in which each part is illuminated by every other part; new parts bring fresh views on everything that preceded. Sartre described every life as being animated by an initial choice that is expressed in values, meanings, interests, and deeds, which he called a fundamental PROJECT. The fundamental project is the way of life that a person creates for himself or herself. It is the continuously recovered sense of whole that develops in time and that constantly synthesizes the past, present, and future of one's life. Each concrete act is a potential symbol of a person's total mode of BEING. Individual acts are meaningful only in relation to the fundamental project of which they are expressions, but the fundamental project can be deciphered and understood only in terms of these individual acts. Only by looking back over a life can one reconstruct the path it has followed and the original choice a person has made. Kierkegaard observed that while life must be lived forward, it can be understood only backward. For Sartre, one must choose between living one's life or telling about it. Each is a distinct dimension of both what my life is and what it is not. While I am alive, my life is more than just my past. It constantly eludes my grasp. In one sense, parts of my life are over. Whether I regret them or feel proud of them, I cannot change them. However, my regret or pride subtly changes with how I integrate my past into my life. My sense of what it means to be alive and what my life means fluctuates in time. I feel most fully alive when I am pursuing some project. When my projects become stale, I may slide toward despair.

MARCEL and Sartre understand that my life is present to my consciousness in the form of a story whose narrative structure I determine. This story is not a chronological inventory of episodes nor a precise reproduction of my life. It is a selective condensation and interpretation, a synthesis that is colored by my attitudes and values at the time I tell it. I add meaning to events that they did not have when I lived them. My life in the story is different from the life I lived, since my telling has been influenced by knowing too much and yet too little. As I tell the story of my life, I must determine the point of the story and if there even is one. Hence, it is true that my past is and yet is not my life. I now know things that I couldn't have known when certain past events occurred; yet next time I may tell the story of my life differently, since the future is open to new, unforeseen developments. Ultimately, the life that I will have in the future, which is permanently unknowable for me, will give meaning to my present and past. My life reveals itself like a melody, with each note reverberating on the ones that preceded and waiting the ones that follow it to achieve their full richness. I must assume responsibility for my life but also accept my freedom to transcend what my life has meant until this moment and to make myself anew. Marcel described the difficulty of getting a grasp of my life. I might keep a diary in which I record the succession of events, thoughts, dreams, and actions that transpire daily. My life would thus be presented as a disparate collection of unrelated material. However, my past is more than this random succession. A diary will likely fail to express the overall coherence I experience and that I describe when I reflect on my past at a distance. Also, though it is closer to actual events of my life than an autobiography, even a diary imposes a structure and meaning to events and feelings. When I read the diary at a later time, I realize that it both is and is not my life.

Human life is lived in the presence of others. Life is not a solitary enterprise with occasional interruptions by other people. One is born into a set of RE-LATIONS with the world. BUBER placed relation at the core of life. Authentic life requires a dialogical relationship with NATURE, with other people, with spiritual beings, and with God. The I–Thou relation offers a deeper dimension of life than the ordinary I–It relations that constitute much of modern life. Marcel likewise described relations with others as constitutive of authentic life. Authentic life transcends manipulative or possessive relations, which are dominated by desires and FEARS, to relations of simply being with another person, of being fully present to the Other, and appreciating the MYSTERY of the Other's life. In the loving relationship each partner helps to constitute the other in an act of creative fidelity. For Sartre, the presence of the Other reveals a dimension of my life over which I have no control. My life is a struggle between the meanings that I give it and those that the Other gives to it.

Consciousness and anticipation of DEATH are an important part of life. Indeed, the affirmation of life in the face of death gives life its special meaning. Nietzsche held that death could be a victorious experience when one ceases to fear or flee it as an enemy secretly sneaking up on oneself and affirms death as the natural consummation of one's life. HEIDEGGER believed that AUTHEN-TICITY requires moving from the notion that one must die to the personal realization that I must die. Such awareness of death enables me to live authentically. Awareness of death awakens me to my life as an individual distinct from the mass and responsible for my own project. By accepting my ANXIETY, by being prepared for death, I am freed to live openly and creatively. For Sartre, death is not something that I experience. Death is the final absurdity, since it stops my project in midcourse and turns the meaning of my life over to the Other. Death makes life into a thing and prevents me from ever looking at my life as a whole. I cannot truly contemplate my own death, since that would require taking on the viewpoint of the Other who survives me. In death, my life has become an object for the Other, reduced to my past. The project that was my life becomes solidified into a story that has ended and is told by another.

For many existentialists, the ultimate meaning of life is a mystery. As Marcel pointed out, a mystery, unlike a problem, is not something that can be solved or fully explained. It is the foundation from which we ask questions. Thus, our view of life is always partial; we remain enveloped by its mystery even as we interrogate it.

Primary Works

Marcel, Gabriel. *Creative Fidelity*. Trans. Robert Rosthal. New York: Farrar, Straus, and Giroux, 1964.

Nietzsche, Friedrich. *The Will to Power*. Trans. Walter Kaufmann and R. J. Hollingdale. New York: Vintage, 1969.

Bibliography

O'Malley, John B. *The Fellowship of Being: An Essay on the Concept of Person in the Philosophy of Gabriel Marcel*. The Hague: Martinus Nijhoff, 1966.

LITERATURE
Jana Sawicki

One finds existential motifs in a wide array of literary texts throughout the nineteenth and twentieth centuries. In addition, nineteenth- and twentieth-century existentialists were profoundly influenced by literary figures and theories. Many thinkers wrote literary works. Many of their writings straddle and interrogate the boundaries between the literary and the philosophical. Thus, while some used literary techniques to convey and explore existentialist themes, others challenge the propriety of prevailing philosophical modes of discourse and use literature to develop alternatives. French existentialists were widely renowned not only for philosophical and literary writings but also for their literary criticism. SARTRE discussed the meaning and social HISTORY of French literature and located existentialism within this history in *What Is Literature*? He also developed a theory of the role of the writer in SOCIETY.

KIERKEGAARD and NIETZSCHE both employed literary techniques. They frequently exhibited a preoccupation with questions concerning style. Kierkegaard employed an indirect method of communication with the reader, and Nietzsche challenged the assumed priority of EPISTEMOLOGY and META-PHYSICS over literature, emphasizing the linguistic character of reality. The starting point of Kierkegaard's PHILOSOPHY was the immediate, concrete experience of the existing individual who is cut off from any absolute perspective on reality and consequently must find his or her own moral and religious TRUTH. He rejected Hegel's one-sided emphasis on speculative and abstract philosophical prose, as well as efforts to sum up reality through a deductive method. He preferred literary forms, stories, or fragments of LIFE, which he found to be more adequate for describing the rich experience of individuals in the agonizing and isolating process of decision and self-formation.

Either/Or contains a series of first-PERSON pieces written by four fictitious authors. Kierkegaard's use of pseudonyms serves several functions. First, it distances the author from the work and thereby discourages the reader from identifying the ideas expressed as those of the author. This aesthetic distancing also stimulates reflection. It helps Kierkegaard present numerous imaginary possibilities for living life rather than attempting to persuade the reader through direct argument of the superiority of his religious path to true CHRISTIANITY. Second, it enables Kierkegaard to multiply perspectives on life rather than occupy the impossible place of an omniscient author. None of the viewpoints presented gain ascendancy. Nor is any one more persuasive than the other. Thus, he rejects the Hegelian idea that all conflicting viewpoints can ultimately be reconciled in a rational system; the reader learns the necessity of choosing his or her way. Finally, multiple pseudonyms exemplify Kierkegaard's view of the relationship between SUBJECTS. Each individual is an isolated CONSCIOUSNESS incapable of knowing others and GOD directly. A certain detachment is built into human RELATIONS. The individual is constantly thrown back on the self and reminded of the difficult effort needed to become an authentic individual and Christian.

Nietzsche was also skeptical of philosophical system building. His *The Birth of Tragedy* offers a theory of the birth and decline of Greek tragedy in which he challenges the prevailing view of the Greek SPIRIT as cheerful and optimistic and replaces it with a complex analysis of Greek literature as a beautiful and creative response to existential suffering, as a dialectical synthesis of Apollonian and Dionysian elements. He holds that the emergence of Platonic philosophy and its emphasis on Socratic dialectic brought the demise of Greek tragedy. Nietzsche's writings are experiments in literary style. Many of his books are collections of aphorisms. He referred to his aphoristic style as the style of decadence, which he used to undermine decadence in lazy and intellectually dishonest readers of his time looking for truth in short, pithy maxims. His writings express a preoccupation with the rhetorical aspects of LANGUAGE. He criticized the naive belief in an unrhetorical, natural language that represents or refers to a fixed OBJECT or thing-in-itself. Metaphysical concepts might be grammatical fictions, that is, effects of language rather than its referents. He emphasized the interpreted CHARACTER of reality and the perspectival character of interpretations and analyzed interpretations and evaluations of existence in terms of their VALUE for life. His *Thus Spoke Zarathustra* could be regarded as designed to introduce an alternative set of terms, values, and questions, to define philosophy as a creative, transformative, and life-affirming mode of being without grounding in metaphysical absolutes.

RILKE's POETRY, novels, and letters exhibit his preoccupation with the difficulties of writing and the relationship between ART, particularly poetry, and life. His poems present terrifying and painful dimensions of EXISTENCE, the centrality of change and finitude, the human desire for TRANSCENDENCE, and the constitutive NATURE of language. He suggests that the poetic act be understood as a form of existential REDEMPTION. Rilke's fictitious diary, *The Notebooks of Malte Laurids Brigge*, is a model of the antihero's search for an authentic relationship to life and DEATH. His masterful *Duino Elegies* reflects an affirmation of life and an earthly spirituality.

KAFKA's novels and short stories recognize the revelatory POWER of extreme SITUATIONS and psychological states. The protagonists in his novels *The Trial* and *The Castle* live in an absurd relationship to the WORLD. Demands for transcendent meaning, justice, and redemption are frustrated. Kafka's predilection for the fragment and the rich ambiguity of his symbols forcefully represent the isolation, alienation, and frustration that accompany the human search for meaning in an apparently godless world.

HEIDEGGER referred to Rilke's *Elegies* as a lyrical version of his philosophical treatise *Being and Time*. In this early work, he portrays humanity as immersed in instrumental relations to a world, as having forgotten the question of what it means for anything to be. Throughout his writings, Heidegger attempts to reintroduce the problem of BEING, to resurrect a sense of ourselves as questioners and interpreters of existence, and to restore to philosophy a thoroughly historical self-understanding. His works reflect an increasing awareness of the historical contingency of current practices and meanings. The philosophical language we have inherited is not an ahistorical language of reason through which we can master reality but, rather, a historical creation of past thinkers. It is subject to question and re-creation. Being is not able to be appropriated in some correct representation or adequate language but is, instead, a source of possibility and destiny. In later writings Heidegger claimed that language was the house of Being. He defends a poetic understanding of language in which the poet-philosopher attends to the power of words to open up new meaning or to restore forgotten meanings.

SARTRE supported his philosophical work through fictional explorations of concrete experiences and situations of the individual. His first novel, *Nausea*, takes the form of a diary and conveys the existential sense of life as a succession of often discontinuous present moments moving toward an uncertain future. The protagonist, Roquentin, is writing a biography, which he abandons upon discovering that all efforts to retell a life, whether one's own or another's, are fictions. Narrative structures place an order on events that can be discerned only in retrospect and that must inevitably falsify the lived experience of the individual who must live life toward an open future. Much of the diary chronicles

Roquentin's discovery of the CONTINGENCY of existence. There are no necessary relationships between events or things. Things overflow their limits, words refuse to stick to them, and nothing can be captured once and for all, not even the self. As the truth of existence is revealed, Roquentin discovers his FREEDOM—he has no fixed ESSENCE and must create himself. At the end of the diary, Roquentin decides to write a novel. Perhaps, one can find salvation from the contingency of existence in art and IMAGINATION.

After World War II, Sartre's emphasis shifted to the moral and political dimensions of individual freedom and RESPONSIBILITY. He became preoccupied with the responsibility of the writer to effect social change by moving the reader to reflect on society and to assert his or her freedom. He distinguished between the theater of CHARACTERS and the theater of situations. He claimed that the existentialist writer must not portray the individual as determined by a character rooted in heredity or the environment. Such approaches exhibit little respect for human freedom. Existentialism is a literature in which the author attempts to explore the possibilities for creative responses to situations, sometimes extreme situations. This idea is associated with Sartre's view developed in *What Is Literature?* that writing is a mode of political action and a vehicle of communication. Thus, he preferred prose over poetry since it is a more direct and transparent medium. An example of a committed literature of extreme situations is his trilogy *Roads to Freedom*. Sartre also wrote three biographies of literary figures, Charles Baudelaire, Jean Genet, and Gustave Flaubert. In the last two he combines an existentialist analysis of the author's life with a Marxist analysis of prevailing historical structures.

Many of BEAUVOIR's early novels were inspired by her desire to develop the ethical and social implications of Sartre's existentialism. She emphasized the importance of political freedom as a condition for self-determination. Her novels provide compelling portraits of the interconnections between the personal and the political. *The Blood of Others* considers the individual's responsibility for others and the meaning of death in both political and personal terms. *The Mandarins* marks the continuation of her earlier explorations of the moral dilemmas facing persons. CAMUS is preoccupied with the absurdity of existence—the universe is indifferent to the human demand for ultimate meaning. His first novel, *The Stranger*, illustrates his philosophy of the absurd through a direct encounter with the experiences of the absurd hero, Meursault, who is a stranger to society because he refuses to play its games. He will not exaggerate his feelings and is honest about his moral indifference. Meursault's indifference mirrors the indifference of the universe as well as the dishonest indifference of the society that is condemning him. When he is condemned to die, he refuses to turn to RELIGION and affirms the value of his life despite its absurdity. Camus' later literary works investigate the themes of social responsibility, metaphysical and social EVIL, the failure of Marxist revolutionary politics, and collective rebellion against absurdity—solidarity.

The literature of the absurd is perhaps the literary movement most directly influenced by existentialism, although it also has roots in expressionism and surrealism. It emerged after World War II as a revolt against rationalism. Two leading absurdist writers, Eugene Ionesco and Samuel Beckett, portray humans as alienated and divorced from life. In this situation human actions become senseless and futile. They ignore or distort structural conventions, reject realistic settings and logical reasoning, and often contain no consistently evolving plot.

Primary Works

Kierkegaard, Søren. *Either/Or*. Vol. 1. Trans. David F. Swenson and Lillian Marvin Swenson. Princeton: Princeton University Press, 1959.
Sartre, Jean-Paul. *What Is Literature?* Trans. Bernard Fretchman. London: Methuen, 1978.

Bibliography

Baron Frank, Ernst S. Dick, and Waren R. Maurer, eds. *Rilke: The Alchemy of Alienation*. Lawrence: Regents Press of Kansas, 1980.

THE LOOK
Thomas R. Flynn

The strength and weakness of SARTRE's early social ONTOLOGY lie in his looking/looked-at model of interpersonal relations. His famous phenomenological description of the look in *Being and Nothingness* constitutes an experiential argument for the reality of other minds. Traditional arguments for the existence of other minds did not account for the certainty with which we believe there are other minds. To explain that certitude, Sartre points to the difference between my experience of being gazed upon by another and my experience of being surrounded by mere bodies. The condition for the possibility of the former experience is my immediate awareness of the other as SUBJECT. I am objectified only by the look of another being-for-itself, not by another being-in-itself. In Sartre's well-known example, a voyeur has objectified a couple through a keyhole. Suddenly, he hears footsteps behind him. In his shame-consciousness he simultaneously experiences the other as subject objectified him as embodied. Even if it happens that he was mistaken, that it was only the rustle of the curtains, the experience is still valid. It reveals his awareness of what it is to be in the presence of another subject, to exist for-another.

Bibliography

Barnes, Hazel. *Sartre*. Philadelphia: Lippincott, 1973.

LOVE
Daniel Berthold-Bond

Existentialists' discussions of love share a number of common themes: the RE-LATION between love and desire, the place of love in self-realization, the status of the other in the relationship of love, and the typology of love as sensual or aesthetic (eros), as friendship (philia), and as the participation in, and imitation of, GOD's love (agape). The possibility of love as a positive, constructive PRO-JECT is emphasized much more by the religious than by the atheist thinkers. Atheists tend to see love as highly problematic, while religious existentialists, however they may differ, describe love as capable of redeeming human existence from ANXIETY and its struggle with meaninglessness.

Love is explored by KIERKEGAARD in his pseudonymous works, as well as in several edifying discourses and journal entries. *Either/Or* offers contrasting portraits of love within its larger task of illuminating the opposition between the aesthetic and the ethical spheres of LIFE. Aesthetic love exists on a continuum between the immediate quest for sensuous pleasure as exemplified by Don Juan, each conquest just the same, each only a reiterated experience of the passing moment of pleasure, and the hypersophisticated and introspective seducer who is motivated not so much by the desire for pleasure as by the desire for the interesting. This more reflective, imaginative aesthetic disposition is characterized by the distanced observation of life and the search for distraction from the ennui of EXISTENCE. The aesthete lives in the world of the IMAGINA-TION, poetizing the self into life in order to keep quotidian reality at bay. In the playful, theatrical, poetic recasting of reality to suit the aesthete's desire for continual novelty, the Other becomes part of the aesthete's game. Love emerges as seduction. The Seducer defines woman as pure BEING for an Other, whose soul must be carefully, artistically produced and shaped into the proper state of emotional receptivity so that he may poetize himself into her feelings. It is not

Cordelia that the Seducer loves but the aesthetic idea of love. Hence, he remains distanced not only from Cordelia but from his own EMOTIONS.

An ethical conception of love is presented in the second volume of *Either/ Or* in the letters of Judge William, who reprimands the aesthete for his inner hollowness and flight from the task of becoming a genuine self. By living in the dream of imagination, he is a purely cryptic individual, a mere hypothesis of a self, existing as a constantly changing series of masks and disguises. By adopting a form of love that fails to make commitments, there is no true resolution or unification of the self. The ethical shape of love is conjugal love: in marriage, first love is transfigured through commitment. Only here may the self gain a victory over TIME, by turning away from the self-consuming nature of living always in the now, of dispersing the self in the continual pursuit of ever new, ever ephemeral escapades. Constituted as duty, love becomes truly self-determining, no longer controlled by the caprice of erotic desire, and through the resolute commitment to the other over time, conjugal love has the power to unify the self. In *Repetition*, the young man cannot sustain his erotic-aesthetic love for a girl due to a sense of a higher calling, a calling to POETRY. The girl is not a reality for him but only the occasion for awakening his poetic impulse. Like the Seducer, the young man is moved by the imaginative idea of love, by which love in a concrete sense is sacrificed, but unlike the Seducer, the young poet is ethically repulsed by the possibility of using the girl as a mere means to his own poetic fulfillment. So he leaves town and begins an experiment in working back to a recovery of his original love. His attempt to poetically reconcile himself with the girl fails, precisely because the poetic demands the TRANSCENDENCE of any particular realization of love. His apprenticeship in religious repetition, in his reading of the book of Job and his yearning for a divine intervention by virtue of the absurd, also fails. He cannot sacrifice his poetry to FAITH. For Kierkegaard, the love of God is no idea but must be concrete.

At times, Kierkegaard's pseudonyms stress that the love of God requires the sacrifice of preferential love for others, demands that we give up everything, let all go, and die to the WORLD. On the other hand, especially in *Works of Love*, Kierkegaard proposes that even eros and friendship may be transformed into genuinely spiritual possibilities of reciprocal devotion and respect. Here, love is no longer an aesthetic CHOICE of the other but an ethical-religious choice, grounded in the love of God. When transfigured in this way, eros, friendship, and love of the neighbor ultimately overlap with the nonpreferential, agape-love of God, which is the mediating force of all authentic love. To live Christianly is to strive to bring into our relations with others the presence and POWER of God's love. The love of God entails the desire to imitate, to seek to transform oneself into the likeness of the beloved. This love is not to be confused with an emotion but is a way of being.

NIETZSCHE's scathing polemic against Christian love emphasizes three themes. First, love of God implies a dying to the world, a cowardly desire to be released from the gravitational pull of life on Earth, and a denial of human responsibility for constructing its VALUES. To love God is to hate the self, which is seen as worthless and impotent. Religious love thus is the will to self-crucifixion, a sort of vampirism that sucks away all that is vital and healthy in the human WILL. Second, religious distrust of the earthly uproots love from its instinctual center in the BODY and transforms it into a passionless ethic of neighbor love. While the command to love thy neighbor might appear to entail an affirmation of the human, in fact it devalues it. We are called to love our neighbor for the sake of God, not because there is inherent value in our neighbor; but to assert the equal worth of all to be loved is to construct a MYTH of homogeneity and to deny the fundamental law of difference between humans, the pathos of distance that separates the weak from the strong, the sick from the healthy. Third, the MORALITY of neighbor love reflects the Christian seduction away from the self, the flight from individual subjectivity into a herd for which all value is already determined by the authority of the absolute Other, God.

Nietzsche grounds love in the domain of the body, the realm of instinct and will. Such does not mean that he privileges erotic or sexual love. His point is that all love originates in instinct and cannot be torn away from this origin without mythologizing it. But he agrees with Christian PSYCHOLOGY that love must be sublimated. The goal of this sublimation is not to suck away the vital force of the erotic but to channel it into creative energy by which the self becomes its own artist. Thus, love is, at its highest, self-love. Even love of fate may be seen as an expression of the value of self-love. In affirming the eternal recurrence of all things, the self seeks to unite an acceptance of fate with the will to self-creation: if all is to recur, then we must will at every moment to create ourselves as works of ART we could live with and love, again and again. Such self-love is far removed from egoism or self-satisfaction; it involves the love of one's possibilities, which prepares one for self-overcoming, transcendence, a perpetual experimentalism and artistic re-creation of the self. Love of possibilities is also seen in Nietzsche's replacement of love of the neighbor with love for the most distant possibilities of man, so that in the midst of a great contempt for man, ZARATHUSTRA finds a love for humankind in terms of its prospects for self-overcoming: what can be loved in humans is that they are an overture to the future. Friendship reflects this self-transcendence. Zarathustra seeks companions, fellow creators with whom he may engage in self-overcoming and self-perfection. My truest friend must also be my truest enemy, as one who is worthy of entering into struggle with me, testing me, strengthening me. Friendship is a dialectical interplay between the mutual creation of higher ideals and the struggle for independence and autonomy.

HEIDEGGER is taken to task by SARTRE for offering a PHENOMENOLOGY of the emotions that omits an account of sexual desire and love, resulting in an implausibly asexual DASEIN. Sartre seeks to recover the body as the original SUBJECT of love. Desire places the self in a conflictual relation with an other; love emerges as the desire to possess the other's FREEDOM so as to affirm my being-for-self. As being-for others, I am subject to the other's LOOK, which inscribes me as an object, as FACTICITY opposed to freedom, as a body for the Other. Love is a project of self-recovery of my subjectivity, or being-for-self, which is possible only through overcoming the autonomy of the other's Look and hence his or her freedom. Here arises a fundamental contradiction in the project of love. On one hand, I desire to remove the other's freedom so as to reaffirm my own, but, on the other, I desire to have the Other affirm my freedom, to love me as a subject, which requires that the Other remain free. Love is the desire to be loved, which is the desire to capture the other's freedom, to enchant and ensnare the other's subjectivity.

Love is defined by Sartre as seduction of the Other by which I attempt to get hold of the other's freedom while at the same time incarnating the Other as flesh, facticity, objectivity, body. The lover's caress is a shaping of the Other into flesh, yet in this act I impossibly require the other's freedom to appear. Thus, love emerges as an unrealizable ideal, doomed to failure. *Being and Nothingness* details the strategies of responding to the unrealizable ideal of love, strategies modeled on Hegel's master-slave dialectic. Masochism and sadism are the two basic responses to the failure of love. In masochism, the self assumes the stance of GUILT before the Other and seeks to make itself into pure body for the other, while in sadism the self strives to incarnate the other's freedom through violence. Masochism fails since I can never complete the project of self-annihilation except in DEATH—I am freedom, despite all attempts to deny it. Sadism fails because the other's freedom always threatens to awaken even in the midst of violence. Even the attempt to achieve a state of indifference to the Other must fail, since desire for the Other is an inescapable ground of my being.

BEAUVOIR does not see love as unrealizable in principle. In *The Second Sex* she stresses that, given the historical place of woman as object, it is extremely difficult for heterosexual love to be realized. Lesbian relations may offer a fuller prospect of healing the wounds of woman's reduction to object-for-man, although women in such relations must still face the temptation to submit to unequal roles and self-enslavement. *The Second Sex* emphasizes the anatomy of woman as being for man. Beauvoir agrees that for love to be possible, it must be an exchange between two equally free subjects; while she is very concerned with the difficulties for achieving this exchange, she does not share Sartre's ontological principle that it is impossible. For Beauvoir, mutual recognition as free beings is achievable: we may love without throwing our LIBERTY into question; to know the Other in love is to reach the absolute, the unification of self and self. But given woman's long apprenticeship in submission, her traditional definition as possession and prey, the fulfillment of the ideal of love is essentially a PROJECT for tomorrow, when humanity lives in its flesh in conscious liberty, and women are no longer objects of a seduction.

TILLICH argues that love is not, first of all, an emotional concept, although emotion or passion is a necessary accompaniment of love. He emphasizes the NATURE of love as a way of being and acting that he terms participation. But first of all, love is a fundamental ontological principle, grounded in being-itself, which is the same as God. Thus, Tillich agrees with Kierkegaard that love cannot be fully understood apart from faith in God and that love of God is the highest expression of human love. Love is the moving power of all life, the longing for connection and participation with the Other. This power and longing, rooted in being-itself, assume four forms: libido is love as need, the desire for connection with what satisfies such essential needs as food, motion, and sexuality; eros is the nature of love that strives for a union with that which is a bearer of values, for example, beauty and TRUTH; philia is a personal relation of the self to an other who is seen as equal to the self, the love of an I for a Thou; and agape, the highest form of love, is the unconditional desire not for one's fulfillment but for the fulfillment of the other. While eros and philia represent opposite poles of love, the one being transpersonal and the other personal, neither is fully possible without the other. Thus, to be incapable of friendship is equally to be incapable of loving the artistic expression of value. Philia and eros may be united with libido, in which case sexual attraction takes on its most authentic expression. Agape, the unconditional desire for the fulfillment of the other, is perfectly realized only by God's love for humans, although agape stands as the model and ideal for all other shapes of love.

Human love for God is erotic, the striving for union with that which transcends us in value. In faith, or ultimate concern, the self strives to give itself to the fulfillment of God's love for humankind. This striving to fulfill God's love through our love for him leads to a final point: love that is healthy is not merely the desire for union with an other but the desire for participation, an active and concernful encountering of the other in which existence becomes transformed into a significant, meaningful reality. Love as participation is a form of healing the self's fundamental anxiety before death, incompleteness, and meaninglessness. Such love, which is fully realized only in the engaged, participatory love of God, is the basis for my courage to be, the resolve and fortitude to affirm my existence in the face of anxiety. Courage is necessary for the risk of love, the opening up of the self to another, while love reinforces my courage to confront anxiety.

For BUBER love implies feeling but is not constituted by it. In *I and Thou* he writes that feelings dwell in man, but man dwells in his love. Buber stresses that the love of humanity is not the love of an abstraction, of the concept of a species-being or humanity in general or the universal neighbor, but is the concrete, direct, engaged love of particular individuals. Love is the relation of I and Thou, never a passive declaration but always a concrete meeting. In the I–It relation, the other remains an object—of desire, of curiosity, of observation; there are no genuine interrelation, no reciprocity, no opening up of two selves to each other. In an I–Thou relation, I address the other and allow myself to be addressed. Dialogical love transfigures reality into a hallowed place.

Primary Works

Kierkegaard, Søren. *Works of Love*. Trans. Howard Hong and Edna Hong. New York: Harper and Row, 1964.
Tillich, Paul. *Love, Power and Justice*. Oxford: Oxford University Press, 1964.

Bibliography

Lampert, Laurence. *Nietzsche's Teaching: An Interpretation of "Thus Spoke Zarathustra."* New Haven, CT: Yale University Press, 1986.

GEORG LUKACS
(1885–1971)
Ilan Gur Zeev

Georg Lukacs was born in Budapest as Gyorgy Bernant Lowinger, the son of Jozsef Lowinger, a wealthy Jewish banker. He is known as an important founder of Western MARXISM, especially his book *History and Class-Consciousness*. His contribution to existentialist thought belongs to an earlier period. The work of the early Lukacs is a reflection of, and a response to, the crisis of modernity, which attained apocalyptic manifestation in the horrors of World War I. He turned to the realm of aesthetic experience as part of the struggle for TRANSCENDENCE. In *Soul and Form* Lukacs formulates the existential predicament of the modern era as one where LIFE is an anarchy of light and darkness: nothing is ever completely fulfilled, and nothing ever ends. Everything flows, and each thing merges into another thing; the mixture is uncontrolled and impure; nothing ever flowers into real life. There is only eternal unfolding of everything. He rejected Hegelian historicism with its promising reconciliation and understood the absolute as NOTHINGNESS that manifests itself in the eternal, basically meaningless unfolding of life possibilities. This conception of the absolute is to be understood as the driving force of every physical movement and cultural development. Accordingly, the question of culture was always identical with the question of life as a most private struggle that has its root in ONTOLOGY. His writings reflect an effort to uncover the ontological conditions of the human life of misery and meaninglessness.

A dialectics of pessimism and utopia is the axis of Lukacs' existentialist thought. His ontology, which presents the absolute as nothingness and the life struggle as its manifestation, is typical to pessimism; there is no place for TRUTH, neither objective nor nonobjective; nor is there a possible meaning for a life struggle that challenges this inevitable reality. Human HISTORY and the life of the individual have neither telos nor meaning. This pessimism does not exclude utopia; it is an outlet to a struggle for meaning in life, purpose, and transcendence. Such is to be seen in his understanding of tragedy. The utopian potentialities depend on the possibilities for tragic life and symbolic representations of the tragedy in a meaningful way. To the SUBJECT, tragedy offers something of great VALUE, his or her subjectivity, while striving to conduct his or her life in conditions that are ontologically and historically never granted to him or her. The essay "The Metaphysics of Tragedy" in *Soul and Form* diagnoses the state of modern culture as being one in which there is no place for tragedy. Life has become a universal leveling process. Tragedy is possible where the miracle of the accident transcends the PERSON and one's life. But in modernity, life excludes accident, miracle, and transcendence; hence, life is nothing more than an endless plain with no elevations that embraces a logic of cheap security.

Lukacs condemns bourgeois culture for preventing a person from dedicating oneself to an ideal PROJECT derived from within oneself and, instead, forcing one to dedicate one's life to something independent from, and alien to, oneself. He distinguishes between authentic and inauthentic life and demands total dedication to a struggle for self-creation of the self, while understanding that even an authentic subject or the struggle for self-constitution as an authentic subject is but an OBJECT and a reflection of ontological conditions and cultural powers. These conflicting concepts might have enriched each other and could have been a central part of a general theory. But he made no effort to avoid contradictions and aporias. In contrast to his later, Marxist period he had no general theory at that time. Yet he did construct his negative utopianism.

Negative utopianism, unlike positive utopianism, does not promise a possible reconciliation of contradictions or an end to suffering, to philosophical problematics, or to history. It refuses to accept the preconditions of these positive alternatives. Negative utopianism understands that there is no place for a positive reality and no possibility of metaphysical reconciliation. Therefore, there is no place for optimism for a better future. Yet, negative utopianism refuses to surrender to the present in all its dimensions. It demands total negation of present reality. It offers self-constitution without optimism and is an imperative that is tragic in its essence since basically it brings to the self destruction of the one who strives for authenticity. It calls for accepting nothingness as the absolute and understanding that principally, under this project, there are no happy end and reconciliation. Accordingly, one has to deny the reality of current life and its limitations and possibilities in order to live. The question of tragedy or the possibility of tragedy thus becomes the question of meaning and ESSENCE. The GOD of destiny and meaning is presented as speechless and unredeemed, and he is contrasted with the gods, who alone have a voice and power in history;

their mastery reduces human beings to puppets. Tragedy appears as a threshold to life-possibilities, that is, to authentic life.

The deepest longing of a person for selfhood, the longing for transcendence and totality, is the metaphysical root of tragedy; therefore, the recognition of DEATH or the transcendence into the totality of nothingness is the essence of authentic life. Thus, the heroes of tragedy always die happy. In contrast to tragedy, the novel is an epic in a world that has been abandoned by God. Lukacs' conclusion is that the highest station an individual can reach in the modern era is insight into the NATURE of the irremediable antinomy of life at present. Negative utopianism is the only gate still open to struggle for authentic life, since there is no *Gemeinschaft*, COMMUNITY, but only capitalist-oriented bourgeois *Gesellschaft*, SOCIETY. The triumph of modernity establishes a locus of a new totality, an omnipotent, spiritless totality. The tragic ETHICS that he establishes reflect a utopian quest for a new totality, while also acknowledging that positive utopia is not to be realized in history. The tragic way is, indeed, a lonesome way.

Primary Works

Lukacs, Georg. *Essays on Realism*. Trans. David Fernbach. Cambridge: MIT Press, 1981.
———. *Writer and Critic*. Trans. Arthur Kahn. London: Merlin Press, 1970.

Bibliography

Joos, Ernest. *Georg Lukacs and His World*. New York: Peter Lang, 1987.

GABRIEL MARCEL
(1889–1973)
Sonia Kruks

Marcel described his childhood as sorrowful, overshadowed by the death of his mother when he was very young. The arid, positivist rationalism and the invincible agnosticism of his father and of the aunt who brought him up were compounded by the dry scholasticism and competitiveness of a lycee EDUCATION, which he endured in misery. He turned to a PHILOSOPHY of inner experience, to a somewhat mystical religiosity, and also to music and the writing of

DRAMA. He converted to Catholicism in 1929. Although it brought about changes of emphasis in his work, it presented no fundamental rupture with his prior thought or life. For much of his life, drama was as important to him as philosophy. Several of his plays were produced in the interwar period, but they never received the acclaim he felt they deserved.

Marcel gave the Gifford Lectures in Aberdeen in 1949–1950 and the William James Lectures at Harvard in 1961. He frequently published his reflections on political LIFE. He defended traditional Catholic VALUES, his sympathies tended to be with the Right, and he was deeply hostile to communism. However, he never joined political organizations and would not even agree to sign petitions or manifestos, since he regarded organized politics as dehumanizing. In his pursuit of ways of grasping religious experience, Marcel developed a powerful critique of Cartesianism, which atheistic French existentialists were also to echo. He was the first who demanded a situated concrete philosophy. Insisting that the concrete, lived experience is the proper starting point for philosophy and opposing abstraction and reductionism, Marcel discussed the relationship of embodiment to consciousness, the interdependence of subjectivity and intersubjectivity, and the links between individual EXISTENCE and the social WORLD—themes that SARTRE and MERLEAU-PONTY later addressed. He elaborated the broad lines of an existential PHENOMENOLOGY well before Sartre started writing. Moreover, he had done so in ignorance of the work of HUSSERL and HEIDEGGER.

Marcel's first major philosophical work, *Metaphysical Journal*, was written over the period 1914–1923 in a deliberately antisystematic, intimate diary form. Central to the work is the distinction between existence and objectivity. There is an absolute priority of existence. To be concerned with existence (rather than to search for objectivity) is to seek to discover the pure immediate, that is, those kinds of immediate experience that are, by their NATURE, incapable of intellectual mediation. Existential philosophy must undertake the delicate, paradoxical task of trying to evoke unthought and unspoken experiences such as of self, LOVE, and FEAR. Yet it must do so without destroying them by turning them into objects of contemplation. The task of philosophy is similar to that of POETRY or drama: to express that which is unexpressed and can be only indirectly expressed.

Objectivist approaches to reality—what in later works he calls the spirit of abstraction—not only are philosophically mistaken but involve an attitude to life, a way of BEING, that is destructive of the distinctly human existence. Scientists treat natural phenomena as constituting an objective order: they regard them as OBJECTS of inquiry laid out for scrutiny before the detached, scientific MIND. Marcel doubts whether this assumption of distance is justified even in the domain of natural science. What is certain is that if we treat our inner experiences in this way or take this attitude toward other people—as do many politicians and social scientists—we destroy what is distinctively human about our existence. The detached attitude of objectivism invites indifference and callousness. It is the ultimate source of violence and oppression in human affairs, the origin of political conflict.

When Descartes writes in the Third Meditation, ''I am a thing which thinks,'' he is stating a paradox that Marcel addresses: how can I be both a thing and yet also a thinking I if, as Descartes asserts, my thinking being is independent of my bodily form? What links these two Its together, assuming their conjunction in my self must be something more than chance? *Metaphysical Journal* approaches this problem from the standpoint of FAITH. The I believe is radically different from the I think. Faith is a wholly personal experience, involving its particular mode of immediate knowing, which Marcel calls MYSTERY. By contrast, the cogito implies the universality and the impersonality of the thinking SUBJECT. The kind of KNOWLEDGE that is accessible to a thinking subject is radically different from the knowledge attained through faith. In opposition to the cogito, Marcel elaborates a relation to the world that posits an existential faith, grounded in the indubitability of bodily, incarnate existence. If there is an indubitable such as Descartes sought to establish, it is an existential indubitable—my existence. Were I to deny my existence, I would not be able to assert any other kind of existence. To say that I exist means that I am more than a CONSCIOUSNESS. It means that I am manifest, having something that enables me to make my particular self known both to others and to myself. That something is not myself as cogito, but my self as BODY. As a bodily existent I feel, I sense my existence. As body I participate directly in the being of the world. To exist does not mean to think or to live as much as to experience.

Participation—a central concept in Marcel's thought—implies a nonobjective relation to Being. Reflective consciousness involves relations that are mediated, distanced; it conceives of the world of objects (including the body as object) as detached from the thinking subject. By contrast, in participation there is no distance, only a copresence, a being with the world that is not translatable into the LANGUAGE of external objects. Participation is beyond judgments of the kind we pass on the objective world. Sensations and feelings are our direct experience of the world, our mode of copresence with it, while judgment requires objectifying reflection. Only at the objectifying level of ideas of feelings can we evaluate our experience or even begin to doubt it. Fundamentally, as my body I participate in Being. While it is possible to say what the phrase ''my body'' or the related statement ''I am my body'' does not mean, it is not possible to give them a positive meaning. To say ''I am my body'' means only that I cannot say that I am anything other than my body. Such is because my relationship to my body, which is immediate, is intrinsically opaque. If I conceive of my body as a body-object, it would be comprehensible, but merely as an instrument whose function was to transmit sensations. If, however, I conceive of my body as a body-subject, all I can say is that it is immediately revealed to me through sensation, but I cannot identify myself with it through logic. My body is a mystery to me.

A problem is posed when I inquire into the world of things, or when I consider people as things, as fully distinct from the inquirer. When addressing a problem, the inquirer assumes oneself to be a detached spectator. To work on a problem is to work on something without according any attention to my relationship with it. Scientific inquiry proceeds in such a detached manner. It speaks about the world in the third person, as "it." A problem-oriented approach invites me to search for solutions and to manipulate the world. Technology is the product of problem-oriented investigation. In later works Marcel is highly critical of the encroachment of technological approaches in human affairs. For example, by treating people as mere data, as the objects of impersonal manipulation, bureaucracy reduces humans to abstractions. By contrast, in exploring a mystery I do not assume myself to be distinct from the data placed before me. Mystery does not mean an encounter with the impenetrable or indecipherable. Rather, mysteries are inaccessible to an objectifying reflection, because no clear distinction can be maintained between what is experienced and the experiencing self. My relation to my body is perhaps the most pervasively encountered example of mystery, but it is but one manifestation of the mystery of Being.

Even before becoming a Catholic, Marcel conceived this ontological mystery in religious terms as an immediate relation to GOD. Mysteries, as immediate experiences, imply our situatedness in Being. The mystery of embodiment involves my SITUATION in SPACE and TIME, but not as objective dimensions. Space and time, insofar as I am situated as a substantial, but finite, body within them, are not independent givens or externalities that define me. That "I am my body" means also that I am one with my daily surroundings and that I am one with my past. The space and time in which I am situated are specifically mine, invoked by my own participation in Being. Space and time and my situation within them pertain to the order of existence and not to that of objectivity. A real meeting of two humans is also a mystery: it is not the encounter of two distinct consciousnesses; nor does it involve the PERCEPTION by each of the other as an object. Other people are, like my body and like God, already present with me. I meet another person, a Thou, within my field of incarnate being and in no way as a threat to myself or as a potential NEGATION of myself. On the contrary, a Thou is integral to my self-fulfillment. Communication with oneself is possible only through communication with another. In the most intense I–Thou relations the boundary between myself and the other person becomes blurred. There is a fertile indistinction, where humans not only communicate but come into existence through communicating with each other.

The kinds of relations that Marcel discusses in early writings are predominantly positive: love, friendship, faith in others, loyalty. The fundamental human relationship involves always two people: the dyad of I and Thou. This dyad is mutually supporting, and the possibility of its existence appears to be independent of the presence of any wider collectivity. Its foundation is Love, a transcendental relation that takes us beyond the experience of self and other and beyond mere desire. Particularly from the early 1930s, Marcel became increasingly preoccupied with what he called (in the title of a play) "the broken world." In his essays "On the Ontological Mystery" and "Outline of a Phenomenology of Having," pessimism and despair become, in an age dominated by technicism and depersonalization, the trials against which we must struggle in faith and hope. In such volumes as *Homo Viator, Man against Mass Society*, or the later collection *Tragic Wisdom and Beyond*, there is less a celebration of communication and love than a struggle to affirm such values in the face of overwhelming threat and against the temptation to despair.

In *Being and Having*, Marcel began to explore the source of such a threat: when we seek to have, rather than endeavoring to be, forms of self-objectification arise. In our relation to our bodies such an objectifying self-relation easily appears. I can conceive of my body as something that I have instead of what I am; thus, my body is conceived as external. But when things are external, they can become separated from me. For the individual whose attitude to one's self and to the world is primarily one of having, life becomes dominated by the fear of loss. *Man against Mass Society* laments that in the modern world technological and bureaucratic approaches to life have come to predominate, along with the predominance of the masses. The SPIRIT of abstraction in its most extreme form enabled the Nazis to declare Jews and others subhuman and systematically to eliminate them. But such a spirit is not confined to Nazism; it is pervasive in the modern world. The crisis is, at root, metaphysical, a crisis of values, and thus is not to be overcome by political or problem-oriented action but only through grace and God's light. The only effective resistance to the forces of EVIL must be to struggle with the evil within ourselves. If there is ever to be peace on earth, each person must be at peace with oneself: each person will have had to overcome one's temptations to evil through inner struggle.

Marcel's phenomenology of having and his account of the insidious advance of the spirit of abstraction and of technical life provide an extended meditation on the subjective experience of modern capitalist society in which humans are depersonalized and are regarded as no more than their technical function in society. He once described himself as a liberal who had become more and more painfully aware of the limits of liberalism. However, the thrust of Marcel's thought runs counter to the foundations of liberalism insofar as the notion of individual autonomy is central to that doctrine. The claim that individuals are autonomous, be it made on either possessive, individualist, or moral grounds, runs counter to participation in the mystery of Being. It involves making an abstraction of each person, advocating an atomic individualism. It fails to realize that subjectivity is never possible except as intersubjectivity. FREEDOM is not to be confused with autonomy. On the contrary, freedom takes us beyond the tension between Same and Other that predominates in the world of having, where autonomy is seen as a self-possession. In the fullest experience of freedom the notion of an autonomous self is revealed to be an abstraction. Freedom does not reside in the untrammeled possession of oneself or in having full control of one's actions. It is an experience of creative communion. Freedom might best be called an open disposition. It is a concrete way of being-in-situation such that I am open to the mystery of Being.

Primary Works

Marcel, Gabriel. *Metaphysical Journal.* Trans. Bernard Wall. Chicago: Henry Regnery, 1952.
————. *The Mystery of Being.* Vols. 1 and 2. Trans. G. S. Fraser. Chicago: Henry Reg-nery, 1960.

Bibliography

Gallagher, Kenneth T. *The Philosophy of Gabriel Marcel.* New York: Fordham Univer-sity Press, 1962.

MARXISM
Frank Schalow

The emphasis that existentialists place on the self and FREEDOM contrasts sharply with the Marxist putting the ideal of social cooperation ahead of the welfare of the individual. Yet existentialists have an interest in social activism. Hence, they have entertained many of the seminal Marxist analyses of HIS-TORY, class structure, ALIENATION, and revolutionary praxis. Some existen-tialists have formed a partnership with Marxism by radicalizing its methodology. For them, Marxism does not constitute a univocal term that can be tied to a monolithic system of thought. Nor can Marxism be identified with the philos-ophy of Karl Marx or a pure strain of communism. Rather, they emphasize the open-ended character of Marxist thinking in its attempt to grasp the contradic-tions of history and the social inequities of capitalism. Some expand the scope of Marxism from a strictly economic focus to a concern for the ontological assumptions on which its revolutionary intent rests.

Perhaps SARTRE best illustrates the attempt to develop a dialogue between Marxism and existentialism, which is vulnerable to two Marxist criticisms, first, ignoring the self's place in SOCIETY and, second, discounting the importance of social revolution. Sartre welcomes the opportunity to clarify existentialism in order to establish its wider political relevance. Existentialism maintains a posture of social activity by emphasizing the human POWER to alter one's circumstances. Thus, he answers the most poignant Marxist criticisms of existentialism. He challenges Marxism to reexamine its own presuppositions. Any future development of Marxism must resist the tendency of closure, of upholding a method that seeks a perfect completion of history. It is necessary to consider Marxism in its essential ambivalence. On one hand, Marxist thought develops a historical vision designed to liberate the oppressed and allow humans to take charge of their destiny. On the other hand, Marxism subscribes to a historical telos that can admit no other culmination to history than that which its theoretical precepts allow. Marxism's primary weakness lies in embracing this historical inevitability. Sartre reexamines the roots of Marxist methodology. Marx applied the dialectical method in order to show how history advances by reconciling socioeconomic contradictions. Presumably, the penultimate historical contradiction or capitalism can be overcome only through a worldwide revolution that redistributes the private ownership of wealth on a public scale. Yet, it is not so much the desirability of this outcome that is questionable, but its necessity. In contrast to the objective telos of communism, it is just as vital to accent the freedom of the PERSON who effects historical change. Persons not only are embedded in history but can also decide to change the course of historical events. Missing in Marxist thinking are the initiative and anticipation by which the self can plot its future possibilities, that is, by undertaking a PROJECT. The freedom of the human project can precipitate a change that Marxists presuppose as the heart of political revolution.

For Sartre, a project is a meaning-giving task that a person undertakes. This undertaking prefigures the human sensuous activity that Marx initially identified, as well as the revolutionary praxis of the proletariat that he later stressed. Human praxis must also include CREATIVITY, anticipation, and IMAGINATION. By unfolding the organizational possibilities of TRANSCENDENCE, individual praxis may break the bonds of social oppression and develop new institutions to promote LIBERTY. Thus, Sartre supplements the Marxist program with a social ONTOLOGY that resurrects the possibilities of freedom and transcendence. He attempts to radicalize Marxist methodology in light of a more encompassing vision of freedom. An appropriate method for writing history balances a regressive approach accenting the plurality of historical interpretations with a progressive approach upholding the convergence of historical TRUTHS. The Marxist ideal of class CONSCIOUSNESS becomes a concrete reality only when developed within an expanding horizon of individual choice. Alienation not only occurs when the capitalist exploits the proletariat but is already endemic to the way humans realize their identity in a social context. A new dialectic of self and history, of liberating praxis and social conflict emerges to reshape Marxism.

MERLEAU-PONTY exposes Marxist thought to its inherent tensions, polarities, and contradictions. Marxism must be recognized for its importance in redefining the philosophical task. He considers the dialectic according to its dual role in crystallizing the philosophical meaning of history and in rooting philosophy in the historical reality of human conflict. Marxism stands apart from Hegelianism by linking philosophical truth to the efficacy of human praxis. Marx maintained that the aim of PHILOSOPHY was to change the world rather than merely to interpret it. An action-oriented philosophy like existentialism can successfully cultivate the nexus between theory and praxis in order to uphold Marxism as a possibility. Merleau-Ponty proposes an adventure with the dialectic in order to revitalize Marxism in terms of its nascent possibilities. Dialectic is not an encompassing program that constitutes the totality but instead is situated in the whole. Emphasizing the situational CHARACTER of the experience of truth provides the key to avoiding one of Marxism's most notorious pitfalls. Specifically, Marxism labors under the paradox that the leaders who spearhead a revolution may themselves perpetuate a new rule or regime that undermines the SPIRIT of the revolutionary movement. Only a philosophy that continually returns to the uniqueness of the moment can purge the dialectic of its tendency toward deification.

Marxism must avoid posing as the only form of political praxis, of reconstituting itself as an ideology that seeks to monopolize the truth. In this respect, the totalizing movement and synthetic vision of Marxism can prove self-destructive. The existentialist contribution to Marxist thought lies in exposing this flaw and in reaffirming the open-ended character of Marxist methodology. According to Merleau-Ponty, it is not Marxist dialectic that is obsolete but, rather, the pretense of achieving a utopian end to history. Thus, Marxism assisted some existentialist thinkers to develop a philosophy of history to match their vision of freedom. These thinkers also clarified ontological freedom, which propels the Marxist quest to overcome social exploitation and tyranny.

Primary Works

Merleau-Ponty, Maurice. *Adventures of the Dialectic*. Trans. Joseph Bien. Evanston, IL: Northwestern University Press, 1973.
Sartre, Jean-Paul. *Critique of Dialectical Reason*. Trans. Alan Sheridan. London: Verso, 1982.

MAURICE MERLEAU-PONTY (1908–1961)
Ernest Sherman

In his short lifetime, Merleau-Ponty was a professor of PHILOSOPHY, a militant political writer, and, with SARTRE, editor of *Les Temps Modernes*. He was raised and educated in Paris, where he attended the École Normale Superieure, graduating in 1930; Sartre and BEAUVOIR were fellow students and friends. Politically, he was at this time conservative, and philosophically, he was an idealist. During the 1930s, his politics shifted to the left; he began to work out an independent philosophic approach, drawing upon Hegel, Marx, MARCEL, Gestalt psychology, HUSSERL, HEIDEGGER, and Scheler. In 1938, he completed *The Structure of Behavior*. During World War II, he served in the army until France's defeat. Returning to Paris, he wrote *Phenomenology of Perception*. Together with Sartre and CAMUS, he wrote and distributed underground literature as part of the Resistance. In the late 1940s and 1950s, Merleau-Ponty and Sartre became the famous exponents of humanist existentialism. Their aim was to establish an existentialist Marxism that would support the Soviet Union as the best hope for proletarian revolution while defending individual FREEDOM against the Communist Party's totalitarian control. For Merleau-Ponty, this ideal dissolved in 1950, when the Soviet bloc initiated the Korean War; he broke with Sartre. His academic accomplishments earned him appointment to the prestigious chair of philosophy at the College de France, a post that he held from 1952 until his death. Merleau-Ponty married and had children.

Inspired by Husserl, Merleau-Ponty maintains that both science and philosophy have lost touch with our everyday life-world, *LEBENSWELT*; hence, it is necessary to undertake a recommencement of our theoretical activity in order to do justice to this concrete sphere. Prior to any reflection we live, move, and have our BEING in the life-world. It gives us a direct and primitive contact with reality; yet the reflective tradition has either falsified or neglected that contact. Thus, if we can suspend our usual formulations and make explicit contact with what we have implicitly assumed, we shall be in a position to reformulate concepts more appropriately, establish the true basis for future conceptualization, and live more fully. For Husserl, PHENOMENOLOGY is a method of resolving philosophical problems by bracketing all presuppositions about reality and intuiting the phenomenal, the bare appearances of things for CONSCIOUSNESS. Once my MIND is able to put the world out of play in a suspended judgment, epoche, I should arrive at the irreducible data of conscious experience and the ESSENCES of these data. Finally, Husserl holds, we should be able to trace all the data back to the structuring activity of our mind. Consciousness is always a consciousness of something—an INTENTIONALITY directed toward a WORLD of things. Although Merleau-Ponty retains the techniques of bracketing and reduction, he interprets their function differently. The role of philosophy and of phenomenology must be thoroughly redefined. While Husserl still hoped to derive the prereflective order from the reflective, Merleau-Ponty holds that consciousness must be dethroned and the life-world installed as the source of everything, including consciousness. He argues that he has inverted Husserl's idealism and established its proper foundation in ordinary worldly EXISTENCE.

No longer to be construed as the INTUITION of data for consciousness, thinking must think of itself as a new type of activity that revives, repeats, and imitates the prereflective scheme of things. Theorizing must suspend previous notions in order to accomplish this end; yet philosophic insight can elucidate, but never supersede, the primacy of PERCEPTION. Thinking must function as a sort of refined extension of perception; as such, it can attain only a maximum reciprocity between the perceiver and the perceived, the explicit and the implicit, the philosopher and the *Lebenswelt*. Phenomenology properly understood is existential phenomenology: we think in order to live more wisely; we do not live in order to think more wisely.

The Structure of Behavior and *Phenomenology of Perception* uncover the NATURE of the life-world through a critique of various philosophic and scientific accounts of it. Behaviorism, rationalism, materialism, and other approaches draw upon lived experience, yet they each suppress or distort its concrete import. Their major blind spot has to do with the centrality of bodily experience. If I examine the naked testimony of my lived BODY, I discover that there has been a tendency to abstract from it in a quasi-disembodied fashion and remove me from that BEING-IN-THE-WORLD that is closest and most real. Thus, owing to his sharp duality of thinking thing and extended thing, Descartes has great difficulties explaining how rational self-consciousness with its clear and distinct ideas is related to an order in which body is a limited thing among things. Indeed, for Descartes, the SUBJECT plays a godlike role. Weighed down by the body's confused and partial ideas of SENSATION, it strives to clarify what should already be perfectly clear. Not located in extended SPACE and TIME, it floats among the extensae like an enigmatic ghost in the machine. In short, rationalism is too loftily abstract, too sublimated.

Nevertheless, despite its failings, rationalism is more faithful to our bodily situation than classical materialism. While the former inflates our common awareness into a pure lucidity, the latter deflates it into a pure opacity—a blankness that leaves room for no awareness whatsoever. Consider the would-be reduction of sensing to particular physical stimuli and responses in the brain. Can this mode of explanation ever be successful? No, because among other errors, it would decompose our sensorimotor relationship with things into a wholly determinate presence of things. Yet if such utter immediacy were actually the case, why would the evident mediation of sensing and thinking be necessary? Flatly coincident with this or that set of facts, I should have neither the need for, nor the possibility of, intending something beyond myself. If Descartes gives us too much light, the antithetical view consigns us to sheer darkness. We need a focus on the mean between these extremes.

Neither totally plain nor totally obscure, neither transparent idea nor occluded materiality, my lived bodily sentience is characterized by an insurmountable ambiguity and indeterminacy, for, though things and we ourselves are accessible to comprehension, we can never wholly comprehend either aspect. As we mediate with the world, we can make surface determinations of its nature; yet our knowledge of it will always be open to further determination. Unable either to fuse with things or divorce ourselves from things, we can merely overlap with things. Sounding the depths of things, we can deepen our acquaintance but never reach bottom. What eluded science and philosophy was self-TRANSCENDENCE: the being-beyond-itself that applies to both humans and every other entity. Wedded exclusively to the logic of identity, the tradition did not realize that this logic was a foreground procedure that could never encompass the background. We are exploratory creatures in a chiaroscuro world. There is a horizon of darkness forever offsetting and interpenetrating our light.

Together with Sartre, Merleau-Ponty had worked to create an independent Left that would combine existentialism and MARXISM. At first he believed that the Soviet Union, as the standard-bearer of the proletarian revolution, was to be favored against the capitalist West, despite human rights abuses. The Korean conflict and the relentless authoritarianism of the Communist Party shattered his FAITH. Abandoning the bulk of Marxist teachings, he called for a new liberalism that would adhere to representative democracy as the best vehicle for change. Neither communism nor capitalism requires uncritical acceptance. We should pursue a nonrevolutionary alternative that learns from both and breaks the deadlock of the Cold War.

What had drawn Merleau-Ponty to Marxism was not merely its humanitarian concern but the concept of praxis—its tendency to analyze HISTORY in terms of that concrete ensemble of activities that links humans to nature and to each other. In the young Marx there was a recognition that these links are neither exclusively subjective nor exclusively objective, neither mental nor physical as such. Cutting across these rigid demarcations, they exemplify, rather, an interworld, an ambiguous, dialectical region in which each aspect overlaps with, and reciprocates with, the rest. Merleau-Ponty saw here an anticipation of his emphasis on the life-world and our intermediate role in it. The older Marx had subordinated dialectic to historical materialism. The ambiguity of the human condition, Marx insisted, was to be once and for all resolved by the objective, material perfection of the classless SOCIETY. When Lenin subsequently elevated the Communist Party over the proletariat, the objectivism grew worse. Reciprocal exchanges between party and worker were hindered by so-called correct, scientific pronouncements from above.

Nevertheless, were not the reductive materialism and dehumanization of the capitalist system more egregious? Did not the so-called free world, led by the United States, carry out a systematic policy of neocolonialism, oppression of the poor, and racism? Perhaps the overthrow of capitalism and the control of production by the proletariat would bring about the most consistent and developed praxis. In fulfillment of Marx's early vision, reductionism would be avoided, and the cultivation of reciprocal dialectical RELATIONS would be maximized. Yes, this was the faith, the dream; when it vanishes, Merleau-Ponty accuses Marxism of being irredeemably materialistic. Marx made the mistake of endowing real humans—workers in a particular historical situation—with an unreal, absolutely objective status. Adapting Hegel's dialectic, Marx imputed to the proletariat nothing less than the total significance of history. Furthermore, to postulate the utopia arising from Marxism is to assume that humanity will acquire a positive, unambiguous meaning. Like the units of matter in classical materialism, the inhabitants of the worker's paradise shall enjoy a collective ''A is A'' identity that lacks nothing and moves toward nothing. Our overlapping relationship to things would be leveled out into a totally determinate presence of things. Instead of historical praxis with its ongoing mediation, we would be compressed into an absolutely self-contained immediacy.

Very well, Marxism in its pure form is to be rejected. But what hybrid of communism and capitalism should we strive for? Why should parliamentary government be the instrument of CHOICE to attain our goals? Merleau-Ponty does not provide a satisfactory answer. He indicates that our praxis is always going to be challenged by some kind of opposition, and since representative democracy is the only known form of government that permits dissent, it is the most appropriate for dealing with these challenges. Political and economic establishments need repeatedly to be criticized and altered. Thus, as long as a political structure tolerates peaceful modification, revolutions should be eschewed. For while every revolution begins as a humanizing force, it is likely to congeal into a counterrevolutionary status quo, thereby provoking another revolution, in an unbroken cycle of violence.

In the 1950s, Merleau-Ponty begins to reexamine the middle way that he had laid out early in his career. Had he reflected sufficiently on prereflective bodily experience? Not yet. The light previously shed on day-to-day existence did not go far enough, for while he had signaled our ambiguous overlapping with things, he had, to some extent, used unambiguous categories to interpret it. He had chiefly failed to apprehend that our bodily being-in-the-world is an expression of a universal Being, a flesh of the world. What is the flesh? Consider my perception of an ordinary cube. Does this entity have a positive, unambiguous meaning as the logic of identity demands? Is it presented to us as an absolutely positive, six-sided object or an absolutely positive set of components to be associated by inference? On the contrary, while I merely see this or that restricted perspective, I am able nonetheless to pick up on the style of the whole. Quite literally, I see through to the whole, because the whole is that latency that appears only in perspective, in depth behind its surfaces. Just as every one of the cube's perspectives cannot be copresent to me here and now, so its total latency retains a hiddenness that can never be totally unhidden.

What is true of the cube applies to my lived body. My carnal selfhood is a self-presence that is an absence from self. Suppose I turn back upon myself with my own body, can I be an absolute immediacy? If I touch one hand with the other, I am both the toucher and touched; but am I the sheer identity of the two? Do I as a sensory being become completely sensible to myself? By no means. Rather, when I focus on the touching hand, I cannot simultaneously focus on the touched hand, and vice versa. No matter how hard I try, I cannot sense both poles at once; I can merely shift from one to the other. The same incompleteness takes place in self-thinking. Even on the ideal levels of reflection and speech, I cannot simultaneously be both the reflector and the reflected-on, the speaker and the listener. I have to play one role at a time. Thus, my limited reflexivity exhibits in an overt manner the same figure-ground pattern, the same unconcealed concealment as things at large. Incapable of being fully present to myself, I am a sensibility that is, in principle, distant from itself, hidden from itself. In my encounter with myself as an incomplete sensible, I am a paradigm of that transcendence that characterizes the sensible world. Hence, as odd as it may seem, if I judge matters from a subject–OBJECT standpoint, the environment is a direct extension of my lived body. The things and I are flesh of each other's flesh: I em-body their elusive depths in my flesh.

Merleau-Ponty's exposition of the flesh renounces the compartments that divide entities up into subject–object, mind–matter, self–other. The flesh is the common transcendent background, the medium within which and against which sensible things emerge. He wishes to abandon even the polarity of whole and part. Fundamentally, my sensory powers are deflected away from themselves and remain latent to me. But granting this state of affairs, it is plain that I am also not totally self-creative: I did not make my body; and in my deeds and sufferings, I am supported by the power of the flesh. When I, as a sensing-sensible thing, turn back upon myself and model other sensible things, I must be the expression of a universal, fleshly coiling over on itself. Through me the flesh of the world must turn to sense itself, think itself, and thereby unveil its latency to itself. Furthermore, since it is one and the same turning that occurs both as part and as whole, we should no longer regard these alternatives as mutually exclusive.

For instance, what happens when my eye senses the world? Surely, it does not exist and function in limbo, as a heterogeneous exception to what it sees. To the contrary, as my particular organ envelops the whole scene, it is at once enveloped by the same scene. If my eye belongs to a seer who captures the visible spectacle, the seer does so only insofar as one's entire body is caught up in the spectacle and is something visible. Accordingly, how can we say that there is a decisive envelopment or capture in any respect? Just the opposite— we are forced to admit the reciprocal insertion and intertwining of what we call part and whole. Like an oscillating circuit, the flesh swings between itself as microcosm and itself as macrocosm, each phase incorporating and being incorporated by the other.

Merleau-Ponty's death prevented his presenting wider implications of the flesh. Still, there are sufficient hints about the conclusion of his inquiry. He would have closed his ontological circle and returned us to our everyday selves. What will that closure entail? He had been concerned with the nature of LANGUAGE. Now, in speaking of the flesh as that which resists classification, he is pushing language to its limit. For if, he conjectures, the flesh is an absolute self-movement and intertwining, then perhaps language is not an assemblage of words in subject-predicate form but a dynamic interplay of verbal elements. He adapts the structural linguistics of De Saussure to his ontology. De Saussure contended that language is not essentially composed of separate words with separate meanings; it is a diacritical system in which each word has meaning only in active interrelationship with all the others. But if that is the case, then the structure of language enunciates the self-mediation of the flesh that occurs on the basic sensible level. While my sensing body and the environment were at first intertwined only in silence, to verbalize the situation makes the flesh's self-mirroring more open and self-conscious. Through philosophic speech is accomplished an intertwined speaking of the universal flesh. Further, when philosophic speech is brought to its full potential, it shall let the flesh speak and be spoken without restriction; at that juncture, human self-activity and the flesh's self-activity shall be fulfilled at one stroke.

What shall this peak experience amount to? Can we glimpse its character? In the beginning is the flesh, and in the end is the flesh. Ever coiling over on itself, ever mirroring itself as microcosm and macrocosm, the oscillating circuit of the flesh can have no static goal. The flesh will everywhere be a self-presence in self-absence. It constitutes an inexhaustible unconcealment of its own inexhaustible concealment. Yet suppose we have through speaking of the flesh managed to circle back to our original place, will that not amount to a peculiar type of open-ended goal? Will I not be so united with the flesh that I enjoy a kind of moving ETERNITY that is ever new yet always the same? Yes, Merleau-Ponty indicates, such will, indeed, be our concrete existential eternity. Once I as speaker attain a rapprochement with the implicit mirroring of the flesh by the flesh, then the speaker and the spoken, the perceiver and the perceived, the explicit and the implicit shall interpenetrate and be virtually indiscernible. Just as the landscape painter can be so caught up in the object of one's inspiration that it becomes impossible to distinguish between what paints and what is painted, so the inspired philosopher can be captivated by the total landscape of the flesh, that one no longer knows who speaks and who listens.

What is the act of painting? Merleau-Ponty's answer to the questions concerning artistic CREATIVITY is that the creativity of the painter cannot be reduced to a lifeless reduplication of things or an equally lifeless reaction to things or even an amalgam of the two. These options are precluded because they are another version of the same subject/object abstractionism that would disembody us in other connections. Specifically, what could be the sense of copying an already determinate objective form, even supposing that such an addition to its identity were possible? Or, how could the private feelings and fantasies of an I-subject ever be geared to the expressive possibilities that reside in the things and in my bodily gestures? Here again the missing link is the mediation of the lived body, or the self-mediation of the flesh of the world, which never stops turning back upon itself and mirroring its inexhaustible concealment. The artist is a privileged vehicle of its universal self-expression. Never content with depicting the figure before oneself, the true artist makes visible its invisible ground. Tuning-in to the perpetual fleshly explosion of Being, the artist's gift is to further that creativity through one's bodily creativity, and vice versa. Thus, the painting of the flesh is imitative of the latter's endless self-relating and self-expressing.

Cezanne is responsible for the revolutionary breakthrough that transformed painting to a self-conscious exercise of its fleshly role. Critics hold that Cezanne is the first of the abstract painters, because he dared to liberate himself from the enslavement to representation and to concern himself with the underlying elements of visibility. This judgment, Merleau-Ponty holds, is misleading, since no painter ever could be a mere copier, though a vast number were led to believe that they were. Whether their approach was figurative or nonfigurative, painters had by definition to deal with the elements in question; Cezanne's unprecedented accomplishment was to do so explicitly and systematically. Cezanne is the painter's painter—he who shows for the first time the naked emergence of things before our eyes, the hitherto secret genesis of vision. His abstraction does not belong to some psychic dimension that is foreign to concrete things. Quite the reverse—both he and the painters after him are communicating the fleshly depth, which is more concrete than its surface-features.

In summary, Merleau-Ponty remained a hybrid figure, an existential phenomenologist and ontologist who never completely sympathized with the revolt against system. Though he shared with the others an emphasis on our free SITUATION in the world, he did not see the latter as a dread-filled encounter with NOTHINGNESS. While we are obliged to take our fate in our hands, we never do so as single ones; rather, we act interdependently and intersubjectively; in the last analysis, we are phases in the universal self-movement of a wider Being, a flesh of the world, which carries out an interminable process of self-intertwining and self-reciprocating. We fulfill ourselves by reaching maximum attunement with it. To become what we are is to develop an enlightened perception of the flesh as that ambiguous cycle that transcends the surface dualities of whole/part, subject/object, TIME/eternity. This vision will not only supply the founding principle of an ETHICS but embody nothing less than an existential eternity. Once we live solely to let the flesh express itself through us, we shall flow with its ever-creative unity.

Primary Works

Merleau-Ponty, Maurice. *Adventures of the Dialectic*. Trans. Joseph Bien. Evanston, IL: Northwestern University Press, 1973.
———. *Signs*. Trans. Richard C. McCleary. Evanston, IL: Northwestern University Press, 1964.
———. *The Structure of Behavior*. Trans. Alden Fisher. Boston: Beacon Press, 1963.

Bibliography

Madison, Gary. *The Phenomenology of Merleau-Ponty: A Search for the Limits of Consciousness*. Athens: Ohio University Press, 1981.

METAPHYSICS
Frank Schalow

Many existentialists redefine metaphysics in order to question the meaning of human EXISTENCE. They emphasize dilemmas, predicaments, and paradoxes of LIFE. The renouncing of traditional metaphysics, however, spawns new challenges. Metaphysics survives as a quest to reestablish the tension between BEING and nothing, life and DEATH, order and chaos, meaning and absurdity. Even when they criticize metaphysics, existentialists seek to recover its importance, to fathom its possibility. The questionable character of human existence supplies a new guideline for addressing a topic as perennial as Being. This self-questioning, which places the inquirer into question, governs the attempt to radicalize the metaphysical PROJECT. Thus, when they address Being, their questioning includes the inquirer's concern for the enigma of human existence. HEIDEGGER epitomizes this attempt to engage the inquirer in metaphysical investigation.

Heidegger emphasizes that humans are drawn toward metaphysical questions. Formally, metaphysics can be defined as the investigation into beings as such and in totality. This definition reflects an ambiguity in metaphysics between emphasizing the constitution of beings in general and considering the highest being, or GOD. Heidegger traces metaphysics back to its roots as an essential possibility of human existence, as radicalizing a natural inquisitiveness inherent in DASEIN. Hidden in traditional metaphysics is the spark of wonder. He explores the dimensions of this wonder, which issue from a fundamental disposition pervading human existence and sparking philosophical inquiry. Humans question due to their condition as thrown into the WORLD and their ANXIETY arising from being thrown. In anxiety, Dasein experiences the slipping away of beings-in-totality and finds itself projected into the nothing. Given its suspension within the nothing, Dasein attains the openness and FREEDOM to raise metaphysical questions. Metaphysics is not an accidental pursuit but a decisive possibility of Dasein.

Dasein is a future-oriented, ecstatic projection of possibilities. Dasein is that entity who understands being in the course of ex-isting or standing out beyond itself. Human existence is the original happening through which metaphysics becomes possible as a thematic investigation into the meaning of being. Heidegger's essay ''What Is Metaphysics?'' shows that being first reveals itself to Dasein on a prephilosophical level through the opposite extreme of absence, through the countermovement of withdrawal, insofar as Dasein surpasses beings-in-totality and endures the nothing in confronting the prospect of its own death. Heidegger carries out an existential analysis of Dasein as the prelude to reasking the question of Being. This inquiry is hermeneutical; the entity who exhibits concern about its own being engages in a process of self-interpretation in order to arrive at clues to reask the question of Being. In *Being and Time*, Heidegger defines human existence as BEING-IN-THE-WORLD or CARE. He examines the relation between Dasein and Being in three stages. First, he describes the essential structures of care as existence, FACTICITY, and falling. Second, he considers the meaning of care as temporality, or how the threefold structure of Dasein's being is unified across the arc of primordial TIME, the ecstases of future, past, and present. Third, he addresses temporality as the transcendental horizon for understanding Being. As finite, Dasein understands Being in temporal terms, that is, as self-emerging presence. In its temporal constitution, Dasein transcends all beings or entities, including itself, to the forefront of world. Through TRANSCENDENCE, Dasein acquires its possibility to understand Being.

Transcendence becomes a focal concept for the existentialists who develop a comprehensive vision of Being to match their concern for human existence. Unlike JASPERS, who envisions transcendence as the tension between infinite and finite, Heidegger maintains that transcendence roots human existence in its finitude, in the there of its situation. Metaphysics presupposes Dasein's finite, temporal existence as being-in-the-world. In *Kant and the Problem of Metaphysics*, Heidegger adopts an ambivalent stance toward metaphysics. On one hand, he retrieves its insights as preserving a concern for Being. He appeals to Kant to distinguish a preliminary inquiry into human finitude that resets the parameters for reasking the question of Being, or fundamental ONTOLOGY. On the other hand, he assigns limits to metaphysics insofar as it shifts the focus from Being to specific beings or entities. Since Plato, the active sense of Being as a mode of uncovering and coming into presence has lost its import in comparison with the demand to define reality in terms of a fixed model.

Though metaphysics and ontology may parallel each other, Heidegger reserves the term ''ontology'' to designate the strategy for uncovering the meaning of Being. Fundamental ontology is the attempt to reformulate the question of Being according to the possibility of its temporal disclosure. The effort to grasp reality in terms of permanent structures such as Platonic forms or Aristotelian substance gives way to a metaphysics of temporal finitude. Such a metaphysics emphasizes the modality of the possible in contrast to the actual, or what can be, rather than what is given as present-at-hand. Beginning in the late 1930s with his lectures on NIETZSCHE, Heidegger construes traditional metaphysics in a much more negative light. He agrees with Nietzsche's assessment that Western history has succumbed to NIHILISM and that with the death of GOD, PHILOSOPHY stands at a crossroads. He maintains, however, that nihilism stems from the forgetting of Being to which Nietzsche contributed. Insofar as Being remains forgotten or unthought throughout the history of metaphysics, beings become the fulcrum of concern in terms of their possibilities for technological use and exploitation. Metaphysics as the forgetting of Being parallels the emergence of technology as the drive to exert domination over all aspects of reality. The dangers of technology cannot be avoided by denouncing it. Technology can be placed within its limits by appropriating the unthought origin of metaphysics and recovering alternative ways in which beings reveal themselves outside the framework of exploitation. In "Letter on Humanism," Heidegger defines Dasein in terms of its ability to dwell in correspondence with Being, to allow its truth to unfold within LANGUAGE. Humanity assumes the role of the shepherd of Being. Thus, metaphysics ceases to be merely an intellectual exercise and, instead, harbors a decision in which the fate of Western humanity hangs in the balance.

The attempt to develop a metaphysics of possibility and existence, in contrast to a metaphysics of actuality and presence-at-hand, emerges in MARCEL's thinking. He emphasizes that the source of meaning arises along an otherworldly axis. He opposes Nietzsche's, Heidegger's, and SARTRE's attempts to circumscribe human concern within the finite horizon of time and history and upholds a spiritual realm adjacent to our worldly endeavors. This domain includes a COMMUNITY of humans who are joined by a shared FAITH and an avowal of ultimate VALUES such as LOVE. He reserves a special place in his metaphysics for the other PERSON, who constitutes a special arc of transcendence that intersects with the absolute and introduces deeper values into life. He diverges from fundamental ontology on two key points. First, human life acquires meaning only by opening forth into a realm beyond itself. Second, what is most heart-wrenching about death is not the prospect of my mortality but rather the finality of suffering the other's loss. Hence, it is incumbent upon me to prevent the other's death from passing the verdict of annihilation and, conversely, to promote the person's remembrance and even renewal beyond this life. Cultivating this optimism in the face of death entails fidelity. In turn, fidelity forms the cornerstone of a metaphysics of hope, which emphasizes the strength of the human SPIRIT and the possibility for its transformation in accord with a greater mystery.

A metaphysics of hope reaffirms the meaning of human existence in light of an ultimacy often disguised in everyday life. Hope holds forth the plenitude and abundance of being in spite of an overwhelming sense of lack that humans experience. NOTHINGNESS may be a key aspect of any encounter with reality but is not the decisive ingredient. Humanity experiences value in seeking the plenitude of being through hope, rather than in the drive to accumulate and possess things. While having remains a preoccupation of life, the self must turn to the mystery of being to find a higher source of meaning. In *Homo Viator* Marcel develops a metaphysics that cultivates the image of humanity as a traveler who undergoes a journey of the spirit that begins in the transitory realm of daily life and leads to a proximity with the eternal God. The destination of Marcel's traveler lies in developing a spiritual community that joins self and other, human and divine. He reinterprets RILKE's POETRY in order to accent humanity's spiritual journey and the search for an ultimate meaning in a way that contrasts sharply with Heidegger's emphasis on being-in-the-world. He remains committed to the MYSTERY of love that shines beyond the darkness of death. His metaphysics stands out by blending existential motifs with the Christian message of faith, hope, and charity.

Sartre's essay "Existentialism and Humanism" distinguishes two varieties of existentialism, atheistic and religious. Sartre identifies his own thought with the former and points to Marcel's and Jaspers' writings as examples of the latter. He denounces the attempt to provide an ultimate ground for reality as metaphysical and describes his approach to being as a phenomenological ontology. In *Being and Nothingness*, Sartre opts for an ontological dualism that divides reality into exclusive spheres of being-for-itself and being-in-itself. Being-for-itself describes the state of consciousness where an individual's identity is always in the process of development and formation. Being-in-itself determines all reality that does not possess the potential for self-consciousness and hence applies to things that already have a fixed identity. He affirms the transphenomenality of Being as the central precept of his metaphysics. Being is transphenomenal in the sense that it exceeds and stands over against CONSCIOUSNESS. Moreover, while Being can be encountered only through its appearances, the diversity of appearances never exhausts Being. Given its transphenomenal dimension, Being defines a limit that consciousness cannot overcome, the unbridgeable hiatus in the rationalistic quest to render reality intelligible. The inherent opacity of the real order counters the spontaneity and purpose of conscious intent.

In confronting the obstacle that reality poses, consciousness becomes vulnerable to ANGUISH and anxiety born of its own finitude. But while an encounter with the transphenomenality of Being may provide such an occasion, the actual experience of anxiety rests on the constitution of consciousness itself. The self is, first and foremost, anxious about the development of its identity through the unfolding of future possibilities, through the exercise of freedom. Being-for-itself faces the insoluble riddle of identity, which can never become a question for being-in-itself. Yet being-in-itself can provide a resistance point against which consciousness discharges its opposition, that is, its negativity or nihilation. Through its nihilating activity, being-for-itself actualizes its nature as possessing spontaneity and conscious intent. Thus, consciousness displays a double INTENTIONALITY, in which it both differentiates itself from being-in-itself and depends on that antithesis in order to be conscious.

Sartre describes nothingness as a worm coiled in the heart of being; he thus emphasizes the upsurgence of possibility that enables the self to undertake its projects from within a SITUATION. Consciousness displays internal negation insofar as being-for-itself opposes its identification with any set of properties. But due to this internal NEGATION, the self experiences the anguish of being who it is not and not being who it is. My self also exudes negativity toward the Other, who as being-for-itself may pose a threat of seeking to reduce me to the status of being-in-itself. Consciousness projects itself into the future through its nihilating activity and thereby experiences anxiety within the depths of its existence. The self can never find an ally in Being but must exist in the perpetual uncertainty of having to re-create who it is. A metaphysical understanding of the self's place within the world remains a possibility, but only in contrast to the rationalist systems of Descartes, Hegel, and HUSSERL.

Primary Works

Heidegger, Martin. *An Introduction to Metaphysics*. Trans. Ralph Manheim. New Haven, CT: Yale University Press, 1959.

Marcel, Gabriel. *Metaphysical Journal*. Trans. Bernard Wall. Chicago: Henry Regnery, 1952.

Bibliography

Samay, Sebastian. *Reason Revisited: The Philosophy of Karl Jaspers*. Notre Dame, IN: University of Notre Dame Press, 1971.

MIND
William Hurst

The Cartesian mind is an inner SPACE, a kind of private room with a window providing a view of the outside WORLD. The room's occupant sometimes moves to the window to observe the street scene below. Noticing passers-by, the occupant might think they are humans, but simply seeing passing figures in no way ensures that there are humans in the street; they might be automatons or puppets. Only a judgment could assure the occupant about what is seen. The I of the seer depends on the I of the judge, if one is to know what one sees. Eventually, this I of the judge, as the principal occupant of the mind that knows, became the Kantian Transcendental Ego, the condition of possibility for the unity of experience. Thus, the unity of the mind is guaranteed by its occupant, the EGO, or perhaps by the Transcendental Ego, which guarantees the unity of the ego itself.

In contrast, SARTRE and MERLEAU-PONTY conceived of the experience of the SUBJECT, as seer and knower, as having been cast out into the world. This subjective experience, referred to as CONSCIOUSNESS, has no inhabitants or occupants, whether the I of the judge or the Transcendental Ego. It is, rather, a mind always already immersed in the world, engaged with OBJECTS and other PERSONS. Its experience intertwines that of others, and its presence to itself is intersected by that of others to themselves. The mind is not a place in which a judgment occurs to deliver the world to a SUBJECT otherwise disengaged from it but is already immersed in that world, exploring and interrogating it. For Sartre the mind has no occupants, and the ego is a transcendent object, like any other. Being both spontaneous and impersonal, the mind is simply a relatedness to objects. This consciousness has no subjective or noetic pole, intending a noema or object. As there is no ego immanent to the mind, so there is no Transcendental Ego as the hidden source of the unity of the ego and of mental life. The ego is an object, like any other; it exists in the world as an object of consciousness. It is therefore transcendent and not immanent to the mind. Sartre's expulsion of the mind's contents included also the UNCONSCIOUS, which he considered to be a variation on the concept of a Transcendental Ego. Thus, Sartre transformed HUSSERL's PHENOMENOLOGY from a description of the contents of consciousness into a description of the existential involvements of humans, leading to an INTUITION of the full range of meanings for a human FREEDOM. To Sartre, Husserl's definition of consciousness as INTENTIONALITY meant that since consciousness is defined essentially as an aiming at objects, it follows that it has no content of its own but is simply a relation to those objects. He agreed with Hegel that the essence of Mind is negativity, or NOTHINGNESS.

According to Merleau-Ponty, the mind is always already immersed in the perceived world as that world unfolds for a subject exploring it and investigating it. He focused on this unfolding of the perceived world, on the kind of experience this affords the perceiving subject, and on the nature of the mind, or consciousness, that is engaged in this experience. He came to understand the role both of the eye and of the mind in the generation of a perceived field, specifically, a visual field. In the opening of a visual field, the perceiving subject experiences a framework for the emergence of visible objects, which can then be explored and examined. The eye itself opens such a field and examines and explores the objects presented within it. Having such a field means that the seer is caught up in the field and cannot be conceived of as outside it, as some kind of invisible seer. A human seer can have a visual field only because that seer is one of the visibles in the field. Without such a position, the human seer would not have been able to adumbrate a perspective but would somehow hover over a scene of flat beings. Having a visual field implies having a perspective, which implies that one has taken up a position within that field and that one is a visible object. Furthermore, in seeing the objects in the field, one is implicitly assuming the perspectives that those objects have on oneself as the seer, because one is engaged at every moment in situating oneself within the field as it evolves. Thus, PERCEPTION places the seer in the midst of the world being perceived.

The world that unfolds for such a perceiving subject is not occupied by flat figures whose NATURE must be discerned by a judgment of the mind; it is, rather, a world of many dimensions through and around which vision and other modes of perception find their way, thus taking the subject of perception far beyond anything that could be considered its own point of looking or perceiving. Perception is necessarily ecstatic; this aspect of it makes a visual field possible. As a visible seer, the human subject experiences a world that includes him or her and therefore turns back upon, and enfolds, the seer. As an explorer of objects that have backs and sides, as well as fronts, the human seer is engaged in the constitution of a perceived world that is enfleshed by the vision of the seer. The object presented is not naked for a neutral vision. The seer is perhaps alienated through a kind of narcissistic immersion in the objects seen. Out of such an immersion, the human subject comes eventually to discriminate what belongs to itself from what belongs to the object seen or perceived. But such discrimination is never accomplished once and for all. Immersion in the world remains always at the source of subjective experience.

As against Descartes, Merleau-Ponty claimed that the judgment of seeing is immersed in the seeing itself. The mind of a human is not isolated in a pure subjective space but is out there, immersed in the world that is being explored by the eye, which, in generating a field of vision, provides the subject with a space in which objects can come to be. In contrast to Sartre, Merleau-Ponty struggled with a Freudian dimension in his thinking, which sought to keep a place for an unconscious. But the unconscious he preserved is neither within nor under the subject, as a kind of transcendental ego; it is to be found in the articulations of our field, in the intertwining of fields, in the subtle interlacing of subjectivities, which allows for the emergence of otherness or alterity both within and for a human subject. Thus, a mind without an occupant is a complex of RELATIONS with others and with oneself that imply that one is always already inserted in the world and is a BEING-IN-THE-WORLD. This is the genuinely human world. The mind that exists behind the window is an invention of a thought that merely attempts to disengage itself from the world.

HEIDEGGER did not devote himself to conceptual analyses of the sort developed here. Both Sartre and Merleau-Ponty employed the notion of the ''there is'' as a significant component of their thinking. Sartre noted that it was more appropriate to say ''there is consciousness,'' than to say ''I am conscious,'' because consciousness is a spontaneous and impersonal presence in the world and has an ego only as one of its intended objects. Merleau-Ponty wrote about the primitive ontological assurance, perhaps resting upon a perceptual FAITH, that ''there is something.'' The ''there'' and the ''there is'' are critically important in the thought of Heidegger; in his early works he attempted to think the nature of the ''there-Being'' as DASEIN, which is, in every case, my own. In later works, Heidegger attempted to come closer to thinking the ''there is.'' The meaning of mind is to be found in the ''there,'' both the ''there'' within which Being discloses itself and the ''there'' that is ingredient in the ''there is.''

In the structure of the ''there'' of Dasein, Heidegger identified as a most essential feature its ecstatic CHARACTER, or its nature of always being outside itself, in the world, as the disclosure of Being. Dasein is not closed in upon itself as a Cartesian consciousness would be. The Cartesian ONTOLOGY is one of substances; the nature of substance is not therefore questioned. Heidegger hoped to destroy such an ontology by putting the being of substance into question. Thus, mind is not to be understood in terms of substance or in terms of subject, to the extent that that concept depends on the concept of substance. The mind is, rather, an aspect of the PROCESS in which Being is disclosed. It takes its essential mode of being from the ecstatic character of Dasein. Moreover, the intentionality of consciousness rests upon this ecstasis of Dasein. Mind is a feature, a component, or an aspect of the disclosure of Being. To be precise, mind comes to itself and understanding, as interpretation, and also as states-of-mind. To the extent that all of these modes of disclosure of Dasein to itself and of Being within the "there" of Dasein are equiprimordial and there are identical with the very nature of Dasein, it might be said that the nature of Dasein is mind.

JASPERS objected to Heidegger's fundamental ontology, because it presented itself as KNOWLEDGE, rather than as PHILOSOPHY. Philosophy, for Jaspers, is an activity through which an individual comes to authentic existence, from out of one's historical SITUATION, and in confrontation with TRANSCENDENCE. Existential concepts are essentially unlike the categories of science in that I cannot think them unless I am in some way in them. While what I am is irrelevant to scientific categories, it is never thus with existential concepts. Moving toward authentic existence is a process in which the mind unfolds from an initial preoccupation with empirical existents to an eventual confrontation with the Encompassing that I am, and from there to a meeting with the Encompassing that is the World, and finally to be a confrontation with the Encompassing that is Transcendence. Philosophical thinking cannot make this happen, but it prepares the way and perhaps helps to create the conditions in the individual for what seems to be a kind of ascesis of the mind.

Jaspers used the concept of horizon to explain the Encompassing, indicating that at each point in one's experience, when one might have thought that everything was grasped or understood, one finds oneself in a new region. The mind emerges in the mode of Consciousness in which one attempts to engage one's abilities to understand oneself and the world in the most general terms, approaching as near as possible to universal TRUTHS. This movement into the mind and its capacity for yielding universal truths follows a preoccupation with grasping oneself as an empirical existent, which means not yet as a historical existent but as one of a category, such as might be presented by a sociological, biological, or psychological study. The mind intervenes eventually and notes the incompleteness of such a grasp, which leaves out essential features. Subsequently, as the individual strives for universal truth, the limits of this mode of the Encompassing are reached, and the individual moves into the mode of the SPIRIT.

In the mode of Spirit, in the Encompassing that we are, I attempt to provide a totality for the various regions of my thoughts and experience. I engage in philosophical thought, seeking ideas that can give coherence and order to the rest of my experience. I recognize that what I seek in this mode is not really knowledge, which belongs to the understanding. In the mode of the Spirit, I come to stand in a kind of rational WHOLENESS, which I recognize eventually to be incomplete, in that it does not account for all that I am. I come face-to-face with my own concrete, historical situation, which might be menaced by disorder, EVIL, sickness, struggle, and DEATH. I see that I am not, as Spirit, or, indeed, as any of the modes of the Encompassing that we are, complete and full, because I exist within the limits of a specific historical situation. As I come to myself in this situation, I begin to move toward an authentic existence. As EXISTENZ, I am called upon to make the fateful decisions in the face of my situation that will make actual all the possible modes of being I might have contemplated in the modes of the Encompassing. In doing so, I realize that, as Existenz, I am not all. I reach the horizon of my own Existenz, and in so doing I encounter the Encompassing that is the World and ultimately the Encompassing that is Transcendence. Jaspers does not consider this to be a program for mental development but, rather, a way of illuminating Existenz in its basic struggle for authentic existence. The philosophizing he proposes always depends on, and promotes, an inner development, from empirical existent to a confrontation, from out of one's historical situation, with the Encompassing that is Transcendence. The mind is present in various modes of the Encompassing that we are and, indeed, as Reason, serves as the bond between the various modes. It must always be understood, however, as never fully graspable within any one mode but as being an expression of the Encompassing that I am, whether as empirical existent, consciousness as such, or Spirit. The mind functions as the principal force in the illumination of Existenz.

Primary Works

Jaspers, Karl. *Philosophy*. 3 vols. Trans. E. B. Ashton. Chicago: Univesity of Chicago Press, 1969/1971.
Sartre, Jean-Paul. *The Transcendence of the Ego*. Trans. Forrest Williams and Robert Kirpatrick. New York: Farrar, Straus, and Giroux, 1987.

Bibliography

Shroeder, William Ralph. *Sartre and His Predecessors: The Self and the Other*. London: Routledge, 1984.

MOOD
Vincent McCarthy

Two principal sources for the discussion of moods are KIERKEGAARD and HEIDEGGER, who seem to focus on mood itself as a manner of being self-preoccupied. Heidegger's discussion is regarded as indebted to Kierkegaard, as an explicitation of Kierkegaard's indirect portrayal of moods in pseudonymous philosophical novels and treatises. Kierkegaard does not define mood. His works depict potential religious PERSONS mired in the illusions of aesthetic existence. He explores their crisis in novels and abstract treatises in which the role and prominence of moods are inescapable and constant. Kierkegaard's interest is to explore the life of SPIRIT in the individual, in contrast to the external manifestation of spirit unfolded in Hegelianism. Almost as a parody of a Hegelian philosophy of world HISTORY, Kierkegaard explores personal upheavals that he sees as invested with enormous importance in the history of the individual. *Either/Or* depicts a moody young aesthete wrestling with self-dissatisfactions, lack of WHOLENESS, painful fragmentation, and the veritable emotional roller coaster that he daily rides. His melancholy afflicts him under two aspects: a bittersweet, unfulfilled longing and a brooding, critical emptiness. In some moments, he is the soul of IRONY, which is the mood of infinite negativity toward the finite world and all its illusions, both sensual and intellectual. ANXIETY is a deeper crisis that discloses the problematic nature of the self to itself, the NOTHINGNESS of its own unactualized potential. Finally, the mood of despair is the recognition of self-caused fragmentation as well as the recognition of one's helplessness to undo it. Such is despair before GOD, and the paradox of acknowledging guilt and helplessness before the deity becomes the means of restoration and even of a higher self.

The four moods, melancholy, irony, anxiety, and despair, color all other experience and one's CONSCIOUSNESS. They arise out of an emotional disequilibrium that reflects a deeper disequilibrium. They can appear to be aimless occurrences, unless they are responded to and their hints allowed to become disclosures. Thus, moods are far more than an affect or emotional upheaval. While not voluntary, a mood requires an act of WILL in order to accept the lesson that it imparts and to surmount it. Moods are often crisis moments that allow a breakthrough to a higher consciousness and higher self-realization. Hence, the four moods of aesthetic existence reveal their inner law and disclose a dialectic toward religious awakening, in response to the stirrings of the spirit. They are completed in a fifth mood, resignation, which belongs to the RELIGIOUS STAGE.

Heidegger's discussion of mood is as the everyday mode of *Befindlichkeit*, translated as state of mind but meaning how one finds oneself. He focuses on anxiety, which he contrasts with FEAR. Mood is not just an emotional experience but a cognitive state whose disclosure one can rise to, as one may rise to respond to anxiety. While distinct from theoretical knowing, mood remains an important form of KNOWLEDGE, a dynamic knowing. Mood is a source of self-knowledge and discloses much that is not accessible to theoretical knowing. It makes the SUBJECT a self-conscious being. Moods are neither voluntary nor involuntary, nor are they random happenings but are events richly rewarding a probing, part of how I am, or my state of MIND. Probing moods may disclose the ontological structure of DASEIN and through Dasein the structure of Being. The subject is always in a mood, and the subject's mood influences how he or she will feel and react to many events. Mood reveals Dasein to oneself as a structure of being-there within a larger structure: BEING-IN-THE-WORLD. The INTENTIONALITY of moods can be probed for further knowledge.

For Heidegger, mood is a disclosure of the self as burden to oneself, even when one tries to evade the disclosure. Mood assails a subject in one's everyday, unreflecting involvement in the WORLD. If moods are not passively endured, they can become deep sources of disclosure. They disclose by turning to or turning away. In a sense, one must give in to mood—exactly what the individual normally does not do. For by giving in, paradoxically, one becomes master of one's moods through knowledge and will. Mood is thereby an intensification of subjectivity, first as feeling, then as enabling a higher self-knowledge about the structure, condition, and intentionality of subjectivity. Anxiety is a fundamental mode of self-knowledge, an experience that can turn a subject from everyday immersion in the world and bring it about that one's being becomes a question to oneself and to all of Being. Unlike Kierkegaard, Heidegger does not explore despair as SIN-consciousness and the intensification of anxiety. He places the power of self-recovery entirely in the hands of the subject.

Primary Works

Heidegger, Martin. *Basic Writings*. Ed. David Farrell Krell. New York: Harper and Row, 1977.
Kierkegaard, Søren. *The Concept of Anxiety*. Trans. Reider Thomte. Princeton: Princeton University Press, 1980.

MORALITY
Robert Holmes

Existentialists view morality against the background of previous philosophies, momentous historical events, or an appraisal of the contemporary Western world. Tending to see humankind as alienated from the world, they take morality, in the sense of accepted VALUES and norms, that need either to be replaced, transcended, or reconstituted. This conviction provides the starting point for existentialist ETHICS. Many view morality and ONTOLOGY as linked, with morality integral to the disclosure and constitution of BEING. Existentialists deny that morality can be based on external authority, human or divine. The challenge to show how meaningful human existence is nonetheless possible is taken up differently by religious and atheistic existentialists.

KIERKEGAARD views morality as practical rather than theoretical and as requiring CHOICES and the cultivation of habits rather than mere acquisition of KNOWLEDGE. People commit themselves to one of three ways of life—the aesthetic, the ethical, or the religious—each with its own values and standards. Only the religious avoids self-deception. The aesthetic represents self-absorption, as in pursuit of sensual pleasure. Its deception is to suppose that one can achieve satisfaction from personal experience alone. The ethical recognizes the need to transcend the self, but its commitment to moral principle fails to acknowledge moral dilemmas that reason and logic cannot resolve. Only by a LEAP of FAITH can one transcend both the aesthetic and the ethical, though retaining what is sound in them, to the religious, understood as a commitment to the personal GOD of CHRISTIANITY.

TILLICH views LOVE as the supreme moral imperative but detaches it from the idea of God as a personal being. God is not a being but Being itself. We have an essential nature, manifesting God's WILL. Hence, estrangement from God is estrangement from our essential NATURE. Here morality has an ontological function. Without it we cannot be fully human. Morality represents consciousness of the imperative of love understood as a manifesting God's will in us. It thus differs from moralisms (systems of rules conditional upon social and cultural circumstances) and moralism (self-righteousness often generated by moralisms). Only through morality can a PERSON become integrated with one's essential nature, hence, be fully realized as a person. The fundamental moral imperative to realize my essential nature does not bind because of any eternal authority—not even that of God. Its unconditionality derives from being freely chosen as an act of self-affirmation. Indeed, morality itself is the pure form of essential self-affirmation. As only love can do justice to the concrete SITUATIONS in which choices must be made, only love serves the end of self-realization. Its rootedness in transcendent, ultimate reality gives morality an irreducibly religious quality.

BUBER sees the world as pervaded by an I–It relationship that relates to persons, animals, and OBJECTS as instruments to be used. This gives the dominant morality an alienating, utilitarian cast that obstructs the natural, direct awareness of persons and things, necessary to our innate desire for relationship, hence, necessary for genuine existence. We must, therefore, move from the controlling, consequentialist outlook toward one that encourages people's natural, basically good tendencies to come forth. The divine is encountered directly in and through I–Thou relations with other persons. This statement implies that relationships that extend to God—not as transcendent being or as a metaphysical ground of being but as a personal God—are at the heart of moral existence.

For SARTRE the self has no predetermined ESSENCE, either in God or in human nature. We create an essence through free choice, action, and commitment. Indeed, for human reality, to be is to choose oneself. But in choosing, we also choose a morality. The commitment to one morality rather than another cannot bindingly be prescribed by ethical theory, because it is we who must, in the end, freely decide whether any such theory is correct. The inseparability of choosing a morality, creating values, and making the self gives free choice a combined moral and ontological function, in which both values and fully actualized persons come into being.

BEAUVOIR distinguishes spontaneous FREEDOM, which one has by virtue of being human, from creative freedom, which one can choose or not choose, pursue or not pursue. Only creative freedom has absolute value. A worthy outlook, in which one assumes RESPONSIBILITY for one's freedom and confronts the fundamental ambiguity of ethics, namely, that we cannot help but treat other persons as means as well as ends—only a life framed by such an outlook is authentic. To fail to accept an authentic life's responsibilities submerges one in the values of one or another type: the subman, the serious man, the nihilist, the surrealist, the passionate man, or the adventurer. Each type constitutes a kind of morality, with its values and standards. Most common is the serious person, who substitutes ready-made values found in society for those of childhood. It is not the specific content of these values which varies greatly, so much as the unreflective, self-deceptive SPIRIT in which they are held that renders serious persons unauthentic.

Beauvoir views moral choice as integrated into human development. For the child, values are given ready-made. But the growing awareness at adolescence that values are nothing more than the creations of other persons, either individually or collectively through custom, generates an ANXIETY that can be dispelled only by assuming responsibility for one's freedom in creating values. We can fail to do this in many ways. The attitudes of the serious, the nihilist, the surrealist, and others are forms of flight from freedom. We commit ourselves to creative, moral freedom only by taking freedom as an absolute end, furthering it in ourselves and respecting it in others. Herein lies the integration of morality and ontology. Choosing freedom implies a bond with other persons. Their free choices not only help determine the future in which realization of my projects can take place but also create the possibility of my life's significance extending beyond my death. To will myself free is to will others free as well.

Primary Works

Beauvoir, Simone de. *The Ethics of Ambiguity*. Trans. Bernard Fretchman. New York: Citadel, 1970.
Buber, Martin. *Between Man and Man*. Trans. Ronald Gregor Smith. New York: Macmillan, 1965.

Bibliography

Burnier, Michel-Antoine. *Choice of Action: The French Existentialists on the Political Front Line*. Trans. Bernard Murchland. New York: Random House, 1968.

MYSTERY
Patrick Bourgeois

Much of twentieth-century PHILOSOPHY has revealed the richness, fullness, and ambiguity of human EXISTENCE, which entails the mystery of BEING at the heart of human existence. Although MARCEL's unique thinking has thematized mystery, this theme is not alien to the philosophy of others. These philosophies rediscover the richness of lived existence underlying any scientific model, which is found only to schematize the concrete, allowing the human gaze to become blinded by the clarity and assurance of these derived, second-level accounts. The philosophy of Marcel most explicitly develops human existence in terms of the mystery of Being.

The mystery of Being in Marcel's philosophy can be related to all of his celebrated themes: presence, recollection and second reflection, creative fidelity, participation. His thinking expresses the question of Kantian limit only obliquely. For Marcel, in this context of limit, the objectivity and characterizability of the problematic are surpassed in the notion of mystery to which access is gained in a second reflection attuned to existence in such a way as to bring it to thought. Existence as mystery is not a problem before me but one that involves me. I cannot abstract myself from the mystery of my being. Thus, this dimension of mystery cannot be considered merely to be a problem that cannot be solved. Rather, I am precisely what (who) is being reflected upon. On this level there is an ontological exigence at the heart of human existence that should prevent me from closing myself off into the problematic and the objective. On this level the Thou is encountered in presence.

If second reflection were to allow itself to begin other than with the realization of the presence of the Other, it would not be possible to get the Other as PERSON back into reflection. This presence is closely linked to availability or readiness for the Other. The unavailable person is not really there for the Other but maintains a closedness and a distraction toward something else. With this move in second reflection to existence as mystery, Marcel has turned toward the fullness of existence, which alludes first reflection and which is irreducible to it. The Thou, as a concretely situated being, cannot be approached in a reflection that is detached and epistemologically oriented, instead of involved and immersed in the concrete SITUATION. Thus, this critique of the primacy of objectivity has overcome the primacy of EPISTEMOLOGY and found its source. But what is more important is the affirmation that existence not only is given but is also giving. Existence is the very condition of any thinking and, as giving, encompasses CREATIVITY.

Giving as creative is a central motif of Marcel's philosophy; as soon as there is creation, we are in the realm of Being. The converse is equally true: there is no sense in using the word ''Being'' except where creation, in some form or other, emerges. On this level all of his celebrated themes, mystery, participation, presence, fidelity, creativity, charity, FAITH, and hope, must be interpreted, for first reflection, oblivious to this level, would reduce them to an abstraction or an objectivity. Thus, discussing mystery is a bringing into focus the attempt to think the WHOLENESS of existence and the questions that most vitally concern human LIFE. It is an attempt to reach the ineffable in a reflection that will never be adequate because of the richness of existence and of being. To undertake this attempt, he invokes faith, which, intimately related to hope and charity, is not exclusive of a philosophical faith in GOD.

Marcel seems to hint at the need for an indirect access to the question of the whole, in thinking beyond the boundaries of KNOWLEDGE and of problematic reflection. Most of his primary reflection on the mystery of Being takes place within a domain that for Kant must remain unknowable. He speaks of the need for images, for MYTH, in order to prevent idolatrizing that which is reflected upon—the price for our human condition as incarnate beings. Further, images may often serve as symbols of something richer, with two levels of meaning. We cannot free ourselves from some key images—for example, that of Heaven as the abode of the blessed—provided that these images are bound up with the conditions of existence of a wayfaring creature and that they cannot be considered as literally true. That Heaven can hardly appear to us as other than the sky; but insofar as the bond that holds us to the Earth is relaxed or changes, it will present a different aspect. We are destined to undergo a transformation the NATURE of which we can foresee only imperfectly. Thus, salvation can be better conceived as a road rather than a state.

Primary Work

Marcel, Gabriel. *The Mystery of Being*. Trans. G. S. Fraser. Chicago: Henry Regnery, 1960.

Bibliography

Gallagher, Kenneth T. *The Philosophy of Gabriel Marcel*. New York: Fordham University Press, 1962.

MYSTICISM
Sonya Sikka

Mysticism is sometimes a form of quietistic contemplation that is wholly detached from the WORLD, has left concepts and images behind, and is beyond TIME and HISTORY and in which individual identity is dissolved in the divine. This ideal runs counter to the SPIRIT of existentialism, with its emphasis on the concrete individual whose decisions and acts are finite and historical. Mysticism also stressed personal experience as opposed to either preconstituted religious dogma or a purely speculative METAPHYSICS. Much of the Western mystical tradition has maintained a relatively open and flexible attitude toward religious theses, doctrines, symbols, or historical narratives, holding these to be limited articulations of a reality that can never be fully comprehended and resists literal expression. These features of mysticism—its emphasis on personal experience in one's relation to GOD and its assertion that all religious formulations are, at best, partially true—often appealed to existentialists whose thought includes a religious dimension.

KIERKEGAARD rejects the mystical ideal. The ideal human EXISTENCE consists in achieving a proper synthesis of ETERNITY and TIME, BEING and becoming, the infinite and the finite. Mystical absorption, as an ecstatic state in which individuality is lost, may involve a rejection of one side of this essential polarity. However, his respect for Johannes Tauler, a fourteenth-century mystic, points to a more positive relation to some tendencies within Christian mysticism, especially the individual's relation to the divine. Against Hegel's rationalism, Kierkegaard insists upon the inwardness and ineffability of this RELATION, which cannot be captured in concepts and transcends the universality of ethical precepts.

The ideal of human existence for JASPERS also consists in achieving a proper synthesis of empirical, actual, and wholly immanent life with the dimension of being human, which is pointed toward TRANSCENDENCE, toward the Encompassing. The former aspect of existence Jaspers names DASEIN; the latter EXISTENZ. Mysticism would appear to annihilate Dasein; but Dasein is a necessary condition for Existenz. Mysticism that involves a flight from time and a dissolution into pure, formless immediacy is inauthentic. Mysticism, in rejecting Dasein, is one extreme; at the other lies positivism, which rejects Existenz. An authentic human existence remains embedded within the empirical world while being pointed toward transcendence. It does not seek timelessness but the eternalizing of the moment within present existence. It also does not seek formlessness, since it recognizes that mediation is the condition for human thought and for the discovery of truth. With respect to the divine, Jaspers' ideal recognizes that the infinite essence of the Encompassing, to which the movement of Existenz is related, ultimately does transcend all finite forms of expression. Religious formulations, including metaphysical theses, are ciphers of transcendence that simultaneously reveal and conceal the encompassing.

Here Jaspers is indebted to mystical THEOLOGY, particularly to Plotinus, Pseudo-Dionysius, Meister Eckhart, and Nicholas of Cusa. There is affinity between his idea of the Encompassing and the Plotinian transcendent. Neither is to be understood as metaphysical entities underlying the world; both are immanent as well as transcendent, depending on the perspective one adopts; both are manifested and dissimulated by finite existents and by the symbols, names, and descriptions through which humans attempt to know the unknowable. Nicholas of Cusa speaks of a coincidence of opposites in GOD, in whom contrasting rational categories are subsumed and transcended, and of a learned ignorance based on the realization that no names or descriptions are adequate here.

A similar stance is evident in HEIDEGGER's writings, whose attitude toward a certain kind of mysticism is positive. His later notion of Being as the other to what-is, which simultaneously conceals and reveals itself in what-is, is close to Jaspers' notion of the Encompassing. Being also cannot be comprehended; it can only be glimpsed in an experience in which the seer is caught up and included in the seeing. This could be described as a form of mystical INTUITION, in that it cannot be fully described in terms of either sense-perception or reason. It also defies literal expression, and the language for what is seen must be poetic, for it can only hint and beckon. Heidegger claims that Being is not God, but the fact remains that what he says about it is, in many respects, the same as what many mystical theologians have called God, or the Godhead.

Primary Works

Heidegger, Martin. *Poetry, Language, Thought*. Trans. Albert Hofstadter. New York: Harper and Row, 1971.
Jaspers, Karl. *Philosophy*. 3 vols. Trans. E. B. Ashton. Chicago: University of Chicago Press, 1969/1971.

MYTH
Mathew Rampley

Myth has exerted considerable fascination for PHILOSOPHY since Plato; modern interest in myth may perhaps be set at 1725, with the publication of Vico's

New Science, which posits myth as typifying a primitive stage of human CON-SCIOUSNESS. Against such a conception, some existentialists state that myth is of continued importance and not an obsolete, historical artifact. Specifically, myth embodies the prereflective LIFE-WORLD, which is increasingly displaced by the modern technological culture. Major existentialists make use of myth, including figures such as Prometheus, Sisyphus, Don Juan, or Abraham in their writings. They consider myth as a narrative intended to help present human EXISTENCE. Mythical narratives frequently offer a useful vehicle for the representation of prereflective existence. The use of myth, however, also occurs on another level in the thought of HEIDEGGER and is based on the idea of an inner spiritual bond between the Greeks and the Germans.

KIERKEGAARD's use of myth stems from a conviction that abstract conceptual LANGUAGE is inadequate to represent the concrete actualities of existence. A central strategy is to illustrate human existence by means of narratives, often centered on mythicohistorical individuals. A mythic narrative is seen, therefore, as having exemplary significance; thus, Don Juan is a powerful illustration of the AESTHETIC STAGE. Similarly, in *Fear and Trembling* the contradictions, complexities, and difficulties of leaping into the religious stage are presented in the myth of Abraham's sacrificing Isaac.

In his early work, Heidegger shows little interest in myth; indeed, he warns against the temptation to read in his analysis of everyday DASEIN a description of primitive historical Dasein bound by mythicopoetic thinking. One element of his later thinking on myth is already apparent in the founding role he accords the Greeks in introducing the question of BEING. In his later thought Heidegger seems to be suggesting a new mythology revolving around a narrative of the loss of Being after Plato and Socrates and its partial recovery in the POETRY of Holderlin. The historical process whereby Western METAPHYSICS has concealed Being attains a mythic significance. The putative recovery of Being in German thought is not seen as a historical event but rather as a destinal one and is related to the early pre-Socratic Greeks as a mythic origin; since then the HISTORY of Western culture has been a falling away. Heidegger's later writings are imbued with a profoundly religious sentiment. Being is an object of awe, of reverence. It is connected to his pagan mythology of the Fourfold of Heaven and Earth, mortals and GODS. This mythology forms a powerful focus of much of Heidegger's later work on poetry, according to which Holderlin, RILKE, and others are consumed with the problematics of saying the Holy when the gods have withdrawn. His final myth, therefore, is of a modernity destitute of gods, the REDEMPTION of which depends on their return.

Despite differences, CAMUS and SARTRE share with Heidegger the conviction of the contemporary importance of myth. In the play *The Flies* Sartre uses material drawn from classical mythology. Camus draws on mythical figures such as Sisyphus, Prometheus, and Don Juan in *The Myth of Sisyphus* and *The Rebel*. Myth for these writers reveals a capacity for universal exemplariness—for Camus, Sisyphus embodies the existential condition of the modern individual. For Sartre myths so sublimate their subjects as to render them universally recognizable. Thus, the mythic accomplishes the task of critical writing, namely, the articulation of the universal particular. In some writings Camus also displays considerable ambivalence toward myths, criticizing them as the sustenance of the poor in SPIRIT. This critique is in the context of his struggle between LOVE and revolt against the world and seems more aimed at inherited, sterile, and unproductive myths. His essay "Prometheus in Summer" argues that myths have no life of their own, that their meaning depends on the use made of them. He then interprets the Prometheus myth as a narrative of endurance in adversity, an interpretation with obvious contemporary political connotations. Prometheus figures prominently, too, in *The Rebel* as a symbol of metaphysical revolt against the absurd and as the symbol of the betrayal of that revolt by the advent of totalitarianism. Thus, myth is not to be seen as a source of authority or reverence but rather as an exemplary narrative embodying the typical universal of the human condition.

Primary Works

Heidegger, Martin. *Holderlin's Hymn "The Ister."* Trans. William McNeill and Julia
    Davis. Bloomington: Indiana University Press, 1996.
Kierkegaard, Søren. *Either/Or.* Vol. 1. Trans. David F. Swenson and Lillian Marvin
    Swenson. Princeton: Princeton University Press, 1959.

NATURE
W. Kim Rogers

Ancient and modern conceptions of nature as a separate, independent domain to which humans, as bodies at least, belong as parts is rejected by the existentialists in favor of an interdependent view of humans and nature. Thus, for BUBER the natural WORLD is not something that exists out there, as a ready-made part of experience. Rather, humans, by seeing, hearing, touching, meet the world that rises up to be met. Only by acting and being acted upon is anything made accessible. Humans experience what belongs to things or, in Buber's terms, the world of It but learn that there can be no experience of a thing in and of itself, for every It is bounded by others. There is not an experience of just this thing but rather of a world of things arranged around one thing or another. Thus, nature presents itself as a manifold through each of the things that humans experience. Buber offers as an example the perception of a tree, of its form and structure, its colors and chemical composition, its intercourse with the elements and the stars. The tree is a bundle of qualities, an object comprising parts, that is, one of many Its. Yet, in Buber's view one can surmount experience and meet the tree as a Thou. Thus, our RELATION to things in nature can also be an I–Thou relation.

Humans experience nature, according to MARCEL, SARTRE, and MERLEAU-PONTY, as the extension of one's BODY and its POWERS. For Marcel the natural world, the world that one senses, is accessible through the body and in the same way as the body. One's body is this world in its nearest approach to oneself. Sartre viewed the body as outlining one's possibilities in the world, living possibilities such as touching, running, dancing, while the world is revealed as an interconnected and unfolding series of instrumentalities and of acts to be performed. The natural world appears as both those objects that have their meaning in themselves and as the others that, being disclosed by one's own activities, have reference to oneself and one's own possibilities. The natural world is also the context in which one finds one's place defined by the spatial order and by the particular nature of the things that surround oneself.

Merleau-Ponty seems to have moved back and forth from viewing the world of one's perceptual experience as the pregiven setting of human LIFE to the view that this world is given and ordered for one in and through one's body and its activities. To this ambiguity of the world's APPEARANCE in one's life there corresponds the ambiguity of the body itself, which is not simply SUBJECT or simply OBJECT. On one hand, in the body–world relation, the body is a point of view on the world, a mediator of a world, and one's vehicle of being in a world. It is one's anchorage in a world. The body is the means by which one turns to, and comes to, awareness of that world in which one as a body at the same time finds oneself existing. On the other hand, as the relations between things or aspects of things perceived always have one's body as their vehicle, the body can be said to be the potentiality of this perceivable world. Thus, things and the world are given me along with the parts of one's body in a living connection identical with that existing between the parts of one's body itself. One's body is the fabric into which all objects are woven, and it is in relation to the perceived world, the given instrument of one's comprehension of that world. The body is the system of the objects of the world that one perceives, that is, of nature. Through the body one is at home in that world, can understand it, and find significance in it.

Thus, the natural world and the experiences and activities of humans are interwoven and dialogical. Nature is not to be viewed as a reality separate from the lives of humans, nor is it reducible to a mere ingredient in human experience. In this the existentialists' views of nature are quite close to what in contemporary physics has come to be called the anthropic principle. The human body has a special position as providing the site and the framework of relations as well as the means for the revealing of nature.

Primary Works

Buber, Martin. *The Knowledge of Man*. Trans. Maurice Friedman and Ronald Gregor Smith. New York: Harper and Row, 1965.
Merleau-Ponty, Maurice. *The Structure of Behavior*. Trans. Alden Fisher. Boston: Beacon Press, 1963.

NEGATION
Thomas R. Flynn

CONSCIOUSNESS, being-for-itself in SARTRE's terms, is the internal negation of being-in-itself, the other major division of being. It is the locus of possibility, of negativity, and of lack. All the ''not'' aspects of human reality, whether the ''not yet'' and ''no longer'' of temporality, the incompleteness of desire, or the otherness of our presence to the world and its objects—these are correlative to the ''productive power of the negative'' that Sartre claims eluded Descartes' cogito and the PHILOSOPHY of consciousness that he originated. Sartre coins the terms ''nihilation'' and ''negativity'' to denote features that exhibit the negativity of consciousness. To nihilate is not to annihilate or destroy. Rather, it is to ''other'' the WORLD and its objects that consciousness constitutes. The otherness of NOTHINGNESS that consciousness entails yields the inner distance between consciousness and its self that is the root of ontological FREEDOM for Sartre. Because consciousness does not coincide with itself, because it ''others'' its very self into a ''circle of selfness,'' it is free.

Primary Work

Sartre, Jean-Paul. *Critique of Dialectical Reason*. Trans. Alan Sheridan. London: Verso, 1982.

FRIEDRICH NIETZSCHE
(1844–1900)
Laurence Lampert

Despite often being maligned and misunderstood, Nietzsche has had enormous influence throughout the twentieth century. Such extreme reactions stem, in part, from his immodesty: he thought that his work represented a turning point in HISTORY. His immodesty, he argued, was not a pose or an aspiration but a fate forced on him by the importance of his ideas. Nietzsche was a student of spiritual revolutions, of the great shifts in human understanding marked by the irruption of a new teaching; he thought his own views were such a teaching. He believed he was kindling a spiritual war that would define the coming centuries and decide the fate of humankind. "God is dead," Nietzsche said and added that GOD deserved to die, because the spiritual force behind the idea of a transcendent god is the judgment that LIFE is no good. The result was that Nietzsche became best known for his NEGATIONS and grasped as one whose essential work was critical or destructive. He wrote his books in such a way as to force his reader to slow down, to make connections, to issue challenges, to think for oneself; he hated reading idlers and would do nothing to help them. His interpretation of other thinkers included a relentless unmasking of how life limited and determined thought, how the particulars of biography and CHARACTER dictated perspective and conviction. Nevertheless, he strove to transcend the limiting effects of his TIME, place, and particularities. He sought a comprehensive, true perspective.

Nietzsche was born in Rocken bei Lutzen, a village in Saxony, where he is buried. He was named Friedrich Wilhelm by his father after the kaiser born on the same day. His father, his grandfathers, and many other forebears were Lutheran ministers. Nietzsche was raised in a fervent, narrow Protestant piety. His father died when he was five; Nietzsche was taken with his younger sister to Naumburg, the provincial center, where he lived with his mother, his father's mother, and his father's two older sisters. By age thirteen, he won a scholarship to the best classical boarding school in Germany, Schulpforta, five miles from home. At University in Bonn and Leipzig, he abandoned THEOLOGY for philology, which influenced his work because it nurtured the ART of reading carefully. He was appointed professor of philology at the University of Basel at the age of twenty-four, even before he received his Ph.D.

While a student, Nietzsche discovered Schopenhauer and first met Richard Wagner. The young professor of philology and the older composer began a close association. But Nietzsche's philosophical maturity required making a clean break with both Schopenhauer and Wagner. Ill health forced Nietzsche to resign his professorship after ten years. He sustained himself for the rest of his working life on a small pension, living frugally. He became a wanderer: winters on or near the Mediterranean—Nice or Rapallo or Genoa or Turin—summers in the high Alpine valleys of Switzerland, at inexpensive boardinghouses. He worked on long walks, penciling his thoughts into pocket notebooks. Later, he copied them out in pen in larger notebooks, expanding, refining, excising, in a neat and legible hand. He suffered a disastrous breakdown in Turin in early January 1889; his work came to an end. The consensus is that he fell victim to tertiary syphilis.

The complete works of Nietzsche in the standard edition contain the eighteen books that he prepared for publication, plus approximately ten volumes of notebooks and eight volumes of letters. The books can be divided into two periods, before and after what Nietzsche regarded as his most important book, *Thus Spoke Zarathustra*. His books begin with *The Birth of Tragedy*, which is a study of high Athenian culture in its decline, focusing on tragedy and Socrates as fateful events in the spiritual history of the West. Socrates was held responsible for the DEATH of tragedy and for the establishment of optimistic rationalism. The last third of the book turned hopefully to Kant, Schopenhauer, and Wagner as modern revivals of the spirit of tragedy against the long-reigning rationalism of Socrates, a hope Nietzsche later abandoned. The book developed a fundamental theme: Apollo and Dionysos as inspiring the beautiful in different forms, the serene, tranquil, controlled, eye-centered wakefulness of Apollo, and the surging, streaming, frenzied, chthonic raging of Dionysos. In later works Dionysos takes over all positive artistic achievements, replacing Apollo most notably as the patron and exemplar of PHILOSOPHY.

Nietzsche published a series of meditations: "David Strauss the Confessor and the Writer," "The Uses and Disadvantage of History for Life," "Schopenhauer as Educator," "Richard Wagner in Bayreuth," which were sustained attacks on the highest ideals of German culture. They were especially untimely because they appeared in the midst of the supposed triumph of German culture, the nationalist euphoria following the victory over France in the Franco–Prussian War. In place of reigning ideals Nietzsche elevated Schopenhauer and Wagner as exemplars of a higher concept of culture; later, he said that these names could be replaced by the name Nietzsche. In works that followed he perfected the aphoristic form, which placed extreme demands on the reader because of its compactness and its apparently casual and chaotic character. Among these works are *Human, All Too Human; Daybreak*; and *The Gay Science.*

Thus Spoke Zarathustra is Nietzsche's most important book. An astonishing departure in style, it is a narrative that flares with metaphors, images, and parables, an apocalyptic work, a fable in which the old Persian prophet ZARATHUSTRA returns to proclaim the DEATH of the old teaching and the appearance of a new one. At first, Zarathustra can announce only its fundamental principle—be loyal to the Earth—and the need for a new teacher, some future SUPERMAN, who alone will know what this new loyalty means. But the book is a DRAMA; it chronicles

Zarathustra's growth, using metaphors of ascent and descent to map his entry into the primary discoveries of the new earthly teaching, on WILL to POWER, eternal return, and the European past, present, and future. Zarathustra is shown becoming the fundamental teacher. The book ends with Zarathustra preparing to return with the new teaching. Nietzsche regarded the book as a triumph, but it made almost no contemporary impact, forcing him to reconcile himself to being born posthumously.

Nietzsche said that after he had looked into the most distant futures in *Thus Spoke Zarathustra*, he was forced to train his eye again for the near and familiar. *Beyond Good and Evil* is the first fruit of this disciplined focus on the present. As with all the post-Zarathustra books it is an introduction to *Thus Spoke Zarathustra*. Nietzsche left behind a rich collection of fragments in notebooks kept from his earliest days. There are extensive notes on some issues treated only skimpily in the books. This is especially true of the notebooks from 1885 onward, which contain valuable reflections on BEING, knowing, NIHILISM, and the history of philosophy. These notes were preparations for what Nietzsche had promised in later books: a new major work that would draw his themes together in an unprecedented form. His legacy was distorted by the publication of a book purporting to be that final major work: *The Will to Power*. The fragments in this collection contain many important matters, but they lack both the order Nietzsche would have given them and the polished form he would have supplied. His letters are of lesser interest because he never developed extended correspondence with friends and associates in which he presented his ideas in a personal form or argued on their behalf. They do, however, have their fascination for his life.

''Is it permitted to say this?''—so Nietzsche often asked before stating an unpermitted view, one that could not be welcomed or easily understood because convention rules the world of ideas. All his books bear the marks of strategic reflection on how to present ideas that were subtle and elusive, distant from held opinions, and upsetting in their implications. What follows are some major points central to grasping his thoughts.

Everything that is, is in PROCESS; there is no discernible goal to the process. Nietzsche defended the ancient view that all is flux. The historic opponents of this view in the West are Plato and those who hold that there is a realm of Permanence, which alone is of ultimate concern to us. Such views diminish the importance of the WORLD of becoming or view it as fallen: they regard the permanent as GOOD and process as bad. The advancement of science helped to make such views increasingly unbelievable, but their demise spreads a malaise or sadness: if only the world of process and becoming exists, how can that satisfy humans? That all will be ruin seems a counsel of despair to a culture raised on the view that only the timeless is ultimately valuable. Nietzsche's moral teaching aimed to restore the innocence of becoming, not only to spare it the moral condemnation it has suffered but to celebrate it and beautify it. If everything that is, is in process, the proper science of beings is natural history, or genealogy.

Nietzsche's view of natural history was evolutionary and nonteleological. He places humans back among the animals while guarding against the vanity that humans are the great objective of animal evolution. The human is not the crown of creation: every living being stands on the same level of perfection. Nietzsche quarreled with the Darwinian principle that life is self-preservation. The principle of life for Nietzsche was not reactive and preservative; fundamentally, life is dynamic, surging, expansionary. He tried to capture that principle in a label: Will to power. With this phrase he attempted to name the process present in all beings and events. But his view of process and his view that everything that exists is singular, one of a kind, mean that any label is a metaphor that limits by stabilizing and generalizing; it is, at best, a convenient abstraction for phenomena that exist as processes of unique events and entities.

Nietzsche set his view of will to power against the then-dominant physics of atomism and mechanism, that NATURE consisted of irreducibly solid particles that bounced around the universe in obedience to laws of mechanical motion. This view, he argued, was anthropomorphic; it humanized and simplified nature via human categories. It subjected nature to a political program of human dominance through technology; it aimed to transcend nature by subduing it. Moreover, it was false. Against atomism and mechanism, he posited will to power as a universal theory. To be is to be a quantum of force; to be an entity is to be a structured, but temporary, equilibrium of force quanta within a field of force quanta. Each force quantum exists as the expression of its force and as resistance to other forces. The whole consists of the relentless expression of force relations existing in dynamic tension. The universe is this total field of forces in uninterrupted flow, congealing temporarily into entities of greater or lesser stability: into stars, say, as dynamic processes of gases. The intelligible character of such a world derives from its tendency to structure. The natural history of the world exhibits that tendency as a hierarchy of structures of lesser and greater complexity. Among these complex structures is the structure for understanding and explanation, the intelligence driven to grasp intelligible structure as far as this is possible.

Nietzsche is famous for his skepticism, for submitting all claims of KNOWL-EDGE to suspicion. He relentlessly uncovered reasons for mistrust: the limitations of our senses; the perspective character of understanding; the necessity that reasoning makes the unlike like, that it categorizes the singular under rules of identity and sameness that have no counterpart in nature; the history of human misunderstanding that exhibits not merely a capacity to be mistaken but a powerful desire to take things other than they are. These and other reasons for mistrust lead to caution and suspicion as confederates of an incautious and passionate desire to understand. But how can it be claimed that will to power is the way of all beings? Nietzsche's reasoning is that the most knowable is the nearest and most intimate: the processes of one's inner life. ''Know thyself'' is the imperative behind all philosophy as it moves from the more knowable to the less knowable, from self to nonself. Further, one can, to a degree, know the processes of one's inner life as the development and ramification of will to power and that one must experiment with this force as the explanation of organic function and of efficient force.

The will to power view refutes not God but the devil. What once took the name God must be seen as demonic from the new perspective, and what was once demonic, fallen under the powers of the Prince of Darkness from the perspective of TRANSCENDENCE, becomes divine or sacred from the new perspective. Nietzsche's view is a vindication of the gods, the earthly gods Dionysos and Ariadne. Once the force of the old view spends itself, more nuance and affirmative judgments can be made—ultimately the judgment that, seen as Will to power, life is good and warrants our saying to it: Eternally return. Nietzsche presented eternal return as his most important teaching. After this thought appeared to him in the summer of 1881, he wrote *The Gay Science*, ending the book with a poetic announcement of the new teaching and introducing Zarathustra as a vehicle for presenting the idea of eternal return. Zarathustra brings a series of discoveries, the most basic of which is that life is will to power.

Humans live an evaluation of the facts, some system of VALUES that gives life Meaning. Zarathustra discovered in the traditional teachings, in the POETRY and thought that created and sustained human cultures something both basic and uniform: a refusal of nature, a hatred of time and beings that expressed itself in what Zarathustra called the SPIRIT of revenge. This spirit framed human values in the dominant cultures. As Zarathustra expressed it, revenge is directed particularly against the passage of time, which deposits into the past everything that has been, leaving it dead and gone, inaccessible to the human will to alter and remake. What is the teaching of eternal return? It can be understood as a literal return: everything that was and is has returned and will return an infinite number of times exactly as it was and is. This view is not presented as a factual conclusion drawn from cosmological investigations. Instead, it arises from reflection on how humans have understood and valued the world until now. Zarathustra aims at reconciliation with time, a reconciliation that refuses any claim that time could be suspended or transcended. But eternal return appears as something higher than any reconciliation, for it does not simply reconcile the one who affirms it to the world as it is. Eternal return expresses the desire that the world as it is be as it is an infinite number of times.

Zarathustra presents eternal return as the new sanity in the face of the old preaching of madness; but in its own way it, too, is a kind of madness, the affirmative madness of a lover: passionate, lyrical, transfiguring, sane, it says to the beloved: Be what you are; be eternally what you are. The affirmation of eternal return arises out of joy: the joyous participant in life, granted the gift of insight into the way of all beings as will to power, wants what was and is repeated into all eternity. The spirit of gravity—Zarathustra's name for the grave, life-denying, avenging teachings that have prevailed—is replaced by the spirit of the dancer, supple, strong, rhythmic, light, joyous, free. Nietzsche also wrote notes that argued that eternal return was the most scientific of all possible hypotheses and supplanted the teleological and mechanistic hypotheses: if the world is infinite with respect to time and finite with respect to possible energy states, the fact that no end state has yet been reached proves that no end state can be reached and that teleological and mechanistic hypotheses are false.

Nietzsche's presentations emphasize the moral element. As the highest possible affirmation of life, it is the highest value, and the highest value arises out of the fundamental fact. Desiring the eternal return is the highest human affirmation of the discovery of what throbs, seethes, spumes, and sprays in the heart of things. Eternal return is the core of Nietzsche's creation of new values, and value creation is a central task of the genuine philosopher. All values are subjective: everything valuable is made valuable by the act of valuing it. But valuing, in its fundamental form of value creation, is not arbitrary; it has an inner logic that a proper physiopsychology can trace and describe. Just as the old values arose plausibly and logically from a disposition of heart and MIND expressed in the word ''revenge,'' so too, values that derive from eternal return have an inner logic and coherence because they arise from the opposite disposition. In addition, the new values have a historical logic that makes them desirable at this point in human history. As the supreme value arising out of the new naturalism, eternal return expresses a new teaching on justice, the human act of giving what is due to other beings. To desire the eternal return of everything that was and is expresses the highest affirmation attainable. Eternal return is the affirmative core of a new human judgment on the natural order. In this teaching an ecological philosophy expresses its loyalty to the Earth. Eternal return is the supreme value that grounds a new culture. Humans have aimed to escape nature or to master it. Eternal return marks a new departure: beyond all reconciliation, it is the unconditional Yes to all that was and is, a new human stance toward the Earth.

Nietzsche emphasizes genealogy, the attempt to recover the family history of the human species. Genealogy traces human origins, following the trail of evolutionary events that produced humans as social animals. Firmly within the tradition, he sketched an evolutionary history of humankind based, as far as possible, on what is documented. The focus of his investigations was the way of life engendered in historic cultures. He concentrated on the Homeric culture, which gave birth to a singular greatness, the artistic and intellectual achievements of classical Athens: Aeschylus, Sophocles, Aristophanes, Thucydides, and the philosophers leading up to Democritus, especially Empedocles and Heraclitus. The center of his attention in the Greek world remained Socrates, whom he viewed as a problem: How could the Socratic view arise and finally hold sway when it represented something so anti-Hellenic? Socrates' anti-Hellenism was optimistic rationalism, the faith that thought, using the thread of logic, could penetrate the deepest abysses of being and even correct it. Reflecting on Plato, Nietzsche again raised Athens' question: Did Socrates corrupt the young after all? Did he deserve his hemlock?

Nietzsche holds that Plato's philosophy opposed the monumental achievements of Homeric culture, which reached their peak in the festivals of tragedy in Athens. The greatness of Attic tragedy consisted primarily in two things: it recognized the human place in a blind and meaningless process that humans cannot master or transcend and that can crush even the purest human aspiration and bring to ruin even the best man; and it affirmed the human and natural seen with this clarity. Its affirmation took the form of the creation of the beautiful. In words, sounds, and images it magnified and beautified the human in nature, elevating it into paradigms of the heroic. Socrates and Plato refused this affirmative vision; in a cultural event of the first magnitude, they set out to replace it with a set of comforting wishes. These included the wish that the whole of nature be lucid and transparent to human understanding, that nature be brought to a standstill in permanent, Platonic ideas that are founded on the idea of the good, a transcendent and ineffable perfection. This was the most dangerous of all errors. Plato also made concessions to the dangerous wish that humans be immortal and, with the help of gods, occupy some paradise beyond the earth.

Plato availed himself of an old right claimed by fundamental teachers, the right to lie. Nietzsche was a student of the noble lies, as Plato called them, equipping his best city with lies of divine origin and divine sanction. He sees in Plato a most effective master of the art of high-minded lying, lying for everybody's good by persuading them that the world is a moral order that rewards goodness and punishes wickedness—beliefs necessary to ground moral behavior. Such salutary lying played a crucial role in the dominant traditions, having been endorsed by Indian, Greek, Persian, and Muslim philosophers. While acknowledging esotericism as an inescapable component of the MYSTERY and enigma of EXISTENCE, Nietzsche in no way endorsed its Platonic form, the elaboration and defense of a true world, higher and different from this world. Untold damage has been done to humanity by the belief that there exists a higher, better world. That damage had been done to Western culture by Platonism, which prepared its decisive event: CHRISTIANITY's capture of imperial Rome. Christianity brought ancient science and philosophy to a premature end centuries before any possible fulfillment. European history became a drama marked by the dominance of Christianity punctuated by occasional renaissances of the Hellenic and Roman spirit.

Modernity in its optimism for mass democracy and enlightenment, its powerful movement for equality and homogeneity, its view that it is the fulfillment of history in freedom and enlightenment, its liberalism is, in Nietzsche's view, the secular heir to Christianity. The lateness and intensity of his assault on Christianity arise from his deepening understanding of its historic offspring, modernity. But modernity is ambiguous, for it also advanced the fight against Plato and Christianity, the fight to recover ancient science and scholarship in a renaissance that would last. Nietzsche recognized that the modern advancement of science had served to move European societies in the direction toward building a culture on the foundation of science, on nature as investigated and brought to light by inquiry. However, the naturalistic view of the world is opposed by the deep wish that the world be otherwise, the wish flattered and nourished by Platonism. For Nietzsche, modern science had succeeded: God is dead, and Platonism lies on the ground. But this success had been a negation. The defeat of old ideals, now known to be impossible and undesirable, and the logic of cultural history dictated that this success be experienced as nihilism. So profound and complete was Nietzsche's anatomy of nihilism that many readers saw him as a teacher of nihilism, even though he claimed to have surmounted it with a new, affirmative teaching. The core of that new teaching is eternal return.

Nietzsche's thought is the first comprehensive response to modernity, to the Europeanization of the globe through the IDEOLOGY and technology of modern Europe. This global SOCIETY is inhabited by the last men described powerfully by Zarathustra: contented, mild, shortsighted, self-satisfied egoists of modern culture, consumers of the modern MYTH that the very meaning of history was to create modern humanity. Nietzsche responded to global modernity with his great politics, the spiritual revolution based on the affirmation of the Earth. Cultural history provides the grounds for his immodest assessment of the importance of his views: they are a historic departure from the old perspectives and an experimental possibility for the future.

Was Nietzsche the turning point in the history of culture that he aspired to be? His own perspective on the dynamics of culture and the role of founding teachers suggests that it is still too early to tell.

Primary Works

Nietzsche, Friedrich. *The Birth of Tragedy and The Case of Wagner*. Trans. Walter
    Kaufmann. New York: Vintage Books, 1967.
———. *The Gay Science*. Trans. Walter Kaufmann. New York: Random House, 1974.
———. *The Will to Power*. Trans. Walter Kaufmann and R. J. Hollingdale. New York:
    Vintage, 1969.

Bibliography

Lampert, Laurence. *Nietzsche's Teaching: An Interpretation of "Thus Spoke Zarathu-
    stra."* New Haven, CT: Yale University Press, 1986.

NIHILISM
Phyllis Kenevan

Nihilism has been defined as the situation where everything is permitted; since there are no absolutes, presumed necessary TRUTHS are not necessary, and there are no goals or VALUES that have intrinsic worth. Consequently, human life appears to be meaningless, without purpose or destiny, haunted by a bleak NOTHINGNESS that no theological or rational assumptions can allay. Humanitarian ideals were dismissed by the nihilist as self-indulgent romanticism. The first nihilists were devoted to destroying the old order so that SOCIETY could be rebuilt along new, progressive lines. Nihilism as a philosophical theme is associated with NIETZSCHE, who used it to signify a pathological state following the decline of the Judaic-Christian tradition, described in *The Gay Science* as the DEATH of GOD. NIETZSCHE was not advocating nihilism; he was diagnosing it as a pathological, temporary condition, a direct result of the failure of CHRISTIANITY, described in his works. That failure was inevitable and justified since Christianity was the chief cause of degeneration in modern LIFE. However, he viewed nihilism as a transition state, the result of using wrong categories to interpret life. What was needed was the creation of new meanings, goals and values that would turn the Western world toward a healthier, more vital direction. That depended on active CHOICE; unless right choices were made, nihilism could destroy humanity.

Nietzsche argued that Christianity provided a temporary relief from the malaise of an evolutionary past that drove suffering inward. The priest, by interpreting suffering in religious terms—as payment for SINS—gave a meaning to suffering, thereby avoiding nihilism. But Christianity carried the seeds of its destruction in its BELIEF in the divinity of TRUTH. The WILL to truth brought its downfall. The claims of a rational, moral order in the universe in unity, divine justice, purpose all failed when put to the test. When the will to truth revealed its failure, intellectual nihilism emerged. In fact, the loss of a goal and unity for all becoming left such a profound disbelief in its wake that not only the world became valueless but humanity also lost FAITH in its own value. "GOD is dead" means there is no longer any Being or absolute truth or MORALITY. The madman who carries his lantern into the market realizes he has come too soon; the self-professed atheists who mock him fail to realize that the moral values they hold no longer have a foundation to support them.

Pathological nihilism, Nietzsche predicted, would take 200 years to run its course. During that time the weak would perish of their decadence, and the strong would struggle and overcome it, ridding themselves of both the old values and nihilism. To those with the rejuvenating power to conquer the decadence of their time would come the realization that nihilism was a result of having measured the value of the WORLD according to categories that referred to a fictitious world and the realization that since those categories no longer applied, there was no reason to devaluate the universe. Nihilism, then, is an interlude between the DEATH of the old and the birth of the new ideals. Once the decadence has vanished, a new order can be built.

KIERKEGAARD sees contemporary nihilism as a failure to distinguish between spurious and genuine Christianity. The malaise, emptiness, and threatening triviality of human EXISTENCE are the sickness unto death or despair that can be cured only by a leap of faith. For the Christian, nihilism is not the threat; the real danger is a weakness of will or a defiance that keeps one from making the commitment toward faith. The state of sin is one in which, with the conception of God, one remains in a state of despair. Only demonic despair might be viewed as a form of nihilism; but to the believer, this nihilism is understood as the deepest state of sin. Even this nihilism is curable, since with God all things are possible.

CAMUS confronts nihilism with the question of whether or not life is worth living. The problem is one of meaning. The world can be a familiar place. But with no recognizable meaning one is an alien. A world in which we are estranged, where we neither remember a lost home nor hope for a future promised land, is Absurd. Hence, why not SUICIDE? But if the universe is silent in regard to our quest for meaning, suicide is not our only alternative. There is a life beyond nihilism, which involves finding our humanity in refusing to be gods. There is more to admire in humanity than to despise; we do not need to come from the Garden of Eden or look for one at the end of HISTORY. The universe may be silent in regard to our questions, but we can find answers in embracing our present. We may resemble Sisyphus, forever rolling a boulder up the mountain, but we may also conclude that life is worthy. Later, Camus sees humanity preparing a renaissance beyond nihilism, away from failed absolutes and embracing our first and last LOVE, the Earth.

SARTRE found no need to defend atheistic existentialism from the threat of nihilism. He admits that it is distressful that God does not exist; nevertheless, that loss does not condemn me to meaninglessness. It does condemn me to choose. I may be left alone and without excuse, but this abandonment is also liberating since it allows me to create my image of what human existence should be. Existentialism thus is optimistic; human NATURE is still to be determined, and DOSTOYEVSKY's claim that if God did not exist, everything would be permitted is, for the existentialist, the starting point. This optimism is born from an honest encounter with the ANGUISH that announces my inescapable FREEDOM. The realization that nothing justifies me in adopting a particular value, that there is no moral ought that I have not propped into place by my own choice could evoke the ANXIETY associated with nihilism. But the real problem is not whether or not God exists; for even if God existed, it would make no difference. The real problem is one of self-confrontation. In action, Sartre sees ground for hope. The problem of meanings and values is one that can be met creatively and responsibly through an honest acceptance of the need for authentic choice. The task of creating meaning and an ETHICS starting from an atheist position is compatible with hope, even when accompanied by anguish, abandonment, and despair. Such is a task that we cannot escape, because if there is no God, then someone has to invent values.

For HEIDEGGER also, nihilism is not a threat. The real danger is that we have forgotten BEING, have even forgotten to raise the question regarding Being. Since everything comes from Being, which both reveals and conceals itself, we may be homeless now, but we are not condemned to find meaning only in ourselves. We need to open ourselves to the MYSTERY of Being, to learn how to question Being and to listen to the silence. If I confine myself to calculate thinking and ignore contemplative thinking, that knows how to think what at first sight doesn't go together, I throw away my essential nature. "Letter on Humanism" argues that speaking against traditional humanism does not mean advocating nihilism or a barbaric inhumanity. On the contrary, it opens up other vistas, especially a HUMANISM that thinks humanity from nearness to Being. Similarly, to speak against logic is not to lose the reign of thinking or to be reduced to the irrational. Logic is not synonymous with thinking; the alternative is not the illogical but a return to the prelogical, to true ontological thought that is presubjective and open to Being. Thinking against values is not to see everything as valueless. What is valued only as an object for human estimation is a subjectivizing of beings into mere OBJECTS. Instead, Heidegger wants to let beings be or to bring the lighting of the truth of Being before such thinking. We are too filled with logic. That is why whatever disturbs prevailing opinion is registered as a despicable contradiction. Furthermore, nihilism is inappropriate because the assumption that God is dead is no more warranted than one that God lives. To be indifferent to the question of whether or not God exists would be nihilistic. To live nonnihilistically, we have to turn to the question of the truth of Being; we must adopt a thinking more rigorous than the conceptual. Such thinking is neither theoretical nor practical—it precedes this distinction. It is recollection of Being, a thinking more original than METAPHYSICS that leaves PHILOSOPHY behind.

Primary Work

Nietzsche, Friedrich. *The Gay Science*. Trans. Walter Kaufmann. New York: Random House, 1974.

Bibliography

Thody, Philip. *Albert Camus: A Study of His Work*. New York: Grove Press, 1957.

NOTHINGNESS
Thomas R. Flynn

Existentialists have stressed the radical CONTINGENCY of human EXIS-TENCE. Human reality is superfluous for SARTRE; under threat of nonexist-

ence in DEATH, according to HEIDEGGER; inevitably facing limit situations
in JASPERS' view. For these thinkers, AUTHENTICITY requires that we accept our finitude with resolute decisiveness, taking full RESPONSIBILITY for
our SITUATION. Inauthenticity, on the contrary, entails flight from finitude
toward such BELIEFS as determinism or personal IMMORTALITY. In *Being
and Time* and other writings Heidegger offers an ontological account of the
nothingness that our experience of dread reveals. Elaborating on KIERKE-
GAARD's description of dread as the awareness of our own FREEDOM, he
interprets this experience of nonbeing as giving us access to the finite BEING
of beings. Heidegger here is an ontologist, a philosopher whose guiding problem
was to gain access to Being. In *Being and Time* this occurs by way of an analysis
of DASEIN's being-unto-death, that is, a phenomenological account of what it
means to be, facilitated by the anguished experience of our finitude, of what it
means not-to-be. The upshot of these descriptions is that Being is finite, and
nothingness is experienced as such. In *Being and Nothingness*, Sartre equates
nothingness with the nihilating CONSCIOUSNESS that secretes negativity as it
constitutes a WORLD. As the internal NEGATION of its OBJECTS, consciousness is the nothingness of things or being-in-itself. Nonbeing is a component of
the real. All forms of the "not" that inhabit our world, including negative
judgments and what he calls negativities—the fragility of a glass or of a friendship—are both correlative to consciousness and symptoms of our contingency.
Though consciousness-relative, negativities are not subjective phenomena. They
presuppose a prejudicative comprehension of nonbeing as transphenomenal.

Primary Work

Sartre, Jean-Paul. *The Psychology of the Imagination*. Trans. Bernard Fretchman. New
    York: Washington Square Press, 1966.

OBJECT
Lawrence J. Hatab

A significant feature in existential PHILOSOPHY is the critique of, and departure from, the standard of objectivity intrinsic to modern philosophy, beginning
with Descartes. In the *Meditations* Descartes dramatized the orientation of modern thought as a reflective separation from tradition, custom, common sense,
PERSONALITY, passion, and normative concerns—for the purpose of articu-

lating and defending the mathematical/mechanistic PROJECT of the New Science. Such a project was geared toward rendering the WORLD as an object, toward an active stripping from thought and experience of all elements that do not conform to a mechanistic model of causality and the bare conception of extended matter in motion. The world is reduced to a scientific object bereft of meaning, purpose, beauty, goodness, sacredness—elements that, at best, are deemed subjective human interpretations and not properties of the world. Implicit and complicit in this reduction are the human reason's manipulation and control of NATURE in modern technology. Concurrent with this development is a disenchantment with bourgeois capitalism and its reduction of human relations to instrumental rationality, monetary value, material possession, and quantitative calculation. Existentialism is frequently a rebellion against modern transformations of the world into nothing more than an object, particularly when humans are submitted to objectification.

KIERKEGAARD refuses to reduce humans to objective properties, emphasizing the subjective experiences of personal life. His notion of subjectivity involves the first-PERSON standpoint. For Kierkegaard, objective categories cannot capture how we exist as subjects because our experience of possibility always exceeds the actuality of objects and fixed conditions. Human EXISTENCE is always becoming and unfinished. Objective categories have their place, but only subjective categories apply to central concerns of human existence. In ETHICS, RELIGION, and other spheres, subjective experiences such as desire, passion, involvement, CREATIVITY, ANXIETY, decision, and commitment are paramount. None of these are characteristic of objects; any attempt to trace them to objective categories betrays an ALIENATION from the human condition. In effect, the modern rational and scientific impulse toward exhaustive frameworks that screen out subjective experience perpetuates a flattened, impoverished, and closed picture of human LIFE.

SARTRE distinguishes between objects and CONSCIOUSNESS, which is nothing like an objective fact because it shows itself as a persistent NEGATION to actualized states in the WORLD. He accepts the BEING of objects and affirms consciousness' essential intentional RELATION to them. Yet he insists on the special features of consciousness that can never be traced to fixed objective states. The objective being of a mountain is a given; but human responses to it, such as seeing it as majestic or as a challenge to climb, exhibit consciousness' free and open project of meaning-making that never resolves itself into something that simply is. Sartre's famous proposition that existence precedes ESSENCE means that with humans there is nothing prior to the existence of consciousness that can define it prior to an individual's CHOICE to live one way rather than another. The being of consciousness is a perpetual negativity, a kind of nonbeing. There is no denying objective conditions of human life, for instance, biological facts about the body and its needs for survival; nevertheless, the FREEDOM of consciousness is shown in the human capacity to resist domination even under pain of DEATH. Included in freedom is anxiety in the face of nothingness. There is a common impulse to deny or conceal the negativity of consciousness and to want to be a kind of object. Persons often resist or mask RESPONSIBILITY for choices by depicting behavior as a consequence of compelling natural conditions or social forces. We also take comfort in the closed assurances of objective explanations of human practices and their HISTORY. Such constitutes a refusal of freedom, BAD FAITH, and a surrender to the seduction of casting humans as objects of scientific analysis. Consciousness is the very antithesis of any object.

HEIDEGGER agrees that modern philosophy and science have erred in restricting thought to methods and modes of objectification. He explores a conception of being that does not split into a polarized framework of SUBJECT and object. He challenges traditional objective ontologies but refuses to restrict his alternative ONTOLOGY to subjectivity or consciousness. Although his notion of DASEIN indicates a priority of human existence, it is such only as the opening to the meaning of Being in general and as the opening of Being in a primal process of disclosure, of coming to presence out of concealment. The meaning of the world and various regions of beings are disclosed to Dasein by way of its finite comportment and fundamental temporality. Dasein's experience of being-toward-death opens up the range of temporal and historical movements within which the world is disclosed. At a fundamental level, Dasein experiences primal moods, nonobjective modes of attunement that exhibit the meaningfulness of the world before one reflects on it or uses it. Accordingly, Heidegger argues that Being can never be reduced to an objective state because the world is first uncovered through meaningful involvement and through CARE. We care about the world before we objectify it.

Thus, Heidegger challenges the metaphysical standard of objective TRUTH, which traditionally has held that truth is independent of human comportment. Since science has to first matter to Dasein, existential conditions are implicated in all forms of truth. The search for truth is a finite, temporal, and historical process of disclosure that cannot be grounded in any condition or state. Beings are disclosed to Dasein, not produced or projected by Dasein. Though departing from objective ontologies, Heidegger refuses to join the side of the subject–object polarity. Subjectivism concedes too much to the modern subject–object bifurcation that thrust apart existential concerns and world conditions into disparate spheres of mere human interests and bare, self-contained objects. Heidegger not only wants to rescue human existence from objectification but also wants to rescue things in the world from being reduced to the status of an object. Even entities in the world have a preobjective meaning and presence that scientific rationality cancels out or conceals. Hence, poets and artists are sensitive to, and uncover, rich dimensions of beings encountered in the world. Heidegger gives much attention to poetic LANGUAGE and its mode of revealing. Such disclosure is grounded in an opening toward, and opening of, a primal presencing that the poet enacts and serves; such is neither a strictly objective nor subjective event.

Primary Works

Heidegger, Martin. *Poetry, Language, Thought.* Trans. Albert Hofstadter. New York: Harper and Row, 1971.

Kierkegaard, Søren. *Concluding Unscientific Postscript.* Trans. David F. Swenson and Walter Lowrie. Princeton: Princeton University Press, 1968.

ONTIC
John Protevi

"Ontic" is the adjectival form of the contrasting term to "ontological" in HEIDEGGER's technical vocabulary, denoting a type of analysis of a BEING. An ontic analysis is concerned with the properties of an OBJECT, taking the Being, or ground of those properties, for granted. An ontological analysis, on the other hand, is concerned with the understanding of Being, the understanding of the ground of the various ways a being can appear. An ontological analysis of a being thus deals with the way it can appear not just as an object with properties—sensation, shared with animals, is just such an ontic revelation—but as a being whose Being is revealed in an understanding of Being. The ontic and the ontological are intricately intertwined. *Being and Time*, the investigation of the horizon for the question of the sense of Being in general—the way in which any being can appear—analyzes DASEIN, that is, that being among whose ontic properties is that of having an understanding of Being—in other words, that being to whom other beings can appear in their Being. Thus, only Dasein is ontological; only it can turn about and deliver an ontological analysis of itself as a being with an understanding of Being, even when that understanding has not been developed into a thematic ONTOLOGY. The ontological analysis of Dasein is thus described in *Being and Time* as having an ontic fundament, the fact that Dasein has the ontic property of an understanding of Being. In *The Metaphysical Foundations of Logic*, Heidegger further describes the intertwining of ontic and ontological by showing the way fundamental ontology, the analysis of Dasein's understanding of Being, develops into its overturning into the discipline of metontology, which investigates beings as a whole. Metontology is a task because Dasein is, no matter how special, one being among the others in the whole of Being, one for whom the fact of EXISTENCE presupposes the factual extantness of NATURE. Fundamental ontology and metontology thus constitute METAPHYSICS, the investigation of Being and beings in their intertwining.

Primary Work

Heidegger, Martin. *The Metaphysical Foundations of Logic*. Trans. Michael Heim. Bloomington: Indiana University Press, 1984.

ONTOLOGY
Lawrence J. Hatab

Ontology is concerned with the question of BEING. Existentialists often challenge traditional conceptions of ontology. For NIETZSCHE, PHILOSOPHY since Plato is based on a preference for being over becoming, for that which *is* over unstable conditions governed by temporality, change, variation, disintegration, and DEATH. Since lived experience is permeated with unstable conditions and therefore cannot measure up to strict conditions of being, traditional philosophy grounds thinking and reality in metaphysical principles, GOD, the soul, or natural laws—which transcend lived experience. Thus, traditional philosophy is based on psychological weakness, on an inability to affirm a temporal WORLD. Consequently, the conception of being is an illusion, a psychological construct meant to ward off negativity and to nurture a sense of security. Often, LANGUAGE permits and fosters this illusion: since nouns can be distinguished from verbs, we are tempted to isolate substances from activities. Things, however, are only what they do; there are no permanent entities behind, or distinct from, the changing streams of events.

KIERKEGAARD partially accepts traditional categories of being but maintains that EXISTENCE is a special category of human LIFE that cannot fall under the rubric of being. Being and existence are not synonymous. Western thought had always distinguished between ESSENCE and existence; essence names what a thing is, its definition or general NATURE; existence indicates that a thing is. Existences are particular, contingent, temporal occurrences, while essences are universal, necessary, eternal conditions. Traditional ontology could be called essentialism, since only essences can be said to truly be. Existent things can be understood only as instantiations of metaphysical principles or universal categories. Philosophy has looked to objective properties for an understanding of humans, rather than the subjective experiences of each PERSON. Kierkegaard's notion of subjectivity involves the first-person standpoint of experiences. Objective categories of being pass over and conceal how I exist as an individual. OBJECTS and objective properties can be said to be, but only the individual SUBJECT exists. Existence is always more than being, in the sense that possibilities always outstrip whatever actualities obtain in an individual's LIFE. Human existence is always becoming and can never be reduced to objective states of being. Objectivity and being have their place, but in questions of human meaning, subjective decisions are paramount. In ETHICS, RELIGION, and other realms, CHOICE, ANXIETY, possibility are crucial. Any attempt to press these experiences into objective categories amounts to ALIENATION from the human condition. Our task in life is to face up to the difficulties and demands of always being thrust out beyond the bounds of fixed conditions.

SARTRE distinguishes two realms of being, the being of objects and the being of CONSCIOUSNESS, which he called a kind of NOTHINGNESS because it shows itself as continual and various forms of negative RELATIONS to things or objective conditions in the world. Phenomena such as desire, denial, CREATIVITY, possibility, and anxiety all show that human consciousness is not an object. Such is the source of his famous statement: existence precedes essence, which holds that with humans, there is nothing prior to a subject's existence that can define it prior to one's choice to live one way rather than another. Traditional essentialism maintained that something prior to individual existence defines what the individual is and gives guidance as to what one will or can be. For Sartre, certain facts about my life can be said to be, for instance, the color of my eyes, but I can never be reduced to a stable state freed from negativity. Since nothing can explain, fix, or predict what human life is or should be, humans are free to define themselves through the project of CONSCIOUSNESS, through the negative relations of consciousness to conditions. Hence, existentialism is a HUMANISM, in the sense that traditional objective explanations of human life are exchanged for a humanistic spirit of self-determination. The meaning of human life is continually created by individuals.

HEIDEGGER's approach to ontology has more in common with the premodern idea that Being is something that presents itself to humans rather than something constructed by or for humans. However, he does not want to restrict his alternative ontological conception to the human sphere, to subjectivity or consciousness. He seeks a general approach to Being. Although DASEIN has priority, it is such as an opening to the meaning of Being, which is partially disclosed through and to Dasein. Dasein's essence lies in its existence, which is meant in the ec-static sense of Dasein standing-out of itself in the world. Thus, what beings are and the question of Being cannot be separated from human existence, since the disclosure of Being is not an objective event but rather is codisclosed through Dasein's MOODS and involvements. Meaningfulness is at the core of Heidegger's conception of Being. Beings are meaningful to Dasein, but this meaningfulness is more Dasein's response to the world than a self-contained sphere distinct from the world. *Being and Time* offers a phenomenological analysis that articulates this correlation of Dasein, world, and Being, climaxing in Dasein's experience of death, which reveals the primal limit situation from which and within which care about the world can find it meaningful. Human being is radically finite in that it is illuminated by limit conditions and NEGATION; it is finite in its temporality and historicality, as a continual unfolding out of a concealed future by way of an appropriated past. Being is more a verb than a noun, a PROCESS of coming to presence out of concealment and back to concealment. The meaning of being opens up to this background process of emergence that is shot through with negation and is missed in ontologies that have focused only on what emerges in the process. Being is the inherently elusive element in thinking and experience that cannot be grounded in any condition or state of beings. Heidegger's refusal to ground Being in the human subject permits him to embrace an ontological realism. Ways in which beings emerge—as finite, plural, temporal, or historical—are disclosed to Dasein and are not produced by Dasein.

Primary Works

Heidegger, Martin. *The Basic Problems of Phenomenology.* Trans. Albert Hofstadter. Bloomington: Indiana University Press, 1982.
Sartre, Jean-Paul. *Existentialism and Humanism.* Trans. Philip Mairet. London: Methuen, 1973.

Bibliography

Sallis, John, ed. *Radical Phenomenology: Essays in Honor of Martin Heidegger.* Atlantic Highlands, NJ: Humanities Press, 1978.

JOSÉ ORTEGA Y GASSET (1883–1955)
Anton Donoso

José Ortega y Gasset was born and died in Madrid. His family owned and operated one of Spain's best newspapers, *El imparcial*. At age fourteen he graduated from preparatory school, at nineteen from the University of Madrid, and at twenty-one from the same institution with his doctorate. A few months after graduation Ortega departed for Germany, where he studied at various universities until 1908. He began teaching at the University of Madrid as professor of metaphysics in 1910 and soon conducted discussions with recognized intellectuals, including UNAMUNO. Although Ortega's earliest political sympathies were toward socialism, in 1912 he joined the Republican Reform Party, as less dogmatic than the Socialist Party in its quest for democracy, universal EDUCATION, secularization, and tolerance.

Ortega's first book, *Meditations on Quixote*, was published in 1914. He continued writing for the newspaper and for two journals he founded, *Espafia* and *El Espectator*. Ortega sailed for Argentina in 1916, where he delivered lectures. The country fascinated him, and he returned on two other occasions, in 1928 for a lecture tour and in 1939–1942 in self-imposed exile. Returning to Spain, Ortega broke with the family newspaper over political matters and became the editorial SPIRIT behind the newly founded daily *El Sol*, probably the finest newspaper Spain ever had. In its pages were published the essays that later constituted his books: *Invertebrate Spain, The Theme of Our Time, The Dehumanization of Art and Ideas on the Novel, Studies on Love*, and *The Revolt of the Masses*. In 1923 there appeared Ortega's most influential and long-lasting journal, *The Review of the West*, published up to the outbreak of the civil war and introducing Spain and Spanish America to the latest in European PHILOSOPHY and science.

By the summer of 1930 Ortega was convinced the TIME had come for a republic. As soon as censorship was lifted, he helped found the Group at the Service of the Republic, which worked for a victory in the municipal elections of April 1931, which led to the voluntary exile of the monarch. In the elections for a Constituent Parliament Ortega won a seat, along with fifteen others affiliated with the group. Dissatisfied with politics, he resigned in 1932. Shortly after the military uprising of July 1936 that began the civil war, Ortega left for France, ill with gall bladder problems. Some say his sympathies lay with the Nationalists, and others that he favored some sort of republic, but he kept his silence to his DEATH. His self-imposed exile took him to France, Holland, Portugal, Argentina, and finally back to Portugal. He returned to Spain in 1945 but was unable to influence the cultural LIFE of the nation because the government saw him as a founder of the republic that led to the civil war, and the church considered him a threat to the spiritual formation of the youth because of his rejection of scholasticism. Ortega's status abroad was growing. In July 1949 he was invited to the United States to participate in the bicentennial of the birth of Goethe, and in September he visited Germany for the same occasion. He lectured in England in 1954 and in Venice in 1955 and was awarded an honorary doctorate by the University of Glasgow in 1951.

Ortega's doctoral thesis was "The Terrors of the Year 1000. Critique of a Legend." The foreign influences on Ortega were French, especially Renan. Except for NIETZSCHE, Ortega did not know any German philosophy. Thus, in Leipzig Ortega began to learn German and to read Kant's *Critique of Pure Reason.* During his brief stay in Berlin he availed himself of the up-to-date-libraries and heard Georg Simmel lecture. During Ortega's second stay in Germany, at the University of Marburg, he studied under Herman Cohen and Paul Natorp. Shortly after his return from his first stay in Marburg, his essay entitled "Adam in Paradise" revealed the use of the term "life" in the sense of biographical life and a stress on the human's environment—the physical, historical, and cultural surroundings. By 1914 in *Meditations on Quixote,* the earlier metaphorical insight became clearer; the concept of my life was defined as "I am myself and my circumstances." In a way, this definition summarizes Ortega's PHILOSOPHY; he spent the rest of his life expanding upon it, often aided by insights from other philosophers, without allowing himself to be exclusively influenced by one thinker. This definition held that human life is a task to be realized, concretely found coexisting with its surroundings, that reason is not antithetical to life but functions in the service of life, and that there are as many true perspectives of reality as there are observers.

Ortega began to formulate his political and social philosophy more systematically in his *Invertebrate Spain.* Its first part dealt with the social forces of association, wherein small groups join in a common goal, and disassociation, where individual groups cease to feel a part of the whole, and each acts on its own rather than cooperatively. Its second part presented his aristocratic theory of SOCIETY: a society is a well-functioning whole to the extent that those who have talent are the leaders of those who do not have talent. He critiqued Spain as being well down the road of disassociation and as rejecting individual excellence for the sake of conserving the status quo. In *The Theme of Our Time* Ortega advocated that reason be placed in the service of life. In other writings he extended his ratiovitalism to ART, the novel, and LOVE. *The Revolt of the Masses* was conceived as a critique of Southern Europe, primarily of Spain; it appeared in book form when Europe as a whole was under the threat of political violence from both the Left and the Right. Despite Ortega's assertion that his analysis was social and not political, his position was often misunderstood. Ortega saw those of mediocre talent, who should be followers, aspiring to positions of leadership on all social levels, for the sake of power rather than of service to the group. One major result was the destruction of the politics of liberalism and a disrespect for the science behind technology, both of which had raised the level of life in Europe. The revolt of the masses indicated that Europe as a group of separate nations was morally bankrupt. The only solution was the formation of an united Europe. This does not mean an increase in state power but a wider goal that includes the goals of previous separate nations.

The posthumously published lecture series *Man and People,* although half completed, was a seeking to understand what society is. For Ortega human life is characterized by (1) not being given ready-made; (2) having to be chosen and hence having RESPONSIBILITY; (3) being untransferable, in the sense of each having to make his or her own CHOICES; (4) being lived in solitude, in the sense of having to choose without society's pressures; and (5) above all, being circumstantial, in the sense of being surrounded by a WORLD. Thus, I am my self and my circumstances. Society will not be understood adequately as long as it is contrasted to the individual. Instead, it must be contrasted to interindividual coliving, to actions performed with foreknowledge, purpose, and responsibility and directed to those we know, rather than performed because of a felt pressure of binding observances and directed to strangers, as is the case in society. Five key studies by Ortega were not published in newspaper installments: *What Is Philosophy?*, *Some Lessons in Metaphysics*, *History as a System*, *Historical Reason*, and *The Idea of Principle in Leibniz and the Evolution of Deductive Theory*. Only *History as a System* appeared during Ortega's life, in a volume honoring Ernst Cassier; the others were found among his papers. In *Historical Reason* Ortega outlined what he saw as the HISTORY of existentialism, which he considered should be the sole basis for philosophizing for the next era. However, he thought existentialism was impossible as a philosophy because EXISTENCE cannot be completely grasped intellectually.

Four attempts have been made to create a philosophy based on life. The first was by Dilthey, but it turned out to be inadequate, as Ortega thought he had shown in his essay in honor of Dilthey's centennial. Ortega was convinced that his idea of life had advanced beyond Dilthey, that his notion of living reason marked a higher level than the historical reason of Dilthey in his effort to show that reason was not solely the pure reason of Descartes and Kant. Dilthey had been unable to free himself from considering life as irrational, a position Ortega thought he had overcome by embedding pure reason in living reason and both in human life. Because of his irrationalism Dilthey was convinced that philosophy was impossible and confined himself to history and PSYCHOLOGY. Ortega stated in *History as a System* that human life is not a thing, not a being, and does not have a NATURE but is a DRAMA, a happening, a task to be accomplished, a novel writing itself, a going-on-being, a history. Alongside pure physicomathematical reason is to be found narrative reason. To understand anything human, a person or a collective, one must tell its history. Human life takes on a measure of transparency only in the light of historical reason. Unlike a tiger of today, which is neither more nor less than the tiger of a thousand years ago, always the first tiger, the human individual does not put on humanity for the first time. Thus, there is no cause to condemn historicism, to be concerned with the mutability of everything human, for this is our ontological privilege and the source of progress.

The second attempt was Ortega's, although he added that he is referring to the chronological priority of his university lectures and not to an adequate publication of his thought, even though he had examined briefly the idea of life in two or three publications. The third attempt was that of JASPERS, who offered a reinterpretation of human life with certain insights. However, his position was flawed because of a lack of philosophical expertise. The fourth attempt was that of HEIDEGGER, concerning whose basic ideas Ortega claimed chronological priority. Ortega did not claim priority to the philosophy of existentialism, which he found flawed because of its extremism of considering life as irrational, but to certain key ideas about life expressed in existentialism.

The first important references to Heidegger in Ortega's work appear in *What Is Philosophy?*, the posthumously published lectures delivered in 1929. Most scholars find in this work Ortega's first effort to be more systematic and precise, concluding that it was the result of his seeing Heidegger as a challenge. Heidegger, in a recent work of genius, Ortega said, has made us note the enormous significance of the statement that to live is to find oneself amid the world. This idea, like all principal ideas in these lectures, Ortega emphasized in his tenth lecture and could be found elsewhere in his published work. Ortega acknowledged his enormous debt to German philosophy but thought he might have exaggerated, so that his own contribution was concealed even from those closest to him.

In *The Idea of Principal in Leibniz and the Evolution of Deductive Theory* Ortega pointed out that in 1925 he had planned a series of publications to which he had proposed the title "Restating the Problem of Being," declaring what this would entail. As it turned out, this was the proposal of Heidegger's book of 1929. Not to have followed through because of timidity, Ortega admitted, is what separates him from Heidegger, whom he admired as an indisputable genius entitled to be considered one of the greatest philosophers. Nevertheless, he could accept almost none of Heidegger's positions on living human reality, "except those that we hold in common." Ortega found erroneous the starting point of attributing to the human person: a comprehension of BEING. He criticized Heidegger for not casting the slightest light on what Being means, for not having posed the problem of Being, for introducing the trivial distinction between the ontological and the ONTIC. To Ortega's four stages, a fifth one should be added, given what he wrote concerning those who call themselves existentialists. Only once did he mention a specific person, SARTRE, whom he admired as having great talent despite the fact that Sartre said and did tasteless things because of existentialism's errors. The philosophy of existentialism Ortega considered an error from the start, for, according to it, a human commits himself or herself by a special act as if living were not always such a commitment, as if the simple act of living were not an inexorable matter of being already committed. Moreover, existence does not designate a human mode of being, for a human is precisely that being who does not exist but lives or is alive. Things exist. To live is to work out my ESSENCE or what I am.

Ortega seems to have linked some of the errors of existentialism to KIERKEGAARD. He admitted that he had never been able to get beyond the fifth page of any work by Kierkegaard without its style making him ill and that Kierkegaard may possess admirable ideas, but his literary posturing kept him from seeing them. Nevertheless, Ortega suspected two things: one, that Kierkegaard was an example of that eternal Christian who, instead of basing his or her CHRISTIANITY on something positive, based it on a negativity, that reason is a limited, tragic thing, and two, what Kierkegaard called existentialist thought, born of his own thought's despair, was probably an exasperated, arbitrary resolve, a kind of direct action that does not involve reflection. Hence, in Kierkegaard what is existential is not philosophy but RELIGION, and in this he is completely right. In any case, Ortega pointed out that his own philosophy was not existentialist but what he called a philosophy of living reason in which reason is substantially and fundamentally vital but is no less reason for all of that.

From youth, Ortega was surrounded by talk of political, cultural, and literary matters. By the time his university studies began, Spain was in turmoil as the result of its humiliating loss of the last of its American and Pacific possessions in the Spanish-American War. The young Ortega agreed with those who favored turning the nation's attention inward to regenerate itself culturally rather than to rearm itself with modern technology. He saw Unamuno as the symbol of a renewed life for Spain. When Ortega returned from his studies in Germany, he was sadly aware of how inefficiently Spanish society functioned, of how far below the level of the times Spanish university education was. He was determined to do his part to raise Spain to the level of the times, to bring the nation once more into the mainstream of European life. This put him at odds with Unamuno, who wanted to preserve the uniqueness of Spanish society against the materialism of Europe. Indeed, Unamuno held that if one and the same country could not produce both a Descartes and a Saint John of the Cross, he would prefer Saint John.

In public lectures that constituted *What Is Philosophy?* Ortega acknowledged that to persuade the people of Madrid to concern themselves a bit with philosophy was the dream of his life. To realize his dream, Ortega had to enter the public forum of the newspaper to reach and aesthetically seduce his readers, who were more interested in the beauty of LITERATURE than in the truth of philosophy. He wrote an original philosophy in Spanish in a literary style that held its own in literature. Ortega the teacher shared the vigorous study methods he had learned in Germany with his students, some of whom eventually joined the Faculty of Philosophy and Letters of the University of Madrid. Nothing, Ortega said, would have been more easy, once he had been appointed to his first teaching post, than to follow the example of the German professor and devote himself exclusively to scholarly pursuits, referring to national matters only obliquely. He realized that if he did this, he would be unfaithful to his destiny. The French, English, and Germans live in already established social environments, unlike the Spaniards. Their societies may not be without faults, but they do possess the necessary operations and services to function well. Eventually, the Spanish philosopher would come to realize that Spain is the first, the whole, the preemptory problem.

As a result, his personal destiny seemed inseparable from that of his country. For many years his work was obsessively concerned with the problems of Spain, a Spain that seemed to have already realized itself in history so that the question remains of whether it can do it again. Hence, Ortega wrote in *Meditations on Quixote* that a people must periodically halt at the crossroads and question its selfhood, to cast light on its historic mission. Such is true of a people and of every PERSON within it, for an individual does not find one's place in the universe except through one's people, in which he or she is immersed like a drop of water in a passing cloud.

Primary Works

Ortega y Gasset, José. *History as a System and Other Essays toward a Philosophy of History*. Trans. Helene Weyl. New York: Norton, 1962.
———. *The Revolt of the Masses*. Anonymous Authorized Translation. New York: Norton, 1957.
———. *What Is Philosophy?* Trans. Mildred Adams. New York: Norton, 1964.

Bibliography

Marias, Julien. *José Ortega y Gasset: Circumstance and Vocation*. Trans. Frances M. Lopez-Morillas. Norman: University of Oklahoma Press, 1970.

PERCEPTION
Patrick Bourgeois

Within existentialism, the interpretation of the role of perception is indicative of the respective philosophical stance toward EXISTENCE. MERLEAU-PONTY's writings include the most explicit treatments of perception in relation to lived existence. Influenced by HUSSERL, perception has come to play a central role for others, such as SARTRE and HEIDEGGER. Sartre focuses on the *percipere* and the *percipi* in *Being and Nothingness*; his focus is on their BEING and the modes of being in RELATION to one another. The being of the *percipere* leads to the for-itself and the prereflective cogito, and the being of the *percipi* leads to the in-itself. For Heidegger any perception of something is concomitantly an awareness of its mode of being, leading to an interpretation of the modes of being in the implicit self-comprehension of one's own being as well as of Being itself.

The primacy of perception is central to Merleau-Ponty's works: *Structure of*

Behavior and *Phenomenology of Perception*. The first describes the scientific treatments of behavior by physiology and experimental PSYCHOLOGY in order to delve into their presupposed conditions and to derive an adequate grasp of behavior. It establishes the fact that these sciences distort behavior, that NATURE and CONSCIOUSNESS reinterpreted can be understood in terms of one another instead of in opposition to one another. The scientific treatments of behavior demand a PHENOMENOLOGY of perception that can reawaken the experience of the WORLD, which, overlooked in ordinary experience, needs to be rediscovered in reflection. The *Phenomenology of Perception* shows that perception emerges within an operative level of vital INTENTIONALITY as an anticipatory orientation of the lived BODY. Human perception is inextricably linked to action, which, as anticipatory in its receptivity of things perceived in the world, has the capacity of orienting oneself in relation to the possible, thus distinguishing humans from animals. The general aspects of human behavior brought together in this corporeally unified, vital intentionality are action, perception, and affectivity, each intertwined with the others, each reciprocally related to the others, and each revealing its aspects of original intentionality as essential features of existence.

Thus, the content of perception emerges within this basic and pervasive activity beneath the intentionality that posits objects, and is constituted in action. For Merleau-Ponty, perception, in its structure and PROCESS and with its operative intentionality, contains an anticipatory attitude toward possible distance perception. The primacy of perception means that perception is irreducible in that it must be accounted for holistically as vital intentionality bringing to LIFE a world of meanings within interactive experience rather than explained via reductionistic accounts. With this thesis he attempts to deal with the perceiving MIND, reestablishing its roots in its body and world at the human level of behavior. The perceived OBJECT as present and living is the origin of objectivity and is not decomposable into a collection of SENSATIONS because in it the whole is prior to its parts. This whole is not an ideal whole but rather occurs in an intentional perceptual experience that gives us the passage from one moment to the next, which thus realizes the unity of TIME and involves a practical synthesis.

Action entails the anticipatory dimension of perceptual experience mentioned before. This experience, as the attuned behavior directed toward a thing within an oriented focus, is selective. Merleau-Ponty thus interprets the anticipatory and sensory aspects of the structure of meaning to emerge within the context of prereflective, vital intentionality. Further, a quasi-manipulative aspect is included within perceptual awareness that is revealed first as I can, rather than as I think, manifesting action as basic intentionality. This practical synthesis and these phases of perception entailed within the structure of behavior are prior to that achieved by the understanding, so that the significance of the thing-perceived is not first and foremost a meaning for the understanding but rather a meaning in relation to this basic level of behavior. Emphasizing the practical as constitutive of human existence, he states that we experience a perception and its horizon in action, not by positing them or explicitly knowing them.

Hence, perceptual objects as simultaneous with the perceiver are constituted in action. The transitional-synthesis on this level brings about the passage from one perspective to the other, retaining, without mediation, a hold on one while anticipating others. Thus, distance cannot be understood by comparing various contents presented in an already constituted SPACE but, rather, in terms of being in the distance that links up with being where it appears. Thus, when Merleau-Ponty refers to the visual experience of an object, like seeing the lamp, he intends to include more than the detached or distant object seen. He aims to include the full ramifications of meaning structure, including the structure of the possible practical dimensions of the response. Thus, to account for the nonvisible sides of a perceptual object, revealing the synthesis as a practical one, he explicates the experience latent within the experience: humans can touch a lamp— not only the side turned toward us but also the other side; one has only to extend one's hand.

Although the thing perceived is for the one perceiving, it is not given exhaustively, even though it is given as a whole, with its unseen or absent side present in the experience of the thing, but present precisely as other side. If it were not for the common sensibility shared by both the body of the perceiver and the object perceived, there would be no perceived object. In this context other objects, just as the other PERSON, can be considered to allow the sentient organism to experience its own sensibility, for, in attempting to draw a commonness between the perceiver and the perceived, between the seer and the seen, Merleau-Ponty is led to their common sensibility, the overlapping or intertwining of touching with touched—the hand in touching can be touched by the other hand—thus becoming the touching touched. In order to sense, it also must be sensible, and this sensibility is shared with the whole sensible realm.

Thus, Merleau-Ponty's view of perception and existence allows to unfold a unique relation between them. Lived existence has been approached from both the epistemic and the ontological perspectives, but only because first the focus was on the concrete dimensions of perceptual existence. This focus allowed two fundamental and originary avenues of approach: first, inquiry into the epistemic aspects of the originary and foundational level of existence; second, inquiry into the ontological aspects of the same originary and foundational level of existence. Both approaches emerge in the development of his view of perception and existence, though he does not explicate the relation between them. Thus, his phenomenology represents an understanding of human perception and existence that rejects a tradition of PHILOSOPHY that begins with the SUBJECT–object split; he attempts to deal with the problems such a beginning entails. In overcoming such a split, he turns more and more to lived existence, the dwelling place of perception, and eventually allows for the ontological approach, which can be integrated with his earlier epistemic approach.

Primary Works

Merleau-Ponty, Maurice. *The Structure of Behavior*. Trans. Alden Fisher. Boston: Beacon
    Press, 1963.
———. *The Visible and the Invisible*. Trans. Alphonso Lingis. Evanston, IL: North-
    western University Presss, 1968.

Bibliography

Madison, Gary. *The Phenomenology of Merleau-Ponty: A Search for the Limits of Con-
    sciousness*. Athens: Ohio University Press, 1981.

PERSON
Richard Polt

The Latin *persona*, corresponding to the Greek *prosopon*, originally referred to
a mask worn by an actor. Roman jurisprudence extended the meaning of the
term to designate the legal SUBJECT of rights and duties. Thus, there are two
main senses in the etymology of ''person'': a role played and person as the
basis of RESPONSIBILITY. Modern philosophers generally focus on the person
as the bearer of responsibility. For most medievals, the person is a rational
individual substance that has a distinctive dignity. For modern thinkers, personhood is based on self-CONSCIOUSNESS and on memory, which provides identity through TIME. Existentialists present the person as a dynamic event rather
than a substance, an event that must be understood in terms of the alternatives
of authentic and inauthentic existence. Selfhood is a DRAMA that unfolds as
one makes choices in one's environment; in ORTEGA's phrase, I am myself
and my circumstance. One's choices can forge an authentic PERSONALITY, a
life that is given integrity and coherence through inwardness, LOVE of fate, or
resoluteness. Existentialists reject as inauthentic any identification of personhood
with one's role in SOCIETY; in HEIDEGGER's terminology, the they-self is
not to be confused with the authentic self.
    For BUBER, human LIFE takes place in a dramatic tension between the
presence and absence of genuine personhood. The poles of this tension are the
two stances intimated by the basic words I–It and I–Thou. Human life fluctuates
between the two poles. To experience the others in the world as an It is to

objectify reality and to distance it from oneself; to experience others as Thou is to enter into dialogue with specific others. The I of the I–It is different from the I of the I–Thou. Buber refers to the I that encounters a Thou as subjectivity, that is, dynamic participation in an interpersonal reality that gives rise to genuine COMMUNITY and selfhood. In the I–It attitude, the I is experiencing and manipulating. Such a person is isolated from interpersonal reality and from the true self, which is experienced merely in terms of what is mine. Thus, the person is not an interior or private phenomenon. One becomes a true person only by meeting others in the world as a Thou. Personhood does not consist in self-consciousness but in a consistent genuineness of one's interactions.

Buber speaks of a unique dynamic center that unifies one's acts and makes one a whole person. This center is not produced by an act of WILL. Unified personality is achieved through trust in reality and the confirmation that comes through acts of commitment and FAITH, acts of personal making present. This conception of the person is not to be confused with a collectivism that abolishes individuality. Even though the meeting with the Thou is essential to being a person, responding to the Thou does not mean losing oneself. The encounter with the Thou does not obliterate the distance between self and other; rather, it lets both self and other emerge as persons through mutual confirmation. The highest of relations is to GOD, the eternal Thou. If humans are to gain the rank of person, they should respond to God as a person, rather than as a mere idea or principle.

MARCEL views humans as voyagers who exceed mere EXISTENCE or trust absorption in the immediate in order to seek BEING or a source of ultimate meaning. My existence includes my incarnation in a feeling BODY and my coexistence with others in a concrete SITUATION. I can reflect on existence through primary reflection or methodical abstraction, which assists in solving certain problems; this reflection is typical of natural science and technology. Secondary reflection arises when I wonder at a concrete MYSTERY that involves me personally. He also distinguishes between a possessive and manipulative stance toward others and a stance that allows the other to be present as a Thou. Genuine personal existence requires love and hope, which transcend the subject understood as a self-contained MIND and will. My acts in the WORLD realize and develop me as a person, although they can never define me; personhood demands that I take responsibility for these acts in relation to the existence of others, developing mutual freedom in collaboration with my fellows. My FREEDOM and self-determination thus involve a link to what transcends me. Only if I remain accountable, faithful, and available to the transformative presence of God and other persons can I maintain contact with reality. Availability is the remedy for the modern broken world, which suffers from a depersonalizing abstraction; abstract categorizations of humans miss the crucial fact that we are seekers who develop ourselves creatively in unique situations and who are capable of intimacy with others and receptivity to God. Abstraction disregards the heart of the person—the mysterious vitality that guides us through life as if through an adventure. LANGUAGE necessarily involves a certain degree of objectification of the other.

BERDYAEV calls himself an existential philosopher in the tradition of Augustine, Pascal, KIERKEGAARD, and NIETZSCHE—prophetic thinkers whose thought expresses their personal being. His writings revolt against the objectifying and standardizing forces that negate the freedom of the person, subordinating it to conformism, necessity, or violence. His thought is directed against global perspectives and everyday routines that enslave the SPIRIT and the inner world. He asserts the primacy of personality as a self-determining and creative force that unifies human existence. A personality is unique but has universal significance; it is finite but has infinite potential. He sees us as dual creatures, torn between attachments to the world of objective necessity and our ties to the realm of personal freedom. Hence, personality is no mere possession but a difficult PROJECT to be realized by the individual: I must achieve my freedom by carrying out with integrity my vocation or destiny. Personality thus manifests an existential purpose, which is also a divine purpose; Berdyaev conceives of personality as the human likeness of God.

Personality is, in part, a persona, a mask by which we both play a role in the objective world and defend ourselves against this world. But a person also longs to transcend solitude through communion with a Thou that is manifested not in a mask but in a face. Like Buber and Marcel, Berdyaev endorses the distinction between the It and the Thou and describes how reciprocal communion gives rise to a WE. He contrasts this community with mere society, which is an impersonal, objective structure. Developed personality requires coexistence and self-surpassing: I must transcend my individuality through loving and sacrificing for other persons, creating suprapersonal values, and acknowledging my dependence on God, the total personality. Such personhood leads to an ethic based on the eternal worth of the person and a political ideal of personalist socialism that exalts the value of the irreplaceable person over the universal order of the whole or abstract being. This perspective necessarily takes issue with MARX-ISM–Leninism, which in its materialist and positivist basis denies the ESSENCE of personality. A genuine revolutionary PHILOSOPHY must be a philosophy of free activity that aims at the realization of personality, guided by the principle of the dignity of the person.

SARTRE distinguishes between being-for-itself, or CONSCIOUSNESS, and being-in-itself, or the nonconscious object of consciousness. Although the for-itself is nothing other than an awareness of the in-itself, it is radically distinct from the in-itself because it is characterized by INTENTIONALITY, or awareness of an object. There is thus an opposition between being conscious and being the OBJECT of another's consciousness—interpersonal relations are inherently conflictual. Others are first manifested to me by their looking at me; such is an objectifying look that tends to reduce me to an in-itself. These relations are struggles between consciousnesses that attempt to objectify each other; none of these struggles can be won, since the for-itself can never be transformed into an in-itself.

As for God, Sartre holds that the concept of an absolute consciousness is an incoherent combination of the in-itself and the for-itself: there can be no absolute consciousness, because consciousness is necessarily related to something other than itself—its object. Even if God existed, it could never provide guidance to us by presenting an objective GOOD, since the for-itself creates all VALUE through its free decisions. This uncompromising emphasis on freedom somewhat divorces consciousness from personality. *The Transcendence of the Ego* argues that the I exists not within consciousness but outside it, in the world. If the EGO were an inhabitant of consciousness, it would interfere with the clarity and spontaneity of consciousness; its acts would no longer be free but would be the products of a preexisting, obscurely understood self. We can explain the unity and individuality of consciousness in terms of intentionality, without appealing to a personal ego that lies at the basis of conscious acts. Consciousness constitutes the ego as an ideal unity of the series of conscious acts; consciousness then attempts to escape its radical freedom, or nonpersonal spontaneity, by identifying itself with this personal ego.

It might seem that Sartre views personality as a stumbling block that consciousness puts in its own path. He consistently holds that it is a mistake to view conscious acts as the effects of a preexisting CHARACTER or ego; however, he supplements this view by examining a different dimension of personhood that is quite compatible with the freedom of consciousness. Personality as a fixed character is a construct that is alien to consciousness; but the person as a project is the realization of freedom and is thus intrinsic to consciousness. In his discussion of existential psychoanalysis in *Being and Nothingness*, the person is understood as an organized unity of freely chosen ends; the person is futural rather than past, freedom rather than substance. In the light of the initial project that constitutes one's self, one evaluates the situation in which one is engaged and gives meaning to the world. Existential psychoanalysis consists in discovering the original project that is at the root of a person's likes and dislikes, habits and propensities—a project that one may be hiding from oneself in BAD FAITH but that is also always open to change. The original project aims at being some particular combination of the for-itself and the in-itself that would remedy the emptiness and indeterminacy of consciousness and furnish consciousness with an essence; in other words, each person desires to be some version of God. This goal is, of course, incoherent and unrealizable—hence, "man is a useless passion." But at the end of *Being and Nothingness* Sartre suggests that it may also be possible to take freedom as the goal of one's project, thus combining personhood with an authentic recognition of the spontaneity of consciousness.

Buber, Marcel, and Berdyaev reject Sartre's view of the person; RELATIONS to others are not necessarily objectifying, the self is constituted in encounters with others, and freedom involves not merely invention and will but discovery and response. Sartre eventually came to see his portrait of human existence in *Being and Nothingness* as too negative and abstract; in later writings, we find the potential to transcend mutual objectification through empathy and the person understood engaged in concrete, historical acts with other persons.

Primary Works

Berdyaev, Nicolai. *Slavery and Freedom.* Trans. R. M. French. New York: Scribner's, 1944.

Buber, Martin. *Between Man and Man.* Trans. Ronald Gregor Smith. New York: Macmillan, 1965.

Marcel, Gabriel. *The Philosophy of Existentialism.* Trans. Manya Harari. Secaucus, NJ: Citadel Press, 1980.

Sartre, Jean-Paul. *The Transcendence of the Ego.* Trans. Forrest Williams and Robert Kirkpatrick. New York: Farrar, Straus, and Giroux, 1987.

PERSONALITY
Abrahim H. Khan

The term "personality" has at least two aspects to its existential meaning complex. One is designated by the Latin *persona*, the mask through which resounds the voice of the actor. Among classical Greek and Latin moralists, such as Cicero and Panaetius, the meaning of persona takes on a moral tone, a sense of being conscious, free, and responsible. From this extended sense, the step is short to the juridical meaning of persona as an individual human with legal and moral rights and RESPONSIBILITIES. The second aspect of the meaning complex designated by persona signifies the human and even divine personality. The resonant idea characterizing this aspect is that of tearing away of whatever has been superimposed, laying bare the NATURE of the role-player, to reach through to that which is one in itself. This idea gained prominence through the use of term "persona" in fourth-and fifth-century theological controversies on the three persons in the Trinity. Boethius is credited with formulating the classical definition of PERSON as an individual substance with a rational nature.

Plotinus was convinced that personality as such must have its ground in a transcendent order. Scholastics followed the Plotinus–Boethius definition of person, with Aquinas defending its application to GOD. Thus, God as creator is not only a Person but a moral Personality. Humans created by and in the image and likeness of a Person are also persons whose personality participates in the Personality of God, through their faculty of CHOICE and self-determination. While Descartes emphasized human CONSCIOUSNESS, Leibniz placed the true ESSENCE of human personality in self-consciousness. Kant deepened the ethical view of personality by defining it in terms of FREEDOM and independence of the mechanism of nature. In Fichte the notion underwent further transformation to become the category of self, which is already a primordial category in the Pietist tradition but becomes a central category in contemporary PHILOSOPHY. The underlying idea is that personality is understood as a rational being responsible for his or her action and capable of organizing LIFE experiences into a whole. Self-consciousness and self-determination come to be features of the second aspect of the meaning complex of personality.

When KIERKEGAARD came to realize that Danish CHRISTIANITY, associated with Hegelianism, threatened to reduce the individual to impotency, to alienate humanity, he reached beyond Kant and through the Pietist tradition to the Christian doctrine of the creature standing in relation to the Creator. Indeed, being self-conscious and self-determinate and hence a bearer of moral VALUES, a human could exercise choice in becoming a genuine person or self. He understood the becoming of such a self as a relation defined in terms of creature and Creator or the temporal and the eternal or necessity and freedom. Essential to the relation and hence to personality was choice. Personality is understood to be finite and has to be infinitized. A finite personality is related only to the environment, containing a multiplicity of determinants, characteristics, and rich concretion. It is dimly present in mood, finds expression in pleasure, and is said to be aesthetical.

However, Kierkegaard holds that when an individual chooses absolutely his or her finite personality, the latter becomes transformed so that its center is no longer in the periphery but in itself. Chosen absolutely, finite personality becomes infinitized or ethical; it is in possession of itself as being free. Genuine personality is formed in degrees by acting to make actual in one's own life what is present as a possible: the more the struggle to choose absolutely, the more the personality is formed concretely. When such choice is lacking, personality despairs and is hardly free. However, when choice of finite personality is unconditional, the act is ethical. Such a discussion underscores the ideas of choice and of transparency, seeing through oneself to give a complete accounting. In the Christian tradition other concepts of personality emerge. According to BERDYAEV, personality is suffering or a refusal of the human SPIRIT to conform to worldly or material values. However, the volitional side of personality—choice, freedom, and self-determination—is echoed in the writings of NIETZSCHE, SARTRE, and recent secular philosophers, who also treat topics such as despair, self-deception, objectivity, subjectivity, consciousness, and EXISTENCE.

A concept of personality, presented by existentialist thinkers, understood as having choice and transparency integral to it, is not the same as the everyday use of personality to signify an individualization and differentiation shaped by one's social group and by the roles one plays in the group. This latter idea of personality, as determined by group affiliation and roles, does not correlate with the question of what it means to be a self, whereas personality understood in terms of choice and transparency does. Personality as choice remains the dominant meaning that contemporary LITERATURE with existential themes reflects. Sometimes usage of the word personality in such literature might seem to suggest a shift away from that meaning, but when conceptual linkages to related ideas are traced, the apparent shift is at a functional level only.

A case in point is BUBER's essay ''The Education of Character.'' He views personality along the lines of individualization, defining it as a spiritual-physical form containing dormant impulses and as a completion. That definition implies the idea of that which is given and has to be cultivated and enhanced. But such a definition seems to serve as a contrast for the conception of CHARACTER to which Buber is drawing attention and understands as a becoming rather than a completion. Personality as a completion, however, has to be understood as having relational structures, spiritual-physical ones, requiring for their actualization the exercise of choice. In this deeper sense, then, personality is also a becoming, has conceptually an ethical mooring, and is no different from the conception reflected in the writings of Kierkegaard. Rather, personality lies between that which one is and that which one can become ideally or hopes to become. This meaning of personality resonates in much of the literature on existential PSYCHOLOGY.

Primary Works

Berdyaev, Nicolai. *Slavery and Freedom*. Trans. R. M. French. New York: Scribner's, 1944.

Buber, Martin. *Between Man and Man*. Trans. Ronald Gregor Smith. New York: Macmillan, 1965.

Kierkegaard, Søren. *Concluding Unscientific Postscript*. Trans. David F. Swenson and Walter Lowrie. Princeton: Princeton University Press, 1968.

PHENOMENOLOGY
Paul Gorner

The term ''phenomenology'' was introduced by the philosopher J. H. Lambert to refer to the study of the sensible APPEARANCES of things. Later, Hegel used it in his *Phenomenology of Spirit* to refer to the presentation of the dialectical unfolding of forms of CONSCIOUSNESS that culminates in absolute KNOWLEDGE. As a movement of PHILOSOPHY, phenomenology belongs to the twentieth century. What unites the philosophers assigned to the movement is more a matter of family resemblance than of common doctrines. Within the movement one can distinguish certain broad types.

What may be called realist phenomenology owed its inspiration to HUSSERL's *Logical Investigations*. This type of phenomenology is characterized by a rich ONTOLOGY that rejects the empiricist restriction of entities or OBJECTS to the physical and the mental. There are material objects and thoughts, feelings, mental acts, but there are also numbers, states of affairs, logical laws, institutions, PERSONS, and works of ART. Such objects are not reducible to some other thing. Following the maxim, To the things themselves, objects of whatever ontological type are to be taken as they present themselves to consciousness and not as some theory or system says they must be. Every entity has its ESSENCE, which is not the reflection of how we use words but objectively exists. Moreover, they are not merely objects of thought but can, in a manner, be perceived. Phenomenology is the study of essences and RELATIONS between essences by means of a kind of nonsensory seeing or intuiting of essences. The essential TRUTHS laid bare are a priori, and because everything has its essence, the a priori is not restricted to the formal but can pertain to anything. There are a priori truths about sensation. Moreover, the necessity that characterizes a priori truths has nothing to do with how we think or how we must think but is purely objective.

However, a priori truths or essential truths do not depend on the actual existence of instances of essences. That the color orange comes between the color yellow and the color red does not presuppose any actual instances of red and yellow. Nor does apprehension of an essential truth necessarily require the experience of actual instances. Imagined instances can provide the foundation just as well. Although emphasis is given to the INTENTIONALITY of consciousness, and intentional experiences constitute much of its subject matter, this is not because it is thought that somehow things other than consciousness depend for their EXISTENCE and CHARACTER on consciousness. Rather, the failure to recognize intentionality, to properly distinguish between consciousness and what one is conscious of, is thought to underlie most forms of reductionism. Thus, the failure to distinguish between the sensations involved in PERCEPTION and the object of perception is responsible for attempts to reduce material objects to bundles of SENSATIONS. The failure to distinguish between thinking as a psychical process and what is being thought about leads to the confusion of laws of logic with psychological laws. Similarly with the reduction of VALUES to feelings.

Whether Husserl was ever a phenomenological realist is a matter for debate. He produced a devastating critique of psychologism, and his doctrine of categorial INTUITION defended the possibility, indeed, necessity, of the intuition of essences; but it is doubtful whether he identified phenomenology with the study of essences. The demolition of psychologism was a necessary preliminary to gaining access to the transcendental dimension of pure consciousness. For transcendental phenomenology, consciousness or subjectivity is the exclusive theme. Objects figure in phenomenological description but purely as intentional objects—as one is conscious of them, as objects of consciousness. Pure or transcendental consciousness is arrived at by a process of reflection on the basis of an operation called the phenomenological or transcendental reduction. This is the suspension or putting out of action of all BELIEFS regarding the real existence and NATURE of all objects of consciousness. Intentionality is not conceived as the way in which a conscious subject relates itself to a preexisting reality but as the medium in which what counts as real is constituted. Transcendental phenomenology is the description, on the basis of transcendental experience, of the constitution of the WORLD in transcendental subjectivity. This is not to say that phenomenologically reduced experiences reach an absolute foundation. The experiences themselves as temporal objects are constituted in time-constituting consciousness.

Hermeneutic phenomenology arises in connection with the belief that the fundamental question of philosophy is the meaning of BEING. Being is what determines entities as entities; it is that on the basis of which entities are always already understood. Being is always the being of entities, but, given that there are different kinds of entities, which entities are to be questioned with regard to their being? There is one entity whose being is such that an understanding of being belongs to this being, an understanding that embraces not just its own being but the being of entities other than itself to which it comports itself. This entity, the human, HEIDEGGER calls DASEIN, whose being is essentially determined by an understanding of being. However, this understanding of Being, which makes possible comportment to oneself and to entities other than oneself, is not the explicit understanding of Being provided by ontology. It is preontological. The working out of the question about the meaning of Being must begin with the analysis of the being of Dasein.

Phenomenology is the method for carrying out this analysis. By phenomenon is meant that which shows itself. Phenomenology is the letting be seen of that which shows itself. But Heidegger calls this phenomenology in the formal sense. Recall the distinction between Being and what is or between Being and entities. The letting be seen of that which shows itself, where that which shows itself is an entity, is phenomenology in the ordinary sense. In the proper philosophical sense, phenomenology is the letting be seen of what at first and for the most part does not show itself but has to be brought out of concealment. This is not an entity but the being of entities. Being is not some great abstraction but that which makes it possible for entities to show themselves or be encountered. So phenomenology is the letting be seen of that which makes it possible for entities to show themselves but which, for the most part, does not show itself. Phenomenology is hermeneutic in that its letting be seen consists in the interpretation of Dasein's understanding of Being. The entity with the understanding of Being is not a transcendental EGO outside the world but an entity whose being is BEING-IN-THE-WORLD. Dasein is not in the world in the sense that something is located in a bigger thing. It is not a subject in the world. Rather, Dasein as being-in-the-world is an attempt to overcome the subject–object dichotomy. By "world," Heidegger means a structure of significance, not something over against Dasein but part and parcel of what Dasein is. Reversing the customary order, theoretical modes of intentionality are seen as grounded in practical modes. Being-in-the-world is not an instance of intentionality but, rather, a condition of the possibility of intentionality. Dasein is essentially the understanding or disclosedness of being whereas Husserlian consciousness is a SUBJECT that relates to objects.

Existential phenomenology attempts to incorporate Heidegger's insights into a phenomenology that has consciousness as its theme. It is exemplified by MERLEAU-PONTY's thinking; some of the ground had been laid by Husserl. Late in his life Husserl developed the way through what he called the life-world, the world of lived experience. The natural sciences purport to describe the world as it is in itself and dismiss the world as we experience it. But the scientist continues to live in the life-world; it is by reference to the life-world that his or her theories are verified. More radically, the concepts employed in the natural sciences are such that they refer to the life-world. Such concepts are the product of a process of idealization and mathematization of structures that the life-world embodies. So it makes no sense to relegate the life-world to the status of subjective appearance. Through Merleau-Ponty's thinking phenomenologists came to see the description of the life-world and its structures and the exposure of the prejudice of an objective world of determinate entities as phenomenology's principal task. Such phenomenology is existential as opposed to transcendental because consciousness of the life-world that it describes is that of the concrete, situated, historical, engaged, incarnate subject in the world rather than that of a transcendental ego. It involves a reduction, a suspension of the objective sciences but not a genuinely transcendental reduction. For the existential phenomenologist the removal from the life-world of the garment of ideas thrown over it by science is not seen as a stage on the way to world-constituting transcendental subjectivity.

Primary Works

Heidegger, Martin. *The Basic Problems of Phenomenology*. Trans. Albert Hofstadter. Bloomington: Indiana University Press, 1982.
Husserl, Edmund. *Logical Investigations*. Trans. J. N. Findlay. London: Routledge, 1970.

Bibliography

Kockelmans, Joseph J., ed. *Phenomenology: The Philosophy of Edmund Husserl and Its Interpretation*. Garden City, NY: Doubleday, 1967.

PHILOSOPHICAL ANTHROPOLOGY
Patrick Bourgeois

Existential PHILOSOPHY is related to philosophical anthropology in two ways. First, it can be seen in two ways to contain a latent philosophical anthropology: an implicit philosophical anthropology within the view of FREEDOM at the heart of EXISTENCE and a philosophical anthropology in the holistic view of humans. Second, it leads directly to a developed philosophical anthropology in the writings of some existentialists. Existentialism pits itself against the tendency of some sciences to reduce the human in order to treat it scientifically. In their opposition to such reductionism, SARTRE and MERLEAU-PONTY develop a latent philosophical anthropology. Merleau-Ponty focuses on the human phenomenon as a unique level of behavior that cannot be understood adequately by reducing it to that of lower animals. He works from within many different expressions of PSYCHOLOGY and human science, explicating from within their limited account how they themselves keep bumping against these limits and working toward a more holistic view of humans in relation to their environment. He develops a view of human BEING-IN-THE-WORLD as a uniquely human BEING.

A central anthropological element common to existential philosophy is the inclusion, at the heart of human existence, of freedom. Freedom is at the core of KIERKEGAARD's account of human existence, whether it is actualized on the level of the aesthetic, the ethical, or the religious. Authentic freedom, however, is actualized only before GOD as purity of heart in a mature response from the core of one's will; inauthentic freedom determines the self before pleasure in the aesthetic mode of existence and before the law for the ethicist. For NIETZSCHE, CREATIVITY, as the highest manifestation of the WILL to POWER in human existence, drives toward self-overcoming in the SUPERMAN and is expressed in the transvaluation of VALUES. Although HEIDEGGER turns to fundamental ONTOLOGY, from which any philosophical anthropology is derivative and upon which it is founded, freedom is at the core of his ontology of the temporality of DASEIN.

Kierkegaard's philosophical anthropology is enframed in a theological anthropology and must be extricated from it to remain strictly philosophical. Such was done by twentieth-century atheistic existential writers, for example, Sartre, who replaced it with freedom itself, which becomes freedom before freedom or for the sake of freedom alone. For Kierkegaard, human existence is a synthesis of the infinite and the finite within the realms of cognition, practical action, and the affective or feelings. Humans are authentically free and maturely human only in purity of heart, when the heart rests only in GOD, when freedom is actualized only before God, or when the will wills the one thing, the GOOD. Such can be achieved only from the gift of FAITH in the tradition of Abraham and developed by St. Paul, a faith that is total commitment to a personal God of the Hebraic-Christian tradition.

In contrast to Kierkegaard's theistic thrust, Sartre considers freedom to be an absolute at the heart of human existence, but it is a freedom before freedom without God. Freedom before freedom must keep freedom from sticking fast to any whatness as role or quality or thinglike existence. Within Sartre's fundamental ontological orientation, the prereflective Cogito is intentional in that it is related in all of its acts of awareness to that which is not itself, so that for-itself can exist only in RELATION to that which is not itself and not its own mode of BEING: in-itself. Further, this prereflective awareness is two-directional in that in every awareness of something there is already an awareness of the awareness, a fundamental self-awareness that is not-positional. It is not a posited self-awareness, not an explicit act of self-awareness, but rather one that accompanies all awareness of specific things, so that there is a basic self-awareness underlying any usual sense of self-consciousness. The ground for the AUTHENTICITY of freedom is latent here, since this prereflective awareness, even in the depth of BAD FAITH, is able to see authentic possibilities. For freedom to be what one is not and not be what one is involves the precise situation of Orestes at the end of Sartre's play *The Flies*, who takes on his own shoulders the burden of Argos and of his crime and thus leaves the people of Argos in a position to move toward their own authenticity of freedom.

BUBER's fundamental insight is the difference between relating to a thing or an OBJECT that is observed and relating to a PERSON or a Thou who addresses one and to whom one responds. He shows that one can relate to a person as a thing and miss the personal dimension of the relation. Such an objective attitude toward another person puts the person in an I–It relationship, which is not a genuine personal relationship since it does not transpire between an I and a Thou but, rather, involves an I with merely an It, even though the It is another person. Within such a relation, the I is entirely alone. The genuine I–Thou relation, being a relationship between persons who are present to one another, is a real address and response. This personal Thou becomes the perspective on the universe in the light of which it is interpreted. Likewise, the I is different, since the whole being is involved in the I–Thou and thus involves a risk not entailed in the I–It relation. This takes on special significance in the religious context. According to Buber, the ESSENCE of biblical RELIGION is the dialogue between persons and God in which each is the other's Thou. God is the only Thou who, by his very NATURE, cannot become an It, even though that is what much traditional THEOLOGY attempts to do. When this fundamental insight is applied to other areas, as psychotherapy, the dialogical situation of speaking to each other is emphasized, as it is in theology and in all areas where Buber reflected, thus showing his philosophical anthropology as personal.

That there is still a need for the legacy of existentialism in a viable contemporary philosophical anthropology is witnessed by the fact that the field of scientific anthropology is still too often ruled by reductionistic behaviorism and scientism. Such science inevitably contains an implicit philosophical anthropology and would profit considerably from becoming explicitly aware of its implications and inadequacies and perhaps improve its very science by philosophical critique.

Primary Works

Buber, Martin. *Between Man and Man.* Trans. Ronald Gregor Smith. New York: Macmillan, 1965.
Kierkegaard, Søren. *The Concept of Anxiety.* Trans. Reider Thomte. Princeton: Princeton University Press, 1980.

Bibliography

Kruks, Sonia. *Situation and Human Existence: Freedom, Subjectivity and Society.* London: Unwin Hyman, 1990.

PHILOSOPHY
Steven Emmanuel

The Greek word *philosophos* is commonly translated as "lover of WISDOM." The word "philosophy" entered the major languages of Europe via the Latin philosophies. During the Enlightenment a uniquely German style of philosophy, grounded in the German LANGUAGE, began to take shape, due largely to the influence of Christian Wolff. Wolff conceived of philosophy as a rigorously scientific inquiry into the essential NATURE of things. Thus, the conception of philosophy as a systematic science was firmly established and found its most developed expression in the work of G. W. F. Hegel, who regarded his own system as the most comprehensive science of all. Hegel's system became a critical point of departure for some existentialists. According to Hegel, the WORLD in its totality forms an intelligible system that can be known through rational reflection. Philosophy's task is to mirror the structure of that system;

its KNOWLEDGE is attained by a PROCESS of abstraction from the particular and the concrete. Such an inquiry must be impersonal, dispassionate, and objective. Existentialists asked whether such a metaphysical outlook adequately accounts for human EXISTENCE.

Though critical references to Hegel's philosophy are scattered throughout KIERKEGAARD's writings, the most serious, sustained critique is advanced in *Concluding Unscientific Postscript*. This work is a polemic against the scientific approach characteristic of speculative METAPHYSICS. The term "philosophy" is understood to be synonymous with the Hegelian philosophy; hence, the terms "philosophy" and "speculation" are used almost interchangeably. The main argument advanced against Hegel's system is that it views existence as something finished and complete. For Hegel, the concepts of contradiction, movement, and transition fall under the rubric of logic. Because logic functions according to the principle of identity and hence recognizes only that form of movement that is characterized by necessity, it annuls the division between thought and BEING, between actuality and possibility. Thus, the speculative view fails to account for the fact that the thinker is constantly in a process of becoming, and such must somehow be reflected in the form of his or her thought. Against the metaphysical attempt to interpret all movement from the point of view of necessity, Kierkegaard stresses the Aristotelian notion of coming-into-being, thus affirming the contingent nature of the transition from possibility to actuality. According to this view, the actual movement of existence is determined not by identity and continuity but by contradiction and discontinuity. The existing individual is inevitably confronted with alternatives that cannot be rationally mediated but require a LEAP.

Moreover, since FREEDOM and CHOICE are fundamental to a PERSON's ethical development, Kierkegaard contends that Hegel's system is essentially devoid of ETHICS. The chief difficulty of existence is that it presents us with the task of becoming a self in the midst of the flux of temporal being, a task that can be accomplished only through an ethical-religious form of striving, through which the individual strives to be related to the eternal in TIME. But speculative thinking ignores the difficulty of thinking the eternal in the process of becoming. In sharp contrast to the dispassionate objectivity of abstract thought and reflection, the decision to commit oneself to an ethical-religious form of LIFE cannot be understood apart from the passion of the individual.

Despite the negative view of philosophy that predominates in Kierkegaard's writings, he also explains that speculation helps us to establish and clarify the categories and concepts by which we choose to order our lives. We must first grasp a concept in the abstract before we can grasp how it manifests itself in existence. The philosophical activities of abstract thinking and mediation are not inherently bad; rather, we must understand their limitations. Hegel's great contribution lies in his abstract thinking. His fault is that he goes beyond the task of attaining clarity on existential issues and reduces FAITH to the realm of conceptual thought. Kierkegaard strives to establish the proper RELATION between philosophy and Christian faith. Though philosophy is not itself a substitute for faith, it can help to clarify the proper object of ethical-religious striving. He endeavored to employ philosophy to clarify the strenuous existential requirements of living within Christian categories. From a theological point of view, it is not reason but REVELATION that makes human REDEMPTION possible. The paradoxical nature of revelation prevents faith from becoming an OBJECT of human knowledge. Here faith is higher than philosophy. Even as reason is employed to clarify the object of faith, there must always be a dialectical relation between thought and existence. Only when this dialectical relationship is recognized can philosophy become valuable in the individual's search for meaning.

NIETZSCHE is also extremely critical of philosophical system building and the inherent tendency of metaphysics to still the movement of the flux. He criticizes philosophers for their lack of historical sense and their failure to appreciate the Heraclitean concept of becoming. Such a theorist is Hegel, who assumes that the world is an interconnected system that can be rationally known. The faith of the metaphysician is parallel to that of the religious believer. Hence, the slogan GOD is dead, which attacks foundationalist thinking, also signals the absence of an absolute framework for interpreting self and world. This perspectivist view indicates that there are no facts, only interpretations. TRUTH and VALUE are grounded in the freedom and RESPONSIBILITY of the individual who takes part in the creation of self and world through one's interpretive activity. At the heart of what it means to be an existing individual is the question of value. For the true philosopher, values are a vehicle for achieving self-awareness. Since there are no objective values, we have the power to be self-legislating. But to do so, we must have the courage to question the prevailing values and to effect a transvaluation of all values.

In ''Schopenhauer as Educator,'' the philosopher is an educator whose mission is to liberate us from the narcosis of modern culture, to clear a path for the development of genius. EDUCATION is an activity that roots out all hindrances, so that what is strong and healthy can flourish. In *Ecce Homo* Nietzsche remarks that the philosopher is a terrible explosive, endangering everything. Elsewhere we are told that the philosopher's task is to demonstrate the need for a transvaluation of values by diagnosing and exposing the illusions of a diseased culture. *Beyond Good and Evil* calls for a new species of philosopher who, in contrast to the traditional dogmatic, is an experimenter who aspires to a higher truth without any pretense to universality. The picture of the philosopher that emerges is of one who strives to remain free and self-asserting by avoiding the pitfalls of formulaic thought. This free spirit thrives under extreme conditions, daring to live experimentally, accepting full responsibility for one's actions. Driven by the desire for self-mastery, he or she overcomes the paradox of radical freedom by having the strength of WILL to live according to self-created values. The philosophical life is a heroic struggle that recognizes the impossibility of conventional happiness.

The philosopher must show by one's actions that the LOVE of truth is fearful and mighty. This passion for truth is a far cry from the scholarly-scientific ideal of German speculative philosophy. Nietzsche asks, How could there be any passion for cold, pure, inconsequential knowledge! His philosophy is addressed to individuals who have the courage to reject the slavish morality of the herd, to overcome those obstacles that prevent them from realizing their will to POWER, to the reader willing to engage in transvaluation. In later writings, this activity is given ideal expression in the life of the SUPERMAN, whose qualities include health and vitality, joyfulness, serenity, honesty, integrity, wisdom, strength, perseverance, hardness, and self-discipline. Such an individual has the courage to affirm every moment of one's life unconditionally, that is, to desire the eternal recurrence of every moment of joy and of suffering. The superman thus points the way to a higher form of humanity.

HEIDEGGER placed emphasis not on existence but on being. By insisting on the possibility of an ONTOLOGY, he appears to be much closer to traditional metaphysics. However, an examination reveals a penetrating critique of that tradition; he calls for a radical reconceptualization of the philosophical task. He points to a fundamental confusion prevalent since Aristotle between the reality of Being and the various modes of being. Philosophical tradition has obscured the real question of philosophy, namely, What is the ground of Being? It has lost touch with the Being of beings. However, it is possible to understand the reality of my being, which Heidegger calls DASEIN, only insofar as it is illuminated by Being. The reality of human existence can be grasped only by returning to the primary source and ground of all Being, by inquiring into the ontological structure of Being. From this standpoint, the HISTORY of Western philosophy represents a series of attempts to explain human reality in terms of one or another finite concept of being.

The question of the meaning of Being is intimately connected to the concept of time. In Greek philosophy the turn away from Being is bound up with the conception of time as a static present. Existential duration and being are seen as a sequence of discrete nows. There is no room in this conception for human temporality or history. The incompatibility of TIME and movement with philosophical speculation is epitomized by Hegel's system, which attempts to bring existence under the constraints of timeless necessity. Though Hegel succeeds in providing a theory of the totality of being, the real task of philosophy is to give an account of the temporality of human being in relation to the ultimate ground of Being. Heidegger reconceptualizes philosophy as a form of meditative thinking that attempts to reveal in language the way things are and in what their essential Being consists. But philosophy that confines itself to the activities of conceptual and representational thinking is inadequate to the task of inquiring into the ontological structure of Being and hence unable to shed light on the nature of human existence. By contrast, meditative thinking is an opening of oneself up to the voice of Being, an attentiveness to the truth of Being as revealed in philosophical conversation. The pre-Socratics were in tune with this way of thinking. According to Heraclitus, the lover of wisdom does not seek to possess knowledge but rather to be in harmony with the Logos, to speak in the way the Logos speaks. Logos is understood as a unifying principle, a gathering-together of being into Being.

Modern language has departed from the task of revealing; it is far removed from the Greek experience of language. When the language of philosophy attempts to represent and clarify, it cuts us off from the source of our inquiry. As a corrective, Heidegger calls us back to Heraclitus. Though we cannot return to his language, we can enter into a conversation with the Greek experience of language as a vehicle for revealing the Being of being. Heraclitus shows us what philosophy is as a distinctive manner of language. Thus, the answer to the question, What is philosophy? consists in a correspondence with the Being of being, a correspondence that is an entering into a conversation with the history of philosophy. In this sense we should understand Heidegger's call for the destruction of the history of ontology: it means going beyond historical assertions about the history of philosophy and opening ourselves up to the voice of Being that speaks through that tradition. This conception of philosophical thinking may seem esoteric. The attempt to follow Heidegger's explanation is further complicated by his innovative use of language. But this is a result of what he was trying to accomplish: to make his language reveal the Being of being. A century earlier, Hegel proclaimed that he had taught philosophy to speak German. It could be said that Heidegger's project was to teach Germans to speak the language of philosophy.

It can be said that Kierkegaard, Nietzsche, and Heidegger conceive of philosophy as an activity aimed at self-transformation. This is reflected in the form and content of their writings. In Kierkegaard and Nietzsche, the conspicuous absence of a uniform authorial voice is intended to prevent the reader from taking a passive stance with respect to their texts. These texts are occasions for the reader to think through the problems of human existence in a new, deeply personal way. Heidegger invites the reader to enter into the ongoing conversation of philosophy, the age-old inquiry into the truth of Being. His task is not to impart truth but to lead the reader to that difficult path along which truth is to be found. This view is shared by BUBER, SARTRE, and JASPERS. We cannot read these authors without being forced to think more deeply about the meaning of philosophy or about what it means for an existing individual to seek the truth.

Primary Works

Heidegger, Martin. *An Introduction to Metaphysics*. Trans. Ralph Manheim. New Haven, CT: Yale University Press, 1959.

Kierkegaard, Søren. *Concluding Unscientific Postscript*. Trans. David F. Swenson and Walter Lowrie. Princeton: Princeton University Press, 1968.

Nietzsche, Friedrich. *The Gay Science*. Trans. Walter Kaufmann. New York: Random House, 1974.

Bibliography

Raymond, Diane Barsoum. *Existentialism and the Philosophical Tradition*. Englewood Cliffs, NJ: Prentice-Hall, 1991.

PHILOSOPHY OF HISTORY
Doug Mann

Philosophers have speculated in a systematic fashion about HISTORY. KIER-KEGAARD's interest in history centered on the problem of Christian FAITH. Although CHRISTIANITY was a way of embracing the eternal, it also had historical incarnation and REVELATION in the LIFE of Christ. He asks whether a historical point of departure can be given for an eternal CONSCIOUSNESS. The eternal, he adds, has no history, for anything historical is a coming into EXISTENCE, and the eternal obviously does not come into existence. But faith is historical, a sort of coming into existence. Faith is in the historical fact that GOD has taken human form, which cancels out all other historical facts. Consequently, each religious follower must renew one's faith in the fact of the God having taken human form in one's lifetime, at a given historical point. But this renewal of faith is a renewal of faith in the eternal. Thus, Kierkegaard's philosophy of history turns the believer away from history, through the LEAP of faith, to the eternal, even though the leap of faith takes place at a historical moment.

NIETZSCHE related to history on two levels: his remarks on history as an intellectual discipline and his views of the history of ART, of PHILOSOPHY, and of morals. The second level constitutes his philosophy of history. He traces the genealogy of morals throughout history in terms of a dialectic between noble morality and herd morality. Noble morality is created by higher SPIRITS out of a sense of strength and the fullness of life. Reacting against noble MORALITY, slave morality creates a table of VALUES that gives the slaves a weapon to brandish against the strength and abundance of life of the nobles, to tame these noble beasts of prey. The slave revolt in morals begins when the members of herd become resentful of their low status and turn the "GOOD" of the masters into an EVIL. Instances of this slave revolt in morals are found among the ancient Jews, in Socrates, Christianity, and the French Revolution. Democracy, socialism, the labor movement, and feminism are also instances of slave morality. At the core of this thinking is a view of the history of morality as structured by the metaphysical monism of the WILL to POWER. Both master and slave are driven to express their will to power in the creation of tables of values. He saw the future as an age of great politics and wars the like of which had not been seen. He announced that the leveling of European man constituted the greatest danger.

Initially, HUSSERL showed little interest in history except in the history of philosophy; by the 1930s, with the advent of Nazi rule in Germany, the problem of history came to the fore in his work. In his work on the crisis of the sciences and of humanity in Europe, he speculated on the structure of history. Yet, his sense of history was in tension with PHENOMENOLOGY's focus on freeing the individual from presuppositions. The phenomenological reduction of these presuppositions, the return of philosophy to the certainty of the Cartesian EGO, left little room for speculation about human coexistence across the ages. In his early *Philosophy as a Rigorous Science* he attacks both historicism for its rejection of the absolute, atemporal validity of all ideas and Weltanschauung philosophy for its acceptance of all ideas as equally valid for their TIME. Against this he places philosophy as a rigorous science that appeals to a systematic ideal. The skeptical subjectivism that arises from historicism can be dispelled if we remember that the science of history cannot distinguish between valid and invalid science, art, or RELIGION, despite the fact that all scientific theories, aesthetic views, and religions are destined one day to pass away. Value judgments about these things are separate from judgments of their historical fact. Studying the comings and goings of worldviews means confining oneself to the finite, abandoning the infinite aspirations of the will to science that has governed the history of Western thought.

In his 1935 lecture ''Phenomenology and the Crisis of European Man,'' Husserl suggests that the crisis of humanity in Europe is spiritual; objective science cannot solve it. The spiritual birthplace of Europe was Greece in the seventh and sixth centuries B.C., when philosophy and science were born. From this birth Europe derived its central telos, a striving toward the infinite that is the purpose of philosophy as a science of the spirit. Unfortunately, modern Europe has been led astray from this telos by naturalism and objectivism. Here he puts forward the idea of the life-world, of common experience, in which we all live before it is covered over by the mathematization of nature initiated by Galileo and continued by modern science. We live in an age in which objective science weaves a web of theory and logic over the subjective, directly experienced life-world. The point of the phenomenological reduction is now to bring us back to the life-world—to throw aside the veil of objectivism and return us to an earlier epistemological, if not historical, stage of civilization. The ''Crisis'' does indicate a three-stage structure of history: (1) before the birth of civilization, (2) from the birth of civilization to the birth of a geometrical-logical worldview, and (3) our civilization of objective science. This structure is part of a dialectic of objectivism and transcendentalism that underlies the history of the West since the Renaissance. This philosophical dialectic involved a struggle between phenomenology and naturalistic PSYCHOLOGY as competing explanations of the human MIND.

SARTRE's initial radical emphasis on FREEDOM seemed to point to history as an arena of freely chosen human PROJECTS. Individual RESPONSIBILITY was the watchword; we showed ourselves to be free by acting and refusing to concede anything to being-in-itself. Humans were in history yet were expected, if they were to avoid BAD FAITH, not to make concessions to the iron laws of history as constraints on their actions. Later, Sartre considered humans as free only insofar as they lived in a SOCIETY without scarcity; until scarcity was eliminated, the project of the individual was limited by the necessity to seek material well-being. In *Search for a Method* he follows Marx in seeing the economic substructure as determining the political and ideological superstructure; his progressive-regressive method was meant to show how the free individual lives within a given society at a given time.

Sartre held that contemporary MARXISM lacked a hierarchy of mediations that would allow us to understand the individual within one's class and society at a given moment in history. Hence, many Marxists see humans as mere products of specific economic structures. He reminded these idealist Marxists that just as we are the products of our class and society, we are also the makers of the world in which we exist. Sartre saw three ideological moments from the seventeenth to the twentieth centuries: those of Descartes and Locke, of Kant and Hegel, and of Marx. These moments corresponded to the march of European society from analytic to dialectical rationalism. At present, the only living philosophy is Marxism, the others being pre-Marxist survivals of earlier class struggles. We can look forward to a post-Marxism, a philosophy of freedom, only after there exists, for one and all, a margin of freedom from the need to produce, from the rule of material conditions. Such can be accomplished only by the proletariat's becoming conscious of itself and thereby becoming the SUBJECT of history. Then history will have one meaning, determined by human freedom.

JASPERS' philosophy of history can be found in its most complete form in his *The Origin and Goal of History*. He speculates that around 500 B.C. (give or take three centuries) we discover an axial period in human development, when the great prophets, philosophers, and sages of antiquity—Plato, Buddha, ZARATHUSTRA, and Confucius— appeared on the stage of world history in three centers of civilization: China, India, and the West. Together with them, reflective thought emerged. These men helped humanity become conscious of BEING as a whole and of the terror of the world. Their radical questions led to a spiritualization of the human race. The breakthrough of the axial period brought forth religious and philosophical ideas that helped to shape the ancient and modern worlds: the Platonic Idea, atman, nirvana, the tao, or the will of the One True God. The ESSENCE of the axial period lay in its being a model for all civilized cultures that came afterward, in its being the spiritual axis of world history.

Jaspers divides history into four periods: the dimly perceived Prehistoric period; the age of Ancient Civilizations; the Axial Period and its progeny; our Scientific-Technological Age. He dismisses five possible factual grounds for the unity of history: human biological unity; psychological or sociological universals; human progress; unity in SPACE and time; local unities. He also dismisses any unity that we might read into history based on a common meaning or goal, such as civilization, LIBERTY, the production of genius. Hence, we must focus on the manifold CHARACTER of these possible sources of unity, comprehending the many diverse forms and lines that make up a picture of the historical. He exhibits historicist assumptions and believes that we can attain TRUTH only from our present position within the historical tradition; our present being is best judged by plunging into the depths of our historical origins. The philosopher of existence requires a universal view of history, which would lead into the unity of the revelation of Being. He shares HEIDEGGER's belief that the modern age is characterized by an absence of involvement with Being and an oblivion to this absence. Yet without historicity, humans would be lost in the particularities of a contingent existence.

Although existentialist interpretations of the past vary, one underlying similarity might be their emphasis on ideas, values, and worldviews as factors giving history structure and meaning.

Primary Works

Husserl, Edmund. *Phenomenology and the Crisis of Philosophy.* Trans. Quentin Lauer. New York: Harper and Row, 1965.
Jaspers, Karl. *The Origin and Goal of History.* Trans. Michael Bullock. New Haven, CT: Yale University Press, 1953.
Sartre, Jean-Paul. *Search for a Method.* Trans. Hazel E. Barnes. New York: Knopf, 1963.

PHILOSOPHY OF RELIGION
Thomas B. Ommen

Philosophy of religion lies between the scientific study of RELIGION and THEOLOGY. Philosophers of religion move beyond empirical description and may affirm the EXISTENCE of, and try to talk about, GOD or transcendent reality. On the other hand, philosophers of religion avoid an appeal to particular FAITH experiences not widely shared by other humans. Thus, when TILLICH relies on philosophy of religion as a part of his theology, he is anxious to defend the rationality and public character of his argument. Existentialist thinking on religion includes theistic and atheistic. At one pole are SARTRE and CAMUS, who viewed religion as a form of BAD FAITH. At the other pole are believers like

KIERKEGAARD, BUBER, Tillich, and BULTMANN, who developed theologies. HEIDEGGER and JASPERS stand between theism and atheism. Neither Jaspers' TRANSCENDENCE nor Heidegger's BEING can be identified with a traditional understanding of God, yet neither philosopher can be described as an atheist. MARCEL, BERDYAEV, and UNAMUNO stand closer to the theologians. But they resisted a theological identification and maintained a distance from any specific confessional stance.

Even Camus and Sartre recognized a need for transcendence that remained unsatisfied. Life without God is marked by absurdity and meaninglessness. But a need for God does not guarantee his existence. For the modern age, God is, in some sense, dead. Buber found such a position to be understandable but superficial. Sartre and Camus may have confused God's eclipse or temporary silence with his DEATH. The real issue is whether it is possible for humans, as Sartre recommends, to forget God and recover creative FREEDOM. The religious relationship, Buber holds, lies deeper than Sartre thought; it emerges in the human condition. Heidegger and Jaspers shared Sartre's sense of God's silence but recognized the permanence of a religious question. The quest for religion is basic to human existence. LIFE is marked by a givenness that is not adequately reflected in creative freedom.

The need for transcendence is often described by Christian theologians in the biblical image of the Fall. Humans have fallen from a state of grace or innocence and live in a state of estrangement. The Fall points not to a specific historical event but to a permanent gap between what we are and what we should be. Tillich pointed to a dim awareness of the unconditional at the depths of every human life. Because humans exist in a state of estrangement from this unconditional ground, REVELATION is needed to overcome the divine/human divide. Tillich and Bultmann found the definitive response to estrangement in Christ. The questions of life point toward the New Being opened up as a human possibility by the Christian message. PHILOSOPHY cannot create the possibility for authentic existence. The resolution of ANXIETY, in Christian terms, requires the grace of God mediated through Christ and interpreted by theology.

Because only faith in revelation can mediate an encounter with God, philosophy is limited to exploring questions that are basic to the human SITUATION. The Christian proclamation can respond to such questions as an answer. Thus, philosophy might highlight the estrangement of the human condition, and the Christian theologian can try to show that religious symbols offer ways of articulating and overcoming that estrangement. Bultmann found in existentialist philosophy the appropriate concepts for characterizing the basic structure of human self-understanding and for interpreting in nonmythological terms the biblical proclamation. But both Tillich and Bultmann agreed that philosophy could not mediate authentic existence; such a possibility emerged for the first time in Christian faith and its theology. For Jaspers, the religious need is expressed in a sense of foundering, which highlights the hopelessness of all attempts to reach the Absolute from within life. It brings humans up against the boundaries of existence and the anxiety these boundaries entail. Concrete religions don't recognize the depth of foundering, because they appeal to various forms of supernatural revelation. CHRISTIANITY removes the real tragedy of existence by promising a definitive salvation. Whatever grace there is in life is far more ambiguous and not available in such positive, explicit forms.

In contrast, Marcel writes that humans live in a broken world. All hope must ultimately be hope of salvation. Human LOVE refuses to accept the death of the loved one; it seeks an answer to the anxiety that death creates. Love raises us above the destruction that marks the world in which we live. Only in God, Berdyaev argued, does a person overcome one's solitude and discover a purpose that matches human aspiration. Nonreligious existentialism leaves humans alone, with no response to the need for spiritual fulfillment. For Unamuno a hunger for IMMORTALITY persists even in the face of the contrary claims of reason. Ultimate NOTHINGNESS would be a worse punishment than Hell. The furious longing to assign finality to the universe, to make it conscious and personal, leads to belief in God. Reason may dismiss such faith, but this only indicates the need to go beyond reason. Reason is the enemy of life.

Existentialist thinkers point to the presence of, as well as the need for, transcendence. The supernatural manifests itself in the natural. The central issue is whether there is an experience of a gift or grace at a deep level of existence that points beyond nothingness and despair. Some take tentative steps in this religious direction. For Heidegger, properly raising the question of God meant finding a more adequate theological approach than metaphysical systems that have been embedded in the forgetfulness of Being. Through a step back to a more primordial thinking, it may be possible to raise again the question of God. A new ONTOLOGY might make possible the reappearance of God or the holy. Jaspers moved very cautiously in a religious direction. In limit situations, humans become aware of a dimension of transcendence; they sense that the limits of the phenomenal world are surpassable. As parts of the world are seen in wider and wider contexts, a sense of the encompassing manifests itself, the source from which all new horizons emerge. Wonder before the all is experienced. Some worldly entity, such as the ocean, may attain a deeper quality; transcendence may shine through, albeit in an uncertain light. Self-transcendence in spiritual terms is a part of life, but this does not make possible a definite determination of the CHARACTER of the transcendent reality toward which human self-transcendence is directed.

Marcel argued that the distinction between the natural and supernatural must be maintained. But the supernatural can be grasped only if there is some basis in the natural for understanding it. In the natural sphere, one finds a restless anticipation of another order. God is present in the spiritual dimension in human existence. At an ontological point in every human the natural and supernatural, divine and human meet. The core experience that pointed ultimately to God was participation. The interaction with the world and other humans and the world carries with it an INTUITION of the ultimate ground of such relationships. The unity, harmony, and assurance found in the symphony of Being can appear to the believer as a mysterious indication of the presence of God. Berdyaev found the heart of philosophy in the idea that the divine and the human exist in reciprocal interaction. The essence of Christianity lies in the notion of the incarnation. God is present when humans are most fully free and have most fully achieved their humanity. He hoped for a new MYSTICISM, fully involved in the world, in which this humanity could be expressed. According to Unamuno, the longing for immortality and for a personalized universe has led humans, in a sense, to create God. He acknowledges that such suggests that God might seem to be a projection of the human mind. He holds that outside the personal relationship with God, from the standpoint of reason, God can appear to be an illusion. But within the relationship, within the concrete longing for God, His existence becomes a reality.

Existentialists share a distaste for the modern dominance of objectifying thought, which is particularly inappropriate in a relationship with God. There is a common conviction that God can never be approached as an object of human KNOWLEDGE. The divine reveals itself in the inner life of the individual but is not there as an object of experience or as a concept of thought. This refusal to treat God as an object led to the critique of natural theology and of efforts to prove God's existence by rational argument. The strongest rejection of rationalism can be found in Kierkegaard's emphasis on Christian paradox and rejection of Hegel's essentialism. Unamuno's work tended in a similar antirationalist direction. Reason was the enemy of life. In contrast, Marcel, Berdyaev, and Tillich tried to reformulate, in nonobjectivist terms, some form of METAPHYSICS. They sought an ontological and existential basis for talking about God.

The critique of objectifying forms of thought led existentialists to stress the individual character of religion. God cannot be there as an object but can be encountered only in the inwardness of personal life. Marcel and Buber moved in a different direction. Although both shared a sense of the priority of I–Thou over I–It relationships and were convinced that God cannot be properly approached and known in third-PERSON terms, they linked the relationship to God to other forms of relationship. Buber called God the eternal Thou who can never be an It. Marcel, appealing, in part, to Buber, stresses the importance of participation. The self exists not in abstract isolation but in an incarnate existence. The individual is always permeable to others. This ontological communion with the world of NATURE and with other humans is the route to transcendence.

Primary Works

Bultmann, Rudolf. *History and Eschatology*. New York: Harper and Row, 1957.
Tillich, Paul. *Systematic Theology*. Vols. 1–3. Chicago: University of Chicago Press, 1955.

Bibliography

Macquarrie, John. *An Existential Theology: A Comparison of Heidegger and Bultmann.* London: SCM Press, 1955.

POETRY
Mathew Rampley

Poetry, ideas of the poetic, and the figure of the poet constitute a recurring motif in existentialist thought. For KIERKEGAARD the poetic, specifically the poet, exemplifies the AESTHETIC STAGE, which leaves the individual dependent on the CONTINGENCIES of EXISTENCE, unable to see beyond his or her immediate desires and needs. This often leads to passive melancholy or despair. Poetry serves to transfigure this despair, but it does not dispel it. Indeed, not only does poetry merely transfigure the ennui of the aesthetic stage, but it also prevents progression to the ETHICAL STAGE. Becoming immersed in poetry may lead to losing the ability to distinguish between reality and poetic fancy. Thus, poetry masks the realities of the aesthetic stage; its figures cover up the ground for the ambiguities and contradictions of the aesthetic LIFE, thereby perpetuating its illusions. Yet, Kierkegaard is also reliant on the poetic. The various stages of existence are illustrated by means of fictional, at times poetic narratives rather than logical analysis.

The early thought of HEIDEGGER displays little concern with poetry. In *Being and Time*, however, he claims that PHILOSOPHY must prevent the most elemental words from being rendered unintelligible by common understanding. Although these elemental words remain unspecified in *Being and Time*, in his later thought they seem to be equated with poetry. In studies of poets, most notably, Holderlin, but also RILKE, Trakl, and Stefan George, he emphasizes the primal role of poetry: all LANGUAGE is originally poetry; nonpoetic language is derivative. A key element is his claim for the neighborhood of thinking and poetry. All great poetry is open to the country of thought. In addition, thinking about BEING is often a form of poetizing. While poetry thus only alludes to Being, it nevertheless plays a founding role in the understanding of Being. Indeed, poetry brings a WORLD into existence, which is consistent with his view that beings emerge only in language. Naming is of central importance in this process, and that naming is seen to occur frequently in poetry, which thus has a pivotal role in the life of a culture, since a world is named and brought into being through poetry. Yet poetry does not directly name Being. Poetry can establish a clearing in which the mapping out of the fourfold of Earth, sky, mortals, and GODS emerges. Heidegger sees this fourfold as constituting the coordinates within which a historical world comes into Being. Although Heidegger offers his thinking on ART, poetry is privileged within the account of the history of Being in Western culture, inasmuch as it takes a central role in the overcoming of METAPHYSICS.

Poetry undergoes a variety of evaluations in the thought of SARTRE. In *What Is Literature?*, he makes a forceful distinction between prose and poetry. Poetry is caught up in a fetishism of language; words lose their original communicative function and are granted a magical autonomy. The poetic attitude considers words as things and not as signs. In *Being and Nothingness* he criticizes poetic metaphor for treating the in-itself as for-itself. Later, this opposition is replaced by one of signification and *sens*, the former denoting language's communicative function, the latter its material aspects. The poetic attends primarily to *sens* rather than communicating any signification. The background of this critique is an engagement with modernism and its fascination with language. Sartre's reservations over modernist poetry are linked to his wider conception of the task of LITERATURE, which is to articulate a PERSON's existential SITUATION and one's FREEDOM. This draws upon his complex view of language, which sees it as a medium of both freedom and alienation.

Sartre views poetry more positively elsewhere. The modernist, poetic fetishism of language is seen as a liberation from ALIENATION. His analysis of black African poetry in *Black Orpheus* discusses the alienation of the African colonized by the language of the French colonizers. The poetry of Africans of the Negritude movement, with its disruption of signification, is an attempt to undermine the language of colonizers in order to restore an authentic voice to the colonized. A similar reevaluation of poetry occurs in *Saint Genet*; the failure of communication in Genet is a refusal to follow the rules of a language imposed by others. In these later works Sartre seems to accept that poetry, while interfering with communication, nevertheless plays an important role. Through its rejection of usual patterns of signification poetry can evoke aspects of lived experience that prose cannot. Not merely the content but the manner of delivery ultimately counts.

JASPERS argues that poetry is a primary form of language; consequently, philosophy, too, is first expressed in poetry. This conclusion suggests parallels with Heidegger but has to be tempered by the differences between the two thinkers. MERLEAU-PONTY is better known for his fascination with painting than for his interest in poetry. If he does not discuss poetry, it is because the poetic is so central to his philosophical PROJECT that its presence is taken as implicit. This is clear from his refusal to distinguish between philosophy and poetry, and his use of a highly mannered style that rejects the canon of philosophical rigor and clarity. Poetry and art in general are an expression of one's style of being and are founded in one's carnal relation with the world. Hence,

Merleau-Ponty avoids the distinction between prose and poetry. This is indicated by his claim that if we wish to understand what happens when we speak, we have to address ourselves to the poet. All linguistic usage thus has a style of the kind more usually attributed to poetry. At the same time he distinguishes between the literary and the rational-scientific. While both are founded on the exploration of ideas, literary ideas cannot be detached from sensible appearance. Implicit in this is a notion of poetic discourse as a more immediate expression of existence than the logicoscientific language dominant in Western modernity.

Primary Works

Heidegger, Martin. *Poetry, Language, Thought*. Trans. Albert Hofstadter. New York: Harper and Row, 1971.
Sartre, Jean-Paul. *Saint Genet: Actor and Martyr*. Trans. Bernard Fretchman. New York: Braziler, 1963.

Bibliography

Bernasconi, Robert. *The Question of Language in Heidegger's History of Being*. Atlantic Highlands, NJ: Humanities Press, 1985.

POLITICAL PHILOSOPHY
Sonya Sikka

The political philosophy of existentialists spans the political spectrum. MARCEL was a monarchist for much of his LIFE, while JASPERS ended as a cosmopolitan liberal. HEIDEGGER became a member of the Nazi party, the NSDAP (Nationalsozialistiche Deutsche Arbeiterpartei), in 1933. Although his period of active support for the Nazis was brief, his thought remained nationalist. SARTRE and MERLEAU-PONTY supported some form of MARXISM for much of their life, while CAMUS was critical of any totalizing IDEOLOGY. ARENDT renewed, in existential terms, much of Greek political thinking. These thinkers have in common a rejection of abstract and supposedly universal political principles and an emphasis on the concrete historical situation in which an individual makes decisions and acts. They also stress the finitude of human KNOWLEDGE and the uncertainty that accompanies this finitude.

In 1933, Heidegger became rector of Freiburg University as a member of the

Nazi Party. His inaugural address as Rector, "The Self-Assertion of the German University," cannot be termed a Nazi speech. Nonetheless, the address has become infamous because of its LANGUAGE and rhetoric, which evoke themes expressed in Nazi propaganda, and because of the amalgamation of these themes with the philosophical analysis of human EXISTENCE in *Being and Time*. Heidegger speaks of the mission of the German people, calling upon teachers and students to stand firm in the face of German destiny. This readiness and resolve to answer the appeal of destiny involve a WILL to ESSENCE and to fulfill the historical and spiritual task of the German people. He calls for a renewal of the Greek ethos, in which knowledge was supposed to shape the spiritual WORLD of a people. He describes this world as the POWER that comes from the most profound preservation of the forces rooted in the soil and blood of a *Volk*. Over the next year, Heidegger gave several shorter speeches and contributed articles to the Freiburg University student newspaper, expressing support for the Nazi regime. After ten months, however, he resigned the role of rector; he was not politically active after 1934.

The analysis of DASEIN in *Being and Time* stresses the primacy of the unique historical SITUATION into which the existing individual is thrown, within which he or she must make CHOICES. Heidegger speaks of the voice of CONSCIENCE, which recalls Dasein from its immersion in the THEY, to its FREEDOM and RESPONSIBILITY. The decision to heed this call is resoluteness. It has been claimed that this mistrust of the ordinary social world and its description of individual resolve and decision in the absence of guiding norms imply a form of arbitrary irrational voluntarism, which might underlie the political decisions Heidegger made. Some of Heidegger's later writings contain further reflections on the role of language, tradition, HISTORY, and place in constituting the identity of a people, focusing specifically on the German people. They have an anticosmopolitan tenor; they often incline toward a Romantic and narrow nationalism and encourage the MYTH of a historical mission for Germany. In Heidegger's defense, however, note that *Being and Time* includes an analysis of authentic being-with, which involves solicitude, the appropriate mode of CARE for the BEING of the other. Also, his discussions of *Volk* are never biologically based; he criticizes biologism.

Prior to World War II, Sartre's concern with politics was minimal. He and BEAUVOIR shared a sympathy with the proletariat, the Russian Revolution, and the Communist Party. However, these sympathies were not accompanied by personal or intellectual commitment. They remained, during this period, disinterested spectators of history. At this time, Sartre's conception of freedom was highly individualistic. For the most part, his antibourgeois sentiments were not yet directed against the oppression of the working classes through the power relations established by capitalism. Rather, they were aimed at the narrow conventionalism of the bourgeoisie, with its tendency to stifle original thought and expression. World War II shook Sartre out of complacency. He spent a year in the French army and another year in a German prisoner of war camp; he was released into occupied France in March 1941. These experiences demonstrated to him the impossibility of separating oneself from the vicissitudes of history and left him with a newly found sense of human solidarity.

Sartre's idea of engagement is the conscious decision to assume one's involvement in history, rather than evading it, and thereby to assume, in every action, social and political responsibility. He does not produce a set of ethical norms to guide decisions, since he rejects the possibility of a stable human NATURE that could serve as a foundation for such norms. He emphasizes the primacy of the concrete and always unique historical situation. Decision must proceed in response to the exigency of this situation. Yet, the explorations into the nature of CONSCIOUSNESS in *Being and Nothingness* do not contain a developed social or political theory and are not much concerned with the contingent events of history. The study does include an analysis of being-for-others, which recognizes the intrinsic connection between self-consciousness and the awareness of being an OBJECT for another. But the fundamental relation underlying being-for-others is that of one individual to another. He does not address the web of institutions and power relations that constitute SOCIETY or the historically determined nature of groups and classes. Moreover, his interpretation of human coexistence suggests that it is essentially conflictual and fraught with contradictions that make genuine COMMUNITY impossible.

Although Sartre's view of interhuman relations remains agonistic throughout his career, his writings after the war acknowledge the possibility of community. They also broaden the question of freedom to encompass that of social emancipation. The journal *Les Temps Modernes*, founded by Sartre, Beauvoir, and Merleau-Ponty after the war, was to be an example of engaged writing. In *What Is Literature?* published in 1947, Sartre writes that the engaged writer knows that words are action. *Les Temps Modernes* was to follow similar principles in its dedication to bringing about change through writing. Over the next decade, the journal published critical articles on the de Gaulle regime, the French policy in Algeria, racism and political oppression in the United States, and the Hungarian Revolution. During this period, Sartre was anticapitalist and antibourgeois; his relations with the Communist Party were supportive, but not uncritical. In 1950, *Les Temps Modernes* published articles against the Soviet concentration camps but did not denounce socialism. While the terror of the Soviet regime posed a problem for both Sartre and Merleau-Ponty, they believed that violence was present in every political regime.

The question then was whether the violence of the Soviet regime could be justified in light of its emancipatory mission. After the start of the Korean War, Merleau-Ponty's answer was: No. In contrast, Sartre declared unequivocal support for the communists and included a fierce attack of the moderate Left. In 1956, however, the Hungarian Revolution led Sartre to break with the Communist Party. It was clear that the Soviet troops and the Hungarian workers were not on the same side, and *Les Temps Modernes* sided with Hungarians who opposed Soviet intervention. From this time, Sartre supported a de-Stalinized form of Marxism. In the late 1950s, he wrote *Critique of Dialectical Reason*, a systematic attempt to combine existentialism and Marxism. He replaced the traditional Marxist theory of historical materialism—which is incompatible with his view of the freedom and spontaneity of consciousness—with his own anthropology and PHILOSOPHY OF HISTORY.

For Merleau-Ponty, too, World War II resulted in a political awakening. In 1945, he assumed the political editorship of *Les Temps Modernes*. His *The Phenomenology of Perception* was published in the same year and can be read as taking issue with a number of Sartre's theses. It questions the dualism of consciousness and BODY that seems to underlie Sartre's being-for-itself. Merleau-Ponty proposes, against such a dualism, the lived experience of the body as the exterior aspect of the person. He also grounds thought in PERCEPTION, where perception is a function of the body in its interactions with the material world. This understanding of the way the person is embedded in the material world shaped Merleau-Ponty's interpretation of Marx's idea of praxis and historical materialism. Society's basic relationship with nature is economic reality. His analysis of how ideology is founded upon this reality extends his analysis of how thought is founded upon perception.

Merleau-Ponty points out, against Sartre's conception of the isolated individual, that we exist in a social world of shared experience and meaning. The commonality of this world is rooted in the commonality of perspectives on the physical world as encountered by the BODY, in shared praxis. This genuinely intersubjective world is also woven by language, which both shapes and articulates perception. Through the dialogue that language permits, our perspectives merge, and we coexist through a common world. Therefore, society is a dimension of human existence. Class consciousness, containing within itself the possibility of solidarity and the desire for revolution, emerges from this social dimension of human existence, rooted in praxis. Yet, it is not produced passively. Human existence both produces and is produced. Perception is already a process of making sense, and this process both constitutes and discovers. Meaning emerges through the interplay of constitution and discovery and therefore through an interplay of freedom and determinacy.

Moreover, Merleau-Ponty views freedom as a feature of certain types of actions, those that overcome the sedimentation resulting from the accumulated weight of the past. The revolutionary movement is a case in point. The meaning of such actions is never wholly transparent. Meaning is an intersubjective process, fraught with obscurity and CONTINGENCY. The individual cannot be certain of the final outcome of one's actions or of the collective struggle in which one is engaged. He attacks Sartre's identifying the working class with the Communist Party, where the party is thought to bring the proletarian consciousness into existence, thus constituting its TRUTH. The truth of the proletariat, however, its meaning in history, can emerge only through an ongoing dialectical exchange between the class and the party. It is impossible to decide a priori what the end of communism will be, independently of proof and of what its history brought to light. The meaning of this movement is contained within the actions and events of its past and present. Its logic appears to have led to an imperialism and oppression that are no better than those of capitalism. Thus, while Merleau-Ponty had previously criticized liberalism for separating the realm of politics from human existence, he turns to a new liberalism, asking if there is not more of a future in a regime that does not intend to remake history but only to change it. His final position appears to be that the free exchange of ideas is at least a prerequisite for emancipation, and a political system that guarantees a minimum of such an exchange is preferable to one that does not.

Camus was born in Algiers. His father was killed in combat in 1914, and he grew up in poverty. He had a deep sensitivity to the plight of the poor and the working class, both their deprivation and the oppressed dignity of their lives. He joined the Communist Party in Algiers in 1934 but quickly became disillusioned and developed a distaste for grand political theories that forget the daily sufferings and hopes of humans and treat live PERSONS as instruments in the realization of a future design. He was active in the French Resistance; his numerous interventions in politics were aimed at particular problems and rarely involved speculation about ethical principles. *The Rebel* contains a systematic account of Camus' mature political position. He was suspicious of Sartre's hatred of his class, his belief in the relativity of all VALUES and the indeterminacy of human nature, and his notion of radical freedom and commitment. Camus criticizes these positions and draws a distinction between rebellion and revolution. The rebel rises up against one's master in order to preserve something in oneself that is worthwhile and that he or she feels is common to oneself and to all persons. Cut off from its roots and merged with political revolution, such rebellion can become totalitarian terror, which recognizes no limits to its knowledge or power. Then, the demand for total freedom turns into complete tyranny.

The rebel thus affirms that there is a nature common to all upon which a minimal transhistorical ethics could be based. Camus rejects the supposition behind absolute revolution, namely, that human nature is absolutely malleable. He also rejects Marxist ESCHATOLOGY, with its messianic mission for the proletariat and its prophetic belief in the necessary coming of a new era. Facts do not support this prophecy, and the belief becomes an excuse for sacrificing the lives of countless individuals for the sake of an uncertain future. Against much contemporary Marxism, he quotes Marx: an end that requires unjust means is not a just end. *The Rebel* ends with a call to moderation that would renounce the desire to be GOD and with an affirmation of the intrinsic value of ART and LITERATURE, beauty and nature.

Primary Works

Camus, Albert. *The Rebel*. Trans. Anthony Bower. New York: Knopf, 1967.
Sartre, Jean-Paul. *Critique of Dialectical Reason*. Trans. Alan Sheridan. London: Verso, 1982.

Bibliography

Kruks, Sonia. *The Political Philosophy of Merleau-Ponty.* Atlantic Highlands, NJ: Humanities Press, 1981.

POWER
Stephen Tyman

Power is a concept diverse in application and elusive. Everything, even EXISTENCE, can be understood as a manifestation of the power to be. In what, then, is power grounded? How might this potential be further explored? Existential thought has repeatedly addressed this question. Power tends to be a relational concept, depending on the context in which it is invoked. Quite often it involves social relations or institutions. Thus, in one major delineation power indicates a factor in a constellation of political affairs, or a measure of social influence. For practical purposes, this suggests a model of command structure sustained by governmental hierarchy backed by an instrument of force such as a constabulary or militia. But to approach the question solely on this level is to accept a circumstantially determined sense of power.

The social dimension of power is often interrogated on a psychological level, for example, in the FEARS of those who choose to acquiesce or the urge to dominance of those who seek to make institutions an instrument of their empowerment. In this light, power often suggests a criticism of social power RELATIONS. Here there is a major tension within existentialism, for individualism is a central existential theme and stands in direct opposition to any kind of collectivism. Hence, SARTRE distinguished between existentialism and MARXISM, declaring the former to be broadly apolitical, while the latter is necessary for describing the sphere of praxis, with its power relations. But such a division is intrinsically uneasy, especially since existential individuation is always understood to be situated and therefore not simply something other than the social and political contexts in which it can be enacted.

A primary aspect of Hegel's analysis of power is the ambiguity with respect to its substantiality, that is, the question of where power is ultimately seated. The issue is examined in the famous dialectic between master and slave in which he shows that the master, in whom power is overtly invested, is locked in a codependent relationship with the slave as the one who recognizes and grants to the master the status of being the powerful one. Power of this sort, however, becomes more the mark of one who becomes dependent on the circumstances sustaining recognition of power than one who retains the inward ability of self-determination. The latter capacity is reserved for the slave, in whose labor the forces of subliminal empowerment are at work, with the effect that the slave achieves power over the self while the master, having become empowered in relation to the slave, is enslaved to that relation and thus powerless to effect self-transformation. Thus, a primary inheritance of existentialism is that power must be treated upon the basis of a relation of the self to itself, a question of self-making. In KIERKEGAARD's formulation, this self-relation is described as informed from within by a deep relation to the power that constitutes the deity. The subjective approach to this deity colors his THEOLOGY. Nevertheless, to conceive the process of self-making as relational to an Absolute, the constituting Power, is to subordinate the relational character of the self to a sense of the Absolute precisely with respect to power. The Absolute is posited not only in the traditional way as inscrutable and beyond reason but also as the source of a paradox, an affliction to reason. Thus, a state of tension seems to exist between the twofold dimensions of self-making: its autonomous power to be what it will be is in conflict with its absolute dependence or powerlessness in the face of the source of BEING.

In the case of nonreligious existentialists, the tension is often expressed in terms of a dialectic between the self and some aspect of its SITUATION, most often a social one. HEIDEGGER describes the existing self confronted with the THEY, which is a kind of inertial undertow against the process of authentic LIFE. Existential power is expressed as an ownmost potentiality to be. But he does not regard this as an utterly self-originating power; DASEIN continues to be thought of as relational to Being, although the relation can be grounded in nothing outside the self, and therefore Being cannot be posited as an independent Power. The poignancy of Heidegger's approach is that, through this way and means, the last vestige of absolutism is expunged, leaving a self seeking to tap its ownmost resolve to be, with no other indications concerning its whence and whither.

In his formulation of the WILL to power, NIETZSCHE asserted the absolute existence of power as equiprimordial with will, with both possessing fundamental ontological status. Power, for Nietzsche, represents a concept that decenters the will by drawing it into the world of manifestation, where it discovers itself in its effects. At the same time, power continues to be thought of in relation to will, that is, as a self-directing, restless phenomenon, a monster of energy. Thus, while will and power essentially inform each other and coexist in a kind of binary opposition, each problematizes the other radically, disrupting the conceptual stability not only of each pole but even of the whole nexus. A pervasive ambiguity and ambivalence here become evident. Yet he emphasized that a purely objective notion of power, force, or energy, lacking the component of will, is an incomplete concept. But with regard to the intelligibility typically sought by those who insist upon the irreducible relevance of subjective factors, questions of meaning and purpose, he is also very skeptical.

Despite the intrinsic instability of the concept of will to power, its legacy has been strong. Many frameworks of explanation, like the sciences, effectively reduce to extrinsic measure all the phenomena of experience. Concepts like the conservation of energy or the various physical forces function to interpret power. Also many points of view opt, instead, for the subjective and inward orientation to power, both as this exists in solitary form and as an intersubjective cultural function. But to take these two approaches together as codeterminative of a single dimension of significance exceeds the bounds of all but a few perspectives. Since Nietzsche despaired of any coalescing of all available perspectives into a single frame of reference, he manages to represent the broadest range of characteristic existential responses to the power question.

Primary Works

Arendt, Hannah. *Between Past and Future*. Harmondsworth: Penguin, 1977.
Nietzsche, Friedrich. *The Will to Power*. Trans. Walter Kaufmann and R. J. Hollingdale. New York: Vintage, 1969.

Bibliography

Allison, David B. *The New Nietzsche*. Cambridge: MIT Press, 1985.

PROCESS
Frank Schalow

The importance of the term ''process'' in existentialist thought becomes evident by contrasting a vision of change, growth, and development that existentialists advocate with a static vision of substance that they reject. They reject the attempt to conceive the identity of the self or the NATURE of reality in terms of an ideal of permanence. They develop a process view, which emphasizes the concrete experience of TIME. The importance that they attach to temporality and the transitoriness of human EXISTENCE sets the stage for their understanding of process.

For KIERKEGAARD, the self unfolds through a dynamic fusion of ETERNITY and time. This dynamic shapes the self's ethical and religious development. The self does not find its identity already given but must instead undergo an abrupt reversal of its priorities or a conversion, in order to realize its uniqueness in harmony with a higher religious vocation. The act of conversion is a spiritual process in which the self experiences a radical transposition of its identity. Rather than narrowly fixating on the satisfaction of desire, the self discovers in GOD the wider compass of all its concerns. The self can be ripe for such a transformation, however, only insofar as it exists as a SPIRIT that fuses opposites, of infinite and finite, eternal and temporal. For Kierkegaard, the development of an ethical or religious commitment requires its reaffirmation or renewal at each step. Even a conversion qualifies as such only to the extent that it resurfaces as a possibility to be fostered anew as the animating spark and governing movement of a PERSON's life. The fact that any conversion requires the conjunction of eternity and time in the moment reinforces the concrete dimension of that process as shaping the self's development. Thus, process distinguishes the self's immersion in the questions of life and its EDUCATION in the school of possibility.

The vision of process as etched in the possibilities of the moment emerges in NIETZSCHE's description of time as eternal recurrence. He repeatedly attacks the metaphysical concept of substance as permanence. Neither the world nor the self can conform to any such thought-construct, for each must exhibit the interplay of opposites that fuels the process of becoming. To affirm suffering and joy together, as well as death and renewal, is the key component in celebrating LIFE. This Dionysian blending of opposites reaches its climax in the eternal recurrence of the same. Time recurs insofar as the self-affirmation of life upholds the moment as including all that has been and prefiguring all that will be. He coins the term LOVE of fate to distinguish the heroic self-affirmation of the individual facing the eternal recurrence. Life can be fully experienced only by appreciating its CHARACTER as a tragic event in the transitory beauty of nature and in the creative rapture of art. He envisions the self as an artistic process of transfiguration whose example resides in the SUPERMAN who channels the basic life-energy or WILL to POWER, in order to create higher expressions of humanity. Such relentless self-overcoming epitomizes the process character of human identity as the drive to rise beyond one's present level.

HEIDEGGER developed an ONTOLOGY of process that criticizes the traditional concept of substance as permanent presence. His aim is to uncover temporality as the movement that shapes the pursuit of selfhood and the disclosure of BEING. *Being and Time* redefines human existence as a projection of the self upon possibilities. DASEIN stands out beyond itself and undertakes the movement of TRANSCENDENCE. Heidegger develops the notion of repetition as the retrieval of the past in future possibilities. Temporality is ecstatic in the sense that the casting forth of its dimensions of future, past, and present enables Dasein to stand out from itself toward possibilities. Process thereby defines the concrete way of addressing being out of the finitude of human existence. Dasein's self springs forth along the arc of temporal transcendence. Temporality displays an elliptical movement insofar as it arises from the future, returns from the past, and breaks through into the authentic present. Ecstatic temporality is in contrast to the derivative view of time as the sequence of nows. Previous philosophers developed a more conventional view of time by giving priority to the now. They forged a concept of substance that abstracts from the dynamism of temporal movement and privileges the present as a form of permanence or endurance. This metaphysical endeavor stems from Dasein's natural tendency to Fall and to flee the inevitability of its own DEATH by taking refuge in a continual present. Conversely, primordial time arises insofar as Dasein anticipates the possibility of one's own death and resolves to act authentically within its SITUATION. Thus, Dasein develops its identity by acting upon the possibilities that arise through the disclosedness of its temporal movement. Dasein exists authentically by reaffirming its uniqueness in the face of death. Self-identity is not a given, but a task that each individual must undertake. Moreover, this task corresponds to the dynamic movement in which human existence stretches itself along in the zone between past and future, birth and death. The active dimension of stretching itself along constitutes Dasein's form of self-constancy, a choosing who it is at each juncture of existence. Temporality temporalizes through self-constancy as a repetition of the past in future possibilities. This temporalizing movement is the dynamic alternative to the fixed identity that previous philosophers attribute to substance.

Existentialists concur in their effort to dissociate process and progress. Change and growth often receive their dynamism through a renewal and reaffirmation of the past, rather than through linear progress. Heidegger suggests that HISTORY entails the transmission of heritage, which recovers the meaning of the past in the future. A worthy existence reintroduces what is old in what is new and promotes development through the appropriation of tradition. The process outlook entails that humans can never grasp the ultimate meaning of events by stepping outside of life into a static eternity. Perhaps the most radical vision of the cyclical reaffirmation of life stripped of teleology occurs with CAMUS' image of Sisyphus pushing a boulder up a hill only to have it crash down again into the valley. Rather than leading to resignation, the emphasis on process can attest to the resiliency of the human spirit.

Primary Works

Kierkegaard, Søren. *Stages on Life's Way*. Trans. Howard V. Hong and Edna H. Hong. Princeton: Princeton University Press, 1988.
Nietzsche, Friedrich. *The Gay Science*. Trans. Walter Kaufmann. New York: Random House, 1974.

PROJECT
Constance L. Mui

Existentialists characterize humans as conscious individuals who give meaning to their own lives through freely chosen projects. Every project expresses one's CHOICE of oneself by opening the PERSON into the future and revealing who that person will become. Moreover, a conscious person is never without a project, regardless of how mundane or inauthentic it may appear. The project of LIFE evoked by CAMUS' Sisyphus was to become an authentic person who boldly accepts life's absurdity but struggles to find happiness in spite of it. Because we are free, we can choose our project in any SITUATION. These projects put us in the continuous PROCESS of defining and redefining ourselves, such that a person's identity is never fixed. The notion that every person is an unfinished project appears in the works of HEIDEGGER and SARTRE.

Heidegger uses the word "project" to describe the structure of one of DASEIN'S existentials, ontological understanding. In *Being and Time*, understanding is introduced along with disposition to represent the three aspects of TRANSCENDENCE, a concept developed to capture Dasein's EXISTENCE as BEING-IN-THE-WORLD. The term "eksistence" literally means standing-out-toward. Thus, the idea of transcendence is already contained in the word existence; Dasein, in order to be, must reach beyond itself toward the WORLD; its most basic awareness is to discover itself already existing in the world. But unlike other OBJECTS in the world, Dasein is unique in that its being is a task that only it can fulfill. Notice that transcendence is an existential that illustrates Dasein's way of BEING. For Dasein to exist as transcendence, as Being-in-the-world, means that it exists in a world-structuring way. The world is not a thing but a unity of RELATIONS that is disclosed in and through Dasein's existence. By virtue of its existence in and as transcending, Dasein realizes its own being in and through the world, which correlatively becomes a relation-whole.

Ontological understanding is that component of transcendence that enables Dasein to know foregoingly its way about the world. It refers to Dasein's primordial and nontheoretical knowing of its possibility, its Being-able-to-be. Understanding has little to do with the theoretical grasping of facts but is rather the primordial awareness of what one can do. Understanding as knowing what one can do reinforces Heidegger's insistence that to be human is not merely to be a knower but to be a maker of both oneself and one's world. Through understanding, things in the world that are ready-to-hand become, for Dasein, things for the sake of; they are further disclosed in their usability and serviceability. Understanding also discloses to Dasein its own being as thrown possibility through and through. Exactly what usability things will have and how Dasein will realize its own Being-in-the-world as Being-able-to-be will depend on the project that lies in the heart of ontological understanding.

Here project is not to be taken in its ordinary sense to mean a chosen goal, such as building a house. The word in German refers to a basic, encompassing plan or design that would exist beforehand to underlie the whole so that all the subsequent parts within the whole may appear intelligible. Project is that feature in understanding that determines Dasein's sense of what it can do and, consequently, the possibilities that are perceived to be open. Put simply, Dasein projects its own possibilities in its concernful dealings with things, based on the primordial, nontheoretical notion that Dasein has of its ability. What Dasein can or will do is largely a function of the particular way in which it is tuned to the world, the specific MOOD or disposition Dasein takes on with respect to the world. Observing this reciprocity between understanding and disposition, Heidegger cautions that neither is to be confused with Dasein's faculties: both are existentials that characterize Dasein's way of being. They have the disclosing function of bringing Dasein face-to-face with its THROWNNESS as being-in-the-world.

Sartre understands the term "project" in two senses. In the first sense, project refers to any freely chosen goal that a conscious being may establish, such as writing a book. In the second sense, the word "project" describes the dynamic, moving CHARACTER of CONSCIOUSNESS as the perpetual pursuit of being. Sartre begins with the theory that consciousness is thoroughly lucid. It is not a substance but a NOTHINGNESS, an explosive upsurge that actualizes itself by surpassing itself toward some object in the world. To substantiate this idea, illustrations of the different aspects of a person's existence as relation of identity denied are provided. One such aspect is temporality. TIME is not something a person confronts out there in the world; one exists temporally, thus bringing time into the world. Moreover, a person does not have a past, present, or future but exists as the internal relation of all three ekstases. This relation can be understood in light of transcendence. As transcendence, the meaning of a person's existence is to move beyond what-it-is (its past actions) toward what-it-is-not (its future possibility). This puts a person at a distance, ahead of its past as the having been. The present is precisely this moving—it is a flight from being (copresent) toward being (future) but is never completely caught in being. Alluding to this temporal aspect of a person's ontological structure as relation of identity denied, Sartre says that consciousness is before itself, behind itself, never itself. The ontological meaning of project is extrapolated from this analysis of temporality. As flight-from-identity a person is never fully defined but is perpetually in the process of freely defining oneself, defying determinism.

When Sartre describes human existence as flight, he does not mean that persons leap blindly or haphazardly into the future, nor does he see it as being simply shoved along by mechanical forces. Flight, as the very being of consciousness, is always focused or goal-oriented. Consciousness does not merely flee its projects; it takes aim at its objects and reveals itself as FREEDOM. Furthermore, to say that consciousness is purely of an object is tantamount to saying that consciousness is nothing more or other than the exhaustive projecting-toward-an-object. This sense of project thus constitutes the dynamic ontological structure of consciousness.

Finally, Part 4 of *Being and Nothingness* focuses on the idea of a fundamental project. Each person, Sartre says, is a totality that is constantly totalizing oneself, a totality in that one's actions form a pattern that reveal who one is. Underlying this pattern is one's fundamental project, one's basic choice of being, a nonthetic or prereflective choice that consistently emerges in one's acts. A fundamental project can include a basic choice of AUTHENTICITY or BAD FAITH, even though it also has a specific content and direction. Most persons initially choose the inauthentic project of appropriation, which prompts one to act in a pattern of bad faith in concrete situations. Appropriation is one's attempts to possess, as consciousness, the substantiality of a thing in order to satisfy one's desire for the being that one lacks. One could change one's behavioral pattern only by changing one's fundamental project. But this would require a radical conversion of one's fundamental project.

Primary Works

Heidegger, Martin. *The Basic Problems of Phenomenology.* Trans. Albert Hofstadter. Bloomington: Indiana University Press, 1982.
Sartre, Jean-Paul. *The Family Idiot: Gustave Flaubert 1821–1857.* Vols. 1–5. Trans. Carol Cosman. Chicago: University of Chicago Press, 1981–1993.

Bibliography

Barnes, Hazel E. *Sartre and Flaubert.* Chicago: University of Chicago Press, 1981.

PROJECTION
Phyllis Kenevan

Projection appears in the ONTOLOGY of HEIDEGGER and SARTRE as part of the description of human EXISTENCE as a temporal process, each moment being a synthesis of past, present, and future. Projection describes the way in which I exist my future possibilities at any moment. Through my projections I find meaning and VALUE; my understanding of both self and world is developed on the foundation of, and through the interpretation of, projections. Heidegger describes projection as the way in which DASEIN exists ahead of itself as CARE. Dasein can be ahead of itself because it has the CHARACTER of projecting itself into future possibilities. Projection is thus a TRANSCENDENCE, opening up meaningfulness or significance that provides the ground for a familiar, intelligible world. These possibilities are projected by the understanding that is part of the equiprimordial structure of Dasein. Understanding as one of the possible modes of cognition is derivative of, and made possible by, this primary understanding, which is a basic mode of Dasein's BEING. Projection is an original transcendence, an opening or disclosure of possibilities that are not grasped thematically, although they provide the basis for all interpretation and knowledge.

Heidegger's approach explains how KNOWLEDGE is possible. On the basis of this projection of possibilities Dasein can understand both its self and the WORLD in which it exists. This original transcendence is a disclosure of possibilities, which is the ontological ground for the ontic interpretation of any specific encounter within the world. This holistic background that makes the world intelligible is not grounded. It is the ground through which I interpret everything. How does it provide that ground, and how does projection operate in the interpretation of specific essents within the world? Our cognitive explanations come from a context of intelligibility that is projected in the understanding. Since Dasein finds itself thrown into a world, already projected into a SITUATION with concrete possibilities limited by that situation, Dasein interprets itself and its world on the ground of the original holistic projection of possibilities.

At the level of practical concerns, whatever I interpret as something will be within the holistic projection of possibilities; the particular situation limits the context of possibilities. Thus, a moving light in the night sky is an airplane, a meteor, or a balloon. I do not hear noises but footsteps, snapping twigs, or dogs barking. I see a hammer as a hammer to pound nails. I understand these entities in terms of the web of relations that they share with other entities. The projected context of meaningfulness, which is not explicit, is the forestructure of our understanding. All understanding is circular, since any interpretation must already have understood what is, in order to be interpreted. No interpretation is without presuppositions, and there is no understanding distinct from interpretation. Interpretation is the concrete working through of the possibilities projected by the understanding. Projections of the understanding thus provide a prestructure that furnishes the ground for interpretation; all interpretation is based on prior understanding. Dasein's understanding of the world is always also a self-understanding; the original disclosure involves both Dasein and world. I project myself into a future within which everything, including myself, has meaning; the world is in the hermeneutic circle, as its horizon. Dasein comprehends itself in terms of that whole system. The world is familiar because

Dasein is in the world, embedded in the referential totality of ends and purposes that make up the meaningful context.

Sartre also described projection as a part of the temporalizing PROCESS that characterizes human existence. CONSCIOUSNESS structures a familiar world, characterized by FACTICITY and transcendence. Facticity refers to my always being in a particular, concrete situation, with a certain BODY, born into a certain social class, at a specific TIME. Transcendence is a description of the way I project future possibilities that go beyond my facticity. There is no moment in my consciousness that is not given meaning by its RELATION to future projections. The future that is projected is the ideal point where, if merged with its past and present, the Self would arise as existence in-itself of the conscious for-itself. The project of the for-itself toward the future is a project toward the in-self. But since the for-itself is always in temporal process, that compression of ecstatic temporality will never occur. Consequently, Sartre calls the conscious self a detotalized totality. ''I am my future'' means that I am always, at all times, projecting myself into future possibilities that give meaning to my present. Although the future projection constitutes the meaning of the present consciousness, it does not predetermine which for-itself is to come. That awareness reveals my FREEDOM. The possibilities of each present are concrete because consciousness arises situated in a world and projects its future in terms of that world, which is invested with possibilities in terms of which consciousness interprets itself. I am always in a particular situation. But within the limits of that situation I am always looking toward a future and projecting what I wish to do. I can reinterpret my past, based on my present projections toward a possible future. My capacity to project possibilities that may lead to reinterpretation is a characteristic of the for-itself. Through this freedom of projection I confer meaning and value on the world.

With his description of an original project, Sartre lays the groundwork for a theory of existential psychoanalysis. The original project refers to the initial CHOICE that constitutes a person's BEING-IN-THE-WORLD. In that sense it is irreducible. The aim of existential psychoanalysis is to look for that original choice that, as a choice of being, decides the attitudes and VALUES of the PERSON. Every one of my actions and passions is influenced by my original project. Finding the original choice is not simple, although it is experienced concretely. Sartre calls it a MYSTERY in broad daylight. It is experienced but not known because reflection can give only a quasi knowledge. Reflection grasps the original project only as it is expressed through concrete behavior, as a preontological or nonthetic comprehension of itself; it is not fixed by concepts. The project can be brought to light by psychoanalysis.

Primary Works

Heidegger, Martin. *The Basic Problems of Phenomenology*. Trans. Albert Hofstadter. Bloomington: Indiana University Press, 1982.

Sartre, Jean-Paul. *The Family Idiot: Gustave Flaubert 1821–1857*. Vols. 1–5. Trans. Carol Cosman. Chicago: University of Chicago Press, 1981–1993.

PSYCHOLOGY AND PSYCHOTHERAPY
Betty Cannon

Existential philosophers have often provided worthy psychological insights. JASPERS wrote a text on psychopathology. BUBER's *I and Thou* may guide one to authentic relationships. HEIDEGGER's analyses were the cornerstones for the work of BINSWANGER. SARTRE's first published work, *Imagination: A Psychological Critique*, was followed by psychological discussions in many other works. BEAUVOIR's *The Second Sex* is a seminal work in feminist psychology.

The significance of existential psychology and psychotherapy as a radical departure from previous approaches can be better understood by considering the basic premises of psychoanalysis and behaviorism. While psychoanalysis and behaviorism differ in many significant ways, they agree on this fundamental assumption: human behavior and psychopathology are determined in the same way that events in the natural world are determined, and the task of psychology is to discover the laws of causality and prediction that govern human interactions and behavior. Both also agree that the NATURE of causality in human affairs can be found in the interplay of hereditary and environmental forces. Existential psychology and therapy, by contrast, introduce indeterminacy and FREEDOM into the heart of social science theory.

While it might be said that psychoanalysis focuses on the past, and behavioral therapy on the present, it is certain that existential therapy focuses on the future in the sense that it is that which I am in the process of becoming that elucidates my present action and my interpretation of the past. Thus, I choose the direction of my LIFE and the VALUES it represents rather than my life's being shaped by hereditary and environmental forces. Such fundamental life CHOICES are not made in a vacuum: circumstances are important, but I choose their meaning and significance. I may, at any moment, through a radical reorientation of my life PROJECT, change that meaning and significance—rewriting both my current and distant HISTORY as I orient myself toward a different future. The significance of this departure from the assumptions of positive science is enormous. Everything looks different: the client–therapist relationship is refashioned in the context of existential encounter. Psychopathology is understood in terms of life choices, past and present. ANXIETY is no longer a neurotic symptom; it may be a normal or creative reaction to the conditions of being human.

As freedom replaces determinism in psychological metatheory, the therapist's task is to understand a particular client's lived experience and to open up the possibility of choosing a different way of BEING in the WORLD. If the analyst can be said to be an interpreter of UNCONSCIOUS processes, and the behavioral therapist a technician of change, the existential therapist is a companion and facilitator with the client of the PROCESS of change. The therapeutic relationship itself, with its authenticity and capacity for allowing the client to confront deep-level existential dilemmas, facilitates change. While existential therapists do not deny the painful nature of their clients' dilemmas, they take a different standpoint on psychopathology than the traditional analyst or behavioral therapist. Indeed, there may be reason to discard the idea of pathology, with its connotations of medical science, in favor of more humanistic notions of human difficulties. If psychopathology as a concept is retained, it must be understood in terms of existential choices and dilemmas, past and present. With regard to etiology, the existential therapist looks not for causes in the scientific sense but for motives and choices. While not denying hereditary or environmental influences, existential therapy maintains that an individual's choice of a way of living these circumstances is important, not their brute existence.

One cannot say that an individual always made good choices, especially if one has been subjected to extreme circumstances. Choice is not necessarily a cognitive deliberation. It is often a gut-level response to a SITUATION. Sartre distinguishes between reflective and prereflective CONSCIOUSNESS. Prereflective consciousness is situationally conscious but not self-conscious in the sense of reflective awareness. Thus, my reflective awareness may be at odds with nonreflective choices, as when a PERSON who wishes to stop smoking continues to smoke. Gestalt techniques are particularly suited to help an individual understand the original choice of a project of being, which lies at the heart of his or her current pathological symptoms. Take a male client whose problem is timidity with authority figures. If this client is asked to role-play a dialogue between himself and one of these figures, say his boss, the client may be able, after a process of recasting one's past, to understand the original choice he made in childhood. It was a good decision in a bad situation. Uncowed by authority figures, he then may be able to make a new choice of a way of being in the world.

The recovery of the original choice reempowers this individual. Because a person is free, he or she is free to do something different. One's psychopathology emanates from an original choice that made sense in the original situation and that now needs revising. Furthermore, all psychopathology must be regarded as individual. Hence, diagnosis, though it may be useful if it allows a therapist to access a phenomenal world different from the therapist's own, is not useful if it clouds attentiveness to the lived experience of the client or if it allows the therapist to keep the client at arm's length. The existential therapist will look for the existential dilemma at the core of the disturbance. For example, depth therapists agree that at the core of narcissistic disorders lies an early injury to self-esteem. From an existential perspective, this bespeaks the importance of the first Others as subjects, not as libidinal objects. The Other as mirror is the Other before whom I discover myself as a particular kind of OBJECT—lovable and valuable or unlovable and worthless. For instance, the narcissist may be seen as a person who has not solved the dilemma posed by the discovery of the other person as another SUBJECT. Instead of respecting and valuing the Other as another freedom, the narcissist tries to curtail the Other's freedom so as to force the Other to mirror the narcissist's grandiosity and hence to counteract the underlying feelings of worthlessness and emptiness. The existential meaning of the narcissist's choice is the appropriation of the freedom of Others in order to counter an originally painful sense of worthlessness.

Writers on existential therapy have indicated that there is a distinction between existential and neurotic anxiety. Neurotic anxiety is a signal that something is being repressed or kept out of awareness. For psychoanalysts it is the sign of the return of the repressed; the individual responds by defending the EGO and relegating the objectionable material to the unconscious. Existential therapists do not deny that clients feel anxiety when they approach understandings about themselves that are uncomfortable and unacceptable to their sense of self. What is overlooked, however, is the fact that existential anxiety is perfectly normal. Hence, the existential themes of therapy are the same themes as those concerns about which existential thinkers have often written: DEATH, freedom, meaninglessness, and isolation.

Consider existential anxiety over freedom. A client has explored the underlying choices constituting his or her difficulties. This client clearly sees what motivated the original choices and seemingly wishes to change. While earlier there may have been anxiety about seeing clearly, that is no longer the case. Then suddenly, the client is very anxious. He or she wishes to go back and revisit early themes, or new difficulties emerge in the client's present life that seem to contradict the new choices he or she is trying to make. If the therapist at this point encourages the client to bring up more childhood material, he or she may be missing the point. Further exploration may show that what is happening is that the client has begun to change and that this is producing the anxiety. Clients at this stage of therapy may say: ''I feel I am on the verge of an abyss'' or ''The ground beneath my feet does not feel solid'' or ''Who will I be if I am not the person I was?'' This is existential anxiety, which is the discovery of my freedom. I am not a person as a table is a table. I may change and change radically. Not only this—the world changes as I change. A world in which I am cowed by authority figures is not the same world as a world in which I see my boss and other authority figures as human like myself.

The discovery of one's freedom may be disorienting in a very profound sense, and it may help explain why a radical reorientation of one's life project is often very difficult. Furthermore, if I was free, and I am free, I am free to change in the future. There is no solid self on whom I can count. Hence, some people prefer the misery they know to this awareness of freedom. Furthermore, with freedom comes RESPONSIBILITY. I can no longer blame my circumstances, my upbringing, my unconscious for my actions. Not that I do not live in certain circumstances, have not suffered a particular upbringing, or have not talked myself into being unaware, on a reflective level, of certain TRUTHS about myself. Yet I can now see very clearly that it is I who am the author of my way of orienting myself in the world and toward others. The discovery leads to a lightness and playfulness in many people who experience it. It also has its accompanying existential anxiety. Never again can I count on a solid self, even a negative self, and an unvarying orientation toward being in the world.

Primary Works

Beauvoir, Simone de. *The Second Sex.* Trans. H. M. Parshley. New York: Vintage, 1989.
Jaspers, Karl. *General Psychopathology.* Trans. J. Hoenig and Marian W. Hamilton. Chicago: University of Chicago Press, 1972.

Bibliography

Boss, Medard. *Psychoanalysis and Daseinanalysis.* Trans. Ludwig B. Defebre. New York: Basic Books, 1963.
Cannon, Betty. *Sartre and Psychoanalysis.* Lawrence: University Press of Kansas, 1991.

KARL RAHNER
(1904–1984)
Tom O'Meara

Karl Rahner, a native of Freiburg in Breisgau, entered the Society of Jesus in 1922 and was exposed to a new dialogue between Catholic thought and modern PHILOSOPHY at the Jesuit schools of Pullach and Valkenburg in the decade after 1924. His superiors sent him to pursue doctoral studies in philosophy from 1934 to 1936 at Freiburg, where he was influenced by HEIDEGGER but studied under Martin Honecker, because of Heidegger's connections with the Nazi Party. The neo-Thomist Honecker did not approve the dissertation combining Thomist and Heideggerian approaches, and the young Rahner left Freiburg without a doctorate in philosophy; he received his advanced degree at Innsbruck, where he began to teach THEOLOGY. *Spirit in World*, published in 1939, received considerable acclaim, as did a PHILOSOPHY OF RELIGION, *Hearers of the Word*, published in 1941. While Rahner's first book drew out the implications of a few pages in Aquinas on EPISTEMOLOGY in a modestly neo-Kantian and Heideggerian way, the second book used the phenomenological interpretation of the conditions of human EXISTENCE to draw out the structures of human LIFE that would influence any divine REVELATION; he concludes that these conditions were those freely employed by GOD in the Judeo-Christian revelation of a free, personal, and historical presence in human life.

A brief, insightful essay on Heidegger's thought appeared in 1940. Since the Jesuit schools were closed during the Nazi period, Rahner worked in theological and pastoral EDUCATION of clergy and laity in Vienna. He taught at Innsbruck from 1948 to 1964. By the 1950s his creative essays on reinterpreting Catholic theology through idealist and existentialist motifs were attracting attention; Rome threatened with censorship. In 1962, however, he was named a theological adviser to Vatican II; his fame and influence took on international dimensions. In 1964 he became the successor of Romano Guardini at the University of Munich, and in 1967 he moved to Munster from which he retired in 1971. During the next decade he continued to participate in conferences and write essays. A major work is his *Theological Investigations*, twenty volumes in the English translation.

Rahner's relationship to existentialism is mainly a relationship to Heidegger, whom he considered a great intellectual master. He also mentioned that what he had learned was a way of thinking, of circumscribing a problem, of seeing its historical and existential dimensions. Rahner understood that the popes after 1863 had kept Roman Catholicism (particularly outside Germany) from any extensive dialogue with modern philosophy. But one's age could not be totally repressed, and the theologies of the present and the future will have roots partly in modern German philosophies. Hence, Rahner drew from transcendental, idealist, and neo-Kantian directions as well as from PHENOMENOLOGY and existentialism. His conversation with existentialism was that of a gifted student of Thomas Aquinas and of a theologian determined to get beyond the prison of neo-Thomism enclosing Catholic religious and intellectual life. What he found objectionable in neo-scholasticism were the realities of the Christian message reduced to Latin propositions, a disdain or hostility toward pastoral life, and a metaphysical assertion of control and monopoly in theology even over the Scriptures and the Fathers of the church. Both God and the human PERSON had been emptied of life, removed from theological MYSTERY or ultimate issues.

Rahner's theology is first transcendental, then existential, and finally historical. In modern theology the SUBJECT and the OBJECT known or loved have their own conditions, their own world: Christian revelation and grace were not deduced from consciousness, as with a century of liberal Protestant theologies; rather, they appeared as a distinct presence of God. But this transcendental approach was evident because grace and revelation touched each individual in an unthematic mode prior to being concretized in RELIGION and revelation. Heidegger's existential suggestions and analogies led Rahner to the following major contributions to an existentialist Catholic theology.

1. A phenomenology of the person as the event of God's word and grace. Some have described Rahner's doctoral thesis as resembling the approach to phenomenology in Heidegger's *Being and Time* and as a move to the texts of Aquinas prepared for a disclosure of the human subject and the WORLD. In *Hearers of the Word* the human person becomes the place of revelation, where transcendental structures of knowing, freedom, and HISTORY both condition and call for divine revelation and grace. Salvation is a primal presence of God, including what emerges as grace and revelation. This divine self-communication comes first in a universal and unthematic way to all; then humans and society make it concrete in individual life and collective religion. His theology is one of experience, not an extraordinary religious state but as a contact by God with all the levels of human personality. This primal self-communication to a person or an age expresses concretely human quests for meaning, entanglements in SIN and FAITH, hope, and LOVE.

2. A supernatural existential. Catholic theology after the 1930s was involved in getting beyond the two-story approach to religion and humanity, grace and nature. Rahner's theology emphasized the mystery of God's loving presence and the depths of each self. Heidegger's existential ONTOLOGY offered a new framework to pass beyond the mechanical theologies of Baroque and nineteenth-century writers to where grace was depicted not as a commodity or an extrinsic force and to recover Aquinas' theology of the supernatural as the formal object of the POWERS of graced life. The development of existentials offered a new framework for the discussions of NATURE and grace. The supernatural existential was the existential correlate to divine self-communication, just as for Aquinas initial justifying, actual grace, habitual grace, and supernatural virtues were all, in their source, Trinitarian life. An existential approach to the active PERSONALITY encountering the divine self-communication amid the existential dimensions of DEATH, sin, culture, and moral decision assisted Roman Catholic theology in becoming less ecclesiastical and more personal. Not only are death, culture, and temporality existential facets of personality, but there is also a supernatural existential, God's constant offer of grace.

3. The historicity of truth. Rahner looked at the history of philosophy and theology positively and rejected Heidegger's view that medieval and modern philosophy was a distortion of the Greeks. Heidegger's theory of TRUTH, revelatory as a process of disclosure, limited by TIME and culture, was present in Rahner's understanding of the history of dogma, of history vitalizing theologies, liturgies, and other ecclesial forms, and in salvation-history and the history of religion. Heidegger viewed truth as a revelatory illumination of beings, as a disclosure of their manner in a particularly historical culture. Rahner used the disclosure motif to explain the unfolding of revelation recorded in the Scriptures.

Different cultural and theological epochs emerged in history, because an incarnational revelation disclosed itself in the forms of an age. There are links between Rahner's view of mystery and Heidegger's thinking. All history is salvation history; the supernatural existential has a history; God's presence works in each individual's story and each religion's history, respecting freedom and struggling against sin. God's acceptance of history implies that the Trinitarian presence of grace has its history in regard to us. One difficulty with Heidegger's thought was that despite its historicity it had a certain timelessness: the radical newness of existential decisions cut the person off from WISDOM, and there was little of human tradition or heavenly ETERNITY to inform or critique decisiveness.

The transcendental and existential dimensions of Rahner's theology were modified after 1965 by the changes set in motion by Vatican II. What was the nature of institutional and theological changes that seemed so numerous? Rahner's theology emphasized the diversity of forms from the beginning as well as the underlying perduring reality; history was not a runaway train of free patterns; nor was it a timeless religious museum. History was necessary for grace and revelation to become concrete in different human cultures. This theology, however, eventually becomes more historical, more an unfolding of a history of salvation in the concrete forms of religion, gospel, church, and sacramentality.

Thus, Rahner used patterns, insights, and terms from neo-Kantian, existentialist, idealist, and Thomist philosophies to interpret for a wide audience a faith in a divine plan and gift, freedom and activity. His system begins with a phenomenological and existential analysis of the human BEING complemented by transcendental and Thomist approaches; he holds that the event of grace and its history owes something to the disclosure of being and truth and their historicity in the epochal moment. Theology could be profound in transcendental and historical dimensions when it offered a new view of the parish and meditations on daily life. Theology was not found in footnoted articles: theologians had serious issues, complex problems, and worldwide audiences. He insisted that he wrote not for scholars but for ordinary Christians, for all religious people to explain the reality of the mystery of a special present of God in each individual life and in the history of humanity.

Primary Works

Rahner, Karl. *The Christian Commitment: Essays in Pastoral Theology.* Trans. Cecily Hastings. New York: Sheed and Ward, 1963.
———. *The Church and the Sacraments.* Trans. W. J. O'Hara. Freiburg: Herder, 1963.
———. *Grace in Freedom.* Trans. Hilda Graef. London: Burns and Oates, 1969.

Bibliography

Lehman, Karl, and Albert Raffelt, eds. *The Content of Faith: The Best of Karl Rahner's Theological Writings.* New York: Crossroad, 1993.

REALISM
Gary Backhaus

Realism is the position that an external, objective WORLD exists independently of our perceptual experience. Some existentialists preempt this position by showing that realism derives from an ill-founded question about reality. NIETZSCHE's WILL to POWER, HEIDEGGER's BEING-IN-THE-WORLD, and MERLEAU-PONTY's Flesh provide grounds that dissolve the tenets of realism.

Nietzsche rejects as a pseudoproblem the conceiving of an independent, objective world structure. Realism is based on a survival function in human evolution that has led to the tendency to think in terms of things. Thinghood is a fiction of humanity that serves its particular species' need for survival. The inclination to believe that there is a real world is related to the will to power. Hence, the real world is merely another interpretive form concerning the NATURE of reality. However, relative to other interpretations commonsense realism is true; it comprises a set of fictions without which our particular type of creature could not survive. Metaphysical realism constructs a conceptual real world over against the apparent world of common sense. It is merely a skeletal interpretation of the very thinghood of common sense; its alleged superiority over common sense is naive. Metaphysical realism is a useless, stultifying PROJECT; what needs to be accomplished concerning thinghood is already found in the commonsense version; metaphysical realism needlessly diverts us from the fundamental project of serving and affirming LIFE.

Nietzsche cannot attack metaphysical realism as being false, because all positions are fictions. Since the positing of a so-called real world behind the scenes of life demeans the life-world and does not promote the serving of life, the dissolution of realism is required. Commonsense realism is the METAPHYSICS of the herd and can lead only to mediocrity and doltishness. Overcoming commonsense realism is required for the transmutation of VALUES, which entails the TRANSCENDENCE of the standpoint of reaction (what we need to know in order to survive) in order to engage in action (what we are capable of accomplishing in the creative affirmation of life).

Heidegger claims that a fundamental ONTOLOGY can be elaborated only by first uncovering the BEING of DASEIN, which asks the question of Being. Dasein's way of being is EXISTENCE, which consists of its interpretation of itself through projecting its possibilities. Dasein is an openness of being-there; its primordial structure is Being-in-the-world. Since Dasein is not a worldless substance that needs proof of an external world, the project of realism is unnecessary. The proofs of the external world elaborated by realism are provided by a being that in its very Being already is what realism deems necessary to demonstrate. The real world refers to intraworldly beings founded upon the worldhood of Dasein. Being-in-the-world does not mean that only when Dasein exists will intraworldly entities exist. But when Dasein does not exist, things are neither intelligible nor unintelligible. Dasein's nonexistence entails that it would be unintelligible to ask whether entities are or are not, for intelligibility is a mode of Dasein's Being-there. The tenet of realism that things exist independent of us is dependent on there being a being that already includes such entities in its Being.

Heidegger traces the ontological source for realism to a derivative mode of Being-in-the-world. Being-already-alongside-the-world is a constitutive mode of Dasein. Dasein is involved with its world in the doing-activities of making and manipulating equipment. Dasein's mode of letting-something-be-involved frees an entity for its readiness-to-hand within the environment. Dasein's dealings amount to a nonthematic, circumspective absorption in familiar references and assignments. But when Dasein becomes fascinated with its environment, it holds back from concernful dealings and encounters entities by beholding them. It is a deficiency of concern by which Dasein places itself in the sole remaining mode of Being-in, the mode of just-tarrying-alongside. In this mode theoretical KNOWLEDGE emerges. Knowing determines an entity as merely present-at-hand. Realism posits a theoretical knowledge of the world as a constant presence-at-hand. However, this theoretical access to the real world not only already presupposes the worldhood of Dasein but is based on a derivative mode of worldhood. Realism, then, makes a philosophical position out of fascination, which is a deficient mode of concernful dealing with the world. Factical being-in-the-world is already being-with intraworldly beings. Even though worldhood is a constituent of Dasein, Heidegger recognizes that Nature remains when no Dasein exists and that Nature is indifferent to our interpretations. Wherever there is a being-in-the-world, beings that are intraworldly are also uncovered. Yet, intraworldly nature is always uncovered from the standpoint of worldhood. The Being of nature is always an interpretation founded upon being-in-the-world. An account of an independent real is a function of the worldly practices in which such claims arise. The tenets of any realism are hermeneutic possibilities of Dasein's historicity.

Merleau-Ponty attacks the causal realism of Cartesianism, which is the ontological bridge between two mutually exclusive entities, thought and extension. By overcoming causal realism, he replaces the bifurcation of reality with the phenomenal world, a perceptual unity prior to its abstraction into CONSCIOUSNESS and things. He calls this primordiality the carnal world, the world of Flesh. Cartesian realism conceives real parts that are mechanistically and linearly caused to perform a particular motion that in turn, effects other real parts to perform a motion. Modern EPISTEMOLOGIES based on Descartes presuppose causal realism in the givenness of SENSATION. The sensory contents of experience are structureless and devoid of meaning, that is, the products of causally real events. Through an existential interpretation of Gestalt psychology, Merleau-Ponty demonstrates the ubiquity of meaning at every level of reality. The sensory contents of experience are not real effects of real events. The BODY is not a thing from which consciousness gains access to the real world.

In *The Structure of Behavior* Merleau-Ponty examines physiological explanations of lived-experience. According to the doctrine of reflex mechanisms of classical physiology, the behavior of the organism only appears to be intentional, that is, meaningful. Using Gestalt psychology's notion of form, he shows that research produced data that weakened the presuppositions of causal realism. He proposes a doctrine of circular causality, which he develops to subtend the antinomy of consciousness and thing. Circular causality engenders a meaningful field whereby the organism and its milieu are two dialectical poles. This gestalt structure is intrinsically meaningful as an existential situation that is primary and antecedent to the SUBJECT–OBJECT dichotomy, which is shown to be an abstraction. Being-in-the-world is a single, circular system of which the lived-body and its milieu are but dialectical moments. There is no real world of things independent of the lived body.

Merleau-Ponty applies the gestalt notion of form to three orders of activity: the physical, the vital, and the human order. The differences between these orders are structural and not substantial. Structural differences involve degrees of integration by which individuality is progressively achieved. This doctrine shows that the soul and body are merely two relational terms in a single dialectic. In the human organism the lower instinctual forms are integrated into higher-level forms that reexpress the lower in symbolic INTENTIONS. This dialectic involves a nonreductive expression of meaning at the highest levels of integration and equilibrium for the human organism in its relation to its environment. Thus, Merleau-Ponty foils the strategy of realism of subtracting consciousness from the world in order to determine the real events or the real world.

The source for Merleau-Ponty's doctrine of the primacy of PERCEPTION, which replaces the dualism that realism presupposes, is the gestalt principle of autochthonous organization. In a perceptual whole the intrinsic relations maintained among the parts are grounded in the phenomena. The phenomenal world is intrinsically meaningful; it need not await an intellectual synthesis to supply it with meaning. The matter of perception is pregnant with form. A lived-body INTENTIONALITY that is an existential structure is already in the world. Such destroys causal realism by robbing it of its real contents; its thesis is but an empty posit. The perceived thing is neither consciousness-of-the-thing nor the thing-itself. The phenomenal world is neither a constituted world nor a real, objective world of nomological explanation. This brute world remains enigmatic to modern science with its presupposition of causal realism.

The brute world can best be characterized by the reversibility thesis. Merleau-Ponty's model for this thesis is the touching of one hand with the other. An essential ambiguity manifests in which the touching hand gives way to being touched as the touched hand begins to touch. This encroachment can never become an absolute identity. There is this essential dehiscence, or reciprocal noncoincidence, which occurs with every form of perception. The Flesh is this fundamental reality of the world folding over upon itself. The perceiver/perceived reversibility is a decentering by which Flesh reveals an indivision of sensible Being that I am and all the rest feels itself in me. Realism is a vacuous term, for the Flesh is the fundamental ontology, which is neither dependent on, nor independent of, conscious subjects. The problem of discovering a reality that is independent of the being who apprehends reality is an ill-formed question.

Primary Works

Merleau-Ponty, Maurice. *The Structure of Behavior*. Trans. Alden Fisher. Boston: Beacon Press, 1963.
Nietzsche, Friedrich. *Daybreak*. Trans. R. J. Hollingdale. Cambridge: Cambridge University Press, 1982.

Bibliography

Madison, Gary. *The Phenomenology of Merleau-Ponty: A Search for the Limits of Consciousness*. Athens: Ohio University Press, 1981.

REDEMPTION
Georg Kovacs

The word ''redemption'' does not seem to belong to the central terminology of existentialism, which focuses on EXISTENCE, ANXIETY, FREEDOM, CHOICE, RESPONSIBILITY, and other such terms. This impression may be accounted for by the assumption that the idea of redemption constitutes a theological concern. How does the question about redemption come about in existentialist thinking and analysis? It is discerned and raised in exposing the dangers and possibilities of recovering oneself, of overcoming or triumphing over the sense of loss and despair experienced at the boundaries of the human condition. Redemption renders viable an optimistic perspective on human reality, on the sense of direction of historical BEING-IN-THE-WORLD. Thus, teachings about redemption emerge in the writings of those who are committed to an optimistic view of the human condition and of those who recognize a religious dimension of being-in-the-world.

The concern with redemption constitutes a significant, decisive element of the final understanding and relating to human existence, the world, the dynamics of HISTORY, and GOD. Redemption stands for more than the optimistic claim that the human being is redeemable, that there is self-improvement in human living, that there are self-recovery from ALIENATION and triumph over adversity. Redemption means the realization of ultimate or boundary situations of human LIFE, such as DEATH, finitude, GUILT, and suffering, as well as seeing true BEING and not NOTHINGNESS in ultimate failure. PERSONS, JASPERS claims, seek redemption and search for TRUTH in conversion. The great universal RELIGIONS offer this alternative, this way of existence that transcends the world and the failure of existence. For Jaspers, all PHILOSOPHY is a transcending of the world and, thus, to an extent, enables humans to determine the future. Philosophy is analogous to redemption.

NIETZSCHE's ZARATHUSTRA teaches of redemption without religious consolation; the movement of redemption is not upward but descending into, and liberating the self from, the impositions of the past under the influence of TRANSCENDENCE. Redemption resides in the will that can transform and thus make the past its own. For CAMUS' Sisyphus, the WILL to be happy against all odds and in spite of the human limits of finitude, which entails the struggle against the overwhelming forces of absurdity, becomes the source of happiness, of introducing meaning into a seemingly meaningless WORLD. For BUBER, one possibility of redemption is the bringing of the world of It into the immediacy of the Thou. God redeems us through the dialogical relation that includes acceptance of his redemption, by the turning of our whole being to fellow humans and to him. BERDYAEV's notion of creative freedom, his teaching on overcoming objectification, and his notion of the human as God's coworker reveal his thinking on the cosmic dimension and historical unfolding of redemption.

A decisive teaching about redemption is found in ROSENZWEIG's *The Star of Redemption*. For the Greeks, for pagan CONSCIOUSNESS, according to Rosenzweig, the cosmos, the gods, and humans exist in isolation from each other. In biblical and Jewish thought, the world, God, and humans are interrelated in their RELATIONS to one another, especially in creation, REVELATION, and redemption. Creation should be thought of neither as a scientific fact nor as a cosmological theory; it is the continuous activity of God as everlasting reality. Revelation is the assurance of God's LOVE that gives birth to the human soul; it is not a set of statements but the inexpressible presence of God; it is God's love giving identity and self-worth to the individual. Human life is meaningful; it is a gift from God. Redemption is understood in the context of creation and revelation. Creation is an incipient revelation of God; the awareness of creatureliness leads to an awareness of God's love as the ESSENCE of revelation. Revelation, including the ever-renewed birth of the soul, instills in the human the hope of redemption, the eternal future of the kingdom. When a person becomes conscious of God's love, he or she experiences the love of the neighbor as a commandment. The love of God expresses itself in the love for the neighbor. In the love of one's neighbor an ensoulment of the world emerges; love endows the other person with spirit and ensouls the world. This ensoulment of the world is redemption. The soul, reawakened in the person, animates the life of the world. The world is already revitalized by God's creation; it is ever growing toward life. Thus, redemption is already implicit in creation. Creation is initial ensoulment of the world; redemption is its complete ensoulment by God.

Humans have a role in redemption. Ensoulment is a reciprocal relation between humans and the world; human deeds of love redeem the world. God is Redeemer in a much more radical sense than he is Creator and Revealer. Yet, God is not only the one who redeems but also the one who is redeemed. In the redemption of the world by humans and of humans by the world, God redeems himself. The person and the world disappear in redemption, but God perfects himself. All merge into the totality of God; only in redemption does God become the one and All. The ultimate goal of redemption, for Rosenzweig, is the perfection of God through the perfection of humans.

Thinking about redemption establishes an optimist perspective on human life and the world; it also exposes the limitations of the traditional philosophical conceptualizations of God. The idea of God as redeemer and as accessible to prayer represents much more than the metaphysical concept of God as the guarantor of the natural order. Thus, the notion of God as the necessary being, in fact, may amount to an idol, to a false image of God. The idea of redemption, as MERLEAU-PONTY seems to acknowledge, may be suggesting that God as redeemer and as accessible to prayer may be closer to the true God than the metaphysical concept of the necessary being. Thus, by thinking of redemption, one may become aware of one's limitations in attempting to think the depth of human reality, the world, and the idea of God.

Primary Works

Jaspers, Karl. *Philosophy*. 3 vols. Trans. E. B. Ashton. Chicago: University of Chicago Press, 1969/1971.
Rosenzweig, Franz. *The Star of Redemption*. Trans. William W. Hallo. Boston: Beacon Press, 1972.

Bibliography

Glatzer, Nahum N. *Franz Rosenzweig: His Life and Thought*. New York: Schocken, 1961.

RELATION
Kurt Salamun

Many positions of existentialism are grounded in a concept of human BEING that stresses specific relations for self-realization. These relations are necessary conditions or constitutive elements for realizing a dimension of humanity such as EXISTENZ, true selfhood, the authentic self, FREEDOM, engagement, and true PERSONALITY. By stressing the relational aspect of the self, these thinkers affirm the unfinished character of human EXISTENCE. In *The Sickness unto Death*, KIERKEGAARD characterizes the human self as a relation that relates to itself insofar as it is a synthesis of the infinite and the finite, of the temporal and the eternal, of freedom and necessity. These oppositional components of the self show the paradoxical structure of human existence. By relation of the self to itself he also refers to a PROCESS of intensive self-reflection, which leads to an awareness of these oppositional components and to self-acceptance. The relational character of the self is constituted not only by a relation to itself but also by a relation to that which has established the relation, GOD.

Another expression of Kierkegaard's conception of true selfhood emerges in his distinguishing three basic modes of existence, characterized by paradigmatic relations. Aesthetic existence is a mode of living in which an individual is permanently related to the WORLD outside oneself, absorbed by external impulses and activities. One's main interest consists in entertainment, enjoyment, excitement. The aesthetic individual lives for the moment; he or she has no coherent life-plan based on self-awareness and reflection. No goal or ideal that springs out of intensive self-exploration and conscious self-acceptance governs one's CHOICES. The meaning one gives to one's LIFE depends solely on external stimuli.

The dominant feature of ethical existence is what Kierkegaard calls subjective reflection as opposed to objective reflection. By objective reflection, as it dominates scientific thought, one can gain KNOWLEDGE of things in the world and of one's objective NATURE. By subjective reflection one is directed to the nonobjective, nonrational dimension of selfhood. Such is not mere contemplation of oneself but a reflection upon oneself that implies a self-conscious choosing of oneself. This choice is a moral act in which an individual takes full RESPONSIBILITY for one's lifestyle. The individual recognizes the relational CHARACTER of one's self and becomes aware that one's selfhood transcends the objectifiable and temporal sphere, to something eternal. The awareness of the imbalance between the polarities infinite/finite, temporal/eternal, and necessity/freedom may stimulate ANXIETY and despair. But it is necessary to go through these existential moods, through which one may encounter that which has established the existential structure of the human; only in this way can one stand before God.

Religious existence consists of a personal relationship between an individual and God. This relationship is the realization of true selfhood in a present moment. As a highly subjective, immediate experience, this relation is intimate and nonobjective. It cannot be communicated as objective knowledge or conceptualized. One cannot know God objectively because God is a SUBJECT and therefore exists only for subjectivity in inwardness. In this highest degree of selfhood a PERSON becomes aware of ETERNITY.

Realizing true human selfhood through relations is also found in JASPERS' thought. He calls true selfhood, that is, the nonempirical, nonobjective dimension of humanity, Existenz. Existenz can be realized only in specific moments of life, either in the experience of boundary SITUATIONS (DEATH, suffering, GUILT, life-struggle) or in existential communication with another person. A person constantly exists in situations, among them boundary situations, which cannot be related to the rational knowledge used to solve problems in normal situations. Boundary situations require a radical change in one's way of thinking. The way to respond to them is not by planning and calculating to overcome them but by becoming the Existenz we potentially are. Experiencing boundary situations is necessarily bound to an intensive process of self-reflection. This process is a nonempirical, nonobjective relationship to one's own self. The act of self-realization of Existenz is accompanied by the awareness of TRANSCENDENCE. One experiences one's self-realization as a gift from a nonobjectifiable being that Jaspers calls Transcendence, which is not grounded in an objective revelation but is manifest only through ciphers. Every attempt to rationalize the reality of Transcendence must necessarily founder. In this context Jaspers presents the conception of a philosophical FAITH in opposition to religious faith.

The relational character of true selfhood is stressed by Jaspers' concept of self-realization through interpersonal communication. Existenz constitutes a threefold relation: the relation of the self to itself, to another person as Existenz, and to Transcendence. A set of moral attitudes is a necessary condition of existential communication: (1) the nonegoistic intention to help a communication partner realize his or her Existenz without using the other as an instrument for one's own self-realization; (2) an open-mindedness and frankness that enable a person to communicate with another person without prejudice and masked purposes. Such often includes the decision to risk the empirical self, that is, to risk a change in habits, opinions, and way of life; (3) a real intention to accept the communication partner in his or her freedom and historicity and specific possibility of self-realization. Jaspers demands complete equality. Communication partners have to accept each other as completely equal in their personal freedom and chance to become Existenz, despite differences such as status, rank, fortune; (4) an intellectual integrity and truthfulness that allow an openness to criticize one's own failings and dogmatized opinions with the same force as the failings and dogmatized opinions of others. Mutual critique and mutual support of communication partners are a loving struggle; (5) the willingness and ability to bear loneliness and the dignity of solitude. One should dare to be lonely and live in solitude as opposed to an attitude of escaping loneliness and social isolation at any price, including self-deception, humiliation, and personal degradation.

In *I and Thou*, BUBER distinguishes between two basic attitudes towards the world: the I–It relationship and the I–Thou relationship. The I–It relation is the objective attitude of experiencing a thing or a person, relating to a thing or an object that one observes and recognizes in its functions, causalities, and utilities. Buber calls this relation the monological principle of encountering the world. The I–It is a necessary attitude toward the others and the world, but it is not a relationship that constitutes true selfhood. Full humanity can be realized only by opening oneself to the I–Thou relationship, which is direct, mutual, and dialogical, in which one's whole being is involved. The Thou in the dialogical relation is wholly present. But it is the fate of humanity that this relation has limited duration: every Thou must become an It again. Only God is an exception that never becomes an It; he is the Eternal Thou.

For Buber, nature and spiritual beings can also be partners in an I–Thou relationship. In the essay ''Distance and Relation,'' he gives the concept of relation a strict ontological meaning. Human life consists of a twofold movement: (1) the primal setting at a distance and (2) entering into relation. Both movements are necessary conditions of self-realization. In interpersonal relations, setting the other at a distance means to see another person in his or her individual and elemental otherness. Such is necessary for realizing the genuine relation that implies the mutuality of acceptance, of affirmation and confirmation of one another. This relation is to be understood as an act where the other becomes a self with me. In MARCEL's view true PERSONALITY is realized by participation in the MYSTERY of being, which can be reached when one enters into dialogical relations with a personal Thou or the Absolute Thou (God). Such concrete approaches to the mystery of being within dialogical relations are necessarily based on personal experiences of LOVE, fidelity, hope, and faith.

The conceptions of self-realization mentioned share a common distinction between an inauthentic and authentic relation. Inauthentic relations are necessary conditions of human life and are normally defined by negative attributes such as being merely objective, public instead of private, abstract instead of concrete, superficial and instrumental, lack of self-awareness and self-reflection, egocentric and egoistic, anti-individual. To transcend inauthentic relations requires a permanent effort by humans who wish to realize their selfhood through authentic relations. HEIDEGGER and SARTRE discuss inauthentic and authentic relations in depth.

In Heidegger's *Being and Time*, the BEING-IN-THE-WORLD of DASEIN is inauthentic when it lives a life of everydayness like the indifferent and anonymous crowd, the THEY. This life includes idle talk, curiosity, and ambiguity.

In this mode of living, Dasein forgets the search for Being itself. It is absorbed in particular beings in its everyday CARE of things and people. Inauthentic being can be transformed into authentic being in those moments when anxiety becomes a dominant mood. This mood results from facing one's own being-in-the-world as a whole, specifically, facing one's death. The insight that one's being is always a being-toward-death may lead to relating authentically to one's life. Facing the possibility of NOTHINGNESS, one may attain a resoluteness that is linked to a call of CONSCIENCE and care. Authentic being means to become one's self in one's concrete singularity, individual responsibility, and care. The relation to others becomes being-for or being-with and care-for, concern-for, or concern-with.

In Sartre's phenomenological ONTOLOGY, CONSCIOUSNESS of one's own freedom presupposes consciousness of the freedom of the Other. Both modes of consciousness, however, are constituted in a permanent conflict and mutual struggle, a struggle that seeks to ontologically dominate the Other. The LOOK of the Other reduces me to an object for the Other. It reifies me and tends to negate my individuality and to reduce my being to being-in-itself. I defend myself by trying to reify the Other, thus reaffirming my subjectivity against the Other. This fundamental human condition is realized in individual PROJECTS, initial choices, and unconditioned actions. Authentic human being lies in the realization of the human condition of freedom. In situations that are permanently in flux, one's choices and actions must be rooted in the consciousness of one's responsibility for those choices and actions. Inauthenticity is a living in BAD FAITH, which is a manner of fleeing from freedom and responsibility. Bad faith tries to escape the elementary ANGUISH that is an inevitable consequence of a person's awareness of one's freedom.

Primary Works

Buber, Martin. *Between Man and Man*. Trans. Ronald Gregor Smith. New York: Macmillan, 1965.
Jaspers, Karl. *Philosophy*. 3 vols. Trans. E. B. Ashton. Chicago: University of Chicago Press, 1969/1971.

Bibliography

Gordon, Haim. *Dance, Dialogue, and Despair: Existentialist Philosophy and Education for Peace in Israel*. Tuscaloosa: University of Alabama Press, 1986.

RELIGION
Georg Kovacs

Existentialists are not engaged in abstract speculation intent in making a final judgment on the contents of the great faith-traditions. Their main intent is the clarification of concrete EXISTENCE, in understanding a way of life as striving for AUTHENTICITY and overcoming the many forms of dispersion and ALIENATION in daily worldly living. Religion, then, is much more than a persistent element of human culture and a fact of HISTORY; it is a way of BEING-IN-THE-WORLD that may contribute to, or distract from, a worthy LIFE. Existentialist thinkers' attention to the question of GOD neither eliminates nor introduces arguments for God's existence. Their suspicion about final systems of thought and otherworldly TRANSCENDENCE raises the question about the place and meaning of God. The decisive issue consists in wondering about the meaning of God in and for human living. The question of God, CAMUS suggests, is connected with the experience of absurdity, with the possibility of finding meaning in a conflicting, paradoxical RELATION between the human nostalgia for clarity and the obscure silence of the WORLD. The absurd calls into question the logic leading to the affirmation of God. Neither the idea of God nor the adoption of religiosity should function as a consolation or compensation of a future illusion for current hardships and for the absence of a profound meaning in the present.

KIERKEGAARD's critique of institutionalized religion was coupled with his notion of the individual's facing religious truths and paradoxes. His attacks on Hegelian system-building and his Socratic irony exposed the pretensions of scientific, calculative rationality as the embodiment of detachment from the dynamic of existence, from the task of becoming an individual. The individual's struggle against anonymity and crowd-mentality, leading to aesthetic dispersion and to the false self-certainty of following a code of rules, spares him or her ANXIETY. Yet anxiety can lead to the LEAP of FAITH in God. Religion is assumed as personal, as RESPONSIBILITY before God, as a concrete living relation with Christ as the paradox of the finite and of the infinite. This perspective may help to recover the lost or diluted inwardness of religion, of becoming and striving for authentic, responsible existence. Thus, the religious way of being is born out of the most personal decision in choosing God (like Abraham) in a personal leap of faith and in putting the concrete, personal relation with God above everything else, in giving oneself to God as the ultimate source. Authentic existence, the life of the responsible individual standing alone and finding one's true self before God, takes place in fear and trembling, in the experience of anxiety. Religion is a way of life of striving for the inwardness of PERSONALITY in enacting the truths of FAITH—the hard, ascetic, daring demands of New Testament CHRISTIANITY. Genuine becoming and finding one's self take place before God, in the life of personal relationship with the absolute. Religious existence overcomes the alienation and fragmentation of the self, the abolition of the individual, the identification of the individual with the general idea of humanity. SOCIETY, marked by crowd-mentality, is a threat to individuality, to the uniqueness and integrity of individual existence. The horizontal dimension of existence, the relation with others and the world, is based on the vertical axis of life, on the personal faith-relation to God. Thus, religion lived as witnessing to the TRUTH of Christianity leads to the inner peace with God and to the true self; it is the way to overcoming alienation and loss of the self. In finite time, the religious individual alone makes a decision for ETERNITY and thus transcends to God in personal relationship and makes the immediate relation to God the central fact of, and guide for, living.

For NIETZSCHE, the overcoming of alienation and NIHILISM is atheistic, or at least antiontotheological; it means the liberation of the individual from the illusion of another, higher world. The experience of the self consists in descending into the depths of human existence and into the unexplored possibilities of the earth, of this world; in the final analysis, one experiences only oneself, not the immediacy of the divine or of an afterworld. Christianity, as vulgarized Platonism, devalues and instrumentalizes this life; it turns the attention from the wealth and depth of yet unexplored meanings of this life, of the present, to the illusory promise of another, higher, transcendent realm, to an afterworld. Rituals, traditions, conformity and mediocrity, and the submission to the burden of religious transcendence suffocate the self. Christianity creates RESENTMENT in the obeying individual and thus destroys the joy and VALUE of this life.

Nietzsche's attack on cultural, historical, and political Christianity claims to bring about the overcoming of nihilism, the creation of new values, the discovery of the potentials of human FREEDOM and CREATIVITY, the joy of living, the affirmation of life returning without end, without being replaced or displaced. His teaching of the eternal recurrence of the same proclaims the self-worth and value of this life, of this world. This way of thinking and living overcomes the consequences of the phenomenon of the DEATH of God, the lack of direction after the rejection of the moralistic God and religious TRANSCENDENCE. It recovers the human self in this TIME without its metaphysical-religious illusion. His insights and LANGUAGE teach the ART of thinking and free inquiry.

According to BUBER, religion is holding fast to the existing God, not to an image of God as a human construct. PHILOSOPHY, especially in the twentieth century, is the intellectual letting go of God. The existence of God cannot be proven; it is not a matter of inference from the world, history, or the self. God is the absolute PERSON, the eternal Thou that never becomes an It, an OBJECT. The holding fast to the living God, facing God as Thou, is not the result of dialectical speculation. It comes about in turning to the Other; through meeting the human, finite Thou one obtains a glimpse to the eternal Thou. Religion, as holding fast to the living God, is connected with human relationships, with the affirmation of the fullness of dialogical living. It is the response of the human to the divine in concrete living, in the process of becoming. Humans can enter into direct relation with God because God enters into direct relation with humans. A person cannot speak to God while ignoring other humans.

SARTRE suggests that human self-understanding includes discarding the idea of God and the recovery of responsibility for one's existence. Human freedom, choosing oneself while acting in a specific situation, cannot be reconciled with a God who determines one's ESSENCE, as held in many religions. The basic nature of human relationships is conflict, not dialogue; intersubjective relations are frequently based on conflicting PROJECTS, leading neither to the other nor to God. The death of God renders possible the liberation of the human to choose genuine, authentic existence. Sartre regards religion as teaching conformity, as preaching resignation to the lower classes of society.

TILLICH's definition of religion as ultimate concern for BEING indicates the depth and existential implications of life as relating to God through faith. A main difficulty of this understanding of religion consists in the fusion of ontological and theological perspectives. To philosophize, MERLEAU-PONTY suggests, means to seek; it does not consist in returning to, or defending, a specific tradition. Philosophy should seek to see. THEOLOGY often uses philosophy for its own purpose and thus ends philosophy; it frequently makes use of philosophical wonder for the purpose of motivating an affirmation that ends the wonder. Philosophy never comes to an end. It arouses us to what is problematic in our existence and in that of the world so that we shall never be cured of searching. Thus philosophy arouses the problem: What is responsible for the birth of God in human CONSCIOUSNESS? The thinker wonders about the constant manifesting of religious phenomena through world history and about the continual rebirth of the divine. The thinker attempts to describe this rebirth. The philosopher tries to understand religion as an expression of consciousness. However, understanding religion and accepting it are not the same.

Primary Works

Buber, Martin. *Eclipse of God.* New York: Harper and Row, 1952.
Kierkegaard, Søren. *Attack upon Christendom.* Trans. Walter Lowrie. Princeton: Princeton University Press, 1968.
Tillich, Paul. *Systematic Theology.* Vols. 1–3. Chicago: University of Chicago Press, 1951–1963.

RELIGIOUS STAGE
Robert L. Perkins

KIERKEGAARD divides the religious stage of EXISTENCE into two expressions that he calls Religiousness A and Religiousness B. His pseudonym, Johannes Climacus, uses an existentially reconstructed Socrates to present Religiousness A, a view of ethical subjectivity that, in its deepest moment, shades over into RELIGION. The figure of Socrates represents the adequacy of human reason and GOOD WILL to resolve all moral difficulties and inadequacies; it embodies the highest moral aspiration of the Enlightenment and idealism. A different position is represented by the Teacher, whom Climacus does not name but whom he identifies as the savior or redeemer. One form of religiousness is not truer than the other; they merely differ. Climacus emphasizes something the historical Socrates apparently did not: we are moral failures. Nonetheless, Climacus maintains the Socratic position that subjectivity is the TRUTH.

There are three successive forms of ethicoreligious pathos. Resignation means that we should relate absolutely to the to the absolute and relatively to the relative. We frequently fail in this moral effort. Suffering is the result of this failure, but religious suffering is, paradoxically, the certainty that we are in a subjective RELATION to the truth. Without the suffering we would be moral philistines. GUILT testifies to the presence of a relationship to the absolute. Guilt is the result of how we exist, what we do and do not do; it is a moral category. This description of moral subjectivity, or Religion A, expresses the universally human. Religiousness A is the second form of the ethical for Kierkegaard; the ethical has subtly shifted over into the religious because of moral failure. Is this failure a lack of capacity, weakness of will, or more serious? Answering the question requires a deeper view of subjectivity.

Climacus claims that the only way subjectivity could be intensified is to think that subjectivity is the untruth rather than the truth. The moral failure recognized in Religiousness A as producing guilt, when understood theologically, is SIN, for which we are responsible and which requires forgiveness. Sin is not merely the failure of the human moral capacity; it is a change in the kind of PERSON I am. Such a view is an offense to the ethical and the universally human, for the ethical implies honesty and integrity. But the offense is far deeper; in Religiousness B it relates primarily to its central figure which is the God-man. Religiousness B is paradoxical for the category of the God-man is a stumbling block to the Jews and folly to the Greeks. It is an absolute paradox; the most reason can do is to understand that it will never understand the paradox. It can be grasped only by a LEAP of FAITH. This ultimate offense arises because human understanding resists anything it cannot comprehend. So on two accounts, morally because of guilt/sin and philosophically because of the God-man, persons are offended. However, if taught by the God-man, persons can accept the forgiveness of sin offered by the God-man.

Religiousness B requires that we LOVE our neighbor as we love ourselves. Kierkegaard presents neighbor love in *Works of Love*, which elaborated an original critique of the ideological attempt to use CHRISTIANITY to legitimate the political, economic, and class structure in Denmark. Such an effort reduces Christianity to the aesthetic, a means ironically used by the upper classes and the official church to dominate the lower classes. Kierkegaard's dying appeal was to the common man on behalf of New Testament Christianity, which offers forgiveness of sins to sinners and can never be used as an instrument of political and social domination against the powerless.

Primary Works

Kierkegaard, Søren. *Philosophical Fragments*. Trans. Howard V. Hong and Edna H. Hong. Princeton: Princeton University Press, 1974.

————. *Works of Love*. Trans. Howard Hong and Edna Hong. New York: Harper and Row, 1964.

RESENTMENT
Laurence Lampert

Resentment was made prominent in moral theory by NIETZSCHE, who regarded it as an essential, though hidden, component of traditional MORALITY. His most complete discussion appears in *On the Genealogy of Morals*. According to Nietzsche, all moral VALUES are subjective, originating in the subject's primary experiences of pleasure and pain. But moral values were accorded objective status as if they were resident in the PERSONS, things, or events. What persons counted as morally GOOD or bad depended on the type of person making the evaluation. There are only two general types of morals; each can be traced to the CHARACTER of human groups. In master morality moral values arose from an experience that was affirmative of itself and the WORLD; it began with the notion of good—what is like me or pleases me—and passed to the notion of bad—what is lower than me, what is base or petty. Such evaluations arose among ruling groups disposed to think well of themselves. In the slave morality moral values arose from a human experience of the self and the world that was negative; it began with the notion of EVIL—what causes me pain—and passed to the notion of good—the cessation of pain. Such evaluations arose among the ruled or the dispossessed, inclined to condemn their lot and those they held responsible for it.

Gratitude is the primary motive for the first set of moral values. Resentment is the primary motive for the second set of moral values. When generated out of resentment, moral values themselves became an instrument for taking revenge on the things resented: on those who oppressed them, on oneself as guilty of being oppressed or enslaved, and ultimately, on LIFE itself. Untold spiritual damage has been inflicted on humanity by values based in resentment. When given sublimated, spiritual expression in moralities and RELIGIONS, resentment taught humans to disparage mortal life and the things of the body and to seek an escape from earthly EXISTENCE in various afterlives. The struggle between the morality of gratitude and the morality of resentment in Western culture led eventually to the victory of the morality of resentment through CHRISTIANITY, which gave it powerful and popular expression.

Primary Work

Nietzsche, Friedrich. *On the Genealogy of the Morals and Ecce Homo.* Trans. Walter Kaufmann and R. J. Hollingdale. New York: Vintage, 1969.

RESPONSIBILITY
W. Kim Rogers

Responsibility is understood by existentialist thinkers as meaning, first of all, responsibility for oneself, that is, choosing oneself as FREEDOM. But freedom is to be discovered only in an action; it is one with the act. Choosing is not something separate from, and prior to, one's acting; it occurs in one's acting. The moment of CHOICE is a nihilating upsurge against all that is just there, and yet one remains in absolute continuity with it. Choosing is one's transcending break with one's given conditions, NATURE, HISTORY; at the same time it is an identifying recognition of these as one's starting points and limits. As KIERKEGAARD indicated, one has one's place in the WORLD, but as freedom one also chooses one's place. One chooses oneself as this individual with particular talents, dispositions, passions, influenced by a particular environment. In choosing oneself, one assumes responsibility for all this.

SARTRE held that for humans, there is no difference between existing and choosing oneself, being responsible for oneself. The self in choosing itself cannot choose randomly, for one finds oneself in the presence of affairs that already have meanings; they are parts of a world that one shares with others. This world includes myself as an OBJECT for other selves. The fully responsible self chooses itself as a self limited by others. Thus, I must accept responsibility for the self I have become, and I am responsible for the self I will become. To exist as a human one must be a self, and at the same time one must choose to be oneself. Thus, for all existentialists, the self is not something one has but a task, a vocation.

Yet, one does not come from nothing; one chooses oneself in the reality to which one belongs and so has oneself as a task that is manifoldly defined. The self is then its own goal, the future being toward which it strives. The self is not a finished product; it is a unique, original PROJECT, a creative PROCESS. Freedom is the taking of responsibility for oneself and thus making and remaking one's future self. Each person is conjointly responsible both to oneself and to everyone else. Choice isolates oneself, for in choosing oneself one detaches oneself from the whole world. Yet, at the same moment, one is choosing oneself back into the world, for it is not an abstract self but the concrete self that is chosen. The responsibility in one's action can give a meaningful fulfillment to the actions of others.

Closely related to these ideas is MARCEL's notion of availability, an aptitude to give oneself, to respond to the appeal of another. BUBER also pointed to the intimate connection between responsibility and response: through a dialogical response to the address of the Other, responsibility emerges. For Marcel meeting the Other should be an act of hospitality, an inviting of the other to share of one's being. A PERSON who is available is with the other person, with him or her with the whole of one's BEING. Such a response affirms the freedom of the other person. If one treats the Other as a Thou, one helps this Other to be free. For Kierkegaard, it is not just an other person to whom the self is responsible, but GOD. The self becomes itself only in and through its relationship to God. To be a self is a demand and a gift that God bestows. This I signifies nothing if it does not become the Thou to whom eternity unceasingly speaks. The self then will be both responding to, and receiving itself through, God's call. The self must choose itself or, better, make itself before God. However, Kierkegaard holds that such must not be understood as an exclusive relationship, for the self's LOVE of God makes possible and is completed in one's love of other humans. In relationships to other humans, the selfishness that is presupposed as existing in every self is overcome when God is the middle term. Unselfish love of the Other is to be found only in a relationship between the self and God and the Other. However, Marcel pointed out, one's responsibility does not stop with loving God and the Other. One does not fully affirm the other unless one loves those whom this Other loves. Love demands for its complete realization unlimited communion, the creation of a COMMUNITY centered upon an absolute Thou.

Primary Works

Buber, Martin. *Between Man and Man.* Trans. Ronald Gregor Smith. New York: Macmillan, 1965.

Sartre, Jean-Paul. *Existentialism and Humanism.* Trans. Philip Mairet. London: Methuen, 1973.

REVELATION
Murray A. Rae

The concept of revelation in religious thought expresses the idea that an understanding of GOD and His message is attainable through a divine act of self-disclosure. Theologians disagreed whether the content of revelation is a series of metaphysical TRUTHS or, rather, the disclosure of God Himself. In the first case revelation takes propositional form and may be objectively examined; in the second it is a personal encounter and address and seeks the response of FAITH and trust. Those existentialists who speak of revelation are inclined to conceive of it as an event of personal address and response rather than as a deposit of propositional truth.

KIERKEGAARD contends that Christian faith involves a subjective, rather than an objective, relation to God. He develops the idea that learning the truth of God and the truth about myself is not an evolutionary PROCESS depending on my epistemological resources but is, rather, a divinely initiated revolution that redemptively transforms me in my ALIENATION and brings me to an unfinished, yet sure, RELATION to God. He calls this revolution conversion and likens it to a new birth. Thus, revelation emerges in an interpersonal encounter and transformation. It elicits the subjective response of BELIEF, LOVE, and trust and remains inaccessible to the rationalist program of detached, objective inquiry. The personal manner in which revelation is apprehended does not mean that revelation has no objective ground.

Kierkegaard's insistence upon subjectivity is not a disposition to ignore facts but a call to passionate concern about them, especially to those facts with direct impact upon the individual's EXISTENCE. The most decisive fact of the Christian's existence is the personally transformative event of God's self-disclosure in Christ. This is expressed within Christian THEOLOGY as the inseparability of revelation and reconciliation. God discloses Himself in the servant form of Jesus of Nazareth with a view to the redemption of fallen humanity. The state of estrangement or alienation into which we have fallen is existence in untruth or SIN and is a manifestation of human freedom. Revelation is directed toward the overcoming of such alienation. Rather than compelling assent, it awaits recognition and free response. The proper response of FAITH and love is to be understood as a gift empowered by God. Responsible speech about God proceeds from attentiveness to revelation; this self-disclosure of God and not human reason is the ultimate criterion of truth and error. It is certainly true that attentiveness to revelation very often requires the abandonment of one's prior categories and assumptions, nowhere more clearly demonstrated for Kierkegaard than in the paradox of the incarnation; but evidence in his journals and later published works suggest that the redemption of reason, rather than its abandonment, is the consequence of a faithful adherence to revelation. He seems to suggest that our thinking and knowing processes find their proper reference through faith in God's disclosure of Himself.

BUBER also held that revelation concerns the conveying of God's personal presence and message rather than the impartation of information about God. Revelation must be understood in the terms of the I–Thou relation. The content of revelation is the message of God rather than a series of timeless truths. Revelation sets a PERSON in a situation of dialogue. Humanity receives in revelation a presence that is characterized by reciprocity and bestows meaning upon the reality of our lives in this world and is directed to the REDEMPTION of the individual and the COMMUNITY. Such presence can never be expressed as a piece of KNOWLEDGE. The basic approach emerging in the Hebrew Bible is that human LIFE includes a dialogue between Heaven and Earth. The Hebrew prophets heard and proclaimed the divine voice, laying bare the consequences of human FREEDOM and calling humans to a radical decision for God. The whole of creation is regarded by the Hebrew Bible as the enunciation of God's glory.

Buber insists that anything in our experience may be the medium of God's self-revelation. Whether we turn to NATURE or to our fellow humans, we are regarding the hem of the garment of the eternal Thou. We do not experience God in these relationships. Experience designates a relation between SUBJECT and OBJECT, and its reference is something that we may speak about. In revelation God makes Himself present. We may not, therefore, speak of revelation in general terms. Revelation as dialogue is always characterized by specific address and concrete response. More particularly, revelation takes place wherever nature as well as SPIRIT is perceived as a gift; revelation yields awareness of a meaningful presence, a new vision of the world as it ought to be, and a powerful impetus to action. Revelation is not only presence but also command.

Although it is true that revelation yields a new awareness of God, it is also true that revelation safeguards the MYSTERY of God. God is disclosed in revelation, but the divine mystery is not exhausted. Buber resists dogmatic or systematic formulations that stand in the place of dialogue. Such formulations contravene the nature of God, who cannot become an It. There are times when God seems to withdraw from the Earth, when the noise of HISTORY seems empty of the divine breath. This has been especially the case in the twentieth century; the question of whether it is possible still to listen for the divine voice is raised with despairing urgency. There can be only one answer to such a cry: the APPEARANCE of God himself, the same God who never actually turns His back. In the meantime our choice is to stand with the psalmist who cries, How long Oh Lord!—or to abandon all hope.

TILLICH considers revelation to be the manifestation of the ultimate ground of BEING, which nevertheless retains its mysterious CHARACTER. Revelation takes place through the mediation of signs or symbols. Anything may be such a sign. Any feature of the created order may be the means by which the individual is arrested by the threat of nonbeing and reassured of the power and stability of the ground of Being. Revelation does not yield knowledge. Rather, through revelation both the reality of the ultimate ground of Being and our relation to it are experienced. Revelation is always directed toward a concrete situation of human concern and has revealing POWER only in this correlation. He emphasizes both an objective and a subjective aspect of revelation. Something occurs that grasps the person; that is the objective side. The person is grasped; that is the subjective side. Without this correlation between the objective occurrence and the subjective reception no revelation can take place. Revelation does not take place apart from the existential questions with which humans are struggling. Using available philosophical or hermeneutical tools, we must penetrate to the heart of the human SITUATION and uncover the most urgent and profound questions of existence. In engaging these questions the answers found in revelation can be heard and appreciated. The awareness of our finitude and of the precariousness of human life poses the question to which God as the ground of Being is the answer. Our experience of sin and guilt finds resolution in the new being that is promised in the Christian understanding of revelation, mediated by Christ. Tillich thus attempts to arrive at a correlation between human questioning and divine disclosure and begins with the identification of those features of human life that constitute a preparedness to receive the divine word. Humans may set out to encounter God in revelation.

Thus, existential thinkers insist upon the relational nature of revelation. They speak of the transformation of existence through personal experience of the transcendent. Revelation is directed toward the establishment of authentic human existence before God; rejection of revelation is a manifestation of SIN. Emphasis is given to both the mysterious character of ultimate reality and the safeguarding of human freedom in the face of revelation.

Primary Works

Buber, Martin. *On the Bible*. New York: Schocken, 1968.
Kierkegaard, Søren. *Works of Love*. Trans. Howard Hong and Edna Hong. New York: Harper and Row, 1964.

Bibliography

Adams, James Luther. *Paul Tillich's Philosophy of Culture, Science and Religion*. New York: Harper and Row, 1965.

RAINER MARIA RILKE
(1875–1926)
Herbert Lehnert

German philosophers interpreted Rilke's mature work as parallel to that of HEIDEGGER, only expressed differently. Heidegger himself placed Rilke's works in the age of the completion of Western METAPHYSICS, closer to NIETZSCHE than to his own thoughts. To interpret Rilke's images in terms of Heidegger's concepts is now seen as a reduction. Nevertheless, existentialist thinkers and Rilke's mature POETRY deal with the question of how to live and to face DEATH without GOD and REDEMPTION. Liberation from existing SOCIETY, ALIENATION, and ANGUISH is central to Rilke's LIFE and works. Originally called Rene, he grew up in a German-speaking, middle-class family in Prague that claimed to be descended from aristocracy. His parents separated when Rene was eight years old. He was deposited in an Austrian military school, from which he was dismissed because of psychosomatic illnesses. This experience led to a hatred of compulsory duty and violence, which predominates in his works. Under the protection of an uncle, who wanted him as a successor for his law practice, Rilke prepared himself for the university and enrolled at the German University of Prague in 1895. He did not take his university studies seriously, neither in Prague nor in Munich or Berlin. Rather, he attained a BODY of KNOWLEDGE by avid reading.

Trying to establish himself as a writer and journal editor, he at first wrote neo-Romantic poems and Naturalistic, one-act DRAMAS displaying poverty and tragic love affairs. The antibourgeois aggressiveness of some early works disappeared in his mature writings, but Rilke continued to reject loyalty to family, country, and the Christian RELIGION. In Munich in 1897, he met the writer Lou Andreas-Salome, one of few German female intellectuals of the time, a former friend of Nietzsche. A relationship developed in May 1897 between the thirty-six-year-old Lou and the twenty-one-year-old Rainer, as she called him. He poured out sentimental love poetry for her. In 1899 and 1900 Rilke traveled with Lou in Russia, briefly meeting Tolstoy. He wanted to regard Russia as a fictional homeland. Another homeland was in his mind when he went to the North German artist colony of Worpswede near Bremen to write a book on the painters living there. After marrying Clara Westhoff, a sculptor, his attempts to support her and their daughter by reviewing for newspapers failed. In 1902 he went to Paris on a commission to write a book on Auguste Rodin, which appeared in 1903. Rodin impressed him by the admonition, Always work and called Rilke's attention to Baudelaire's writings. Also in 1903 he finished *The Book of Hours*, a collection of seemingly pious Jugendstil poems with a Russian monk as fictive author. The poems reflect monistic, rather than transcendental, BELIEFS and represent a transition between the wordy rhyming of his early years and his valid work. Its third part condemns big cities and the alienated human EXISTENCE in them. The VALUE of the individual is to be rescued by the call for one's own DEATH. The book was a success and made him well known. In 1906 Rilke settled in Paris, employed for a time as secretary by Rodin. He separated from his wife and daughter after 1910.

Rilke's mature work begins with *New Poems*. The word ''new'' in the title suggests not only a new period in his ART but the difference from traditional poems. The poems in *New Poems* are traditional in that they are rhymed, most have stanzas, and many follow the sonnet form. But the deviations from the traditional mode of poetry suggest parody. Form-CONSCIOUSNESS, though strong, is constantly undermined, not only by enjambments that hold or quicken the flow of the verses but also by surprising word use. Most of the poems present themselves as if they were describing an OBJECT: an animal, a merry-go-round, a picture, a sculpture, a remembrance, an image from HISTORY, a biblical scene. Yet this object or theme loses its place in human knowledge, history, or experience, its temporal place. The poems assume that the world does not have a sense in itself. While the art-thing in the poem appears present, these game words are allusive, open avenues of insights other than the usual concept of the object at hand, sometimes even alien to it. The conventional substance of the object is dissolved, transformed into a web of correspondences that forms the new poem.

This artistic overcoming of dissolution, the transformation of the temporal into timeless art, took the place of redemption in Christian THEOLOGY. Artistic transformation of temporal life into lasting form affirms the monistic principle that death is merely the other side of life. Equally important was Rilke's belief in the value of erotic LOVE without an object. Such intransitive love is to induce artistic sensibility. In *Requiem for a Friend*, he asserts total existential FREE-

DOM for the artist, freedom even in love. In spite of Rilke's monistic and artistic proposals, the FEAR of death remained strong in his life and works. It found a reflection in *The Notebooks of Malte Laurids Brigge*. A young, poor Danish nobleman who came to Paris in order to write, much like Rilke, attempts to use his imagination to convert his impressions of anonymous city life, misery and poverty, reading experiences, and his personal recollections into timeless art. But this new interpretation of the world and life eludes Malte, because the task requires total alienation from society. Malte considers even great art, such as Ibsen's and Beethoven's, to be subverted by fame. The book ends with Malte's rewriting of the parable of the prodigal son as one who does not want to be loved. Only God could overcome the gap between the people wanting to love the returning son as theirs and his desire not to recognize any binding relations, while living among people and creating his childhood anew.

Rilke's *The Life of Mary* includes poems with a slightly ironic respect for religious tradition. Its origin in 1912 overlaps with the beginnings of his principal work, *Duino Elegies*, named because he was then a guest at the castle of Duino at the Adriatic Sea. The elegies are written in free verse with allusions to classical hexameters and blank verse. The lament of the writer who has to live alienated from alienating society was to be overcome at the end by jubilation and praise over the transforming POWER of poetry. The work remained a fragment for eleven years. Although the elegies do not mention the poet as its central SUBJECT, the work is a combination of images and poetic reflections about the conditions of CREATIVITY in a time of rapid change in which humans must find a new mode of accepting death. The poet's task of artistic perfection is constantly subverted by the fragile, mortal human condition. Consciousness removes humans from the origins of authentic creation, from the openness of the source of creativity. The resulting despair is mitigated by the transformation of words and images into permanent art-things.

Rilke's poems written after 1911 tend to reflect the somber note of the first elegies. At the outbreak of World War I, he was traveling in Germany and was forced to remain there. The despair about his inability to return to Paris is reflected in somber poems written during the war. His despair intensified when he was, for a short time, inducted in the Austrian army. Friends provided for a sinecure in Vienna and eventual discharge. In 1922 he finished the *Duino Elegies* while living in a small medieval castle in the Valais, provided by a Swiss friend. The fifth elegy, written last, demonstrates, by the image of Parisian street artists, how, with concentrated effort, meaninglessness may revert to the empty abundance of artistic ability. Artistic accomplishment transcends the fear and meaninglessness of death and penetrates human suffering. The condition of the aesthetic justification of the world is to accept it with its woes. There are to be no easy comfort, no redemption of the individual soul, no sinless state.

In 1922 Rilke wrote a series of very loosely composed sonnets, *Sonnets to Orpheus*, dedicated to Orpheus, who sings after he had sung among the dead. The sonnets contain poems with comments on modern life, like the demand that machines should serve, not dominate. Other poems praise nature and flowers. One poem discredits humane penal practices. Between 1923 and 1926 Rilke wrote reflective poems and poems praising NATURE in German and French, some simple, and some at the margin of comprehensibility. He died a painful death from acute leukemia. Only Rilke's mature work qualifies as being akin to existentialism. In it appear his sense of total freedom, his rejection of traditional human bonds, his concern with death, unconsoled by traditional religion, the idea of a principal difference between human consciousness and primitive forms of living existence, his lament of the human condition.

Primary Works

Rilke, Rainer Maria. *The Book of Hours*. Trans. Stevie Krayer. Salzburg: Salzburg University Studies in English Literature, 1995.
———. *Duino Elegies*. Trans. David Young. New York: Norton, 1978.
———. *Sonnets to Orpheus*. Trans. M. D. Herter Norton. New York: Norton, 1962.

Bibliography

Fuerst, Norbert. *Phases of Rilke*. New York: Haskell House, 1974.

FRANZ ROSENZWEIG (1886–1929)
Zeev Levy

Franz Rosenzweig was born in Kassel, Germany, in a liberal-assimilated Jewish family. During childhood he received limited guidance in JUDAISM. In 1905 he commenced academic studies in Munich and Freiburg and finished them in Berlin; he studied medicine, HISTORY, and PHILOSOPHY. He completed his studies in 1912, writing his doctoral dissertation on the POLITICAL PHILOSOPHY of Hegel under the instruction of F. Meinecke. At this period of his LIFE, several close friends and relatives converted to CHRISTIANITY. Rosenzweig also considered converting since by embracing German culture he considered himself to be virtually Christian. After a nightlong discussion during July 1913 with his relative Eugen Rosenstock-Huessy, who had already converted, he decided to convert but wanted to do so not as a pagan but as a Jew who knows why he abandons Judaism for Christianity. However, after attending the High Holiday services in a small orthodox synagogue in Berlin, he changed his MIND. As a Jew he felt himself close to GOD and in no need of a mediator—Jesus—to reach God.

This return to Judaism determined much of his subsequent life. In Berlin, Rosenzweig met and became a student of Hermann Cohen in 1913 and made the acquaintance of MARTIN BUBER. As a German soldier during World War I on the eastern front, he was impressed by the AUTHENTICITY of the Jewish population. He began writing *The Star of Redemption* on military postcards while still a soldier and completed the book in 1919. He married his wife, Edith, in 1920; in 1922 his son, Raphael, was born. Rosenzweig settled in Frankfurt, where he organized, together with other Jewish intellectuals, the Free Jewish Study-Center. In 1921 he contracted a rare fatal illness that slowly led to total paralysis. He lived for eight more years, during which he continued his literary and scholarly activities.

At first, Rosenzweig was immersed in Hegel's philosophy; however, when his dissertation appeared in book form in 1920, one can already detect indications of his imminent existentialist turn. *The Star of Redemption* stresses the need of a new thinking: philosophy has nothing more to say unless it attains help from THEOLOGY, but theology is useless unless it relies on philosophy. Instead of dealing with concepts, philosophy ought to deal with man or, more precisely, men. One must emphasize the philosopher's subjective position. Objective thought must be replaced by subjective belief. As against the idealistic tradition that considered man to be a part of totality, Rosenzweig underscored the individual living here and now.

Rosenzweig is unique among existentialists in constructing a system that aims at synthesizing philosophy and BELIEF. He employs the dialectical method of Hegel, while condemning the idealistic foundations of Hegel's philosophy. He rejects conceptual abstraction and advocates empiricism, but he formulates an elaborate thought-structure. Man, however, is central to his system. He postulates pluralism, namely, the independent existence of three elements—God, WORLD, Man. The three elements are equivalent from the point of view of his method: each is independent of the two others, but God is superior to Man or World. Each element displays a distinctive feature: God is not a concept but a real BEING, a personal God. Man is distinguished by his individuality and by his relationship to fellow beings. The world is the meeting point between the particular and the universal.

The three elements form the subjects of METAPHYSICS, metalogic, and metaethics, but they can be conceived only by their activities—Creation, REVELATION, REDEMPTION. These are not abstract concepts but real activities. We encounter them in three configurations: the fire, the rays, and the star that symbolize the eternal life (Judaism); the eternal way (Christianity); and the eternal TRUTH (the merger of both). In the end of days both Judaism and Christianity will be superseded by absolute truth. Each one of these nine notions is also analyzed by three criteria: MYTH, LANGUAGE, and ART, as conceived in three different eras—antiquity, modernity, and the age of science. Finally, all this is carried out by thinking, which is replaced by belief, giving birth to believing thought. Rosenzweig illustrates this complex structure by two triangles, one for the elements and one for the activities. Blended together, the two triangles form the Star of David. This speculative construction underscores that neither of the elements can be derived from the two others: each one exists independently. Likewise, the three activities operate in full FREEDOM.

The relations between the elements and the activities are necessary: the relation between God and the world is manifested in Creation, between God and man in Revelation, while the relation between man and World can achieve Redemption. Creation and revelation are God's acts, but redemption is man's activity. Man transfers God's LOVE of man to the world, namely, to the world of his fellowmen, in accordance with the biblical verse Love thy neighbor as thyself. God is active, the world is passive, but man is both passive—receiving God's love—and active in communicating it to his fellowmen. Creation is an attribute of God, an integral part of his divine essence, while revelation is not an attribute but an activity whose chief content is love. Can revelation become an OBJECT of thought? This question leads to an important concept: orientation. It implies that revelation does not refer to man in general but addresses man as a concrete, distinct PERSON. Revelation does not blur man's authentic existence.

Consider the twofold meanings of belief and revelation. In its first sense belief means acceptance of facts given by experience and endorsed by thought. The second sense of belief is to conceive of those aspects that cannot be confirmed by thought in principle; in this sense it means FAITH. For Rosenzweig belief in the first sense is no less important than the second one. It expresses the priority of EXISTENCE over thought. The same holds for the two meanings of revelation. In its first sense God reveals Himself objectively, by creation. In the second sense God reveals Himself subjectively, by His love of man. This love is superbly expressed in *The Song of Songs*. God's love then evokes man's response, namely, his communicating this love to his neighbors. Personal revelation is of utmost importance. It expresses God's dialogue with man and entails man's dialogue with other men.

Redemption is a result of human activity, namely, to transfer God's love of man to other men; the meaning of redemption is to redeem the world of men in daily human existence. By means of love man overcomes the temporality of life and the finality of death. The merging of philosophy (thought) with theology (belief) culminates in anthropology. Hence, a distinctive feature of this dialectics: Whereas in Hegel's philosophy the antithesis mediates between the thesis and the synthesis, in Rosenzweig's thought thesis and antithesis are equivalent. While, according to Hegel, every synthesis may become the thesis of a new dialectical triad, Rosenzweig's synthesis completes the process. In the process of redemption God also redeems himself. Against Hegel's claim that all reality is part of thought, Rosenzweig's philosophy postulates that existence is prior to thought. This priority can be experienced only by belief; belief thus precedes thought.

Notwithstanding the turn toward belief, thought is not discarded. The priority of existence cannot be corroborated by thought but is a matter of belief, yet this conclusion is the outcome of thought. Belief and thought are both necessary in order to comprehend the whole of reality. Thought, belief, and believing thought are also distinguished by characteristic means of expression. The instrument of thought is mathematics, which symbolizes the latent elements of the world prior to revelation. The instrument of belief is grammar, manifested by speech; it expresses the miracle of the world being revealed at present. The instrument of believing thought is liturgy, especially prayer, whose task is to elicit the future in the present. Thus, Rosenzweig's existentialism is optimistic, full of hope. He begins his book by discussing death, especially FEAR of death; he terminates the book by speaking about the Gate that shows the way into life.

Rosenzweig did not consider *The Star of Redemption* to be a Jewish book. Nevertheless, Judaism plays a predominant role. Israel is outside the stream of history to which all other peoples and RELIGIONS are subordinated. While Christians are converts to Christianity, and conversion takes place at a certain time by baptism, a Jew is born a Jew and belongs to the realm of ETERNITY from birth. Ethnicity acquires a theological VALUE. The Jew experiences eternity through one's religious calendar, whose language is the liturgical chorus. This calendar is indifferent to history, unlike the Christian calendar.

Rosenzweig was opposed to assimilationist trends because he conceived of Judaism not merely as a religious denomination but as an ethnic-religious entity. He was also opposed to Zionism because the unique ESSENCE of the Jewish people emerged outside the land, in exile. Because a Jew is nowhere at home, he is at home everywhere. Hence, only in the Diaspora can Judaism fulfill its spiritual mission. Rosenzweig's attitude to Zionism was less a matter of adversity than of indifference. After all, if a Jew is at home everywhere, this evidently includes Palestine. But Zionism aspires to reintroduce the Jewish people into the course of history and to settle it on its ancient soil; this aim Rosenzweig rejected as a betrayal of Israel's spiritual freedom for the sake of earthly, temporal interests. The same holds for the Hebrew language. It is not a dead language, like Latin or Greek, but a living language; like the Jewish people it is also not subjected to history. It is the Holy Language and therefore ought not to serve temporal purposes.

Primary Works

Rosenzweig, Franz. *On Jewish Learning*. New York: Schocken, 1965.

———. *The Star of Redemption*. Trans. William W. Hallo. Boston: Beacon Press, 1972.

Bibliography

Glatzer, Nahum N. *Franz Rosenzweig: His Life and Thought*. New York: Schocken, 1961.

JEAN-PAUL SARTRE (1905–1980)

Thomas R. Flynn

Playwright, novelist, essayist, philosopher, and polemicist, Sartre personified French letters for a third of a century. After World War II, he became the model of the existentialist philosopher, committed to giving the bourgeoisie who constituted his chief readership a bad conscience. Sartre was born at Thiviers in south-central France. After attending Lycées in Paris, he graduated from the École Normale Superieure and passed his *agrégation* in 1929. While at the École he met Raymond Aron and SIMONE DE BEAUVOIR, his lifelong companion. After several years of teaching in Lycées interrupted by military service and incarceration in a German prisoner of war camp, he abandoned the classroom for LIFE as an author. With Beauvoir, Aron, MERLEAU-PONTY, and others, he founded the influential review *Les Temps modernes*, which first appeared in October 1945. That year he refused the Legion of Honor. He refused the Nobel Prize in 1964.

Sartre's philosophical works can be divided roughly into two periods, separated by his experience during World War II. His publications of the 1930s and 1940s, beginning with *The Transcendence of the Ego* and culminating in *Being and Nothingness*, are existential, phenomenological studies of CONSCIOUSNESS and BEING. They show little political commitment but exhibit an underlying moral concern. His novels, plays, and short stories of this period, most notably *Nausea* and the plays *The Flies* and *No Exit*, exemplified artistically the theses and themes of his philosophical writings. An increasingly complex relation between PHILOSOPHY and imaginative LITERATURE continued in his postwar plays. He addressed the problem of committed literature in a series of essays originally appearing in *Les Temps modernes* and published subsequently as *What Is Literature?* The second portion of Sartre's career, influenced by Marxist theory and practice, includes existential psychoanalyses of Baudelaire, Genet, and Flaubert and his autobiography, *The Words*; here psychological descriptions and social criticism intermingle. The major philosophical work of this period is the *Critique of Dialectical Reason*. His three-volume study of Flaubert, *The Family Idiot*, is arguably the culmination and the synthesis of its individualist and socialist periods. During both periods, Sartre wrote numerous essays.

Existentialism has strong ties to imaginative literature. One could trace the evolution of Sartre's political and philosophical views through his stories, novels, and plays. His first novel, *Nausea*, describes the experience of CONTINGENCY and FREEDOM, which ground Sartre's phenomenological ONTOLOGY in *Being and Nothingness*, published five years later. Mathieu, chief protagonist in the trilogy *Roads to Freedom* (1945–1949), incarnates the abstract freedom of the prepoliticized Sartre. The ambiguities of political realism and idealism emerge in the play *Dirty Hands* (1948) and the biography *Saint Genet* (1952). Sartre's last major play appeared in 1959, *The Condemned of Altona*; it describes the power of the practico-inert—a thesis central to *Critique of Dialectical Reason*, published the following year. *What Is Literature?*, while carefully distinguishing literature from propaganda, insists that the themes and theses of the writer in our time should challenge the ALIENATION of work and exhibit the individual as creative action. These two sides of freedom, the negative and the constructive, remain integral to Sartre's theory of human reality.

At least four theses reveal themselves at every stage of his development: (1) Sartre is a philosopher of the IMAGINATION, (2) a dualism of spontaneity and inertia pervades his thought, (3) freedom is both a fact and a VALUE, and (4) the individual enjoys a primacy that is ontological, epistemological, and moral. These features lend a coherence to Sartre's work.

1. Imaging consciousness, discussed in Sartre's early *Psychology of the Imagination*, becomes paradigmatic of consciousness. The nihilating character of the imaging act and its totalizing freedom analyzed in that essay emerge as essential features of being-for-itself in *Being and Nothingness*. Sartre accepts HUSSERL's thesis on INTENTIONALITY that all consciousness is consciousness of an other; in HEIDEGGER's words, human reality is already in-the-world. In defense of Husserl's claim, Sartre insists that intentionality overcomes the illusion of immanence (the belief that our consciousness is populated by images and other subjective phenomena) and frees us from philosophies of the inner life. Sartre's criticism of Husserl is that he failed to be true to his insight, falling victim to the illusion of immanence at least with regard to the imagination.

Psychology of the Imagination defines the image as an act that intends an absent or nonexistent OBJECT in its corporality by means of a physical or psychical content that is given not for its own sake but only as an analogical representative of the intended object. Despite the inevitable substantive, images, like EMOTIONS, memories, percepts, and other conscious phenomena, are not lodged in consciousness. They are acts, ways of BEING-IN-THE-WORLD. Imaging derealizes the perceptual mode, converting the perceived object or its psychical content into an analogon of the imagined one. This is especially fruitful for analyzing aesthetic works such as paintings and artistic performances; it enables Sartre to distinguish and relate the physical artifact to the aesthetic object and enrich the latter by the synthesizing act of imaging consciousness. He asks at the end of *The Psychology of the Imagination*, What kind of consciousness makes imaging possible? He answers, One that can totalize the entire perceptual world in order to hold it at bay, to nihilate it with respect to the imagined object, to constitute itself as other than its object, to be the locus of possibility, negativity, and lack. Thus, consciousness is able to imagine because it can nihilate the world as a totality and surpass it, in other words, because it is transcendentally free.

Sartre sees *The Family Idiot*, written at the end of his life, as a sequel to *The Psychology of the Imagination*. A central issue of this work is the meaning of Flaubert's CHOICE of the imaginary. As with other SUBJECTS of his existential psychoanalyses, Baudelaire and Genet, Sartre is concerned with the existential PROJECT, which gives meaning and direction to one's life as an ongoing totalization. He is convinced that every PERSON comprehends prereflectively the meaning and direction of one's actions, though one may not know reflectively that meaning. This implies that I am always responsible for my acts and that BAD FAITH is possible. The question is why Flaubert became a novelist and, specifically, the author of *Madame Bovary*. By a subtle use of historical materialism and existential psychoanalysis, elaborated as the progressive-regressive method, Sartre examines childhood and family RELATIONS that necessarily mediate socioeconomic conditions and individual projects. Flaubert's choice of the imaginary is part of a bad-faith project to derealize and demoralize the bourgeoisie who, living in the imaginary world of Second Empire pretense, found in *Madame Bovary* their resonance: the unreal was addressing the unreal. Sartre sees an objective neurosis in French SOCIETY in the 1830s and 1840s that left its artists no choice but neurotic art, a complex of attitudes that entailed detachment, solitude, derealization, failure, misanthropy, and NIHILISM. Flaubert chose the life of a neurotic who lived a life of the imagination in order to be able to write.

2. The dichotomy that pervades Sartre's thought is spontaneity versus inertia. He avoids the Cartesian ontology of MIND and matter by denying that consciousness is a substance and embraces a dualism of spontaneity and inertia: being-for-itself and being-in-itself in *Being and Nothingness*; praxis and practico-inert in his later thought. The for-itself is a pure, spontaneous upsurge, an internal NEGATION of the in-itself. The latter is characterized as an inert plenum, opaque, solid, beyond becoming, knowing no otherness, not subject to temporality, self-identical. Consciousness is metaphorically a hole in being-in-itself; it is self-transparent, unstable, in constant flux; it introduces otherness by nihilating the in-itself. Consciousness totalizes and temporalizes the world that it constitutes; it is non-self-identical. The major consequence of these claims is that human reality is infected with otherness. Human reality is in the manner of

not-being it, that is, as the determinate, internal negation of whatever feature we might ascribe to it. Thus, the waiter is a waiter, not as a stone is a stone but in the manner of not-being a waiter, of being other than his social function. To say that circumstances leave him no choice but to be a waiter is bad faith. He chooses to remain a waiter every time he answers the alarm clock and dresses for work. It is the SITUATION of not-being this waiter that constitutes his identity. The otherness that consciousness introduces into the world affects every aspect of human reality, including that inner distance that marks consciousness itself.

Human reality is free because one is not a self but a presence-to-self. Non-self-identity or self-presence is the ontological basis of freedom. The duality of spontaneity-inertia qualifies the relationship between consciousness and the self, whether as I, the subject, or as me, the object of actions and events. The self is the product of my reflective consciousness and of others' objectifying gaze. In either case, the self is being-in-itself, and human reality is a self only in the manner of not-being it, that is, in internal negation of that self. If reflective consciousness constitutes a self, prereflective consciousness is a dynamic relationship of determinate otherness to that self. Because we are always present-to-self but not identical with it, we are free to reconstitute or reappropriate that self as we choose. This is the ontological foundation for Sartre's motto: You can always make something out of what you have been made into.

Search for a Method and *Critique of Dialectical Reason* adopt the economic and class factors that characterize historical materialism. But the duality of spontaneity-inertia continues. Praxis, whether individual or group, is originative; the practico-inert is at best the locus of past praxes, which, by its inertia, deforms, deflects, or preserves. Speaking, playing, and working, for example, are praxes, whereas LANGUAGE, games, and the corporation are practico-inert. Sartre's shift to praxis entails a growing sense of the dialectical nature of human activity as well as the possibility of a group praxis that involves positive, mutual reciprocity—something explicitly denied in *Being and Nothingness*.

3. The term "freedom" undergoes an evolution in Sartre's thought. The original, noetic freedom of his early phenomenological studies, the freedom to give meaning-direction to whatever situation you find yourself in, persists. We are condemned to be free in his later works as well. But after World War II, he holds that one is obliged to WILL the other's freedom at the same time as one's own; one cannot be free in a concrete sense unless everyone is free. The latter claim becomes the maxim of his ethic of disalienation. The essay "Materialism and Revolution" distinguishes between the individualism of the rebel and the collective sense of the revolutionary. The revolutionary philosophy that he proposes requires the elucidation of the new ideas of situation and being-in-the-world. Physical work provides the worker's first experience of freedom. Labor, which he subsequently describes as the basic form of praxis, our fundamental being-in-the-world, implies an ideal of mutual dependence and collective action: what the worker hopes for is that the relationship of solidarity that one maintains

with other workers will become the model of human relationships. Once we adopt the viewpoint of labor, freedom places itself on the level of solidarity.

Sartre adopts this model when, in the *Critique of Dialectical Reason*, he discusses the emergence of freedom in group praxis. Human reality is being-in-situation. Situation is an ambiguous mixture of FACTICITY and TRANSCENDENCE, of objective conditions and one's manner of coming to terms with them. *Being and Nothingness* insists on one's choosing the meaning-direction of whatever situation one might find oneself in. Later he comes to regard his earlier view as excessive. In *Anti-Semite and Jew* he argues that the only way to destroy anti-Semitism is to liberate both anti-Semite and Jew from their exploitative situations. The anti-Semite's situation must be modified from top to bottom. In short, if we can change the perspective of CHOICE, the choice itself will change. Thus, one does not attack freedom but brings it about that freedom decides on other bases and in terms of other structures. This insistence on the bases and structures of choice constitutes a thicker sense of freedom in Sartre's later thought. Although he leaves the conditioning role of these bases and structures ambiguous, this expanded understanding of situation does respect the social and historical dimensions of freedom.

The freedom that emerges from Sartre's postwar writings cannot be built on the ocular ontology of *Being and Nothingness*: there is no such thing as plural gaze. Concrete freedom is conditioned by a practical equivalence among participants in a common task. Each must be liberated from the objectifying gaze of the Other; objectification must be rendered nonalienating. But that Other is now conceived as integral to a socioeconomic system that depends on exploitation. The freedom of mutuality and positive reciprocity demands a radical change in the socioeconomic condition of contemporary Western society—nothing less than the dismantling of class distinctions and the state apparatus.

4. Both Sartre's existentialism and his individualism are significantly modified by becoming dialectical, which means that each accommodates a collective and totalizing component that seems to ill fit them. He calls his blend of these elements dialectical nominalism. A threefold primacy of the individual emerges: ontological, epistemological, and moral. The ontological principles of dialectical nominalism claim that there are only individuals and real relations between individuals. There is no collective consciousness or superorganism over and above the individuals that constitute it. Such implies accepting the purely psychological explanations of social phenomena favored by methodological individualists. He introduces the functional concept of the mediating third into his social ontology precisely to respect the qualitative difference between individual and society, while preserving the values of AUTHENTICITY and individual RESPONSIBILITY. The mediating third party denotes the group member. The reality of practical relations simultaneously constitutes the group and modifies the members. As Sartre explains, in group formation the multiplicity of other praxes is interiorized as mine: every ''there'' is ''here''; every ''other'' is ''the same'' in practice, without resorting to an abstract idea or to nominalist stipu-

lation. Such entails an ontological change. As long as a person is mediating as third between pairs, the ensuing group can support predicates such as right and duty, function and POWER.

Sartre summarizes the ontological primacy of praxis thus: the original foundation of unity, of action, and of finality is individual praxis as the unifying and reorganizing transcendence of existing circumstances toward the practical field. Other elements in his social ontology, namely, the practico-inert, seriality, the pledged group, and the institution, are either forms or deformations of free, organic praxis. Praxis also enjoys an epistemological primacy since it exhibits translucency. Comprehension that accompanies praxis is not a special faculty or an abstruse ART. I practice comprehension every TIME I play tennis, drive on a crowded street, or hold the door for someone with an armload of packages. Sartre argues that the impossibility for a union of individuals to transcend organic action, as a strictly individual model, is the basic condition of historical rationality. Constituted dialectical reason, as the living intelligibility of all common praxis, must always be related to its ever-present, but always veiled, foundation, constituent rationality, or organic praxis. No doubt, one can make some sense of social reality by appealing solely to the practico-inert. But that intelligibility will be abstract and analytic, not dialectical; it misses the dynamic, totalizing nature of social reality. In Sartre's study of Flaubert, the principle of progressive-regressive intelligibility is dialectical: a person totalizes one's age to the extent that one is totalized by it.

Frequently, the moral primacy of praxis comes to the fore. Sartre's theory of history and society reveals the responsibility that sustains all social situations, even the most necessary laws and institutions. Marxist economism has attenuated this responsibility; Sartrean HUMANISM emphasizes it. If social causation is ultimately attributable to individuals-in-relation, then so, too, is social responsibility. If individual praxis is transparent, then collective bad faith is always possible, and inauthenticity is ascribable to societies. Still, in principle it should always be possible to find acts of oppression sustaining structures of exploitation. Sartre would agree: in the end, you can always find someone to blame. He would strenuously deny that that someone is always someone else!

One can distill Sartre's thinking into several standard containers: PSYCHOLOGY, ontology, ETHICS, politics. Sartre's work will ultimately transcend these categories. But they assist in comparing his views with those of other philosophers.

Sartre's chief contributions to psychology, made in the 1930s and 1940s, stem from a rigorous application of Husserlian intentionality to the imagination and the emotions as well as from appeal to his ontology of being-for-itself and being-in-itself for treating such matters as the NATURE of the self, the mind-body problem, other minds, and action theory. His method is phenomenological; he describes the givens of conscious life in their various modes of givenness: images as derealized percepts, emotions as forms of failure behavior generating a magical world, and percepts as presenting the world according to practical concerns. *Being and Nothingness* sketches an existential psychoanalysis that seeks to discover the fundamental PROJECT that defines a person's unified way of being-in-the-world. His biographies and autobiography are applications of this psychoanalysis. *Being and Nothingness* is subtitled *An Essay on Phenomenological Ontology*. In it being-in-itself, being-for-itself, and being-for-others are grasped through phenomenological descriptions. His descriptions of NOTHINGNESS and negation are striking and reveal the power of the phenomenological method, which forges strong links between the ontological and the psychological. Some of Sartre's most arresting arguments are convincing descriptions of our experiences. Such an approach could pass for ontological idealism, were it not for his insistence on the intentionality of consciousness. He distinguishes ontology from METAPHYSICS, which deals with ultimate causes and cannot surpass the merely hypothetical.

One can distinguish three stages in the development of Sartre's ethical thought. The first, an ethics of authenticity, characterizes his vintage existentialism. It stresses radical freedom and responsibility, criterion-constituting choice, authenticity, and bad faith. His second, dialectical ethic, one of disalienation, is more consequentialist in nature. It underscores the need for revolutionary activity that would violate bourgeois VALUES in order to bring about a society where equality and genuine ethical relations were possible. The work he was composing with Benny Levy at the time of his death was to be an ethic of the WE. In the last interview he gave, he promised that this new position would stress communal values that his earlier work had ignored and face up to the conflict between fraternity and violence that had plagued his thought for decades.

Though Sartre always tended toward the political Left, his sympathies were more with the less regimented Italian than with the pro-Stalinist French Communist Party. Occasionally, he recommended that workers align themselves with the Party as their only option. But he strenuously refused to join any party, regarding it as incompatible with the role of an intellectual. He was uncompromising in his criticism of capitalist and bourgeois thought and life but could equally be critical of socialists' and communists' vested interests in the political realm. In later years he supported a kind of anarchism as the ideal relation of equality and mutuality among brothers and sisters in a nonexploitative, stateless society.

Primary Works

Sartre, Jean-Paul. *Critique of Dialectical Reason*. Trans. Alan Sheridan. London: Verso, 1982.
———. *The Family Idiot: Gustave Flaubert 1821–1857*. Vols. 1–5. Trans. Carol Cosman. Chicago: University of Chicago Press, 1981–1993.

———. *The Psychology of the Imagination*. Trans. Bernard Fretchman. New York: Washington Square Press, 1966.

Bibliography

Flynn, Thomas. *Sartre and Marxist Existentialism*. Chicago: University of Chicago Press, 1984.

SENSATION
W. Kim Rogers

Sensation as understood by modern philosophers is a subjective entity but also an objective product, like a message present in my CONSCIOUSNESS that I have received from some outside source by which some quality of the sender becomes known. Existential philosophers reject this understanding of sensation.

MARCEL gave a reductio ad absurdum argument to end speculations about sensations understood through the analogy of the emission and reception of a message—the view that stimuli are sent from an unknown source external to one's consciousness and interpreted by a physical receiving instrument that translates sensations into OBJECTS in consciousness. For such a process to occur there must be a substitution of a set of given signals for another set of given signals, and for this to happen there must be an awareness of both sorts of signals, of their differences, and of their correlation. Yet, the physical event that produced the stimuli is not given as such to one's awareness: thus, it cannot be the text that one is to translate. Nor am I aware of the stimuli as such, for example, a certain pattern of light waves. These light wave patterns are translated into chemical changes by the nerve endings at the rear of the optical organ; the changes are translated into microelectrical pulses sent to the optical center of the brain, where they are translated into sensations of colors and shapes that consciousness translates into objects of experience. However, these sensations are not to be found in consciousness, and there is no awareness of the preceding electrical pulses or of chemical changes in the optical organ. For such a translation PROCESS to occur there would have to be postulated the EXISTENCE of intermediary, unsensed sensings or mediating awareness of which we are unaware—which is nonsense. Thus, the attempt to understand sense experience through the model of the reception of a message is hopelessly incoherent. We must also give up the accepted opposition between an outside and an inside that called for the use of such a model. We must, rather, Marcel declared, recognize in PERCEPTION the role of the non-mediatizable immediate.

SARTRE similarly insisted that sensation as an intermediary between consciousness and the WORLD is a creature of reason, a daydream of the psychologist that must be rejected. Perception of objects requires that we say, with HUSSERL, that the presence of the world and of objects to us is necessary. The perception of a quality, for example, white, involves not just one's consciousness of an object's being white but also the impossibility of oneself being a color. Consciousness of white is also consciousness of one's not being the color white. The perceptive field refers to a center objectively defined by that reference and located in the field oriented around it, namely, the BODY, which is also what I am, the perceiving SUBJECT. The centering body I am is for me an inapprehensible object—or rather, not objectifiable at all. It is my being-in-the-midst-of-the-world, which is indicated to itself by the distance and orientation of objects in the world. It is possible, of course, to see and touch parts of my body either directly or through some secondary means—in this case there is a distance between myself and the present perceived object. I cannot see myself seeing, though I may see some bodily part or parts of the seen. One's body is, however, not only one's capacity to perceive others but also and foremost oneself acting in the world. One can be a perceiver only in and through one's PROJECTS of action. It is impossible to separate sensation from action, and vice versa.

MERLEAU-PONTY also discards the modern meaning of sensation but retains the term with a radically altered meaning. The sentient being and the sensible object are not related to each other as two mutually external terms, nor can it be that one suffers while the other acts or that one confers significance upon the other. Sense experience is a bodily transaction with the world that is literally a form of communion. Each phenomenon on its APPEARANCE sets an obscure problem for one's body to solve and vaguely beckons to one's whole body as a system of perpetual POWERS. What is called an experience of it is one's full bodily coexistence with the phenomenon. Sense experience is a vital communication with the world that makes it present as a familiar setting for our LIFE.

Primary Works

Husserl, Edmund. *Cartesian Meditations: An Introduction to Phenomenology.* Trans. Dorian Cairns. The Hague: Martinus Nijhoff, 1960.

Merleau-Ponty, Maurice. *The Visible and the Invisible.* Trans. Alphonso Lingis. Evanston, IL: Northwestern University Press, 1968.

LEV SHESTOV
(1866–1938)
Peter Royle

Lev Shestov was the son of a wealthy Kiev textile manufacturer. After studying mathematics and law at the universities of Moscow and Kiev, he worked in his father's company, then began a life of travel that saw him established at different times in Italy, Switzerland, Germany, and France, with several protracted sojourns in Russia. In 1896, while in Rome, he married a medical student, Anna Eleazarovna Berezovsky; they had two daughters. He moved in brilliant intellectual circles, cultivating interests in music, LITERATURE, POETRY, and PHILOSOPHY, the last of these gradually becoming his absorbing concern. He had close friends such as Bulgakov, BERDYAEV, and HUSSERL, with whom he strongly disagreed on philosophical matters but whom he respected as his most challenging adversary. From 1920 until his DEATH, Shestov resided in France.

Throughout his LIFE Shestov was a strong antirationalist, which emerges in his early writings on Shakespeare, NIETZSCHE, Tolstoy, and DOSTOYEVSKY, whom he regards as having penned, in *Notes from Underground* and *The Dream of a Ridiculous Man*, the most compelling critique of reason ever enunciated. As Shestov's thought matures, it becomes ever more religious; the RELIGION he espouses is not the Judaism into which he was born but CHRISTIANITY—however, with a difference. The TRUTH, he believes, has been divined by only a few individuals in the course of HISTORY, and those who have glimpsed it have not been able to hold onto it and act in accordance with it on a regular basis. Such is, in part, because the truth, vouchsafed only by FAITH, is rooted in the experience, cultural traditions, and INTUITIONS of the Jewish people, whereas historical Christianity has been contaminated by the rationalist thought of ancient Greece. Faith is not imperfect KNOWLEDGE but belongs to a different order, in which miracles are not scandalous but simple, everyday occurrences and in which GOD, as in the Bible, enters into a direct dialogue with humans.

Certain quotations that he repeats lead to the heart of Shestov's thought, for example, the quotation from Seneca about God's always obeying, having commanded only once; or Luther's about the monster without whose killing man cannot live; or Spinoza's ethical principle not to laugh, not to lament, not to curse, but to understand. The poisoning of Socrates is a historical event that is mentioned many times. The quotation from Seneca reveals that for the ancient

Greek world and its Western heirs the commander of the universe is not God but Necessity, whose chief lieutenant, enjoining resignation and obedience in the ethical realm, is Reason. The laws that govern us are inflexible, and God may have created them, but if so, he is now as much their prisoner as we are: He has commanded only once. God may be omniscient, but, according to the rationalist tradition, His omnipotence is purely verbal, as there are many things He cannot do: He cannot undo the past, He cannot fly in the face of reason and logic, He cannot be EVIL, He cannot endow stones with CONSCIOUSNESS, He cannot save humans against their WILL. For God two plus two equals four, and the logical laws of contradiction and identity obtain just as much as for us; He is impotent even in the face of individual historical events, such as the poisoning of Socrates.

According to Judeo-Christian belief God can intervene in the WORLD, but, Shestov claims, even Western philosophers whose religion demanded that they pay lip service to miracles have regarded them as, at best, an embarrassing vestige of primitive belief or, at worst, a scandal. For Luther, as for St. Paul, "whatsoever is not of faith is sin." The Catholic Church, against which Luther rebelled, had become, in his eyes, an institution not only arrogating to itself the POWER of the keys to the kingdom of Heaven given to Peter but attempting to use this power not for the greater glory of God but for its own selfish and therefore satanic ends. Instead of preaching salvation through faith, it had become, during the Middle Ages, a rationalistic, logic-chopping, and arid, corrupt institution. Faith, Luther taught, was the opposite of reason; it meant abandoning oneself to the will of a free God and thereby negating the work of the serpent in Eden. The Fall of the human race had occurred because Adam had eaten the fruit of the Tree of Knowledge. Evil had come into the world with the knowledge of GOOD and evil. Spinoza's ethical principle is seen by Shestov as the inevitable outcome of centuries of pernicious rationalism.

The ideas that God is identical to natural law, that we should therefore bow to Necessity and LOVE intellectually a God incapable of love himself, that happiness is not the reward of virtue but virtue itself are anathema to Shestov. Happiness has nothing to do with the stoic resignation of the school of Athens; to lead a rich, satisfying life means precisely to laugh, to lament, and even to curse. One of his heroes is the biblical Job, who had the courage to defy his comforters and to express misery and incomprehension of his fate to God. In Job's story, God does not act in accordance with human canons of goodness. Hence, we must seek that which is higher than the good. We must seek God. The frequent allusions to the poisoning of Socrates are at first puzzling. Socrates is perhaps the wisest man who ever lived; but his WISDOM is an Athenian, rationalistic one and therefore false. Unfortunately, Socrates' noble bearing in the face of death has given weight to the rationalistic views he espoused, leading to indifference in the face of injustice.

Thus, our world is not a just or rational place. Our reason is incapable of penetrating its MYSTERIES. True faith demands not that we accept injustice in the belief that because it exists, there must be a good reason for it, but that we ask God to annul it; if He sees fit to do so, He can resurrect the dead and wipe out the past. Failure to react thus and to let ourselves be beguiled by the siren voice of philosophy or reason is to be transformed, like those transfixed by the look of Medusa, into stones endowed with consciousness. Humans are made in the image of God; they will be free despite the Fall if they have the courage to exercise their FREEDOM by asking God for what they want. Shestov grasps the difficulty of faith in a good God firmly and, true to the picture of God of the Bible that he sees, states that He is arbitrary and that freedom is caprice. To the rationalist objection that we have to respect natural laws such as the law of gravity and that freedom is the recognition of necessity, he replies that it is not freedom but rationality that recognizes necessity. Freedom can express itself only irrationally. Freedom is emancipation not through reason but from it. For irrational freedom to result in human fulfillment and creativity involves our individual participation, through the communion of faith, in the creativity of God.

Furthermore, truth is neither approximation of thing and intellect, as for many philosophers, nor the unconcealedness of HEIDEGGER. It is not knowledge; it is not one. In absolutizing truth, we relativize BEING. Truth is created; there are truths that are born in time, such as Socrates was poisoned in 399 B.C., and truths that are presumably eternal. God, although He deceives us when it suits Him, is the source of truth but not rational truth. My truth is ultimately incommunicable as it is not universal. Shestov agrees with Heidegger that truth is to be seen rather than intellectually apprehended, but only up to a point: to see is to be separate from. Of ultimate truth, we must believe that we have seen it, when a light suddenly dawns on the soul. In the course of a lifetime such moments are few and far between. Yet, if my truth is incommunicable, why bother to try to express it? There is always the hope that its expression will produce an INTUITION of the same truth in some of those who listen; but, ultimately, I do it for myself, as without expression my truth, like love, will fade away, and I will have no memory of that which is of supreme importance.

Shestov's attitude to LANGUAGE appears to be ambivalent, as do his attitudes to science and philosophy. Contrary to Hegel and received opinion, Shestov maintains that human progress is to be seen not in the evolution from particular to universal thinking but in the opposite, the movement toward the singular and concrete. It might be expected that he would try to escape the limitations of language by writing POETRY, but he does not. Whereas some Romantics exalted poetry as the expression of a primitive communion, the notion of such a communion does not find favor with Shestov, for whom salvation is necessarily individual and personal. He tries to communicate, knowing that he will be misunderstood. Like a prophet crying in the wilderness, he writes in prose. Toward logic he has a similar ambivalence. He does not deliberately contradict himself, but he is not unduly worried by self-contradiction. We are free to make deductions or not. The principle of contradiction is not always false (how could it be?), but it can be established only by a will and may be overridden by a superior will.

All philosophies, Shestov holds, contain contradictions and are equally arbitrary. He does not maintain that contradictions are or are not a sign of truth, only that they do not necessarily rule against it. Where possible, they should be avoided; otherwise they should be faced. In METAPHYSICS they are unavoidable. Philosophy, while an admirable activity, can easily become the preserve of charlatans; it is doomed to failure as long as it persists in the pursuit of coherence and the construction of systems. Its true vocation is not the persuasion of multitudes but, as Plato saw, the preparation of the individual soul for death. Life is like a dream, from which death will be the awakening. He does not reject science, which is not, like philosophy, primarily logical and a prioristic but inductive and descriptive. He objects to scientism and the determinist BELIEF that because things happen, they happen of necessity. If it is reasonable to accept the operation of laws in the natural sphere, it is reasonable, too, as the inexplicable regularity of the results of flipping a coin will show, to believe that they issue from the fiat of an Almighty will; they can therefore be suspended or abrogated.

Reason need not, anymore than any existent, justify itself, only its pretensions to primacy. Will, not reason, is the fundamental metaphysical principle. If Shestov's philosophy is essentially incommunicable, as he declares all philosophies to be, it will be said perhaps that it is of importance only to himself. Though not a philosopher of the traditional system-building school, the school of Athens, he is a highly distinguished historian of ideas and a brilliant critic. He may not aim at logical coherence, but his thoughts are certainly consistent. He has the gift of empathy and insight and a genius for illuminating, in the work of others, the most private struggles and obsessions, not in a scientific or pseudoscientific manner but in soteriological terms of universal import. In the final analysis, Shestov's importance lies in the extremity of his antirationalism and the lucid, largely dispassionate arguments that he adduces in defense of it.

Primary Works

Shestov, Lev. *Athens and Jerusalem*. Trans. Bernard Martin. New York: Simon and Schuster, 1968.
————. *In Job's Balance*. Trans. Camilla Coventry and C. A. Macartney. Athens: Ohio University Press, 1975.
————. *Speculation and Revelation*. Trans. Bernard Martin. Athens: Ohio University Press, 1982.

SIN

Vincent McCarthy

KIERKEGAARD and TILLICH employ the term "sin" as an existential concept. BUBER makes several references to sin. The ESSENCE of their discussions have parallels in terms such as ALIENATION, estrangement, and inauthenticity. For all three, the meaning of sin is ontological and existential: sin is the theological term for a problem in one's BEING. Such is in contrast to the conventional theological understanding of original sin ascribed to humankind: sin entered the world in the deed of Adam, and all humans are heirs to this original deed. Kierkegaard does not deny or omit the role of Adam but focuses on the Adam-like first sin of all humans. Tillich treats the biblical story as symbolic; it seems to depict sin as a necessary given, something that Kierkegaard would deny. Kierkegaard's emphasis on the universality yet CONTINGENCY of sin appeals to the MYSTERY of sin, which emerges in the dizzying moment of ANXIETY.

Kierkegaard's discussion of sin occurs in *The Concept of Anxiety* and *The Sickness unto Death*, both of which analyze and prescribe for the fragmented self. The former's subtitle announces it as a psychological investigation oriented toward the dogmatic problem of original sin. Kierkegaard's analysis begins with the first sin, or original sin. By this he means not the traditional notion of a sin inherited from Adam. Kierkegaard argues that every PERSON's sinfulness begins with a first sin that must be understood as one's own deed. The story of Adam and Eve is the story of their sin and the historical entry of sinfulness into humanity; it is not the story of everyone's coming to sin. Every sin, including original sin, is one's own, just like Adam's sin. Anxiety explains the dizzying Fall, from which one awakens to discover that one has sinned and is responsible for it. Anxiety is a MOOD that discloses the underlying state of sinfulness from which one is called to recover.

The Concept of Anxiety analyzes the state of sinfulness and prods the reader toward overcoming it. In *The Sickness unto Death* despair is both a synonym for the state of sin and, paradoxically, the action verb of recovery: to despair of illusionary self-fulfillment in aesthetic categories; to despair as acknowledging one's GUILT and taking on the painful sin-consciousness of inability to restore oneself, with the corollary need of divine grace. The discovery of sinfulness through anxiety poses the alternative of remaining in sin or choosing to overcome it. *The Sickness unto Death* is an analysis of sinfulness through discussing the elements that constitute the dynamic synthesis of human being: finitude and infinitude, possibility and necessity. Sin-consciousness is an advance beyond guilt-consciousness in that it is an assuming of RESPONSIBILITY for the shattered, fallen human condition of sin before GOD, considered as the Constituting POWER of the human synthesis and the sole source of reconstitution. The sickness unto DEATH is despair, a heightened form of anxiety. For to take on the CONSCIOUSNESS of being a shattered self, in addition to the experience of being shattered, is unbearable agony to one who does not repent. Despair is thus the state of continuation in sin and the act of will that can lead to vanquishing sin. Sin is avoidance of one's authentic possibility of being a repentant, restored self, grounded in a God-relationship. Despair is the state of being cut off from the future, from possibility. Without a sense of future, as growth in a God-grounded life, one is condemned to an ever-repeating, unsatisfying present. Despair can become a defiantly willed state, which amounts to SUICIDE of the SPIRIT. The life of poetic imagination, with fantasies of fulfillment grounded in sensuality or in intellectuality, is the principal object of criticism, because the fantasies are usually overlooked, regarded as harmless or even admired. Sin is thus the shattered self, with the self understood religiously: grounded in spirit and destined for a greater, evolving life of spirit.

Tillich does not regard the state of Adam pre-Fall as perfection but rather as dreaming innocence. This opens the way for the analysis of restoration from sinfulness that eventually can lead to a higher perfection. EXISTENCE is a state of estrangement; it is not only a universal condition but also a natural one. Sin expresses the personal side of the natural condition of estrangement: one bears personal responsibility in one's estrangement by having acted to turn away from that to which one belongs; one bears guilt for this ongoing state at least to the extent that one does not turn back (to God) and overcome estrangement. The marks of estrangement are unbelief, concupiscence, and hubris: unbelief as turning away from God and the disruption of cognitive participation in God; concupiscence as the temptation to make oneself the center; and hubris as self-centeredness to the point of self-deification.

HEIDEGGER's *Being and Time* has the secular synonyms of thrownness and fallenness; both are tied to the anxiety experience. The principal difference in his secular analysis is the absence of anything like sin-consciousness pointing to the need for divine action or cooperation in overcoming the condition. JASPERS describes a similar condition as shipwreck but has a God-synonym in the Encompassing. Buber in *Two Types of Faith* appeals to what he calls traditional Jewish doctrine in defining sin as the disturbing of the fundamental God/human person relationship. Sin is recognized by the fact that one cannot direct one's heart to God. In *Good and Evil* he associated sinfulness with disposition or a state of heart. Purity of heart becomes the dividing line between the godly and the ungodly, far more decisively than action that may be sinful because it violates a divine edict. Purity or impurity of heart is a metaphor for not just the disposition but CHOICE of the WILL. Hence, Buber finds the locus of sin in the will. EVIL is defined as indecision and lack of direction in one's LIFE, far more than any substantive act. The corollary is that GOOD is a decision of the whole soul and is directedness. Only good can be done with the whole soul: if the soul comes together in wholeness, it does the good; if the soul is dispersed, in its lack of direction it is evil.

Primary Works

Buber, Martin. *Good and Evil*. New York: Scribner's, 1952.
Kierkegaard, Søren. *The Concept of Anxiety*. Trans. Reider Thomte. Princeton: Princeton University Press, 1980.

Bibliography

Perkins, Robert L., ed. *The Concept of Anxiety: Volume 8 of International Kierkegaard Commentary*. Macon, GA: Mercer University Press, 1985.

SITUATION
Stephen Tyman

The concept of situation acquires a central meaning in existential thought. The term has come into prominence through the work of JASPERS and SARTRE. In Jaspers' thought the concept of situation begins with a principally personal resonance in the invocation of the situatedness of the thinker. This recognition has a confessional savor, expressing his sense of the limitations and the committedness of the authentic reflection to which existentialism aspires. But AUTHENTICITY of this sort is hard won. Against this kind of thought, Jaspers finds arrayed a powerful web of illusion in the form of a spurious self-certainty that he associates with the putatively unsituated EGO cogito of Cartesianism. Far from being an isolated, intellectual aberration, Cartesianism represents a continuing, subtle, and alluring temptation for thinking to step out of its skin and to carry on as if the posture of reflection could somehow be brought fully under control or made a nonissue through being protoscientifically secured. The Cartesian supporting apparatus can come to be so insidiously presupposed as to be no longer thematic, and all attention, projecting outward from this inexplicit mind-set, can come to rest undisturbed in the OBJECT of a KNOWLEDGE whose procedures seem obvious. Thinkers with this mind-set are reassured at every turn by their success, measured, to be sure, in the very terms they have projected, in controlling and manipulating an objective WORLD. Against this background, any thinking that would reacquaint itself with its primordial situation must undertake an act of self-abnegation and enter into a state of unknowing with regard not only to the world but even to its innermost motivations.

Only from within this frame of MIND can one hope to encounter the elusive cipher that Jaspers calls TRANSCENDENCE, which has the paradoxical quality of being both infinitesimally near and infinitely far from the personal seat of reflection; it both participates in the essential figure and delineation of the human situation and delimits this situation by providing its impenetrable boundary. In the latter sense, Jaspers speaks of the ineffability of the Godly, a vanishing point that human self-reflection seems unable to do without, even while never achieving a stable and repeatable relationship to it; nor can one grasp it through an adequate concept. Situation thus carries a resonance of displaced spirituality, unable in GOOD CONSCIENCE to resort to the self-assurance of an unquestioning FAITH but equally unable to function apart from an existential commitment. The latter is not so much devoted to the accidental characteristics of one's peculiar context but rather to the redeemability of the accidental in relation to a human SPIRIT needful of the accidental for its self-expression and development.

The ambivalence contained in Jaspers' conception of situation has been carried into the discussions of hermeneutic PHENOMENOLOGY, for example, by HEIDEGGER. The work of Sartre, however, poses an existential challenge to the theme of distraught and distended transcendence that Jaspers applied to the problem of situated thought. Sartre does not think Jaspers goes far enough in grasping the fundamental sense in which this concept must undermine the whole transcendence motif. In *Search for a Method*, he declares that KIERKEGAARD asserts unrelentingly the irreducibility and specificity of what is lived. This constitutes the core of what Jaspers inherited from the Dane. However, this legacy included also a tendency to seek repose in personal subjectivity, which is nothing other than an attempt to escape the world of concrete historical circumstances. Thus, Jaspers succumbs to a surreptitious wish to resuscitate the transcendent, for he flees from the real movement of praxis and takes refuge in an abstract subjectivity whose sole aim is to achieve an inward quality.

Sartre takes seriously the themes of historical materialism presented by the Marxists. Of particular importance are the factors of distortion in the human self-conception: exploitation, ALIENATION, fetishism, and reification. These factors constitute a kind of indigestible residuum for what Sartre calls the intellectualist idea of a knowledge. The problem is that they are centered behind the back of the knower and therefore may predispose the outcome of knowledge without the knower knowing it. The great virtue of MARXISM is that it has drawn attention to this spectrum of issues and dislodged the Enlightenment image of an essentially intellectual humanity from the center stage of cultural HISTORY. This does not mean that existentialism has nothing important to add to Marxist analysis. Indeed, existentialism provides an ontological framework registered fundamentally in the problematics of meaning that Marxism must always presuppose even with regard to its central concepts, such as the function of labor in the establishment of the human ESSENCE. By bringing into play the projection-analysis, Sartre reintroduces into Marxism a problematized and highly self-referential analysis of the dynamics of meaning. This necessarily deals with purely cognitive elements—universals—that, if left to themselves, would be misleading. But without this dimension Marxism itself would be shorn of all meaning. The salient point for Sartre is that the situating factors of human existence cannot be cognized independently of a free human intelligence. Hence, existentialism has something to contribute even while it profits by proximity to Marxism.

From a broader perspective, Sartre's concept of situation can be expressed in terms of his commitment to reintroduce into the dynamics of human self-recognition a sense of the unsurpassable singularity of each LIFE. In effect, this serves to highlight one more feature of the inner tension present in the concept since Jaspers: that transcendence cannot be thought merely as one pole or dimension of the human situation but, rather, that the human situation is already fundamentally self-transcending to the core. Transcendence itself is shot through with situatedness. Thus, it would be safe to say that within existentialism the figure of transcendence has haunted the sense of situation as ineluctably as the latter has done to the former. The result is that the two motifs form a kind of bipolar field within which existential options and orientations are arrayed.

Primary Works

Jaspers, Karl. *Philosophy*. 3 vols. Trans. E. B. Ashton. Chicago: University of Chicago Press, 1969/1971.
Sartre, Jean-Paul. *Search for a Method*. Trans. Hazel E. Barnes. New York: Knopf, 1963.

Bibliography

Samay, Sebastian. *Reason Revisited: The Philosophy of Karl Jaspers*. Notre Dame, IN: University of Notre Dame Press, 1971.

SOCIETY
Rivca Gordon

BUBER sees the social realm as the potential for realizing a true, free society in the SPIRIT of dialogue. For ARENDT society is essentially a negative realm that destroys the FREEDOM that emerges in the political realm. SARTRE holds that society reveals negative aspects and positive possibilities. These and other existentialist thinkers agree that there is no individual for oneself, nor is there a human COMMUNITY for itself. There is an internal, dynamic relation between the individual and the community that should be described from the perspective of freedom.

Sartre's early ONTOLOGY, in *Being and Nothingness*, describes human BEING as primarily being-for-itself. However, human EXISTENCE also has a social dimension: being-for-others. A PERSON is thrown into a WORLD where others already exist. Thus, one belongs to a nation, a class, a family—with their customs, culture, LANGUAGE, and instruments. This belonging is factual; it cannot be deduced from the ontological structure of the for-itself. The Other is simply there, in the world, as a permanent and primal given. What characterizes all human relationships in society is a constant conflict of subject–object RELATIONS, or a double relation of looking-looked: I am an OBJECT seen by an Other who is a SUBJECT, or the opposite. This gap between the Other and myself cannot be liquidated. A unity of for-itselves is an impossibility. Two kinds of pluralities can emerge: the WE and the Us. The We is a plurality of subjects, who without a previous relationship have assumed a common PROJECT. They feel a harmonious nearness between themselves; they understand themselves as a We-subject. Yet this experience is temporal and passing; it is not more than a subjective event that occurs on the psychological level. Why? Because there is no necessary condition that all who are present are experiencing this happening or are conscious of it. A unity of CONSCIOUSNESS into an intersubjective totality or a synthetic whole is impossible. Although I sometimes do experience a situation of sharing action with others, the original conflict, which is in the ESSENCE of human relations, is indestructible.

The Us does have an ontological status, connected to my being-for-others. The APPEARANCE of the third as external subject, who is looking at the act of at least two persons, causes an essential change in the situation: the conflict disappears, and an external mutuality encompasses the two, as if glueing them together into a We-as-object in relation to the third. Yet a totality like this can exist only before a look that is separated from this totality, only before a third for-itself. The We-as-object cannot be a basis for a worthy society, since it is based on the look of the third. The for-itself as being-for-others is not a genuine social agent, and the double relation of looking-looked does not allow the coming into being of either a true social sphere or real social wholes.

In *Critique of Dialectical Reason*, Sartre presents a broader social ontology, based on Marx's thought. A person is a practical organism that exists with other such organisms in a material world, in a social realm, and in a historical context. Society, which constantly develops, is a dynamic plurality of humans who through their individual praxis totalize their society within the encompassing, inert materiality. Thus, the praxis of persons constantly constructs the human community. Society is the integration of all of these individual praxes; but this integration never creates a hyperorganism. Mutual relations between three persons, in which the mediation of the third person is crucial, are the basis for all social relations. Going beyond *Being and Nothingness*, the basis of these three-person relations is praxis. At times an external threat can unite a series of persons into a forged group, in which unity and seriality blend. A more positive mutuality is a transcending of the collective, in which each third person encourages the free activity of Others. Such is the basis of a true group.

Humans find themselves in serial existence. Groups and communities are established, develop, and disintegrate on the basis of mutual praxes seeking ways to cope with need. Society was crystallized from these manners of coping. Sartre sees today's society as capitalist and oppressive. The working class, as a product of this society, is struggling to attain a LIFE of free praxis and positive mutuality. A revolutionary praxis may establish a true we that will destroy the negative structures of exploitation and oppression, which often bring ALIENATION, racism, and other EVILS. His vision was of a genuine socialist society in which solidarity, CREATIVITY, and generosity would result from genuine praxis, based on freedom.

Buber firmly rejects two major, modern social doctrines: Individualism, which abandons or rejects all possibilities of genuine community, and Collectivism, which ruins friendship and the realm of the interhuman. Societies established upon such doctrines ignore genuine dialogue and I–Thou relationships, which should guide every person's life. A society whose members are guided in their lives by I–Thou encounters and by the genuine dialogue that they establish with others will be a worthy community. Such will be a community of freedom, of mutual sharing, of a genuine we. In such a community, GOD may be present as a Thou, and God's presence may influence the emergence of dialogue. By relating to others as a Thou, persons can help to sanctify society. In contrast, a society in which I–It relations prevail will tend toward elevating the masses; in pursuing this goal, it will benefit from the profound separation and alienation between members of society; aloneness and objectification will characterize human relations.

Buber believes that a genuine society elevates both the person and the community. The test of such a society is in the everyday, concrete event. To fulfill the demands of the test, freedom, creativity, dialogue, RESPONSIBILITY, and spontaneity should repeatedly emerge in the lives of a society's members. The immediate meeting with others in society is where dialogue, sharing, and freedom should prevail. Genuine members, who live a life of dialogue, can help to unite a society into an authentic we. Elements of such a community emerged in early Hasidism—despite its later failure, in which many offshoots embraced fundamentalism and fanaticism. For Buber, the political realm is the enemy of the genuine community and of the life of dialogue. He distinguishes between what he calls the political and the social principle. A true society is built upon small communities that unite for a shared goal. It is not a politicized society. In contrast, the politicized society, which prevails today, is an expression of the surrender of the community and the victory of lust for POWER and deceit. We cannot today cancel the political realm but must enedeavor to redeem it by dialogue, EDUCATION, personal responsibility, and the reestablishment of genuine communities.

Arendt points to, and discusses, three realms of human activity: the private, the social, the political. In ancient Greece the two important realms were the private and the political realms because in the political realm freedom could be lived, and excellence could be achieved, and in the private realm a person could rest from one's struggles as a free person and conceal oneself from the demanding light of the political realm. The polis, the political realm, comes into being in that SPACE between persons in which they discuss, decide, and act upon principles of living together. Thus, justice can be struggled for and attained by free people who exist in the polis. The pursuit of justice within the polis can bring immortal glory. The lawgiver Solon attained glory through activities in the polis. In the private realm, in one's house, where the Greek person had no need to appear before one's peers, one rested and attended to one's biological needs. Hence, the private realm was always hidden from the eyes of the public. In ancient Greece it was totally separated from LIFE in the polis.

Society is that realm that has come into being once matters of the private sphere emerge into the light of the public realm. One of the results of this rise of society, Arendt explains, is a ruining of the privacy of the private realm. An additional result is the attempt to transform the political realm into a function of society. When such occurs, persons acting in the political realm become solely concerned with economic policies and with personal and general interests; they do not relate to principles and the pursuit of justice. With the rise of society in the eighteenth century, socialization of humans began; the individual became central and the supposed source of everything. The equality of peers in the polis was transformed into the equality of persons in a society. Such a transformation led to the demand that persons conform to the interests of their society. Widespread conformism, however, ruins freedom and the pursuit of excellence. Persons no longer grasp themselves as political beings. Instead, the masses and the mob become social and political forces. The political realm, where words and deeds are respected, shrinks and almost vanishes; in its stead rises the demand to constantly gauge the fickle views of the masses. Arendt concludes that the ultimate victory of the social realm can bring about a destruction of the space needed for the freedom of the political realm to emerge. With that destruction, those things that are worthy in themselves, such as the pursuit of justice, which need that space so as to come into being, may also vanish.

Primary Works

Arendt, Hannah. *The Human Condition*. Chicago: University of Chicago Press, 1968.
Buber, Martin. *Paths in Utopia*. Trans. R.F.C. Hull. Boston: Beacon Press, 1958.
Sartre, Jean-Paul. *Critique of Dialectical Reason*. Trans. Alan Sheridan. London: Verso, 1982.

Bibliography

Hinchman Lewis P., and Sandra K. Hinchman, eds. *Hannah Arendt: Critical Essays.* Albany: State University of New York Press, 1994.

SOLIPSISM
Robert Richmond Ellis

Philosophers distinguish between metaphysical and epistemological solipsism. Whereas metaphysical solipsists hold that the only real existent is the self, the epistemological school advances the modest claim that the self is the source of all KNOWLEDGE of EXISTENCE. Although few existentialists make explicit references to solipsism, most implicitly reject it and recognize an interrelationship between the subjective and objective dimensions of reality. Descartes introduced solipsism into formal philosophical discourse through his methodological doubt. Although he rejected solipsism, philosophers continued to be troubled by the concept. Kant declared that solipsism was a scandal to PHILOSOPHY. Schopenhauer indicated that the solipsist was a madman shut up in an impregnable blockhouse.

SARTRE rejected solipsism, holding that realists and idealists have both failed to resolve the problem of solipsism as it relates to the BEING of the Other because they have attempted to distinguish between the self and the Other through an external NEGATION. In so doing they have known that the Other is not themselves, in the way that a table is not a chair; but they have neither proved nor disproved that the Other exists as a for-itself. Several recent philosophers understood that the being of the Other cannot be revealed through an external negation. However, they viewed the relationship between the self and the Other as one of knowledge to knowledge rather than being to being. According to Sartre, consciousness is apodictically certain that the Other is a for-itself insofar as it experiences itself as an OBJECT of the Other's LOOK. Through the look the NOTHINGNESS of the for-itself is objectified and transformed into a for-others. The objective structure of the psyche, or the me, is thus ultimately constituted by the Other. This egological object is and is not the for-itself to the extent that the for-itself exists only through a process of internal negation, that is, through a negation of itself as not being the object of which it is conscious. This experience proves to the for-itself that the Other must be an intentional CONSCIOUSNESS like itself. In his analysis of the relationship of the for-itself of consciousness to the in-itself of the world, Sartre thoroughly refutes solipsism. In contrast to the Other, the in-itself does not reveal itself through an act of objectification. Rather, it is the condition of the existence of the for-itself. From the moment of its upsurge in the WORLD, the for-itself is aware that it is no more than a relationship to a being that it is not. The intentional act of consciousness thus involves a concomitant realization of the being of the world and of its own nonbeing vis-à-vis the world. Were the world not to exist, as the metaphysical solipsist asserts, consciousness would disappear.

UNAMUNO articulates a theory of being-for-others similar to Sartre's. For him the knowledge that consciousness has of itself is ultimately an internalization of the meaning that the Other ascribes to it. In certain passages he implies that the only real being is the hunger of consciousness for the being that it lacks. Although this is suggestive of metaphysical solipsism, Unamuno recognizes a corresponding hunger in other consciousnesses and things and even in GOD. In the thought of CAMUS the existence of the Other and of the absurd universe that oppresses humans is undeniable. In the thinking of Buber the very question of solipsism is impossible. He maintains that in the beginning is the RELATION and that the Other is a reality central to the relationship of the individual and the divine. In the thought of KIERKEGAARD there is a recognition of the Other and of the interpenetration of the world of SOCIETY and the world of the individual believer.

Primary Work

Unamuno, Miguel de. *Tragic Sense of Life*. Trans. J. E. Crawford Flitch. New York: Dover, 1954.

Bibliography

Barnes, Hazel. *Sartre*. Philadelphia: Lippincott, 1973.

SPACE
William Hurst

Space within existentialist thought is a fundamental characteristic of BEING-IN-THE-WORLD, to be distinguished from objective space as a kind of container of objects related to one another through the distances of such a space.

Existentialist thinking does not remain with the givens or the prejudices of a WORLD by attempting to create a conception of it out of an experience of a SUBJECT that exists outside it. The subject of PERCEPTION is always situated and always a perspective on the world, which is always already constituted.

MERLEAU-PONTY attempts to think the emergence of objects and of objective space from the more primitive experience of the world being given to the subject in the hold it takes, or has already taken, on the world, as a living BODY belonging to the world. The subject of such an experience, the subject of lived space as opposed to the space thought about by physicists and geometers, is anterior to the thinking subject but is always presupposed by positions taken by a subject or by any directions encountered within the world of its perception. Lived space implies that directions arise out of a point of view of the perceiving subject that has always already taken hold of the world and has given itself a space to inhabit. Distance is not an objectively calculated dimension of an OBJECT within one's visual field but an intrinsic characteristic of the spatiality of the perceived world. Depth is not reducible to breadth, through the intellectual coordination of APPEARANCES. To see a man at 500 yards is an immediate perception of depth and not the appearance of a small man in front of whom there is a multitude of objects of a size greater than his, leading me to conclude that he is at a distance. Furthermore, as an intrinsic characteristic of lived space, to which I belong, from which I cannot detach myself by becoming a worldless subject, and to which my perceptual fields give access, depth perception is a temporalizing process. To perceive something at a distance is to coexist with it and with the other things in such a way that all are included in the same temporal wave.

A perceptual field does not evoke, within Merleau-Ponty's thought, an objective field whose limits can be objectively identified. What is behind me is a part of my visual field, as is the sound of a record player from the next room that I cannot see. What I am seeing is, in very significant ways, being formed by the things that are behind me, as by the sounds that I hear emanating from things I do not behold. Such ideas clarify what Merleau-Ponty was approaching by his notion of a preobjective experience out of which objects come to be within objective space. Thus, space is an attribute of BEING, in that being is fundamentally situated, and of EXISTENCE, whose mode of being is spatializing, in that it has always already taken hold of the world in such a way as to give meaning to directions of top and bottom, up and down, right and left, far and near, directions that are features of the temporalizing thrust of subjectivity.

The priority that Merleau-Ponty gave to temporality as that dimension of existence structuring all experiences, including the spatial, seems consistent with HEIDEGGER's position in *Being and Time*, although his focus on bodily existence and perception is different. Heidegger attempts to show that space is derived from temporality, although it is equiprimordial with it. Distances flow from the fallenness of DASEIN; the principal distances generated as Dasein comes to itself are the distances of TIME—of its past, present, and future. These are to be understood not as objective time-categories but rather as dimensions of Dasein, which give an opening or a place for beings to be. Each of these dimensions of time is taken up within the lived present of Dasein; together they open up a place within which beings can become present. Thus is the spatiality of Dasein derived from the temporality of Dasein. In later writings, Heidegger stated that he had not succeeded with this interpretation. The important point is that the there of being, which gives Dasein a world and allows for the spatiality of that world to come into being, is fundamentally the temporal dimension of Dasein; it emerges from the ecstaticohorizontal structure of Dasein.

Sartre approached the question of space in his discussion of determination and negativity. As the for-itself is the source of all RELATIONS, it is also the source of all determinations, beginning with the creation of an all and a this. As a totalizing totality, the for-itself, in its ecstatic mode of not being what it is and of being what it is not, brings about a differentiation between an all and a this. The all of being reveals itself to the for-itself as the ground against which all the particular beings that at any moment the for-itself is not can also come to be or reveal themselves. The for-itself is at the same time a TRANSCEN-DENCE toward the totality of what is, as the ground of any particular being, and a transcendence toward the particular being that it is not. The differentiation between the all and the this, which comes to be as a multiplicity emerges from a unified ground, or as a continuous ground passes into discontinuous figures, is space. The spatializing being is the for-itself, as copresent to the whole and to the this. Thus, space is not a being; it is the unique way in which beings that have no relation can be revealed. It is pure exteriority. The for-itself, through its spatializing of being-in-itself, makes it possible for beings to be because it creates a gap or a nothing as a there within which beings can reveal themselves.

Space, Sartre holds, depends on temporality and on a being whose mode of being is temporalization. Space is not an a priori form of our sensibility; it is the way in which a temporalizing being loses itself ecstatically in order to realize being. Space is not a form precisely because it is nothing, bringing only NE-GATION to the in-itself through the for-itself. This negation brings about dif-ferentiation between the whole and the this, between the discontinuous and the continuous, between the ground and the figures. By denying exteriority to itself and apprehending itself as ecstatic the for-itself spatializes space. Put otherwise, by denying extension to itself and apprehending itself as pure interiority, there is extended being, revealed against the NOTHINGNESS of the for-itself. Such extension, as it is differentiated in relation to the for-itself that detotalizes itself as a totality, thus revealing the totality of the in-itself, is constituted by this differentiation as spatial.

Primary Works

Heidegger, Martin. *The Basic Problems of Phenomenology*. Trans. Albert Hofstadter. Bloomington: Indiana University Press, 1982.

sed cry of an anguished CARE for the things of this world no longer
tes the spiritual turning but a more direct apprehension of a genuinely
al affect.

ough this spiritualization of the ontological difference, Marcel rejoins the
hysics of light in GOOD CONSCIENCE. Yet he was wary of final so-
embedded in conceptual formulas. He resolved to hold the bright prin-
f spiritual plenitude to the discipline of the epithet Tragic WISDOM. The
of the tragic echoes Nietzsche, who, in this invocation, embodies the
ancy of a spirituality mostly distraught, distended, and disturbed and cer-
not available in any easy representation.

ry Works

aev, Nicolai. *The Divine and the Human*. Trans. R. M. French. London: Geoffrey
   Bles, 1949.
l, Gabriel. *Creative Fidelity*. Trans. Robert Rosthal. New York: Farrar, Straus, and
   Giroux, 1964.

ography

on, Haim, and Jochanan Bloch, eds. *Martin Buber: A Centenary Volume*. New York:
   Ktav, 1984.

SUBJECT
Lawrence J. Hatab

---

raditional terms, TRUTH has mainly been restricted to standards of objec-
y, independent of human desires, needs, and aspirations. Descartes and oth-
maximized this criterion by strictly separating subject and OBJECT so that
gs in the WORLD could be purged of human meaning, interest, or inter-
tation and thus be reduced to properties that accord with the mechanistic
ntation of modern science. Existential PHILOSOPHY launched a critique of
ectivist standards of truth. KIERKEGAARD claimed that truth is subjectivity.
begins with the unique personal experiences of individual lives and claims
t philosophy has canceled out such subjectivity by subordinating human ex-
nce to objective universals. He disdains all forms of abstraction applied to
mans, including social and cultural identities, since they pass over the sheer

---

Merleau-Ponty, Maurice. *The Structure of Behavior*. Trans. Alden Fisher. Boston: Beacon
   Press, 1963.

SPIRIT
Stephen Tyman

The concept of spirit came into modern currency through the work of Hegel,
for whom it had been the one absolute ontological category. Yet it was not clear
by the middle of the nineteenth century whether Hegelian spirit was a theistic
or atheistic term. Even in rejection, one had to choose which Hegel one would
react against. Some thinkers' intent was to supply a spiritual want for which the
modernism that Hegel had come to represent was notorious. Others, such as
SARTRE and NIETZSCHE, cast aside much pertaining to spirit. In these instances existentialism is construed as antithetical to the classical issues of RE-
LIGION, which are taken to provide only a thin veneer of comfort and meaning
over the harsh reality of an absurd EXISTENCE. However, even where spirit
is most under attack, the existential response attempts to preserve beneath the
rejected term the deep stratum of subjective LIFE pure and unsullied by the
distortions of conventional religious IDEOLOGY. This spirit of HUMANISM
adds poignancy and complexity to any existential critique of religion.

Existentialist thinkers endeavored to reconnect spiritual doctrine with its experiential core and to explore the possibilities this reveals. This brings the group
of spiritually oriented existentialists into a sometimes precarious proximity with
MYSTICISM, even with gnosticism. The central problem is one of isolating an
experience that is uniquely spiritual and of forging some consistent and repeatable means of access to it. For KIERKEGAARD, spirit represents the ontological dimension of absolute BEING, definitive alike of Creator and creature. The
focus of his interest is the question of how one may, as creature, come to
function in a distinctively spiritual way or, as he put it, to relate absolutely to
the absolute. The problem entails the task of edification, which differentiates
and recenters the activity of spirit in relation to the general morass of human
behavior. The task is rendered difficult by the fact that spirit itself is thinkable
only dialectically. One who seeks out the ways of spirit must brave the paradox.
In *Fear and Trembling* this paradox is described in the account of Abraham's
FAITH following the command to sacrifice Isaac in Genesis. The essay demonstrates the incommensurability of the demands of faith with the resources of
reason, as illustrated dramatically in Abraham's INTENTION, in obedience to

God's command, to sacrifice the son he was nevertheless convinced, by divine promise, would become the father of his seed. Such involves the paradox of the manifest and the unmanifest, for spirit, not originally manifest, seeks to become manifest. Thus, as it comes into realization, spirit is always already what it is not; that is, it is only a shadow or distortion of itself. This prevents the entailments of spirit from being definitively encased by any concept or held in any act of KNOWLEDGE; to think otherwise, Kierkegaard declared, is to yield to the heresy of gnosticism.

BUBER sought access to the spiritual dimension through a God-relation mediated by compassion and interhuman RELATIONS. MYSTERY emerges in the authentic meeting of two selves, in the I–Thou. By acknowledging and standing within this mystery of relationship, one gives sway to the way of existing that is called spiritual. This relationship stands in contrast to the I–it, which is increasingly omnipresent in a technological world, dominated by calculable relationships. This contrast is further developed in *Two Types of Faith*, where spirit is described as completely incalculable, announcing a different kind of intelligibility in human affairs, an intelligibility of the heart.

The exploration of the gnostic connexus in a more solitary setting emerges in the work of BERDYAEV. He is acutely aware of the tensions between the elements of thought and the spiritual dimension, in which and of which he attempts to think. While thought thrives in the medium of concepts, enjoys the clarity brought by their circumscriptive subordination of all to the ideal, and is enjoined by the desire for reasons and grounds, its passive representations can only distort and refract, but not cocreate, a WORLD. Consequently, a slavish adherence to a monolithic rational order is no advantage. Spirit must assert its FREEDOM in the face of any ready-made order it encounters. In so doing, thought brings into play meaning that lies beyond the confines of this limited world, although it simultaneously disrupts the continuities of this life, even to the point of DEATH. Nevertheless, the syntheses of cognition are indispensable for attending to the various dimensions of a spiritual life that remains essentially alien to this order. Thus, spirit announces itself in a perpetual conflict with the conditions of its manifestation.

Berdyaev sees the world as an alien order: the realm of Caesar. He writes that spiritual knowing is divine-human, knowledge neither by reason nor by feeling but by integral Spirit. This spiritual gnosis associates more with the IMAGINATION, symbol, and MYTH than with institutional science. Berdyaev associates this corridor of thought with the primitive notion of the UNCONSCIOUS. But psychological theory has failed to provide an adequate anthropology, being unable to locate at the crux of human CREATIVITY the point of the convergence of the human and the divine. This crux remains a paradox, caught in the irreducible interplay between the finite and the infinite, TIME and the eternal, GOD and humanity. This consideration tells against any existentialism that would be a humanism; for not only is humanity never representable

as complete, but its essential freedom is so far fr[...] logical vacuity of simple self-making that its sou[...] picture of fullness functioning creatively and abund[...] to have the divine image in order to have the hum[...]

But it is not sufficient to identify this core elem[...] the heart of the human enterprise; some measure of [...] structure is required as the leitmotif of any human v[...] cryptic formula for the God–human relation: ''The c[...] which is in humanity as a particular reality.'' Havin[...] fessed that a considerable ambiguity reigns with r[...] Berdyaev tended toward a mysticism not of the quie[...] the active type. He was astute in recognizing how su[...] way into the mainstream of Western European cultu[...] The continuity of a praxis with such extensive unde[...] record of engagement with the world constituted t[...] particularity. Yet, to reach actively back into the orig[...] Godhead, is, at the same time, to dissolve every last [...] and the manifest.

MARCEL, as his thinking matured, used the term '[...] substantive, preferring instead formulations like ''spir[...] Marcel's reticence concerning the use of spirit as [...] stemmed more from his distrust of LANGUAGE than [...] issues or the methods of ONTOLOGY and METAPH[...] writing was to reintroduce the spiritual factor of myste[...] these disciplines. He pursued the spiritual nexus in term[...] human experience, requiring the vigilance of constan[...] nounces itself without entirely coming to presence. Exp[...] tery full of unexplored potentialities. The tendency to f[...] of experience through reifying its relations and articula[...] danger; there seems to be a tendency to seek to have [...] experience.

As for Marcel's commitment to the spirit, he seemed [...] suppleness without loss of resoluteness. What for him [...] the hypostatizing proclamation of spirit as real but, rathe[...] highest calling and capacity in the workings of hope. [...] throughout his writings and was counterposed to the t[...] become an existential theme. Hope, for Marcel, holds [...] makes human illumination possible; accordingly, it revea[...] tive act of spirit. Hope is the affect that emerges from th[...] spirit to its essential calling and hence is, rather than ang[...] logical. He suggested a reading of HEIDEGGER's famou[...] the ONTIC and the ontological, which he suspected Heide[...] let the ontic be called the illumined, and the ontological [...]

specificity of individual experience. Even the cognitive subject found in the writings of Kant is not the personal subject and amounts to another kind of object. Subjective experience is permeated by possibility and thus always exceeds the actuality of objective conditions. Human LIFE is always becoming and unfinished; we directly experience such openness all the TIME; hence, my EXISTENCE cannot be described by the objective analyses of the sciences.

Special categories apply in personal subjectivity: desire, passion, CHOICE, ANXIETY, commitment. None of these categories can be captured by, or reduced to, objective truths and explanations. Kierkegaard is not denying that there is objective truth; he is arguing that human concerns are not and cannot be governed by objective criteria, universal truths, or any other warrants outside of an individual choice to adopt a certain manner of living. The subjective phenomenon of choice displays unstable, precarious, and nonuniversalizable features that belie traditional assumptions about human NATURE and practice. The exclusivity and ambivalence of important life choices will never be amenable to straightforward, objective criteria that claim to organize and resolve indigenous complexities and tensions. In crucial human matters only individual experiences pertain; hence, a significant array of philosophical topics are divorced from objective analysis and compressed into the sphere of subjective orientations. Thus, he initiates a major existential theme: protecting the individual from being subsumed under objectifying forces, which include scientific explanations, metaphysical formulations, social conditions of conformity, and mass consciousness.

SARTRE distinguishes between objects and CONSCIOUSNESS. When discussing the subjectivity of consciousness, he stresses the primacy of the prereflective consciousness in lived experience and action. Consciousness cannot be an object because it shows itself as a perpetual negative relation to actualized conditions, displayed in phenomena such as denial, hope, and IMAGINATION. He accepts the BEING of objects and affirms their correlative role in the makeup of consciousness. Yet he insists on the special features of consciousness that can never be reduced. Consciousness always transcends objective states in its responses to the world—such as anticipation, refusal, interpretation, innovation. Sartre claims that existence precedes ESSENCE: nothing prior to the existence of a PERSON can define it prior to the individual's choice to live a certain way. Neither a divine mind nor scientific laws nor material or social conditions determine in advance what a human being is. The being of human consciousness is an intrinsic negativity, a NOTHINGNESS that cannot be fixed or universalized. The correlate of nothingness is the radical FREEDOM of consciousness, its open PROJECT to create meaning and resist forces of objectification. Full RESPONSIBILITY for human existence is on the subject. Consciousness is fundamentally free: since there is no fixed human nature, persons create themselves through their choices. Humans are not determined by extraconscious conditions such as biochemical processes, environmental forces, or unconscious drives. A Kantian rational freedom is superseded by a wide-open process of meaning-making that is not grounded in, or answerable to, rational constructs or faculties.

HEIDEGGER agrees that modern objectivism is an inadequate ONTOLOGY and that human existence exhibits a negative TRANSCENDENCE that continually exceeds completed states of actuality. He wants to explore a notion of Being that does not traffic in bifurcated conceptions of subject and object—be it the scientific model that privileges objectivity or the existentialist who privileges subjectivity. He seeks to undermine objective ontologies, but not by turning to the human sphere, subjectivity, or consciousness. DASEIN is, indeed, connected with human existence. Dasein is the opening to the meaning of Being and the opening of Being as a process of disclosure, of coming to presence out of concealment. The meaning of the world is shown through Dasein's CARE. Dasein cares about the world while recognizing the radical finitude of being shown in being-toward-death. Since Being is not a strictly positive condition, it cannot be grounded in any condition or state of being—including consciousness or subjectivity.

Though departing from objectivism, Heidegger does not want to jump to the other side and rest with a counterobjective, existential subjectivity, because even existential subjectivity concedes too much to the modern subject–object binary that split apart existential concerns and world conditions into disparate spheres of human meaning and neutral objects. An emphasis on the existential subject is flawed: things in the world need rescuing from objectification, too. Nature and other things we encounter have a preobjective meaning that modern science and rationality conceal. Hence, poetical language opens up rich dimensions of the world. Beings are disclosed to Dasein, not projected by Dasein. Dasein is thrown into the world and is immersed in circumstances and a historical heritage. In Descartes' writings the conscious MIND becomes the grounding subjectum; subsequently, the subject has been associated with the human self. Heidegger seeks to avoid all groundings of Being, even if such are associated with human thought and experience. Even existential subjectivity suggests, for Heidegger, a grounding reminiscent of the modern subjectum, and that cannot do justice to world experiences.

Primary Works

Heidegger, Martin. *Basic Writings*. Ed. David Farrell Krell. New York: Harper and Row, 1977.
Kierkegaard, Søren. *The Concept of Anxiety*. Trans. Reider Thomte. Princeton: Princeton University Press, 1980.

Bibliography

Lauer, Quentin. *The Triumph of Subjectivity*. New York: Fordham University Press, 1958.

SUICIDE
Stuart Charme

Suicide, the willful termination of one's LIFE, has been an important concern for existentialists; ordinarily, it reflects a decision that one's own life or human life in general is not worth living. CAMUS' *The Myth of Sisyphus* claims that suicide represents the single most serious, important, and urgent philosophical question, which must be answered before any other question is considered. MARCEL suggests that contemplating the possibility of suicide represents the beginning of any real metaphysical thinking, since the FREEDOM to kill oneself forces one to confront the reality of human EXISTENCE. In most cases, the temptation to exercise this freedom is derived from ANGUISH and despair. These feelings or MOODS may be a response to the collapse of one's systems of meaning and the inability to feel at home in the universe. Though most existentialists insist on the absence of any permanent or fixed meaning that might justify human life or alleviate despair, they do not recognize suicide as an appropriate response to the radical absurdity of life. Lack of justification for one's life does not mean that it is not worth living. Rather, what is needed in the face of life's pain and suffering is a heroic commitment to affirm one's life and to engage in the difficult task of creating meaning for it.

DOSTOYEVSKY's novel *The Possessed* presents the character Kirillov. Rather than being led to suicide out of despair, Kirillov concludes that suicide is the ultimate expression of freedom in a world where GOD does not exist. The absence of transcendent ethical codes means that all people have become gods with absolute control over their own lives or DEATHS. In suicide, Kirillov attempts to affirm the ability of humans to conquer their FEAR of suffering and death as well as their fear of God's judgment in an afterlife. NIETZSCHE, too, stressed the importance of mastering one's fear of death by actually willing one's death, but ZARATHUSTRA's teaching about voluntary death is not an inducement to suicide. One is liberated from death when one embraces it as a natural ending to the life one has personally created. Suicide, on the contrary, is a sign of weakness and failure to live passionately and creatively. CHRISTIANITY has encouraged this no-saying attitude toward life by institutionalizing suicide through its idealization of martyrdom and asceticism. Nietzsche's idea of eternal recurrence makes it imperative to joyfully redeem one's life by giving it a meaning that is worth reliving endlessly.

Though Kirillov may have been right that suicide offers the thrill of human freedom's ultimate expression, SARTRE points out that this violent turn of freedom against itself is an attempt to destroy freedom by escaping into the existence of an OBJECT or thing. The fallacy of suicide is that it undermines the temporal quality of human existence. The meaning or VALUE we attribute to the events and experiences in our lives is always open to revision in the future. But suicide cuts off the very future that would give meaning to this life. Someone who survives a suicide attempt may later decide that the choice of suicide was a mistake or an act of cowardice and thereby begin to reclaim the will to live. Or one may decide to attempt suicide again. The meaning of the successful suicide's life is no longer open to one's revision. It has been handed over to the others who remain alive.

MARCEL contrasts suicide, which represents a refusal to find meaning or hope in life, with self-sacrifice or martyrdom, in which one gives up one's life for something regarded as having greater meaning or value. He believed that such ultimate sacrifice is rooted in hope and bestows fulfillment on a life in the moment that one gives one's life away. Although Sartre regards suicide as a manifestation of BAD FAITH, grounded in an attempt to permanently escape the anguish of freedom and an indeterminate future, nonetheless, in extreme situations such as may arise in war, he acknowledges that an authentic life may end in suicide if that is the only way to avoid torture and the possibility of betraying one's cause or comrades. There may be SITUATIONS where all possible actions to transform an oppressive situation have been so radically blocked that suicide represents the only remaining form of protest and revolt.

Primary Works

Dostoyevsky, Fyodor. *The Possessed.* Trans. Constance Garnett. Greenwich, CT: Fawcett, 1966.
Sartre, Jean-Paul. *Existentialism and Humanism.* Trans. Philip Mairet. London: Methuen, 1973.

SUPERMAN
Laurence Lampert

The term "superman" was used by NIETZSCHE in *Thus Spoke Zarathustra*. In German, it is *Ubermensch*, also translated as "overman." The term acquired connotations that are very different from Nietzsche's sense and that played no part in his views. It was one of Nietzsche's words for a high human type with a noble historic mission and had a strictly limited range in his writings. It appears as a central notion only in the first two parts of *Thus Spoke Zarathustra*. There, the superman is proclaimed as a future teacher whose way is to be prepared by ZARATHUSTRA and his followers. Just what his teaching will be cannot be said beyond the assurance that it will be loyal to the Earth. As the drama of the book unfolds, Zarathustra becomes the heralded teacher by discovering and embracing the WILL to POWER and eternal return. Nietzsche ceased to use the term after *Thus Spoke Zarathustra*, though he did not abandon what it stood for: the highest human spirituality and spiritedness marked by a willingness to take RESPONSIBILITY for a comprehensive interpretation of things.

Bibliography

Lampert, Laurence. *Nietzsche's Teaching: An Interpretation of "Thus Spoke Zarathustra."* New Haven, CT: Yale University Press, 1986.

TELEOLOGY
Gail Weiss

Teleology might seem to be opposed to existential thought because it connotes the EXISTENCE of a final purpose or end. Yet, as religious existentialists have demonstrated, to accept a teleological conception of existence is not incompatible with the claim that humans are free to choose their existence. A question is raised at the outset of KIERKEGAARD's *Fear and Trembling*: Is there a Teleological Suspension of the Ethical? Is it possible that GOD, who provided us with commandments that define an ethical existence, could also command us to set those commandments aside for a higher purpose? He considers Abraham's being asked by God to sacrifice his son Isaac as a paradigmatic example of this paradox. Why would God command Abraham to perform such an unethical act? How could Abraham, as an ethical individual who loves his son more than his own LIFE, be willing to act as God requested? Why has Abraham's willingness to sacrifice Isaac confirmed his place in HISTORY as the father of FAITH, rather than relegating Abraham to the label of attempted murderer? If there is no teleological suspension of the ethical realm, then Abraham was wrong to do what God requested; he should have refused to sacrifice Isaac. Indeed, there is no rational justification for the sacrifice of Isaac; God's request violates the ethical laws that God has set forth. Moreover, Abraham's test of faith can be a test only for one who exists as an ethical individual, who accepts and lives by the universal precepts that define the ethical realm. The solution to this paradox is no real solution because the paradox is preserved and affirmed as faith.

Through posing and answering the question, Is there a teleological suspension of the ethical?, Kierkegaard provides a basis for distinguishing between a violation of the ethical for aesthetic or unethical reasons and a suspension of the ethical realm for the sake of a personal relationship with God. To claim that a personal relationship with God is the ultimate goal of human existence, a goal that can be achieved only in and through faith, in no way implies that one is unable to make CHOICES or lacks FREEDOM. Yet there is no recipe for faith; it is not always possible for one knight of faith to recognize another knight of faith. The existential movement toward God is taken in FEAR and trembling, and the outcome is always uncertain. There is no final outcome since one's commitment to God must be renewed again and again; one can never rest on the laurels of previous spiritual achievements but must strive to intensify one's relationship with God. The challenge of faith is to remain absolutely committed to obey God unconditionally without being able to justify that commitment or even to rationalize the sacrifices required. Abraham's willingness to set aside the ethical laws for God is the most individuating moment of his existence. By passionately affirming a higher purpose to existence than the ethical and by choosing the path of faith without knowing what further sacrifices it may require, he enters into a direct relationship with God. To choose God does not mean that one has answers to the basic existential questions. As Kierkegaard indicates, it is fruitless for Abraham to ask, Why me? Such a questioning would vitiate the absolute character of his faith. Although God's omniscience may allow God to foresee where my choices will lead, I must choose either the uncertain path of faith or the equally uncertain path that leads away from God.

BUBER believes that God provides all of creation with a final end or purpose, although we are unable to know with certainty what that purpose is. To have unconditional faith means to accept God as both source and end of all existence without questioning God's WISDOM. Yet, only by spontaneously entering into an I–Thou relationship with another BEING can God's presence be discerned. The I–Thou relationship hallows an individual's life; it is the way in which we allow God to enter our lives. Hence, individualization can never be the goal of human existence. Movement toward God must always involve a movement toward the WORLD and an affirmation of COMMUNITY. The teleological dimension of human existence involves making oneself open to participation in I–Thou relationships; doing so will anchor one more firmly in existence and bring one ever closer to God. These relationships, moreover, cannot be planned in advance but must be spontaneously entered into. No one of the parties in that relationship can determine if, when, where, and how it may occur.

Primary Work

Buber, Martin. *Between Man and Man*. Trans. Ronald Gregor Smith. New York: Macmillan, 1965.

Bibliography

Perkins, Robert L, ed. *Fear and Trembling* and *Repetition: Volume 6 of International Kierkegaard Commentary*. Macon, GA: Mercer University Press, 1993.

THEOLOGY
Thomas B. Ommen

In the most comprehensive sense, theology means an attempt to think and speak about GOD. Ordinary LANGUAGE about God is not theology, which must include critical and reflective thought. Yet, many philosophers who have critically reflected on the problem of God would not classify their work as theology. The key issue is whether a thinker reflects critically on God from within a particular COMMUNITY of FAITH or speaks from a more external, independent standpoint. MARCEL was a believing Catholic but did not want to be considered a theologian. He did not see his work as a justification of the TRUTH of theological claims. The same is true of UNAMUNO and BERDYAEV. Both were Christian believers but strove to maintain their independence from any particular confessional stance. In contrast, BULTMANN and TILLICH speak from and to a specific community of faith; they attempt the justification of particular religious claims, and they describe their work as theology. BUBER did not want to be called a theologian, in part, because the label implied an objectifying and logical stance over against God. But Buber spoke from his Jewish tradition. Some view him as a theological embodiment of that tradition. Existentialist theologians are united in the protest against abstract essentialist forms of PHILOSOPHY and theology that inadequately capture the dynamics of human LIFE. They formulate interpretations of basic religious notions such as God, SIN, and REDEMPTION. These religious realities are reinterpreted in existential terms to make them more relevant to contemporary life.

The twofold movement of theology between SITUATION and tradition was characterized by Tillich as the method of theological correlation. Theology uses existential categories to interpret the situation, the basic CHARACTER of human self-understanding in any historical period. This situation can be illuminated in a number of ways, but existentialist philosophy and PSYCHOLOGY were for Tillich particularly helpful. An analysis of the situation uncovers questions to which religious tradition can relate. Philosophy might, for example, highlight the ANXIETY that marks the human condition, and the theologian can then try to show that religious life offers ways of articulating and overcoming that anxiety. Tillich is identified with the notion of theology as correlation, but analogous PERCEPTIONS can be found in the work of other theologians. Bultmann found in existentialism the appropriate concepts for characterizing the structure of human self-understanding and for interpreting in nonmythological terms the biblical proclamation.

Existentialist theologies challenge objectifying and abstract modes of thought. For existential thinkers, life and thought are inextricably related. Truth must be apprehended on an inner, personal level. KNOWLEDGE properly terminates in the question of the meaning of that knowledge for the individual knower. They suspect grand conceptual schemes unrelated to the concreteness of life, hence, KIERKEGAARD's attack on the impersonality of Hegel's idealism. For Kierkegaard, TRUTH was not so much an object of thought as a property of particular relationships. Christian truth was constituted by inwardness; an objective knowledge of the truth of CHRISTIANITY was untruth. For Buber, only in the I–Thou relationship are the whole person involved, and the fullness of truth made accessible. The dominance of the I–It, of controlling and manipulating knowledge, has been a temptation of our scientific age. Existentialism appealed to Tillich because of its powerful protest against the power of controlling knowledge and the mechanical and objectified world to which it has led. REVELATION, for Tillich and Bultmann, never comes in the form of objective knowledge or as a cosmic PROCESS that takes place outside faith. Revelation is an event in the experience of the believer, communicated especially by the oral word of proclamation. One can speak about revelation only on the basis of a deep personal relationship. Bultmann distinguished such understanding from a theoretical or existential understanding. One might develop a theoretical understanding of the notion of revelation, but this would be different from an inner, personal experience of revelation.

If life cannot properly be treated in objective terms, this is even more the case with God. Existentialists contrast the God of the philosophers with the God of faith. God is reached not through reason but through faith, although Tillich tried to translate this insight into a new form of ONTOLOGY. For Kierkegaard, God is a SUBJECT and therefore exists only for the individual in a subjective, personal relationship. God cannot be related to directly, and this makes divine reality obscure from a rational point of view. If God were there like a giant green bird in a tree, belief in God would be easier. For Buber the Eternal Thou cannot by its NATURE become an It. There is a close connection between the relationship to God and the between that emerges in human dialogue. Dialogue is not merely an aspect of human existence but the way a PERSON comes to the fullness of authentic being. Also, in each Thou we address the Eternal Thou.

Thinking of God as an OBJECT alongside other objects, albeit the highest objects, was, for Tillich, the mistake of supernaturalism. At the other extreme, naturalism identified God with ESSENCE or POWER of the universe. Tillich sought a position between these extremes. God is the ground or depth of BEING. If God is reduced to an object, he ceases to be God. For Bultmann objectification occurs in what he called MYTH. God's acts are mythically portrayed as objective occurrences in SPACE and TIME. Bultmann found such an objectification of the divine at the center of New Testament proclamation and argued for demythologization. Myth must be interpreted in terms of the self-understanding it expresses; its real intention is to reveal the authentic reality of humans. Acts of God are never there in HISTORY but occur in the inner life of the believer. They are invisible to the nonbelieving, secular eye. Efforts to make God objective reflect the sinful attempt to attain security in the relationship to the world and to God and thus to avoid the LEAP of faith and the confrontation with paradox that it entails.

Buber distinguished his version of existentialism from that of SARTRE at this point: RELIGION is not something that can be rebelled against and then left behind. It is a permanent feature of human existence. AUTHENTICITY cannot be secured by creative FREEDOM alone; we are established by a power outside ourselves. Christian theologians generally portray this human sense of incompleteness as a consequence of the Fall. The Fall refers not to an actual event in time but, as Tillich puts it, to the pervasive sense of an ontological gap between human existence and human essence. We are not what we should be, and there seems to be no finite power that can make us whole. Only those who have experienced the shock of transitoriness, the threat of nonbeing, can understand what the notion of God means. The tragic bondage of estranged existence pushes humans to search for that which transcends existence, although it appears within existence. For Bultmann, anxiety is a fundamental experience aroused by the sense of being thrown into a WORLD in which we are not at home. We normally respond to anxiety by trying to achieve a sense of security. But anxiety has no finite resolution. The situation cannot be overcome by an act of resolve or courage. Anxiety points humans toward God. Through Christ, humans are delivered not only from the illusions of worldly, self-actualized security but from the anxiety produced by the anticipation of DEATH.

The turn to tradition, particularly in its textual forms, has generated existential methods of interpretation. The interpretation of religious tradition has been prompted, in part, by what Buber called the eclipse of God. Christian existential theologians have sought new hermeneutical strategies for formulating key themes. Tillich maintains that religious realities like sin and judgment have become vacuous and irrelevant. They have not lost their truth, but their expressive power has dimmed. They can be regained only if they are reinterpreted using the insights into the human condition that existentialism provides. With such a reading, texts like Job and Ecclesiastes might appear in a new, more illuminating light. For Bultmann, the interpreter of Scripture must be open to the claim of the text, willing to hear it as a summons to a new self-understanding. History is more than a set of objective facts; it is an event in the life-experience of the interpreter. A personal relationship to history is a necessary presupposition of historical understanding when serious LITERATURE like Scripture is the focus of interpretation. Reflective understanding involves a clarification of the interpreter's preunderstanding of the meaning of existence.

Thus, existentialist thinkers provided a conceptuality for interpreting both the nature of human existence and key symbols of religious tradition. A way of approaching God has been sought that avoids the distortions of objectifying ways of thinking. Existentialist interpretations of basic religious symbols have tried to locate a self-understanding in them that is accessible to our nonmythological age.

Primary Works

Bultmann, Rudolf. *History and Eschatology*. New York: Harper and Row, 1957.
Tillich, Paul. *Systematic Theology*. Vols. 1–3. Chicago: University of Chicago Press, 1951–1963.

Bibliography

Clayton, John P. *The Concept of Correlation: Paul Tillich and the Possibility of Mediating Theology*. New York: De Gruyter, 1980.

THEY
John Protevi

The "They" is a term in HEIDEGGER's philosophy denoting the anonymity of the everyday being of DASEIN. No one maintains his or her self in everydayness but goes along doing and thinking what they say is to be done and thought. In *Being and Time*, Heidegger asks, Who is that being that is in the way of BEING-IN-THE-WORLD? The analysis proceeds by way of the everyday BEING of Dasein, the way it is proximally and for the most part. The self that remains identical beneath changing experiences is a thing present-at-hand,

an answer inadequate to the investigation of the Being of Dasein. Perhaps everyday Dasein is precisely not its own self. The answer is that the who of everyday
Dasein is the they. Heidegger lists several traits of the relation of Dasein to the
others in the they. Dasein is subjected to the others in their averageness, which
levels down the possibilities of Being. This handing over of RESPONSIBILITY
for everyday decisions disburdens Dasein and creates a vicious circle: it more
easily accommodates itself to the they. The they is an existential structure of
Dasein, a primordial phenomenon of its Being. Since the they-self concerns itself
with the public world according to the categories of a sedimented ONTOLOGY,
renewing the question of the sense of Being entails a turning from the inauthenticity of the they-self to the authentic self, which takes responsibility for its
thoughts, words, and deeds.

Bibliography

Dreyfus, Hubert L., and Harrison Hall, eds. *Heidegger: A Critical Reader*. Oxford: Basil
    Blackwell, 1992.

THROWNNESS
John Protevi

Throwness in HEIDEGGER's analysis of DASEIN in *Being and Time* denotes
the FACTICITY of being handed-over. It is the fact that Dasein does not choose
to be yet nonetheless is, without fully understanding the origin of its EXIS-
TENCE or its ultimate destination. In this involuntary ignorance Dasein experiences its existence as a task that is revealed in moodfulness. Dasein is as
being-attuned, as always in one MOOD or another, even if in bored everydayness. This finding oneself in a mood reveals Dasein's BEING as a task, even
though the they-self seeks to avoid this recognition by falling into absorption
with the things of the WORLD. This very absorbing evading serves to reveal
the there and Dasein as being there. Thus, in throwness we are handed over
to our Being as a task, as something we must do, although the whence and
wherefore of this being-handed-over remain hidden. Facticity is the CHAR-
ACTER of our Being as something to which we are handed over. Hence, facticity is something that must be taken over: one must achieve the proper
RELATION to throwness. The improper relation is falling, being lost in the
publicness of the THEY. Proper, authentic relating to throwness is resolute open-

ness, the mood that runs forward to the point of view of one's own DEATH, thereby revealing the situation in all its starkness and freeing Dasein to realize its relation to others with whom it shares the situation.

Bibliography

Sallis, John, ed. *Radical Phenomenology: Essays in Honor of Martin Heidegger*. Atlantic Highlands, NJ: Humanities Press, 1978.

PAUL TILLICH
(1886–1965)
Jeff Owen Prudhomme

Paul Tillich was born in Starzeddel, Germany (now part of Poland). His father was a Lutheran pastor. He attended the universities of Berlin, Tübingen, and Halle, where he wrote a dissertation on Schelling and received his licentiate in THEOLOGY. He wrote a second dissertation on Schelling for his doctorate of PHILOSOPHY from the University of Breslau. After ordination he undertook pastoral service in a working-class section of Berlin. He served as an army chaplain in World War I. From 1919 to 1924 he was privatdocent at the University of Berlin. He taught briefly at Marburg and then at Dresden and Leipzig before becoming professor of philosophy and cofounder of the Institute of Social Research at Frankfurt in 1929. After a brief first marriage, Tillich remarried and had two children. In 1933 he was suspended by the Nazi government. He was allowed to leave the country for a temporary position arranged by Union Theological Seminary and Columbia University. Tillich remained in the United States and became a citizen. This transition initially slowed his work, as it forced a restatement of his thought in a new LANGUAGE and intellectual context.

Tillich chose the motif of being "on the boundary" to organize his autobiography of that name, as his LIFE and thought moved between disparate realms: between his attraction to NATURE and his attraction to urban life, between the cultural heritage of his homeland and the greater openness of his adopted land, between his ecclesiastical affiliations and his appreciation of culture. His thought sought to navigate between theology and philosophy, RELIGION and culture, and to chart their intersection. Such is reflected in its apologetic and systematic CHARACTER. His theology was apologetic in the sense of being open to the existential SITUATION and in the way it spoke to this situation. His thought was systematic not solely in building systems but also in the way he faced methodological issues confronting theology, in his consistent methodical procedure, and in his treatment of issues in cognizance of their interconnection within an overarching context.

Writing during the 1920s and 1930s on the PHILOSOPHY OF RELIGION, Tillich describes religion as a pure state of being-grasped by the unconditioned. FAITH is the orientation toward the unconditioned that is effective in all functions of the human SPIRIT. Faith is not a state of being grasped or overwhelmed by a particular thing or state of affairs, by any conditioned reality, but by that which grants BEING to any particular being, by that which transcends every conditioned thing or state of affairs—the unconditioned. Tillich immediately confronts the predicament of reflection upon religion: religion intends the unconditional, yet reflection upon religion makes this intention relative and thereby treats the unconditional as conditional. In the philosophy of religion reflection treats an OBJECT that strives not to be an object of philosophy, an object that claims to be elevated above philosophy. If philosophy ignores this resistance on the part of religion, it loses the object it intended to grasp. Yet if it acquiesces, it obviates its own justification as philosophy of religion and endangers the justification of all reflection: if there is an area closed off to philosophy, then philosophy could not draw the boundaries between this and other areas of reflection.

In response to this predicament, Tillich appeals to what he calls the systematic use of paradox. Every assertion, by saying something about something, involves the schema of SUBJECT and object, which is the form of conditioned being. Thus, in order to speak of the unconditioned, of what is beyond the subject–object structure, assertions about the unconditioned must use the form of assertion in a way that exposes its very inadequacy—they must use the form of systematic paradox. Every assertion about GOD takes the form of an objective assertion but can be true only as a paradoxical assertion. A positive paradox marks the opening of the religious to philosophical reflection, for it means that philosophy of religion is not based primarily upon a critical decision about the nature of religion but upon the experienced paradox of the irruption of the unconditional into the finite structure of being. This relationship entails that there is a critical moment intrinsic to faith, a critical moment against the conditioned reality through which the unconditioned is experienced. This critical moment offers a validation of doubt that is beyond any simple NEGATION of faith.

In *Dynamics of Faith*, Tillich defines faith as the state of being ultimately concerned. The term ''concern'' has both a subjective and an objective meaning; concern can signify both an act of the self (the act of caring) and the object intended in that act (the object of concern). In the term ''ultimate concern,'' Tillich sees these two sides to be united: faith is both the centered act of the self and the referent of this act, the ultimate or unconditioned itself. Faith, as a centered act of the self, cannot properly be confined to any one aspect or mode of being of the self or their summation; it is operative in all functions of spirit and is not reducible to any one in particular. If faith is no longer seen as a cognitive endeavor, then cognitive uncertainty or doubt cannot stand as an opponent to faith. Faith entails the participation of the whole self in ultimate concern and thus does not deal with theoretical certitude about a given or even probable state of affairs but with existential certitude about the ultimacy of one's ultimate concern. It is existential doubt, as the doubt concerning the very meaning of one's EXISTENCE—in distinction from scientific-methodological doubt and skepticism—which is implied in faith. Such doubt exposes the risk present in faith, yet it does not represent an annulment of faith. Through courage, faith can accept the risk inherent in itself as ultimate concern.

In *The Courage to Be* Tillich presents an analysis of three different types of ANXIETY: of fate and DEATH, of GUILT and condemnation, and of emptiness and meaninglessness. He interprets three epochs of human HISTORY in terms of the predominance of one type of anxiety. In our modern age, anxiety of meaninglessness predominates: the awareness of the threat of the loss of all meaning. Such a threat of radical existential doubt would seem to undo the very possibility of faith, for any concrete reality in which one finds ultimate meaning could be dislodged in its certitude by the despair of meaninglessness. Tillich's response is absolute faith, which does not seek to avoid the anxiety of meaninglessness but rather accepts this despair. It is the acceptance of oneself as accepted not by anyone or anything in particular and despite one's very despair about the meaning of this acceptance. Such faith is absolute in the literal sense of being disconnected from any finite, conditioned reality—for any such concrete reality is dislodged in its claim to ultimate meaning by the radicalness of the despair of meaninglessness. The concept of God that corresponds to absolute faith is the concept of the God beyond or above God, beyond the disappearance of any particular deity in the anxiety of doubt. For such a God there can be no concrete realization in a symbol; nevertheless, absolute faith is the state of being grasped by the God beyond God, who is the source of the most extreme form of the courage to be.

REVELATION designates the way the unconditioned, which, as such as remains concealed, is given in the religious act. Revelation occurs upon natural things or events that become bearers of revelation—or symbols. Symbols point beyond themselves toward something else; they participate in the reality they intend. In contrast to signs, the connection of symbol to referent is not established by convention. Symbols are rooted in the LIFE of a COMMUNITY and are capable of opening up dimensions of the WORLD and possibilities of our selfhood of which we were not previously aware. Religious symbols are characterized by their referent, which is a matter of ultimate concern, the unconditioned. Religious symbols represent, or give concrete, objective form to, that which transcends ultimately every such representation or objectification.

Tillich addresses the truth of religious symbols through subjective and objective criteria. The subjective or pragmatic criterion asks whether the symbol is able to express an ultimate concern for someone. The objective criterion asks whether the ultimate intended in the symbol is the ultimate. This criterion expresses the self-critical principle in religious symbols and counteracts the idolatrous tendency to elevate the finite, conditioned, symbolic material to the level of ultimacy itself. Thus, the most true symbol would be the most radically self-negating, which recognizes the conditional status of its own materiality and denies its ability to represent the unconditioned—and so points the more clearly to the unconditioned.

Tillich's major English-language work is his three-volume *Systematic Theology*; this is one of several systems. His earlier *System der Wissenschaften* offers a comprehensive presentation of the sciences and situates theology within this context. He divides the sciences as (1) sciences of thought or ideal sciences such as mathematics and logic, (2) sciences of being or empirical sciences such as physics and psychology, (3) sciences of spirit such as the humanities. Norms, as the synthesis of formal principles and material content, provide an indication of the standpoint of the thinker, an indication that is required of the human sciences. The object of the sciences of spirit is the self either as it receives reality or as it shapes reality. METAPHYSICS seeks the unconditioned basis of the conditional forms of the theoretical sphere, and ETHICS seeks the unconditioned in the practical. Theology enters into this scheme by virtue of the distinction of the two possible attitudes of the sciences of spirit: theonomy, direction toward the unconditioned for the sake of the unconditioned; and autonomy, direction toward the unconditioned for the sake of providing a foundation for the conditioned. In the broadest sense, one could speak of theology as theonomous metaphysics and theonomous ethics, not as distinct sciences alongside others but as a different attitude within the same scientific endeavor.

The hallmark of *Systematic Theology* is its method of correlating the ontological and the religious, which reflects Tillich's exposure to HEIDEGGER. The method of correlation proposes to analyze the human situation in order to expose the questions implicit there and then to interpret religious symbols insofar as they respond to these questions. Correlation entails the reciprocal illumination of the philosophical and the religious without equating them or reducing one to the other. It interprets the content of faith through the mutual interdependence of existential questions and theological answers. This interdependence means that the questioning is not silenced or stilled, for the answers make sense only in terms of the questions, and the questions drive toward their answers. *Systematic Theology* proceeds by elaborating, through existential-ontological analysis, the questions implied by the human condition and then shows how Christian religious symbols respond to these questions. The basic question can be put as the question of Being. Hence, each volume develops the correlation in terms of a distinct moment of the question of Being. The first volume correlates the question of the ground of the self-world structure with the symbol of God. The second correlates the quest to be anew amid existential estrangement with the symbol of Jesus as the Christ, who, as someone not estranged while yet living under the conditions of estrangement, is able to overcome that estrangement. The third volume correlates the quest for essential being amid the ambiguous mixture of ESSENCE and existence in life with the symbols of the divine Spirit, the Kingdom of God, and Eternal Life.

System der Wissenschaften identifies ethics as the correlative endeavor to metaphysics on the part of practical reason; ethics unites the formal aspects of law with the content expressed in communal solidarity as it seeks the unconditioned in action. There can be theological ethics only insofar as one posits an unresolvable conflict between autonomy and theonomy. Theonomous ethics do not represent a separate division of ethics in relation to a particular religious confession but, rather, ethics undertaken with the theonomous attitude. In later writings, Tillich describes the essence of the ethical as the inherently religious task of actively being and becoming a fully centered self in a community. The religious dimension of the moral imperative, as the command to be the self one most truly is, lies in its unconditional character. This command exposes the split between our actual and essential selfhood but cannot heal this rift. Grace, the acceptance of one's essential selfhood as an unearned gift, in at least a fragmentary way reunifies the self and constitutes the religious or transmoral dimension in moral motivation. The transmoral conscience recognizes the motivational insufficiency of the moral imperative and accepts that it must break with any formal legalism by following the principle of LOVE in unity with a sense of the right TIME. In so doing, the transmoral CONSCIENCE aims to fulfill the essence of MORALITY by reconstituting it on a higher level, yet it faces the risk of degenerating into a form of anomie.

Tillich's political writings, which, in part, led to his suspension from his professorship by the Nazi government, are characterized by his espousal of religious socialism and by the continuing affinity with ontological concerns. Religious socialism was Tillich's response to his sense of the kairos in post–World War I Germany. The awareness of the kairos is the sense that the moment is pregnant with possibility, a possibility of unconditional significance and a possibility for which one must be open as to a demand and promise. This sense of the fullness of time is combined with the notion of the demonic, as a creative, yet ultimately form-destroying, expression of the unconditioned. The new possibility demanded by the situation of that time was religious socialism, the reinterpretation of socialism in terms of theonomy and the awareness of the kairos. Tillich did not seek to connect socialism to a church, nor did he connect Christian religious symbols to specific policies or parties but rather sought to grasp and interpret the theonomous or unconditional element in the current political situation. Religious socialism offered a means of resistance to the destructive tendencies of capitalism and nationalism. He did not see religious socialism as a viable possibility in America, nor did he so clearly again give a reading of the kairos. He did remain politically active.

Tillich's proposal to interpret the social-political realities of his time from the point of view of theonomy connects to his theological interpretation of culture. He holds that the unconditioned is equally the foundation of both religion and culture and thus can come to expression in two forms—directly in a religious form or indirectly in a cultural form. Consequently, the unconditioned can be interpreted in both a church theology as well as a culture theology. Both religion and culture use conditioned cultural forms to express the unconditioned, but the intention of religion is the unconditioned, whereas culture intends those conditioned forms themselves: culture is religious in its import or substance, but not in its intention, whereas religion is cultural in its form but not in its intention. Tillich distinguishes the depth content, or the unconditional significance, from the form and the surface content, through which the import or what is depicted comes to expression. He envisioned an interdependence of ecclesiastical theology and theology of culture. Church theology tends toward irrelevance and antiquarianism as it clings to past cultural forms that may express the unconditioned to only a small religious community. Cultural theology has contemporaneity and immediate relevance that allow it to address a larger community, yet it tends toward faddishness. Ecclesiastical theology can thus give cultural theology the normative viewpoint to resist being swept up in the latest fads, and the theology of culture can keep church theology open to the present situation in its fullness.

In summary, Tillich conceived of theology in a universal manner, not tied to a religious community, both in the way he saw religious symbols as capable of responding to existential-ontological questions and in the way he sought the theonomous depth of secular culture. His phenomenological approach to the essence of religion and his manner of addressing existential concerns with a sense of their timely and historical character enabled him to appeal to a contemporary audience of broad intellectual interests.

Primary Works

Tillich, Paul. *The Courage to Be*. New Haven, CT: Yale University Press, 1952.
———. *Morality and Beyond*. New York: Harper and Row, 1963.
———. *Systematic Theology*. Vols. 1–3. Chicago: University of Chicago Press, 1951–1963.

Bibliography

Adams, James Luther. *Paul Tillich's Philosophy of Culture, Science and Religion*. New York: Harper and Row, 1965.

TIME
Phyllis Kenevan

Time is crucial to understanding an existentialist account of both self and WORLD. Even though there is a common focus on inner time, there are significant differences. KIERKEGAARD combines finite, horizontal temporality with vertical, spiritual ETERNITY, linked to the incarnation of Jesus. NIETZSCHE introduces a concept of eternal return. HEIDEGGER and SARTRE concur in finding the essential character of human EXISTENCE to be an ekstatic, temporalizing PROCESS.

Kierkegaard describes finite, human BEING as existence, in contrast to GOD's being as eternity, signifying the incommensurable difference between human and divine. The self is a structural synthesis of possibility and necessity rooted in the temporal moments of future and past. Although humans are confined to temporal existence, the hope of eternal LIFE is found in time. Because existence is eternity in time, an either-or choice becomes crucial. In eternity there is no either-or. But with the eternal in time and the FREEDOM to choose, human existence is characterized by the ANGUISH of existential CHOICE, for along with CONTINGENCY, temporality, and change, human life is also SPIRIT and so destined for eternity. Since the eternal is immanent in the temporal order, it has to be confronted in time through an act of FAITH, which is itself a temporal event. The LEAP of faith is faith in a paradoxical historical event, the incarnation, which is a synthesis of time and eternity. Faith in this paradox makes the believer contemporaneous with Christ, a temporal, historical act that has eternal import. Though temporal and transient, the instant of faith is decisive. Kierkegaard calls it the fullness of time, a moment in which time and eternity touch one another. The instant posits the temporal, where time intersects eternity, and eternity, permeates time.

In the moment of incarnation, God, the eternal, becomes temporal; in the moment of faith, the human, temporal individual becomes eternal. The incarnation makes the eternal historical, and the historical eternal. The moment of God's incarnation is not an ordinary historical event; it is an eternal or absolute fact. Thus, time and eternity touch, and the temporal becomes permeated with eternity. Only through this RELATION with God does the individual become an authentic temporal self. Kierkegaard describes three different positions in the gradual movement toward greater accentuation of the eternal. The lowest stage is Paganism, an imperfect form, where the temporal itself has little meaning, and the eternal is conceived as an abstraction. In JUDAISM, there is recognition of a TRANSCENDENCE above and beyond the temporal order, but PERCEP-

TION of eternity remains partially abstract. In CHRISTIANITY the highest stage is reached: eternity enters HISTORY, and time and decisions in time acquire infinite weight for the individual. Doubt can be ended only by an individual's act of WILL. KNOWLEDGE is of no use, since the question is how, as an existing individual, one relates to the Absolute.

The problem of BELIEF is therefore not epistemological but a problem of relationship between the Eternal God and the temporal human. Psychologically, one experiences time according to the mode of existence one has chosen, differentiated by Kierkegaard as aesthetic, ethical, and religious. When one lives aesthetically, unconscious of being spirit or of having an eternal soul, time is experienced in a staccato fashion. The moment becomes everything, but it passes; boredom threatens; hence, life is a racing to fill passing moments. There is no continuity in the CHARACTER since repetition is boring, and the constant search for something new to fill each moment fragments time and the self. In the ethical mode time is experienced as continuity, because living under universal moral law, the individual can make commitments, which connect past resolutions and future intentions to present choices. Repetition is desirable; time is experienced as cohesive and constructive. Until one chooses the ethical-religious mode, however, one does not reach full consciousness of being spirit and therefore eternal. Once the leap is made, the finite, temporal individual becomes contemporaneous with Christ and, as spirit, eternal within time. All, however, comes from God. Finite existents share in being by receiving their temporal existence and eternal spirit from God. If you have passion, either you are a believer, or you are offended. The possibility of offense is unavoidable since the required belief, that God entered into existence in time as a particular man, is a paradox that crucifies reason. Only faith can overcome the possibility of offense.

Nietzsche writes that time, space, and causality are metaphors of knowledge, the means by which we explain things to ourselves. Time is nonsense and exists only for a being capable of SENSATION. NATURE's infinity has no boundaries; the finite is only for us. Time is infinitely divisible; what is there is always there. There are no goals in infinite time and SPACE. As finite beings, however, we have to believe in time, space, motion, even though we grant them no absolute reality. Historically, humanity's defense against the fleeting of time, with its condemnation to ephemeral finitude, has been the promise of eternal life in a world beyond time, where gods mete out justice. By the end of the nineteenth century, however, Nietzsche's madman warned that God was dead, and because of that DEATH and the loss of that consolation, rancor, RESENTMENT, and NIHILISM would follow.

Against the threat of human degeneration, Nietzsche offered his thought of eternal recurrence, which means that I live innumerable times. This life as it is lived now and has been lived has nothing new in it; the events of my lives follow the same succession and sequence in repeated cycles. Yet, eternal recurrence is a cure for nihilism, because to freely will its necessity is to affirm oneself and one's life. Affirmation of eternal recurrence by the creative will is a triumph of health over the pathology of nihilism. Furthermore, the idea of eternal recurrence is a supreme challenge, because it transforms eternity into time. Eternity becomes this life, this Earth, in the present moment. Thus, eternal recurrence is a synthesis of being and becoming; it makes becoming, or temporality, eternal. The thought of eternal recurrence transforms the destiny of humankind. It finalizes the death of God and offers REDEMPTION from revenge over the will's aversion to time. This point is crucial since rancor over one's finitude demoralizes humanity. But not everyone has the spiritual strength to embrace the thought of eternal recurrence; those unable to bear it would perish, and those who found salvation in it would be the chosen of the future. Thus, the idea would become instrumental in the future evolution of human life. Nietzsche stressed belief in eternal recurrence, not the need to establish its TRUTH. Since those who could not bear the idea would die off, and those who could, would be driven upward, the consequences of this belief would be overcoming nihilism and creating new VALUES. This world, here and now, would be joyfully affirmed; every moment would be eternity.

In *The Phenomenology of Internal Time Consciousness*, HUSSERL accounts for time as the basic form of all experience. Time is lived experience, which is primarily the present now. The present now, however, is not a discrete instant; it is all three dimensions of time, since the present moment carries retentions of the past and protensions of the future. The past is retained as past in the present along with anticipations of the future as future. This tridimensional present becomes a past retention for the succeeding present. This account of present CONSCIOUSNESS as a synthesis of all three temporal dimensions became a basic tenet for Heidegger and Sartre. Heidegger distinguishes between the time of physics, measured or clock time, and primordial temporality, the latter belonging to the fundamental being of DASEIN, who is historical, since it is grounded in ekstatic temporalizing. That grounding makes it possible for Dasein to be a BEING-IN-THE-WORLD, since the horizon of that temporalizing is the horizon of the world. Such is a departure from the underlying assumption that beings are simply given in time. We are not temporal because we stand within history; we exist historically because we are temporal. How does Heidegger arrive at primordial time? He begins with an analysis of human existence in the everyday involvements of ordinary life and explains that involvement by characterizing human life as CARE, a description that reveals the human existent as thrown, or already there, and as projecting possibilities ahead of itself and absorbed in entities in the midst of the world.

This horizontal extension, constituting a field, is not recognized as such by ordinary, everyday awareness, which experiences time inauthentically as an unbroken procedure of nows. The time of being-with-one-another-in-the-world reckons time and measures it by the clock. The happening of the world is always encountered in the present, for the clock shows us only the now, never the future or the past. Time is interpreted as present, the past is no-longer-present, and the future is not-yet-present. Everything flows from an infinite future to an irretrievable past. In other words, ontologically, the world as phenomenon is a mode of being of existing humans. Since the everyday mode of being grasps everything in terms of the world, it takes time not as its own being but as external and public. Time, thus temporalized publicly, is world time, interpreted as an aspect of the world itself. Only an authentic awareness of one's being can explain how inauthentic public time is possible.

Care can be accounted for only because the primordial self, open to Being, is dispersed in the horizontal ekstatic unity of past, present, and future. That authentic self is individuated by its projection toward the future, which reveals its uniqueness and finitude. In the AUTHENTICITY of what Heidegger calls the moment of vision, present awareness is pulled out of its absorption and lostness in a public self and recalled to its authentic self in ekstatic temporal unity. Time, then, can be accounted for only through going further than the ONTIC facts of human historicity; the answer lies in the ontological constitution of the being of the historical SUBJECT. In inauthentic historicity that primordial, ekstatic extension is dimmed down, hidden, which explains why, along with the disclosure of world, there is also a disclosure of world time. Things in the world are experienced as in time, which is neither objective nor subjective, although world time is more objective than any possible OBJECT, for it is the condition of the possibility of objects being given. What, then, is time? The full answer to that question has to be deferred until the meaning of Being is clarified. What remains clarified is that the ekstatic unity of temporality is leveled down and covered up by public world time. Phenomenological analysis, however, reveals Dasein's being as historical; consequently, every factual science and history itself is dependent on that historicity. The ontological project of Dasein's historicity reveals both its rootedness in temporal ekstases and its projection of a temporal horizon, which gives, at the same time, the horizon of the world.

Sartre refers to conscious human being as for-itself to differentiate it from all nonconscious being, in-itself. In the upsurge of the for-itself as presence to being, there is an original dispersion in three temporal ekstases. Sartre calls that dispersion a detotalized totality, or spontaneous absolute. Through that ekstatic dispersion a meaningful world is projected as temporal horizon or circuit of the self. The relation of consciousness to others and the world is therefore always temporalized. The three ekstatic elements of time—past, present, and future— are structured moments of an original synthesis, each with its own temporal character. The past that I was, is what it is, like things in the world. I am my past in the sense that I have to be what I was. I cannot change the past, although I can change its meaning. The present moment of this temporal dispersion is a flight. My present consciousness is not what it is, and it is what it is not. The future is my possibility of presence to being and constitutes the meaning of my present consciousness. It also completes, as possibility, the ideal limit of my Self. That ideal limit of the temporal stretch that I am completes the circuit of the Self.

Always in process, I am separated by a psychic distance from my past and at a psychic distance from the future states that I will be. Only at death will there be a compression of the ekstases: I will be wholly past, an in-itself, no longer the past of a for-itself. Original temporality, of which we are the temporalization, is not the same as what Sartre calls psychic temporality. The latter is our subjective experience of time revealed through reflective consciousness. Pure reflection is the discovery of the historicity that it is, but while this is the original form of reflection, it is revealed only through a modification of impure reflection. Impure reflection is given first in daily life and constitutes the succession of psychic facts that make up the psyche, a virtual and transcendent identity, composed of states, qualities, and acts that form character and habits. There can be reflective self-knowledge of the EGO, but it is knowledge of a self viewed as in-itself. Purified reflection, on the other hand, won by catharsis, is recognition rather than knowledge, it discovers the for-itself in its reality, in its original nonsubstantiality. Purified reflection reveals a self always at a distance from itself, in the future, in the past, in the world, as a historicity in progress. Original temporality, which purified reflection grasps through this quasi knowledge, temporalizes itself.

Psychic time as impure reflection is a projection into the in-itself of that original temporality. It is a virtual being that accompanies the ekstatic temporalizing of the for-itself. Consciousness arises always situated in a world, where things appear as permanences existing in time. Since I am a temporal dispersion, I reveal things in time, even though these things are not, in their being, temporal. When I reflect that the tree outside my window has a past, it is a memory of my past presence to the tree, as a copresence with a former state of the tree, that makes time appear as external. Thus, my consciousness projects a continuity of my present and past, as the continunity of the present and past of objective time. World time is my projection of temporality into being. When I am unreflective and unconscious of my temporality, I discover it only outside myself, reflected by the world as objective time. That is how external objects appear to be in time. There is no transcendent or absolute meaning to history; rather, history is the way in which each person and each concrete collectivity lives its history. History is pure subjectivity.

Primary Works

Husserl, Edmund. *The Phenomenology of Internal Time Consciousness*. Trans. J. Churchill. Bloomington: Indiana University Press, 1964.
Kierkegaard, Søren. *Concluding Unscientific Postscript*. Trans. David F. Swenson and Walter Lowrie. Princeton: Princeton University Press, 1968.

Bibliography

Lampert, Laurence. *Nietzsche's Teaching: An Interpretation of "Thus Spoke Zarathustra."* New Haven, CT: Yale University Press, 1986.

Spiegelberg, Herbert. *The Phenomenological Movement*. The Hague: Martinus Nijhoff, 1965.

TRANSCENDENCE
Gail Weiss

Any discussion of the term "transcendence" for existentialist thought must include the term with which it is most often contrasted: IMMANENCE. The distinction between immanence and transcendence is fundamental, in particular, for SARTRE and BEAUVOIR. In *Being and Nothingness*, Sartre identifies being-in-itself with immanence and being-for-itself with transcendence. Being-in-itself is characterized by its solidity, passivity or pure thereness, and its resistance to change. As transcendent, being-for-itself is dynamic, open-ended or future-oriented, and continually redefining itself. Humans are both immanent and transcendent, even though human existence is identified as being-for-itself. This is because we share with other OBJECTS a physical EXISTENCE that is identified with being-in-itself. Immanence refers to the FACTICITY of the SITUATION, those aspects of our situation that are given and that remain fairly constant over TIME. For example, a PERSON's date of birth and the circumstances surrounding that birth constitute immanent features of that person's existence.

Sartre holds that the past belongs to the domain of immanence insofar as it is incapable of being changed. He acknowledges, however, that we are always free to reinterpret that past from a new perspective. All that is nonhuman belongs to the immanent domain of being-in-itself. Yet, objects in the WORLD are transcendent in the sense that they exist apart from our CONSCIOUSNESS of them. What separates human transcendence from nonhuman existence is the distinctive ontological structure of human consciousness, which alone is conscious of its consciousness. This consciousness of consciousness is nonpositional or a nonthetic consciousness. It is nonthetic because it is not oriented toward any specific object but is rather always already operating on a prereflective level in everyday existence. Both thetic consciousness and nonthetic consciousness are intentional; that is, both have the structure: consciousness of. Insofar as consciousness is intentional, it exhibits transcendence, because it is always directed toward some object that lies outside itself.

Consciousness, Sartre argues, is empty; it has no content of its own. The content of consciousness comes from outside consciousness, and the transcendence that he attributes to consciousness derives from the fact that the very structure of consciousness involves a projection beyond itself. Just as the object may be regarded as transcendent to our consciousness of it, so, too, we must recognize consciousness as transcendent in relation to the objects, events, memories, and other phenomena with which it is concerned. To say that human consciousness is transcendent does not mean that we are able to attain clear or perfect insight into our conscious existence. Consciousness is translucent, not transparent; this translucence is due to our inability to make our present nonthetic awareness the subject of reflection. When I attempt to grasp the nonthetic domain, I always find myself reflecting upon a moment that has just past. Nonthetic awareness is ongoing and cannot be captured in a single act of attention.

Sartre associates human transcendence with a horizon of possibility that characterizes our existence from one moment to the next. To be a transcendent BEING is to possess FREEDOM, specifically, the freedom to change one's situation by drawing upon the future to establish a present that differs from the past. An immanent being has no future. It has no situation. The only future it possesses is one that humans ascribe to it; it does not share our temporality, and hence its LIFE or duration lacks significance. Although the transcendence of consciousness is a source of freedom and RESPONSIBILITY, in the absence of an immanent domain, there would be no facticity, and without facticity there can be no situation. Without a situation, there would be nothing for consciousness to be conscious of; hence, transcendence and immanence are interdependent.

In *The Second Sex*, Beauvoir takes up the Sartrian distinction between immanence and transcendence and explores the ways in which social attitudes and conventions have influenced our understanding of these terms. She argues that transcendence has come to be seen as a positive term associated with males, and immanence has developed more negative connotations and is associated with females. Although all humans are both immanent and transcendent, and both immanence and transcendence are indispensable aspects of human existence, historically, societies have tended to regard males as more transcendent beings than females. Accepting Sartre's distinctions, she claims that men are viewed as dwelling more in the transcendent realm of consciousness than women, who are seen as more tied to their bodily existence. The early pages of *The Second Sex* focus on the ways in which anatomical differences between males and females give rise to a situation in which women are forced to pay more attention to their bodies than men. The monthly menstrual cycle and the demanding processes of reproduction and lactation, which often wholly occupy the life of the woman experiencing them, have no direct counterpart in the male's existence. Even for the female, the mysterious workings of her BODY may resemble an alien spectacle in which she is merely a bystander rather than an active participant. In a certain sense, then, the female's body may appear as a transcendent object that escapes her conscious awareness and control. For this reason, a woman often experiences her body as a burden, an immanent reality that consumes and constrains her existence.

From the standpoint of SOCIETY, Beauvoir maintains, to exist as a transcendent being is to be free to pursue an intellectual life that is not so tied to bodily needs and demands. While men are often described in terms of their intellectual achievements, women tend to be defined through their domestic activities. The danger of viewing women as more immanent than men is that fewer opportunities are made available to women to develop their capabilities; not surprisingly, women are often led to view themselves as intellectually inferior. Thus, women may come to believe that they are less transcendent than men; yet, to accept this view would mean that one accepts an ontological difference between male and female consciousness—a difference neither Sartre nor Beauvoir recognizes. So, for Beauvoir, all humans are equally transcendent, even though men are more encouraged to develop the possibilities inherent in that transcendence than women, who are encouraged to remain within a sphere of immanence that restricts them from fully realizing their potential.

In *Philosophy of Existence*, JASPERS contrasts the conception of transcendence in RELIGION with the transcendence that characterizes philosophizing. Whereas religion understands transcendence as a supernatural, determinate object, such as GOD, the transcendence experienced through philosophizing reveals Being; this latter is not an object but an eternal reality in which one's own being is encompassed. Being itself is reality, a realm of possibility that takes us beyond, and is more primordial than, thought. He also distinguishes between transcendence and immanence and argues that to realize the freedom of our existence, we must move from the immanent domain of being that is known to the unknowable realm of transcendence or Being itself. Only in making this LEAP, from the knowable to that which cannot be known, can we aim at EXISTENZ. Existenz is not something we achieve once and for all but can be understood as the locus for the authentic self, a self that exists as a potentiality rather than a possession. This authentic self gives unity to our existence, and, therefore, only through transcendence can this unity be experienced. Unlike the transcendent object of religion, which most often has a definitive NATURE, the transcendence we encounter through philosophizing is not tied to any type of being or experience. Instead, like the fleeting I–Thou relationship, we can encounter transcendence at any place or time, and, when we are open to this encounter, the experience of transcendence gives us access to a reality that lies beyond that place and time.

Primary Works

Beauvoir, Simone de. *The Second Sex*. Trans. H. M. Parshley. New York: Vintage, 1989.
Jaspers, Karl. *Philosophy of Existence*. Trans. R. F. Grabau. Philadelphia: University of Pennsylvania Press, 1971.

TRUTH
Alfons Grieder

Some novel conceptions of truth emerged in existentialist thinking. The correspondence theory of truth, perhaps the most important of the traditional conceptions, may be characterized thus: (1) the truth-bearers are propositions, statements, judgments, BELIEFS, and the like; (2) a proposition or statement is true if, and only if, what it asserts is the case; or alternatively, a PERSON's belief is true if, and only if, what the person believes to be the case is the case. Thus, truth consists in some correspondence with facts, with what is the case. Another traditional theory, the coherence theory of truth, has found less acclaim, as coherence with a particular whole of propositions is considered neither necessary nor sufficient for a proposition to be true.

The correspondence theory of truth fails to respond to some well-known connotations of the word ''true.'' We may speak of a true friend or of true meaning. Christ is reported to have said: I am the truth. Here truth is not what pertains to propositions but what somebody is or perhaps a way of LIFE. A truth may be lived and made one's own. We may say of a man who acts in accordance with his moral outlook that he is true to himself: his action agrees not merely with his standard but with a standard that is judged to be properly his, part of himself. Existentialists made two distinctive contributions: (1) they introduced and explored some hitherto neglected conceptions or senses of truth, existential truth, truth as unconcealment and as a fundamental determination of a person's BEING, and (2) although the correspondence theory of truth was rejected as inadequate, attempts were made to understand it in light of the newly elaborated conceptions of truth, by pointing out its derivative CHARACTER and by comparing it with other senses of truth.

KIERKEGAARD draws a crucial distinction between subjective and objective truth. The latter is roughly in line with the correspondence theory. Although objective truth is an indispensable guide to humans in their conduct of life, he calls it inessential and contrasts it with the essential, subjective truth. Subjective truth is an individual's way of relating to something objectively uncertain, by believing in it, holding passionately onto it, and appropriating it. Whoever has this relationship to something or somebody can be said to be in truth, irrespective of whether what he or she relates to actually exists in the usual, objective sense. What is decisive are the individual's attitude and commitment in the face of an objective uncertainty. The focus is not on what is said but on how it is said and on the relationship the speaker existentially sustains to the content of one's utterance. The thought-content of the utterance may be paradoxical and even contradictory, and the individual may be aware of this yet still be in truth.

Kierkegaard points out that his definition of subjective truth can also serve as a definition of FAITH; he adds that where there is no risk, there is no faith. Subjective truth is a venture of faith that belongs to an existing individual. Christian faith constituted Kierkegaard's paradigm of subjective truth. The Christian believer cannot fall back upon objective truth and evidence concerning GOD. On the contrary, God, having become man, having been born into, and died in, this world, must appear paradoxical. That the eternal truth has come into being in TIME—this is the paradox. The individual, failing to take the extreme risk and to hold passionately onto God, in the face of paradox and absurdity falls into untruth and is in SIN. Christian faith would be unrealizable as subjective truth if the God were known objectively and with certainty. Furthermore, the fact that eternal truth can appear as only a paradox to the finite believer increases the inward intensity of faith. Since existential truth and reality cannot be directly communicated, the opposition to the correspondence theory is acute. Existential truth is essentially secret; there are no town criers of inwardness. Indirect communication is the subjective thinker's style; it is also the appropriate mode of communication between humans as spiritual beings. Concern with the communication of objective results tends to prevent the appropriation of inward truth.

JASPERS elaborated a conception of multiple truth, bringing together (1) pragmatic truth, (2) truth of consciousness-in-general, (3) truth of SPIRIT, (4) truth of EXISTENCE, and (5) truth of TRANSCENDENCE. Pragmatic truth of an opinion or belief consists in its usefulness for life. Truth of consciousness-in-general is the correctness of a proposition or judgment, but such that it can be made compellingly evident for anybody able to understand the truth claim concerned. The truths of science are of this type. Truth of spirit is defined as the participation in, or producing of, ideas or as conviction of ideas. The idea of the university as an institution directed to the search for, and transmission of, truth may guide and unite a range of human activities; in this case truth of spirit consists in being convinced of that idea and pursuing it. Truth of existence is characterized as awareness of what it is to be oneself or, more elaborately, as the coincidence of a person's effective communication, attitude toward one's tasks, and penetration of the limiting SITUATIONS. Truth of Transcendence is seen as a kind of coincidence of the finite person with Transcendence, be it in philosophic thought, in the reading of the cipher-writing, or when actualizing oneself in existence.

Jaspers' conception of truth forms part of his PHILOSOPHY of the Encompassing. To each of the basic senses of truth corresponds a mode of the Encompassing. All are indispensable, but each is limited and needs complementing by the others. Real truth emerges only where all these senses and types of truth are present as a whole and linked with each other. Reason is a bond uniting them and enabling us to remain open in our search for being and for ourselves. Humans do not possess truth in this embracing sense once and for all; we have to strive for it again and again. As an existing being I may experience truth in my faith; but my existential truth is without objective certainty and proof and need not be such truth for another. Yet Jaspers resists relativism and commits himself to the thesis of one truth—emerging in communication. Existential truth and truth of Transcendence are founded in an I–Thou relationship.

Although Jaspers' five types of truth are interdependent and have a common element, they are heterogeneous. Truth of consciousness-in-general comes closest to the correspondence conception of truth but restricts it considerably as the requirement of compelling evidence is added to that of correctness. It is doubtful whether scientific truths are of this type. It is widely accepted that the laws and theories of the empirical sciences cannot be proved and are not compellingly evident. To take usefulness as a criterion of truth seems equally questionable; a belief may be incorrect yet useful, while some correct beliefs may be practically useless. Spiritual truth represents an uneasy mixture of Kantian ideas, the Hegelian idea, and the Hegelian spirit of TIME. The coincidence involved here is quite unlike that of truth of consciousness-in-general. It consists in participating in a spiritual-historical whole, accepting its ideas, and letting oneself be guided by them. As to Existence and Transcendence, Jaspers holds that they are non-objects par excellence that cannot be experienced as realities in the WORLD; truth regarding them cannot be adequately expressed in propositions and in accordance with rules of ordinary logic. Thus, philosophy cannot be restricted to the realm of consciousness-in-general and cannot be scientific.

HEIDEGGER's earlier conception of truth, developed in *Being and Time*, differs from the later one, which emerged after the mid-1930s. *Being and Time* puts forward the following theses: (1) in its primordial sense, truth is DASEIN's disclosedness, which goes hand in hand with the uncoveredness of entities within the world; (2) Dasein is equiprimordially both in the truth and in untruth; and (3) the truth of assertions, the truth most familiar to us, originates in primordial truth, in disclosedness. Asserting is a way in which Dasein comports itself toward things. That an assertion is true signifies that it uncovers some entity. Taking his clue from the Greek *aletheia*, Heidegger gives the word ''true'' the twofold meaning of uncovering and uncovered. Hence, he says that Dasein is true and, further, that Dasein, disclosed to itself and disclosing entities in the world, is in the truth. Taken in the first sense, as being-uncovering, truth is an existential. It is an ontological determination characterizing Dasein's existence and BEING-IN-THE-WORLD. Connected with this first sense is truth as being-uncovered or uncoveredness and as a determination of the being of things in the world, also of Dasein. Whatever is true in this sense has been taken out of its hiddenness.

For Heidegger, truth and untruth belong together in several respects. Truth as being-uncovering and being-uncovered is possible only where beings are hidden to begin with. Furthermore, just because whatever is disclosed is disclosed in a certain respect, it remains hidden in other respects. Dasein is proximally and for the most part absorbed in the world. As such it discloses what there is, including itself, in a specific manner. For instance, certain entities are disclosed primarily as ready-to-hand, while what they are in themselves may remain more or less hidden. Being absorbed in the world, Dasein is dominated by the way things are publicly interpreted in idle talk and concealed in ambiguity. As absorbed in the world, Dasein is in untruth, not only with regard to other beings but, above all, with regard to itself. It is estranged from itself and fails to recognize, explore, and realize its potentiality-for-being. Authentic existence, on the other hand, is characterized by an authentic disclosedness, by a resoluteness that brings Dasein before the primordial truth of existence and reveals its factical potentiality-for-untruth.

Heidegger remarks that truth of assertion comes last, when considered existential-ontologically; but for us it comes first and is closest, so much so that it effectively covers up the primordial phenomenon of truth. He attempts to elucidate the derivative character of truths of assertion, starting from Discourse as a particular way in which Dasein discloses things. He is aware that his account of truth commits him to the claim that there cannot be truth unless there is Dasein; in fact, any assertion whatsoever can be true only as long as Dasein exists. Already, *Being and Time* spoke of the there of Dasein as the clearing and of truth as that basic character of Dasein according to which it is its there. For the later Heidegger truth is primarily the truth of Being and what is proper to Being. Human ESSENCE is said to consist in standing out into the openness of the truth of Being. Dasein is the guardian of Being, used by Being to disclose beings and the Being of beings: without the truth of Being, no Dasein; without Dasein, no truth of Being. Unconcealment and concealment go hand in hand; the opening of Being is also called the opening of the concealment of Being. Truth is thought as happening; in the ways in which it happens originate the crucial decisions and the epochs of the HISTORY of Being. European history from the early Greeks is essentially a history of the forgetfulness of Being. In Plato, Heidegger sees the transition from *aletheia* to truth as correspondence; the Cartesian quest for certainty, the Nietzschean will to power, the reign of modern technology mark subsequent ways in which truth happened.

In none of his writings published during his life does SARTRE systematically deal with truth. In the posthumously published *Truth and Existence* he adopted a predominantly ontological, rather than epistemological, approach, utilizing and, to some extent, questioning the framework of *Being and Nothingness*. He views truth as unveiling and ontologically prior to prepositional truth as well as to particular truths. Truth as the unveiling of being is inseparable from the for-itself, its PROJECT and FREEDOM: CONSCIOUSNESS exists as this revelation of Being. In this fundamental sense, truth is an event, both a human enterprise and a history of Being. Whatever is thus revealed is present—not simply given. Truth appears as illuminated Being, at the end of an operation and in the light of a project. However, all truth is inhabited by ignorance, not only because it is ignorance having become truth but also because all unveiling takes place

against a horizon of ignorance and cannot u
always has a side to it that escapes the unve
in three ways: (1) as my truth, unveiled by n
for others as well; (3) as pure abstract staten
ization of a certain unveiling.

Thus, Kierkegaard, Jaspers, Heidegger, an
notion of truth. They showed that humans,
themselves and open toward what is other th
the orthodox truth-theories and the paradigm

Primary Works

Heidegger, Martin. *Poetry, Language, Thought.*
   Harper and Row, 1971.
Jaspers, Karl. *Philosophy.* 3 vols. Trans E. B. A
   Press, 1969/1971.
Sartre, Jean-Paul. *Truth and Existence.* Trans. A
   sity of Chicago Press, 1992.

Bibliography

Kaufmann, Walter. *Nietzsche: Philosopher, Psyc*
   ton University Press, 1974.

MIGUEL DE UN
JUGC
(1864–19

Robert Richm

Miguel de Unamuno y Jugo was born in B
he was six; he was raised by his mother in
At the age of sixteen he completed seconda
sity studies in Madrid, where he discovered
cialism. He abandoned religious practices a
PHILOSOPHY. In 1884 he received his de
In 1891 Unamuno was granted a chair in Gr

materialism. For him, the dynamic of history and of all being was neither ideas nor things but consciousness. Nothingness has not only an existential but a logical priority over being. However, there exists in Unamuno's thought a certain ambiguity regarding nothingness. He speaks of the anguished INTUITION of nothingness. Yet often he describes nothingness not ontologically but metaphorically as a something that is, when compared with the totality of being to which it aspires, like nothing. Moreover, he envisions the dissolution of death as a return to absolute nothingness. Thus, though consciousness is a kind of nothingness, only consciousness can lay claim to the title of being. In this context being is ultimately the desire for being. At times, however, he speaks of a nothingness of things, as if an intentionality in NATURE was propelling it toward an ontological fulfillment. This INTENTIONALITY is not a by-product of human intentionality but rather a bond between humans and the world. This particular intuition remains underdeveloped. Yet it removes him from the confines of existential SOLIPSISM, indicating the possibility of a new dialectic that would not subordinate humans to external forces of history but would nevertheless account for the workings of a history beyond their own.

Primary Works

Unamuno, Miguel de. *Selected Works*. 7 vols. Ed. Anthony Kerrigan. Princeton: Princeton University Press, 1967–1984.
———. *Tragic Sense of Life*. Trans. J. E. Crawford Flitch. New York: Dover, 1954.

Bibliography

Ellis, Robert Richmond. *The Tragic Pursuit of Being*. Tuscaloosa: University of Alabama Press, 1988.

UNCONSCIOUS
Stuart Charme

The idea that the human psyche includes mental activities that escape conscious awareness has been referred to by philosophers, psychologists, and writers over the last three centuries, but Sigmund Freud is credited with the first systematic theory of the unconscious that claimed scientific validity. Freud suggested that psychic activity is rooted in the flow of instinctual energy that is constantly seeking release. The unconscious consists of instinctual wishes and feelings that have been repressed in order to conform to the demands of civilized LIFE; it may also include the memory of traumatic events that have been repressed, so as to prevent further pain, GUILT, or ANXIETY. This concept of the unconscious is necessary to unravel the meanings of neurosis, verbal slips, acts of forgetting, dreams, religious ideas and rituals. These phenomema can be seen as disguised expressions of repressed psychic material that has remained active and is looking for release. A major goal of psychoanalysis is to decipher these symbolic disguises of the contents of the unconscious. Relief from neurotic symptoms was possible if repression was overcome, and previously unconscious thoughts and feelings were brought into the full light of CONSCIOUSNESS.

NIETZSCHE and DOSTOYEVSKY emphasized the weakness and superficiality of ordinary rational consciousness. They recognized that the vitalizing POWER within humans includes warring instincts and EMOTIONS that consciousness neither understands nor controls. Yet, the response of many existentialists to Freud's theory of the unconscious has ranged from ambivalence to hostile rejection. While they acknowledge the brilliance of Freud's discovery of human meaning in bizarre symptoms and his appreciation for the influence of thoughts and feelings that are not accessible to ordinary consciousness, they object to the metapsychological theory he developed to explain such phenomena.

Existentialist objections to the concept of the unconscious are, first, that the theory is deterministic and implies that FREEDOM is an illusion. If the true origin of our thoughts and behavior is rooted in biological instincts and childhood experiences that are now lost to us, then a free act is impossible. The recognition of the freedom of consciousness and of the PERSON as a vital factor in any account of human thought and behavior has been eliminated. Second, the theory of the unconscious is mechanistic. What initially may have begun as a set of metaphors for understanding psychic functioning became a mechanical view of the psyche in which psychic energy or instincts were managed by different parts of the psyche. Even the meaning of unconscious shifted from an adjectival quality of certain psychic processes to become an independent thing, system, and locality. Freud's theory reifies all of human consciousness into an inner landscape or storehouse where some parts are visible while large portions are obscured, hidden in darkness, or buried. In addition, the psyche supposedly includes some kind of psychic apparatus that manages the unconscious and mechanically transforms instincts into behavior, thoughts, and emotions according to rules outside consciousness. It offers the analyst an excavation site where repressed memories can be dug up and examined.

Existentialists rejected this view of the psyche as a container whose contents are either visible or hidden. In most cases, their views of human consciousness are rooted in PHENOMENOLOGY and its principle of the INTENTIONALITY of consciousness, which is always actively engaged in the construction of one's sense of reality, not passively recording mental pictures and storing them for later reference. For existentialists, the task of creating meaning for the individual components of one's LIFE as well as for one's life as a whole makes human EXISTENCE unique. Ultimately, consciousness assigns the meaning to events in one's past that will become the background for one's actions in the present. If meaning is a RELATION of consciousness to the WORLD, then unconscious meaning is a contradiction. Even in the case of neurotic symptoms or behaviors, existentialists demand an account that recognizes the role of intentionality in creating the meaning of such behavior. Causal explanations acknowledge only a unidirectional effect of the past on the present and overlook the dialectical relation of past and present. Not only does one's past influence one's present psychological state, but one's present state of consciousness determines which way of construing the past one accepts. The same type of trauma early in life may produce very different reactions in different people depending on the subsequent individual PROJECTS they undertake. Similarly, the meaning of a particular past event may undergo radical changes at different points in a person's life. Indeed, one goal of psychoanalysis is to invest one's past with a new set of meanings. By translating human meanings into biological forces, Freud's metapsychology results in a dehumanized view of the psyche.

MARCEL, MERLEAU-PONTY and others rejected the idea of causal relations between consciousness and the BODY, between the mental and the physical. For Marcel the unconscious represents those ideas, feelings, and forms of being with which we have no dialectical communication. There will always be parts of one's existence that exceed what a person could bring to light about oneself. Merleau-Ponty contended that Freudian concepts of unconscious complexes, repressions, and regression can be explained in terms of fragmented streams of consciousness, which he called separated dialectics. Consciousness and behavior are ordinarily organized in ways that progress beyond infantile attitudes and patterns. In some cases, however, isolated systems of behavior persist that a SUBJECT refuses to admit or integrate as significant to the rest of one's life. Under such circumstances, a person's consciousness becomes infantile consciousness or returns to a more primitive way of organizing conduct. In addition, he felt that the human body itself expresses an intentionality apart from consciousness. It is not that unconscious memories contained in the psyche erupt into the body from TIME to time. Rather, certain stimuli may evoke a particular traumatic body memory. Nonetheless, SARTRE, Marcel, and Merleau-Ponty do not see all psychological phenomena as conscious in the sense that people always know their desires or feelings. Since meaning structures are not always accessible to reflective knowledge or awareness, people may often be unable to understand or verbalize their needs and desires.

Sartre eliminated the need for the unconscious by distinguishing between consciousness and KNOWLEDGE. Consciousness refers to the whole psychological realm of subjectivity as distinct from purely physical relations between objects. Hence, unconscious feeling is a misnomer for a feeling that has been kept from awareness or conceptualization, but it is still an element of consciousness. In Sartre's analysis, Freud fragmented the psyche into one part that I am and another part whose existence is mere conjecture and whose contents can only be passively received. To explain the process of repression, Freud assumed that one part of the psyche operates as a censor, determining what will be allowed into consciousness and what should be repressed. This function was later subsumed under the idea of the superego. But, Sartre indicated, the censor must be conscious of those memories or feelings that need to be repressed. Some part of my consciousness must have access to those aspects of myself that I do not want to see or remember, if only in order to conceal them more effectively. Thus, what is repressed is not really unconscious to the censor. Sartre concluded that a person is always aware, in some sense, of what has been repressed but has refused to notice it. If this were not the case, there would be no reason for consciousness to experience anxiety or pleasure when a disguised expression of some repressed desire or memory appears in a dream or slip of the tongue. Nor would patients have any reason to resist the psychoanalyst's suggestions about the meaning of their symptomatic behavior or feelings.

After resistance finally collapses in a successful psychoanalytic treatment, a patient's INTUITION that the analyst's interpretation is correct likewise implies some prior awareness of that material. Sartre argued that psychoanalysis unnecessarily destroyed the unity of each person by splitting the psyche into conscious and unconscious. Ultimately, this solved nothing since the problem of self-deception was merely pushed back to the level of the censor, which existed in BAD FAITH. Sartre accepted the facts of repression, displacement, and disguised symbolization within the psyche, but he treated them as intentional acts within the dynamic, dialectical nature of the psyche, not mechanical processes of the unconscious.

Other existentialists have complained that Freud's view of the unconscious is not so much wrong as it is incomplete. While recognizing the divided NATURE of the self and irrational elements that are hidden from consciousness, religious existentialists criticized Freud for neglecting the noninstinctual, nonsexual, nonneurotic parts of the unconscious. BERDYAEV refers to the spiritual dimension of the unconscious that is the source of CREATIVITY, IMAGINATION, and intuition. He preferred Jung's model of the unconscious, which includes a core that is the source of meaning and spirituality. For Buber, Freud's theory of the unconscious was objectifying and reductive. By treating the unconscious as a portion of an individual's psychological functioning, it failed to grasp the person as a whole and destroyed the unique MYSTERY that appears only in relation.

Primary Works

Dostoyevsky, Fyodor. *The Brothers Karamazov*. Trans. Richard Pevear and Larissa Volokhonsky. New York: Vintage, 1991.

Marcel, Gabriel. *The Mystery of Being*. Vols. 1 and 2. Trans. G. S. Fraser. Chicago: Henry Regnery, 1960.

Bibliography

Cannon, Betty. *Sartre and Psychoanalysis.* Lawrence: University Press of Kansas, 1991.

VALUE
David Detmer

The traditional philosophical distinction holds that there are only two possibilities concerning values. One is that values are subjective, meaning that they do not exist apart from human CONSCIOUSNESS. Things are valuable only because we value them. Therefore, there can be no genuine KNOWLEDGE of values—no discoverable TRUTH about value judgments. The other possibility is that values are objective, meaning that values exist in their own right apart from human consciousness; therefore, it is possible, in principle, to judge about value questions. Hence, genuine knowledge of values is possible; when we are in possession of it, we judge things to be valuable because they *are* valuable. Existentialists criticize objectivism and place a great emphasis on personal CHOICE. They favor a preference for FREEDOM, AUTHENTICITY, and individuality, which harmonize well with a subjectivist outlook. However, they also retain a strong sense of moral RESPONSIBILITY.

KIERKEGAARD claims that a PERSON's allegiance to one set of values over another can stem only from free choice. He describes three different modes of EXISTENCE: the aesthetic, the ethical, and the religious. Once one has chosen the aesthetic mode of existence—of pursuing sensual pleasure—one will encounter and feel bound by aesthetic values. Similarly, the choice of the religious mode causes religious values to be experienced as having a binding quality. The same reasoning applies to choosing the ethical existence and ethical values. But how should we choose between these ways of existing? Kierkegaard's answer is that we must choose in the absence of any objective reasons. While there are aesthetic reasons for choosing aesthetic values, ethical reasons for choosing ethical values, and religious reasons for choosing religious values, there are no reasons accessible for choosing one of the modes of existence. This fundamental choice is a LEAP.

But such does not mean that fundamental choices are beyond evaluation. Rather, Kierkegaard holds, in evaluating such choices we must shift our focus away from objective factors and toward subjective factors—the sincerity, honesty, CREATIVITY, integrity, and passion with which one chooses. However, one should not characterize Kierkegaard's view as one in which there is no place for reason, objective truth, and personal responsibility. Consider the following. (1) Kierkegaard's definition of subjective truth is an objective uncertainty held fast in an appropriation-process of the most passionate inwardness. (2) His limitation of the relevance of subjective truth and subjective values to SITUATIONS of objective uncertainty suggests that situations of objective certainty might call forth other values. (3) Once one has chosen a mode of existence, one directly experiences values appropriate to it as binding. (4) Though there are no reasons external to the framework of a particular mode of existence for choosing one of them over the others, he suggests that reasons can be found from within any given mode for abandoning it in favor of another. Indeed, he shows in detail how the aesthetic LIFE tends, on its own terms, to fail and thus may motivate a conversion to the ethical life and how the limitations of the ethical mode may lead to a conversion to the religious life. (5) Finally, Kierkegaard often uses rational arguments in defense of his doctrine of the subjectivity of the fundamental choice of mode of existence.

NIETZSCHE declares that the philosopher's task is to create values. Genuine philosophers are commanders and legislators. However, he rejects a central tenet of orthodox ethical subjectivism, namely, the fact/value distinction. According to this distinction, a major reason for regarding values as subjective is simply that they are not facts; they lack the hardness and givenness of facts and thus, unlike facts, are subject to various interpretations. But Nietzsche insists that facts are precisely what there is not; only interpretations exist. Yet, he seems to reject radical subjectivism, noting that the claim that everything is subjective is itself merely one interpretation among others and one moreover, that involves the invention of the SUBJECT and its projection behind what is given in experience. Thus, he distinguishes between interpretation and invention or projection. The former he regards as necessary and irreducible and thus defensible; the latter he repeatedly and vehemently rejects as intellectual dishonesty and cowardice. Nietzsche holds that the prevailing values of the present are bankrupt and must be replaced. His call for value-creation is not an indiscriminate ethical subjectivism, since he regards the values of the present to be indefensible and undoubtedly would not regard just any values that might be created in the future to be defensible. Rather, he consistently advocates values of intelligence, creativity, sexuality, strength, pride, this-worldliness, WHOLENESS, and the dominance of excellence over mediocrity. He holds that we are currently living in a nihilistic epoch in which intellectual timidity, obedience, chastity, meekness, humility, otherworldliness, and equality are the dominant values. He regards the defense of the currently dominant antilife values as a spiritual sickness that must quickly be stamped out.

Both HEIDEGGER and SARTRE argue that the notion of an objective world, stripped bare of everything that humans have projected onto it, is empty at best and unintelligible at worst. We gain our knowledge of the world through our engagement with it. Consider an example from Sartre. Suppose I go to a café and search for my friend Pierre, whom I hope to find there. When my thorough careful search for Pierre reveals his absence, I reluctantly conclude that he is not in the café. This story illustrates the inadequacy of the traditional subjectivism-objectivism dichotomy. It seems odd to say that Pierre's absence exists objectively in the world, in part, because the encounter with Pierre's absence depends on my being engaged in the PROJECT of looking for him. Billions of other people are also absent from the café—would we say that all of these billions of absences objectively exist in the café? Note that Pierre's absence is not projected upon the café by some subjective act of consciousness. Rather, in a very real sense, this absence is found or discovered in the café. Had Pierre really been there in the café, an exhaustive search for his presence would have rendered the discovery of his absence impossible. His presence would have precluded any social construction of his absence.

What is true of Pierre's absence is, for Sartre, also true of values. Values are not objective in the sense that they exist apart from our engagement with the world, nor are they subjective in the sense of being human projections onto the world, which our encounters with the world can in no way falsify. Indeed, a major part of Sartre's existential psychoanalysis is devoted to showing that the fundamental project in which most people are engaged and that determines the values they choose cannot possibly succeed. Sartre's alternative is to advocate freedom and authenticity as the supreme values in the sphere of ETHICS. Sartre defines authenticity as a true and lucid consciousness of the situation. Such a consciousness includes an awareness of the futility of an ideal fundamental project, as well as an understanding of the ineliminable dimension of freedom in human experience. Moreover, freedom and authenticity are adequate to account for the dimension of justice and of social responsibility in our value-experience, since (1) authenticity reveals to me the freedom of others as well as my own freedom, (2) my own freedom is intimately bound up with the freedom of others, and (3) the ontological freedom that pervades all conscious experience is foundational to, and explains the urgency of, practical freedom in the political and economic spheres. Note that Sartre retains a strong sense of individuality. Authenticity demands it. Individuals who lucidly recognize, and do not flee from, their freedom of thought and action reveal their individuality. Also he never renounces his support for play, in which a free individual engages in creative activity.

Primary Works

Kierkegaard, Søren. *Stages on Life's Way*. Trans. Howard V. Hong and Edna H. Hong. Princeton: Princeton University Press, 1988.

Nietzsche, Friedrich. *Beyond Good and Evil*. Trans. R. J. Hollingdale. Harmondsworth: Penguin, 1973.

Bibliography

Detmer, David. *Freedom as a Value*. La Salle, IL: Open Court, 1988.

WE

Peter Royle

Only a solipsist would deny that ''we'' exist in the sense that I inhabit a WORLD shared by others; but the question that exercises many existentialists is whether this we has any ontological status, or whether I exist in irremediable separation from my fellow humans. For HEIDEGGER DASEIN is a being-with. In my encounter with the world I encounter others who are also in it. Even if I experience solitude, my sense of lack points to my essential BEING as a being-with-others. In everyday life I exist dispersed in the THEY. I speak as they do, think as they do, eat as they do, dress as they do; only by facing resolutely my own DEATH can I achieve AUTHENTICITY.

For BUBER the world of we is reality, but to enter it a PERSON must open oneself by engaging in dialogue with another being. The difference between I–It relationships and I–Thou relationships is significant. I–It relationships are perfectly proper, for example, in the realm of science, while I–Thou relationships are a different sphere of knowing. This second kind of KNOWLEDGE may actualize a we. This we does not deprive a person of one's separate identity but is a dialogue among persons who retain their otherness.

For MARCEL, the we raises the problem of authenticity, as it seems almost impossible to reconcile sincerity, conceived of as faithfulness to myself, with fidelity to a freely espoused commitment to another, whether human or divine. True EXISTENCE lies in my RELATION not with the Other, but with a Thou. Moreover, humans have a dual ESSENCE: FREEDOM and NATURE. They seem to be able, qua freedom, to conform or not to their essence qua nature. The I who relates to the human Thou is relating to that person's freedom. What is more, such a relation helps the Thou to be free. Furthermore, we free persons can, ideally, overcome our separation and our NOTHINGNESS through communion and a common participation in BEING. Such occurs through a free act of commitment, which is a response to an invitation extended by the Other. This realization of a we transforms the Other into a Thou and enables me to realize my higher nature through an act of FAITH that may become an enduring commitment. The conflict between sincerity and fidelity is thereby overcome. In practice it is not so easy, as both the I and the Thou remain free to respond to solicitations of their natures.

For SARTRE the we, as SUBJECT, has no ontological existence. There is not, at least initially, a being-with-others, but a being-for-others, in which I am radically objectified by the Other's LOOK unless I, in turn, look at, and objectify, him or her. At this level, the essence of our relations is necessarily conflict. As I am free through and through, human reality is a construction of itself in this conflict. Yet he believes that the human condition can be characterized as solidarity in solitude. This formulation was accepted also by CAMUS, yet there are differences. Whereas for Camus VALUES, like mathematical truths, are a priori, and their recognition, together with that of the we, is the fruit primarily not of courage but of clarity of vision, for Sartre values are not discovered but created—and so is the we. In all SITUATIONS where it emerges a we has to be constructed. Further, unlike Camus, for whom, at least in his earlier writings, humans are essentially GOOD, Sartre distinguishes between those who are good and those who are bad and leaves room in his vision of the world for genuine heroism. The bad person remains mired in egoism and BAD FAITH, whereas the hero endeavors to transcend the egoism/altruism dichotomy through the creation of a we. In the ONTOLOGY presented in *Being and Nothingness* there is an us but not a we. Initially, I exist in the face of an Other. In the course of my inevitable conflict with the Other, singular or plural, the Third may supervene, converting us both into his or her plural object. I thus experience myself as lumped together in an us, which is my personal apprehension of the them constituting the object of the Third. This us to which I now belong is radically objectified by the look of the Third. Because human reality has a ternary structure, this us can exist. This us, however, cannot be converted into a we on the ontological level, as my apprehension of it is strictly mine and not ours, and any movement on my part to transcend the Third will reestablish me in my unique singularity. A psychological we exists, which I experience in the use of tools designed for anyone or in following, for example, arrows and signs in the subway, but it can have no objective correlative on the level of ontology.

In Sartre's ontology the second person is little more than a regulative concept or ideal to which, in my desire for authenticity, I may aspire but the reality of which is problematic. Personal relations with a preferred Other may even get in the way of authentic political activity, as can be seen in his play *Dirty Hands*. In *Critique of Dialectical Reason*, written later, a more optimistic view emerges. Although for historical reasons, having to do with the capitalist economic order, we are, for the most part, alienated from one another, we are capable, in the formation of groups, of constructing a genuine we. These groups are practical and are created out of serialized collectivities by a common PROJECT fusing into wholes in apocalyptic moments, such as revolutionary uprisings. Leadership of such a revolutionary group rotates from one regulative third to another and can be assumed by virtually any member of the group. Yet the totalized group, once it is formed, is not a definitive ontological or ONTIC totality: it is a detotalized one, with the result that, if it is not to disintegrate rapidly, it will have to be kept together by oaths, terror exercised on its behalf by its members, and social and political institutions subject to solidification, embourgeoisement, decay, and degeneration. Thus, in establishing the we, there can, indeed, be solidarity, but it will necessarily be, at the deepest level, solidarity in a solitude whose effects can be as dangerous as they are unpredictable.

Primary Works

Buber, Martin. *The Knowledge of Man*. Trans. Maurice Friedman and Ronald Gregor Smith. New York: Harper and Row, 1965.
Sartre, Jean-Paul. *Critique of Dialectical Reason*. Trans. Alan Sheridan. London: Verso, 1982.

Bibliography

Gordon, Haim. *Dance, Dialogue, and Despair: Existentialist Philosophy and Education for Peace in Israel*. Tuscaloosa: University of Alabama Press, 1986.

WHOLENESS
Richard Polt

The existentialist discussion of wholeness can be seen as harking back to classical ideals of the just or virtuous soul, a soul that lives a LIFE distinguished by wholeness. However, classical ONTOLOGY tends to conceive of wholeness on the model of an intact and well-functioning natural BEING or manufactured item. Still, it was partially recognized even in ancient thought that the wholeness of the life of a PERSON acting in a COMMUNITY is qualitatively different from the wholeness of other kinds of beings. Existentialists stress this qualitative difference: human wholeness cannot be understood as a self-contained, self-sufficient totality or as the complete actualization of a preestablished potential. Rather, human wholeness must be compatible with the free, open-ended, situated CHARACTER of human life.

At an important juncture in *Being and Time*, HEIDEGGER introduces the demand for wholeness in terms of a methodological problem. In order to carry out a thorough interpretation of DASEIN, we must get the whole of Dasein into view. However, Heidegger's previous analyses have shown that Dasein's EX-

ISTENCE always involves the projection of future possibilities: existence necessarily includes potentiality and the not-yet. Hence, it seems that it is, in principle, impossible to grasp Dasein as a whole, for its way of being is incomplete, unfinished, unsettled. He confronts a problem: How can one develop an interpretation of existence without doing violence to existential FREEDOM, whose open-endedness would seem to be foreign to all closed schematization and conceptualization? DEATH does not remedy the incompleteness of Dasein, for as soon as I am dead and no longer subject to the incompleteness of projection, I no longer exist. The moment of dying cannot make existence into a whole. Thus, the phenomenon of death drives home the point that my way of Being is intrinsically unfinished.

In response to this aporia, Heidegger develops a concept of death that is quite different from the common concept of death as the cessation of life. His concept preserves the unfinished, projective character of existence while discovering an intrinsic boundedness, or finitude, which provides wholeness within this very projection—a kind of wholeness proper only to Dasein. We must recognize that Dasein's not yet is a special kind of unfinishedness, unlike that of an unripe fruit, a half-eaten loaf of bread, or a waxing moon. Dasein's not yet is a Being-toward-the-end that continually characterizes human existence. My existence is oriented by possibilities in terms of which my WORLD and my identity make sense—which include the distinctive possibility of the impossibility of my existing. This possibility is death. As opposed to demise or the actual event of Dasein's passing into nonexistence, death is essentially a possibility, and I must relate to it as a possibility. The special wholeness provided by death consists in the fact that I am not guaranteed unlimited options, that existence is constantly susceptible to closure, and that, therefore, my choices give shape to my life. An authentic relation to death accepts and embraces this distinctive wholeness through anticipation. For Heidegger, anticipation does not mean brooding about one's demise but rather acknowledging the finitude of one's possibilities and thus achieving practical clarity about which possibilities are truly important. In an authentic RELATION to death, I am liberated by opening myself to ANXIETY. I am individualized and torn away from the THEY, for my mortality faces me not as just anyone but as an existing individual. Such an ontological structure that provides wholeness to my existence indicates an authentic, whole way of existing.

Many elements of MARCEL's portrayals of the human quest can be understood in terms of the search for wholeness. He holds that genuine wholeness can be discovered through a movement of secondary reflection that reintegrates or reunifies what primary reflection has sundered. Primary reflection, however, is a necessary and valuable stage in my emergence from prereflective existence. In prereflective existence, I am absorbed in the immediate reality of my EGO and its circle of needs and possessions. I do not extend my consciousness beyond my identity here and now. However, as a human, I am called to move beyond prereflective existence. The egoistic state is fundamentally deluded, because the true center of my existence lies outside the circle of my private satisfactions. Whether I like it or not, I can be myself only intersubjectively, in my interactions with others. I can thus become dissatisfied with ordinary satisfactions and feel transcendence as a requirement.

Primary reflection expresses this requirement by dividing my contingent, empirical existence from my ties to a greater reality. I thus distinguish between my BODY and my MIND, the exterior and the interior, the particular and the universal aspects of my existence. I learn to think in the abstract, using well-defined techniques to solve problems. Thus, primary reflection is initially liberating. However, when taken to an extreme, it runs the risk of excessive rationalization and alienation. The result is a disengaged, merely spectatorial or technical attitude to one's environment. On a social level, excessive primary reflection leads to our broken world, deprived of a living center. Such a world has the unity of a bureaucratic, systematized state that organizes individuals into a collective. But this is a broken unity, for it is a far cry from genuine wholeness. The unity of the broken world is an atomizing unity that does not embrace its members as persons in a community. Secondary reflection is a recuperative movement that wins back on a higher level the unity dissolved by primary reflection, achieving an awareness that the wholeness of the person is a precondition for primary reflection. The key to secondary reflection is an appreciation of the embodied self that is involved in its surrounding world. Such is neither a return to prereflective existence, engrossed in its satisfactions, nor an embrace of TRANSCENDENCE as an escape from my incarnate life but a recognition that transcendence deepens and broadens my life.

In secondary reflection, I achieve true intimacy with myself and my body to the point where I can say, I am my body. I also participate authentically in my situation by becoming open to encounters with others. I thus attain an existential wholeness that is not autonomous or self-contained but open and exploratory. I become capable of sensing the unity of my being, a unity that binds together past and future and provides deep fulfillment. This fulfillment is not a matter of totality, self-sufficiency, or perfection. It is best understood on the model of LOVE, which is fulfilled through its participation in something beyond itself— ultimately, an eternal GOD and the promise of IMMORTALITY. Marcel's understanding of existential integrity is paralleled by his understanding of PHILOSOPHY and TRUTH. Truth is manifest within an intelligible background that is an essentially uncompleted structure. Hence, a philosophy is always provisional and in PROCESS. Its wholeness lies not in any systematic explanatory force but in its connection to the developing life of the philosopher.

Heidegger's and Marcel's portraits of existential wholeness are, in some respects, strikingly different. Heidegger finds wholeness in the solitary acknowledgment of my mortal finitude. For Marcel, wholeness demands a connection to intersubjective and transsubjective realities—ultimately, to God and the possibility of immortality. Marcel's position depends on an understanding of personality as fulfilled through interpersonal encounters, an understanding that he shares with BUBER and BERDYAEV. While Heidegger would deny that his position denigrates intersubjectivity, his account of authenticity and temporality is explicitly based on an individualizing moment. What is shared by Heidegger, Marcel, and other existentialists is the attempt to think of human phenomena, such as wholeness, in a way that does justice to the distinctive character of human life.

Primary Works

Buber, Martin. *Between Man and Man*. Trans. Ronald Gregor Smith. New York: Macmillan, 1965.
Marcel, Gabriel. *Creative Fidelity*. Trans. Robert Rosthal. New York: Farrar, Straus, and Giroux, 1964.

Bibliography

O'Malley, John B. *The Fellowship of Being: An Essay on the Concept of Person in the Philosophy of Gabriel Marcel*. The Hague: Martinus Nijhoff, 1966.

WILL
Stephen Tyman

Through German Idealism the concept of will achieved independence from the devotional context of its medieval treatment. Despite the radical break contained in the secularization of free will, a continuity remained in the concept's being teleologically oriented. The issue of an ontological negativity carried over into post-Kantian Idealism, where it became associated with self-creation through exploration of the potentials of will. Existentialism frequently focused upon the problem of will, in which respect it was abetted by phenomenological characterizations. Without the idealistic commitment to the ascendancy of the rational, the landscape of the will was utterly transfigured. KIERKEGAARD managed a detailed psychological exploration of the dynamics of the inner modulations of will while remaining within the Christian tradition. He attempted to refocus the role of will in an existential relation to the Creator. For Kierkegaard, the central problem relates to the question of how and by virtue of what capacities one actively solicits the dimension of the self through which the God-relation may be pursued. His answer is traditional: this is the function of FAITH, the active self-orientation of the will. But the nexus of faith/will is unique in his usage. Faith is no longer thetic; it is no longer thought in terms of a set of BELIEFS. Instead, it is an existential CHOICE, the LEAP to a positive potential-to-be the other side of which is despair.

Kierkegaard concluded that only where radical EVIL is possible is radical GOOD also possible, and the latter can be grounded in universal reason no more than the former; both issue from the paradox that the individual is higher than the universal. Faith thus expresses the choice that disposes absolutely the meaning of one's EXISTENCE. Choice extends beyond worldly affairs and terminates solely in the SPIRIT, its effects reaching into the afterlife. Since it is the destiny of spirit to endure, the failure to achieve peace portends eternal discomfiture. This stresses the burden of will: anything short of complete grace is experienced as gnawing despair, which, in its most deeply experienced form, despairs at not being able to be rid of existence, not being able to die. Through reflection on the unconscious dimension of despair Kierkegaard analyzes the will-factor in its negative moment. The analysis begins with the profound connection between what has been willed and the disposition of personal self-consciousness. But to arrive at the TRUTH, an inversion is required to permit the understanding to get past itself to the will that already informs it.

Kierkegaard asks, Can one be in despair without knowing it? The answer is both yes and no. If despair is simply a description of one's state of MIND, not to feel oneself to despair would be not to despair. However, as it happens that later developments cast previous states of mind in a new light, the authority of these earlier states is called into question. Thus, despair in its existential sense can function unconsciously. When it does obtrude into CONSCIOUSNESS, either retrospectively, as when one concludes that an earlier episode in one's life has exhibited unconscious despair, or in the present moment as an immediate affect, despair, in effect, announces that the factor of consciousness has all along been refractive of the deeper dimension of will. It is this same dimension, when despair is surmounted, that issues in faith. To thinking, however, this is available only as a paradox. The originary source of thought itself is within the paradox; it is the passion of reason. To take up the task of willing in a central way and thereby to awaken the sleeping consciousness is the focus of much of Kierkegaard's writing.

For NIETZSCHE, human self-making was posed with no sustaining TELEOLOGY. He strove to set forth the dimension of will in light of its autonomous potentials, in a way that escapes both RELIGION and the rationalism that had conspired so fundamentally to distort this phenomenon. This orientation to will is preoccupied with the goal of finding a means to circumvent what is called the veil of consciousness. The task suggests that normal awareness is regarded as a surface phenomenon, and through discipline of the will, one seeks access to hidden layers of the psyche. The depth dimension was named for the Greek god of passion, Dionysos. *Thus Spoke Zarathustra* presents the archetype of the master of manifestation through disciplined will. In another dimension of his thought he attempted to render the will in a more programmatic way. In *The Will to Power*, will becomes a term fraught with intimations of the absolute, as if it were a thing unto itself, even though per hypothesis it functions only through the very particulars that manifest it. The tensions in this position were never fully resolved, which only serves to highlight the intrinsic difficulty of combining a critique of rationality with an overture toward the Dionysian forces of will. The point was to bring forth the primal will and to make it serve as the enlivening agent in thought.

HEIDEGGER's infusion of the dynamics of willing into PHENOMENOL-OGY lies in the factor of angst as the ontological mood serving as clue to the existential matrix of care and in the characterization of presence through the category of fallenness. At the heart of this analysis lies a recognition that the way one conceives oneself to have one's BEING will, in large measure, depend on decisions modalizing in advance the character of the possibilities from which one chooses. When they are inauthentic, choices flow from an uncritical sense of group-identification; when they are authentic, choices involve a resolute self-assertion. Heidegger assigns a central role to CONSCIENCE in the disposition of individual will. Through conscience one affirms that one's choice is not merely self-relational but interwoven through the larger factor of Being. Indeed, at the level of its root experience there is not even so much as a well-formed conscience itself, but rather a mere disposition to conscientiousness, a wanting-to-have-a-conscience that longs to hark to its call. In his later reflections one senses the tension between the active and the passive faces of will or between the existential and the phenomenological dimensions of the discussion. Perhaps the most definitive Heideggeriain statement on the question came in the essay ''Who Is Nietzsche's Zarathustra.'' where he declared that no amount of learning will ever uncover what it means that Being manifests as will. What it means can only be asked in thinking.

Primary Works

Kierkegaard, Søren. *Fear and Trembling and The Sickness unto Death*. Trans. Walter Lowrie. Princeton: Princeton University Press, 1954.
Nietzsche, Friedrich. *The Will to Power*. Trans. Walter Kaufmann and R. J. Hollingdale. New York: Vintage, 1969.

Bibliography

Gardener, Patrick. *Kierkegaard*. Oxford: Oxford University Press, 1988.

WISDOM
Mark Peterson

Wisdom carries two connotations in existential texts. It is used in a casual way to describe sound judgment or KNOWLEDGE leavened by experience and as a reference to the extrarational or even mystical knowledge described by religiously oriented writers. BUBER's description of the I–Thou relation could be an example of the second, more religious sense of the term. Wisdom is not an explicit point of interest in the HISTORY of PHILOSOPHY since Descartes, when knowledge and epistemic questions become the major focus. Wisdom became dislocated from the main stream of philosophic interest into the religious or theological sphere. Since then wisdom seemed related more to questions of GOD and the extranatural, while knowledge was the approach taken to questions of science and earthly LIFE.

Wisdom, as the English rendering of *sophia*, implies a capacity of understanding different from philosophy's normal definitions of understanding. For the ancient Greeks wisdom was taken to mean a practical application of intelligence—it seems to have possessed the sense of delighting in the application of intellect to any OBJECT of interest. Wisdom was a virtue, an excellence, a skill, the LOVE of a thing well done, well made, or accomplished with excellence. From the Western philosophical view of wisdom found in Socrates, a thread runs to KIERKEGAARD and NIETZSCHE. Existentialism, to the degree that it speaks about a dimension in human experience beyond what is available in SENSATION, opinion, and knowledge, is a return to wisdom and a turn away from logical TRUTH functionality as the object of philosophy.

Wisdom in the Socratic sense is easier to define negatively. It does not seem to be the same as knowledge, BELIEF, or experience, and while it seems commensurate with a lifetime of experience, it seems less than perfectly commensurable with mere knowing. It is Socratic to note that knowledge alone is not a sufficient cause of wisdom, yet neither is experience. Wisdom for Socrates meant recognizing one's own ignorance, knowing when you do not know, and the kind of piety that results. Something akin to this Socratic view of wisdom appears in Nietzsche and Kierkegaard, specifically, in their respective critiques of reason as the sole basis for grasping lived experience. In Nietzsche it is his opposition to, and attack upon, the content and methods of traditional philosophy. In Kierkegaard it appears in his rejection of the belief that everything can be mediated by thought—specifically, in his attack on Hegel's system. More positively, wisdom is the POWER of the individual to sustain the irrational, absurd paradoxes of life and understanding in passion. The crux of both views is an attack on the idea that a full understanding of life and the self is available through the channels offered by reason alone.

Existential writers have often pursued their goals by appropriation of paradox as a way of moving beyond the normal philosophic range of rational syllogism or truth-functional argument. They emphasize a way of suspending or violating the normal process of reason. Thus, in ''Why I Am So Wise'' in *Ecce Homo*, Nietzsche answers the question by emphasizing his skill at revaluation of VALUES and at reversing perspectives. He submits that holding contrary perspectives simultaneously, what in another LANGUAGE might be called sustaining the paradoxes of EXISTENCE in a single moment, is central to his worldview. Wisdom is a triumph over ressentiment or, explicitly, a kind of spiritual hygiene in which one is no longer trapped by the expectations and presuppositions of others but is freed to engage in a constant process of self-overcoming. In *Human, All Too Human* Nietzsche says that Socrates is distinguished by the gay seriousness and a wisdom full of pranks that constitute the best state of the soul of man.

Kierkegaard criticizes reflection, doubt, and understanding as easy to achieve but as lifeless. His writings confirm wisdom as distinct from, and more than, knowledge—as a kind of understanding that involves the paradox of disrupting the mediation of reason without abandoning it. In *Fear and Trembling* he seems to indicate that passion like Socratic wisdom can help one to sustain the paradox between the limits of understanding and knowing the truth. Passion is the essential mode of critiquing the overarching, overwhelming mediation that is the centerpiece of, and greatest danger posed by, the Hegelian system, and the reason it exalts. The passion of FAITH, for instance, is not an uninformed, childish, and irrational mode of knowledge but one fully informed by the very impossibility of what is being asked of it. Yet with passion we are able to move beyond the reflection and limits of understanding to a kind of knowledge denied to, or that escapes from, the mediation of reason. The critique of reason in *Concluding Unscientific Postscript* or the paradoxes of knowledge in *Philosophical Fragments* display the limits of rationality as a mode of living. That critique of reason invites explicit comparison to Socratic wisdom.

Additional attempts to impart a form of Socratic wisdom in the critique of reason and the illumination of human existence are found in other existential writings. Here are a few examples. SARTRE's poignant descriptions of human existence in his philosophical writings and in his novels and plays, in which the prevalence of BAD FAITH is described and analyzed, are wise. Wisdom is also found in CAMUS' analysis and description of the human condition as resembling Sisyphus' absurd determination. Much wisdom emerges in KAFKA's writings, which move the absurdities of contemporary existence to the center of life's stage and thus often throw the meaning of a reader's own life into perspective.

Primary Works

Jaspers, Karl. *Way to Wisdom.* Trans. Ralph Manheim. New Haven, CT: Yale University Press, 1954.

Kierkegaard, Søren. *Concluding Unscientific Postscript.* Trans. David F. Swenson and Walter Lowrie. Princeton: Princeton University Press, 1968.

Nietzsche, Friedrich. *On the Genealogy of Morals and Ecce Homo.* Trans. Walter Kaufmann and R. J. Hollingdale. New York: Vintage, 1969.

WORLD

W. Kim Rogers

Western thought began with the natural world as its OBJECT, treating it as composed of bodies that are independent and self-sufficient, with humans as their knowers. For existentialism the starting point is human LIFE, which is a being-in-relation. KIERKEGAARD declared that human EXISTENCE is merely one's RELATION to others and that what one is, is by virtue of this relation. ORTEGA held that existing is first and foremost coexisting. However, while self and others are so connected, they also exist in mutual externality. BUBER held that the principle of human life is a twofold movement. The first movement is the formal setting at a distance, and the second entering into relations.

But what are these others with which a self is essentially correlated? They are all the affairs that make up the world. A PERSON, Ortega held, is a part of a dual fact whose other part is a world. Between the world and self, there is no priority. Nor is the one or the other nearer to us. HEIDEGGER expressed a similar position in *Being and Time*: BEING-IN-THE-WORLD describes human existence. The world-structure is that wherein human existence already is; ontologically, world is a characteristic of human existence. The world belongs to that which constitutes being-human. SARTRE has written of humans and the world that they are relational beings, indeed, that the principle of their BEING is the relation. MERLEAU-PONTY held that humans are through and through compounded of relationships to the world.

Existentialists focus on three questions: What is meant by a world; that is, what is worldly about the world? What does it mean to say that one experiences an objective world that surrounds one as a perceptual whole? If the world can be changed, why ought it to be changed, and whose RESPONSIBILITY is it to change it? As to the meaning of world, if, as Heidegger wrote, DASEIN is being-in-the-world, then world means the there, wherein a person has one's own mode of being and is oriented in each of one's PROJECTS. The world is the primordial totality of those relationships wherein human existence, in relation to a possibility of its being pertaining to that being, inasmuch as this very being is at issue, lets entities show themselves in its concern, so those entities, becoming involved thus with human existence as a project, are discovered in their serviceability or unserviceability. World is not a being but rather that wherein beings present themselves to one another and which enables humans in their concrete behavior to seek comportment with other beings. In contrast, Ortega described the world as a vast enigma in which one finds oneself as one who, shipwrecked, must swim; for we are living in what is foreign to us. The world in which one lives is pure problem. From this perspective of radical solitude the world appears as the Other, as foreign and enigmatic. The world is all the rest of things beyond the boundaries of the organism, against which the organism in its self-isolation is pitted; it thus assumes the character of absolute otherness.

In response to the second question, as sensing SUBJECTS we both have a world and are aware of our selves as parts of the world. Each person experiences the world in particular aspects that are exclusively one's aspects of always the same world. Observers, however, are interchangeable because each of them can direct oneself to the one world that encompasses everything. The relation between the individual and the world is not the result of putting together fragmentary aspects; the relationship rather constitutes the ground of all discrete experiences, which can be understood only as so many delimitations of this totality. Sartre sensed the need for an explanation of how the world, which in its totality can never as such be presented in the individual's experience, nevertheless can belong to human experience and can be the ground of all one's experiences. He held that the presence of a conscious being to being as totality comes from the fact that, insofar as the self makes itself be as an upsurge against all that is not itself, all beings stand before it as an all that the self is not. The self, by denying that it is any and every other being, establishes a world.

Merleau-Ponty affirmed of the world that it is not an OBJECT of human making—as the outcome of a series of syntheses—but is the first object for all one's thoughts and PERCEPTIONS, in relation to which one is constantly situating oneself. The world is what we perceive. Yet, how is it possible for me to experience the world as an existing object, since none of the perspectives of it that I perceive exhaust it, since its horizons are always open? His answer is that the world is, in the full sense of the word, not an object. But, then, is the world I experience only an ever-shifting liminal phenomenon, a mere apperceived horizon of latent experienceables? Merleau-Ponty suggests that we not look for a creative thought that embodies the framework of the world or illumines it, for in looking for what makes that experience possible, we should be unfaithful to our experience. The world is not what is thought of but what is lived through. Our relation to the world cannot be further clarified by analysis.

The world is a MYSTERY that cannot be dispelled by some solution; it is on the hither side of all solutions.

For Ortega, the appearance of the world in human experience ought not even be approached in individual terms; for the world is not found first in the life of a person. Rather, the world that arises for our experience and action is essentially world-for-us; from birth it is a world composed of humans; one understands everything through them. Before humans have to do with the world of things, they have to do with other humans; they see those things through their relations with others. To the givenness of the world of things belongs the sense of it as something for others and shaped by others as well as oneself.

BERDYAEV saw the world as historically related to human destiny. The world should change and will be changed. He was concerned with both the world's present alienated form and its future, eschatological transformation. This world in which humans live today is not ultimate reality but only a phase of it in which humans are alienated from themselves, the world, and God. We find ourselves in an abstract, depersonalized world of mere things in which technique and functionality reign. The world we live in, characterized by objectivity, where everything is defined from without, determined, and impersonal, is a false world. Personality suffers abandonment, loneliness, and strangeness in a world that confronts one as a problem to be solved. In contrast, the true world is supportive of PERSONALITY. It is spiritual; human FREEDOM and creativeness are realized in it. At each moment of one's life, what is needed is to put an end to the old world and begin the new. Every creative act is eschatological; in it there are the end of the world of objectivity and determinism and the beginning of a different world. Human freedom is realized in the world's transfiguration, its being released from the spell of objectivity. Freedom means the breaking through by the creative act of the closed circle of objectification, the irruption of personality into the objectivized world. The end of the false world is a divine-human act that proceeds from the freedom both of GOD and of humans. The new world cannot be established by human strength alone, but it also cannot be established without the creative activity of humans. God expects from humans their participation in the work of creation. He awaits the works of human freedom. The world that God created is a world of possibilities; it is not a ready-made, finished world. In it the creative process has to be continued through human acts.

Thus, existentialists relate to the world not as independent of human actions and experience. The worldliness of the world consists in its being the human environment without which humans cannot exist.

Primary Works

Berdyaev, Nicolai. *Slavery and Freedom*. Trans. R. M. French. New York: Scribner's, 1944.

Ortega y Gasset, José. *What Is Philosophy?* Trans. Mildred Adams. New York: Norton, 1964.

Bibliography

Allen, E. L. *Freedom in God: A Guide to the Thought of Nicolas Berdyaev.* New York: Philosophical Library, 1951.

ZARATHUSTRA
Laurence Lampert

Zarathustra was a Persian prophet who is believed to have lived around 1000 B.C.; he founded the Zoroastrian religion. Zarathustra entered modern PHILOSOPHY in *Thus Spoke Zarathustra*, NIETZSCHE's most important work, as the prophet of Nietzsche's teachings. In Nietzsche's view, Zoroastrianism had an unparalleled impact on WORLD HISTORY through its influence on biblical RELIGION and Greek philosophy. In *Thus Spoke Zarathustra*, Nietzsche allows this monumental historical figure to return in order to make amends. Moved by truthfulness or honesty, Nietzsche's Zarathustra overcomes the views that he had been the first to proclaim and arrives at the new views on the human place in the universe. This mouthpiece gave graphic representation to Nietzsche's views on the self-overcoming of MORALITY. The old view that morals are written into the NATURE of things is overcome by the moral imperative of truthfulness that insists on seeing things as they are and living in accord with the way things are.

Bibliography

Lampert, Laurence. *Nietzsche's Teaching: An Interpretation of "Thus Spoke Zarathustra."* New Haven, CT: Yale University Press, 1986.

SELECTED BIBLIOGRAPHY

Adams, James Luther. *Paul Tillich's Philosophy of Culture, Science and Religion*. New York: Harper and Row, 1965.

Al-Hibri, Aziza Y., and Margaret A. Simons, eds. *Hypatia Reborn: Essays in Feminist Philosophy*. Bloomington: Indiana University Press, 1990.

Allen, E. L. *Freedom in God: A Guide to the Thought of Nicolas Berdyaev*. New York: Philosophical Library, 1951.

Aloni, Nimrod. *Beyond Nihilism: Nietzsche's Healing and Edifying Philosophy*. Lanham, MD: University Press of America, 1991.

Archer, David. *Marxism and Existentialism: The Political Philosophy of Sartre and Merleau-Ponty*. Belfast: Blackstaff Press, 1980.

Arendt, Hannah. *Between Past and Future*. Harmondsworth: Penguin, 1977.

———. *Crises of the Republic*. New York: Harcourt Brace Jovanovich, 1972.

———. *Eichmann in Jerusalem*. Harmondsworth: Penguin, 1977.

———. *The Human Condition*. Chicago: University of Chicago Press, 1968.

———. *Men in Dark Times*. New York: Harcourt Brace Jovanovich, 1968.

———. *On Revolution*. Harmondsworth: Penguin, 1963.

———. *The Origins of Totalitarianism*. New York: Harcourt Brace Jovanovich, 1951.

Barnes, Hazel. *An Existentialist Ethics*. Chicago: University of Chicago Press, 1967.

———. *Sartre*. Philadelphia: Lippincott, 1973.

Baron, Frank, Ernst S. Dick, and Wauren R. Maurer, eds. *Rilke: The Alchemy of Alienation*. Lawrence: Regents Press of Kansas, 1980.

Barret, William. *Irrational Man*. London: Heinemann, 1961.

Bartsch, Hans Werner. *Kerygma and Myth: A Theological Debate*. Trans. Reginald H. Fuller. New York: Harper and Row, 1961.

Beauvoir, Simone de. *Adieux*. Trans. Patrick O'Brien. New York: Pantheon, 1984.

———. *All Said and Done*. Trans. Patrick O'Brian. New York: Warner Books, 1975.

———. *The Blood of Others*. Trans. Yvonne Moyse and Roger Senhouse. Harmondsworth: Penguin, 1964.

———. *The Ethics of Ambiguity*. Trans. Bernard Fretchman. New York: Citadel, 1970.

———. *Force of Circumstance*. Trans. Richard Howard. Harmondsworth: Penguin, 1968.

———. *Letters to Sartre*. Trans. Quintin Hoare. New York: Arcade, 1992.

———. *The Mandarins*. Trans. Leonard M. Friedman. London: Collins, 1957.

———. *Memoirs of a Dutiful Daughter*. Trans. James Kirkup. Harmondsworth: Penguin, 1963.

———. *Old Age*. Trans. Patrick O'Brian. Harmondsworth: Penguin, 1977.

———. *The Prime of Life*. Trans. Peter Green. Harmondsworth: Penguin, 1965.

———. *Quiet Moments in a War: The Letters of Jean-Paul Sartre to Simone De Beauvoir, 1940–1963*. Trans. Lee Fahnestock and Norman MacAfee. New York: Scribner's, 1993.

———. *The Second Sex*. Trans. H. M. Parshley. New York: Vintage, 1989.

———. *A Very Easy Death*. Trans. Patrick O'Brian. Harmondsworth: Penguin, 1969.

Belmore, H. W. *Rilke's Craftmanship*. Oxford: Basil Blackwell, 1954.

Berdyaev, Nicolai. *The Beginning and the End*. Trans. R. M. French. New York: Harper and Row, 1957.

———. *The Destiny of Man*. Trans. Natalie Duddington. London: Geoffrey Bles, 1949.

———. *The Divine and the Human*. Trans. R. M. French. London: Geoffrey Bles, 1949.

———. *Dostoievsky*. Trans. Donald Atwater. New York: Sheed and Ward, 1934.

———. *Dream and Reality*. Trans. K. Lampert. London: Geoffrey Bles, 1950.

———. *The End of Our Time*. Trans. Donald Atwater. New York: Sheed and Ward, 1934.

———. *The Fate of Man in the Modern World*. Trans. Donald Lowrie. Ann Arbor: University of Michigan Press, 1962.

———. *Freedom and the Spirit*. Trans. O. F. Clarke. New York: Scribner's, 1935.

———. *The Meaning of the Creative Act*. Trans. Donald Lowrie. New York: Collier, 1962.

———. *The Meaning of History*. Trans. George Reavy. Cleveland: Living Age Books, 1962.

———. *The Origin of Russian Communism*. Trans. R. M. French. London: Geoffrey Bles, 1955.

———. *The Realm of Spirit and the Realm of Caesar*. Trans. Donald Lowrie. New York: Harper and Row, 1952.

———. *The Russian Idea*. Trans. R. M. French. Boston: Beacon Press, 1962.

———. *Slavery and Freedom*. Trans. R. M. French. New York: Scribner's, 1944.

———. *Solitude and Society*. Trans. George Reavey. Westport, CT: Greenwood Press, 1976.

———. *Spirit and Reality*. Trans. R. M. French. London: Geoffrey Bles, 1934.

———. *Truth and Revelation*. Trans. R. M. French. London: Geoffrey Bles, 1953.

Bernasconi, Robert. *The Question of Language in Heidegger's History of Being*. Atlantic Highlands, NJ: Humanities Press, 1985.

Blocker, Gene. *The Metaphysics of Absurdity*. Washington, DC: University Press of America, 1979.

Blondel, Eric. *Nietzsche: The Body and Culture, Philosophy as a Philological Genealogy*. Trans. Sean Hand. Stanford, CA: Stanford University Press, 1991.

Bonhoeffer, Dietrich. *Christ the Center*. Trans. Edwin H. Robertson. San Francisco: Harper and Row, 1978.

———. *The Cost of Discipleship*. Trans. R. H. Fuller. New York: Macmillan, 1949.

———. *Ethics*. Trans. Neville Horton Smith. New York: Macmillan, 1955.

———. *Works*. 16 vols. Ed. Wayne Whitson Floyd, Jr. Minneapolis: Fortress Press, 1995– .

Boss, Medard. *Psychoanalysis and Daseinanalysis*. Trans. Ludwig B. Defebre. New York: Basic Books, 1963.

Bourgeois, Patrick L. *The Religious within Experience and Existence*. Pittsburgh: Duquesne University Press, 1989.

Bree, Germaine. *Camus and Sartre: Crisis and Commitment*. New York: Dell, 1972.

Brunner, Emil. *Revelation and Reason*. Trans. Olive Wyon. London: SCM Press, 1947.

Buber, Martin. *A Believing Humanism*. Trans. Maurice Friedman. New York: Simon and Schuster, 1967.

———. *Between Man and Man*. Trans. Ronald Gregor Smith. New York: Macmillan, 1965.

———. *Eclipse of God*. New York: Harper and Row, 1952.

———. *Good and Evil*. New York: Scribner's, 1952.

———. *I and Thou*. Trans. Ronald Gregor Smith. New York: Scribner's, 1958.

———. *Israel and the World: Essays in a Time of Crisis*. Trans. Olga Marx. New York: Schocken, 1948.

———. *The Knowledge of Man*. Trans. Maurice Friedman and Ronald Gregor Smith. New York: Harper and Row, 1965.

———. *Moses: The Revelation and the Covenant*. New York: Harper and Row, 1958.

———. *On the Bible*. New York: Schocken, 1968.

———. *On Judaism*. Trans. Eva Jospe. New York: Schocken, 1967.

———. *On Zion*. Trans. Stanley Godman. New York: Schocken, 1973.

———. *Paths in Utopia*. Trans. R.F.C. Hull. Boston: Beacon Press, 1958.

———. *Pointing the Way*. Trans. Maurice E. Friedman. New York: Harper and Row, 1957.

———. *The Prophetic Faith*. Trans. Carlyle Witton-Davies. New York: Harper and Row, 1960.

———. *Tales of the Hasidim*. 2 vols. Trans. Olga Marx. New York: Schocken, 1947.

———. *Two Types of Faith*. Trans. Norman P. Goldhawk. New York: Harper and Row, 1961.

Buber, Martin, and Franz Rosenzweig. *Scripture and Translation*. Trans. Lawrence Rosenwald with Everett Fox. Bloomington: Indiana University Press, 1994.

Bugenthal, James F. *The Search for Authenticity: An Existential-Analytic Approach to Psychotherapy*. New York: Irvington, 1989.

Bultmann, Rudolf. *Essays*. Trans. James C. G. Grieg. London: SCM Press, 1955.

———. *Existence and Faith*. Trans. Schubert M. Ogden. London: Hodder and Stroughton, 1961.

———. *Faith and Understanding*. Trans. Louise Pettibone Smith. London: SCM Press, 1969.

———. *The Gospel of John: A Commentary*. Trans. G. R. Beasley-Murray. Oxford: Basil Blackwell, 1971.

———. *History and Eschatology*. New York: Harper and Row, 1957.

————. *The History of the Synoptic Tradition.* Trans. John Marsh. Oxford: Basil Blackwell, 1968.

————. *Jesus Christ and Mythology.* New York: Scribner's, 1958.

————. *Jesus and the Word.* Trans. Louise Pettibone Smith and Ermine Huntress Lautero. New York: Scribner's, 1958.

————. *New Testament and Mythology.* Trans. Schubert M. Ogden. Philadelphia: Fortress Press, 1984.

————. *Primitive Christianity in Its Contemporary Setting.* Trans. R. H. Fuller. Cleveland: William Collins, 1956.

————. *Theology of the New Testament.* 2 vols. Trans. Kendrick Grobel. New York: Scribner's, 1951, 1955.

Burnier, Michel-Antoine. *Choice of Action: The French Existentialists on the Political Front Line.* Trans. Bernard Murchland. New York: Random House, 1968.

Camus, Albert. *Caligula and Three Plays.* Trans. Stuart Gilbert. New York: Knopf, 1958.

————. *Exile and the Kingdom.* Trans. Justin O'Brien. New York: Knopf, 1958.

————. *The Fall.* Trans. Justin O'Brien. New York: Knopf, 1957.

————. *A Happy Death.* Trans. Richard Howard. New York: Knopf, 1972.

————. *Lyrical and Critical Essays.* Trans. Conroy Kennedy. New York: Knopf, 1969.

————. *The Myth of Sisyphus and Other Essays.* Trans. Justin O'Brien. New York: Knopf, 1955.

————. *Neither Victims nor Executioners.* Trans. Dwight MacDonald. New York: Liberation Pamphlet, 1961.

————. *The Plague.* Trans. Stuart Gilbert. New York: Knopf, 1948.

————. *The Rebel.* Trans. Anthony Bower. New York: Knopf, 1967.

————. *Resistance, Rebellion, and Death.* Trans. Justin O'Brien. New York: Knopf, 1961.

————. *The Stranger.* Trans. Stuart Gilbert. New York: Knopf, 1955.

Cannon, Betty. *Sartre and Psychoanalysis.* Lawrence: University Press of Kansas, 1991.

Caputo, John. *The Mystical Element in Heidegger's Thought.* Athens: Ohio University Press, 1978.

Carr, Edward Hallet. *Dostoevsky.* London: Unwin, 1962.

Clarke, Oliver Fielding. *Introduction to Berdyaev.* London: Geoffrey Bles, 1957.

Clayton, John P. *The Concept of Correlation: Paul Tillich and the Possibility of Mediating Theology.* New York: De Gruyter, 1980.

Collins, James. *The Existentialists: A Critical Study.* Chicago: Henry Regency, 1952.

Contat, Michel, and Michel Rybalka. *Sartre on Theatre.* Trans. Frank Jellinek. New York: Pantheon, 1976.

Cumming, Robert Denoon, ed. *The Philosophy of Jean Paul Sartre.* New York: Vintage Books, 1972.

Dallmayr, Fred. *The Other Heidegger.* Ithaca, NY: Cornell University Press, 1993.

Daly, Mary. *Beyond God the Father: Toward a Philosophy of Women's Liberation.* Boston: Beacon Press, 1973.

————. *Gyn/Ecology: The Metaethics of Radical Feminism.* Boston: Beacon Press, 1978.

Danto, Arthur. *Nietzsche as Philosopher.* New York: Columbia University Press, 1980.

Detmer, David. *Freedom as a Value.* La Salle, IL: Open Court, 1988.

Diaz, Janet Winecoff. *The Major Themes of Existentialism in the Works of Jose Ortega y Gasset.* Chapel Hill: University of North Carolina Press, 1970.

Dobson, Andrew. *Jean-Paul Sartre and the Politics of Reason.* Cambridge: Cambridge University Press, 1993.

Dostoyevsky, Fyodor. *The Brothers Karamazov.* Trans. Richard Pevear and Larissa Volokhonsky. New York: Vintage, 1991.

———. *Crime and Punishment.* Trans. Constance Garnett. Cleveland: Fine Editions Press, 1947.

———. *The Gambler; Bobok; A Nasty Story.* Trans. Jessie Coulson. Harmondsworth: Penguin, 1966.

———. *The House of the Dead.* Trans. Constance Garnett. New York: Dell, 1959.

———. *The Idiot.* Trans. David Magarshack. Harmondsworth: Penguin, 1955.

———. *Notes from Underground; White Nights; The Dream of a Ridiculous Man.* Trans. Andrew R. MacAndrew. New York: Signet, 1961.

———. *The Possessed.* Trans. Constance Garnett. Greenwich, CT: Fawcett, 1966.

———. *A Raw Youth.* Trans. Constance Garnett. New York: Dell, 1961.

Dreyfus, Hubert L., and Harrison Hall, eds. *Heidegger: A Critical Reader.* Oxford: Basil Blackwell, 1992.

Ehrlich, Leonard. *Jaspers: Philosophy as Faith.* Amherst: University of Massachusetts Press, 1975.

Ellis, Robert Richmond. *The Tragic Pursuit of Being.* Tuscaloosa: University of Alabama Press, 1988.

Elrod, John W. *Kierkegaard and Christendom.* Princeton: Princeton University Press, 1981.

Fell, Joseph P. *Heidegger and Sartre: An Essay on Being and Place.* New York: Columbia University Press, 1979.

Floyd, Wayne Whitson, Jr., and Charles Marsh, eds. *Theology and the Practice of Responsibility: Essays on Dietrich Bonhoeffer.* Valley Forge, PA: Trinity Press International, 1994.

Flynn, Thomas. *Sartre and Marxist Existentialism.* Chicago: University of Chicago Press, 1984.

Foucault, Michel, and Ludwig Binswanger. *Dream and Existence.* Ed. Keith Hoeller. Atlantic Highlands, NJ: Humanities Press, 1993.

Freund, Else. *Franz Rosenzweig's Philosophy of Existence: An Analysis of ''The Star of Redemption.''* The Hague: Martinus Nijhoff, 1979.

Frie, Roger. *Subjectivity and Intersubjectivity in Modern Philosophy and Psychoanalysis: A Study of Sartre, Binswanger, Lacan, and Habermas.* Lanham, MD: Rowman and Littlefield, 1997.

Fuerst, Norbert. *Phases of Rilke.* New York: Haskell House, 1974.

Gallagher, Kenneth T. *The Philosophy of Gabriel Marcel.* New York: Fordham University Press, 1962.

Gardener, Patrick. *Kierkegaard.* Oxford: Oxford University Press, 1988.

Glatzer, Nahum N. *Franz Rosenzweig: His Life and Thought.* New York: Schocken, 1961.

Gogarten, Friedrich. *Christ the Crisis.* Trans. R. A. Wilson. Richmond, VA: John Knox Press, 1970.

———. *Demythologizing and History.* New York: Scribner's, 1955.

———. *Despair and Hope for Our Time.* Trans. Thomas Wieser. Philadelphia: Pilgrim Press, 1970.

————. *The Reality of Faith: The Problem of Subjectivism in Theology.* Philadelphia: Westminster Press, 1959.

Goldman, Lucien. *Lukacs and Heidegger.* Trans. William Q. Boelhower. London: Routledge and Kegan Paul, 1977.

Gordon, Haim. *Dance, Dialogue, and Despair: Existentialist Philosophy and Education for Peace in Israel.* Tuscaloosa: University of Alabama Press, 1986.

————. *The Other Martin Buber: Recollections of His Contemporaries.* Athens: Ohio University Press, 1988.

Gordon, Haim, and Jochanan Bloch, eds. *Martin Buber: A Centenary Volume.* New York: Ktav, 1984.

Gordon, Haim, and Rivca Gordon. *Sartre and Evil.* Westport, CT: Greenwood Press, 1995.

Gray, Rockwell. *The Imperative of Modernity: An Intellectual Biography of Jose Ortega y Gasset.* Berkeley: University of California Press, 1989.

Hammond, M., J. Howarth, and R. Keat. *Understanding Phenomenology.* Oxford: Basil Blackwell, 1991.

Heidegger, Martin. *Basic Concepts.* Trans. Gary E. Aylesworth. Bloomington: Indiana University Press, 1993.

————*The Basic Problems of Phenomenology.* Trans. Albert Hofstadter. Bloomington: Indiana University Press, 1982.

————. *Basic Writings.* Ed. David Farrell Krell. New York: Harper and Row, 1977.

————. *Being and Time.* Trans. John Macquarrie and Edward Robinson. Oxford: Basil Blackwell, 1962.

————. *Discourse on Thinking.* Trans. John M. Anderson and E. Hans Freund. New York: Harper and Row, 1969.

————. *The Fundamental Concepts of Metaphysics.* Trans. William McNeill and Nicholas Walker. Bloomington: Indiana University Press, 1995.

————. *Holderlin's Hymn "The Ister."* Trans. William McNeill and Julia Davis. Bloomington: Indiana University Press, 1996.

————. *An Introduction to Metaphysics.* Trans. Ralph Manheim. New Haven, CT: Yale University Press, 1959.

————. *Kant and the Problem of Metaphysics.* Trans. Richard Taft. Bloomington: Indiana University Press, 1990.

————. *The Metaphysical Foundations of Logic.* Trans. Michael Heim. Bloomington: Indiana University Press, 1984.

————. *Nietzsche.* Vols. 1–4. Trans. David Farrell Krell. New York: Harper and Row, 1979–1987.

————. *On Time and Being.* Trans. Joan Stambaugh. New York: Harper and Row, 1972.

————. *On the Way to Language.* Trans. Peter D. Hertz. New York: Harper and Row, 1971.

————. *Parmenides.* Trans. Andre Schuwer and Richard Rojcewicz. Bloomington: Indiana University Press, 1992.

————. *Poetry, Language, Thought.* Trans. Albert Hofstadter. New York: Harper and Row, 1971.

————. *The Question concerning Technology and Other Essays.* Trans. William Lovitt. New York: Harper and Row, 1977.

————. *What Is Called Thinking?* Trans. Fred D. Wieck and J. Glenn Gray. New York: Harper and Row, 1968.

———. *What Is a Thing?* Trans. W. B. Barton, Jr., and Vera Deutsch. South Bend, IN: Regnerey/Gateway, 1967.

Huertas-Jourda, José. *The Existentialism of Miguel de Unamuno.* Gainesville: University of Florida Press, 1963.

Husserl, Edmund. *Cartesian Meditations: An Introduction to Phenomenology.* Trans. Dorian Cairns. The Hague: Martinus Nijhoff, 1960.

———. *The Crisis of the European Sciences and Transcendental Phenomenology.* Trans. D. Carr. Evanston, IL: Northwestern University Press, 1970.

———. *Formal and Transcendental Logic.* Trans. Dorian Cairns. The Hague: Martinus Nijhoff, 1969.

———. *Ideas.* Trans. W. R. Boyce Gibson. New York: Collier Books, 1962.

———. *Ideas pertaining to a Pure Phenomenology and to a Phenomenological Philosophy.* Trans. F. Kerstein. Dordrecht: Kluwer, 1982.

———. *Logical Investigations.* Trans. J. N. Findlay. London: Routledge, 1970.

———. *Phenomenology and the Crisis of Philosophy.* Trans. Quentin Lauer. New York: Harper and Row, 1965.

———. *The Phenomenology of Internal Time Consciousness.* Trans. J. Churchill. Bloomington: Indiana University Press, 1964.

Ilie, Paul. *Unamuno: An Existential View of Self and Society.* Madison: University of Wisconsin Press, 1967.

Ingarden, Roman. *The Cognition of the Literary Work of Art.* Trans. Ruth Ann Crowley and Kenneth R. Olson. Evanston, IL: Northwestern University Press, 1973.

———. *The Literary Work of Art.* Trans. George G. Grabowicz. Evanston, IL: Northwestern University Press, 1973.

———. *Man and Value.* Trans. Arthur Szylewicz. Munchen: Philosophia Verlag, 1983.

———. *On the Motives Which Led Husserl to Transcendental Idealism.* Trans. Arnor Hannibalsson. The Hague: Martinus Nijhoff, 1975.

———. *Ontology of the Work of Art.* Trans. Raymond Meyer with John T. Goldthwait. Athens: Ohio University Press, 1989.

———. *Time and Modes of Being.* Trans. Helen R. Michejda. Springfield, IL: Charles C. Thomas, 1964.

———. *The Work of Music and the Problem of Its Identity.* Trans. Adam Czerniawski. Berkeley: University of California Press, 1986.

Izenberg, Gerald. *The Existentialist Critique of Freud.* Princeton: Princeton University Press, 1976.

Jaspers, Karl. *Existentialism and Humanism: Three Essays.* Trans. E. B. Ashton. New York: R. F. Moore, 1952.

———. *The Future of Mankind.* Trans. E. B. Ashton. Chicago: University of Chicago Press, 1961.

———. *General Psychopathology.* Trans. J. Hoenig and Marian W. Hamilton. Chicago: University of Chicago Press, 1972.

———. *The Great Philosophers.* Trans. Ralph Manheim. New York: Harcourt, Brace, and World, 1962–1966.

———. *The Idea of the University.* Trans. H.A.T. Reiche and H. F. Vanderschmidt. London: Peter Owen, 1960.

———. *Man in the Modern Age.* Trans. Eden Paul and Cedar Paul. London: Routledge and Kegan Paul, 1951.

————. *Nietzsche and Christianity*. Trans. H.A.T. Reiche. Chicago: Henry Regnery, 1961.

————. *Nietzsche: An Introduction to Understanding His Philosophical Activity*. Trans. C. Wallraff and F. Schmitz. Tucson: University of Arizona Press, 1965.

————. *The Origin and Goal of History*. Trans. Michael Bullock. New Haven, CT: Yale University Press, 1953.

————. *The Perennial Scope of Philosophy*. Trans. Ralph Manheim. New York: Philosophical Library, 1949.

————. *Philosophical Faith and Revelation*. Trans. E. B. Ashton. Chicago: University of Chicago Press, 1967.

————. *Philosophy*. 3 vols. Trans. E. B. Ashton. Chicago: University of Chicago Press, 1969/1971.

————. *Philosophy of Existence*. Trans. R. F. Grabau. Philadelphia: University of Pennsylvania Press, 1971.

————. *The Question of German Guilt*. Trans. E. B. Ashton. New York: Dial Press, 1947.

————. *Reason and Anti-reason in Our Time*. Trans. Stanley Fine-Goodman. New Haven, CT: Yale University Press, 1952.

————. *Reason and Existenz*. Trans. William Earle. New York: Noonday Press, 1959.

————. *Strindberg and van Gogh*. Trans. O. Grunow and D. Woloshin. Tucson: University of Arizona Press, 1977.

————. *Tragedy Is Not Enough*. Trans. H.A.T. Reiche. Boston: Beacon Press, 1952.

————. *Way to Wisdom*. Trans. Ralph Manheim. New Haven, CT: Yale University Press, 1954.

Johnson, Roger. *The Origins of Demythologizing: Philosophy and Historiography in the Theology of Rudolf Bultmann*. Leiden: E. J. Brill, 1974.

————. *Rudolf Bultmann: Interpreting Faith for the Modern Era*. London: Collins, 1987.

Jones, Malcolm V. *Dostoyevsky: The Novel of Discord*. London: Elek, 1976.

Joos, Ernest. *Georg Lukacs and His World*. New York: Peter Lang, 1987.

Kafka, Franz. *America*. Trans. Willa Muir and Edwin Muir. Harmondsworth: Penguin, 1967.

————. *The Castle*. Trans. Willa Muir and Edwin Muir. Harmondsworth: Penguin, 1957.

————. *The Complete Stories*. New York: Schocken, 1946.

————. *The Trial*. Trans. Willa Muir and Edwin Muir. Harmondsworth: Penguin, 1953.

————. *Wedding Preparations in the Country and Other Stories*. Harmondsworth: Penguin, 1978.

Kaufmann, Walter. *Nietzsche: Philosopher, Psychologist, Anti-Christ*. Princeton: Princeton University Press, 1974.

Kelsey, David H. *The Fabric of Paul Tillich's Theology*. New Haven, CT: Yale University Press, 1967.

Kierkegaard, Søren. *Attack upon Christendom*. Trans. Walter Lowrie. Princeton: Princeton University Press, 1968.

————. *Christian Discourses*. Trans. Walter Lowrie. Princeton: Princeton University Press, 1971.

————. *The Concept of Anxiety*. Trans. Reider Thomte. Princeton: Princeton University Press, 1980.

————. *The Concept of Irony*. Trans. Howard V. Hong and Edna H. Hong. Princeton: Princeton University Press, 1989.

————. *Concluding Unscientific Postscript*. Trans. David F. Swenson and Walter Lowrie. Princeton: Princeton University Press, 1968.

————. *Either/Or*. Vol. 1. Trans. David F. Swenson and Lillian Marvin Swenson. Princeton: Princeton University Press, 1959.

————. *Either/Or*. Vol. 2. Trans. Walter Lowrie. Princeton: Princeton University Press, 1959.

————. *Fear and Trembling* and *Repetition*. Trans. Howard V. Hong and Edna H. Hong. Princeton: Princeton University Press, 1983.

————. *Fear and Trembling and The Sickness unto Death*. Trans. Walter Lowrie. Princeton: Princeton University Press, 1954.

————. *For Self-Examination and Judge for Yourself!* Trans. Howard V. Hong and Edna H. Hong. Princeton: Princeton University Press, 1990.

————. *Philosophical Fragments*. Trans. Howard V. Hong and Edna H. Hong. Princeton: Princeton University Press, 1974.

————. *The Present Age and Of the Difference between a Genius and an Apostle*. Trans. Alexander Dru. New York: Harper and Row, 1962.

————. *Stages on Life's Way*. Trans. Howard V. Hong and Edna H. Hong. Princeton: Princeton University Press, 1988.

————. *Training in Christianity*. Trans. Walter Lowrie. Princeton: Princeton University Press, 1967.

————. *Works of Love*. Trans. Howard Hong and Edna Hong. New York: Harper and Row, 1964.

Kockelmans, Joseph J., ed. *On Heidegger and Language*. Evanston, IL: Northwestern University Press, 1972.

————. *Phenomenology: The Philosophy of Edmund Husserl and Its Interpretation*. Garden City, NY: Doubleday, 1967.

Kruks, Sonia. *The Political Philosophy of Merleau-Ponty*. Atlantic Highlands, NJ: Humanities Press, 1981.

————. *Situation and Human Existence: Freedom, Subjectivity and Society*. London: Unwin Hyman, 1990.

Lacoue-Labarthe, Philippe. *Heidegger, Art and Politics*. Trans. Chris Turner. Oxford: Basil Blackwell, 1990.

Laing, Ronald David. *The Divided Self*. Harmondsworth: Penguin, 1979.

Lampert, Laurence. *Nietzsche's Teaching: An Interpretation of "Thus Spoke Zarathustra."* New Haven, CT: Yale University Press, 1986.

Lauer, Quentin. *The Triumph of Subjectivity*. New York: Fordham University Press, 1958.

Lehmann, Karl, and Albert Raffelt, eds. *The Content of Faith: The Best of Karl Rahner's Theological Writings*. New York: Crossroad, 1993.

Levinas, Emmanuel. *Beyond the Verse*. Trans. Gary D. Mole. London: Althone Press, 1994.

————. *Ethics and Infinity*. Trans. Richard Cohen. Pittsburgh: Duquesne University Press, 1985.

————. *Existence and Existents*. Trans. Alphonso Lingis. Dordrecht: Kluwer, 1978.

————. *In the Time of the Nations*. Trans. Michael B. Smith. London: Althone Press, 1994.

————. *Nine Talmudic Readings*. Trans. Annette Aronowicz. Bloomington: Indiana University Press, 1990.

———. *Otherwise than Being or beyond Essence*. Trans. Alphonso Lingis. The Hague: Martinus Nijhoff, 1981.

———. *The Theory of Intuition in Husserl's Phenomenology*. Trans. Andre Orianne. Evanston, IL: Northwestern University Press, 1973.

———. *Totality and Infinity*. Trans. Alphonso Lingis. Pittsburgh: Duquesne University Press, 1969.

Lowrie, Donald. *Rebellious Prophet*. New York: Harper and Row, 1960.

Lukacs, Georg. *Essays on Realism*. Trans. David Fernbach. Cambridge: MIT Press, 1981.

———. *German Realists in the Nineteenth Century*. Trans. Jeremy Caines and Paul Keast. Cambridge: MIT Press, 1993.

———. *The Historical Novel*. Trans. Hannah Mitchell and Stanley Mitchell. Boston: Beacon Press, 1962.

———. *Writer and Critic*. Trans. Arthur Kahn. London: Merlin Press, 1970.

Macann, Christopher. *Critical Heidegger*. London: Routledge, 1996.

Macquarrie, John. *An Existentialist Theology: A Comparison of Heidegger and Bultmann*. London: SCM Press, 1955.

———. *Heidegger and Christianity*. New York: Continuum, 1994.

Madison, Gary. *The Phenomenology of Merleau-Ponty: A Search for the Limits of Consciousness*. Athens: Ohio University Press, 1981.

Malantschuk, Gregor. *Kierkegaard's Thought*. Princeton: Princeton University Press, 1974.

Marcel, Gabriel. *Being and Having*. Trans. Katherine Farrer. Glasgow: University Press, 1949.

———. *Creative Fidelity*. Trans. Robert Rosthal. New York: Farrar, Straus, and Giroux, 1964.

———. *Homo Viator*. Trans. Emma Craufurd. New York: Harper and Row, 1962.

———. *Man against Mass Society*. Trans. G. S. Fraser. Chicago: Henry Regnery, 1962.

———. *Metaphysical Journal*. Trans. Bernard Wall. Chicago: Henry Regnery, 1952.

———. *The Mystery of Being*. Vols. 1 and 2. Trans. G. S. Fraser. Chicago: Henry Regnery, 1960.

———. *The Philosophy of Existentialism*. Trans. Manya Harari. Secaucus, NJ: Citadel Press, 1980.

———. *Presence and Immortality*. Trans. Michael A. Machado and Henry J. Koren. Pittsburgh: Duquesne University Press, 1967.

———. *3 Plays: A Man of God; Ariadne; The Votive Candle*. New York: Hill and Wang, 1965.

———. *Tragic Wisdom and Beyond*. Trans. Stephen Jolin and Peter McCormick. Evanston, IL: Northwestern University Press, 1973.

Marias, Julien. *José Ortega y Gasset: Circumstance and Vocation*. Trans. Frances M. Lopez-Morillas. Norman: University of Oklahoma Press, 1970.

Marsh, Charles. *Reclaiming Dietrich Bonhoeffer: The Promise of His Theology*. Oxford: Oxford University Press, 1994.

May, Rollo, Ernest Angel, and Henri F. Ellenberger, eds. *Existence: A New Dimension in Psychiatry and Psychology*. New York: Basic Books, 1958.

McBride, William L. *Sartre's Political Theory*. Bloomington: Indiana University Press, 1991.

Merleau-Ponty, Maurice. *Adventures of the Dialectic*. Trans. Joseph Bien. Evanston, IL: Northwestern University Press, 1973.

———. *Humanism and Terror: An Essay on the Communist Problem.* Trans. John O'Neill. Boston: Beacon Press, 1969.

———. *In Praise of Philosophy and Other Essays.* Trans. John Wild, John O'Neil, and James Edie. Evanston, IL: Northwestern University Press, 1988.

———. *Phenomenology of Perception.* Trans. Collin Smith. New York: Humanities Press, 1965.

———. *The Primacy of Perception.* Trans. James Edie. Evanston, IL: Northwestern University Press, 1964.

———. *Sense and Non-Sense.* Trans. Hubert L. Dreyfus and Patricia Allen Dreyfus. Evanston, IL: Northwestern University Press, 1964.

———. *Signs.* Trans. Richard C. McCleary. Evanston, IL: Northwestern University Press, 1964.

———. *The Structure of Behavior.* Trans. Alden Fisher. Boston: Beacon Press, 1963.

———. *The Visible and the Invisible.* Trans. Alphonso Lingis. Evanston, IL: Northwestern University Press, 1968.

Morreal, John, ed. *The Philosophy of Laughter and Humor.* Albany: State University of New York Press, 1987.

———. *Taking Laughter Seriously.* Albany: State University of New York Press, 1983.

Needleman, Jacob. *Being-in-the-World: The Selected Papers of Ludwig Binswanger.* London: Souvenir, 1975.

Niebuhr, Reinhold. *An Interpretation of Christian Ethics.* New York: Meridian Books, 1956.

Nietzsche, Friedrich. *Beyond Good and Evil.* Trans. R. J. Hollingdale. Harmondsworth: Penguin, 1973.

———. *The Birth of Tragedy and The Case of Wagner.* Trans. Walter Kaufmann. New York: Vintage Books, 1967.

———. *Daybreak.* Trans. R. J. Hollingdale. Cambridge: Cambridge University Press, 1982.

———. *The Gay Science.* Trans. Walter Kaufmann. New York: Random House, 1974.

———. *Human, All Too Human.* Trans. Marion Faber with Stephen Lehmann. Lincoln: University of Nebraska Press, 1984.

———. *On the Genealogy of Morals and Ecce Homo.* Trans. Walter Kaufmann and R. J. Hollingdale. New York: Vintage, 1969.

———. *Thus Spoke Zarathustra.* Trans. R. J. Hollingdale. Harmondsworth: Penguin, 1971.

———. *Twilight of the Idols and The Anti-Christ.* Trans. R. J. Hollingdale. Harmondsworth: Penguin, 1968.

———. *Ultimately Meditations.* Trans. R. J. Hollingdale. Cambridge: Cambridge University Press, 1983.

———. *The Will to Power.* Trans. Walter Kaufmann and R. J. Hollingdale. New York: Vintage, 1969.

Nucho, Fuad. *Berdyaev's Philosophy.* London: Victor Gollancz, 1967.

O'Malley, John B. *The Fellowship of Being: An Essay on the Concept of Person in the Philosophy of Gabriel Marcel.* The Hague: Martinus Nijhoff, 1966.

Ortega y Gasset, José. *The Dehumanization of Art and Other Essays.* Princeton: Princeton University Press, 1968.

———. *History as a System and Other Essays toward a Philosophy of History.* Trans. Helene Weyl. New York: Norton, 1962.

———. *Man and Crisis*. Trans. Mildred Adams. New York: Norton, 1962.

———. *Meditations on Quixote*. Trans. Evelyn Rugg and Diego Marin. New York: Norton, 1963.

———. *Mission of the University*. Trans. Howard Lee Nostrand. New York: Norton, 1966.

———. *On Love*. Trans. Toby Talbot. New York: Meridian Books, 1957.

———. *Phenomenology and Art*. Trans. Philip W. Silver. New York: Norton, 1975.

———. *The Revolt of the Masses*. Anonymous Authorized Translation. New York: Norton, 1957.

———. *What Is Philosophy?* Trans. Mildred Adams. New York: Norton, 1964.

Ott, Hugo. *Martin Heidegger: A Political Life*. Trans. Allen Blunden. London: Harper-Collins, 1993.

Perkins, Robert L., ed. *The Concept of Anxiety: Volume 8 of International Kierkegaard Commentary*. Macon, GA: Mercer University Press, 1985.

———, ed. *Fear and Trembling* and *Repetition: Volume 6 of International Kierkegaard Commentary*. Macon GA: Mercer University Press, 1993.

———, ed. *The Sickness unto Death: Volume 19 of International Kierkegaard Commentary*. Macon, GA: Mercer University Press, 1987.

———, ed. *Two Ages: Volume 14 of International Kierkegaard Commentary*. Macon, GA: Mercer University Press, 1984.

Pinkus, Theo. *Conversations with Lukacs*. London: Merlin Press, 1974.

Rahner, Karl. *The Christian Commitment: Essays in Pastoral Theology*. Trans. Cecily Hastings. New York: Sheed and Ward, 1963.

———. *Christian in the Market Place*. Trans. Cecily Hastings. New York: Sheed and Ward, 1966.

———. *The Christian of the Future*. New York: Herder and Herder, 1967.

———. *The Church and the Sacraments*. Trans. W. J. O'Hara. Freiburg: Herder, 1963.

———. *Do You Believe in God?* Trans. Richard Strachan. New York: Newman Press, 1969.

———. *Everyday Faith*. Trans. W. J. O'Hara. New York: Herder and Herder, 1968.

———. *Foundations of Christian Faith: An Introduction to the Idea of Christianity*. Trans. William V. Dych. New York: Seabury Press, 1978.

———. *Grace in Freedom*. Trans. Hilda Graef. London: Burns and Oates, 1969.

———. *The Love of Jesus and the Love of Neighbor*. Trans. Robert Barr. New York: Crossroad, 1983.

Raymond, Diane Barsoum. *Existentialism and the Philosophical Tradition*. Englewood Cliffs, NJ: Prentice-Hall, 1991.

Rilke, Rainer Maria. *The Astonishment of Origins*. Trans. A. Poulin, Jr. Port Townsend, WA: Graywolf Press, 1982.

———. *The Book of Hours*. Trans. Stevie Krayer. Salzburg: Salzburg University Studies in English Literature, 1995.

———. *The Book of Images*. Trans. Edward Snow. San Francisco: North Point Press, 1991.

———. *Duino Elegies*. Trans. David Young. New York: Norton, 1978.

———. *New Poems*. Trans. J. B. Leishman. New York: New Directions, 1964.

———. *The Notebooks of Malte Laurids Brigge*. Trans. Stephen Mitchell. New York: Vintage, 1985.

———. *Selected Poems*. Trans. C. F. MacIntyre. Berkeley: University of California

Press, 1940.

———. *Sonnets to Orpheus*. Trans. M. D. Herter Norton. New York: Norton, 1962.

———. *Stories of God*. Trans. M. D. Herter Norton. New York: Norton, 1963.

Rockmore, Tom, and Joseph Margolis, eds. *The Heidegger Case*. Philadelphia: Temple University Press, 1992.

Rosenzweig, Franz. *On Jewish Learning*. New York: Schocken, 1965.

———. *The Star of Redemption*. Trans. William W. Hallo. Boston: Beacon Press, 1972.

———. *Understanding the Sick and the Healthy*. Trans. T. Luckman. New York: Noonday Press, 1953.

Sallis, John, ed. *Radical Phenomenology: Essays in Honor of Martin Heidegger*. Atlantic Highlands, NJ: Humanities Press, 1978.

Samay, Sebastian. *Reason Revisited: The Philosophy of Karl Jaspers*. Notre Dame, IN: University of Notre Dame Press, 1971.

Sartre, Jean-Paul. *The Age of Reason*. Trans. Eric Sutton. Harmondsworth: Penguin, 1961.

———. *Anti-Semite and Jew*. Trans. George J. Becker. New York: Schocken, 1974.

———. *Baudelaire*. Trans. Martin Turnell. New York: New Directions, 1967.

———. *Being and Nothingness*. Trans. Hazel E. Barnes. New York: Washington Square Press, 1966.

———. *Between Existentialism and Marxism*. Trans. John Mathews. New York: Morrow Quill, 1979.

———. *The Communists and Peace*. Trans. Martha H. Fletcher and Philip R. Berk. New York: Braziler, 1968.

———. *Critique of Dialectical Reason*. Trans. Alan Sheridan. London: Verso, 1982.

———. *The Devil and the Good Lord and Two Other Plays*. Trans. Kitty Black. New York: Knopf, 1960.

———. *Essays in Aesthetics*. Trans. Wade Baskin. New York: Washington Square Press, 1966.

———. *Existentialism and Humanism*. Trans. Philip Mairet. London: Methuen, 1973.

———. *The Family Idiot: Gustave Flaubert 1821–1857*. Vols. 1–5. Trans. Carol Cosman. Chicago: University of Chicago Press, 1981–1993.

———. *Iron in the Soul*. Trans. Gerard Hopkins. Harmondsworth: Penguin, 1963.

———. *Life/Situations*. Trans. Paul Auster and Lydia Davis. New York: Pantheon, 1977.

———. *Nausea*. Trans. Lloyd Alexander. New York: New Directions, 1959.

———. *No Exit and Three Other Plays*. New York: Vintage, 1949.

———. *Notebooks for an Ethics*. Trans. David Pellauer. Chicago: University of Chicago Press, 1992.

———. *The Psychology of the Imagination*. Trans. Bernard Fretchman. New York: Washington Square Press, 1966.

———. *The Reprieve*. Trans. Eric Sutton. Harmondsworth: Penguin, 1963.

———. *Saint Genet: Actor and Martyr*. Trans. Bernard Fretchman. New York: Braziler, 1963.

———. *Search for a Method*. Trans. Hazel E. Barnes. New York: Knopf, 1963.

———. *Situations*. Trans. Benita Eisler. Greenwich, CT: Fawcett Crest, 1966.

———. *Sketch for a Theory of Emotions*. Trans. Philip Mairet. London: Methuen, 1971.

———. *The Transcendence of the Ego*. Trans. Forrest Williams and Robert Kirkpatrick. New York: Farrar, Straus, and Giroux, 1987.

————. *Truth and Existence*. Trans. Adrian van den Hoven. Chicago: University of Chicago Press, 1992.

————. *The War Diaries*. Trans. Quintin Hoare. New York: Pantheon, 1984.

————. *What Is Literature?* Trans. Bernard Fretchman. London: Methuen, 1978.

————. *The Words*. Trans. Bernard Fretchman. Greenwich, CT: Fawcett, 1964.

Schacht, Richard. *Nietzsche*. London: Routledge and Kegan Paul, 1983.

Schaeder, Grete. *The Hebrew Humanism of Martin Buber*. Trans. Noah J. Jacobs. Detroit: Wayne State University Press, 1973.

Scharlemann, Robert P. *Reflection and Doubt in the Thought of Paul Tillich*. New York: Harper and Row, 1976.

Schilpp, Paul Arthur, ed. *The Philosophy of Jean-Paul Sartre*. La Salle, IL: Open Court, 1981.

————, ed. *The Philosophy of Karl Jaspers*. La Salle, IL: Open Court, 1981.

Schilpp, Paul Arthur, and Maurice Friedman, eds. *The Philosophy of Martin Buber*. La Salle, IL: Open Court, 1967.

Schilpp, Paul Arthur, and Lewis Edwin Hahn, eds. *The Philosophy of Gabriel Marcel*. La Salle, IL: Open Court, 1984.

Schrag, Calvin O. *Existence and Freedom*. Evanston, IL: Northwestern University Press, 1961.

Schroeder, William Ralph. *Sartre and His Predecessors: The Self and the Other*. London: Routledge, 1984.

Schwarzer, Alice. *After ''The Second Sex'': Conversations with Simone De Beauvoir*. Trans. Marianne Howarth. New York: Pantheon, 1984.

Shestov, Lev. *All Things Are Possible and Penultimate Words and Other Essays*. Athens: Ohio University Press, 1977.

————. *Athens and Jerusalem*. Trans. Bernard Martin. New York: Simon and Schuster, 1968.

————. *Dostoevsky, Tolstoy and Nietzsche*. Trans. Bernard Martin and Spencer Roberts. Athens: Ohio University Press, 1969.

————. *In Job's Balance*. Trans. Camilla Coventry and C. A. Macartney. Athens: Ohio University Press, 1975.

————. *Potestas Clavium*. Trans. Bernard Martin. Chicago: Henry Regnery, 1970.

————. *Speculation and Revelation*. Trans. Bernard Martin. Athens: Ohio University Press, 1982.

Small, Joseph. *Jose Ortega y Gasset, Existentialist: A Critical Study of His Thought and Its Sources*. Chicago: Henry Regnery, 1949.

Spiegelberg, Herbert. *The Phenomenological Movement*. The Hague: Martinus Nijhoff, 1965.

Thody, Philip. *Albert Camus: A Study of His Work*. New York: Grove Press, 1957.

Tillich, Paul. *Biblical Religion and the Search for Ultimate Reality*. Chicago: University of Chicago Press, 1955.

————. *Christianity and the Encounter of World Religions*. New York: Columbia University Press, 1963.

————. *The Courage to Be*. New Haven, CT: Yale University Press, 1952.

————. *The Dynamics of Faith*. New York: Harper and Row, 1957.

————. *The Eternal Now*. New York: Scribner's, 1962.

————. *A History of Christian Thought*. London: SCM Press, 1968.

————. *Love, Power and Justice*. Oxford: Oxford University Press, 1954.

————. *Morality and Beyond*. New York: Harper and Row, 1963.

————. *My Search for Absolutes*. New York: Simon and Schuster, 1967.

————. *The New Being*. New York: Scribner's, 1935.

————. *On the Boundary*. New York: Scribner's, 1966.

————. *Perspectives on 19th and 20th Century Protestant Theology*. London: SCM Press, 1967.

————. *The Protestant Era*. Trans. James Luther Adams. Chicago: University of Chicago Press, 1957.

————. *The Religious Situation*. Trans. H. Richard Niebuhr. New York: Meridian Books, 1956.

————. *The Shaking of the Foundations*. New York: Scribner's, 1962.

————. *Systematic Theology*. Vols. 1–3. Chicago: University of Chicago Press, 1951–1963.

————. *Theology of Culture*. New York: Oxford University Press, 1964.

————. *What Is Religion?* New York: Harper and Row, 1969.

Unamuno, Miguel de. *Selected Works*. 7 vols. Ed. Anthony Kerrigan. Bolingen Series 85. Princeton: Princeton University Press, 1967–1984.

————. *Tragic Sense of Life*. Trans. J. E. Crawford Flitch. New York: Dover, 1954.

Van Kaam, Adrian. *Existential Foundations of Psychology*. Garden City, NY: Doubleday, 1969.

Wahl, Jean. *Philosophies of Existence*. New York: Schocken, 1969.

Willhoite, Fred H., Jr. *Beyond Nihilism: Albert Camus' Contribution to Political Thought*. Baton Rouge: Louisiana State University Press, 1968.

Wolin, Richard. *The Heidegger Controversy: A Critical Reader*. Cambridge: MIT Press, 1993.

————. *The Politics of Being*. New York: Columbia University Press, 1990.

Wood, Douglas K. *Men against Time: Nicolas Berdyaev, T. S. Eliot, Aldous Huxley, and C. J. Jung*. Lawrence: University Press of Kansas, 1982.

Yalom, Irvin D. *Existential Psychotherapy*. New York: Basic Books, 1980.

Young-Bruehl, Elizabeth. *Hannah Arendt: For Love of the World*. New Haven, CT: Yale University Press, 1982.

INDEX

A posteriori, 129

A priori, 32, 43, 184, 193, 196, 224, 226, 350, 372, 442, 487

Abraham. *See* Bible

Absolute, 6–7, 29, 35, 105, 135, 137, 153, 161, 168, 185–86, 198, 201, 209–10, 218, 223–24, 229, 241, 243, 247, 255, 267, 269, 271, 276–77, 279–80, 282, 293, 298, 308, 324–26, 346, 348, 350–51, 354, 357, 361, 364, 373, 375, 394, 399, 402, 404, 406, 408, 415, 429, 443, 449, 452, 460, 464–65, 467–68, 477, 479, 492–93, 497

Absurd, 5, 44, 68–71, 79, 95–96, 104–5, 113–14, 119, 135, 149, 153–54, 188, 191, 210, 237–38, 255–57, 265–66, 268, 271–73, 275, 296, 314, 326, 364, 379, 395, 401, 440, 443, 449, 473, 495

Adam. *See* Bible

Aeschylus, 322

Aesthetics, **1–4**, 22, 116, 138, 206, 213, 218, 239–41, 270, 274–75, 279, 305, 348, 361, 367, 397, 401, 405, 413, 420, 431, 452, 465, 483–84

Aesthetic stage, **4–5**, 10, 20, 39, 75–76, 138, 141, 171, 190, 213, 240–41, 254, 274–75, 305, 307, 313, 353, 367, 397, 405, 465, 483–84

Africa, 253, 368

Agnosticism, 43, 281, 371

Algeria, 68, 72, 371

Alienation, **5–8**, 62, 133, 164, 198, 223, 253, 271, 273, 286–87, 302, 307, 329, 333, 348, 368, 395, 401–2, 408–9, 411–13, 431, 434, 437–38, 478, 487, 490, 498

American Revolution, 19

Amsterdam. *See* Holland

Anaximander, 178–79

Andreas-Salome, Lois, 412

Anguish, **8–10**, 39, 42, 153, 170, 215, 222–23, 254, 258, 260, 265–66, 299, 326, 328, 400, 411, 446, 449–50, 464, 477, 479

Anouilh, Jean, 114

Antigone, 114–15

Anxiety, **10–12**, 20, 21, 65–67, 72, 76, 81, 83, 88–89, 102, 111, 119, 125, 155–56, 161–62, 166, 171–72, 175–77, 204, 208, 210, 213, 226, 228, 258, 268, 274, 278, 296, 299, 305–6, 308, 326, 329, 333, 364–65, 385–87, 394, 397,

Leipzig, 59, 192, 317, 458; of Madrid, 335, 339, 476; of Marburg, 175, 336, 458; of Moscow, 42, 427; of Munich, 225, 235, 388, 411, 414; of Salamanca, 476; of Strasbourg, 259; of Tubingen, 53, 64, 458; of Vienna, 58; of Zurich, 48, 58

Value, 1, 5, 9, 21, 24, 27–30, 44, 60, 69, 71, 75, 83, 85, 97–98, 104, 111, 116–18, 129, 136, 139, 142, 144, 147, 159–60, 162, 165, 169–70, 173, 182, 186–88, 197, 218, 220–21, 250, 265–68, 270, 276, 278, 280, 282, 285, 298, 305, 307–8, 321–22, 325–27, 329, 345–46, 348, 350, 353, 357, 360–61, 363, 373, 382, 384, 386, 391, 402, 405–6, 412, 417, 419, 424, 450, 466, **483–86**, 487, 495. *See also* Ethics
Van Gogh, Vincent, 21, 99
Vatican II, 388, 390
Vico, Giovanni Battista, 312–13; *New Science*, 313
Vienna. *See* Austria
Vologda. *See* Russia
Voltaire, Francois Marie Arouet de, 28

Wagner, Richard, 21, 317–18. *See also* Nietzsche
We, 105, 186, 194, 240, 345, 424, 436–37, **486–88**
Weber, Max, 168
Wholeness, 11, 44–45, 60, 140, 160, 221, 303, 305, 310, 433, 484, **488–91**
Will, 4, 7, 16, 18, 21, 85, 87–88, 91, 110–13, 136–37, 147–48, 153, 161–62, 168, 185–86, 208, 210, 214, 230, 236, 238, 240, 266, 276, 305–8, 321, 325–26, 344, 347, 353–54, 357, 361, 370, 375, 395, 404, 421, 428, 430, 432, 449–50, 465–66, **491–93**; Will to power, 2, 90–92, 98, 136–37, 147–48, 185–86, 214,

319–21, 353, 358, 360–61, 375–77, 391, 451, 475. *See also* Nietzsche
Wisdom, 31, 69, 118, 136, 139, 187, 191, 355, 358, 390, 428, 446, 452, **494–96**
Wolff, Christian, 355
World, 3, 5, 9, 11, 13–17, 19, 21–24, 27–28, 31, 33–34, 37, 40–41, 43, 45–46, 48–54, 56–61, 64–67, 69–71, 74, 77, 79–81, 84, 86, 88–90, 92–93, 95, 97–99, 101–2, 105–6, 108, 110–13, 115–18, 122, 224–36, 140, 144, 148–49, 152, 155–56, 162–63, 165, 168–69, 171–77, 182–83, 186–88, 190–91, 194–95, 199–202, 206–7, 209–12, 214–15, 218–19, 222–24, 226–30, 232–33, 235, 237, 240–41, 247–49, 251–58, 265–66, 268, 271, 274–76, 281–85, 289–97, 299–306, 311–16, 319–23, 325–26, 328–30, 332–34, 337–38, 341, 343–46, 351–52, 355, 357, 361–62, 365–68, 370, 372, 375, 377, 379–80, 382–89, 391–97, 399, 401–3, 405–7, 409, 412–13, 415–17, 419–21, 424, 426, 428, 434, 436, 440–42, 444–48, 452, 454–55, 457, 460–61, 464–69, 473–75, 478–79, 481, 484–87, 489–90, **496–99**
World War I, 54, 59, 279, 413, 415, 458, 462
World War II, 15, 27, 42, 59, 68, 115, 158, 172, 206, 226, 229, 259, 272–73, 289, 370, 372, 418, 421. *See also* Holocaust

YMCA, 42

Zarathustra, 318, 362, 395, 449, 451, 493, **499**. *See also* Nietzsche
Zionism, 15, 58–59, 233–34, 417; Zionist Congress, 59; Zionist Movement, 58, 234
Zoroaster, 230, 499
Zurich. *See* Switzerland

ABOUT THE CONTRIBUTORS

Nimrod Aloni, *Beit Berl College, Israel.*

Gary Backhaus, *Philosophy, Morgan State University.*

Jane Bennett, *Politics, Goucher College.*

Robert Bernasconi, *Philosophy, Memphis State University.*

Daniel Berthold-Bond, *Philosophy, Bard College.*

Gene Blocker, *Philosophy, Ohio University.*

Patrick Bourgeois, *Philosophy, Loyola University.*

Andrew J. Burgess, *Philosophy, University of New Mexico.*

Betty Cannon, *English, Colorado School of Mines.*

Stuart Charme, *Religion, Rutgers University.*

Houston Craighead, *Philosophy, Winthrop College.*

Daniel O. Dahlstrom, *Philosophy, Catholic University of America.*

David Detmer, *English and Philosophy, Purdue University, Calumet.*

Anton Donoso, *Philosophy, University of Detroit, Mercy.*

Robert Richmond Ellis, *Los Angeles.*

Steven Emmanuel, *Philosophy, Virginia Wesleyan College.*

Wayne Whitson Floyd, Jr., *Dietrich Bonhoeffer Works, Philadelphia.*

Thomas R. Flynn, *Philosophy, Emory University.*

Roger Frie, *New York.*

Mordechai Gordon, *Nyack, New York.*

Rivca Gordon, *Beer Sheva, Israel.*

Paul Gorner, *Philosophy, University of Aberdeen, Scotland.*

David J. Gouwens, *Divinity, Texas Christian University.*

Alfons Grieder, *Social Sciences, City University, London.*

Ilan Gur Zeev, *Education, Haifa University, Israel.*

Lawrence J. Hatab, *Philosophy, Old Dominion University.*

Robert Holmes, *Philosophy, University of Rochester.*

William Hurst, *Philosophy, Dominican College.*

Malcolm Jones, *Slavonic Studies, University of Nottingham, England.*

Phyllis Kenevan, *Philosophy, University of Colorado.*

Abrahim H. Khan, *Religious Studies, University of Toronto, Canada.*

Georg Kovacs, *Philosophy, Florida International University.*

Sonia Kruks, *Political Science, Oberlin College.*

Laurence Lampert, *Philosophy, Indiana University.*

Herbert Lehnert, *Irvine, California.*

Zeev Levy, *Philosophy, Haifa University, Israel.*

Doug Mann, *Philosophy, University of Waterloo, Canada.*

Vincent McCarthy, *Saint Joseph's University, Philadelphia.*

Jacob Meskin, *History, Rutgers University.*

Adrian Mirvish, *Philosophy, California State University, Chico.*

John Morreall, *Religious Studies, University of South Florida.*

Constance L. Mui, *Philosophy, Loyola University, New Orleans.*

Tom O'Meara, *Religious Studies, University of Notre Dame.*

Thomas B. Ommen, *Religious Studies, Villanova University.*

Michael Oppenheimer, *Religion, Concordia University, Canada.*

Robert L. Perkins, *Philosophy, Stetson University.*

Sylvia Walsh Perkins, *Philosophy, Stetson University.*

Mark Peterson, *Philosophy, University of Wisconsin, Washington County.*

Richard Polt, *Philosophy, Xavier University.*

John Protevi, *Philosophy, Louisiana State University, Baton Rouge.*

Jeff Owen Prudhomme, *Charlottesville, Virginia.*

Murray A. Rae, *University of Auckland, New Zealand.*

Mathew Rampley, *The Surrey Institute, England.*

W. Kim Rogers, *Philosophy, East Tennessee University.*

Peter Royle, *Modern Languages and Literatures, Trent University, Canada.*

Theodore Runyon, *Theology, Emory University.*

Kurt Salamun, *Philosophy, Karl Franzens Universitat Graz, Austria.*

Jana Sawicki, *Philosophy, Williams College.*

Frank Schalow, *Philosophy, Tulane University.*

Ernest Sherman, *Philosophy, Pace University.*

Sonya Sikka, *Philosophy, University of Ottawa, Canada.*

Peter Simons, *Philosophy, Universitat Saltzburg, Austria.*

Stephen Tyman, *Philosophy, Southern Illinois University.*

Gail Weiss, *Philosophy, George Washington University.*

Douglas Kellogg Wood, *West Topsham, Vermont.*

ISBN 0-313-27404-5

90000>

EAN

9 780313 274046

HARDCOVER BAR CODE